S

Race and Ethnicity
Finding Identities and Equalities

Leo Driedger

Second Edition

OXFORD
UNIVERSITY PRESS

OXFORD
UNIVERSITY PRESS

70 Wynford Drive, Don Mills, Ontario M3C 1J9
www.oup.com/ca

Oxford University Press is a department of the University of Oxford.
It furthers the University's objective of excellence in research, scholarship,
and education by publishing worldwide in

Oxford New York

Auckland Bangkok Buenos Aires Cape Town Chennai
Dar es Salaam Delhi Hong Kong Istanbul Karachi Kolkata
Kuala Lumpur Madrid Melbourne Mexico City Mumbai Nairobi
São Paulo Shanghai Taipei Tokyo Toronto

Oxford is a trade mark of Oxford University Press
in the UK and in certain other countries

Published in Canada by Oxford University Press

Statistics Canada Information is used with the permission of the Minister of Industry,
as Minister responsible for Statistics Canada. Information on the availability of the wide range
of data from Statistics Canada can be obtained from Statistics Canada's Regional Offices, its
World Wide Web site at http://www.statcan.ca, and its toll-free access number 1-800-263-1136.

National Library of Canada Cataloguing in Publication Data

Driedger, Leo, 1928–
Race and ethnicity : finding identities and equalities / Leo Driedger.—2nd ed.

First ed. published 1996 under title: Multi-ethnic Canada.

Includes bibliographical references and index.

ISBN 0-19-541746-1

1. Multiculturalism—Canada. 2. Canada—Ethnic relations. I. Title.

FC104.D755 2003   305.8'00971   C2002-906140-7   F1035.A1D75 2033

Cover design: Brett Miller
Text design: Valentino Sanna, Ignition Design and Communications

1 2 3 4 - 06 05 04 03
This book is printed on permanent (acid-free) paper ∞.
Printed in Canada

CONTENTS

List of Figures

List of Tables

Preface

The focus of this book is unabashedly multiethnic and pluralist. I agree with William McNeill that polyethnicity is the trend in industrial urban societies, and the unitary nation-state with its yearning for a homogeneous ethnic society is both misguided and out of date.

The challenge is to provide theoretical and conceptual frames of the field, which are diverse and proliferated. Unfortunately, the classical theorists such as Karl Marx, Emile Durkheim, and Max Weber provide little guidance in ethnic relations. Only Weber wrote briefly on ethnicity. Although American social science research has existed much longer, Park and the Chicago School focused so heavily on race relations and assimilation that research in ethnic pluralism was neglected. Thus, in a more multicultural Canada, we are faced with finding new theoretical perspectives, adapting and adjusting what research there is as best we can to fit our more polyethnic society. Such theoretical pioneering is both difficult and fraught with problems.

But the 1995 Quebec Referendum, where we almost lost Canada as we knew it; the fighting and negotiations between Afghanis, Israelis, and Palestinians, all remind us that polyethnic societies do not come easily. Alas, mediation and murder too often seem to be bedfellows.

The last challenge is to find what empirical research we can, and fit it with conceptual frames for new light. Much empirical research has been done, and especially during the 35 years following the studies launched by both John Porter and the Bilingual and Bicultural Commission in the 1960s. Canadian publications on race and racism have escalated particularly in the last 10 years. Having studied in the interdisciplinary program at the University of Chicago, I wanted to blend the sociological, anthropological, psychological, economic, political, and historical contributions to give ethnicity a rich conceptual frame, as well as a broad context for understanding thiscomplex phenomenon. Although this volume is focused on sociology, I hope the reader will detect other disciplinary uses and appreciations as well. This complexity, of course, makes the whole enterprise of definitions and careful thought even more difficult in postmodern settings.

In addition to the many people whose writings stimulated me and who are listed in the references, I convey special thanks to the anonymous readers who helped improve this work. I also wish to thank Darlene Driedger, who processed many drafts. Oxford editors Megan Mueller and Phyllis Wilson deserve special thanks for unfailing encouragement smoothing the way.

Leo Driedger
University of Manitoba
2003

PART I

Finding a Theoretical Focus

This study is divided into five parts, each of which fits together into a larger whole. Theory is designed to give the reader an overall view of the larger questions that we face, such as ethnic persistence, the influences of industrialization, and how ethnicity changes. This requires an empirical social context such as a demographic history, and a sense of which groups are located in the various regions. As we examine the larger patterns, we soon see that the dimensions of ethnic identity and solidarity need to be studied, including language, religion, and nationality. Soon we see that these ethnic populations are stratified by power, status, segregation, and race. Prejudice, discrimination, and racism are usually present, so human rights and freedoms must be explored. That is a brief summary of how the five parts fit together into a logical whole.

Part I is devoted to finding a theoretical focus. In Chapter 1 we review the classical social theorists to remind us of what they said about ethnicity and race. Industrial change greatly affects the various identities of the peoples who enter Canada as immigrants. What happens to their heritage, culture, and religion? To what extent must they reorganize to retain their cohesion and identity? There are many theories that explore loss of identities, and others focus on solidarity and persistence. In Chapter 2 we end with a proposed model that is an attempt at presenting the complexity of the many dimensions of identity and change.

CHAPTER 1

Ethnic Pluralism
and Industrialization

Canada is a multiethnic nation with a variety of ethnic, racial, religious, and political identities. Some societies have more diverse populations than others; Canada is among the most polyethnic. But except for Weber, the classical theorists were little concerned with ethnic minorities. However, early American scholars such as Park and Thomas of the Chicago School were intensely interested in race and ethnic relations. Let us review their contributions to gain some perspective on ethnic pluralism and industrialization.

Chicago historian William McNeill (1986) addressed scholars at the University of Toronto saying that 'polyethnicity is normal in civilized societies, whereas the ideal of one ethnically unitary state was exceptional in theory and rarely approached in practice. Marginality and pluralism were and are the norm of civilized existence' (1986:4, 6). He claims that 'the idea that a government rightfully should rule only over citizens of a single ethnos took root haltingly in Western Europe, beginning in the late middle ages; it got into full gear and became fully conscious in the late eighteenth century and flourished vigorously until about 1920' (1986:7). Since then it has weakened in the West, but it still finds fertile ground in the ex-colonial lands of Africa and Asia.

McNeill (1986) shows that before 1750, conquest, disease, and trade all contributed to the reinforcement of polyethnicity; but between 1750 and 1920, especially in Western Europe,

the triumph of nationalism introduced the contrasting ideal of ethnic homogeneity, or mono-ethnicity, within a geographic or sovereign boundary. Ironically, this nationalism—particularly in England and France—fed the monoethnic ideal while overseas wars and the expansion of world commerce were mixing peoples more vigorously than ever before. In Latin America, people of mixed American, African, and European heritage constitute a large proportion of the populations. In North America, English and French nationalism greatly influenced the United States and Canada, but the different histories of the two countries require separate analysis.

McNeill (1986:59–85) argues that since 1920 the multiethnic norm has reasserted itself, so that we are now back to recognizing the factors which promote ethnic mixing and which are the norm of civilized societies. Industrialization, urbanization, and modern communication all encourage polyethnicity, whereas the earlier practice of encasing each ethnic group within its own separate state fell painfully short of expectations for the reduction of ethnic and class frictions. Since World War II Western Europe has been reorganized into transnational affiliations within the United Nations, NATO, the former Warsaw Pact, and the European Common Market. McNeill (1986:70) suggests that new ideas, demographic changes, military organization, and the intensification of communication and transport have all helped to undermine the recent past's ideal of ethnic unity. Hitler's passion for racial unity and his genocidal campaign to accomplish homogeneity have shown where such ideals of monoethnicity can lead. Sharp declines in birth rates in Europe after the war led to the recruitment of workers under the *gastarbeiter* policy, which brought many south Europeans into the north. The two world wars scattered Caucasians around the world, and to this day peacekeeping and jockeying for political power bring many of them together through military operations. The North American Free Trade Agreement (NAFTA) will add to interchange. Modern communications and transportation make it relatively easy for immigrants to continue to stay in touch with their kin by telephone and air travel. Thus, ethnic communities are becoming somewhat more detached from geographical territory. Ethnic ties and religious networks have become more portable, just as the world religions of Buddhism, Confucianism, Christianity, and Islam did.

Joane Nagel (1984) sounds a similar theme, pointing out the ethnic revolution in many parts of the world with its 'secession, organization, devolution and genocide representing the many faces of ethnicity'. Nagel (1984:418) sees 'the pervasive presence of ethnicity underlying such political issues as East-West relations, North-South inequalities, human rights abuses, and short- and long-term political stability'. Quebec's passing Bill 101 making the French language official in Quebec in 1977; the long-standing conflict between Protestants and Catholics in Northern Ireland; conflicts between Israel and the Palestinians; terrorists and the Afghanistan war; attempts of aboriginals to entrench land claim rights in the Canadian constitution are but a few of the ethnoreligious conflicts in the news today.

In this volume we will focus on polyethnicity in North America, specifically in Canada. We agree with McNeill and Nagel that our societies have always been multiethnic, that the drive of North Europeans for monoethnicity does not bode well in a global village of the future, and that we should now concentrate on Canadian ethnic pluralism and see what we can

learn from it in the quest for a more just and humane society.

In Chapter 1 we want to find a theoretical focus by first looking at what the classical theorists such as Weber, Durkheim, and Marx had to say about ethnicity. Max Weber is most helpful because he wrote about race, and the role of culture, language, nationality, and religion in industrial society. Weber's analysis of the characteristics of ethnic groups and identity will naturally lead into an examination of what is meant by ethnicity. In Part II we will discuss the influence that European scholars had on American sociologists, especially those of the Chicago School (Persons, 1987). Ethnic and racial studies were central to the research at the University of Chicago, and the Chicago perspective in turn influenced early Canadian sociologists (Shore, 1987).

Scholars have not linked the study of ethnic relations sufficiently to classical theorists such as Weber, Durkheim, and Marx. One of the reasons is that very few of the classical theorists dealt with the category of ethnicity at all, so there is little natural, ready-made material that can be easily used. Max Weber is one of the few scholars who explicitly addressed the issue, and he only discussed it briefly. The writings of Weber and Marx were left unfinished, but even if they had completed the larger studies that they planned, it is doubtful that ethnicity would have had an important place. When nationalism in northern Europe was on the rise, ethnicity did not seem to be the most pressing issue among the many that required research.

However, the classical social theorists dealt with many issues of identity, solidarity, conflict, and social inequalities of concern to scholars of ethnic relations today. We will begin by using important material that Weber wrote about ethnic relations, and we will use Durkheim's and Marx's contributions on how industrial change affects ethnicity. These theorists lived in England, France, and Germany, the most industrial countries of the day, and sought to understand the dehumanizing effects of industry. They help us to understand industrialization as one of the major factors influencing changes in all aspects of life, including ethnicity.

MAX WEBER AND ETHNIC IDENTITY

Max Weber (1864–1920) spent most of his life in Germany, one of the most highly industrial northern European countries. Germany had only recently emerged as a national power from the multiethnic Austro-Hungarian empire with a variety of languages, cultures, and ideas, so we would expect Weber to be aware of the benefits of diversity. He examined values, leadership, religion, ethnicity, and other non-economic factors that he felt were crucial in the rise of industrialization because he wanted to understand the role and importance of values, ideology, and symbols in shaping the industrialization process.

While Weber did not research ethnicity extensively, he had plans to do so and left us an outline on 'Ethnic Groups', which is useful in providing a conceptual frame (Weber, 1978:379–98). A careful study of his outline shows that Weber saw race, culture, tribe, nationality, and religion as the central foci that define ethnic identity. In his treatise on ethnic groups, he mentioned the need to develop a more careful analysis of the complex phenomenon of ethnicity, but he died before he could do so. Let us use his five points to define and clarify the concept of ethnic identity.

Race and Biological Inheritance

Race, Weber's first ethnic identity factor, is based on heredity and endogamous conjugal groups. Whether or not racial heredity becomes an important feature for delineating social circles depends largely upon social and regional settings and values. All kinds of visible differences can serve as sources of repulsion and contempt, or affection and appreciation. Biological physical differences can be the focus of consciousness of kind:

Strikingly different racial types, bred in isolation, may live in sharply segregated proximity to one another either because of monopolistic closure or because of migration. . . . Almost any kind of similarity or contrast of physical type and of habits can induce the belief that affinity or disaffinity exists between groups that attract or repel each other (Weber, 1978:386).

There is a biological unity of humankind, in that no other species of the genus *Homo* now exists, and our species is restricted to its own members (Kallen, 1995:13). But there is the all-too-human tendency to emphasize and exaggerate differences.

There is no such thing as a 'pure race'. Since the discoveries of Gregor Mendel (1822–84), the science of genetics shows that there are variations within the species *Homo*:

It is clear from these genetic data that primary divisions of humankind are distinguishable from one another. The evidence of physical features, skeletal features, and many genetic markers combine to indicate clearly that there are differences among populations of the same human species that are drawn from the three major geographical breeding grounds of human populations: Africa, Asia, Europe. These biogeographical divisions (races) are commonly identified as Negroid ('Black'), Mongoloid ('Yellow'), and Caucasoid ('White') (Kallen, 1995:15).

Within any human society, the social construction of the concept of race can reflect ideological, political, economic, and cultural biases of those who have authority because they have the power to define. Thus, racial categories often do not remain neutral. Their social relevance then lies not in themselves, but the use to which they are put by those in power to differentiate. Ideologies of racism may develop where, in a system of dominance that socializes and communicates differences based on biological features, minorities become less valued (Henry et al., 2000:14).

Intermarriage becomes a factor, depending on how important physical racial features are to a group, and whether they encourage physical attraction or segregation. When racial features become important in distinguishing groups, then the offspring of intermarriage by individuals from different races may not be fully accepted by one or both groups. This does not sanction intermarriage and the resultant mixed offspring as fully in social circles as endogamous marriages would. In Chapter 10 we will expand on the whole concept of race and its relevance in the discussion of ethnic identity.

Culture and Consciousness of Kind

Although racial differences are based on heredity, Weber (1978:387) says social circles 'may be linked to the most superficial features of historically accidental habits just as much as to inherited racial characteristics'. Cultural differences in clothing styles and grooming, food and eating habits, and the division of labour between sexes can all be the focus of a consciousness of kind that can become either shared characteristics of identity or barriers between groups.

Any cultural trait, no matter how superficial, can serve as a starting point for the familiar tendency to monopolistic closure. . . .
But if there are sharp boundaries between areas of observable styles of life, they are due to conscious monopolistic closure, which started from small differences that were then cultivated and intensified; or they are due to the peaceful or warlike migrations of groups that previously lived far from each other and had accommodated themselves to their heterogeneous conditions of existence. . . .
Such a belief can exist and can develop group-forming powers when it is buttressed by a memory of an actual migration, be it colonization or individual migration. The persistent effect of the old ways and of childhood reminiscences continues as a source of native-country sentiment (Heimatsgefühl) among emigrants even when they have become so thoroughly adjusted to the new country that return to their homeland would be intolerable (Weber, 1978:388).

Heimatsgefühl, or feeling at home in a culture, is a key factor because humans want to live by habit rather than decide constantly what to do next. It is comfortable to sense a 'consciousness of kind' where you are accepted as you are.

After having discussed race and culture as major foci for ethnic identity, Weber presents his definition of ethnic groups:

We shall call 'ethnic groups' those human groups that entertain a subjective belief in their common descent because of similarities of physical type or of customs or both, or because of memories of colonization and migration; this belief must be important for the propagation of group formation; conversely, it does not matter whether or not an objective blood relationship exists. Ethnic membership (*Gemeinsamkeit*) differs from the kinship group precisely by being a presumed identity, not a group with concrete social action, like the latter (Weber, 1978:389).

Weber stresses the importance of a belief in a common ethnicity, no matter how artificial the origin of this belief may be. This belief in common ethnicity often delimits social circles where shared sentiments of likeness emerge and are groomed. When the memory of group experiences remains alive, there is the potential for a powerful sense of ethnic identity, involving 'persistent ties with the old cult, or the strengthening of kinship and other groups, both in the old and the new community' (Weber, 1978:390).

In the process of group identification, a sense of ethnic honour can develop as a part of the subjectively believed community of descent: 'Behind all ethnic diversities there is somehow naturally the notion of the "chosen people," which is merely a counterpart of status differentiation' (Weber, 1978:391). The idea of a chosen people permits anyone to claim this right, no matter what the quality of his or her identity may be. Being one of 'the chosen' encourages differentiation into ingroup and outgroup categories. Any cultural traits—including beards, hats, hairdos, etc.—can then become differentiating symbols of the ingroup. Hutterites, Lubavitcher Jews, and the Amish are but a few examples of groups who use clothing as symbols of identity. These distinguishing features are often used as blood disaffinity (*Blutsfremdheit*) symbols, regardless of their importance in objective reality. Thus, it is common to think of *Kulturgemeinschaft*, a cultural *Gemeinschaft*, a shared culture, as a central feature of ethnic group identity. In Chapter 8 we provide specific Canadian examples of typical ethnic cultural communities.

Tribe: The Emergence of a 'People'

Many tribal groups simply refer to themselves as The People, and the Inuit are our best Canadian example. It is no wonder that the Inuit preferred their own name to the European nickname 'Eskimo', taken from a native Indian word meaning 'eaters of raw meat'. Isolated in the Arctic, far away from other humans, they were The People; there were no others until the Europeans came. Tribe implies the emergence of political organization on a small scale, usually a subdivision of a larger whole. The 12 tribes of Israel became subparts of The People of Israel. This subdivision is similar to that which occurred in the classic world: 'The three Doric *phylai* and the various *phylai* of the other Hellenes' in Greece were similar tribal subdivisions (Weber, 1978:393). Such divisions can soon be symbolized as analogous to blood relationships, political artifacts that create feelings of affinity akin to blood relationships.

Tribes have been formed by families banding together in the past, engaged in common political action to defend themselves or to get some work done. Thus, the memory of their Tribe having lived through common political experiences becomes a social construct, or a memory of cohesion and solidarity that they identify with. In such political actions, they develop a sense of moral duty to other members of their People. The tribe represents an elementary stage of organization around symbols and memory that is more diverse than family blood relationships. When the Europeans came to North America, aboriginals had formed many tribes, many of which still perpetuate their memory and organization in most parts of Canada. They feel special obligations toward each other because of a feeling of affinity that began in the past.

Stories, a form of oral history usually told by the tribal elders, where written language has not yet been developed, are an important part of perpetuating the shared memory of their origins. Stories of the origins of cults that were central to the tribe's beginning, shared places which symbolize these beginnings, and leaders who were central to preserving these memories are all part of the collective memory of The People as a tribe. Religion and shared religious beliefs are important because questions of origin—where they began, why they began, and what sustained their cohesion as The People—are difficult to answer, so that beliefs in being a chosen People show the belief in oracles, gods, or cults as a logical progression of symbolism. Memories, epic tales, and legends often become religious beliefs. Studies show that religion is an important part of tribal consciousness. In Chapter 7 we deal more deeply with the development of the sense of the sacred.

Nationality: The Notion of a 'Volk'

Lest we think that only food-gathering tribal peoples are preoccupied with common descent, we must recognize that urban industrial humans share the same need for nationality and cohesion on a larger scale, which likewise perpetuates the symbols of common descent. People living in modern nations have even less claim to blood relations, but according to Weber (1978:395), they also promote the 'vague connotation that whatever is felt to be distinctly common must derive from common descent'. They perpetuate the concept of 'Volk', or People, on a much larger national scale. Why do Canadian youth travelling abroad often carry the maple leaf flag on their backpacks?

'Today, in the age of language conflicts, a shared common language is pre-eminently considered the normal basis of nationality. . . . Indeed, "nation-state" has become conceptually identical with 'state' based on common language' (Weber, 1978:395). In reality, modern states usually have different language groups within them, so that often nationalism is seen to include an insistence on one common language so that a national identity (*Nationalsgefühl*) can be perpetuated. In Canada, French Canadians are a problem for nationalists, even though Canada is now officially a bilingual country. Many Ukrainians, Germans, Italians, Chinese, and aboriginals still speak their own languages at home; thus multilinguistic tendencies survive. The various languages then take on their own prestige rankings, so that for many, the English language has higher prestige than does French (especially outside of Quebec), while the French language has higher prestige in the province of Quebec.

Weber defines nationality as being oriented toward a common language and culture, which is a problem when applied to multiethnic societies like Canada and the United States. He admits that feelings of identity subsumed under the term *national* are not uniform but may derive from diverse sources including customs, shared political memories, religion, language, and race. Nations have political power, which makes them unique, but how this power is used in moulding ethnicity in a country varies enormously. In Canada we can no longer assume, as they did in Europe, that people of one nation share a common language, religion, or customs. Canada does not have a state religion, but allows freedom of religious expression in many forms. Politically, Canada is not subject to a king, as were many Europeans in the past, but is symbolically related to the British crown only. Canadians choose between many political philosophies, parties, and leaders who change frequently. French Canadians have also retained their distinctive

identity, as have the aboriginal peoples and many other ethnic and visible minorities. This is why Canada has wrestled and continues to wrestle with how to govern such a pluralistic people. What does 'The People' mean in Canada, or is it still possible to think in such terms? What is Canadian national identity, and how can this diversity be ordered? A monoethnic ideal does not seem possible, so Pierre Trudeau called for a bilingual and multicultural Canada. While the Meech Lake Accord seemed to include French Quebeckers in the Canadian constitution, they could not agree to such an accord. In Chapter 5 we focus on the importance of language and a bilingual Canada and Quebec's insistence on special status in Canada as a nation within a nation. Quebec separatists, of course, want Quebec to separate as a distinct nation.

Religion: An Ideological Symbol System

In his ethnic identity discussion, Weber included religion under culture and tribe, where we have also included it in our review. However, Weber wrote a half-dozen volumes on the role of religion in society; it deserves special discussion as a fifth focus in his characterization of ethnic identity. It is especially important to see the place of religion not only in tribal folk societies, but also in the industrial urban setting that he dealt with extensively.

Reinhard Bendix (1977:43) suggests that 'Weber emphasized both the importance of ideas for an understanding of the economic behavior and the social foundation of such ideas if they were to have an effect upon human conduct'. Weber's emphasis on ideas had already become apparent in his early studies of the Junkers in eastern Germany. Ideas and actions were not simply the product of their economic interests, as the Marxists had maintained, but a part of a larger social value system.

We want to cultivate and support what appear to us as valuable in man: his personal responsibility, his basic drive toward higher things, toward the spiritual and moral values of mankind, even where this drive confronts us in its most primitive form. Insofar as it is in our power we want to create the external conditions which will help to preserve—in the face of the inevitable struggle for existence with its suffering—the best that is in man, those physical and emotional qualities which we would like to maintain for the nation (Weber, 1894:159).

It is clear, however, that Weber wanted both lines of inquiry—values and materialism—examined, as he clearly stated later in *The Protestant Ethic and the Spirit of Capitalism* in 1904:

> It is of course, not my aim to substitute for a one-sided materialism an equally one-sided spiritualistic causal interpretation of culture and history. Each is equally possible, but each, if it does not serve as the preparation, but as the conclusion of an investigation, accomplishes equally little in the interest of historical truth (Weber, 1904:183).

This double emphasis was the guiding consideration of Weber's work on the sociology of religion, and it is well expressed by Otto Hintze (1931:252):

> [M]an develops his capacities to the highest extent only if he believes that in so doing he serves a higher rather than a purely egoistic purpose. Interests without such 'spiritual wings' are lame; on the other hand, ideas can win out in history only if and insofar as they are associated with real interests. . . . Wherever interests are vigorously pursued, an ideology tends to be developed also to give meaning, reinforcement and justification to these interests. And the ideology is as 'real' as the real interests themselves, for ideology is an indispensable part of the life process which is expressed in action.

Weber spent enormous time and energy writing his well-known volume, *The Protestant Ethic and the Spirit of Capitalism*, as well as his volumes on religion in China, India, and Palestine, and a general sociology of religion. Like Durkheim, he sensed that religion played an important part in society; unlike Marx, who dismissed religion as 'an opiate of the people', Weber placed ideology—whether religious or political—in an important place. In his discussion of ethnicity, Weber included religion along with language, race, tribe, and culture as one of five important characteristics in the formation of ethnic identity. In Chapter 7 we discuss how the sacred is perpetuated by groups such as the aboriginals, Hutterites, and Jews. We expect that similar patterns of perpetuation occur among many minorities where both religion and ethnicity act as foci for solidarity and identification.

Weber recognized ethnicity as an important social category and phenomenon that he wanted to expand and develop later. Race, culture, and religion have been used extensively as characteristics of ethnicity in the literature. Weber clearly delineates race as having a biological base, and that is how we will treat it as well, including the social consequences of biological diversity in the human population. Weber's second, third, and fourth categories (culture, tribe, nation) represent three parts of 'ethnicity'. Culture includes the languages citizens speak, the food they eat, the fashions they wear, and the way they behave socially. Tribe and nation are two social organizational features. Tribe has to do with the smaller more intimate *Gemeinschaft* of family and kinship organization. Nation involves organization related to larger macro political and economic activity of more diverse and heterogeneous populations. Religion, the last of Weber's five dimensions of identity is ideological. Jewish, Hutterite, Mormon, Mennonite, and Quebec Roman Catholic religious groups represent distinct ideological, cultural, and organizational life in Canada. Thus, biological, cultural, organizational, and ideological bases for social behaviour are clearly present in the Canadian population. The title of this volume, *Race and Ethnicity:*

Finding Identities and Equalities, means that we will make biological distinctions when we use the term *race.* When we use the term *ethnicity,* we will deal with cultural, organizational (tribe, nation), and ideational (religion) values, attitudes and behaviour of Canadians. Since this is a sociological work, each of the categories have to do with the social, socio-psychological, cultural, and organizational dimensions of human interaction.

Since most Canadians were white Caucasians when ethnic studies began in Canada, the early research emphasis was much more on 'ethnicity' than on 'race'. That has changed to greater emphasis on 'race', as immigrants of other races have come to Canada more recently. These 'changing visions in ethnic relations' are dealt with extensively by Driedger (2001:421–51) in the *Canadian Journal of Sociology,* one of the suggested readings at the end of this chapter. When industrialization and urbanization set in, however, these ethnic boundaries are subject to extensive change. Of the process of industrialization, the classical theorists, Marx and Durkheim, had much more to say than they did about ethnicity.

INDUSTRIAL CHANGE: A MAJOR CLASSICAL CONCERN

The classical theorists, while less interested in ethnicity than industrialization, were deeply concerned with the impact of industry on society. They thought it promoted mechanical materialism and undermined social solidarity. These foci are relevant in our discussion of ethnicity because stratification and secularization affect ethnic values such as culture, religion, consciousness of kind, a sense of being a People, and how we relate as racial groups. Marx was concerned with stratification, power, and the potential for alienation; Durkheim probed the role of secularization and what this does to social cohesion and sacred values. Stratification and secularization affect ethnic identity, which is the point of discussing industrialization here.

Over the past century, most Western countries have increasingly modified laissez-faire industrial capitalism by a greater emphasis on the social needs of all citizens. There are at least five basic tenets of early capitalism: 1) individual enterprise, 2) the profit motive, 3) private property, 4) competition, and 5) inheritance, all of which have been greatly modified. Industrial capitalism, in the days of Marx, was designed to give individuals freedom to do business without government interference. Making a margin of profit was most important to the industrialist, so that often factory workers became mere tools in making money. The profits belonged to the owner, and he could pass them on as an inheritance to whomever he wished. Those individuals could freely compete in the marketplace, seeking to gain an advantage over others. In the fray of competition there was a tendency to focus on private gains so extensively that workers and other people often were of secondary importance. This excessive individualism was of great concern to the classical theorists. It is relevant to our study because we propose that ethnicity is, for many people, a way to nurture a consciousness of kind and a distinctive identity that focuses not on material but on human needs.

Marx: Materialism and Stratification

Let us briefly focus on materialism and stratification, two concerns of Karl Marx in the industrial process. Marx spent his early years in Germany, and the latter part of his life in Britain. Marx (1818–83) was among the first to be concerned with the capitalist industrial scene in England, Germany, and France. Industrialization was greatly enhanced by steam power: the exploration of new lands had resulted in the emergence of numerous colonial powers in Europe, and raw materials from these colonies were increasingly processed in north European factories. More and more peasants were moving off their lands into urban areas where factories gobbled up their labour skills. Both Marx and Durkheim were profoundly influenced by industrial change, and both were greatly preoccupied with analyzing what was happening to the human factor during this social upheaval. The various social theorists turned to different parts of the problem. Marx was preoccupied with the effects of economic materialism and its resulting human alienation; he saw a solution only in a complete restructuring of the political economy:

> Marx was profoundly opposed to mechanical materialism. . . . Marx's main criticism of capitalism was precisely that it makes man a prisoner of material interests. Socialism was for him that social order which would liberate man from slavery to greed as well as to blind economic forces. For him, man should become a being who is much, rather than one who has much (Fromm, 1956:xv).

According to Fromm, the often-mistaken interpretation of Marx's works—that he was a materialist interested in promoting satisfaction in material goods—is opposite to Marx's concerns.

Marx viewed not only the product, but also the process of production under the capitalist system as alienating. Workers who had only their labour to sell tended not to identify with the end result; in the process of producing the product, they took little pride in their work because, aside from their wages, the profits they generated benefited only the bourgeoisie, the owners of the capitalist process. Industry also tends to focus attention on machines, schedules, and the mechanical process, distracting from concerns of human fulfilment, creativity, and pride in the product of individuals' skills. As a result the worker feels homeless, work becomes external to him, and he does not fulfill himself in his work. 'His work is not voluntary, but imposed, forced labour. It is not the satisfaction of a need, but only a means for satisfying other needs' (Marx, 1844:85–6).

This work for someone else does not belong to the worker but to the owner. Spontaneity is lost. Marx thought that as the person becomes poorer in himself, he feels he belongs less to himself than to someone else, or he is dependent on machines which are not emotionally satisfying. In the process, money becomes the object of all work because it alone will buy the necessities of life. As a result of the worker's alienation from this work, money tends to have more and more power over him. Thus, Marx concludes that 'all human servitude is involved in the relation of the worker to production, and all types of servitude are only modifications or consequences of this relation' (Marx, 1844:92–3).

While Marx was concerned that industrial materialism not become an alienating factor for humans, he was also concerned with the way in which industrial capitalism stratified humans into the rich and the poor, the powerful and the powerless, the bourgeoisie and the working proletariat. While Hegel used this dialectic in philosophical terms, Marx gave it a concrete empirical context in which the economic classes of the bourgeoisie were pitted against the proletariat masses. The owners of capital, whose major interest was a margin of profit, the accumulation of capital, and investment in more industry, came into conflict with the labourers, who needed to labour in order to earn wages to subsist. Thus, Marx thought, the struggle between the two opposites, the two classes, was inevitable. The process promoted 'the mass of misery, oppression, slavery, degradation, and exploitation; but with this too grew the revolt of the working-class, a class always increasing in numbers' (Marx, 1867:801–4).

Marx concluded that capitalism and its alienating processes were the villains. Thus, it must be exterminated by a structural overthrow of the bourgeoisie, the proponents of capital. Through the ages, the economically and politically powerful had often enslaved the masses, and capitalists enslaved the proletariat in his day. There was but one way to root out this cancerous plague, and that was to overthrow the bourgeoisie by the revolt of the masses. Ironically, communist experiments in eastern European countries, which were designed to replace oppressive capitalist systems, also became oppressive and have been toppled recently. Marx spent much time analyzing the failures of capitalism, but too little time developing effective alternatives.

Since the capitalist structure could not be reformed, Marx proposed that we begin afresh. What his new society would be like, and how it would operate, he addressed only in general communal terms:

> [T]he empirical world should be arranged in such a way that man experiences and assimilates there what is really human, that he experiences himself as man. If the enlightened self interest is the principle of all morality it is necessary for the private interest of each man to coincide with the general interest of humanity (Marx, 1845:307–8).

> Communism is the positive abolition of private property, of human self-alienation, and thus the real appropriation of human nature through, and for man. It is therefore the return of man itself as a social, that is, really human being. . . . Religion, the family, the State, law morality, science, art, etc., are only particular forms of production and come under its general law (Marx, 1844:114–5).

Industrialization affects the maintenance of ethnic identity enormously. We agree with Marx that materialism and stratification, the results of industrialization, tend to undermine community and social relations. Ethnicity remains an important part of industrial modern societies. Many people find ethnic identity an important way of fighting alienation because it enhances consciousness of kind, a sense of belonging to 'a people' who care; it promotes meaningful communities and networks which provide support; and it stimulates a vision and hope for ideology and symbolic interaction.

Durkheim: Cohesion and Sacralization

It is not surprising that, in the midst of the European industrial revolution, scholars would also search for the factors that provide cohesion and solidarity during periods of social change. While Marx focused on the macro economic industrial trends toward materialism and stratification, Emile Durkheim (1858–1917) devoted himself to looking at elements of social cohesion and sacralization. What are the sustaining ties of community during the decline of the religious dogma of the old Catholic world, and where will new guides for the future lie?

Durkheim spent most of his time in France. 'The third Republic was the eighth regime since 1789. There had been three monarchies, two empires, and three republics in the period between 1779 and 1870, and these eight regimes had produced fourteen constitutions' (Bellah, 1973:xvi). French society had for a long time been enfeebled by an excessive spirit of individualism which influenced Durkheim to seek the sources of social cohesion and solidarity.

The social milieu and the industrial and political revolutions of Durkheim's time tended to weaken the structures of belief, authority, and community within which human beings had lived for centuries, even millennia (Nisbet, 1974:14). Durkheim was deeply concerned with the effects of the increasing emphasis on individualism. Individuals everywhere were dislocated from traditional associations and communities. Durkheim rejected this extreme individualism and saw it as leading to the destruction of community, values, and the social order. He focused on the coherence of society and the factors of collective solidarity. Alienation, anomie, and disintegration spelled non-society.

Durkheim saw the crises of the modern age basically in terms of a disintegration of the roots of stability and authority (Nisbet, 1974:9). The marks of conservatism are clear in Durkheim's life and work and may likely have sprung from his own Jewish heritage where the sense of community was strong. While scholars such as Gabriel Tarde and Herbert Spencer focused on individuals, Durkheim, in contrast, saw society as the most important centre of attention.

Ferdinand Toennies's *Gemeinschaft und Gesellschaft*, which Durkheim reviewed, was published in Germany in 1889. Toennies's discussion of community surely influenced Durkheim's thinking. Four years later (1893), Durkheim introduced the concepts of mechanical and organic solidarity in his first published work, *The Division of Labor*. These two polarities tend to convey the evolutionary trend of the time, and he did not use them again in his later works. He labelled labour in folk and rural societies *mechanical* solidarity; because adherents of such communities tend not to think about their structures very much, but follow tradition mechanically and without much evaluation. However, as industrial change sets in, societies are forced to develop new forms of social structures such as associations, which depend more on *organic* or cohesive values and norms more rationally agreed upon and adhered to in free association. Later his books such as *Suicide* (1897) and *Elementary Forms of Religious Life* (1912) continue the search for factors that support social solidarity.

Durkheim advocated the need for intermediate associations that would act as a buffer between the traditional folk norms and values that had formerly been adhered to mechanically and the emerging rational bureaucratic institutions that were a result of the Industrial Revolution. These associations, often centring on occupation, would permit human beings to 'regain the reinforcing sense of membership in society—lost, as Durkheim so forcefully stated in *Suicide*, through the acids of modernity' (Nisbet, 1974:138). If Durkheim's argument holds, then 'the crowning need of contemporary society is for centres of authority and solidarity in which the present anomie and egoism leading to suicide and other forms of deviant behavior will be checked' (Nisbet, 1974:139).

Durkheim 'traces the idea of contract back to the aboriginal relationship between a people and its god, back to the overriding, overpowering condition Durkheim calls the Sacred' (Nisbet 1974:78). He focuses on some god or sacred things that are deemed antecedent to—and in control of—the contradictory parties. Solidarity becomes a contract between humans and the sacred realm. As humans later turned to agri-

culture, they added *land* and a sacred trust to their concept of sacred *descent*. Patriarchs eventually became trustees of the people, charged with perpetuating their sacred history.

Our first human notion of force was expressed in religious terms, which are social terms in Durkheim's view:

> Our analysis of the facts has already enabled us to see that the prototype of the idea of force was the *mana, orenda,* the totemic principle or any of the various names given to the collective force objectified and projected into things. The first power which men have thought of as such seems to have been that exercised by humanity over its members (Durkheim, 1912:363).

Primitive people began to feel the awesome force of the entire community to create and hold a sense of loyalty and obligation, which in turn developed into rituals and rites as an expression of their relationships.

Robert Nisbet (1974:164–5) succinctly summarizes Durkheim's treatment of religion and its function in society: 1) religion is necessary to society as a vital mechanism of integration for human beings and as a means to unify symbols; 2) religion is a seedbed for social change, which both Durkheim and Weber say in their discussions of Protestantism; 3) more important than creed or belief, religion's most enduring elements are in ritual, ceremony, hierarchy, and community; 4) there is a link between religion and the origins of human thought and reason. Religion stimulates the search for knowledge and answers deep questions. Durkheim saw religion as a consecration of community, a respect for society.

While some scholars saw religion as a crutch for primitives who had not yet separated empirical reality from myth, Durkheim thought that the sacred would remain for all time, that it would vary from age to age, and that it would manifest itself differently among the different peoples. It is in this larger sense of the sacred that ethnicity can be viewed as 'sacred' in modern society. Religion may be an important distinctive element, as being Anglican can be for Anglo-Saxons, or it may be a more pervasive, undifferentiated whole linking religion as the defining factor of community, as it is for Hutterites. But ethnicity for secular Jews, non-religious Ukrainians, or other groups may still carry many non-religious elements of sacredness: their attachments to a heritage, a culture, a myth, a set of norms, a consciousness of kind, or values with a particular cultural, social, and communal focal point.

For both the religious and the non-religious, Durkheim suggests that morality based on a system of rules of conduct is crucial. The mechanical rules of the past cannot be forgotten as traditional baggage enslaving the individual, as some proponents of individualism such as Spencer have advocated. Rather, norms of obligation and duty must always be present, albeit often in changed and sometimes new forms. The pre-eminent attribute of morality is its capacity to inspire the individual to a sense of obligation. Here we shall see to what extent ethnicity has played, and still plays, such a role of obligation and sense of morality. Is it disappearing in the rise of industrialization? Is it adapting and changing? To what extent is it and will it remain a driving force in Canadian society?

Durkheim sees the family, religion, and socialization as integrating forms of solidarity. In this volume we propose that ethnicity, especially in North America, can also be a form of identification with a heritage, culture, language, religion, or race. Such solidarity is evident in French rural Quebec, in the northlands where the aboriginal people are a majority, and in many rural or agricultural areas where Ukrainians, Germans, Scandinavians, and others seek to maintain ethnic enclaves. For Durkheim, the attachment to meaningful groups is crucial to an integrated society.

Both Marx and Durkheim were concerned with the effects of industrialization on the quality of human existence. Marx observed increased stratification, alienation, and misuse of power, and suggested that the power relationships and the social structure must be totally changed. Durkheim observed the decline of social solidarity and cohesion when the sacred became profane, and how the threat of anomie increased with industrialization. While they did not apply their findings to ethnicity, their relevance to modern ethnicity is quite obvious. While Marx proposed communism, Durkheim and Weber explored the roles of religion, social cohesion, and identity. Only Weber briefly examined the role of ethnicity in the industrialization process. However, American scholars in Chicago applied many of these European principles and theories to their multiethnic society.

ETHNICITY AND THE CHICAGO SCHOOL

While European sociologists did not focus extensively on ethnicity, early American sociologists fortunately did; they also took the changes in industrialization and urbanization into account. The first Department of Sociology in North America was established in 1892 at the University of Chicago, where the *Journal of American Sociology* has published since 1895. Extensive immigration to the United States from southeastern Europe began in the 1880s and continued until restrictive legislation occurred in the 1920s. Anglo-Americans became increasingly apprehensive about the ability of these immigrants to be assimilated, and about their effect on the American identity. Large influxes of Germans into Pennsylvania, earlier, had fostered similar apprehensions. Pressures toward Anglo-Americanization began to mount, especially during World War I. These immigrants from Europe also came to Chicago and the mid-West, and soon southern blacks also arrived.

Although the early Chicago sociologists, sometimes referred to as 'The Chicago School', are best known for their studies in urban sociology, a number of them also did extensive research in race and ethnic relations. They were among the first scholars to try to study these many immigrants in the city objectively, and in a climate of goodwill. Those particularly concerned with ethnic studies included faculty members William Isaac Thomas, Robert Ezra Park, and Louis Wirth and their students Edward Reuter, Franklin Frazier, Emory Bogardus, Everett Stonequist, and Everett and Helen Hughes (Persons, 1987:33). Because Thomas and Park emphasized quite different interests in ethnic studies, we will review their respective pluralist and assimilationist contributions and will also discuss the contributions of two of their students: Charles Dawson and Everett Hughes, who were located at McGill University and who influenced Canadian ethnic studies.

Thomas and Immigrant Reorganization

While Park has often been considered the central figure in the Chicago School of sociology, W.I. Thomas was a dominant influence in introducing ethnic and racial studies (Persons, 1987). Thomas studied sociology in Germany before he finished his Ph.D. in sociology at Chicago in 1896. He was a member of the Chicago faculty for twenty-two years, until a scandal forced his resignation. This early resignation was unfortunate, because he would likely have moved ethnic studies much more in the direction of ethnic identity and pluralism.

Thomas and Znaniecki's major five-volume study, *The Polish Peasant in Europe and America,* was published between 1918 and 1920, was to be the first of a series of studies on ethnic groups, a project abandoned after Thomas left the University of Chicago in 1922. The work traced the experience of immigrating peasants when they left Poland and arrived in American cities such as Chicago. Ferdinand Toennies's *Gemeinschaft-Gesellschaft* continuum was of considerable interest to these Chicago scholars, and Thomas and Znaniecki wanted to plot the changes which occurred when Polish peasants moved from a closed peasant *Gemeinschaft* to a more open urban Chicago *Gesellschaft.*

Thomas and Znaniecki assumed that there would be a change from a *Gemeinschaft* to more *Gesellschaft* forms of ethnic organization if Toennies's theory was correct. This change they

called ethnic reorganization, in which traditional Polish culture and values would be blended with the new American experience into a reorganized Polish-American *Gemeinschaft*. They found that the Polish family was the main primary group with strong social bonds and mutual obligations and respect. Families rallied to help each other in case of trouble. When family solidarity waned, the community unity was exposed to social disorganization, which today we would see as secondary relations in a *Gesellschaft* society. Thomas and Znaniecki found that peasant family solidarity suffered as individualism increased, when these families moved to cities. They also found that in succeeding generations family structures changed into smaller units that provided less support.

The enormous influx of immigrants into America left many Americans uneasy about the extent to which the United States would change culturally, religiously, economically, and politically. By the twenties, there was a great Americanization movement to force assimilation on these new immigrants. This movement grew so strong that by the end of the 1920s laws were passed to severely restrict further immigration into the United States. At the same time, an Americanization research program was launched. *Americanization Studies* produced 10 volumes on immigrant schooling, predominantly immigrant neighbourhoods, transplanted traits, land ownership by immigrants, health, their aged, the immigrant press, the law as it applied to immigrants, and adjustments to industry to accommodate the immigrants. W.I. Thomas was asked to write a volume that was to become *Old World Traits Transplanted* (1921).

In this volume on immigrant traits, Thomas resists the Americanization pressures for immigrants to give up their 'alien' values and patterns of life, but he clearly takes a modified pluralist approach. He refutes the demand for immigrant cultural extinction and tries to show that this demand would lead only to disorganization and problems. Although the term *cultural pluralism* is not found in it, the book strongly supports a multiethnic policy of forbearance, rather than suppression, of cultural differences (Young, 1971:xiv). Thomas again deals with modified pluralism when he discusses immigrant heritages, ethnic types, the potential for demoralization, immigrant institutions and communities, and the need for reconciliation of heritages. In Part III of our text we devote three chapters (Chapters 5 through 7) to ethnic solidarity and identity.

Had Thomas been able to remain at the University of Chicago, his influence in pluralism and modified forms of ethnic change might have been more clearly developed to modify Robert Park's assimilation theory, which we will discuss next. Thomas rejected the Americanization forces and thought it imperative that continuity between the immigrant's former and present lives should be integrated into a new identity. He insisted that continued use of the native language, participation in immigrant organizations, and an active immigrant press during the transition period helped to maintain stable personalities and to avoid demoralization (Persons, 1987:55). Thomas's focus on social psychology was also important because he might have been able to develop further attitudinal and symbolic features of ethnic change, especially in the city.

Robert Park and Race Relations

While Thomas and Znaniecki studied the adjustment of foreign immigrants, Robert Park focused more on race relations based on his experiences in the American Deep South. Park had studied philosophy in Europe and was also greatly influenced by Georg Simmel and studies of social conflict. Park was particularly interested in urban ecology and change, including superordination and subordination and had spent considerable time at Alabama's Tuskegee Institute working with blacks in the southern United States.

As a former newspaper writer, Park saw social relations as a dynamic process of society. In this process the social relations cycle of interaction involved a sequence of stages from the initial social contact (which often resulted in conflict) to competition, accommodation, and, finally, the fusion or assimilation of ideas, cultures, or populations. Like Simmel, Park thought that this competition often took the form of relationships of superiority and subordination that he had observed between blacks and whites in the South. Slavery and caste systems were extreme forms of human stratification. Although Thomas and Park worked together, their interests were quite different. Thomas focused on the extent of ethnic solidarity maintained by immigrants, while Park examined the industrial urban process of change whereby ethnic and racial groups would assimilate into the mainstream.

Park wrote the seventh volume in the *Americanization Studies* series, titled *The Immigrant Press and Its Control* in 1922; it is still one of the best of its kind. He traced the history of the foreign-language press in the United States, describing its contents, range of material, and assessing its function in preserving the cultural heritage of groups. It is interesting that, although he found 1,052 periodicals published by the foreign-language press in 1920, he nevertheless chose to discuss immigrants in assimilationist terms, and the ethnic press as a means of preventing assimilation. His figures for the period between 1884 and 1897 show a steady increase in the number of foreign-language newspapers and periodicals: well over 1,000 until 1920, involving 31 different ethnic groups (Park, 1922: 310, 318).

During the decade of the First World War (1910–20), there was a shortage of white labour, and a large influx of blacks into Chicago from the rural South posed another problem. This time it was not foreign immigrants but blacks that sparked research in race relations. In 1919, one of the most destructive American race riots erupted in Chicago; there had also been race riots in 1917 and 1918 (Raushenbush, 1979: 94). 'Thirty-eight individuals were killed, hundreds injured, and some thousand rendered homeless. Order was restored by the state militia' (Persons, 1987:64). The governor commissioned Charles S. Johnson to investigate. The outcome was the publication of *The Negro in*

Chicago, one of the most important studies by the Chicago School (Raushenbush, 1979:95), in which Johnson applied Park's social relations cycle to race relations.

In 1923, racial tensions involving Japanese on the West Coast also required study, and Park was asked to make a survey so that the race relations cycle could again be tested. Although blacks, and to some extent Japanese as well, had assimilated culturally, they did not fuse or assimilate as the race relations cycle predicted. They tended to remain in various states of conflict or competition because their racial visibility became a barrier to assimilation and whites often did not allow them free access to jobs and equality. It was Emory Bogardus, a student of the Chicago School, who substantially modified the cycle in an attempt to measure degrees of nearness and farness in what became the well-known Bogardus Social Distance Scale. This scale was designed to measure the degree of acceptance and rejection of minorities by others. It became evident that, while white Poles studied by Thomas had a better chance of integrating, blacks—who were physically visible—had more difficulties even though they might want to integrate and were already culturally assimilated.

'By 1937, Park had so far modified his theory of the ethnic cycle as to concede that any of three configurations could prevail when the cycle was concluded: a caste system as in India; complete assimilation as in China; or a permanent unassimilated racial minority as with the Jews of Europe' (Persons, 1987:73). His training in philosophy at Heidelberg and the models he observed in European nation-states were related more or less to assimilated populations, which led him to look for homogeneous ethnic populations. American blacks had been stripped of their cultures as slaves, so they were wholly assimilated culturally. Many black Chicago students were also questioning the applicability of the race relations cycle of American blacks, so that by 1930 Park increasingly left more room for pluralist options; by 1937 he had abandoned the inevitable outcome of fusion or assimilation,

although he did not go as far as Horace Kallen in the direction of pluralism.

Students of the Chicago School

Park influenced large numbers of students, many of whom are still well known in sociology.

The forty-two theses or books written about race, culture and ethnic relations by students while Park was teaching at Chicago constitute a special chapter in the history of American sociology. . . . Park wrote an introduction or a foreword for Jesse F. Steiner, *The Japanese Invasion*, 1917; Maurice T. Price, *Protestant Missions as Culture Contact*, 1924; Louis Wirth, *The Ghetto: A Study in Isolation*, 1926; Pauline V. Young, *The Pilgrims of a Russian Town*, 1932; Charles S. Johnson, *Shadow of the Plantation*, 1934; Romanzo Adams, *Interracial Marriage in Hawaii*, 1937; Bertram Doyle, *Etiquette of Race Relations*, 1937; Everett Stonequist, *The Marginal Man*, 1937; Donald Pierson, *The Negro in Brazil*, 1938; and Andrew Lind, *Island Community*, 1939 (Raushenbush, 1979:99).

Some of Park's black students (such as Franklin Frazier) did not, however, share Park's initial assumption that the ethnic cycle would culminate in assimilation. Frazier's major work, *The Negro in the United States* (1949), emphasized much more the first stages of conflict and competition, including exploitation. Frazier's last stage was characterized by a bi-racial system of social organization, with each race involved in its own set of social relations. This was really a form of pluralism. Frazier also distinguished acculturation from assimilation, which was more like Thomas's modified pluralism (Persons, 1987:74). He saw that race relations had stopped short of the full assimilation projected by Park, and made the distinction between ethnic and race relations. Frazier worked more with Bogardus's last stages in his scale of rejection of racial groups by the major-ity white society.

Of Park's Chicago students who did impor-tant work in ethnic and race relations, Carl Dawson and Everett Hughes, both came to Montreal to begin sociology in Canada. Carl Dawson, a graduate of Chicago, came to McGill University in 1922 to found what later became the Department of Sociology. Dawson had studied with Park when Park and Roderick McKenzie formulated their theories on human ecology. Dawson began his research related to ethnicity in Montreal and later turned to research of ethnic groups on the western Prairies.

> By 1931 the proportion of Montreal's residents who were neither British nor French extraction had risen to 135,262 (13.5 percent) from a percentage of 4.5 in 1901. Despite the change in racial compo-sition, very few studies of how immigrants had adapted to life in the city existed. . . . Dawson was eager to use Rockefeller funds to study immigrant groups and their assimilation . . . following the same lines as Park's program in Chicago (Shore, 1987:233).

In Canada, too, there were fears of cultural dis-unity, especially as large numbers of immigrants entered eastern cities and the West. The British, who were the majority in Canada at that time, pushed hard for restricting immigration to groups from Britain and the countries of north-ern Europe. Thus, some studies made by McGill researchers were quite controversial because Dawson and his associates were seen as being too sympathetic to a variety of immigrants.

Like the 10 *Americanization Studies* made in the United States, a 'Canadian Frontiers of Settlement' series of 9 volumes was launched in the 1930s. Dawson wrote 2 volumes in the series and is best known for his *Group Settlement: Ethnic Communities in Western Canada* (1936). It includes a study of five groups in the West, including the Doukhobors, Mennonites, Mormons, German Catholics, and

French Canadians a study in which he tried to apply Park's assimilation race relations cycle, but which seemed to make Dawson aware that although many of these groups changed con-siderably over time, their distinctiveness did not seem to disappear. One of the great laborato-ries for examining the natural history of groups' interaction was the Canadian West, with its dis-tinctive bloc settlements that enabled the immi-grants to maintain their language, culture, and institutions. These settlements were cultural islands, segregated from each other.

At McGill during the 1920s, 25 per cent of the faculty of arts, 40 per cent of the law stu-dents, and 15 per cent of the students in medi-cine were Jewish so that McGill began to make restrictions on the number of Jews admitted. In Montreal, Jews were adapting, but not neces-sarily assimilating (Shore, 1987:247, 248). The British, of course, were a minority in Montreal; they, too, kept distinct boundaries between themselves and the larger majority of French Canadians. Some of Dawson's students began to use sources and metaphors like 'mosaic' and 'patchwork quilt', when they referred to ethnic and racial groups in Montreal.

It was to this Montreal setting that Everett Hughes came in 1927 to join Dawson at McGill after finishing his Ph.D. at Chicago in 1928. While Dawson never learned French, Hughes did; the two divided their research, with Hughes studying Quebec, and Dawson studying the West. In his eleven years at McGill (he returned to teach at Chicago in 1938), Hughes quickly discovered that the Chicago theories did not fit well into the study of the French-Canadian experience. Hughes broke decisively with the Chicago ethnic assimilation doctrines. In their study of the small city of Cantonville, Helen and Everett Hughes were impressed with how the French and English remained segregated and how industrialization did not change that segregation. Since then, their *French Canada in Transition: The Effects of Anglo-American Industrialization Upon a French-Canadian Town* (1943) has become a classic. Horace Miner, a student of Hughes at McGill, studied St Denis, a rural parish, as a village counterpart that was not influenced by industry. He published his findings in 1939 as *St. Denis: A French-Canadian Parish*.

The studies of Hughes and Miner broke new ground in that they did not follow the Parkian race relations cycle, but rather followed the ethnographic methods of Robert Redfield (the anthropologist at Chicago) and his study of villages in Mexico. Ethnic communities were studied in their own right, without the imposition of a deterministic assimilation process. These studies were more akin to some of the interests of Thomas and Znaniecki in Polish communities. 'When near the end of his life Robert Park remarked that the United States was becoming a nation of federated ethnic groups rather than of geographical territories, he both repudiated the thrust of his own work and forecast a new uncertain age of ethnic relations politics' (Persons, 1987:150). Perhaps he did not repudiate the assimilation cycle, but he did leave room for modified pluralism.

SUMMARY

According to McNeill (1986) polyethnicity is normal in urban industrial civilization and that ethnic pluralism seems to be on the rise.

While the classical sociologists did not focus explicitly on ethnicity, Max Weber does provide a concise outline, which we use as our conceptual frame to introduce the field. Weber defines the area in five categories including inheritance, culture and consciousness of kind, the emergence of tribe and 'a People', the notion of 'Volk', and nationality, and religion as an ideological symbol system. In our study of ethnicity, some of these characteristics will apply more to a particular group or country than will others. Ethnicity is a complex phenomenon that requires a multi-dimensional approach. Indeed, Weber himself wanted to analyze and study the concept more thoroughly, but never returned to it.

While Durkheim and Marx said little about ethnicity, they were highly interested in the effects of industrialization and sought to find alternative means of counteracting its dehumanizing influences. As industrialization increases, so does specialization and bureaucratization. This increase leads to more involved stratification of groups. Majorities tend to dominate over minorities, resulting in conflict. While Marx was concerned with industrial conflict, Durkheim wanted to find the sources of solidarity and cohesion: religion, culture, and social institutions seemed important.

The Chicago School produced some of the leading early sociologists in North America, and race and ethnic relations were an important part of their studies. While Thomas focused on immigrant pluralism, Park introduced the race relations cycle of assimilation. These two foci of ethnic interests were continued by the graduates of Chicago who came to Canada. Dawson tended to follow the Parkian assimilation interests, while Hughes followed the interests of Thomas and Redfield, focusing on pluralism again. McGill, like Chicago in the United States, was at the forefront of early sociology in Canada, and ethnicity was an important emphasis from the beginning of formal studies in each country.

HIGHLIGHT 1.1 ETHNIC AND RACE RELATIONS

Canadian society can be described, at one level, as a complex network of relations among ethnic groups which occupy unequal economic, political and social positions in Canadian society. Within this complexity three main axes of ethnic differentiation are identifiable: the relationship between natives and non-natives, between English and French and between the colonizing (or "charter") groups and other immigrants and their descendants. These distinctions are relevant not only to the private experiences of individuals but also to public issues....

The relations among ethnic groups must be understood in terms of the access to and control of the society's resources and of the functioning of rules and practices that may benefit or disadvantage particular groups. Inequality among groups can result from several factors, including the circumstances of their arrival in Canada (e.g., establishment of a colony by a European power; individual or family immigration); their size; their visibility; their internal economic political and social organization; the direct or indirect support received from other groups or countries; and the power and status of the country of origin in the international order.

Groups who have achieved control over certain resources (e.g., capital or institutional authority) will protect their gains and attempt to extend them. They are likely to try to deny access to power and control to other groups, and the institutional and bureaucratic barriers are designed to preclude or defuse attempts by such groups to bring about change. The relatively disadvantaged may indeed pressure for change in the economic or political situation, but their chances of success depend on the very factors which brought about inequality. As a result, improvements in the situation of disadvantaged minorities are frequently very slow.

Aboriginals and Canadian Society

The relationship between native peoples and the rest of Canadian society is characterized first by "marginality" and dependence. The historical settlement and expansion of English and French societies led to the displacement of the native population. Land was the main concern of the successive Indian Acts and of the treaties. Total control of Indian Lands in 1850 and then, through the British North America Act, to the federal government. Through Indian treaties from 1850 to 1921 large tracts of land in central and western Canada were surrendered in exchange for reserve lands, money and promises of social assistance.

An objective of the Indian Act of 1876 and of its subsequent versions was the control and management of the native population. For this purpose, it defined "status Indians" as those registered in 1874, their closest dependants in the male line, and their wives and children. It also established a bureaucracy for the administration of native affairs which was staffed almost entirely by non-natives. Recently, this situation has begun to change: native people have been recruited in the government bureaucracy; the administration of native affairs has been decentralized; and moves in the direction of Aboriginal self-government have been undertaken, although progress in that direction is encountering considerable resistance, including from provincial governments. . . .

However, in their efforts at social, economic and political organization, native people will have to overcome the legacy of marginality and dependence. They will also have to transcend the numerous cleavages within the native population arising from different cultural and linguistic backgrounds, from the division of status Indians into some 592 bands, and the division of status from non-status Indians.

Francophone-Anglophone Relations

After the Conquest, the British progressively constructed a society parallel to the one that the French had already established. The institutions of the two subsocieties are crucial for their respective members because they provide them with economic and political opportunities and because they embody their language, cultural values and traditions. As a result, the two groups have struggled, unequally, for the control of cultural, economic and political institutions.

The competition between the English and French societies has always been manifested in the struggle over the control of government institutions. The Quebec Act of 1774, the 1791 Constitutional Act, the Act of Union of 1841, the BNA Act and its modifications, the 1982 patriation of the Constitutional Constitution and the Meech Lake Accord of 1987 have all been concerned with the distribution of powers and the symbolic recognition of the language and culture of both groups. The issues of job distribution, of control of economic institutions, of culture and of the size of their respective populations have been reflected in conflicts over policies dealing with matters such as immigration, international relations, industry and trade, education, family allowances, language of education and work, and mass communication.

Of course, issues change with time and circumstances, but the fundamental questions of political power, population size, access to capital for development, and of the cultural character of the society and its institutions will always be there as long as the two groups are in the same society. The competition is unequal, however, largely because of differences in population and wealth, and because of the Conquest and its implications, the British influence in the shaping of Canadian society and government institutions, and the anglophone character of North American society.

Immigrants and Canadian Society

The decrease in British representation led to a concomitant decrease in their control of the economy or of the political system or to a change in the status of Canada as a "white" society. Other European immigrants do not share equality with the charter groups. John Porter in *The Vertical Mosaic* argued that the crucial fact of Canadian life was the "exclusion of minority groups from the main loci of decision making within the corporate sector of the economy."

In politics the composition of federal Cabinets since 1867 has reflected only the struggle to balance English and French interests. The decision by certain groups, e.g., Finns, Ukrainians and other central and eastern European immigrants, to become engaged in radical political activities has reflected their decision to challenge what has been called "the notion of Canadian society on the one hand and the existence of ethnic groups as something independent of the society on the other."

Conflicts between immigrant and charter groups are a result of unequal access to employment and education, and unequal security and social respect. Several groups have been the victims of systematic exploitation, discrimination and social exclusion, but their situation has largely improved as a result of their own individual and collective efforts, and because of legislation and economic prosperity.

For the first generation of immigrants the structure of social networks and organizations is formed largely for adaptive purposes, i.e., to advance or defend shared interests and to provide social support. The structure tends to weaken in succeeding generations if the group has achieved some measure of economic advancement and assimilation. . . .

Visible Minorities

The visibility of certain group adds a dimension to the question of their full incorporation in Canadian society. Racism in Canada has been well documented in historical studies of immigration. Canadians manifest an ostrich-like approach to the problem, although studies reveal that prejudice and discrimination are a reality in Canada. To the extent that negative attitudes and behaviour exist, it is more difficult for visible than for other minorities to avoid being subjected to them. . . .

The multiculturalism policies and programs of the various levels of government have been a step in the direction of recognition and incor-poration into Canadian society. But their aim has not been to restructure institutions to reflect the composition of the population. What such a restructuring would entail has by and large yet to be defined and whether or not it should be attempted remains a highly controversial question.

SOURCE: Excerpt from 'Ethnic and Race Relations' by Raymond Breton copyright © 2002 Historica Foundation of Canada/The Canadian Encyclopedia. Reprinted by permission of Historica Foundation of Canada.

CRITICAL THINKING QUESTIONS

1. How did Max Weber basically define the area of ethnicity at the beginning of the twentieth century? Do his five major areas and characteristics still apply today?

2. In what ways did classical sociologists Marx and Durkheim have very different perspectives on how to deal with industrial change?

3. What do we mean by 'the Chicago School'? Compare the different emphases of W.I. Thomas and Robert Park.

4. Students of the Chicago School, Carl Dawson and Everett Hughes, were among the first to introduce sociology in Canada. Compare and discuss their contributions to the study of ethnicity.

SUGGESTED READINGS

Berry, John W., and J.A. Laponce (eds), *Ethnicity and Culture in Canada: The Research Landscape* (Toronto: University of Toronto Press, 1994). This is a state-of-the-art review of research on Canada's multicultural society, by 19 authors.

Burnet, Jean R., and Howard Palmer, *Coming Canadians: An Introduction to a History of Canada's Peoples* (Toronto: McClelland and Stewart, 1988). These authors provide an informative introduction to the Generation series, which included 14 histories of minorities in Canada.

Driedger, Leo, 'Changing Visions in Ethnic Relations', *Canadian Journal of Sociology* 26:421–51.

Magocsi, Paul Robert (ed.), *Encyclopedia of Canada's Peoples* (Toronto: University of Toronto Press, 1999). This 1,350-page volume contains entries on all peoples in Canada including their origins, arrival, settlement, economic, and institutional development.

CHAPTER 2

Theories of Ethnic Change and Persistence

Although Weber elaborated the potential racial, cultural, religious, tribal, and national diversities of our modern age, he and other classical theorists were also concerned with the impact of industrialization on humanity. Poverty, economic, and political forces beckon the many groups into the mainstream; for many, these temptations are irresistible. Early sociologists of the Chicago School worked to understand these forces. W.I. Thomas focused on the adjustments of Polish immigrants in Chicago and found that changes to language, culture, and institutions occurred, causing reorganization. Robert Park focused more on the forces of industrialization and urbanization and tried to understand these dynamic forces of change (Persons, 1987). In this chapter, we want to explore what happens to immigrants who enter North America, and the changes that they undergo.

Many theories have been developed to explain what will happen to ethnic groups in an industrial-technological society. The first two theories to be discussed, assimilation and amalgamation, assume that the urban industrial forces of technology and majority power will cause loss of ethnic identity. The third and fourth theories, modified assimilation and modified pluralism, admit that the technological forces will change ethnic minorities, but predict that minorities will retain ethnic characteristics partially or in changed forms. The remaining two theories, ethnic pluralism and ethnic conflict, emphasize that ethnic solidarity and identity can be maintained despite industrialization in both rural and urban environments.

SORTING THEORIES OF ETHNIC CHANGE

While the classical social theorists were relatively unconcerned with ethnicity in Europe, early sociologists in America and Canada have been greatly interested in ethnic change because most residents in North America are the descendants of immigrants who came relatively recently (Halli and Driedger, 1999). They have faced enormous ethnic changes in this relatively short period. Fortunately, early sociologists of the Chicago School such as Robert Park, Louis Wirth, W.I. Thomas, Florian Znaniecki, Robert Redfield, and others did considerable research on immigrants during the industrial boom in Chicago (Persons, 1987). The logical questions were, what will happen to these newcomers, and how will they change as a result?

These Chicago scholars of the 1920s and 1930s, influenced by writings of European sociologists, sought to systematize the insights of Europeans and thus establish a more rigorous investigation of their own contemporary urban community (Persons, 1987). Studies of race and ethnicity were at the centre of their interests. 'The rapid influx of immigrants, as well as the increasing expansion of the metropolitan area, had precipitated the emergence of a type of community the understanding of which was critical for grasping the structural transformation that modern civilization was undergoing' (McGahan, 1986:16). Park and his associates, like Durkheim and Toennies, were also concerned with the disintegrating influences of city life and its related problems:

Transportation and communication have affected what I have called the 'mobilization of the individual man'. They have multiplied the opportunities of the individual man for contact and for association with his fellows, but they have made these contacts and associations more transitory and less stable (Park, 1967:40).

Park saw a decline in the neighbourhood as a socially significant unit and the weakening of the family as an important support group. The rise of delinquency and crime, he thought, were a result of the breakdown of social networks and the traditional ethnic community. He also thought that increased freedom of movement in the industrial arena encouraged weaker ties to primary group values. Park therefore encouraged urban empirical research, and as a result many scholars who came out of the Chicago School fanned out into the rest of North America seeking to better understand the many changes taking place (Driedger, 1996). As indicated in Chapter 1, many Chicago sociologists assumed that there would be assimilation, but they were not sure of what these European minorities would assimilate into. The melting pot and Anglo-conformity are two potential outcomes.

Assimilation: The Melting Pot

Weber, Durkheim, and Marx all agreed that the pervasive force of industrialization tends to attract workers and capitalists alike into the economic work arena, where making a living becomes a primary goal. All three agreed that industry was a major force of change, but they proposed different solutions as to what should be done about it. At the same time, the theory of evolution was becoming more popular so there was the tendency to think, like Darwin and Spencer, that mankind was evolving. Liberalism and the Enlightenment, with its stress on freedom, added to the buoyant hope that the goodness of humans would triumph and that Utopia might be close at hand (Kymlicka, 1989).

Industrialization brings us back to concerns with classical materialism, where the focus increasingly is on machines and what they can produce, rather than people and what they need. When the focus is on family and neighbourhood, it helps to promote the culture, religion, and social solidarity of a community. Industrial machines are impersonal means to make a living, which are often set-up away from homes, schools, and churches where they do not disturb quiet human activity. These machines can turn attention and activities toward: 1) individual enterprise, 2) the profit motive, 3) private property, 4) competition, and 5) inheritance, which draw humans away from the social human activity concerns of culture, religion, human interaction and solidarity.

It is not surprising that, for theorists of assimilation, all humans of whatever culture, language, or belief would be drawn into the industrial fray by the promise of better things for the well-being of all. The arrival of immigrants to the shores of America provided the opportunity for a new beginning; it offered new freedoms to experiment and let the human spirit be creative (Halli and Driedger, 1999). The immigrants did not wish to be dominated by a majority group, as many had already been, so they were similar to the Americans who had fought to become independent from the British. Unlike these earlier Americans, however, they were wary of domination by their fellow Americans. Thus, the tenets of free enterprise, individual initiative, competition, private property, and the profit motive fit well into a laissez-faire style of capitalism. According to the melting-pot theory, many immigrants would no longer wish to continue the traditions of the restricted old world, but would opt for the opportunities of the new. Openness to abandoning the restrictive past for future opportunities is common in the melting-pot theory of ethnic change.

Americans often refer to their country as a melting pot. They broke free of British dominance two hundred years ago and created a nation ostensibly dominated by no one group. All groups contributed to the American dream, with its new constitution, multitude of cultures from many

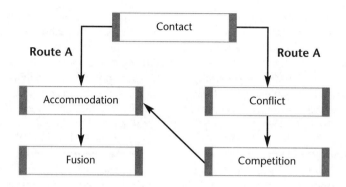

FIGURE 2.1 Park's Assimilation Cycle

parts of the world, and system of free enterprise. Independence and freedom were popular watchwords. It was a new nation, a new culture, a new continent: a pot to which all might contribute. Assimilation theory suggests that immigrant groups will be synthesized into a new group. This evolutionary process results in a melting pot different from any of the groups involved and different from the original melting pot.

A chief advocate of this process was Robert Park. He suggested that immigrants came into contact with the new society and either took the route of least resistance (contact, accommodation, and fusion) or a more circuitous route (contact, conflict, competition, accommodation, and fusion) (Shore, 1987) (see Figure 2.1). Whereas the latter route could take longer and could entail considerable resistance on the part of the immigrant, the end result would be the same—the loss of a distinctive ethnic identity. The new culture and values would emerge.

There were a sufficient number of minorities who did assimilate, as Park predicted, to keep American researchers preoccupied with documenting the progress of their assimilation. For 50 years, these scholars tended to ignore groups that retained a separate identity and to regard their separateness as a relatively insignificant factor in the total pattern of minority-majority relations. The assimilational theory was so influential when combined with the evolutionary thinking of the

day, that it was forgotten that such well-known pluralist studies as Thomas and Znaniecki's *The Polish Peasant in Europe and America* (1918), Louis Wirth's *The Ghetto* (1928), and Harvey Zarbaugh's *The Gold Coast and the Slum* (1929) illustrated considerable resistance to assimilation.

The theory of assimilation was, and is, attractive because it is dynamic. It takes into account the enormous technological change that dominates our North American societies. Furthermore, numerous studies show that many North European groups such as the Dutch, the Scandinavians, and the Germans fairly quickly lose many of their distinctive cultural traits such as ethnic language use. However, in the eyes of some, melting-pot assimilation is too deterministic. That is, as a macro theory it may explain a general process for some groups, but it does not take into account the many dimensions of cultural change. Not all of these forces may be changing in the same direction; the targets of change may be quite different. Nor does it sufficiently take into account the fact that the distinctiveness of all groups may not disappear; Park's cycle does allow for some groups not to follow to the end of fusion, but it implies that industrial momentum will eventually sweep everyone into fusion with the general society. Park and his associates did not focus very much on what was meant by fusion.

Herberg (1955) contends, however, that in America the Protestants, Catholics, and Jews have never 'melted'. Nor have they in Canada. Certainly the French in Quebec are a bulwark against assimilation, whose prophesied synthesis is not happening in Canada. The racial component, well represented in Canada by our aboriginal peoples and in America by blacks, aboriginals, and Asians is not melting very noticeably either. To what extent other ethnic groups such as the French, Chinese, and Italians are melting is the subject of much research, and it is as yet incomplete. Even in the United States where the melting-pot theory is often applied, more and more scholars are having doubts about its application to all ethnic groups (Driedger, 1996; Kallen, 1924; Nagel, 1984; Reitz and Breton, 1994).

Canada's relatively open immigration policy has proved the potential for many peoples to contribute to a melting pot. At the time of Confederation, however, the two founding peoples represented most of the population; their historical influence has been much stronger than any of the other groups that followed. Early British and French influences have tended to dominate early Canadian history and the lives of more recent immigrants. The two charter groups have fought hard not to assimilate either culturally or linguistically; from the beginning, the Canadian melting pot has contained ingredients that don't melt easily.

The synthesis of British, French, Germans, Ukrainians, Italians, Canadian aboriginals, and others into a recognizable national character has been slow. Some scholars think it is this melting process, more than any other, that is needed to develop a spirited Canadian nationalism. The Americans, on the other hand, have stressed assimilation more than the Canadians, and have evolved a stronger feeling of nationalism than Canadians have been able to achieve.

Amalgamation: Conformity to a Dominant Group

A second possibility in the process of minorities losing their traditional identity is joining or amalgamating with a dominant group. In Canada, the British represent the largest group, so we could call this process Anglo-conformity. While industrialization has escalated during the past several centuries, nationalism has greatly influenced North American ethnic development as well. McNeill (1986) shows that nationalism rose in Western Europe between 1750 and 1920, especially in the most successful capitalist countries of Britain and France who were also the most influential European players in the development of Canada and America. The American Revolution culminated in a new nation in 1776, severing colonial ties with Europe and freeing the Americans to follow a melting pot policy. In Canada, however, the French—largely in Acadia and Quebec—and the British, especially after the war of 1759, considered Canada in colonial terms (Breton, 1984). The influence of British nationalism and colonialism was greatly strengthened with the coming of the British Empire Loyalists to Canada.

McNeill (1986) suggests that the triumph of nationalism in Europe introduced the ideal of ethnic homogeneity within a geographic boundary; this rising emphasis on national sovereignty sought to bring about monoethnicity within its boundaries. McNeill sees this as an intrusion into the polyethnicity that we would normally expect in civilized industrialized countries. The British and French, driven by the capitalist need for profits and colonization, greatly influenced North America. They fought many wars in an attempt to gain world dominance over resources. These wars had strong repercussions for Canada, especially in 1759, when the British finally conquered the French in Canada. Later the British and French again sought to gain monoethnic dominance in western Canada, where the British gained strong footholds after the Riel rebellions of 1870 and 1885.

While monoethnic nationalism may be the most efficient way for economic capitalism to flourish with its motives of individual enterprise, competition, and profit, it is often directly contradictory to philosophies of political democracy and Christian religion—also important in Western civilization. Democracy emphasizes universal suffrage and cooperation, not the competition of individuals for profit. Christianity emphasizes brotherhood and sisterhood, human equality, and the welfare of all. While laissez-faire capitalism may allow monoethnic dominance, political and religious values make such dominance unjust.

The emphasis on immigrants amalgamating into a monoethnic culture has influenced Canadian thinking greatly during the past. It is the product of an evolutionary perspective that assumes that ethnic groups are constantly changing from their present minority cultural and structural status to join the majority culture, which in Canada is represented by the British. This theory tends to be deterministic and assumes that the temptation to join the majority will be too much for any minority group to resist. Even if they resist, minorities may still have to live and compete by the rules set up and enforced by the majority. This practice indoctrinates them into the ethos of the majority, and assimilationists predict that minorities will disappear into the dominant group.

There is a great deal of evidence in Canadian history that many British leaders had an Anglo-conformity model in mind when they thought of the aboriginal people, the French, and other immigrants (Breton, 1984). Lord Durham assumed that others would assimilate to a British legal, political, economic, and cultural system (Stanley, 1960). Leaders such as Durham seem to have hoped that somehow even the French would finally amalgamate into the dominant culture although not without conflict and competition. They assumed the desirability of British social institutions and expected all others to learn the English language. For them, the core of nationalism was to remain English while French institutions, language, and history had to take a lesser role (McNeill, 1986). This attitude was also dominant in Western Canada, where the French and British developed their cultures, both having approximately equal numbers in early Manitoba. Soon, however, the languages and schools of other immigrants on the Prairies took second place to the English. Canada did not sever its ties with the British as the Americans did, so

the British colonial influence lasted longer and helped mould Anglo-conformity to a much greater extent than occurred in the United States.

Berry, Kalin, and Taylor's (1977:36–8) national sample shows that 81 per cent of their respondents of British origin identified themselves as Canadian. They also found that 'Canadian' was the most popular response in the most easterly Atlantic Provinces where the population is mainly of British origin. The use of the term *Canadian* varies by subgroups. This suggests that respondents of British origin chose to relabel their loyalties by adopting the 'Canadian' label. As the largest and most powerful group, the British can afford to abandon the 'ethnic' label, hoping that others will join them under a new national label strongly influenced by British history, culture, and language. This is an interesting modification of Anglo-conformity, which nevertheless would favour a new Anglo-conformist Canadian identity. Other groups would be encouraged to join or unite with the British to merge into a single 'Canadian' amalgam structured and shaped by British values.

Modified Assimilation

The two theories of ethnic adjustment discussed so far are essentially ideal types of assimilation in which ethnic groups give up their identity. Weber liked to work with ideal types because they allowed him to delineate and distinguish complexes of social action so that research could proceed in an orderly way. As we all know, however, ideal types rarely exist in real life because social behaviour is usually more difficult to classify in practice than in the ideal. Thus, two modified versions (Modified Assimilation and Modified Pluralism) have been developed by Milton Gordon, in *Assimilation in American Life* (1964), and by Nathan Glazer and Daniel P. Moynihan in *Beyond the Melting Pot* (1963). These versions lean to the assimilationist and pluralist sides respectively, but take numerous modifications into account. These modified versions can be applied very usefully to real ethnic group studies in North America (Driedger, 1996).

Gordon suggests that assimilation is not a single social process, but a number of sub-processes that he classifies under the headings 'cultural' and 'structural'. Cultural assimilation includes the incoming group's acceptance of the modes of dress, language, and other cultural characteristics of the host society. Structural assimilation concerns the degree to which immigrants enter the social institutions of the society (e.g., political leadership) and the degree to which they are accepted into these institutions by the majority. Gordon suggests that assimilation may occur more readily in the economic, political, and educational institutions than in the areas of religion, family, structure, and recreation. As Newman (1973:85) points out, however, 'Gordon contends (that) once structural assimilation is far advanced, all other types of assimilation will naturally follow.'

Gordon's multivariate approach forced scholars out of their unilinear rut. Each of the seven stages or types of assimilation he established, however, tended to be oriented toward either an assimilationist or an amalgamationist target. He saw seven distinctive forms of assimilation for ethnic groups in the process of decline: cultural, structural, marital, identificational, attitudinal, behavioural, and civic (see Table 2.1).

Gordon's major contribution is his complex multilinear, multidimensional view of the assim-ilation process. It has been seen as a considerable improvement on Park's assimilation cycle. Although Gordon was primarily concerned with assimilation as such, and though he did not dwell on pluralism, he did not negate pluralist expressions in religion, the family, and recreation.

Application of the seven assimilation variables to such ethnic groups as blacks, aboriginals, French Canadians, and Scandinavians results in varied patterns that are most interesting. Most blacks in Toronto and Halifax and most blacks in America, for example, have undergone complete cultural assimilation: their former African languages, customs, and religion have been lost. They have not, however, assimilated with respect to the last five variables: intermarriage with whites is limited; they are identifiable racially; there is considerable prejudice and discrimination against them; and they have limited access to civic power (Henry et al., 2000). Aboriginals in northern Canada have hardly assimilated with respect to any of the seven variables, but this situation changes somewhat when they migrate into southern cities (Frideres, 1998).

One group, the Icelanders in Manitoba, has assimilated a great deal. Few Icelandic cultural and ethnic institutions remain; they intermarry freely; they attract little prejudice and discrimination; and some are entering positions of civic influence (Driedger, 1975). Most French

TABLE 2.1 The Seven Assimilation Variables Developed by Gordon

Subprocess or Condition	Type of Assimilation
Change of cultural patterns to those of host society	Cultural or behavioural assimilation
Large-scale entrance into primary group level of cliques, clubs, and institutions of host society	Structural assimilation
Large-scale intermarriage with host society	Marital assimilation
Development of sense of peoplehood based exclusively on host society	Identificational assimilation
Absence of prejudice from host society	Attitudinal assimilation
Absence of discrimination from host society	Behaviour receptional assimilation
Absence of value and power conflict	Civic assimilation

Adapted from *Assimilation in American Life: The Role of Race, Religion and National Origins* by Milton M. Gordon, p. 71. Copyright Oxford University Press, Inc.

Canadians in Quebec, in contrast, have not assimilated according to Gordon's criteria. They retain their language, culture, and French institutions. Most marry within the group. They have even achieved considerable civic power. Gordon's variables are useful, because they show that individuals of some groups assimilate more than others. The degree of variation depends on the ethnic group and its location and varies considerably (Gagnon, 1993; Guindon, 1988). We see that the process is complex, varied, and multilinear; it adds interest to multiethnic comparative research, as Weber advocated.

Modified Pluralism

In contrast to assimilationist thinking, Glazer and Moynihan (1975) distinguish four major events in New York's history that structured a series of ethnic patterns that reflected modified pluralism rather than modified assimilation in that city. In contrast to assimilation where the goal is loss of identity, theories of pluralism focus on retention of separate identities. The next three theories focus on retention of identities. The first, in New York, was the shaping of the Jewish community under the impact of the Nazi persecution of Jews in Europe and the establishment of the state of Israel. The second was a parallel, if less marked, shaping of a Catholic community by the re-emergence of the Catholic school controversy. The third was the migration of southern blacks to New York following World War I and continuing after the fifties. The fourth was the influx of Puerto Ricans following World War II. These migrations introduced the element of race.

Glazer and Moynihan claim that the melting pot did not function in New York. They further claim that, throughout America's history, the various streams of population separated from one another by origin, religion, and outlook seemed always to be on the verge of merging, but that the anticipated co-mingling was always deferred.

Glazer and Moynihan suggest that the blacks are often discriminated against, and that their

assimilation is not tolerated by the majority. The Jews, with their distinct religion, do not wish to assimilate because they are proud of their distinct identity. The Puerto Ricans and Irish Catholics represent combinations of these voluntary and involuntary pluralist variations. Over time they change, but they remain distinct ethnic groups. Modified pluralism takes account of this process of change, as do the assimilationist and amalgamation theories, but it also provides for degrees of pluralism often demonstrated in North American groups such as aboriginals, Italians, French Québécois, Jews, Amish, Mennonites, Muslims, Asiatics, and many others.

This summary focuses on Glazer and Moynihan's theory that, while all groups change, those that are able to shift from traditional cultural identities to new interest foci may maintain their distinctive identities. This formulation recognizes change and maintains that identification can be shifted. It also suggests that some groups may change more than others and implies that the outcome may be a pluralist mixture differing from the Anglo-conformist target. Indeed, Glazer and Moynihan contend that traumatic experiences such as conflict encourage the development of a sense of identity among minorities and may form the basis of a viable Canadian pluralist theory. Although their theory is very general and its dimensions require expansion, it does focus on the dynamics of change that influence the development of group identities.

The French in Quebec are an example of selected change, a form of Glazer and Moynihan's modified pluralism. They are changing from a dominantly rural, religion-oriented population to an increasingly urban, industrial people (Guindon, 1988). Nevertheless, this enormous shift in value orientations does not seem to have affected their determination to survive culturally, religiously, and structurally in North America. This modified pluralism takes account of change, which the assimilationist and amalgamationist theories stress, but it also provides for degrees of pluralism often demonstrated in Canadian groups such as the Japanese, Chinese, Mormons, Mennonites, and many others.

While French Québécois in Quebec rely on linguistic, cultural and institutional completeness for their territorial solidarity, the Jews—who are almost exclusively urban—fortify their identity with a distinctive religion, symbolic means of identification, and strong family ties. Many Jews readily change cultural distinctiveness, but often change to ideological, symbolic, and institutional means of modified identity.

The Ethnic Mosaic:
Multicultural Pluralism

Whereas proponents of the melting pot and Anglo-conformity assume that minorities will assimilate and lose their separate identities, scholars of pluralism and conflict focus on the alternative options of solidarity and identity that are available to minorities (Berry and Laponce, 1994:3–16; Driedger, 1996:25–49). Like Max Weber, advocates of these theories assume that there are alternatives to losing oneself in the industrial arena, and that many individuals and groups have the creativity and resources to fight modern alienation, by maintaining their ethnic *gemeinschaft*. In particular, Durkheim worked at questions of social cohesion and solidarity, which many ethnic scholars have also explored.

Ideal cultural pluralism may represent different ethnic groups that over time maintain their own unique identities. Cultural pluralism is often viewed as an arrangement in which distinct groups live side by side in relatively harmonious coexistence. 'The author of this view of pluralism was a Harvard educated philosopher of Jewish immigrant stock named Horace Kallen', who espoused pluralism for three main reasons (Newman, 1973:67). He argued that there are many kinds of social relationships and identities that can be chosen voluntarily, but that no one may choose his ancestry. Further, each of the minority groups has something of value to contribute to a country, and that the American constitution carried with it an implicit assumption that all people were created equal, even though there might be many distinct differences. Kallen wished to refute the ideas of assimilation and the

melting pot that had gained considerable contemporary influence. Since then numerous sociologists have proposed plural theories of ethnic and religious identity (Dashefsky, 1975a; Mol, 1985). Part III (Chapters 5 through 7) will discuss multiethnic identity and solidarity.

Dashefsky (1975a) developed a fourfold model of ethnic identity that included two sociological perspectives—the sociocultural and interactionist—and two psychological approaches — group dynamicist and psychoanalytic—in the study of ethnic identity. The sociocultural is especially important in the study of recent immigrants, Indian and Inuit aboriginals, northern Europeans on the Prairies, French Québécois in Quebec, and smaller groups like the Hutterites. We devote all of Chapter 5 to the French in Quebec. The symbolic interactionist focus is more useful in exploring the identity of urbanites such as the Jews, Chinese, and Japanese; racial and visible minorities who have come to Canada more recently. Hans Mol (1985) has posited that the role of religion and the process of sacralization are ideological and symbolic interactionist forms of identity.

Whereas the preceding discussion of assimilation tends to emphasize the overwhelming influence of technology and urbanization as the master trend that sweeps away all forms of ethnic differentiation before it, cultural pluralism tends to focus on countervailing forces such as democracy and human justice that presuppose that all people are of equal worth and all should have the freedom to choose their distinct quality of life. Assimilation theories envision the disappearance of immigrant and racial groups; identity theories, in contrast, suggest that there may be greater resistance to assimilation and amalgamation than had formerly been thought. In fact, the trend toward permissive differentiation seems to be set. In North America we have accepted pluralist religious expressions, which were hardly tolerated in Reformation Europe. The same is now true of the political scene, where a diversity of political parties and ideologies exist and are accepted by society. Multiculturalism in Canada is now also recognized federally, albeit ambiguously and not without some resistance.

Conflict: The Dialectic of Incompatibles

Assimilation and amalgamation theories perceive society as changing toward melting-pot or Anglo-conformist goals. They view group conflict as a temporary phenomenon that will improve after minorities have had sufficient time to adjust to the new situation and the new order. Both theories treat social change and conflict as a temporary dislocation in the normal ordered state of a uniform nation-state (Driedger, 1989, 1996). The theories of modified assimilation and modified pluralism allow for a greater measure of inherent conflict in the social system. Gordon's modified assimilation allows for different rates of assimilation that can bring about disjuncture and stress; Glazer and Moynihan's modified pluralism suggests that the minority becomes very much a part of the industrial urban process of change which involves conflict and turmoil as new forms of identity emerge. The counterculture in pluralism becomes a subcultural antithesis to the larger society. Simmel (1955) contended that both conflict and consensus are ever-present in society, and Coser (1956) and Dahrendorf (1959) tended to follow this view. In general, these theorists assume that all social phenomena reflect a combination of opposed tendencies. In Western countries race is certainly a factor. The nature of this conflict varies, however, depending on the group's aspirations.

Theories of ethnic conflict also have many dimensions and components related to change that need to be explored. The conflict focus, although concerned with structure and institutions, emphasizes the processes of ethnic group relations. Since conflict suggests the meeting of people with dissimilar or opposite values and norms, it includes the processes of competition, confrontation, and a dialectic of opposites. Dahrendorf defines social conflict as consisting of 'all relations between sets of individuals that involve an incompatible difference of objectives

with regard to positions, resources or values' (1959:135).

Our discussion of the assimilationist-pluralist range of options suggests that the two opposite ideal poles are seldom if ever present in reality. The majority of activity occurs between these two extremes and shows varying degrees of conformity to the majority or separation into a distinctive identity. In the middle we find considerable conflict between the two tendencies; as a result we have a range of outcomes depending on which pole is stronger and more influential. Examples of the entire range of ethnic identity, or the lack of it, can be found in Canada. In this volume we focus on ethnic identity and solidarity to explore what forms of pluralism and multiculturalism exist in Canada.

The various theories of conflict are too many, and too complex, to discuss here in detail. However, we wish to touch on at least three aspects that are useful in our discussion of ethnic conflict. First, John Jackson (1975) suggests that, contrary to Park's assumption that minorities tend to move through his race relations cycle, some might remain very much in a state of conflict without advancing to competition, accommodation, and eventual fusion. Jackson tried to show in his study of French-English relations in an Ontario community that conflict was a normal and natural outcome of structural processes—of the interplay of power and position, and of boundary maintenance activity. It was not a pathological phenomenon to him. Other examples also suggest that the separatist revolution in Quebec, the aboriginal quest for land rights, and the race relations between whites and visible minorities demonstrate a constant potential for conflict. Examples of such ethnic countercultural conflicts include Hutterite expansion into Alberta farmlands and the province's subsequent restrictive legislation, the conflict of French and other ethnic groups over language rights and education during the Manitoba School question (Clark, 1968), Bill 22 and the conflicts of Italians and recent immigrants with the Quebec government over English education in Montreal, and conflict among blacks, Asians, and those of European ancestry.

A second way is to view conflict as Marx did in *The Communist Manifesto* (1848) in which he saw 'the history of all hitherto existing society as the history of class struggles'. This was an adaptation of the Hegelian dialectic's emphasis on the struggle of opposites; the dialectical movement of conflict between a thesis and an antithesis would result in a form of synthesis. Marx saw the struggle for control over the economic and political institutions of a society as a pervasive conflict; it could involve revolution and the overthrow of existing structures so that those who are powerless might gain greater participation in their destiny. Most ethnic groups in Canada do not aspire to such an extensive power struggle, although the separatist movement is a form of institutional conflict that seeks to gain sovereign control of Quebec's structure and economic, political, and social institutions by a referendum to secede.

Third, Edna Bonacich (1972) has expanded the Marxian argument and has applied it directly to ethnic relations and the 'cultural division of labour' approach. She claims that ethnic solidarity is a derivative of the dual labour-market exploitation that arises when immigrants enter lower-paying jobs that others are reluctant to do and, as a result, have little opportunity for advancement. Hechter (1978) suggests that minorities tend to be at the periphery of the industrial power centre and to be exploited by those in power; thus class distinctions emerge, and polarities for conflict develop. Norbert Wiley (1967) attempts to separate the structural, cultural, and social-psychological dimensions of the social class issues and suggests that minorities who remain within the ethnic subculture will have limited opportunities to achieve socioeconomic mobility (Isajiw, Sev'er, and Driedger, 1993). John Porter (1965:73–103) was also concerned that a preoccupation with ethnic identity would restrict mobility and opportunity. Most of these scholars see ethnic identity in stratification terms and expect that these class and ethnic strata will inevitably be in conflict.

FINDING A CONCEPTUAL MODEL

In discussing the six theories of ethnic change and persistence our focus is on ethnic identities, inequalities, and their varieties of modifications. Let us begin by developing the theories' opposite tendencies on a continuum, and then offer a more complex model using more dimensions and variations as pattern variables to sort and fit it all together. We will use two continua, each with opposite polarities. In this model we will combine a conformity-pluralism continuum with a voluntary-involuntary continuum (Driedger, 1996).

The assimilation and amalgamation theories are represented on the left at the conformity (assimilation) end of the first horizontal continuum, where ethnic groups lose their distinctive identity and become part of a melting pot or conform to a dominant group. The pluralism theory is represented on the right at the opposite end of the continuum, where ethnic groups voluntarily retain their separate identity or are forced to remain separate. Modified assimilation and modified pluralism theories both fall in the middle; the first represents modification of assimilation and the second, modifications of pluralism due to change.

In many respects a continuum with two polarities is simplistic and unidimensional because it does not take into account numerous other dimensions that should be added. Furthermore, it is difficult to include conflict theories unless additional dimensions are added to provide more contrast. Such elaborate patterns can become too rigid, locking us into social structures that do not include change and conflict sufficiently. Nevertheless, we shall use a second vertical voluntary-involuntary continuum, which does illustrate interesting pattern variables when contrasted with the horizontal conformity-identity continuum. The resulting four-cell model is shown in Figure 2.2. Other axes could also be added, but handling two at a time is complex enough, and the model does permit us to include conflict points as a third dimension, making it much more dynamic and interesting.

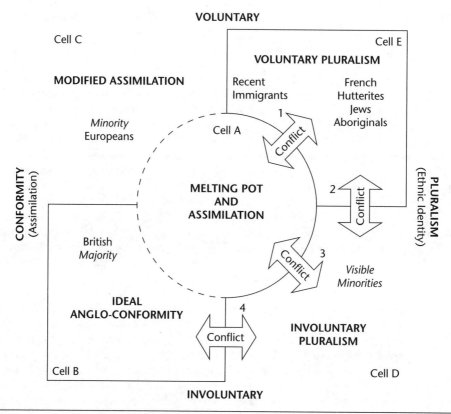

FIGURE 2.2 A Conformity-Pluralist Conceptual Model

Conformity-Pluralist Model

Using the model in Figure 2.2 runs the risk of students hypostasizing the cells and not recognizing that the model contains a number of ideal-typical distinctions. These cells do not represent a substance or concrete reality, which can be embodied or personified. When we place ethnic groups into these cells, we must realize that particular ethnic groups might move from one cell to another over a course of generations, or that some individuals of a particular ethnicity might 'fit' into one cell and others into another, even at the same point in time. These cells become 'helps' or types that often are too rigidly drawn. The student must allow for approximations of 'fit', and considerable movement within the total model in a fairly fluid and flexible way,

without being too rigid about movement from one point to another. With these cautions, let us follow through the construction of the various parts of the model.

We begin with the round Cell A in the middle, which acts as a watering hole to which all the animals must eventually come. If you have been on an African safari, you will have seen that when the elephants are in the hole, all others wait patiently (no matter how thirsty). After the big ones have finished and departed, the rest drink what is left. There is much jostling for position, and many leave, not well watered.

Wsevolod Isajiw (1978) has suggested that the centre of Canadian society is the marketplace where all groups, including the various ethnic groups, must meet to make a living. Everett Hughes (1952) says that indigenous people cannot always supply the whole working force in any industrial society, so immigrants are usually brought in to augment the labour pool. In the industrial process, the many peoples in a country mix with each other. Some, however, will be closer to the centre of power and have more influence than others, while these others will find themselves in layers or concentric zones of less power and influence and farther removed from the centre (Driedger, 1996). This centre of activity we have labelled the melting pot as Cell A, the place where Park's assimilation is most influential (see Figure 2.2). Various ethnic groups try to influence control over the industrial cell while others seek to separate themselves from it. Still others try to enter the industrial fray, but are often repelled or rebuffed. Of the six theories discussed earlier, at least one fits into each part of the model.

We agree with the classical theorists and the assimilationists that the capitalist political economy tends to draw all citizens into the middle of the economic arena because they need to earn a living in the economic fray. This sphere seeks to attract the majority and minorities alike, seeking to plot a new target of assimilation where the outcome will be a melting pot. The many groups will become not British, French, and Chinese, etc., but Canadians: a new entity different from any one of the ethnic contributors. Industry provides the crucible in which the many peoples meet to forge a living.

Thus, industrial changes to both societal structures and values tend to create a free-for-all where new needs for *gemeinschaft* are created. The four cells (B, C, D, E) created by the intersection of our conformity-pluralism and voluntary-involuntary axes show that various means are used by different groups to preserve ethnic values important to them within new structures. Let us think of the four corners of the model (B, C, D, and E) as four ways in which different groups attempt to create new means of dealing with industrial alienation.

As illustrated in Cell B, the largest mostly white (British) or most powerful group will try to shape society by leavening the whole (Cell A) so

that its own language, culture, morality, and institutions are dominant and often may force such conformity upon other minorities. Thus, the line between their goals (Cell B) and national economic and political values (Cell A) tend to be blurred (perforated line between Cells A and B). It is a nationalistic attempt at getting others to conform or assimilate or skew into the dominant form (Cell B of the model). Like all ethnic groups, the dominant majority wants to preserve and perpetuate its own cultural ethos; as the majority, it has the power to influence and sometimes dominate. The French were in such a position in early Acadia, but with their defeat in 1759, the British became both the numerically and politically dominant group in Canada. At the turn of the century, the British represented almost two-thirds of the population of Canada, but by 1995 they had declined to 28 per cent of the total population; they remain the largest group, but not a majority.

In Cell C are located the older, mostly northern European white groups such as the Scandinavians, Dutch, and Germans who have lived in Canada for a number of generations. Most of them have adopted the English language and are now beginning to conform and accommodate themselves voluntarily to an assimilationist goal in the centre (Cell A) where they compete quite well economically. Using Gordon's seven indicators, northern Europeans are losing some of their cultural and structural accommodation to the forces in Cell A. Being Caucasian like the two largest groups, the British and French, they are subject to little prejudice and discrimination, and some are beginning to enter civic positions of power. With some exceptions, these Canadians follow the line of least resistance, as assimilationists would predict. They are modified assimilators because Gordon's seven factors of assimilation are hard at work. Depending on the group, some ethnic features are more in the process of assimilation into Cell A or amalgamation with the British in Cell B than others. Studies show that the Scandinavians in particular are assimilating into Cell A and amalgamating into Cell B quickly (Driedger, 1996; Isajiw, 1981).

Voluntary and Involuntary Pluralism

The minorities in Cells E and D deal with voluntary and involuntary forms of pluralist identity—the focus of this volume (Driedger, 2001). In Part III, we focus on the various dimensions of voluntary ethnic identity and solidarity located in Cell E. In Part IV, dealing with ethnic and racial stratification, we concentrate on social distance, the focus of Cell D.

Whereas Cell C represents intermediary forms achieved by conforming voluntarily to modified assimilation, Cell D is an intermediary process closer to the pluralism pole. In this cell, individuals and groups often remain pluralist involuntarily since they are forced to remain isolated because of race. Many visible minorities like Asians, South Asians, and blacks would like to participate more equally in the centre of the industrialization process but are often prevented from doing so fully because of racial prejudice and discrimination. They are likewise kept in their place by the majority groups of Cell B, as well as by other Caucasian pluralists of Cell E. It is this group that faces the greatest potential for conflict because Canadian and American charters grant them equal rights ideologically, but in real life this is often not the case. Democracy and Christianity also say they should be equal, yet visible minorities often find themselves discriminated against in the marketplace for reasons that are contradictory to these principles of equality. Social and economic reality does not necessarily match national ideals. We will enlarge on these three points of conflict later.

Cell E represents Voluntary Pluralism, in which individuals and groups voluntarily withdraw into their pluralist corner, seeking to remain separate from industrial amalgamation into the national melting pot—and the French of the Québécois 'nation' are the best example. In many ways these people are traditionalists, but their traditionalism takes a number of pluralist forms. We will discuss four distinct forms of pluralist groups: rural French habitants, religious minorities such as Hutterites and Jews,

first-generation immigrants like Italians and Greeks, and non-urban aboriginals.

First, the large French population (25 per cent) highly concentrated in Quebec has always made up a very substantial sociocultural tile in the mosaic; it has not melted, nor has it assimilated into the larger industrial pot (Cell A). The rural French habitants of the nineteenth and early twentieth centuries in Quebec isolated and segregated themselves in rural Catholic parishes away from the industrial fray. One of the reasons that multiculturalism has been established in Canada is because of the preponderance of the French Québécois in Quebec. They were the first European settlers and have from the beginning insisted on another option besides Anglo-conformity. They support Franco-conformity.

Second, religious minorities such as the Hutterites and the Jews are also placed in Cell E. The Hutterites on the Prairies are a rural example of traditional pluralism focused clearly on a separate Protestant religious ideology. Their case is characterized by extensive boundary maintenance and social control in segregated areas. This form of pluralism has lasted for 470 years, since the Protestant Reformation of which the Hutterites are a remnant (Driedger, 1999).

The orthodox Lubavitcher Chassidim Jews in Montreal are an excellent example of urban pluralism (Shaffir, 1993). Jews in general represent a distinct religious tradition different from the large Christian majority in North America. Lubavitcher Chassidim Jews are careful to delineate ritualistic, cultural, and scriptural boundaries to separate them from Gentiles as well as other Jews of less traditional practice. Mennonites especially, have urbanized recently and continue forms of religious Anabaptist renewal as outlined by Driedger (2000a). Religion is a second factor ideologically important to the maintenance of ethnic identity and solidarity in the pluralist Cell E.

Recent first-generation immigrants are a third example of a pluralist group. Portuguese and Greeks have come to urban centres recently. Southern and eastern Europeans such as Italians and Ukrainians with their distinct languages and cultures use cultural residential segregation as a spatial means of boundaried separation in both rural and urban areas. The Ukrainians have the advantages of a separate orthodox religion, which Italians—who are mostly Roman Catholic—do not have. Rural ethnic bloc settlements, especially in Western Canada, are common voluntary segregated examples where the Ukrainians settled in the Aspen Belt, stretching from Manitoba's Inter-Lake region to Edmonton. Rural hinterlands often supply migrants to the city; some of these migrants tend to perpetuate the urban village way of life. An example of this may be seen in the north end of Winnipeg, until recently the stronghold of east European Ukrainians, Poles, and Jews (Driedger and Church, 1974). Kalbach (1990) found historical Jewish and Italian settlement patterns in Toronto and traced how they shifted over time. Balakrishnan and colleagues (1987, 1990, 1992, 1995) have documented such residential segregation in Toronto, Montreal, and Vancouver. Institutional completeness (Breton, 1964; Driedger, 1982a, 1996) is important so that ethnic schools, churches, and associations can enhance identity. The maintenance of a separate language and culture is difficult and unlikely without a sufficiently large ethnic concentration in a given area. Minorities need territory, and they need to control this territory so their offspring can perpetuate ingroup heritage within it. This can best be done in tightly knit communities. Community space thus becomes an arena in which ethnic activities occur and are shared. We have placed recent immigrants in Cell E, but close to Cell B, because some will most likely enter modified forms of assimilation as the generations remain in Canada.

Fourth, rural Indian reserves also demonstrate ethnic territorial segregation. Many aboriginals live in the Canadian northlands, isolated from other Canadians. Some of them are still in a food-gathering economy and wish to retain a sacred way of life, which we will also deal with in Chapter 7. We have placed these aboriginals in Cell E, but near Cell D, because they are to some extent also a visible minority. Rural and reserve Indians, however, usually wish to retain

their distinct ethnic identity by staying close to the land. Increasingly, aboriginals enter southern Canadian cities, and many of these could be placed in Cell D, where their visible distinctiveness keeps them from entering the industrial workplace in Cell A as freely as they would like. Individuals of all of these groups are changing, and as these individuals change, groups also become remoulded and reorganized so they too change, and several generations later may move to a modified, less boundaried form or cell.

Racial and Ethnic Conflict

Lest we think of these cells too rigidly, and tend to draw boundaries too firmly, we need to immediately build into the model change factors, and conflict is one good way of doing this. Industrialization, which influences all of us who are engaged in making a living at the waterhole in Cell A, creates many conflicts. The Jewish working mother has to leave her family home and work behind a computer all day, ruled by machines for hours, before she returns home to continue making a Jewish home, such as teaching the children their prayers and making kosher foods to observe their ethnoreligious rituals.

Our model clearly demonstrates at least four points of conflict (1, 2, 3, and 4). The major point of conflict is between those in Cell E and Cell A; three points of conflict also involve Cell D as visible racial minorities in this cell come into contact with those in Cells A, B, and E.

When ideal pluralists such as the French, Hutterites, Jews, recent immigrants, and aboriginals (Cell E) seek to retain their culture and ethnic institutions, while earning a living in the melting-pot economy (Cell A), there is bound to be a variety of conflict that we have labelled as our first point of stress. Now that the constitution has declared Canada a bilingual country, French language rights are guaranteed. While such rights are easier to maintain in the province of Quebec, where French Québécois are a majority and have control over their provincial government, these language rights raise much conflict elsewhere, where the French represent only a small portion of the population. The Hutterites and Jews seek to retain their distinctive religious traditions in a sea of increased secularization in the larger society. Their youth do not find it easy to identify with their family traditions when many of their peers are different. First-generation immigrants often have severe conflict with the mainstream, and their children are seduced away from their language, culture, and traditions. The aboriginal land claims represent but one point of conflict with the rest of Canada; constitutional guarantees are slow in coming, and untreatied land is increasingly being invaded without legal settlement. There is a dialectic between those in Cell E, who voluntarily wish to retain a separate ethnic identity, and the assimilatory influences of the melting pot in Cell A.

In Cell D, visible minorities such as blacks, Asians, South Asians, and urban aboriginals are in conflict at three different points (2, 3, and 4) (Driedger and Halli, 2000). With some exceptions, these non-Caucasians would likely be in closer contact and integration with those in Cells E, A, and B, but they are often unable to do so because of prejudice and discrimination. We will deal with these conflicts in more depth in Chapters 8 through 12. The voluntary pluralists in Cell E want to retain a separate identity, unlike the visible minorities in Cell D, who often do not, so their goals of relating to the melting pot are very different. These voluntary pluralists are also mainly Caucasians, while most visible minorities are distinguishable by their Mongoloid or Negroid skin colour. Most Jews, Hutterites, French, and recent immigrants want their children to marry their own kind so they can perpetuate their distinctive identities, while many visible minorities do not share this desire. In fact, most of the groups in Cell D want to get rid of such barriers and often see the protectiveness of ideal pluralists as racist. They have different goals; voluntary pluralists don't want to melt, while visible minorities usually do (although there are always exceptions). According to Jackson (1966), these voluntary Cell E pluralists remain in a position of conflict in Park's assimilation cycle and do not proceed toward fusion

and the melting pot because they are committed to distinctive sociocultural and/or religious values incompatible with others.

One of the greatest points of conflict is at point 3, between visible minorities in Cell D and those assimilated visible minorities in Cell A of the melting pot. Most Marxists and neo-Marxists see access to the labour market as the major form of conflict in society in general and see the plight of visible and racial minorities who are unable to compete for jobs in the melting pot as but one version of this class conflict. As we will demonstrate, there is always the potential for racial prejudice and discrimination as visible minorities try to enter the industrial melting pot to earn a living in a market of scarce resources and positions. As Bonacich (1972) suggests, these visible minorities are part of a cultural division of labour; they are in a dual labour market that exploits those who have to take lesser jobs because of their visibility and provides them with less opportunity for advancement. Since blacks are such a large part of the American population, such racial conflicts have been common with them. In Canada, however, visible minorities represent only about 10 per cent of all Canadians, so such conflict has been more dormant. Many recent immigrants, however, are visible minorities; this fact is leading to increased conflict in cities especially. We have placed these visible minorities in Cell D because they are involuntarily kept from assimilating into the melting pot as quickly as many of them would like. They are on the pluralist end of the continuum because of their racial visibility, and others keep them from accommodating.

The fourth point of conflict is between visible minorities in Cell D and the largest, most powerful ethnic group in Cell B, who generally try to persuade others into amalgamating with their British culture, institutions, and values. The conflict between these two cells is clearly a point of class conflict and power. Hechter (1978) suggests that minorities generally are at the periphery of the industrial power centre and tend to be exploited by those in power. Many visible minorities, therefore, may tend to see their relations with the British as a class struggle with the largest, most influential group in power. They see themselves as an exploited minority that finds it hard to enter civic, political, and economic arenas where they can have more influence. Norbert Wiley (1967) suggests that such minorities are forced into ethnic and racial subcultures with limited opportunities to escape the socioeconomic mobility trap. John Porter (1965:73–103) was concerned with similar stratification problems that would limit mobility for some ethnic groups more than others. Racial stereotypes remain with us, making these forms of stratification difficult to combat (Driedger and Halli, 2000; Henry et al., 2000)

The conceptual model we have just discussed is one way of trying to order some of the dimensions into a logical whole so that various relationships can be compared and observed, which structural functionalists often call for. It is not without its limitations but it can generate additional insights that are not so easily apparent when the individual parts remain separate. Such a model has limitations because we can never include all the factors that operate. In this model we dealt with only two axes, leaving out others that also play a part. We do try to include conflict as a third dimension to make it more dynamic. Models can be useful, but they can also become restrictive, and for some they are too static. So again, try not to hypostasize too much, which is especially the case with 'ideal ethnic types'. We turn to them next.

IDEAL ETHNIC TYPES

Traits and features can be wrapped into symbolic characters that can be used as prototypes. Many sociologists have developed individual types that can be fitted into our model, especially into the pluralist and modified pluralist cells to illustrate additional information and insights. Let us discuss three ideal ethnic types to enrich our *Verstehen* or in-depth understanding of some of the more subtle aspects of being ethnic. It is interesting to see how many scholars used this device, and the material of some sociologists

can easily be adapted to create other individual types, even though these sociologists did not do so themselves. Georg Simmel and W.I. Thomas were adept at creating individual types and many sociologists followed their lead.

The Tradition-Directed Ethnic

In *The Lonely Crowd*, David Riesman (1950) developed three types: tradition-directed, inner-directed, and other-directed persons. The tradition-directed person represents the majority of the people from those parts of the world where industrialization has not yet become a major factor. This includes non-urban people in Africa and Asia, where birth and death rates are high and where spatial and social mobility is low. In industrialized countries, it includes many rural people. As these people are introduced to the industrial environment, they move through an inner-directed phase in which they become conscious of their traditional state and begin to become aware of other non-traditional forms of existence. Their rising awareness causes them much inner turmoil and evaluation. Riesman's other-directed third type includes one who has become urbanized, lives in an industrial environment, and is oriented toward secondary others who have entered his social arena and influenced his values (Driedger, 1989). Rural French Québécois, the Hutterites, and northern aboriginals in the pluralist Cell E of our model are clearly tradition-directed types. Orthodox Jews and many Muslim recent rural immigrants are also urban tradition-directed types.

In his discussion of the tradition-directed person or society, Riesman (1950:26–8) describes it as a type of social order which is relatively unchanging: 'The conformity of the individual tends to be dictated to a very large degree by power relations among the various age and sex groups, the class, castes, professions and so forth, relations which have endured for centuries and are modified but slightly, if at all, by successive generations.' The ingroup culture controls behaviour minutely: there is intensive socialization and a careful and fairly rigid etiquette.

Little energy is directed toward finding new solutions for age-old problems or toward developing new agricultural techniques or the like. Usually the tradition-directed ethnic is found in a rural, agriculture, or food-gathering society, although these values are also brought to the city by ethnic villagers (Gans, 1962). The tradition-directed society is in many ways similar to Redfield's (1953) folk society and Toennies's (1957) *gemeinschaft* community.

Perhaps the best example of the tradition-directed ethnic in Canada is the Quebec rural habitant whose ancestors lived in the area for four hundred years. This person faces limited geographical mobility, a traditional French culture and language that has not changed greatly, a conservative Roman Catholic religion, slowly changing agricultural methods, and a general orientation to the local values of the community (Miner, 1939). Although change takes place slowly, it is at a pace that can be integrated fairly readily into the traditional lifestyle.

Numerous other tradition-directed ethnic communities in Canada include the Hutterites on the Prairies (Driedger, 1997; Hofer, 1988; Hostetler, 1974); the northern food-gathering Inuit and Indians (Dickason, 1992); and numerous rural bloc settlements of the Ukrainians, French, Mennonites, Doukhobors, and others. These communities have not yet been greatly influenced by industrial, urban technological change; instead the changes have been accepted into a context of traditional values that have integrated the new trends into stable, slowly changing structures.

Herbert Gans (1962) shows how some tradition-directed persons migrated to the city and transplanted their values, culture, and institutions by forming urban ethnic villages. Often these enclaves show their origins through names like 'Little Sicily' or 'Little Italy'. Such tradition-directed urbanites may be recent immigrants who came to Toronto, for instance, from rural areas such as those of Italy, Greece, Turkey, or Portugal.

The tradition-directed ethnic type, as Riesman suggests, is oriented to traditional ethnic and cultural values; he is reluctant to change, and his major reference group is his traditional ethnic heritage. He is located most often in isolated and rural areas, but may also reside in the city as an ethnic villager. The tradition-directed type is clearly located in the pluralist Cell E of our model.

The Marginal

Park's (1950:348) ideal marginal person is typical of many people in the involuntary modified pluralist Cell D. While teaching in Chicago in the 1920s, Park observed the migration of blacks from the rural American tenant farms of the South into northern cities. This change of residence and the concomitant breaking of home ties with traditional rural values and norms resulted in great cultural upheavals that led to change and sometimes to disorganization and conflict. 'It is in the cities,' he writes, 'that the old clan and kinship groups are broken up and replaced by social organizations based on national interests and predilections' (Park, 1950:353):

> There are no doubt periods of transition and crises in the lives of most of us that are comparable with those the immigrant experiences when he leaves home to seek his fortune in a strange country. But in the case of the marginal person the period of crises and marginality tends to become a permanent personality characteristic. Ordinarily the marginal person is a mixed blood, like the Mulatto in the United States or the Eurasian in Asia, but that is apparently because persons of mixed blood live in two worlds, in both of which they are more or less a stranger (Park, 1950:356–7).

> It is the mind of the man that the moral turmoil which new cultural contacts occasion, manifests itself in the most obvious forms. It is in the mind of the marginal man 'where the changes and fusions of culture are going on' that we can best study the processes of civilization and of progress (Park, 1950:356).

In his earlier essay, 'Human Migration and the Marginal Man' (1928), Park thinks of the marginal person as a racial or cultural hybrid: one who lives in two worlds, in both of which he is more or less a stranger; one who aspires to, but is excluded from, full membership in a new group. The marginal person is between two cultures, and not fully a part of either. 'Park's excluded marginal man was depicted as suffering from spiritual instability, intensified self-consciousness, restlessness, and in a state of malaise' (Levine, Carter, and Gorman, 1976:830). He thought of him as a person who could not cope in the new situation, a potential deviant who might look for outlets of expression in unacceptable ways. This type grew largely out of Park's concern with blacks in the rural American south as well as the urban north, especially Chicago.

Canada is now in the midst of an enormous influx of migrants who are bringing tremendous changes to cities like Toronto. As Asians and West and East Indians of diverse races, cultures, and religion enter, there is much potential for conflict and marginality. The dynamics within Cell D add to marginalization; Isajiw (1978) and Hechter (1978) consign many racial minorities to the periphery of industrial power and opportunities. Because of their visibility and race, many of these minorities find it difficult to compete for jobs in the centre (Cell A), which again places them near the margins (Driedger, 1989). The stratification system clearly places the British at the top of the order, and visible minorities tend to fall toward the bottom.

The Broker or Middleman

Having established clear ethnic types in the two pluralist and modified pluralist cells of our model, we can find changed types who emerge out of these two cells in contact with the industrial melting pot in Cell A.

A broker or middleman is one who enters the industrial fray in Cell A from Cell E. The Jews are the best example of North America's middlemen. Pierre van den Berghe claims that every country has its middlemen: 'Turkey has Armenians and Greeks; West Africa has Lebanese; East Africa has Indians and Pakistanis; Egypt has Copts; Indonesia, the Philippines, Malaysia, Vietnam and Thailand have the Chinese' (van den Berghe, 1981: 137). These are minorities who compete well economically and therefore also are fairly well-to-do socioeconomically. When they compete in the melting pot economically, they seem to be able to separate their economic and social lives, and retain their separate ethnic identity.

Van den Berghe (1981:138) suggests that there is a cluster of characteristics of middlemen minorities (MM) that are remarkably uniform from society to society. He discusses the ideal type in three categories: the characteristics of these groups themselves, the nature of the larger society in which they live, and the particular economic niche they fill. According to van den Berghe, MMs arise from voluntary immigrants who enter a country without having been enslaved previously, but who are often propelled by difficult economic or political situations in their previous homeland to pursue brighter economic prospects in the country of destination. MMs usually maintain strong extended families, perpetuate endogamy, and try to perpetuate their own cultural, institutional, and spatial identity so that they acculturate more slowly than most other groups.

Van den Berghe (1981:138) classified MMs as an urban petty bourgeoisie social class, better off than the majority of the population but often far from wealthy. This better-than-average socioeconomic status often provides them with many advantages in competition with their neighbours. MMs often hold ethnic values such as thrift, frugality, lack of ostentation, and postponement of gratification. Jews, Chinese, Japanese, East Indians, and Mennonites come readily to mind, and most of these can be recognized by their distinctive religion or visibility.

Van den Berghe (1981:139) makes it clear that the host societies in which MMs survive are often complex stratified agrarian societies with mercantile capitalist economics. Existing and potential markets, trade, and supporting agencies provide opportunities for exchange and expansion for those who have the skills and drive to exploit them. The special characteristics of MMs are usually visibly successful; they tend also to become the targets of discrimination when economic times are difficult.

Georg Simmel's 'the stranger' is similar to the middleman. The concept of 'the stranger' unifies the two characteristics of fixity and transience (Simmel, 1950:402). Simmel thought that the stranger could retain a separate identity by controlling his behaviour with others, often by being physically near them to perform economic functions, for example, but distant with respect to their values. On the other hand, the stranger could often be far away from his reference ingroup when performing his duties in urban society, but could still retain a symbolic feeling of nearness and belonging to his ingroup.

Simmel's stranger is a rich concept because it raises major questions such as how can a person retain a 'ground' of identification, as Lewin (1948) would put it, within his own social psychological world and at the same time relate securely to others. We would expect that when the stranger or middleman enters the strange environment of others, he is secure only if he is grounded in a reference group or if he is socially and psychologically motivated by the norms and networks of such a group. This raises many related questions; what must be the nature of such a reference group; how often and how much must an individual contact the reference group to sustain his/her separate identity; what must be the quality of such sustenance; and can an individual make only occasional forays into the strange world on business or can he work outside his group consistently, with occasional refresher periods with his own reference group through telephone, mail, and modern communication networks? How important is spatial proximity for ongoing ties, or can *gemeinschaft* networks be maintained through modern communication networks?

It must be remembered, of course, that these three images of the ethnic individual are all ideal types; as Max Weber (1946) pointed out, the degree to which they are reflected in any society may be partial and never complete. The task then is to examine Canadian society to find which of these ideal types may be most applicable. Indeed, depending on which ethnic group we examine, it may well be that each of the ideal types is applicable to some of the groups within Canada. Our analysis suggests that the rural Québécois habitant and the prairie Hutterite are represented best by the tradition-directed ethnic type; on the other hand, the urban Jew in Montreal and Toronto seems to be typical of the middleman or stranger type. Visible minorities can often be seen as marginals when they find it more difficult to compete in the industrial marketplace where status and prestige are important to finding acceptance and jobs.

We have discussed functional structures and conflicts that occur. Recently some scholars contend that postmodern changes need to be dealt with more, which is a very different emphasis. Postmodernists see life in a much more fluid way, and are often impatient with being boxed into unnecessary structures and overly focused goals, which we turn to next.

POSTMODERN CALLS FOR DIVERSITY

Vaclav Havel, the playwright and president of the Czech Republic, gave a speech in Independence Hall in Philadelphia in 1994 titled 'The Need for Transcendence in the Postmodern World', which is on the Internet (Driedger, 2000b). He begins by saying, '[I]f the modern age began with the discovery of America, it also ended in America.' The sixteenth century of the development of technology that led to land discoveries and the printing press, spawned new land discoveries, the reformation, and the beginnings of capitalism that helped launch the beginning of the modern age. Havel continues:

The modern age has ended . . . we are going through a transitional period, when it seems that something is on the way out and something else is painfully being born. It is as if something were crumbling, decaying, and exhausting itself, while something else, still indistinct, were arising from the rubble.

. . .

The distinguishing features of such transitional periods are a mixing and blending of cultures and a plurality or parallelism of intellectual and spiritual worlds. These are periods when all consistent value systems collapse, when cultures distant in time and space are discovered or rediscovered. They are periods when there is a tendency to quote, to imitate, and to amplify, rather than to state with authority or integrate. New meaning is gradually born from the encounter, or the intersection, of many different elements. Today this state of mind or of the human world is called postmodernism. For me, a symbol of that state is a Bedouin mounted on a camel, and clad in traditional robes under which he is wearing jeans, with a transistor radio in his hands and an ad for Coca-Cola on the camel's back (Havel, 1994).

We seem to be well into a new wave, a new revolution, illustrated by a dozen review essays of debates on postmodern experiments, published in the 1996 journal of *Contemporary Sociology* (Driedger, 2000b). Sociologists cover the entire range, from those who think postmodernism is only a blip that will soon fade like ethnomethodology, and others who think it is a new major revolution spawned by the computer, similar to that of the sixteenth century land discoveries, reformation and beginnings of capitalism, which followed the discovery of the printing press. Lawrence Cahoone's (1996) 700-page anthology of 42 contributors is a good attempt at going back to premodern times, tracing the rise of modernization, into the present postmodern era. Thus, we could think of all these changes as premodern, modern, and postmodern. Cahoone (1996) organizes his *From Modernism to Postmodernism* edited volume by focusing on modern civilization and its critics, which deals with many philosophers and early

sociologists who tried to sort premodern, modern, and postmodern changes.

Futurists Alvin and Heidi Toffler (1995) have in their many books sketched the super struggle that is happening in the 1990s. 'A new civilization is emerging in our lives, and the blind everywhere are trying to suppress it' (Toffler and Toffler, 1995:19). The first wave of change—the agricultural revolution—took thousands of years, beginning some 10,000 years ago. The second wave came with the Industrial Revolution, which occurred during the second half of the past millennium. The third wave—the information revolution—arrived after World War II, accelerating enormous change in a few decades.

Marshall McLuhan claimed that it was Gutenberg's invention of the printing press in the late 1400s, where print technology modified our form of perception, shifting emphasis from the ear to the eye, with significant consequences for individuals and cultures. Soon after the invention of the printing press, a series of revolutions occurred in the early sixteenth century, with the Protestant Reformation, the Peasant Revolt, European discoveries of new continents, and what Max Weber called the Spirit of Capitalism.

The electronic new third-wave information era first crept upon us via the invention of the telegraph, telephone, radio, television, and computers; it blossomed forth at the end of the twentieth millennium in fax, email, the Internet, and more technology. The complexity of the new system requires more and more information exchange among its units—companies, government agencies, hospitals, associations, institutions, even individuals. This creates a ravenous need for computers, digital telecommunications networks, and media (Toffler and Toffler, 1995:32). Let us examine some of the themes.

Challenging the Enlightenment and Reason

The single most significant figure in these developments was Friedrich Nietzche (1844–1900). He announced that nihilism, where traditional beliefs and values are unfounded and that existence is senseless and useless, was inevitable. He denied that there was objective ground for truth and moral values, and thought that conditions in society were so bad that destruction was desirable. Nietzsche devoted his life to exposing the hollowness of Enlightenment hopes, starting a debate on the lack of reality, or a multiplicity of realities, or an anchorless sense of reality (Lyon, 1994:7). His slogan 'the death of God' meant that we can no longer be sure of the Enlightenment; he claimed that humanism found itself in crisis precisely because it replaces God with humanity at the centre of the universe. He saw Western civilization as being in a twilight stage, but he worked at opportunities for reconstruction.

Uprootedness from tradition, ties with the family, kin, and neighbourhood—torn by lack of conventional regulation and new mobility— were major concerns of Emile Durkheim. They resulted in a sense of uncertainty and loss of direction, leaving individuals on their own. He labelled it normlessness or *anomie*. Max Weber was perhaps the most pessimistic about technological rationality, which was focused on utilitarian ends where a sense of ultimate purposes of action would evaporate. Technology that was supposed to free humans could enslave them and hasten the inhumane. Weber (1958) saw bureaucratic technology potentially as an 'iron cage', from which humanity would find it difficult to extricate itself.

Skeptics of Linearity and Science

In his speech at the centennial celebrations of the University of Chicago, Andrew Abbott (1997:1149–82) is critical of the way scientific sociology is going, and he calls for a return to earlier 'Chicago School' preoccupations with time and space. Abbott (1997:1161) suggests that 'the Chicago School made a decisive advance by joining the scientific and the surveying traditions via the central idea of contextuality'. He sees the decline of the early Chicago School research of multiplicity in varied contexts, with the rise of monies for opinion polling

and market research. Sociology followed individual preferences rather than more complex search for why events were happening. The image of probable causality was borrowed from the physical sciences so that 'by the 1970s many sociologists imagined the social world as a kind of general linear reality'. Today, the variables paradigm is old and tired, exhausted because it has not renewed itself. It has lost its excitement where the fun is over, mostly filling in the details. 'Games in networks' seems to hold some hope, while the postmodern scholars are inviting us to leave our iron cages of the variables paradigm, getting us out of our linear rut, in search of new life.

Critique of the Metanarrative

As if challenges to enlightened reason and the hopes of science were not enough, postmodernists also attack linear metanarrative thinking, well engrained in Western thought as history— a storylike moving toward goals, hopes, destiny. Jean-Francois Lyotard (1926–) published his treatise on postmodernism as 'incredulity regarding metanarratives, grand stories about the world and the place of inquiry in it' (Cahoone, 1996:481). What is required is unanimity between rational minds, also part of building enlightenment with the use of metanarratives. Lyotard suggests this process lacks credibility because science attributes 'progress' to itself, but it in turn presupposes it. Borrowing from Wittenstein, Lyotard sees this as 'language games', which are based on attempts at legitimation. Lyotard, however, suggests that the notions of justification, system, proof, and unity of science no longer require metanarratives because they cannot be justified anyway. Science plays its own language game; it is incapable of legitimating its own game, nor is it able to delegitimize the other language games.

Thus, anthropologists are increasingly aware of the importance of foundational myths in that they are more than stories or primitive cultures, but they embody the central core of a culture's values and beliefs and are in that sense fundamentally religious (Grenz, 1996:44). Modern thinkers claim to have replaced myths with rational postulates, but postmodern thinkers assert that the Enlightenment project is itself dependent on an appeal to narrative, a meta-narrative that has over many years gained enormous credence in the modern Western world, but is increasingly faced with problems all around that it too cannot solve. Post-moderns have given up on appealing to a central legitimating myth, because all myths in the end have become tired, including the grand narrative of science, the Enlightenment, and political ideologies. The fall of Marxism in Eastern Europe is the most recent example of the delegitimized metanarrative.

Poststructuralists and Deconstruction

As alternatives to metanarratives and linear thinking, postmodernists like Derrida take us back to smaller units, inviting us to examine the language we use to reconstruct reality.

Algerian-born French philosopher Jacques Derrida (1930–) is one of the two most famous instigators of what is called postmodernism in contemporary philosophy (the other being Foucault) (Cahoone, 1996:336). Derrida is a poststructuralist, and has a difficult writing style. His *The End of the Book and the Beginning of Writing* seemed to have its ideas in reverse (Derrida, 1974). Is it not writing first, and then a product—the book? That of course is the point! Derrida focuses not on the product, the structure, but the process of putting words together, the reflection on their combinations, the managing of context. Language is the problem, and what does it mean? Thus, writing is a 'game' that we enter into, an adventure, a moving thought process that leads into new signs not seen in the same way before. Books are only end products of such processes, which have been stored in libraries as objects of knowledge. Writing, on the other hand, is a creative process that has much more potential for action, movement, thought, reflection, consciousness, experience, effectivity, beyond language itself.

'Derrida's primary goal is to divest us of logocentrism by showing the impossibility of drawing a clear line between reality and our linguistic representations' (Grenz, 1996:148). Especially with respect to written language texts, he wants to wean us from too quickly assuming that we can discover the meaning of the text, because he thinks the Western philosophical tradition is hopelessly logocentric or objectivistic, fixed on an ultimate grounding. 'Derrida interpreted the meaning of signifiers—words and sounds—as in a state of flux and contestation . . . an act of power, the capacity of a social group to impose its will on others by freezing linguistic and cultural meanings' (Seidman, 1994:202). The first term in the dualities (good and evil) were considered superior, and Derrida exerted his energies toward undermining the hierarchical dualities in Western culture (strong and weak; tall and short).

Celebrating Diversity, Pluralism, Difference

While Derrida wants us to examine how language locks us into power systems, he also extends this to cultural differences, claiming that Western thought has again put us into national and cultural 'iron cages' as Weber would put it. Difference, diversity, and cultural pluralism are all around us, which many, now that the world is becoming a global village, are becoming aware of. Isajiw (1999) actually titles his book *Understanding Diversity*. David Hall (1991) makes some useful comparisons between China, which draws heavily from its classical premodern past, and the modern West, which left too much of its past. While the modern West concentrates on identity, being, and permanence, the Chinese find it easier to think difference, change, and becoming than do most of us (Hall, 1991:60). Hall claims that Confucianism and Taoism share the desire to find a means of thinking difference, which is more postmodern than Western thought.

Chicago historian William McNeill (1986:4, 6, 7) addressed scholars at the University of Toronto saying that 'polyethnicity is normal in

civilized societies, whereas the ideal of one ethnically unitary state was exceptional in theory
and rarely approached in practice'. Marginality
and pluralism were and are the norm of civilized
existence. He claims that 'the idea that a government rightfully should rule only over citizens
of a single ethnos took root haltingly in western
Europe, beginning in the late middle ages: it got
into full gear and became fully conscious in the
late eighteenth century and flourished vigorously
until about 1920.'

Joane Nagel (1984) sounds a similar theme,
pointing out the modern ethnic revolution in
many parts of the world with its 'secession,
organization, devolution and genocide representing the many faces of ethnicity'. Nagel
(1984:418) sees 'the pervasive presence of ethnicity underlying such political issues as East-
West relations, North-South inequalities, human
rights abuses, and short- and long-term political stability'. We agree with McNeill and Nagel
that our societies have always been multiethnic,
that the drive of North Europeans for monoethnicity does not bode well in a global village of
the future, and that we now concentrate on ethnic pluralism (Driedger, 1996).

SUMMARY

In this chapter we have addressed the extent to
which ethnic groups persist and maintain their
solidarity, and the changes that occur in the
process of industrialization. We discussed six
theories of change, developed a conceptual
model seeking to integrate some of the ideas,
and dealt with postmodernism, which is asking
new questions.

Proponents of two of the six theories of
change (assimilation and amalgamation) assume
that the industrial magnet is irresistible, requir-
ing minorities either to assimilate with others
into a melting pot, or to amalgamate into Anglo-
conformity. Proponents of two other theories
(pluralism and conflict), however, propose that
minorities can retain their identity through a

variety of traditional and ideological means to
build a pluralist society in which they remain in
conflict either voluntarily or involuntarily.
Scholars of two other theories claim that there
are modified means of survival between the
assimilationist and pluralist poles. Cultural and
structural dimensions do not change at the same
pace, nor do the various groups hold to or aspire
to the same ends and goals. As a result, a variety
of differentiations must be considered.

To illustrate the complexity of the processes
and the diversity of factors operating, we
showed what could be done when just the two
conformity-pluralism and voluntary-involuntary axes were plotted together in one diagram.
Five cells were created, each representing one
of five theories discussed; conflict theory was
also accommodated at the boundaries of each.
Furthermore, we found that ethnic groups
could be placed into each of the cells to
illustrate that Canadian ethnic groups fit all the
theories and cells.

Recently, the computer in the twentieth century has launched the electronic wave of postmodern fax, email, and the Internet. Opinion
regarding the postmodern revolution is deeply
divided. Some say it is only a blip that will soon
go away, others are threatened and are determined to fight it, while many of us recognize that
new times have come and we are trying to
understand what it is all about. Postmodernists
challenge our preoccupation with reason and
have given up on the Enlightenment. More and
more skeptics are wondering whether science
has caged us into the false hope of a linear line
to progress. The metanarratives of evolution,
science, technology, progress, when balanced
with evidence of more crime, poverty, family
violence, also cloud our enthusiasm for an age of
machines. Poststructuralists call for deconstruction and the need to celebrate difference, diversity, and pluralism. In this book, we will first
focus on structural-functional concerns for solidarity and then we explore diversity, with which
postmoderns are preoccupied.

HIGHLIGHT 2.1 CHANGING VISIONS IN ETHNIC RELATIONS

The study of ethnic and race relations in Canada evolved into three major visions and debates after World War II. In the pre-seventies the British and French charter peoples assumed monolingual/monocultural states, and expected that others would assimilate and amalgamate losing their separate identities. Beginning in the 1970s, this was expanded to official bilingual and multicultural visions. By the 1980s, ethnic and demographic diversity had expanded to include debates of equal rights for all, without prejudice or discrimination. National surveys of peoples, search for identities, development of supports such as organizations, journals, conferences, publications, textbooks, schools, and new measures to ensure equality for all needed study and action.

Sociology in Canada before 1970 focused on the two European founding peoples, who were dominant, and Porter's classic 'Vertical Mosaic' centred around the power of the British and French charter groups. Other minorities were seen as entrance groups, and latecomers to the system. Two British and French "nations" within the bosom of one country created conflict, when the rural French in Quebec woke up, and wanted more of the industrial urban dream. A Bilingualism and Biculturalism Commission in the 1960s began much study, research and exploration, where all soon learned that sharing of influence and power needed to be spelled out in official bilingualism. In the process they discovered 'other groups' which had grown to one third of the population, who also aspired to identities which needed to be included.

Trudeau's declaration of Canada as bilingual and multicultural, resulted in an explosion of multicultural research, expanding the ethnic tent especially to other white Europeans. Bilingualism officially expanded national language use to both English and French, new immigration laws opened Canada more widely to non-European immigrants, literature and publications were developed, many national research surveys were launched, ethnic identity research escalated, organizations were organized to support diversity, so that multiculturalism was celebrated as a new vision, expanding the ethnic tent to all.

While in the seventies, white European heritage scholars studied their own ethnic identities and solidarity, by the eighties this shifted to racial 'visible minorities', whose population had doubled, and was about to double again in 2020. Research and publication on aboriginals, race, rights and freedoms became another major area of research, which focused on individual, rather than on collective group rights. The basic assimilation research by Park, and group reorganization research by Thomas in Chicago, and the first Dawson and Hughes contributions on solidarity and assimilation in Canada, are still two major areas of ethnic and racial research in 2001. Ethnic scholars are now working on all three (charter rights, multiculturalism, human rights) fronts, and it will be interesting to see what new debate might emerge in the first decade of 2000.

Two collections of writings, *Ethnicity and Culture in Canada*, edited by John Berry and J.A. Laponce (1994), and the *Encyclopedia of Canada's Peoples*, edited by P.R. Magocsi (1999), are good examples of how far multicultural research in Canada has come. Ethnicity is likely to be to the twenty-first century what class was to the twentieth. It was assumed that ethnicity would be weakened by industrialization, but globalization has weakened the nation-state, the poor in the overpopulated South are increasingly migrating North, continuing the need for "meaningful" communities in urban countries, mixing within borders different races, religions, languages and customs (Berry and Laponce, 1994). Clash of cultures create new problems where everyone is ethnic in multiethnic settings. 'An on-line search of the computerized UBC card catalogue indicates that out of 398 books entered since 1978 with either "multiethnic" or "multicultural" in their titles, multicultural accounted for 90 percent of the total' (Berry and Laponce, 1994). This 'Third Force' is largest and growing, where 'mono' has changed to 'bi', and all are heading toward 'multi'. The twins of diversity and conflict will be exciting research in the next century, as the hundreds of entries in the *Encyclopedia of Canada's Peoples* well illustrate (Magocsi, 1999).

SOURCE: Leo Driedger, *Canadian Journal of Sociology* 26 (2001). Reprinted with permission of Canadian Journal of Sociology.

CRITICAL THINKING QUESTIONS

1. What are the basic differences between the ethnic assimilation and multicultural pluralism perspectives?

2. Why does Driedger place assimilation and pluralism at opposite ends, and then fill in modified types? What are the basic differences in the five types? Define and discuss.

3. Identify Milton Gordon's seven types of modified assimilation and discuss.

4. What is the difference between modified assimilation and modified pluralism? How useful are these two types? Is it important to differentiate these two processes? Why?

5. Discuss the role of conflict in ethnic change. What conceptual sense can you make of these many diverse ways of looking at subgroups in a larger society?

6. Present the basic parts of Driedger's conformity-pluralist conceptual model. Show that you understand the complexity of it. Discuss.

7. What do we mean by postmodernism? What are some basic characteristics? Is this a useful way of dealing with change?

SUGGESTED READINGS

Anderson, Alan B., and James Frideres, *Ethnicity in Canada: Theoretical Perspectives* (Toronto: Butterworths, 1981). This is a first attempt at integrating theoretical perspectives on ethnic identification, persistence, change, and policies in Canada.

Cahoone, Lawrence (ed.), *From Modernism to Postmodernism: An Anthology* (Oxford: Blackwell, 1996). Forty-two contributors discuss the premodern, modern, to postmodern range of changes that are taking place, so the reader can gain some perspective on what is happening.

Kymlicka, Will, *Finding Our Way: Rethinking Ethnocultural Relations in Canada* (Toronto: Oxford University Press, 1998). Kymlicka takes a look at the merits of multiculturalism, the limits of tolerance, and crossroads in race relations.

Persons, Stow, *Ethnic Studies at Chicago, 1905–45* (Urbana: University of Illinois Press, 1987). Persons presents a comprehensive look at the development and accomplishments of social scientists at the University of Chicago, before Canadian scholars studied such questions.

PART II

Providing an Empirical Context

Having spent considerable time working on conceptual and theoretical issues in Part I, it is time to provide more concrete empirical data, to give the reader hard numbers on what kinds of people we are talking about. Demography is a way of sorting human populations, and it usually is helpful to trace population growth historically. In Chapter 3, we begin with immigration, tracing a hundred years of selection of immigrants, where they came from, how these sources have changed over time, and what the current Canadian population looks like. How many are foreign-born, rural, or urban? We end with demographic ethnic types such as the aboriginals, charter Europeans, other Europeans who came, and end with discussing more recent visible Third World minorities.

In Chapter 4 we learn that these immigrants, using linguistic and cultural criteria, have formed a variety of multicultural regions over time. Canada is a country of ethnic regions. The aboriginals are strong in the Northlands, the French dominate in Quebec, Atlantic Canada is mostly anglophone and anglocultural, and there is a bilingual French and English belt in eastern Canada. Ontario is anglophone and multicultural, and the West is mostly multicultural. This macro demographic and ecological examination of all of Canada reveals that we are indeed a country of many languages and cultures, working together.

A Demographic History

In Part II we present general empirical evidence of the diversity of the Canadian population. We have the opportunity to use more than one hundred years of census data, the best general longitudinal comparable statistics available. Our plan is first to present a demographic history of the many peoples who entered Canada, tracing immigration patterns over time. We present factors that influenced ethnic groups in Chapter 3. In Chapter 4 we explore the various regions of Canada, showing that linguistic and cultural patterns vary considerably. Canada is made up of many ethnic regions, forming a multiethnic Canadian mosaic.

IMMIGRATION AND DEMOGRAPHY

It is important to trace the components, trends, selection, and origin of Canada's immigrants over time. We can then explore rural-urban, and demographic types such as aboriginals, charter Europeans, and other immigrant and racial groups.

Births have been the most important population growth factor shaping Canadian demography. In Figure 3.1 we show the indicators of population increase through natural increase (births minus deaths) and net migration (immigration minus emigration) between 1871 and 2001. We expect natural increase to rise with some modifications, such as a dip downward during the Depression of the 1930s, when eco-

nomic and social hardships resulted in fewer births. Figure 3.1 shows the baby boom and a sharp rise in births after World War II. The birthrate has turned downward since the 1970s, with birthrates decreasing dramatically so that the natural population increase is not as great as in the past (Grindstaff and Trovato, 1994; Halli and Driedger, 1999; Krotki and Reid, 1994; McVey and Kalbach, 1995; Statistics Canada, 2001).

The migration factor is considerably less predictable than natural increase, but it is important to ethnic population growth. Figure 3.1 shows two periods of net emigration before the turn of the century; more people left Canada, especially for the United States, than entered Canada through immigration. The second brief net emigration period occurred in the 1930s, which, together with a decline in birthrates, brought a sharp dip in the total population growth pattern during the economic depression.

There were also two peak immigration growth periods in 1901–11 and 1951–61, when immigrants into Canada affected total population growth substantially. The second growth period during the 1950s occurred during the baby boom, so that net immigration and natural increase combined to escalate growth during a very dynamic period of economic expansion and ensuing, considerable social change. In Figure 3.2 we present the extent of immigrants arrivals in more detail.

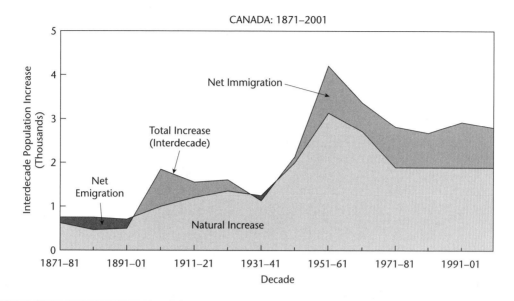

FIGURE 3.1 Components of Population Change, 1871–2001

SOURCES: Dept. of Employment and Immigration. Immigration, 1984 (Ottawa: Minister of Supply and Services Canada); Warren E. Kalbach, 'Growth and Distribution of Canada's Ethnic Populations, 1971–1981', in Leo Driedger (ed.), *Ethnic Canada* (Toronto: Copp Clark Pitman, 1987), p. 90; *Quarterly Demographic Statistics*, Vol. 6, No. 4. (Ottawa: Statistics Canada, 1992); *Canada Year Book 2001* (Ottawa: Statistics Canada, 2001).

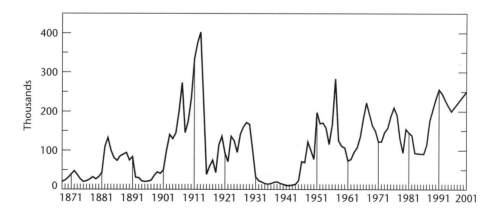

FIGURE 3.2 Number of Immigrant Arrivals, Canada, 1867–2001

SOURCES: Canada Censuses, Department of Manpower and Immigration Annual Reports. *The Effect of Immigration on Population* (Ottawa: Information Canada, 1974), p. 6; Jane Badets and Tina Chui, *Canada's Changing Immigrant Population*, Catalogue 96–311E (Ottawa: Statistics Canada, 1994), p. 6; Citizenship and Immigration Canada, *Immigration Statistics 1992*, Catalogue MP22–1/1992 (Ottawa: Public Works and Government Services Canada); Sergio Marchi, *A Broader Vision: Immigration Plan*, Annual Report to Parliament, 1996 (Ottawa: Citizenship and Immigration Canada, 1996), pp. 22,23; *Canada Year Book 2001* (Ottawa: Statistics Canada, 2001), p. 107.

Canadian Immigration Trends

Immigration exceeded the natural population increase during the two decades, 1901–11 and 1911–21. The 1,759,000 immigrants who came to Canada during the decade of 1901–11 increased the population by 28 per cent. This is an enormous increase when we consider that almost two million new immigrants had to be integrated into the Canadian population, which in 1901 was only 5,371,000, in one decade. Almost as many (1,612,000) entered during the decade of 1911–21, increasing the Canadian population by another 21.2 per cent (Kalbach, 1987:84). During the peak year of 1913, just before the First World War, more than 400,000 immigrants arrived in that single year. The First World War, however, brought immigration into Canada down sharply. This mass migration—mostly from Europe—was possible when the Canadian West was opened up to agriculture. Lands freed through treaties with the aboriginals and the building of the railroad during the 1880s opened up opportunities for agricultural homesteaders. Another 1,203,000 immigrants entered Canada after World War I (during the decade from 1921–31), but since the Canadian population had grown to 8,788,000 in 1921, these immigrants increased the population by only 12.6 per cent.

As shown in Figure 3.2, similar large numbers of immigrants again entered Canada after World War II, with 1,543,000 immigrants arriving from 1951 to 1961; 1,429,000 from 1961 to 1971; 1,447,000 from 1961 to 1971; and also a million and a half from 1971 to 1981; and from 1981 to 1991. The total number of immigrants admitted into the country annually fell from 129,000 in 1981 to 84,000 in 1985. Since 1986, however, levels have risen to 253,000 in 1992 and then dropped again to 218,000 in 1994, and up again by 2001. Since the Canadian population had reached 30 million by 2001, these substantial immigrant numbers still increased the total Canadian population only by 5 to 10 per cent per decade (Badets and Chiu, 1994). Most of these immigrants came from Europe in the past, but since the sixties, many more have come from other parts of the world such as Asia. These immigrants have tended to enter metropolitan cities, and since many represent visible minorities we need to examine this trend as well.

Selection of Immigrants

Canadian immigration policy has evolved over more than one hundred years. From 1867 to 1895, it began with a free-entry period of laissez-faire, on the assumption that the forces of supply and demand for population would spontaneously produce equilibrium. From time to time Orders-in-Council excluded the destitute or restricted Chinese immigrants. Clifford Sifton changed this policy between 1896 and 1914, when he aggressively promoted immigration, especially to Western Canada, to provide an opportunity for the development of primary resources (Department of Manpower and Immigration, 1974:3–16). Free land was offered first to northern European immigrants and, when this did not produce enough response, to eastern and southern Europeans as well. Group immigration was also encouraged, making possible the entrance of substantial numbers of non-English and non-French immigrants to Canada. Between the two world wars (1914–45), a period of uncertainty developed and was exacerbated by the Depression. The First World War had virtually cut off immigration, and the 1930s Depression and the Second World War also discouraged immigration greatly. Both wars created sharp sentiments against Germans, such as the Hutterites and Mennonites who were briefly restricted as immigrants. Also during the Second World War, the Japanese deportation and relocation took place.

The second great flowering of immigration began after the Second World War; from 1946 to 1961, many Canadians wished to rescue their relatives from the chaos in Europe. As a result, two categories of immigrants became major concerns: those who were sponsored by relatives, and those who were resettled displaced persons or refugees. Restrictions on Germans, Japanese, and Asians were increasingly lifted. Two million immigrants came to Canada during these years, an average of 130,000 a year (Department of Manpower and Immigration, 1974:27). After such a large influx of immigrants, and as socioeconomic needs left by the Second World War waned, there were again sentiments after 1961 favouring a more rational policy for selecting immigrants. This train of events persuaded the government to begin a policy review in a White Paper on immigration in 1966. As a result a point system was developed.

When Prime Minister Pierre Trudeau announced the federal multiculturalism policy of 1971, he also linked it with bilingualism. The need to accommodate Quebec nationalism and the separatists was actually first priority, so that the French language could be legally raised to equal status with English. To maintain French in Quebec its government was also concerned about francophonizing newcomers to the province (Richmond, 1994:180). When multiculturalism programs began in the 1970s, they focused primarily on the needs and interests of European immigrants who wanted to preserve their cultural traditions, ethnic organizations, heritage languages, and boost historical and cultural activities which governmental funding assisted. By the 1980s, there was growing evidence of racism with extremist anti-Semitic, anti-Asian, and white supremacist groups on the rise. By 1985 Bill C-85 was passed to deal with employment equity and affirmative action, and by 1988 this came into force (Richmond, 1994:181). Affirmative action is designed to help those who are less able to upgrade their education and job skills, the better to compete in the marketplace. Bill C-93 was passed in 1988, with new programs to combat racism, and by 1990 Bill C-63 was introduced to establish the Canadian Race Relations Foundation. Implementation however, has been postponed because of budget cuts. This shift in policy from European to visible minority immigrants and their needs, was originally brought about with the introduction of the point system for the selection of immigrants to Canada, which allowed people from around the world to apply. Since then many non-European, non-white immigrants have come to Canada in the eighties and nineties.

As Table 3.1 shows, three categories for the selection of immigrants were developed (Independent, Nominated, and Sponsored). Citizens of Canada who had close relatives such as parents, brothers, or sisters could sponsor them to come to Canada if the sponsor was willing to take care of their maintenance for at least a year. (It was felt that newly sponsored immigrants should not become an economic burden to Canada.)

Applicants who had no relatives in Canada could apply for entry as Independents, subject to competition under a point system. As Table 3.1 shows, a total of 100 points could be earned through education, personal qualities, occupational demand, occupational skill, age, arranged employment, and knowledge of the official languages. The number of points required to gain entry varies, depending on the government's desired control over immigrants. Fifty or 60 points are usually required for entry.

Nominated immigrants, the third category of selection, are judged on characteristics from both the Independent and the Sponsored categories. A Nominated applicant can earn up to 70 points under the Independent point system and can also earn up to 30 points if he or she has a Canadian relative not as closely related as those required for sponsorship.

Figure 3.3 shows how this new selection process has affected entry into Canada and what the immigrant trends have been. The number of immigrants has varied annually from just under 75,000 in 1961 to 250,000 in 2001. The number of immigrants who were sponsored and nominated (Family Class) during these decades has fluctuated between 30,000 and 110,000. Immigrants in the Independent category have fluctuated the most in number, ranging from a low of 35,000 in 1961 to a high of 150,000 in 1967. The Canadian government

TABLE 3.1 Summary of Factors Used for the Selection of Immigrants to Canada, 1985

Factors	Range of Units of Assessment That May Be Awarded
INDEPENDENT APPLICATIONS	
Education	0–12
Personal suitability	0–10
Occupation	0–10
Specific vocational preparation	0–15
Age	0–10
Experience	0– 8
Arranged employment	0–10
Knowledge of English and/or French	0–15
Levels of control	0–10
Potential maximum	100
NOMINATED RELATIVES	
Long-term factors (as for independent application)	1–70
Short-term settlement arrangements provided by relative in Canada	0–30
Potential maximum	100
SPONSORED DEPENDANTS	
Close relative in Canada willing to take responsibility for care and maintenance	Units of assessment not required

Note: Independent Applicants and Nominated Relatives, to qualify for selection, must normally earn 70 or more of the potential 100 units of assessment.

SOURCE: *The Revised Selection Criteria for Immigrants* (Ottawa: Canada Employment and Immigration Commission, 1985).

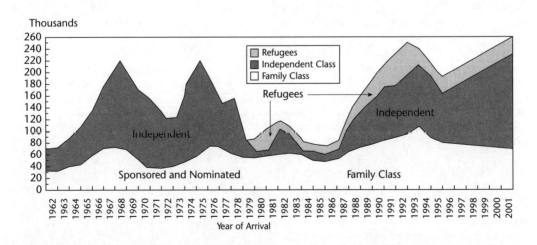

FIGURE 3.3 Immigrant Arrivals by Entry Class, 1961–2001

SOURCES: *Immigration to Canada: A Statistical Overview* (Ottawa, Employment and Immigration Canada, 1989), pp. 8, 25, 31, 47; Citizenship and Immigration Canada, *Immigration Statistics*, 1992, Catalogue MP22–1/1992 (Ottawa: Public Works and Governmental Services Canada); Sergio Marchi, *A Broader Vision: Immigration Plan*, Annual Report to Parliament, 1996 (Ottawa: Citizenship and Immigration Canada, 1996) pp. 22 and 23; *Canada Year Book 2001* (Ottawa: Statistics Canada, 2001), p. 107.

can control the Independent immigrant category by raising or lowering the number of points required to enter, depending on the country's economic and social needs.

Of the 250,000 immigrants who entered Canada in 2001, almost half or 111,000 were in the Family Class including sponsored and nominated persons. Refugees in 2001 were down to 26,000 from 1991 when there were twice as many (53,000), so this category also fluctuates depending on world conditions. The Independent Class has recently included an economic class of 16,000 entrepreneurs in 1992, 35,000 in 1993, and 24,000 in 1994. In 1992 the 15,697 entrepreneurs included 8,000 from Hong Kong, which has recently become a part of China, 1,900 from Korea, and 1,400 from Taiwan, all of which are part of the emerging industrial Pacific Rim countries that are increasingly competing in the world market. These entrepreneur immigrants with capital, flowed predominantly into Quebec (5,661), British Columbia (3,908), and Ontario (3,557). Of the 250,000 immigrants who came to Canada in 2001, 60 per cent came to Ontario (149,000).

This new selection policy was designed to give applicants from all countries of the world a chance to compete for entry into Canada. Formerly, northern Europeans were strongly encouraged to come, and others were often discouraged through Orders-in-Council or other restrictions. Since the implementation of the new policy, the selection process has increasingly encouraged immigrants from the Third World. The Sponsored category still favours northern Europeans—the bulk of Canada's present population who encourage relatives to come. The Independent category provides opportunities for all immigrants.

Origin of Immigrants, 1926–80

Prior to the Depression, immigrants were largely from northern European countries, especially Britain, Germany, the Netherlands, and the Scandinavian countries. Of the immigrants who arrived in Canada before 1961, 90 per cent were born in Europe. This proportion fell to 69 per cent for those who arrived between 1961–70; to 36 per cent for those who immigrated between 1971–80; and to one-fourth for those who arrived in 1981–91. Since then, however, the origins of immigrants have become more varied. Almost one-half (47.8 per cent) of the immigrants between 1926 and 1945 came from the British Isles but this proportion has declined since then; between 1976 and 1980, only 14.1 per cent came from the same source; and by 1981–91 the British proportion dropped to 7.5 per cent (Badets and Chiu, 1994:20). From 1926 to 1945, approximately three-fourths (72.2 per cent) of all immigrants were from northern Europe, but by 1981 to 1991, this proportion had declined drastically to only 12.4 per cent.

A basic shift in immigration patterns has taken place during the last 50 years. Central and East European immigrants had already begun to arrive in Canada during the great influx just before the First World War, and represented approximately one-fifth (19.1 per cent) of the immigrants in 1926 to 1945. However, this proportion declined drastically after the Second World War. Southeastern and southern Europe became an important source of immigrants immediately after the Second World War, representing about one-fourth of all immigrants during 1955 to 1970 and declining again to 8.8 per cent by 1976 to 1980. The most recent source of large immigrant groups has been Asia. Almost none (0.8 per cent) came from Asia between 1926 and 1945, but by 1976 to 1980, almost one-third (31.7 per cent) of all immigrants came from the Far East and by 1991 this had grown to half (49.7 per cent) (Badets and Chiu, 1994:20). This dramatic increase in immigrants of another race, usually of different religions and very different cultures, marks a major shift from the large proportions of northern European immigrants in the past (Driedger, 2001). Why has this major shift occurred, and what will be the consequences for the Canadian population?

TABLE 3.2 The Leading Source Countries of Immigrants, Selected Years

1951	1960	1968	1976	1984	1993	2000
Britain	Italy	Britain	Britain	Vietnam	Hong Kong	China
Germany	Britain	United States	United States	Hong Kong	India	India
Italy	United States	Italy	Hong Kong	United States	Philippines	Pakistan
Netherlands	Germany	Germany	Jamaica	India	Taiwan	Philippines
Poland	Netherlands	Hong Kong	Lebanon	Britain	China	Korea
France	Portugal	France	India	Poland	Sri Lanka	Sri Lanka
United States	Greece	Austria	Philippines	Philippines	Vietnam	United States
Belgium	France	Greece	Portugal	El Salvador	United States	Iran
Yugoslavia	Poland	Portugal	Italy	Jamaica	Britain	Yugoslavia
Denmark	Austria	Yugoslavia	Guyana	China	Poland	Britain

SOURCES: Department of Manpower and Immigration, *The Immigration Program*, Vol. 2, *A Report of the Canadian Immigration and Population Study* (Ottawa: Information Canada, 1974), p. 84; *1976 Immigration Statistics*, Table 3; and Employment and Immigration Canada, *Annual Report to Parliament on Future Immigration Levels*, 1985 (Ottawa: Minister of Supply and Services Canada, 1985). Statistical Appendix; Immigration Statistics Employment and Immigrant Canada, 1986–90; *Facts and Figures: Overview of Immigration* (Hull: Citizenship and Immigration, 1994), p. 3. *Facts and Figures 2000, Immigration Overview*, CIC.

Recent Leading Source Countries 1980–2000

Since the recent changes to the Immigration Act in 1976 (proclaimed in 1978), immigrant patterns based on the country of origin have changed substantially. As seen in Table 3.2, in 1951, 9 of the top 10 source countries were European; 6 of these 9 were northern European. Immigrants from the tenth country, the United States, were largely of original European stock as well. This trend remained roughly the same during the 1960s, although Hong Kong ranked in the top five in 1968. The order changed considerably in 1976, when 6 of the top 10 countries of origin were non-European. Immigrants from Britain were still most numerous, followed by American immigrants in second place. By 1984, six years after the new Immigration Act had been proclaimed, 2 Asian countries—Vietnam and Hong Kong—ranked first and second; Britain had dropped to fifth place, and 7 of the 10 leading countries of origin were in the Third World. This continued into the nineties when Britain dropped to ninth. By 1993, the 7 top donor countries that were sending visible minorities to Canada were Asian. Many immigrants from all over the world were now able to compete with Europeans in gaining entrance through the point system.

By 2000, the population of thirty million Canadians was still mainly Christian Caucasians of European ethnic stock representing several European languages and cultures. More recent immigrants of Mongoloid and Negroid races, whose religions are primarily Buddhist, Muslim, or otherwise non-Christian, brought with them quite different languages and cultures, which is making the Canadian population more heterogeneous. Since the accumulated European ethnic stock is so large, however, the proportion of immigration from Third World countries will increase only modestly in the general population. With the economic downturn in the 1980s, the government's immigration quotas dropped to about 70,000, tending to restrict opportunities for large increments in immigrant growth. In the nineties, with an economic upturn, immigration quotas have in-creased again, and this is slowly changing Canada from a dominant north European population to one that is more diverse.

HIGHLIGHT 3.1 THE IMMIGRATION PLAN FOR 2002

The government remains committed to investing in Canada's economic and social development through immigration. A planning range of 210,000 to 235,000 is confirmed for 2002. Refugees will account for more than 10 percent of newcomers to Canada in that year. Skilled workers, business people and provincial or territorial nominees, together with their families, will again make up about 60 percent of the movement in 2002, and family members of Canadian citizens and permanent residents, slightly more than one-quarter.

This is consistent with the planning range announced earlier for 2002 and reaffirms the long-term objective of moving gradually to immigration levels of approximately one percent of Canada's population, while bearing in mind Canada's absorptive capacity. The skilled workers, business immigrants, family members and refugees who enter Canada through our immigration program are in-creasingly important to maintaining a strong and skilled labour force. These same people also strengthen Canada's social fabric and cultural diversity.

Temporary residents are also a key element of Canada's growth. The immigrant program provides for the temporary entry of skilled foreign workers and business people essential to economic development, foreign students drawn by the reputation of Canada's universities and colleges for excellence in education, research and training, and tourists eager to experience the many attractions of this country.

The commitment to immigration is inseparable from Canada's determination to deny access to those who pose criminal or security threats to Canada and other countries, and who might abuse immigrant, refugee or temporary entry programs for illicit and fraudulent ends. Investigation and interdiction abroad, screening at border and airport entry points, and removal activities in Canada are necessary adjuncts to an open immigration policy and the levels planning process.

Pursuant to immigration legislation, the Social Union Framework Agreement and federal/territorial immigration agreements, consultation is essential to immigration planning, and various federal/provincial/territorial forums exist to that end. In addition, as part of the Multi-year Planning Process, Citizenship and Immigration Canada (CIC) and the provinces and territories are working to establish a joint planning table to address common concerns and challenges related to immigration planning. Consultations with other parties who are increasingly interested in participating in immigration planning will continue.

The scope of the policies and procedures required to enhance public safety and security, and concomitant pressures on the fiscal framework, will have an important effect on future planning, as will the nature of migration flows in the coming years, and other program pressures. Given the current level of uncertainty, it would be premature to announce a planning range for 2003 at this time without further consideration and consultation to ensure that supports are in place to move to higher immigration levels.

SOURCE: *Pursuing Canada's Commitment to Immigration—Citizenship and Immigration Canada, 2002.* Reproduced with permission of the Minister of Public Works and Government Services Canada, 2002.

THE CANADIAN POPULATION

Having discussed general Canadian demo-graphic trends, let us now focus on 110 years of ethnic population growth, the foreign-born population in Canada over time, and rural-urban distribution.

Ethnic Population 1871–91

In Table 3.3 we see that the 1871 census reported that Canada had a population of 3,486,000, comprised largely of the British (60.0 per cent) and the French (31.1 per cent), the two charter groups who together represented 91.7 per cent of the population. This census was taken in five of the provinces in confederation at that time, representing a small part of what is now eastern Canada. It did not include the majority of aboriginals in the Northwest, and most of the existing provinces have been enlarged since. This population grew by about one million per decade, and the ethnic proportions remained roughly the same until the beginning of the great immigrant influx after 1901.

Since the turn of the century ethnic proportions have changed considerably, largely because of new immigration patterns. In 1901, the British population was still in the majority at 57.0 per cent and the French population remained at 30.7 per cent. By 1991, the single response (those who reported a single ethnic origin) population of the British had declined to 28.1 per cent and the French population had dropped to 22.8 per cent, so that the two charter groups now represent just over one-half of the Canadian population. Other ethnic populations grew from 22.3 per cent in 1901 to 27.5 per cent in 1991. Twenty-two per cent chose multiple responses. None of the ethnic groups now represents a majority, and the diversity of others is clearly on the rise. It is not surprising that thoughts of multiculturalism currently make more sense than they did much earlier (Krotki and Reid, 1994).

The Foreign-Born Population

We expect that the foreign-born population—immigrants who have spent at least some of their formative years outside Canada and who are first generation Canadians—will be most eager to continue the linguistic and cultural patterns of their mother countries. In 1901, there were 700,000 foreign-born immigrants in Canada representing 13.0 per cent of the population before the great immigrant influx (McVey and Kalbach, 1995). By 1921, there were almost two million (1,956,000) foreign-born immigrants who represented almost one-fourth (22.3 per cent) of the population in Canada after the great immigrant influx of 1911 to 1920. By 1991, the Canadian foreign-born population had grown to over four million (4,420,000), but the proportion had declined to 16.5 per cent, largely since immigration rates have declined proportionately.

The foreign-born population is not, however, evenly distributed across Canada. Almost half (46.3 per cent) of the foreign-born immigrants resided in Ontario in 1901; this proportion fell close to one-third (32.0 per cent) in 1911. By 1991, it had grown to over one-half (54.3 per cent), and we project that it will continue to grow in 2001. This shows that new immigrants have been disproportionately attracted to the industrial heartland of Canada, except from 1911 to 1931 when the Sifton immigration policy funnelled immigrants to the agricultural West. The Prairie provinces received the largest proportion of immigrants during this period. While the Ontario foreign-born population curve is U-shaped, the prairie curve is more bell-shaped. As the figures for 1951–91 show, immigrants after the Second World War have clearly gone to the cities of the industrial belt in Ontario.

The proportion of foreign-born immigrants in the Atlantic provinces and the Yukon, Northwest Territories, and Nunavut is negligible. Quebec, the second largest province, has been able to attract only a small portion of immigrants ranging between 9.2 per cent and 14.2 per cent: considerably less than half of the

TABLE 3.3 Population[a] of British Isles, French, and Other Selected Origins, Canada, Selected Years: 1871–2001

Ethnic Group	1871[b]	1881	1901	1921	1941	1961	1981[f]	1991[f]	2001[g]
Total[c]	3,486	4,325	5,371	8,788	11,507	18,238	24,084	26,994	30,007
British Isles	2,111	2,549	3,063	4,869	5,716	7,997	9,674	7,595	7,000
English	706	881	1,261	2,545	2,968	4,195		3,958	
Irish	846	957	989	1,108	1,268	1,753		726	
Scottish	550	700	800	1,174	1,404	1,902		893	
Other	8	10	13	42	76	146		2,018	
French	1,083	1,299	1,649	2,453	3,483	5,540	6,439	6,147	6,000
Other European	240	299	454	1,247	2,044	4,117	4,627	4,146	4,000
Dutch	30	30	34	118	213	430	408	358	
German	203	254	311	295	465	1,050	1,142	912	
Greek				6	12	56	154	151	
Hungarian[d]			2	13	55	126	116	101	
Italian	1	2	11	67	113	450	748	750	
Jewish	1	16	126		170	173	264	246	
Polish			6	53	167	324	254	273	
Portuguese								245	
Scandinavian	2	5	31	167	245	387	283	174	
Ukrainian			6	107	306	473	530	407	
Other	4	7	37	18	10	88	452	278	
Asian/African		4	24	66	74	122	533	1,552	3,000
African								26	
Arab								144	
Chinese		4	17	40	35	58	289	587	
East Indian							121	325	
Japanese			5	16	23	29	41	49	
Other			2	10	16	34	82	421	
Aboriginal		40	105	114	126	220	413	471	800
Other[e]	52	84	72	39	64	242	559	1,191	2,000
Black				18	22	32	45	225	
Other				21	42	210	514	966	
Multiple Groups[f]							1,839	5,806	7,200

Notes:
[a] Numbers rounded to the nearest 1,000.
[b] Four original provinces only.
[c] Excludes Newfoundland prior to 1951.
[d] Includes Lithuanian and Moravian in 1901 and 1911 and Magyar in 1981.
[e] Includes 'not stated' prior to 1971. In 1971 'not stated' cases were computer-assigned.
[f] Somewhat different ethnic divisions where multiple origins have been separated into special categories.
[g] 2001 population projections, since ethnic data are not yet available.

SOURCES: Dominion Bureau of Statistics, *1961 Census of Canada, Bulletin* 7:1-6 (Ottawa: The Queen's Printer, 1966), Table 1; Statistics Canada, *1971 Census of Canada, Bulletin* 1.3-2 (Ottawa: Information Canada, 1973), Table 1; D. Kubat and D. Thornton, *A Statistical Profile of Canadian Society* (Toronto: McGraw-Hill Ryerson, 1974), Table f-10. Reprinted from Warren E. Kalbach, 'Growth and Distribution of Canada's Ethnic Population, 1871–1981' in Leo Driedger (ed.), *Ethnic Canada* (Toronto: Copp Clark Pitman, 1987), p. 87; *Ethnic Origin: The Nation*, Census 91, Catalogue 93-315 (Ottawa: Statistics Canada, 1993).

TABLE 3.4 Percentage Urban[a] for Selected Ethnic-Origin Populations in Canada 1871–2001[b]

Year	Total	Ethnic Origin (%)						
		Aboriginal Peoples	German	French	British	Italian	Chinese	Jewish
1871	19.6	1.7	11.1	18.8	22.3	53.5		67.2
1881	25.7	0.6	16.4	23.1	28.8	61.3		79.5
1901	37.5	5.1	28.0	33.7	41.8	65.4		94.2
1911	45.4	3.7	33.5	40.9	50.4	69.8		94.0
1921	49.5	3.7	33.2	47.7	53.7	79.3		95.7
1931	53.7	3.9	36.9	54.0	57.5	81.6		96.5
1941	54.3	3.6	36.4	54.9	58.3	80.9		96.0
1951	61.6	6.7	44.2	59.9	65.7	88.1		98.7
1961	69.6	12.9	61.8	68.2	71.2	94.7		98.8
1971	76.2	30.1	68.8	75.9	75.9	96.6		98.8
1981	75.6	36.4	68.3	73.3	74.5	94.9		98.5
1991	76.5	42.3	68.2	72.8	72.6	93.9	97.9	98.5
2001	77.0	48.0	68.0	72.5	71.0	93.0	98.0	98.6

Notes:

[a]Definition of *urban* is that in effect at the time of the particular census.

[b]2001 percentages are projections.

SOURCES: Censuses of Canada, 1871–1991.Reprinted from Warren E. Kalbach, 'Growth and Distribution of Canada's Ethnic Population, 1981' in Leo Driedger (ed.), *Ethnic Canada Identities and Inequalities* (Toronto: Copp Clark Pitman, 1987), p. 93. *Profile of Urban and Rural Areas*, Part B, Canada, Provinces and Territories (Ottawa: 1991 Statistics Canada, 1994).

26 per cent share they would normally be expected to attract. Compared to Ontario, Quebec's inability to attract new immigrants has continued to erode the Quebec proportion of the Canadian foreign-born population recently. Since about 82 per cent of the population in Quebec is French, this does not bode well for Quebec's political future in Canada. Earlier, Quebec was able to make up for lack of new immigrants by much higher birthrates, but recently births have declined dramatically as more Quebeckers become urban.

Rural-Urban Ethnic Distribution

Our discussion of the foreign-born suggests that many immigrants have moved to industrial areas recently; we should, therefore, examine the rural-urban ethnic distribution. In Table 3.4 we see that only about one-fifth (19.6 per cent) of the Canadian population was urban in 1871; by

2001, the trend had reversed to more than three-fourths of the population being urban. The British and French charter populations have remained very close to the rural-urban national average with the British somewhat above and the French somewhat below it.

The aboriginal peoples have always been a much more rural population, first as food-gathering people, and more recently living on reserves. The aboriginals are among Canada's most rural population, although many have moved off the reserves and into the cities during the past three decades, so that by 2001 almost half of them were urban. In the next section of this chapter, we will discuss the aboriginals as a distinctive ethnic type in many respects.

The Italians, along with others such as the Greeks and Portuguese who moved mostly into the city, represent more recent immigration after World War Two; by 1961 almost all of them (94.7 to 96.6 per cent) were urban, and that continues into 2001. The Chinese are almost all urban. The Jews arrived earlier and have always been the most urban ethnic group in Canada, with almost all of them (94.0 to 98.8 per cent) living in cities as early as 1901. Both the Italians and the Jews have always been much more urban than the national average, and both groups have also been most heavily located in the largest cities of Montreal and Toronto. Urbanization has increased for all groups, but the differences between rural aboriginals and urban Jews are very great. We expect that this range of differences will also be found with respect to other characteristics.

DEMOGRAPHIC ETHNIC TYPES

The general demographic data we have examined so far suggest that some groups can best be understood as ethnic types when attempting to summarize some of the population's diversity. We begin with the earliest native Indians and Inuit and move on to the French and British who later traded and settled in this vast territory. Many other Europeans eventually followed; recently, Third World immigrants have entered the mosaic. The aboriginals, the charter Europeans, the non-charter Europeans, and the more recent visible minorities provide ethnic foci.

The Aboriginals

Anthropologists tell us that the earliest *Homo sapiens* came to the two Americas at least 12,000 years ago, probably via the Bering Strait. The native Indians were here when our European ancestors were still barbarians roaming the European continent. Some aboriginals remained food gatherers, but others turned to agriculture; by the early 1500s, the Spanish conquistadors found the great civilizations among of the Maya, the Aztec, and the Inca in Central and South America.

The French and the British did not find such great civilizations among the aboriginals of the territory that is now Canada. The Hurons and Iroquois had begun farming (Price, 1979:1–20)

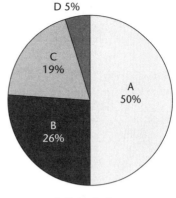

A Status Indians
B Metis
C Non-Status Indians
D Inuit

FIGURE 3.4 Aboriginals in Canada by Type, 1996 (%)
Note: Status Indians are sometimes referred to as registered or legal Indians.
SOURCE: *Canada Year Book 2001* (Ottawa: Statistics Canada, 2001), p. 107.

and the aboriginals of the West Coast were engaged in large-scale fishing (Frideres, 1998) but neither had advanced to the state of their South American counterparts. Aboriginals of the central plains and the northlands were food gatherers, the image often perpetuated in Canadian history. Canadians tend to see a very limited part of the many diversified aboriginal groupings throughout the two Americas. Too often, we tend to forget that the first aboriginal *Homo sapiens* lived in the region of what is now Canada twenty-five times as long as any Europeans have lived there.

Although the aboriginals were the majority until the Europeans arrived, they had declined to 799,010 in 1996, representing less than 1.7 per cent of the total population of Canada (see Table 3.5). The 1996 census found that half of the aboriginal people (50 per cent) were status Indians—aboriginals with whom the government had made treaties, and 26 per cent were Metis, representing a mixture of Indian and French or British ancestry (see Figure 3.4). Figure 3.4 also shows that non-status Indians,

TABLE 3.5 Total Population by Aboriginal Group, 1996

	Total Population	Aboriginal Population				Non-Aboriginal Population
		Total[a]	North American Indian[b, c]	Metis[b]	Inuit[b]	
Canada	**28,528,125**	**799,010**	**554,290**	**210,190**	**41,080**	**27,729,115**
Newfoundland	**547,155**	14,200	5,430	4,685	4,265	532,955
Prince Edward Island	**132,855**	950	825	120	15	131,905
Nova Scotia	**899,965**	12,380	11,340	860	210	887,585
New Brunswick	**729,630**	10,250	9,180	975	120	719,380
Quebec	**7,045,080**	71,415	47,600	16,075	8,300	6,973,665
Ontario	**10,642,795**	141,520	118,830	22,790	1,300	10,501,275
Manitoba	**1,100,295**	128,680	82,990	46,195	360	971,615
Saskatchewan	**976,615**	111,245	75,205	36,535	190	865,370
Alberta	**2,669,195**	122,835	72,645	50,745	795	2,546,360
British Columbia	**3,689,755**	139,655	113,315	26,750	815	3,550,100
Yukon Territory	**30,650**	6,155	5,530	565	110	24,475
Northwest Territories	**64,125**	39,695	11,400	3,895	24,600	24,430

Notes:

[a] The total of North American Indian, Metis, and Inuit do not equal the total aboriginal population because 6,415 persons reported identifying with more than one group.

[b] Single and multiple responses have been combined.

[c] Users should note that the counts for North American Indian may be affected by the incomplete enumeration of 77 Indian reserves and settlements in the 1996 Census, depending on the geographic area under study.

SOURCE: Statistics Canada, 1996 Census Nation Tables.

who have not entered into treaties with Canada, ranked third at 19 per cent. The Inuit (5 per cent) who came to Canada later than the Indians and who live in the most northerly parts of Canada, represent only a very small proportion of the aboriginal category.

The census in 1996 counted aboriginals in each of the 10 provinces and 2 territories, but over one-half live in the 4 most westerly provinces. Only 4 per cent of aboriginals live in the Atlantic Provinces, and only 6 per cent live in the territories. About one-fourth live in Ontario and about one-tenth in Quebec. Aboriginal peoples are one of the most rural ethnic groups in Canada: 6 in 10 aboriginals live in rural areas, and only about one-fourth (24 per cent) live in cities larger than 100,000. The 1996 census shows that 70 per cent of non-status Indians live in urban areas and 60 per cent

of Metis are urban; in contrast only 20 per cent of Inuit and 30 per cent of status Indians are city-dwellers.

The status Indians in the 1996 census represent half of all aboriginals, and they are most heavily located on the prairies (38 per cent). Of the non-status Indians, 34 per cent are located in Ontario, presumably drawn to industrial work opportunities; approximately one-fourth (25 per cent) are in British Columbia, where few treaties have been signed; and nearly another fourth (24 per cent) live on the Prairies. The Metis represent 15 per cent of all aboriginals, and two-thirds (66 per cent) live on the Prairies, where the British and French first opened up the West to the fur trade. About two-thirds (63 per cent) of the Inuit reside in the Yukon, Northwest Territories, and Nunavut, and nearly one-fifth (19 per cent) live in northern Quebec, which

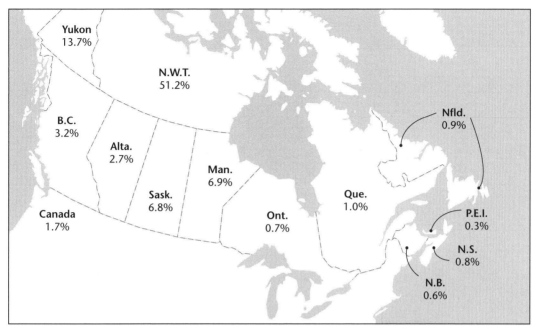

FIGURE 3.5 Aboriginal Percentage of Total Population Located in Provinces and Territories, 1991
SOURCE: *Ethnic Origin: The Nation*, Catalogue 93–315, 1991 Census (Ottawa: Statistics Canada, 1993), pp. 40–1.

was their original hunting grounds and still is for many. The Inuit represent only 5 per cent of all aboriginals.

Figure 3.5 shows the proportions of aboriginals in the total population of the provinces and territories. Aboriginals represent 51 per cent of the population in the Northwest Territories and Nunavut combined; this is the only region in which they are a majority. They still represent 14, 7, and 7 per cent of the total population in the Yukon, Manitoba, and Saskatchewan respectively. There are relatively few (less than 1 per cent) located in the Atlantic provinces and Quebec, the eastern regions which were first occupied by the Europeans. We conclude that the aboriginals of Canada represent a special demographic type because they have lived here much longer than anyone else, are closer to a food-gathering lifestyle, are racially Mongoloid, and are located largely in the Canadian Northwest.

HIGHLIGHT 3.2 THE INDIAN ACT

The Indian Act, first passed in 1876, is the legislation that has intruded on the lives and cultures of status Indians more than any other law. Though amended repeatedly, the act's fundamental provisions have scarcely changed. They give the state powers that range from defining how one is born or natu-ralized into 'Indian' status to administering the estate of an Aboriginal person after death.

The 1876 Indian Act rested on the principle 'that the aborigines are to be kept in a condition of tutelage and treated as wards or children of the State' (Department of the Interior, 1877:xiv). The act gave Parliament control over

Indian political structures, landholding patterns, and resource and economic development. It covered almost every important aspect of the daily lives of Aboriginal peoples on reserves. The overall effect was to subject Aboriginal people to the almost unfettered rule of federal bureaucrats. The act imposed non-Aboriginal forms on traditional governance, landholding practices, and cultural practices.

The Indian Act provided a means of removing political sovereignty from indigenous people by introducing a system of indirect rule and segregation (Fleras and Elliott, 1992). The sweeping regulations under the act included prohibitions against owning land. Early clauses, which have only in recent years been eliminated, controlled every aspect of the lives and lifestyles of Aboriginal peoples, from denying them the right to vote to prohibiting them from purchasing and consuming alcohol (Bienvenue and Goldstein, 1985).

For example, the Indian Act of 1876 and various amendments up to the 1930s decreed that:

- The majority of Aboriginal people living on reserves could not vote in federal elections. (This was not changed until 1960.) Those who wished to have the franchise were forced to give up their status and lose all the benefits conferred by the Indian Act, including rights to land, homes, and community (Sharzer, 1985).
- Aboriginal people could not manage their own reserve lands or money and were under the supervision of federally appointed Indian Agents.
- All chiefs and band councillors were to be elected for three-year terms. Exclusionary and sexist, the act also decreed that only men were to be allowed to vote in band elections. (Aboriginal women were not given the right to vote in band elections until the 1951 Indian Act.)
- Protected reserve lands were to be converted to provincial lands upon the enfranchisement of an Indian.

- Aboriginal peoples did not have power to decide whether non-Indians could reside on or use reserve lands.
- Public authorities were given the power (in 1911) to expropriate reserve land without a surrender, as long as the expropriation was for the purpose of public works.
- No Aboriginal peoples could develop land without the agents' consent.
- For an Indian to be intoxicated on or off the reserve was an offence punishable by one month in jail.
- The sale of agricultural products was prohibited without official permission.

In 1885, a pass system was instituted by the federal government, prohibiting Aboriginal people from leaving their reserve without the written authorization of their agent. This move was designed to restrict parental visits to residential schools. The Indian Act was also amended to authorize the arrest of Indians found on reserves other than their home reserve. This amendment, supported by missionaries, had the effect of prohibiting communal sun dances, thirst dances, and ghost dances. This ban was extended to all forms of Aboriginal dances in 1906.

Another example of the concerted attack on Aboriginal cultural practices was the 1884 amendments to the Indian Act that banned the West Coast potlatch and other ceremonies. Potlatch 'giveaways' were deemed incompatible with Euro-Canadian practices and the concept of private property. Using ritual, ceremony, and celebration, the potlatch provided a central organizing framework in which new leaders were installed, wealth was distributed, names were given and recorded, political councils were held and decisions made, history instruction was provided, and spiritual guidance was given. The Aboriginal peoples were not only denied an opportunity to participate in an important ceremonial festival but lost control over their political life (Ponting and Gibbons, 1980).

The Indian Act of 1927, in recognizing the failures and inadequacies of the coercive assimilationist strategy, tried to bolster it by providing even stronger measures to intervene in and control the affairs of Aboriginal societies. This included further efforts to develop an agricultural economy, in the expectation that social and cultural change would follow in its wake. In responding to Aboriginal political organizations pursuing land issues, especially in British Columbia, the act also made 'raising a fund or providing money for the prosecution of any claim' a crime unless permission was obtained.

By the beginning of the twentieth century, the administration of 'Indian affairs' had assumed a format that continued with few changes until after World War II. The Indian Act provided the Department of Indian Affairs with exclusive jurisdiction over Aboriginal people and gave its officers the authority to supervise most facets of their lives.

In summary, the Canadian government, through the Indian Act, imposed a form of institutionalized racism in the relationship between Canada and its Aboriginal peoples (Frideres, 1993; Bolaria and Li, 1988). The act was designed to promote coercive assimilation, in which Aboriginal peoples were expected to adopt the cultural attitudes and norms of the dominant culture and give up their own cultural traditions, histories, values, customs, and language (Richardson, 1993; Bolaria and Li, 1988). Aboriginal social and political institutions were systematically dismantled.

The Indian Act also set out to define 'who was an Indian'. Yet, as Daniel Raunet pointed out, 'to ask the question in legal terms is in itself discriminatory. . . . People do not need legislation to know their origin or place on this earth' (in Ducharme, 1986). For the White lawgiver, the Indian was a person registered in an 'Indian Register'. Indian women who married non-status Indian men simply lost their status. These legal definitions relating to identity totally ignored the fact that Aboriginal peoples were not a monolithic group but represented extraordinarily diverse and distinct populations with different customs, traditions, histories, cultures, and languages (Ducharme, 1986).

The Indian Act persists as an essentially repressive instrument of containment (Fleras and Elliott, 1996). Founded on the ethnocentric certainties of the nineteenth century, it continues to interfere profoundly in the lives, cultures, and communities of First Nations peoples today.

SOURCE: Frances Henry and Carol Tator, 'The Colour of Democracy', 2nd edn (Toronto: Harcourt Brace, 2000).

The Charter Europeans

One year after the British established the first permanent European settlement in North America at Jamestown (now Maryland) in 1607, the French established the first European settlement in Canada at what is now Montreal, some 150 years before the British settled permanently in Canada. Early French explorers such as Cartier in the 1530s and Champlain in the 1600s were the first European explorers to come to what is now Quebec in eastern Canada. The Vikings came to explore and settle Newfoundland about AD 1000, but our knowledge of these settlements is limited and it is unlikely that the historical European continuity of these Scandinavians is evident in our population today. Thus, the first Europeans to settle in Canada were the French, who today are recognized as one of the two charter-group partners.

In 1871, shortly after Canadian confederation, the first census was taken. We see in Table 3.4 that of the approximately 3.5 million people who lived in Canada, almost all (92 per cent) were either of British (61 per cent) or French (31 per cent) origin. A further 6 per cent of the population was German. The 1871 census did not include the estimated one-half million native Indians scattered over the northwestern territories because the census included only the four original provinces of the East, a fraction of the territory that is now Canada.

Thus, it seemed logical that the Canadian confederation in 1867 would be a union between two European origin peoples, the British and the French. The British North America Act of 1867 legalized the claims of the two original European migrating groups for such historically established privileges as the perpetuation of their separate languages and cultures. The Royal Commission on Bilingualism and Biculturalism continued to support and encourage the charter-group status of the French, even though immigrants of other ethnic origins comprised one-third of the Canadian population by 1991.

During the 125 years following 1871, a considerable demographic shift occurred, with a decline in the British charter majority proportion from 61 to 28 per cent in 1991 (see Figure 3.6). Now none of the ethnic groups is a majority. Immigration from Britain after the turn of the century has continued to add to the British charter group, but considerable numbers of immigrants from other countries have diminished the British total proportion by 1991. Although the British majority tried very hard to make Canada a unilingual and unicultural society, the country was bilingual and bicultural in 1871. However, since no ethnic group was a demographic majority in the 1990s, suggestions of building a multicultural society are more viable, especially since Canada is now legally and officially bilingual and multicultural.

When we consider that the British group comprises the English, Scottish, Irish, and Welsh, the category of British ethnicity becomes more diverse. The English population in Canada has usually been twice as large as the Scottish, Irish, and Welsh combined. The mixed British-French category of 1,522,075 shows that intermarriage is also taking place between individuals of the two charter populations. In 1991 the people who intermarried represented 6.3 per cent of the total Canadian population.

While the smaller French charter group maintained roughly one-third of the Canadian population since 1871, their proportion has begun to drop: by 1991 they represented closer to one-fourth (23 per cent) of the total. Caldwell and Fournier (1987:12) clearly show the recent decline of Quebec's population growth rate. During the 1921–31 decade, the Quebec population growth rate was greater than Canada's (21.8 to 18.1 per cent); during 1941–51 the two were even (21.7 and 21.8 per cent); during 1971–81 Quebec was falling behind dramatically (12.9 to 6.8 per cent). Quebec has had difficulty getting its share of immigrants in the past, and recently the birthrate has dropped much more than in the rest of Canada (Caldwell and Fournier, 1987:22–35). Since a large majority of those with French origins reside in Quebec, indications are that the proportion of the French charter minority will continue to decline. This decline in the French population in Canada will result in a decline in their political power as well, although their proportionate population has not declined for as many years as that of the British.

The British still represent a majority in only the three most easterly Atlantic provinces. However, their proportions have declined in each of these provinces since 1901, most dramatically in Ontario (from 79.3 per cent in 1901 to 30.0 per cent in 1991). The French are a very large majority in Quebec (80.2 per cent) and have held this majority over time with a slight drop.

The Multi-European Entrance

While non-charter Europeans represented only about 7 per cent of the Canadian population in 1871, they have immigrated in increasing numbers. Charter groups were still a dominant majority in 1901, but they dropped to one-half. While the French population declined to less than one-fourth by 1991, the proportion of British origin dropped to slightly over one-fourth.

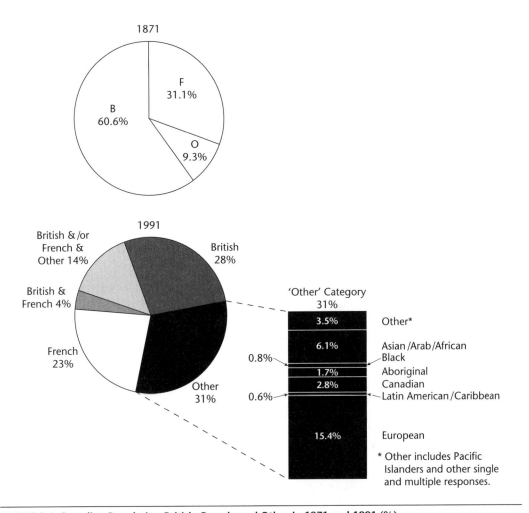

FIGURE 3.6 Canadian Population British, French, and Other in 1871 and 1991 (%)

SOURCE: Statistics Canada, 1871 and 1991. Reproduced with permission of the Minister of Supply and Services Canada.

The other European groups entered Canada well after the coming of the charter groups. Many of the Germans came to Ontario about 150 years ago, but the majority of the others came to open up the West and encountered a country where the charter groups had earlier established the political and economic patterns. The position to which ethnic groups are admitted and the level at which they are allowed to function in the power structure of a society is described as entrance status by Porter (1965).

This non-charter–group presence mushroomed after the turn of the century and before the First World War into one of the largest world migrations from northern, and later eastern, Europe to North America. These European groups, numbered 4,146,601 in 1991, representing 15.4 per cent of the Canadian population (see Table 3.6).

Although the large French population has always tended to resist a national unilingual and unicultural Canada, these large migrations of Europeans into Canada, especially into Western

TABLE 3.6 Ethnic Origins in Canada, 1991

	Single Response N	%	Multiple Response N
Total Canadian	21,183,910		5,810,130
European	**17,888,365**	**59.0**	
British	7,595,120	28.1	6,436,870
English	3,958,405	14.7	4,646,720
Irish	725,660	2.7	3,057,695
Scottish	893,125	3.3	3,355,240
Other	33,860	.1	
French	6,146,601	22.8	242,580
Other European	4,146,065	15.4	4,229,675
Dutch	358,180	1.3	603,415
German	911,560	3.4	1,882,220
Scandinavian	174,373	.6	542,825
Hungarian	100,725	.4	112,975
Polish	272,805	1.0	467,905
Ukrainian	406,645	1.5	647,650
Balkans	131,440	.5	67,210
Greek	151,150	.6	40,330
Italian	750,055	2.8	397,720
Portuguese	246,890	.9	45,295
Jewish	245,840	.9	123,725
Other	396,400	1.5	
Asian/African	**1,633,660**	**6.1**	
Arab	144,050	.5	50,830
West Asian	81,660	.3	16,315
South Asian	420,295	1.6	68,080
East Indian	324,845	1.2	54,435
East and S.E. Asian	961,225	3.6	105,840
Chinese	586,645	2.2	66,000
Filipino	157,250	.6	17,725
Indo-Chinese	116,535	.4	14,355
African	26,430	.1	13,160
Pacific Islands	7,210	.0	4,605
Latin American	**177,930**	**.7**	
South and Central	85,535	.3	34,445
Caribbean	94,395	.4	72,225
Aboriginal	**470,615**	**1.7**	**532,060**
Native Indian	361,375	1.3	418,605
Other	109,240	.4	113,455
Other	**989,715**	**3.6**	
Black	224,620	.8	127,045
Canadian	765,095	2.8	267,935
Multiple Origins	**5,810,130**	**21.5**	
		100.0	

Note: This table includes all specific groups for whom single responses exceeded 100,000. There is double counting of groups in the multiple-response category.

SOURCE: Statistics Canada, 'Ethnic Origin', The Nation, 1991 Census of Canada, Catalogue 93–315, February 1993.

Canada, have created other non-charter majorities in some of the Western provinces. Thus, we propose that in Western Canada, the non-charter European entrance can be seen as another ethnic type of milieu, especially on the Prairies where wheat has replaced fur as the dominant focus of commerce. Certainly, Sifton's immigration policy in the early 1900s was a major factor in the creation of this European non-charter majority in the West. Later we will examine in more detail how this has contributed to much alienation in the West and has led to Western attempts at raising new political parties to counter the eastern Canadian dominance of the charter groups in Ontario and Quebec. Although these non-charter European entrants are too diverse to be considered a 'Third Force' as Paul Yuzyk (1975) suggests, ethnic factors often combine with economic and political issues, making it difficult to see which of the factors, including the ethnic one, is most salient.

Visible Third World Minorities

Earlier, immigrants from northern Europe were encouraged to come to Canada, but recently more immigrants from southern Europe, South America, Asia, Africa, and the Caribbean have come as well. Table 3.3 shows that in 1951, shortly after the war, the leading source countries of immigrants were in Europe, but by 1993 northern European immigrants had been replaced by immigrants of other racial, cultural, and religious backgrounds from the Third World. The change in Canadian immigration policy to a point system was designed to provide these immigrants a better chance to enter Canada. In Table 3.2 we saw that six immigrant source countries in 2000 were Asian.

Closer examination of Table 3.6 shows that the category of non-charter and multiple origin Canadians had grown to almost half (49.1 per cent) in 1991; of these 1,633,660 (6.1 per cent) came from Asian backgrounds. The Chinese—586,645 (2.2 per cent)—represent the largest group, followed by East Indians or South Asians (1.6 per cent). These immigrants stand out

among the predominantly northern European Canadian population as visible minorities whose Asian ancestry is physically apparent. Their racial, religious, linguistic, and cultural diversity is readily apparent. These Canadians are still a relatively small proportion of our population, but their numbers and percentages are growing, so that Canada is becoming more heterogeneous ethnically and racially.

Most of these recent immigrants settled in only a few urban centres, especially Toronto, Vancouver, and Montreal. More than 90 per cent of the Asians are urban; 95.4 per cent of the Chinese live in urban centres of 100,000 or more. Only the Jews, who have lived in Canada for a longer period of time, are more urban than these recent visible arrivals. In contrast, Germans are only 68.2 per cent urban, and only half live in larger urban centres. Again we see a considerable difference between early northern European immigrants and more recent Asian arrivals, so that we will consider them as distinctive Canadian ethnic types. After the Second World War, large numbers of southern Europeans such as the Italians, Greeks, Portuguese, and Spanish arrived. These Canadians are also mostly urban, and they also reside in larger metropolitan centres, especially Toronto and Montreal. Although southern and northern Europeans are all Caucasians, southern Europeans are to some extent more visible because of their darker physical features and distinctive Mediterranean cultures. Many of them arrived from countries less industrialized than northern Europe and they tend on average to be of lower socioeconomic status.

To illustrate the largest concentrations of visible minorities, we present these minorities in Table 3.7 in the three largest metropolitan centres—Toronto, Montreal, and Vancouver. Of the 11.2 per cent classified as visible minorities in Canada, they are most visible in Toronto and Vancouver, where almost one-third (31.6 per cent and 31.1 per cent) of the population is visible minority. The 12.2 per cent who are visible in Montreal are closer to the national average. Chinese (7.9 per cent), South Asians (7.8 per cent), and blacks (6.5 per cent) are the largest

TABLE 3.7 Visible Minorities in Toronto, Vancouver, and Montreal, 1996

| | Census Metropolitan Area | | | |
| | Canada | Toronto | Vancouver | Montreal |
			(%)	
Total population ('000)	28,528	4,233	1,814	3,288
Visible minority population	11.2	31.6	31.1	12.2
Black	2.0	6.5	0.9	3.7
South Asian	2.4	7.8	6.6	1.4
Chinese	3.0	7.9	15.4	1.4
Korean	0.2	0.7	0.9	0.1
Japanese	0.2	0.4	1.2	0.1
Southeast Asian	0.6	1.1	1.1	1.1
Filipino	0.8	2.3	2.2	0.4
Arab and West Asian	0.9	1.7	1.0	2.2
Latin American	0.6	1.5	0.8	1.4
Visible minority, n.i.e.[a]	0.2	1.1	0.4	0.1
Multiple visible minority[b]	0.2	0.6	0.6	0.1

Notes:
[a] Not included elsewhere. Includes Pacific Islanders and other respondents likely to be in a visible minority group.
[b] Included respondents who reported more than one visible minority group.
SOURCES: Statistics Canada, 1996 Census of Population; Jennifer Chard and Viviane Renaud, 'Visible Minorities in Toronto, Vancouver, and Montreal', *Canadian Social Trends* (Toronto: Thompson Educational Publishing, 2000), p. 22.

groups in Toronto. Chinese are the largest visible group in Vancouver, followed by South Asians (6.6 per cent). Blacks (3.7 per cent) represent the largest visible minority group in Montreal. These numbers illustrate that visible minorities are drawn most heavily to the largest cities.

SUMMARY

The purpose of this chapter is to prepare an empirical demographic context so that the reader may get a sense of how the general Canadian population has grown during the past century. We trace natural increase and immigration, as well as the origin of immigrants. We find that the recent selection system has resulted in many more immigrants from the Third World, in contrast to the earlier predominance of northern European immigrants.

Although in 1871 Canada was made up largely of the British and French charter groups, by 1991 and 1996 others represented one-third of the population. Since immigrants have come

to Canada each year, a considerable foreign-born population has continued to replenish existing ethnic diversity. Ontario has always attracted the largest percentage of the foreign-born, with over half of all immigrants residing there in 1991. Whereas at the turn of the century large numbers of European immigrants helped to open the West to agriculture, since the Second World War south Europeans and Third World immigrants have been drawn to the metropolitan centres.

Four ethnic types clearly emerged: the aboriginals, the charter Europeans, the non-charter Europeans, and the visible Third World minorities. Aboriginals represent only 2 per cent of all Canadians now, and over half of them have signed treaties and live mostly in the Northwest. The British and French, who represent the original European charter groups, now comprise less than half of the Canadian population and hold the most political and economic power. Other Europeans who came to pioneer in the West continued to strengthen the European presence in Canada. Since the advent of the new immigration policy, many Third World visible minorities have arrived from Asia, bringing greater ethnic diversity racially, religiously, culturally, and linguistically. These new visible minorities have entered the larger metropolitan centres of Toronto, Montreal, and Vancouver, and have changed the ethnic makeup of these cities considerably.

Using the models we developed in Chapter 2, we see that all these peoples will need to meet at the economic watering hole (Cell A) to survive, that Canada is indeed made up of dominant Europeans, and that many minorities (Cells D and E) will need to find ways of survival. We are reminded by the postmodernists that in this enormous diversity differences are very real, where a linear monoculture is hardly possible (nor desirable) without conflict. Reason may not always prevail, rational science may not be enough, and the metanarrative will have to include others. Much deconstruction may be necessary to reconstruct a new order, to make these differences work in a plural society and world.

CRITICAL THINKING QUESTIONS

1. Many want to come to Canada. How do we select who may come? Discuss the system we use.

2. How has the origin of the immigrants who came to Canada changed over the past hundred years? How do we classify them? Where do they come from?

3. Provide a demographic profile of the ethnic makeup of Canada in 2001. Which groups dominate?

4. Where in Canada do most immigrants tend to go? Who gets the most immigrants? Which cities attract immigrants most?

5. Discuss ethnic demographic types such as aboriginals, charter groups, Other Europeans, visible minorities. Which groups concentrate where? Do regions vary demographically?

6. How plural has Canada become demographically, compared to earlier? What trends do you see?

SUGGESTED READINGS

Dickason, Olive Patricia, *Canada's First Nations: A History of Founding Peoples from Earliest Times*, 3rd edn (Toronto: Oxford University Press, 2002). Sorting the complex, rich histories of 55 aboriginal nations is a gigantic task that Dickason attempts in this 576-page volume.

Frideres, James, *Native Peoples in Canada: Contemporary Conflicts*, 4th edn (Toronto: Prentice-Hall, 1996). Since 1974, this author has studied Native histories, acts, treaties, land claims, organizations, demography, urbanization, and politics of Canada's aboriginals.

Halli, Shiva, and Leo Driedger (eds), *Immigrant Canada: Demographic, Economic and Social Change* (Toronto: University of Toronto Press, 1999). More than 20 demographers and ethnic scholars discuss immigrant theories, policies, and the economic, social, and demographic impact that immigrants have on Canada's population.

CHAPTER 4

Multicultural Regionalism

Our discussion of Canada's population patterns over time illustrates that the aboriginals possessed the land first, followed by the French, the British, other European groups, and Third World immigrants. The proportions of various groups increased at different times; by 2002 the many ethnic groups were not evenly distributed throughout Canada. The British, for example, dominate in the Atlantic provinces but are a small minority in Quebec, while the French dominate in Quebec and, except for New Brunswick, are a small minority elsewhere. Other Canadians tend to be the majority on the prairies, and in southern British Columbia, but are very sparsely represented in the five most easterly provinces. Aboriginals dominate in the Northlands. Ethnically, the various Canadian regions are very different and we need to examine these regional differences.

REGIONALISM: A SENSE OF PLACE

In 1936 Howard W. Odum (1936:8) proposed using 'region as a tool for analysis' because it can be used as 'a *gestalt* in which all factors are sought out and interpreted in their proper perspective and in a framework for social planning'. Samuel E. Wallace (1981:431), in his presidential address to the Mid-South Sociological Society, suggested that the conception of the American South as a distinctive region was well established by 1800. Wallace claims that each section of the country has different needs, interests, and ambitions, even different theories and forms of government, and in the South ethnicity and race relations play an important part. He goes on to say that 'the South is a region, a society, a set of institutions, an attitudinal stance, a people, a symbol, an idea' (Wallace, 1981:432, 438).

Wallace laments that sociological theories and models of the last two or three decades have been devoid of any sense of place, and he wonders whether that is why they downplay the importance of regions. Regionalism persists because 'to be identified with space means to treat space as part of the self—not simply something to use, abuse, destroy, deface, or pollute' (Wallace, 1981:438). In America's Deep South, the sentiment toward the land and symbolism of the land are still important; I suggest in many Canadian regions this sense of sanctified and hallowed ground is also emerging. Wallace claims that 'we lose explanatory power and we also lose history when we abandon the concept of regionalism. . . . Functionalists occupied no space, so they also included neither past nor future in their models. Regionalism, however, can develop only over time' (1981:439).

Ralph Matthews (1980:43-61) follows the same argument: 'There has been virtually no sustained attempt to develop a "regional sociology".' He is impressed with the overriding concern of Canadian sociologists for the nature of Canadian unity and identity. John Porter in *The Vertical Mosaic* provides no analysis of the regional basis of the Canadian elite; indeed, he declares, 'it has never struck me that regions provide basic group identities in Canada' (1975:6). In his view, modernization tends to obscure a sense of place. Matthews (1980) tries to outline the significance of regional considerations and to prepare the ground for an explanation of regional differences in an attempt to develop a theoretical and analytical framework capable of providing insight into the various divisions in Canada.

For sociologists, however, regions are mostly containers in which important social, political, and economic interaction and structure may be found. Richard Simeon (1979:293) says, 'We must first recognize that in no sense is region an explanatory variable; by itself it doesn't explain anything; nothing happens because of regionalism. If we find differences of any sort among regions, it remains for us to find out why they exist; regionalism is not an answer.' Matthews adds, 'We must delve more deeply into their nature and causes' (Matthews, 1980:50). Some studies (Driedger, 1977b) have focused on language and ethnicity in the various Canadian regions. Ralph Matthews, in his call for a Canadian sociology of regionalism, talks about 'distinctive regional cultures' (1980b:49, 51) and suggests that at least socioeconomic, political, and cultural or group identity factors must be considered. Simeon and Elkins (1979) have formed a fourfold typology based on efficacy and trust in politics with significant differences in various regions of Canada. They controlled separately for social class, education, party identification, sex, age, and size of community, and found that substantial regional differences remained after the controls had been introduced (Simeon and Elkins, 1979:43). They conclude that there are 'distinctive regional cultures'.

Many social factors contribute to distinctive Canadian regions, but here we briefly discuss the original cultural ethos that differentiates regions and the linguistic worlds created by migrants who occupy these regions. Tracing these two factors in at least six regions of Canada we find very different ethnic combinations that indeed form quite different Canadian ethnic regions.

Linguistic Demography

Sapir (1949) suggests that language is a structural symbol system into which children are socialized. He uses The Whorf hypothesis that goes further, to say that this structure of symbols provides an entry into a world of symbols. Language also becomes restrictive because the organization of these symbols directs our thinking toward some ways and not others. Language thus becomes a window through which we look at the universe in a certain way, a form of Weltanschauung, or conditioning to see the world in a distinctive way (Shibutani and Kwan, 1965:61). While most European languages have grown out of a similar language pool, other language complexes in Asia, Africa, and the aboriginal Americas are quite different structurally and in their origins. According to Whorf, immigrants who come to North America from the Third World will see the world in quite different ways. Indeed, when the Europeans came to the Americas, they contacted aboriginals who had very different worldviews.

Scholars have devoted considerable attention to the relationship between language and the ethnic identity of immigrant groups in multilingual settings. They have frequently claimed that preservation and continued use of the traditional mother tongue is an important—if not the most—important component of ethnic identity. Factors such as urbanization, secularization, internal migration, widespread exogamy, industrialization, and others are cited as influential in this general process of linguistic change.

In the 1960s and early 1970s in Canada, it was mostly social psychologists and psycholinguists who began to study the context and dynamics of language groups. They concentrated mainly on English and French as official languages, dealing with questions of bilingualism, second language, learning, and the like (see, for example, Berry and Wilde, 1972; Bourhis, 1994; Boyd, 1999; Clement, 1974; Cummins, 1994; deVries, 1999; Taylor and Gardner, 1970). Similarly, demographic studies based on census data concentrated on the official languages with some reference to non-official language groups which where frequently lumped into the category 'Others' (Henripin, 1974; Lieberson, 1970).

The 1975 study conference, The Individual,

Language and Society in Canada (Coons, Taylor, and Tremblay, 1977), was an early interdisciplinary effort by psychologists, sociologists, and sociolinguists to deal with different aspects of the languages-in-contact situation, including non-official languages. While psychologists mainly brought to the meeting their research on official languages (Berry, 1977; Gardner, 1977), sociologists stressed the broader multilingual and regional dimensions of linguistic research in Canada (Driedger, 1977a; Jackson, 1977). They saw competence in the traditional mother tongue and its continued use as one of a number of ethnic identity factors including religion, endogamy, parochial education, participation in voluntary associations, etc. (Driedger, 1978; Isajiw, 1981; Reitz, 1980). Later sociological studies have increasingly focused on language as one important variable related to ethnic identity (Berry and Laponce, 1994; Bourhis, 1994; Cummins, 1994; deVries, 1999; deVries and Vallee, 1980; Edwards, 1985; Isajiw, 1981).

Several Canadian studies have demonstrated the importance of controlling for immigrant generation and community size in the analysis of language maintenance. For the urban context, O'Bryan and colleagues (1976) sampled 10 groups of adult speakers of non-official languages in five Canadian metropolitan centres and found a fairly rapid decline in traditional mother tongue competence from first- to third-generation Canadians. Fluency in the respective languages was fairly high for the first generation (between 56.0 and 80.7 per cent), but it had virtually disappeared by the third generation. These ethnic groups were able to maintain 'some knowledge' (38.7 per cent) of their ethnic language only into the third generation (O'Bryan, Reitz, and Kuplowska, 1976:45–6). DeVries and Vallee amply describe this phenomenon as 'the levelling effect of the third generation' (1980:132).

Breton, Isajiw, Kalbach, and Reitz (1990) found the same decline when they studied three generations of six groups in Toronto. Those studies in Toronto reveal a similar pattern of progressive linguistic assimilation with succeed-ing generations, although the patterns of shift differ significantly among the ethnic groups surveyed. Whereas there is still some ethnic language knowledge in the third generation (mostly skills in reading and writing), verbal interaction has virtually disappeared. Breton and colleagues (1990:34–91) concur with Gans (1979), and suggest a progressive change in language function from instrumental to expressive or symbolic use.

Comparable studies for rural environments have shown that ethnolinguistic or ethnoreligious groups in more segregated rural enclaves have been somewhat more successful in maintaining ethnic languages (Anderson, 1980; Anderson and Driedger, 1980). Although an extremely high proportion of all respondents was still competent in an ethnic mother tongue (though most of them were bilingual), the actual use and the desire to speak it was consistently lower and varied significantly among the different groups—most markedly among the three German groups (Hutterites: 100 per cent; Mennonites: 68.9 per cent; and Catholics: 29.0 per cent) (Driedger and Hengstenberg, 1986:90–109).

Macro-level surveys of the type discussed in the preceding paragraphs include questions on ethnic origin and aspects of traditional mother tongue competence and use: they are powerful instruments for determining the linguistic condition of large groups (Lieberson, 1966; Lieberson and Waters, 1990). A number of previously mentioned sociological studies of specific groups and geographic locations in Canada, as well as studies that are based on census data (deVries and Vallee, 1980; Henripin, 1974) have yielded valuable insights into the relationship between ethnic identity and language maintenance. However, inherent constraints on form, number, and content of questions on language and the resulting need for categorization and standardization tend to obscure the fact that language is 'a highly complex phenomenon comprised of many physiological, psychological, social and other attributes' (Khubchandoni, 1976:97). Consequently, macro-level data need to be interpreted in a socio-psychological context, taking into account

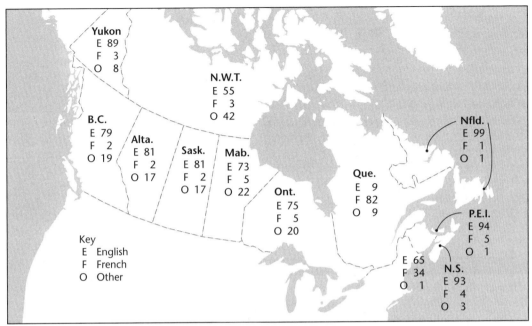

FIGURE 4.1 English, French, and Other Mother Tongues by Provinces, 1991 (%)

SOURCE: Brian Harrison and Louise Marmen, *Languages in Canada*, Catalogue 96–313E (Scarborough, ON: Prentice Hall and Statistics Canada, 1994), pp. 8, 15, 24.

the historical tradition and the language specific peculiarities of the different ethnic groups.

In 1971, Prime Minister Trudeau proclaimed Canada a bilingual and multicultural nation. How do Canadian demographics conform to governmental policy? In the 1991 census 16,311,200 Canadians (60.4 per cent) reported their mother tongue to be English; 6,562,100 (24.3 per cent) reported it to be French; and 4,120,800 (15.3 per cent) claimed a non-official mother tongue. Thus, 85 per cent of the Canadian population reported one of the two official languages as their mother tongue.

These official-language Canadians are not, however, distributed evenly across the country. Figure 4.1 shows that, in the three most easterly provinces (Newfoundland, Nova Scotia, and Prince Edward Island), more than 90 per cent of Canadians learned English as their mother tongue. In the four most westerly provinces and region (British Columbia, Alberta, Saskatch-

ewan, and the Yukon) roughly 80 per cent or more of Canadians learned English as their mother tongue. In the interior provinces (Manitoba and Ontario) more than 70 per cent claim English as their mother tongue. Two-thirds (65 per cent) of the population of New Brunswick, more than half (55 per cent) of the population of the Northwest Territories and Nunavut, and only 9 per cent of the population of Quebec report an English mother tongue. Thus, in each of the 12 regions (except Quebec) more than half the population had learned English first.

French, the second official language, was the mother tongue of 82 per cent of the people in Quebec. One-third (34 per cent) of the population learned French first in New Brunswick, but five per cent or less learned French first in each of the other provinces and regions (Harrison and Marmen, 1994). French ranks first in Quebec and second in three other provinces (New Brunswick, Prince Edward Island, and Nova Scotia).

The greatest concentration of Canadians who learned a non-official mother tongue first is in the Northwest Territories and Nunavut, where 42 per cent of the population learned a non-official language first. Most of these people had learned an aboriginal language first. Non-official mother tongues rank second in the Northwest Territories (42 per cent), Manitoba (22 per cent), Ontario (20 per cent), British Columbia (19 per cent), Saskatchewan (15 per cent), and the Yukon (8 per cent). After English, the aboriginal languages rank second in the northern territories, and German ranks second in the prairies and British Columbia. Ukrainian ranks third in the Prairies and Chinese ranks third in British Columbia. French ranks fourth in the Prairies (Harrison and Marmen, 1994). It is clear that the two official languages dominate in the six most easterly regions; in the six most westerly regions, however, English dominates, followed by other non-official languages.

The extent to which Canadians actually use their mother tongues at home shows even more clearly that Canada is a bilingual country. In Quebec the match between the French mother tongue and the use of French at home is identical (82 per cent). However, in each of the other eleven regions, there is more use of English and less use of French and other languages than their mother tongues suggest. Except for New Brunswick, where one-third (31 per cent) of the population speaks French at home, French is hardly used at all outside Quebec. Only 3 per cent of the population of Ontario and less than 3 per cent of the population elsewhere use it in the home. Those who speak non-official other tongues at home represent 32 per cent of the population of the Northwest Territories, 10 per cent in Manitoba and British Columbia, 5 to 8 per cent in Alberta, 12 per cent in Ontario, Saskatchewan and Quebec, and less than 2 per cent elsewhere. French is the dominant language used in Quebec, and English is used in the rest of Canada. The ethnic linguistic demographics tend to conform quite well to official bilingual national policy.

Original Ethnic Cultural Ethos

While the linguistic demographics confirm that Canada is largely bilingual, we find that culturally the nation is much more ethnically diverse. While immigrants came to Canada largely from northern Europe before the First World War, and from eastern and southern Europe between the two world wars, many others have entered since the Second World War, making the population more culturally diverse.

Comparing Figures 4.1 and 4.2, we see the proportion of British descendants is lower in Figure 4.2 in each of the twelve regions of Canada. On the other hand, the proportion of French, non-charter, and multiple response descendants is higher in Figure 4.2. This comparison shows that the country is moving increasingly toward bilingualism (Figure 4.1), but remains much more differentiated and multicultural in its ethnic origins (Figure 4.2). Let us look at the general regional picture before we discuss ethnic regions.

The first observation in Figure 4.2 is that the aboriginals are a majority in the Northwest Territories and Nunavut, and the French are a huge majority in Quebec. The British are a majority in the three most easterly provinces. Multiple-response and non-charter Canadians are a majority in the five most westerly provinces and the Yukon. These regional tendencies are not surprising when we consider that the aboriginals still dominate the Northwest Territories and Nunavut, their original lands. The Prairies are dominated by European agriculturalists who were part of the great immigration in the 1910–20s, and the eastern regions are occupied by the two charter peoples in Quebec and the Maritimes. Figure 4.2 includes Asians and Africans as Visible Minorities (VM).

Our task later in this chapter is to examine these six regions of Canada, which we suggest are ethnically distinct because of their historically unique demographic and ecological features brought about by immigration and other factors over the past. We also suggest that ethnicity, as a major factor in distinguishing these regions, affects the nation politically, economically, and socially.

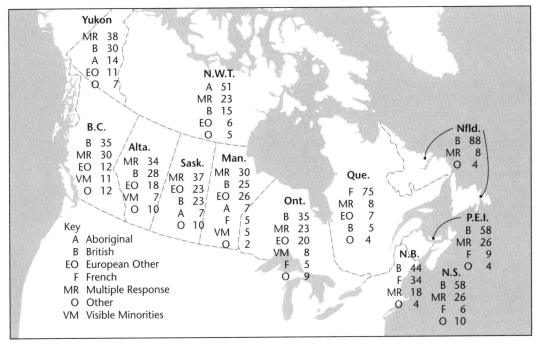

FIGURE 4.2 Ethnic Origin of Canadian Population by Provinces and Regions, 1991

SOURCE: *Ethnic Origin: The Nation*, Catalogue 93–315 (Ottawa: Statistics Canada, 1993); 1991 Census, pp. 12–27.

CANADIAN ETHNIC REGIONS

In our analysis of the various regions, we have plotted the Northlands, the Atlantic region, Quebec, the Bilingual Belt, Upper Canada, and the West as shown in Figure 4.3. The regions vary from unicultural and monolingual in the East, to multicultural and multilingual in the Northwest. High concentrations of the aboriginals in the North, the 'other' ethnic groups in the West, the French in Quebec, and the British in the East represent an interesting mix of cultural values and linguistic patterns.

In sketching the historical, ecological, demographic, political, and economic macro-structures within each region, our underlying assumption is that these six regional ethnic structures in Canada will be quite different, and that they will have different languages, cultural needs, abilities, and aspirations because of these variations. We begin with the aboriginals who

still occupy 80 per cent of Canada in the northerly parts. The Europeans began to invade in the southeast and moved westward to occupy all of the Canadian south, increasingly displacing the aboriginals toward the north. We shall trace these patterns of invasion and succession historically in the six regions.

The Northlands: Multilingual and Multicultural

The Northlands constitute about four-fifths of Canada's territory, a staggering 3,000,000 square miles. Its boreal forests, tundra, and Arctic desert stretch from the Yukon through the vast Northwest Territories and Nunavut to Labrador, and include the northerly two-thirds of British Columbia, the Prairie provinces, Ontario, and Quebec. Relatively few people inhabit this space, which has a population density of about 0.23 persons per square mile. Of this population, a

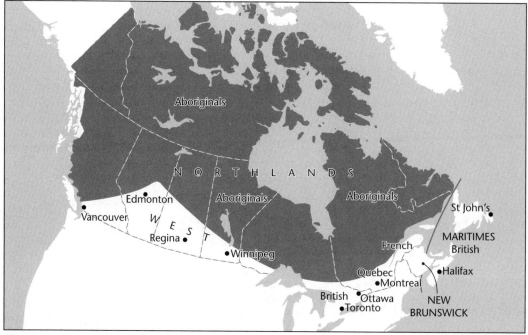

FIGURE 4.3 Cultural and Linguistic Regions, Canada

SOURCE: Leo Driedger and Neena Chappell, *Aging and Ethnicity: Toward an Interface* (Toronto: Butterworths, 1987), p. 49. Reproduced by permission.

majority (51 per cent) are of Native Indian or Inuit origin. Their ancestors arrived here some 14,000 or more years, having come over the Siberian land bridge from Asia after the last ice age. The proportion of people of aboriginal origin increases as we move northward. However, more non-aboriginal people are eroding this northern aboriginal majority as industry seeks to exploit renewable and non-renewable resources.

The population of this region has a very high proportion of rural, non-farm residents. Of this group, the Native Indian and Inuit component far outnumbers the non-aboriginal one. Most people of non-aboriginal ancestry, on the other hand, live mostly in the region's few small cities and towns and on work sites connected with construction, metal mining, or oil exploration and extraction. Even in the towns and settlements where aboriginal people share space with non-aboriginals, the two groups are clearly segregated.

Politically, a large portion of the Northwest Territories is not formally organized, possibly because the way of life in the North does not require it. Recently Nunavut became an organized territory in the eastern half of the Northwest Territories, where the Inuit are a majority. The northern parts that belong to the six most westerly provincial political jurisdictions are largely neglected and ignored. As industry and the southern economic system extend into the north, even more need for political and economic organization will likely develop. The development of a northern oil pipeline is a good example of how the ecology and demography of the region is changing as a result of political and economic decisions to develop an oil industry in the north. The language of communication used in this economic extension is mostly English. If aboriginals wish to benefit from this economic development, they will need to learn one of the two official languages, probably English, in order to get a job.

HIGHLIGHT 4.1 NUNAVUT: DECOLONIZING THE NORTH

The principle of aboriginality as a new paradigm for redefining aboriginal peoples-government relations has gained both constitutional and legislative strength in Canada's Arctic. The old paradigm of treaties, reserves, and outdated colonialism was never practical for the circumpolar peoples, given geographical and demographic considerations (Quassar, 1998). The evolving paradigm is squarely rooted in the principle of aboriginal self-determination over their cultural and social affairs. It is also grounded in the notion that control over material resources and economic self-sufficiency are key in giving practical effect to self-governing initiatives. But the gap between the ideal and reality may prove especially daunting in the implementation, and this Case Study will highlight some of the difficulties in putting an Inuit government into practice in Canada's North.

The Nunavut Nation
The Inuit of the Canadian Arctic have undergone considerable change in response to political and social pressures. Once isolated and without a common awareness for collective action, the Inuit have taken steps since the early 1970s to redefine themselves in relationship with each other and with the Canadian state. In the Eastern Arctic, Inuit aspirations were couched within the framework of Nunavut, the Inuktitut word for 'our land' and also the name of a group of Inuit living in the Eastern Arctic. To date, the concept of Nunavut remains unrecognized in the constitution; nevertheless, the process of defining it and its ratification in 1993 allow us some glimpse into the magnitude of the task that awaits implementation of Nunavut government on 1 April 1999.

The Eastern Arctic Inuit themselves number about 20,000, scattered across a tract of land the size of Argentina. Unlike status Indians in the South, the Inuit were the undisputed landlords of the North, having never entered into treaty arrangements with federal or provincial governments. Legally, however, the Inuit possessed the same status as aboriginal peoples elsewhere in Canada because of a 1939 Supreme Court ruling. Until the 1970s the Inuit did not share a common sense of peoplehood. Political, geographic, dialectical, and jurisdictional problems militated against promotion of a shared and united front under the aboriginal banner. This inability to foster a pan-Inuit identity and aboriginality undermined efforts to exert pressure on central authorities to negotiate territorial self-determination.

The Vision of Nunavut
The vision and struggle for Nunavut gathered momentum during the early 1970s. This redefining process was derived from aboriginal movements in Canada and the United States as well as throughout the world. In 1976, the Inuit Tapirisat submitted its first proposal for the establishment of Nunavut. The plan sought to establish a single Inuit homeland across the Arctic, covering nearly 2,000,000 km of land and adjacent offshore areas, modelled largely on the Cree land claim settlement negotiated with the Quebec government as part of the James Bay agreement. Eight years later, in 1984, the agreement still unsigned, another group, the Inuvialiut Inuit, signed a second land claim settlement in the Western Arctic, including $152 million in cash, 91,770 km of land, and various guarantees, consultation rights, and developmental funds (DIAND [Department of Indian Affairs and Northern Development], *Information*, October, 1996). Having settled their grievances, the Inuvialiut Inuit were free to align themselves with either the more limited proposals of the Denendeh in the Western Arctic or the broad

vision of the Nunavut of the Eastern Arctic. For various political, geographical, and cultural reasons, the Inuvialiut cast their lot with the Denendeh.

What exactly does the Nunavut vision consist of? Nunavut conjures up the same emotional appeal that 'mon pays' does for the Quebecois. The sustaining vision of Nunavut is a society with full control over its culture and language, its resources, and its environment. Proposals for Inuit public government, in which all residents have voting rights regardless of racial or cultural background, rather than aboriginal self-government, reflect the unique demographics of the North, with its high density of indigenous peoples compared to nonindigenes (numbering about 5,000). Equally important is the settlement of Nunavut land claims for securing rights to wildlife and mineral harvesting. The need for such an overarching plan was evident; the social and economic needs of the Inuit were desperate in some cases and forecast to worsen if current trends continued. Forces that were undermining efforts at culture and language preservation were increasingly difficult to control without redefining the government structures of the territorial system. In addition, a diversified economic base was required to meet the material needs of a growing population.

A Vision Realized

The vision of Nunavut came to fruition in May 1993 when the Nunavut Act and Nunavut Land Claims Agreement were signed by federal, territorial, and the Tungavik Federation, making it the largest comprehensive land claim settlement to date in Canada (DIAND, May, 1997). Under the terms of the agreement, the Inuit will receive ownership of 350,000 km of land, including access to 36,000 km of mineral rights. The agreement provides financial compensation of $1.14 billion to be paid out over 14 years. A $13 million Training Trust Fund will be established to ensure the Inuit have the skills to implement the terms of the settlement. A key benefit will be a new type of land-sea resource management structure, with Inuit comprising half of the representatives in these decision-making bodies. The final agreement of a Nunavut Territory and a 'public' government, which will cover about one-fifth of Canada's land mass and came into effect 1 April 1999. The Nunavut Assembly will not resemble aboriginal self-government in the 'sovereign' sense, but will operate as part of Canada's Parliamentary system, with the Inuit in effective control by virtue of the fact they comprise 85 per cent of the population.

To be sure, formidable problems threaten to derail the implementation process, including a continued dependency on federal funding to underwrite the costs of putting the vision into practice. With a population base of around 25,000 including 3,500 in the capital, Iqaluit, Nunavut simply does not have the critical mass of tax base to be self-sufficient and will continue to rely on Ottawa for 98 per cent of its funding (Henton, 1998). The combination of soaring costs of living and deeply anchored social problems will also hinder progress and elicit criticism (Smith, 1995; Andersen, 1998). Still, the fact that the Inuit have already begun to implement wildlife-harvesting rights and participate in environmental exercises suggests that the vision of Nunavut is rapidly becoming a practical reality in a country that itself is still in the process of society building (Legare, 1997; Amagoalik, 1998).

SOURCE: A. Fleras and J.L. Elliott, *Unequal Relations* (Scarborough, ON: Prentice-Hall Allyn and Bacon, 1999), pp. 264–6. Reprinted by permission of Pearson Education Canada Inc.

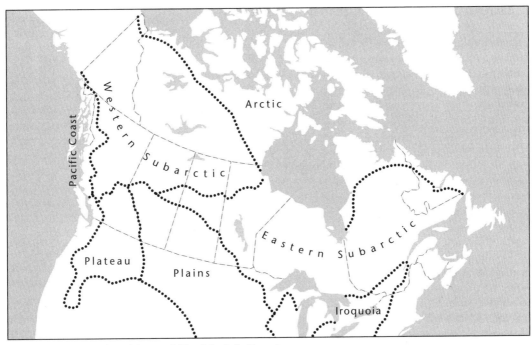

FIGURE 4.4 Early Cultural Areas of Aboriginals in Canada

SOURCE: John Price, *Indians of Canada, Cultural Dynamics* (Toronto: Prentice-Hall Canada, 1979), pp. 52–3.

The issues that attract the most attention and concern for aboriginals in the Northlands have to do with aboriginal rights, the settlement of land claims, and a voice in deciding their own fate. Roughly 3 in 10 claimed a native language (most commonly Cree, Ojibway, and Inuktitut), as their mother tongue in 1991; 86 per cent of those who used their mother tongues at home most often (Harrison and Marmen, 1994:29). The Inuit and status Indians use theirs most; the non-status Indians use theirs least. Less than half of the status Indians living off reserves used their mother tongues at home. Their substantial numbers and isolation in the Northlands have made it possible for the aboriginal peoples to maintain their languages to a greater degree than have the aboriginal peoples in other regions.

In Figure 4.4, Price (1979:52–3) shows the original cultural areas of the aboriginals with the Inuit still located in the northerly Arctic cultural area, and the Native Indians still heavily con-

centrated in the western and eastern subarctic areas. Price (1979:34–5) also shows that the Eskimo-Aleut language families were located roughly in the Arctic, the Athapascan language families in the western subarctic, and the Algonquian language families in the eastern subarctic cultural areas. The area designated as the Northlands in Figure 4.4 includes the three Arctic, western, and eastern subarctic cultural and linguistic aboriginal areas.

'The Arctic is an unusual cultural area in that it has such a severe climate for humans that it was occupied very late in human history and by only one society, the Inuit, who are relatively homogeneous. Inuit culture extends along the coastlines from the eastern tip of Siberia through northern Alaska and Canada to Greenland' (Price, 1979:41). The population of the Inuit in the Canadian Arctic is 0 to 10 persons per hundred square kilometres. They have traditionally lived in igloos in winter and hide tents in summer, used stone lamps to toast their food, and used kayaks and sleds for transportation. Many still live in this fashion, although others have moved to villages near industrial developments.

The subarctic is the largest cultural area in the Northlands, stretching from the interior of Alaska, across the Yukon, the Northwest Territories, Nunavut through northern Ontario and Quebec, and into the Atlantic provinces. It is an area of boreal forests with long, cold winters. Population densities range from 0 to 60 persons per hundred square kilometres. They used to hunt in semi-nomadic bands, are members of the Athapascan and Algonquian language families, roast their meats, live in earth lodges in winter and in bark and hide wigwams in summer, and use the canoe in summer and toboggan in winter for transportation (Price,

1979:42). While some Indians still live in this fashion, most now live in villages near urban and mining projects operated by southern Canadians and use the snowmobile a lot.

The aboriginal residents were the people who lived here first, and they occupy the majority of our land area. Treaties have not yet been made in many areas. They are, however, a very small per centage of our population and are economically and politically powerless. They are also multilingual and multicultural. The trend seems to be for the aboriginals to come south into more urban settings, and there is strong evidence that they adopt English very quickly; only 33 per cent of the aboriginal people in urban areas use their mother tongues (Vallee and deVries, 1975). The Northlands could best be described as multicultural and multilingual.

HIGHLIGHT 4.2 CANADA'S FIRST NATIONS

If any one theme can be traced throughout the history of Canada's Amerindians, it is the persistence of their identity. The confident expectation of Europeans that Indians were a vanishing people, the remnants of whom would finally be absorbed by the dominant society, has not happened. If anything, Indians are more prominent in the collective conscience of the nation than they have ever been, and if anyone is doing the absorbing it is the Indians. Adaptability has always been the key to their survival; it is the strongest of Amerindian traditions. Just as the dominant society has learned from the Indians, so the Indians have absorbed much from the dominant society, but they have done it in their own way. In other words, Indians have survived as Indians, and have preferred to remain as such even at the cost of social and economic inequality. In the Canadian multicultural mosaic, the Aboriginal people are reported to be the least happy with their lot. In part, this is a reaction to cultural loss, par-

ticularly evident in the realm of language. Of the fifty or so aboriginal tongues spoken in Canada at the time of contact, several are now extinct (Beothuk, Huron, Neutral) and most of the others are endangered, some seriously. Cree, Ojibway, and Inuktitut appear to have the best chances of survival. On the other hand, Aboriginal spiritual beliefs have displayed a remarkable vitality and indeed have been enjoying a renaissance. An expression of this has been the introduction of Aboriginal elements into Roman Catholic ritual, a movement that began in the prairie West, particularly in Edmonton. Recently there has been a convergence of Aboriginal and science-based knowledge that holds exciting promise for both the Aboriginal and non-Aboriginal communities. All this has gone hand in hand with the rise of political activism and the campaign for self-determination and self-government. This is the opposite of a separatist movement; what Indians are asking for is full and equal participation in the Canada of today and of the future; this was the clear message of the *Report of the Royal Commission on Aboriginal Peoples.* . . .

The reaffirmation of Aboriginal identity has not been a sudden development; Amerindians have always had a clear idea of who they are. What is new is the demand for recognition of this by the dominant society. Several factors have contributed to this development, some of them of comparatively long standing, and others very recent.

First of all, there has been the growing international recognition of Native art, especially since World War II. West coast art has long been appreciated—dating back to the days of first meetings in the eighteenth century, in fact—but that of other regions has been slower in gaining acknowledgement. In the 1940s, largely through the efforts of Toronto artist James A. Houston, Inuit learned printmaking. Carving in soapstone and ivory and the creation of tapestries were also encouraged; with the support of the Canadian government, the Hudson's Bay Company, and the Canadian Handicrafts Guild and the development of co-operatives to handle production and marketing, Inuit art became known worldwide. Another success story that developed somewhat later, that of Eastern Woodlands art, favours painting over printmaking, although both forms are practised. Crafts such as porcupine quill work, beading, embroidery, and leather work have also come into their own and are much in demand. This flowering of Native arts and crafts illustrates very well the Aboriginal capacity to use new techniques to bring traditional arts, whose antiquity approaches those of Europe, Africa, and Australia, into the contemporary world. In the literary, musical, and theatrical arts also, Native expression is winning respectful attention. The message is clear: Canada's first peoples, far from being interesting relics of the past, are a vital part of Canada's persona, both present and future.

It was only a matter of time for this growing cultural self-confidence to express itself, and to be listened to, in other arenas as well. A key area is education, and Natives have demonstrated their effectiveness in taking control of the schooling of their children. The justice system has been slower to respond, but there, too, the Native input is becoming more evident as it becomes more sure of itself. If one were to pinpoint the moment of truth for this cultural momentum, it would be when Elijah Harper said 'No' to the Meech Lake Accord. The occasion could not have been more appropriate: not only was the whole nation watching and listening, but a good part of the world as well. Harper rose to the occasion, withstood the pressures mounted to bring him into line, and spoke for himself and his people. He even took himself by surprise: 'I never realized that I would have such an impact on this country.' Canada's Natives had finally caught the attention not only of their fellow Canadians but of the international world as well. And they had fundamentally altered the nation's course of events. The standoff at Oka quickly followed, as Amerindians took a determined position against an ancient wrong. The point was emphasized when 300 indigenous leaders held a summit of their own concurrently with the Summit of the Americas, at Quebec City in April 2001. AFN National Chief Coon Come was invited to attend the general summit, but without provision for him to meet with the top leaders of the Americas. Still, this set a precedent that indicated that the message is being heard: no longer will Aboriginal people stand meekly by as others run things to suit themselves, without taking into serious account the people who were on the scene first. As the case of Canada so well illustrates, its confederation may be young, but it has components that are ancient.

SOURCE: Olive Patricia Dickason, *Canada's First Nations*, 3rd edn. Copyright © Oxford University Press Canada, 2002. Reprinted by permission.

The Québécois Heartland: Francophone and Francocultural

Although Jacques Cartier explored the St Lawrence River as early as 1534, it was Samuel de Champlain who established the first permanent European settlement in Canada on the north shores of the St Lawrence at Montreal in 1608 (Trudel, 1985:315). While this first settlement was originally designed to control the French fur trade, it later developed into the settled French Quebec Heartland, a French colony that Champlain had dreamed about. This French settlement in Canada occurred 60 years before the founding of the Hudson's Bay Company by the British in 1670, and 150 years before the British settled in Upper Canada in the 1700s (Guindon, 1988).

For our purposes the discussion of the modern French Heartland comprises all the parts of Quebec that we have not included in the Northlands. It encompasses much of the area on both sides of the St Lawrence and the Gaspé. Hundreds of thousands of people in the region east of Montreal trace their ancestry to settlers in the seventeenth and eighteenth centuries. A very high proportion (95.5 per cent) are of French ethnic origin, and 84 per cent speak French exclusively (Henripin, 1993). Small enclaves of people of non-French ethnic origin and language live in the region, but it is one of the most culturally and linguistically homogeneous parts of Canada.

The social and cultural worlds which people experience directly are French and Québécois. Even in urban places like Quebec City, Chicoutimi, and Trois-Rivières, a person could live out his life in a virtually exclusively French-speaking milieu without hearing or using English. Most stimuli that come from the broader North American context are conveyed in the French language (Guindon, 1988). For instance, football and baseball games, late-night movies, and other American, British, and Canadian media offerings either originate in the French language or have it dubbed in.

A measure of French dominance in this region is seen in the fact that the population of the eastern parts of Quebec shows a net shift from English to French (deVries, 1999; deVries and Vallee, 1980). Because much of this region is economically underdeveloped, it receives very few immigrants. The language support system for the French is very strong in all sectors—with one exception: the economy. Much of the economic sector is bilingual or English at the upper levels of management, although this is changing (Gagnon, 1993). With its high degree of *de facto* French unilingualism and uniculturalism, it would appear that *within the region* itself, language is not a burning issue for the majority of French speakers, although some express concern for the French language in the Bilingual Belt or for the over-representation of English in the economic sector (Guindon, 1988).

In the Québécois Heartland, 82 per cent of the population report French as their mother tongue and 83 per cent also speak French in their homes (Harrison, 1999; Harrison and Marmen, 1994). English is declining as the home language in Quebec, falling from 13 per cent in 1971 to 8 per cent in 1991. The number who are bilingual rose from 2,065,100 in 1981 to 2,413,000 in 1991: more than half (55 per cent) of the bilinguals in Canada, their largest concentration is in Montreal (Harrison and Marmen, 1994:36). The numerical increase in bilingualism among the Québécois French mother tongue group was much greater, totalling more than one-quarter of a million. However, the proportion of Quebeckers who are bilingual increased from 29 per cent in 1981 to 35 per cent in 1991 (Harrison and Marmen, 1994:36).

One of the reasons the English language has persisted in Quebec is that the economic elite were English and tended to use English in their industrial connections with the larger North American scene. However, Toronto is increasingly becoming Canada's dominant financial and industrial base, which means that business headquarters and offices are increasingly shifting to Ontario. Therefore, the power of the English business elite in the province has declined. The use of the French language is a second factor that has encouraged greater French linguistic and cultural influence in Quebec, including provincial legislation that favours the French language. The influence of the Parti Québécois and French nationalists has resulted in some English interests leaving Quebec, which is increasingly adding to an emphasis on French language and culture.

The six million French Québécois living in Quebec represent the largest ethnic regional block in Canada. With their long history in Canada, their renewed emphasis on French identity, the new emphasis to promote French in Canada, and provincial legislation to promote French language and culture, this will remain the strongest single ethnic region if Quebec remains a part of Canada.

With increasing urbanization, multiculturalism with a strong French emphasis is also emerging in Quebec. This is because Montreal will most likely continue to flourish and draw some immigrants who, together with the British minority, will push for multiculturalism. The influences of American investment will likely keep the city multicultural, as will the influence from the rest of Canada.

It is interesting to note the aspiration of French Québécois. They created an early, rural, French Catholic community life in this region; as they became more urban, however, they lost their rural and religious community ties. They seem to have transferred their allegiance from religion to language. Whether language is sufficient ground for a claim to distinctiveness remains a question. At the same time that French Québécois dominate the region, they seem to resort increasingly to provincial legislation to restrict other languages in favour of French. In this practice, they are similar to the British in the past, who relied on language legislation in the West. Quebec's language legislation may help the provincial French majority, but it does little for the others who may desire multiculturalism. This raises the suspicion that neither the British nor the French are interested in multiculturalism, and that both want linguistic dominance (Dion, 1975). The reluctance of leaders in Quebec and of many French-speaking federal cabinet ministers to support multiculturalism furthers the suspicion that they desire French dominance in the region and might want to limit other cultural and linguistic identities, a form of Franco-conformity.

Atlantic Canada: Anglophone and Anglocultural

As far as we know, the Viking Norsemen were the first Europeans to touch North America in about AD 1000 in the Newfoundland area. There is some evidence that they may have settled briefly, but the probability that their progeny is now part of the Canadian population is remote. In 1497, John Cabot left Bristol and landed somewhere on the coast of what is now Newfoundland, claiming it for England. In 1534 Jacques Cartier charted the St Lawrence, bringing Indians back with him to France (Parsons, 1985:253). In 1604, Samuel de Champlain sailed to Acadia with a plan to establish a French colony in the Annapolis Valley of what is now Nova Scotia. Atlantic Canada was visited early by many European explorers; conflict and some evictions took place, especially as the British and French sought to gain control over the new territory.

The most easterly three Atlantic provinces (Newfoundland, Nova Scotia, and Prince Edward Island) exhibit British unilingualism and uniculturalism, with a few small French enclaves. Atlantic Canada is anchored in the east by Newfoundland, which was a British colony until it entered the confederation of Canada in 1949. Eighty-two per cent of Newfoundlanders are of British origin, and 99 per cent reported English as their mother tongue in 1991 (Harrison and Marmen, 1994:10). Over half of the population of Prince Edward Island (54 per cent) and Nova Scota (58 per cent) claimed to be British in 1991, and almost all (93 to 94 per cent) reported their mother tongue to be English (see Figures 4.1 and 4.2).

Their long history is largely British and demographically they are English (Theros and Elliott, 1999). Very few immigrants enter these provinces, leaving the population mainly of British origin. This region represents only 6 or 7 per cent of the Canadian population, so its impact on the total mosaic is small. It is highly unlikely that residents of this region will push for a heterogeneous mosaic. Their aboriginal population is very small. Their black population is English-speaking and small, and multiple responses are growing.

In many ways this region resembles the French Heartland. First, it is underdeveloped economically and has attracted comparatively small numbers of immigrants. Second, apart from the native aboriginals who were here when the Europeans arrived, scores of thousands of people in Atlantic Canada descended from ancestors who settled the region several hundred years ago. As in the French Heartland, some of these ancestors—the Acadians—were French-speaking; the great majority, however, were from England, Ireland, Scotland, and Wales. Thus the British-Canadian character is even more dominant here than it is in parts of Upper Canada.

Survey results suggest that the majority of the people in this region favour two official languages for Canada, certainly more so than in Upper Canada and the West (Vallee and deVries, 1978:762). Multiculturalism and official language policies must seem rather remote to the great majority of people in this eastern area, where the British-Canadian culture and the English language are so dominant. This is the most unilingual and one of the most unicultural regions in Canada; because they are located in the extreme east with its British history, we expect that these Canadians will tend to see Canada very much from an early British perspective.

New Brunswick, which is usually considered part of the Maritimes, has a more mixed French and British history, with the northern third hugging southern Quebec largely French, and the southern half largely English. New Brunswick's Bill 88 calls for a bilingual civil service and for effective equality between the two linguistic groups (Chevrier 1983:39). Implementation is slower than Acadians would like however. They

have four French-language community colleges (Bathurst, Campellton, Dieppe, and Edmundston) (Denis 1999:200). The northern third of New Brunswick benefits greatly from the media services (TV, radio, newspapers) of Quebec, and is able to maintain some of these in its own province as well, but with considerable financial difficulty (Li, 1999:200; Theberge, 1987:36). In many ways the French in New Brunswick are part of a larger bilingual and bicultural belt that requires further examination.

The Bilingual and Multicultural Belt

While the British in the Atlantic provinces are segregated from the French in the heartland of Quebec, these two charter peoples have come into contact frequently ever since they invaded this land from the east. The Hudson's Bay Company, founded by the British, and the Northwest Trading Company, founded by the French, frequently fought to control trading territories as they moved west into the aboriginal lands in pursuit of trade. The remnants of these contacts are still evident in what Joy (1972, 1992) calls a bilingual belt which stretches from Moncton, New Brunswick westward, to Sault Ste Marie on Lake Huron in Ontario. This belt does not conform neatly to any of the provincial territories we have today, but we shall follow it westward from New Brunswick.

New Brunswick is really the only region that approaches the bilingual and bicultural model. In Figure 4.2 we see that 44 per cent of the population of New Brunswick are of British origin, and one-third (34 per cent) are French; one-fourth (22 per cent) claim other origins. As seen in Figure 4.1, two-thirds (65 per cent) of the population claim English as their mother tongue, and one-third reported French (34 per cent). Only 1 per cent learned a non-official tongue first. The French live in the northern half of the province, adjacent to Quebec, and the British live in the southern half in a fairly segregated fashion similar to Atlantic Canada. This province represents only 2 to 3 per cent of the population of Canada.

This bilingual and bicultural region in New Brunswick is the remnant of the earlier Acadian settlements in eastern Canada, and the result of subsequent contacts and invasions that have followed. According to Joy (1972) the likelihood that the French in northern New Brunswick will retain their French language and culture is high; the region hugs the underbelly of the French Quebec Heartland, from which it can continue to receive sustenance from the much larger viable French language and culture in the north. Joy (1972:6) designates Moncton, located in the middle and on the east side of New Brunswick, as the most easterly pole of his Soo-Moncton bilingual line. Joy claims,

> four regions make up an area 1,000 miles long, bounded on the West by a line drawn from Sault Ste. Marie through Ottawa to Cornwall, and on the East by a line from Edmundston to Moncton. Within these limits French is a language in general use; outside this area, it is rarely heard (1972:23).

We have plotted this Soo-Moncton bilingual belt in Figure 4.5 to illustrate the thrust of French exploration and settlement into the West. The early French drive into the West reached into St Boniface and other parts of Manitoba first by trade, and then by settlement. However, the French settlement thrust was halted in the West after the defeat of the Louis Riel struggles in 1870 in Manitoba and 1885 in Saskatchewan. The French presence, though, is still evident.

The region we call the Bilingual Belt straddles the boundaries of Quebec with New Brunswick and Ontario and includes the large metropolitan areas of Ottawa and Montreal. In every region that we have defined for this study, there are important internal variations that we cannot explore because of the limitations of space. Internal variation is nowhere greater and more important than in the Bilingual Belt. For instance, the Montreal metropolitan area, with over 3,000,000 inhabitants, is usually analyzed as a distinctive language zone (Lachapelle,

1979). Obviously, there are very important differences between the Quebec, New Brunswick, and Ontario parts of this zone. These and other variations are not examined here. Rather, we focus on the similarities in pattern shared by all parts of this region.

One is impressed with the sheer magnitude of the language populations in the Bilingual Belt. Sharing this geographical space are 1,223,485 unilingual English; 1,891,095 unilingual French; and 1,633,580 officially bilingual speakers. Because of the salience of English-French language issues in this region, it is often overlooked that in it there are a half-million persons with mother tongues other than English or French, the largest portion of whom are what we have termed unofficially bilingual or English.

Two striking and related sociological features of this region should be noted. One is the high degree of segregation between language categories. The other is the large number of parallel institutions providing strong support for the English and French. There are English and French school systems, universities, hospitals, undertakers, radio and television networks, and the like (Vallee and Dufour, 1974).

The limited information available shows that some languages other than English and French fare as well as, or even better than, those in some other multicultural areas in terms of schools, press, radio, organizations, and so on (Secretary of State, 1972). It should be noted that the degree of maintenance or retention for languages other than English and French is higher in the Quebec portion of the Bilingual Belt than it is for Canada as a whole. That is, the tendency for people with mother tongues other than English or French to also speak that mother tongue most often at home is stronger in this region than in all others (deVries and Vallee, 1980).

In Figure 4.5, we see that the Soo-Moncton Bilingual Belt has raised the bilingual populations in each of the three provinces it affects. Approximately one-third of the population in Quebec (35 per cent) was officially bilingual (English and French); almost one-third of New Brunswick's population (30 per cent) in 1991

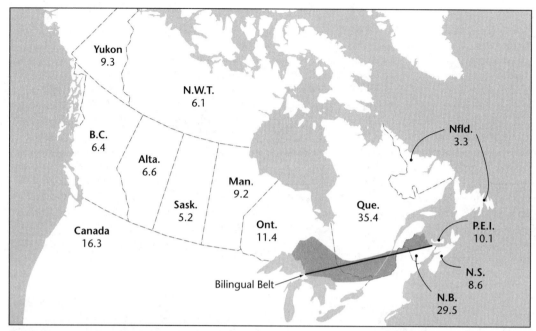

FIGURE 4.5   Canadian Population Who Are Officially Bilingual, by Provinces and Territories, 1991 (%)

SOURCE: Brian Harrison and Louise Marmen, *Languages in Canada*, Catalogue 96–313E (Scarborough, ON: Prentice-Hall and Statistics Canada, 1994), p. 36.

was bilingual; and one-tenth of the population in Ontario (11.4 per cent) was officially bilingual in 1991. Between 1981 and 1991, bilingualism rose in every province, but the heart of official bilingualism is in this Soo-Moncton Bilingual Belt region. The number of officially bilingual people increased from 7.6 per cent in 1981 to 8.5 per cent in 1991 among anglophones and it increased from 36.2 to 38.9 per cent among francophones during the 1981–91 decade. This increase occurred most noticeably in the Bilingual Belt region, where opportunities for the use of both official tongues are best (Harrison and Marmen, 1994:39). In 1991, 4 million Canadians could speak both official languages. More than one-third of Quebec's population can speak both official languages. Bilingualism is related to proximity to the Quebec French Heartland, and rates of official bilingualism drop as distance from Quebec increases. More than half the English mother

tongue group is bilingual in Quebec (Harrison and Marmen, 1994:38). Citizens in the rest of Canada outside the Bilingual Belt have not seen official bilingualism as one of their priorities and are not as willing to put forth the effort to accomplish bilingualism.

Language conflict in this region draws world-wide attention for the obvious reason that Quebec is probably one of the very few regions in the world where English speakers feel threatened by language legislation. In New Brunswick and Ontario, French speakers have to fight to acquire or retain language rights, particularly in the educational system. There is a substantial body of literature on these language conflicts (Jackson, 1975; Joy, 1992; Juteau-Lee and Lapointe, 1977). The only points we want to make here are: 1) that this is the only part of Canada where the Official Languages Act designating English and French as the official languages of the country is likely to produce the results desired by legislators; and 2) despite the general acceptance of the ideology of bilingualism and multiculturalism *de facto*, multiculturalism probably has a bright prospect for realization insofar as cultural maintenance and development depends on language, for in this region continental European and Third World languages show a fair degree of staying power.

Upper Canada: Anglophone and Multicultural

The first United Empire Loyalists settled in Upper Canada, the southern part of Ontario in 1784, shortly after the American Revolution. In those early days the British in Upper Canada were surrounded by potential enemies with the Americans to the south (whom they had to battle in the War of 1812), the larger French settlement to the east, and the many aboriginals to the northwest. At that time it was not clear that York (now Toronto) and southern Ontario would become the stronghold of the British establishment (Armstrong, 1981:274).

The region we have labelled Upper Canada comprises all of Ontario outside the parts we have included in the Bilingual Belt and the Northlands. At one time Upper Canada referred to a political entity settled and controlled by British immigrants and United Empire Loyalists, and separate from what is now the province of Quebec, then called Lower Canada.

One outstanding sociological feature of the region is the dominance of southern Ontario, in particular that portion stretching along the shore of Lake Ontario from Oshawa through Toronto to Niagara Falls. This portion has about one-fourth of the entire Canadian population and within it is concentrated the financial and manufacturing core of the country. Its economic dominance continues to make it a magnet for most of the immigrants who have come to Canada since World War II.

In many ways the ethnolinguistic profile of Upper Canada is similar to that of the West. As Figures 4.1 and 4.2 show, in both regions there are substantial numbers whose origins are other than English or French. However, Upper Canada did have a higher proportion of people of British origin than the West. Many of its smaller cities, towns, and rural areas still retain some British-Canadian flavour of the past.

Although English unilingualism in this region is as high as in the West (73 to 83 per cent), Ontario has a longer anglophone British history. Very strong objections have been raised to the establishment of French-language educational and media institutions at local levels. This has been the case even where the French presence goes back several generations (e.g., Penetang, Welland, and Windsor). It appears that the idea of an officially bilingual country is acceptable to many people in this region provided that French language rights are given concrete recognition in Canada as a nation.

Institutional supports for non-English languages and cultures are many and varied especially in cities like Toronto. Even more than in the West, the stronghold of multiculturalism, one is impressed with the array of ethnic and foreign-language radio and TV programming, newspapers, shops, and the like. The trend is toward multiculturalism as an ideal, particularly in the larger cities where those of British origin are a declining proportion of the population.

Because Ontario is the industrial hub of Canada, it tends to set the economic pace for the country. With a concentration of the British economic elite (Porter, 1965) and with more than one-third of the entire Canadian population, this region tends to be a magnet that has enormous political influence in Canada. The attractiveness of urban industrial activity tends to draw immigrants and migrants from all directions. Thus, the use of English in the economic process will likely gain strength. More study is needed to see to what extent economic and political elites are moving increasingly into Toronto, and the extent to which persons of non-British stock are able to enter the economic and political arena. Have the French, the Germans, the Ukrainians, the Italians, and the Jews broken into this power elite? Is learning French a factor in gaining a place within the economic elite?

Recently this urban industrial area has attracted many immigrants into its labour market so that over half of the population is foreign-born. These immigrants represent many cultures from northern and southern Europe and the Third World. Thus, the urban areas of Ontario are changing from highly British cultural areas to multicultural and multiracial areas where many languages are used. These new immigrants, however, are competing for jobs and are learning English. Although the British culture is not threatened in Upper Canada, multiculturalism is certainly on the rise.

In Ontario approximately 85 per cent of the people use English at home (Harrison and Marmen, 1994:10). Only about 3 per cent speak French at home. Although the population of Ontario has made some efforts to become bilingual in French and English, the English language is dominant and other languages constitute a small minority. This region could best be described as anglophone with strong multicultural trends.

Although the linguistic and cultural conditions of the West and Upper Canada seem to be similar, they are very different historically. The West has been strongly multicultural and multilingual throughout its comparatively short history. Because it is less industrialized however, it does not attract great numbers of immigrants; except for Alberta. Consequently, its cultural diversity is not increasing. In Ontario, however, with a very strong influx of new Third World immigrants, multiculturalism and multiracialism are growing.

The West: Multicultural and Anglophone

The many wars and animosities between the British and French during the colonization of early North America spilled into the settlement of the West. The French settlers who expanded westward from the Quebec heartland extended their Bilingual Belt well beyond Sault Ste Marie to St Boniface, now part of Winnipeg. Louis Riel, a French Metis, was a leading force in convincing the East to recognize Manitoba as the fifth province in Confederation, as it did in 1870. Both the British Hudson's Bay Company and the French Northwest Company extended their fur trade to the forks of the Red and Assiniboine rivers, where they established their forts. The first of 11 treaties was signed with the Indians of the West in 1871 in Fort Garry, when Manitoba was a new province. Because the population was half French and half English, Manitoba was declared a bilingual province. After the defeat of Riel in St Boniface in 1870, however, the French ceased to expand westward. Soon other European immigrants converged on the West so that the French proportion of the population declined (Driedger, 1996).

The West, which includes the southern portions of the four most westerly provinces (British Columbia, Alberta, Saskatchewan, and Manitoba), was the domain of food-gathering aboriginal peoples and it was settled in the last century by immigrants of many European origins. This is the only region where no group is in the majority, although the British form the largest group. The region is highly rural involving agriculture and fishing; it includes a multitude of substantial enclaves of British, German, Ukrainian, French, and smaller ethnic groups. Although the Hudson's Bay Company, administered from Britain, traded in the area for 200 years previous to Manitoba's entry into Confederation (1670–1870), a diversity of European ethnic groups settled the region and began social institutions.

Although many ethnic groups seek to maintain their ethnic languages, the language used at home by the majority (86 to 93 per cent) is English (Harrison and Marmen, 1994:10). Many of these groups promote British, Ukrainian, German, French, and other cultures because no one group dominates the region culturally. Many of the people in the region desire a form of unofficial bilingualism that includes English and their own ethnic tongue (O'Bryan, Reitz, and Kuplowska, 1976). Few Westerners aspire to learn French, and Gagnon (1974) and Gagnon (1993) found that positive attitudes to a language were important in attempts to learn it. Most Westerners consider official bilingualism

(French and English) an impractical imposition because the French are only the fourth-largest population on the Prairies. The need for French is limited, so there is little motivation for those who do not speak it to learn it (Gardner and Smythe, 1975).

One hundred years ago, when the European population in Manitoba was half French and half British, the potential for a bilingual province looked bright (Flanagan, 1991). However, because the British refused to support Riel, and the French did not immigrate in numbers sufficient to reinforce their proportion of the population, the demographic mass swung in favour of the British. Since then the mass migrations of other ethnic groups into the West have turned the region into a multicultural region. With the rise of other ethnic groups, the demographic change is being reinforced by increasing political and economic activity by all groups in all provinces. The ethnic diversity of provincial cabinets is evidence of this multicultural approach to life in this region. The official working language is English; other languages such as French, German, and Ukrainian are kept up by many groups as part of their ingroup cultural heritage. History bears out that French and languages other than English have not been encouraged and have often been systematically legislated against by provincial governments, especially in Manitoba and Saskatchewan.

Three-fourths or more (73 to 83 per cent) of the population in the four most westerly provinces reported their mother tongue as English, less than 1 in 20 (2 to 5 per cent) claimed the French mother tongue (Harrison and Marmen, 1994:24). Up to one-fourth in Manitoba reported a non-official mother tongue (15 to 22 per cent) (Driedger and Hengstenberg, 1986). English is clearly the language of a large majority, and non-official languages run a strong second. In fact, the German mother tongue ranks after English, followed by Ukrainian and French. The West is clearly an English-language region.

Culturally the West is strongly diversified with strong multiple responses (MR). As seen in Figure 4.2, well over half of the population in the West reported non-charter ethnic origins. Less than 5 per cent reported French as their ethnic origin, and less than half (23 to 35 per cent) reported British origins in 1991 (Harrison and Marmen, 1994). The charter groups do not dominate in the West as they do in the East. Except for multiple responses, the British are the largest group; the French rank fourth in size after the British, Germans, and Ukrainians. The West is made up of many ethnic groups, largely from northern and eastern Europe, who were part of the great migrations before and between the great wars. The West is the most multicultural region of Canada with high European other (EO) and multiple responses (MR).

Official bilingualism and biculturalism (meaning English and French language usage and culture) seems unrealistic for the West. A more appropriate formula would be multiculturalism and anglophone. English is spoken and accepted by most Westerners. Because no group dominates the region culturally, nor has the right to such a claim historically, demographically, economically, or politically, it is realistic to promote a variety of cultures and languages.

The concept of Canada as an officially bilingual country does not have much of an appeal to the majority of people in this region (Driedger, 1996). According to one study, the goal of 'unofficial' bilingualism—the combination of English with any other language—is more acceptable than that of English-French bilingualism (O'Bryan, Reitz, and Kuplowska, 1976). In other words, the French and their language are regarded as another minority in the region with no stronger claim to official recognition than other groups such as Germans, Poles, or Ukrainians (Vallee and deVries, 1978:162f).

It would appear that language, as such, is not a major issue in this region and that the vast majority assume that English is and ought to be the only official language for the West. On the other hand, there is a strong resistance to the idea that any one culture should be regarded as the official one. The ideal is that of multiculturalism, brought to the West by thousands of immigrants who form an ethnic mosaic. The bulk of new immigration that might replenish the older ethnic enclaves is, however, flowing into Upper Canada (Driedger, 1996).

Dawson's *Group Settlement: Ethnic Communities in Western Canada* (1936) is a good example of research about the West, using the Chicago School's approach. He examines the Prairies as an ecological area into which a multitude of ethnic groups entered, establishing their many communities. He then selects five groups (the Doukhobors, Mennonites, Mormons, German Catholics, and French Canadians) and devotes the entire volume to various topics: their settlement, invasion, and succession; their means and modes of living; their resistance to secularization; their community building; their establishment of organizations; and their social adjustment and persistence. Dawson's emphasis on ethnicity and religion is similar to many other studies made by sociologists of the Chicago School, who sought to research the patterns of settlement, the forms of community organization, and the extent to which these new immigrants persisted or assimilated (Driedger, 1984: 168–71). The focus was on a variety of distinctive groups living first in rural segregated bloc settlements, and later converging upon emerging urban areas (Anderson, 1972, 1980).

To understand the Canadian West, we must first discuss the unique diverse regional context and assumptions of other regions. From the Western view, we must ask such questions as why the East sent two armies to suppress Riel; why land claims with aboriginals are not being dealt with; why the West produced so many new political parties (such as the Progressive, Social Credit, CCF, and Reform); and why there was so much western opposition to a new constitution. While economic and political modernity factors are certainly relevant, we propose that traditional factors of counter-modernity (such as ethnicity and religion) are important.

Reginald Bibby (1995:37) found in his national surveys of Canada in 1975, 1980, 1985, 1990, and 1995 that more than half (55 per cent) of all Canadians endorsed official bilin-

gualism in 1995, a rise from 49 per cent in 1975. He found that official bilingualism was accepted by most of the population in Quebec (81 per cent in 1995), and that it was least accepted on the prairies (36 per cent in 1995). Almost half of the people outside Quebec (46 per cent in 1995) endorsed official bilingualism. In each of the regions, however, acceptance of bilingualism increased between 1975 and 1995.

Bibby (1995:39) also found that a majority in Canada (56 per cent) preferred an ethnic mosaic (multiculturalism), while only half as many (27 per cent) preferred to see a Canadian melting pot (amalgamation or assimilation) in 1985, but this changed to 44 per cent and 40 per cent by 1995. This did not vary as much by regions, with over half of the Canadians in all regions favouring the mosaic in 1985, and all regions except Atlantic dropping below 50 per cent by 1995. Berry and colleagues (1976) found similar tendencies in their 1974 Canadian national sample, as did Driedger and Reid (2000). Canadians have adopted a policy of diversity in religion and politics for years, and the same choice is also increasing with respect to language use and cultural pluralism. However, Canadians in the various regions seem to see the ethnic future of Canada differently. Some want more pluralism, others more assimilation, and still others prefer modifications or variations in between.

SUMMARY

As Prime Minister Trudeau announced in 1971, Canada is officially bilingual, with French the dominant language in Quebec and English dominant in the rest of Canada (Driedger, 2000b). Although official bilingualism is increasing in all of Canada, the region surrounding the federal government in the Ottawa-Hull centre is actually practising official bilingualism best. Unofficial bilingualism (English and another language) is practised most in the northwest.

Aboriginals still dominate in the vast Northlands of Canada where multilingualism and multiculturalism reign. Remnants of aboriginals still remain in the northern parts of the Prairies. Unilingualism and uniculturalism is dominant in French Quebec, part of the first European settlement along the St Lawrence River. Such single linguistic and cultural British dominance is also evident in Atlantic Canada, especially in Newfoundland, which was a British possession until recently. Joy's Bilingual Belt represents the remnants of old Acadia especially in New Brunswick, stretching east and west from bilingual Ottawa. In anglophone Ontario and the West multiple ethnic responses are now the largest category. Visible minorities are on the rise in urban Ontario, along with remaining aboriginals in the western half of Canada.

Indeed, we found that Canada is predominantly bilingual and multicultural. Canada is multicultural both in governmental policy and in fact, although not all residents recognize this reality equally. Likewise, many people recognize that Canada is officially bilingual, but that there are great variations in the numbers who actually know and use two official languages. A sense of place has been developed historically, linguistically, and culturally in many distinct regions of Canada.

The different ethnic and racial demographic patterns in each of the six regions, shows how difficult it is to try to develop a single structural model like we designed in Chapter 2. It is clear that the British are more dominant in the Atlantic and Upper Canada regions, so processes illustrated in Cell B are more common there, while in Quebec where the French are dominant, Cell E comes into play more. Visible minorities are most heavily located in Ontario and British Columbia, so two other regions are more actively in play in Cell D. The Inuit and Native Indians in the Northlands, actually fit into two cells; Cell E because they want to retain their identities, and Cell D because, like other visible minorities, they are often discriminated against. As we move through the chapters, we hope that the reader will increasingly see the multiple dimensions that are at work in a very diverse society. At the same time as we examine this structurally, we look through the postmodern lens and see that there is diversity everywhere, that it is hard to work only in a rational linear way, and that deconstruction and reconstruction among such diverse populations is constantly ongoing.

CRITICAL THINKING QUESTIONS

1. What is meant by 'region as a sense of place'? What does it mean demographically, linguistically, culturally, ethnically?

2. Sketch a linguistic map to show the diversity of languages spoken by the aboriginals of Canada.

3. Outline the six Canadian ethnic regions that Driedger discusses. What linguistic and cultural combinations did he find?

4. How diverse were the aboriginal cultures originally, and how did the environment shape these cultures? Illustrate.

5. How is history a factor in shaping the Maritime, Quebec, and Upper Canada regions? Compare. Discuss.

6. What does it mean to say that the West is multicultural and anglophone? What indicators can you use to describe the region?

SUGGESTED READINGS

Berry, John W., Rudolf Kalin, and Donald Taylor, *Multiculturalism and Ethnic Attitudes in Canada* (Ottawa: Minister of Supply and Services, 1976). Three psychologists analyze the first national survey of Canadian attitudes on multiculturalism.

Fleras, Augie, and Jean Leonard Elliott, *Multiculturalism in Canada: The Challenge of Diversity* (Toronto: Nelson, 1992). These authors discuss the dimensions of multiculturalism, including linguistic, political, educational, legal, and cultural diversity.

Kalbach, Madeline A., and Warren E. Kalbach (eds), *Perspectives on Ethnicity: A Reader.* (Toronto: Harcourt, 2000). Twenty contributors discuss ethnic issues under general topics of the changing Canadian mosaic, ethnic integration and persistence, power and inequality, prejudice and discrimination.

Dimensions of Identity and Solidarity

I n Part I we presented the theoretical background for this volume; in Part II we sketched the larger empirical demographic and regional context for studying Canada's people. In Part III we will devote three chapters to developing the dimensions of ethnic identity and solidarity. The voluntary ethnic identity (Cell E) part of the Conformity-Pluralist conceptual model, which we presented in Chapter 2, will be our focus here. In Chapter 5 we focus on the unique Québécois 'nation' within a 'nation' of French peoples in eastern Canada. They were the first Europeans who came here, and the French language is a sacred part of their heritage. In Chapter 6, the focus is on general theories of ethnic identity, identification factors, and ethnocultural dimensions of identity for others who voluntarily wish to retain their heritage (Cell E). In Chapter 7 we discuss how groups like Jews, Hutterites, Mennonites, French Catholics, and others construct a 'sacred reality' (a 'sacred canopy') around religion, heritage, culture, language, and family to continue their traditions without assimilation.

We begin in Chapter 5 by creating the Québécois setting, tracing the origins of New France. We sketch the demographic and regional setting in Quebec, and review the development of the French ideologies that have been nurtured in the east for four hundred years. The French language is a very important symbol system, where French has become an official second language of Canada, and we trace the continuity and changes that have occurred. Excellent studies of the early French habitants by Miner and the effects of industrialization by Hughes help illustrate how much effort goes into creating a 'Québécois nation' within the larger Canada. Prime Minister Trudeau had a very different vision of what should become of the French, but René Lévesque wanted separation so French Canadians could create their own sovereign state. There has been much conflict, and these ideologies continue to be fought in the bosom of Canada.

CHAPTER 5

Language and The Québécois 'Nation'

Canada is unique on this continent because it contains within its borders six million francophone citizens, most of them located in the province of Quebec. These French Québécois represent a large bloc (23 per cent) within Canada, but are a small francophone island in the continental sea of 270 million anglophones (McRoberts, 1990:98; Taylor and Sigal, 1982: 59–70). French Quebeckers are distinctive in that all five of Weber's markers of identification apply to them. They are of Caucasian European origin, their French culture provides a consciousness of kind, they are largely Roman Catholic, they have emerged as a distinctive 'people', and they still think of themselves as a 'Volk' or 'nation'.

French Québécois are the best example of an ethnic 'nation' that has maintained its identity for almost four hundred years. They are the reason that Canada is now constitutionally bilingual. They have made plural options increasingly possible, and multiculturalism a national option (Breton and Savard, 1982; Guindon, 1988). Let us examine their origins, region, ideologies, language, and culture to see why they are the major voluntary pluralist force in cell E of the Conformity-Pluralist model, resisting assimilation and amalgamation.

THE QUÉBÉCOIS SETTING

New France was one of the first European settlements in North America. In its demographic and regional setting a francophone system emerged, which has become Canada's second official language (Burnet, 1988:13–16).

The Origin of New France

Almost four centuries ago, Samuel de Champlain founded what is now Quebec, only a year after the first permanent European settlement was founded in Williamsburg, Virginia, in 1607. New France was a French colony, the first European settlement in what is now Canada. No more than 10,000 French immigrants came to settle along the St Lawrence River (Rioux, 1971:12). These French settlers who came to be called 'habitants', had to defend themselves against the Iroquois Indians in a harsh environment. As rural, unlettered settlers they began to develop a 'little' tradition, which became very important after the 1760 conquest. They adapted to the new environment and were left to their own devices after the conquest by Britain. The 'great' tradition cultivated in schools and by the elite was represented by French military, clergy, and businessmen who were mostly interested in the fur trade and profit. After the conquest most of them left the St Lawrence region and returned to France, and it took several generations for new leaders to emerge from within the habitant nation (Guindon, 1988:3–17).

According to Jacques Henripin (1993), the largest waves of immigration had come in 1663 and 1671, so that by 1700 the French settler population was about 15,000. They were divided into 82 parishes: 48 on the left and 34 on the right banks of the St Lawrence River. By 1771 the agglomerations of Quebec City, Montreal, and Trois-Rivières were beginning to emerge as urbanized areas. Two classes developed—the elite and the habitants. The elite consisted of the administrators and higher clergy who had arrived recently and lived in the urban areas, while the habitants had lived in small, rural, strip villages for generations. The elite used France as their reference point, while the rural habitants soon developed their own French-Québécois characteristics and formed their own indigenous lifestyle. Even some of the village French priests began to have their differences with the elite clergy linked to France. It was the habitants who continued the Quebec nation after the conquest (Juteau, 1992:323–34).

The Demographic and Regional Setting

The French settled on both shores of the St Lawrence, which today is part of the province of Quebec. While the British first settled in Virginia in 1607, in Canada they were fur traders for the Hudson's Bay Company that began in 1670 in the Canadian northwest. The British did not settle permanently in Canada until the mid-1700s. Thus, the French settlers on the St Lawrence were for about 150 years the first and only European settlers in what is now Canada. They were starting to develop a French colony that was really the beginning of a new nation called New France. The original 10,000 French settlers grew so that before the conquest, and even after 1760, the French settlers were a large European majority in Canada (McRoberts, 1990). The British conquerors after 1760 were faced with integrating a very large bloc of French habitants who had lived here for many generations in segregated, contiguous, solid French communities, unbroken by non-French settlers. The French habitants were basically the sociocultural society that could most naturally rule themselves as a Quebec nation. However, the conquest interrupted this natural development of a uni-ethnic people. About 1000 of the elite leaders—including administrators, businessmen, and the educated elite—returned to France, leaving the less educated rural habitants to their oral traditions (Rioux, 1971:30). Many habitants were not entirely displeased with the departure of these French elite colonists, although future prospects without experienced leaders would not be easy.

The French settlements along the St Lawrence were fashioned after the Old French feudal system with some modifications (Guindon, 1988:3–24). A feudal estate was granted to a seigneur, who then was obligated to get settlers and to develop the land. A rang system was developed in which settlers received a strip of land, called a rang, on the waterfront. The rang was 200 to 250 metres wide and extended away from the water in a long narrow strip into the treeline. New France literally was the opening up of a river civilization, first along the south shore and later along the north shore. Later, tributary rivers were settled so that:

> [t]oward the end of the French regime, one had only to take a canoe trip along the St. Lawrence and the Richelieu rivers for an almost complete enumeration of Canadian homes; the waterfront or shoreline was synonymous with settled country (Deffontaines, 1965:4).

This rang system had several advantages in the pioneer setting. It allowed settlers to have large narrow land tracts extending away from the river. The layout of the lots afforded protection because the farmyards were lined along the river not far from each other. This fairly close proximity provided more protection and social contact, and they also had access to the river for transportation and fishing. Indians, home and forest fires, famine, sickness, and the long cold winters were all a threat (Guindon, 1988:3–17). Mutual aid and protection were more readily available because of the ecological layout. Later, roads that each habitant had to keep passable followed the river; eventually modern highways, electricity, telephone, and bus services followed the same river shore.

Soon Catholic parishes were established, with churches also lining the river shore at intervals. These churches were named after saints such as St Denis and St Pascal. Soon stores, commerce, social halls, and agencies surrounded these churches and the elderly moved closer to church, leading to the establishment of these parish centres as villages and towns. Professionals such as doctors, lawyers, and notaries joined some of the centralized settlements (Guindon, 1988). With this rural social order, residents of these seigneurial systems were slow to consider going to the city and urbanization did not develop quickly. After the conquest, however, the Quebec population became more rural (Rioux, 1965:34). By 1871, only one person in five lived in the city. Today if you take a car going northeast from Montreal along the north shore toward Quebec City, you will find that the population becomes increasingly francophone. Beyond Quebec City, toward Sept Isle and Labrador, only French radio can be heard. French Canadians are still segregated in rural eastern Quebec.

After the conquest Quebec became more isolated and more homogeneous than before. In 1760, one-fourth of the Quebec population was not engaged in agriculture; by 1825, 88 per cent of the population was rural. In 1871 four-fifths of the population was still rural. High birthrates doubled the rural habitant population every 25 years, and it was largely illiterate: 'barely ten percent had learned, imperfectly, to read and write' (Rioux and Martin, 1964:36). The French revolution occurred shortly after the conquest, which isolated Quebec even more, and it influenced the Quebec habitants very little (Guindon, 1988:4–11).

'By 1840 Lower Canada contained 500,000 French-speaking people and 75,000 English-speaking people' (Rioux, 1965:45). A rebellion had taken place in 1837 and 1838, after which Lord Durham was sent from Britain to assess the problems. When he came, he found 'two nations warring in the bosom of a single state: [he] found a struggle, not of principles, but of race . . . every contest is one of French and English in the outset, or becomes so ere it has run its course' (Wade, 1968:197). Durham's remedy was simple, namely to assimilate the

French of Lower Canada into English-speaking Upper Canada. He wrote:

> I entertain no doubt of the national character that must be given to Lower Canada; it must be that of the British Empire; that of majority of British America; that of the great race which must, in the lapse of no long period of time, be predominant over the whole of the North American continent. . . . Much as they struggle against it, it is obvious that the process of assimilation to English habits is already commencing (Wade, 1968:212).

Durham unabashedly proposed assimilation after the rebellion; in particular, he proposed Anglo-conformity, an amalgamation into the dominant group. The *Act of Union* in 1840 was supposed to bring about the anglicization of French-speaking Lower Canada. Three decades later, the 1870–85 Louis Riel affair opened up the same French-English conflict in the West; it was dealt with by sending armies from the East to ensure Anglo-conformity.

The Development of Ideologies in Quebec

Marcel Rioux (1973) analyzing the development of the various ideologies of francophones in Quebec, suggests that three ideologies have appeared in Quebec since 1840: 1) the conservative ideology, 2) an ideology of confrontation, and 3) the affirmation of Quebec by development and participation. Let us look at each briefly.

After the rebellion of 1837–8, the Québécois sensed that they were to become a minority. They no longer sought to become an independent society, but turned their attention to the preservation of their religion, language and culture. Rioux (1973:263) calls this practice the conservative ideology. It marked a time of tragic contraction when the Québécois gave up their sense of nation, but became an ethnic group that wanted to maintain its heritage. The English sought to divide the French along the St Lawrence from those in Acadia to dissipate their demographic strength. The clergy and the Catholic parish turned inward, seeking to promote their religious ideology with less emphasis on the larger political aims. The church helped to build an ideology of conservation of tradition. Demographically, politically, and religiously, the Québécois reserved control. The English, however, dominated Quebec's commerce, industry, and finance from Montreal (McRoberts, 1990:98–107).

During the 15-year tenure of the French prime minister, Wilfrid Laurier (1896–1911), Quebec had begun to change extensively. In 1871 Quebec was 77 per cent rural; by 1911, it was half urban (Henripin, 1993:304–18). As Montreal's English commerce and industry developed, many rural Québécois had moved to the city to find work as labourers. The French habitants were poorly educated in their Catholic schools, and they were not encouraged to enter higher learning. Therefore, they were destined for only lower-status jobs with little opportunity for promotion and upward mobility. The conservative ideology lasted until the end of the Second World War, but between the wars changes had taken place that provided opportunities for a new ideology (Guindon, 1988:18–24).

Rioux (1965:73–84) called the period after the Second World War 'the springtime of Quebec'. The war effort had escalated the industrialization and urbanization process in Quebec as well as elsewhere in Canada. With the death of the Conservative premier Duplessis in 1959, the Liberals and Jean Lesage came into power in 1960, starting the 'quiet revolution' in Quebec. Quebeckers began to shrug off the fatalism of their conservative ideology and began what Rioux (1973:269–73) calls the ideology of contestation and recoupment. The population involved in agriculture dropped by 64,000 and numbers in non-agricultural occupations increased 79,000 to 237,000 between 1911 and 1951 (Keyfitz, 1965:227). In 1960 the Liberals began to modernize the state, and instilled the hope of change. Québécois turned from seeing themselves as only an ethnic group

that wanted to preserve its culture and language to a French society that wanted to compete in the larger marketplace. This ideology of recoupment tended to discredit the traditional power elites and the ideology of conservatism and turned Quebec's attention to the future.

While the first ideology was directed toward the past, the second was turned toward the present and called for an update. Rioux (1973:274) believes the third ideology of René Lévesque and the separatist movement combines the old and the new in what he calls the ideology of development and participation. This ideology recognizes Quebec as a culture different from others in North America, and reaches back to the earlier visions of a Quebec that hoped for independence and a separate nation before the union and confederation. It calls for a Quebec with a unique culture, language, religion, and traditions, but also for an independent economic and political society that can control its own destiny. The third ideology is most radical because it no longer wishes to be dominated by the rest of Canada. Thus, separatism calls for drastic structural and political changes to liberate Quebec (McRoberts, 1990:110–17).

The referendum over which René Lévesque presided called for sovereignty-association with Canada and was defeated by Quebeckers by a 60-40 margin in 1980 (Guindon, 1988:112–24). In a second referendum (30 October 1995) the sovereigntists lost only by a margin of 1 per cent. Talks about another referendum continue. What new ideology will now follow is hard to predict. The latest separatist ideology and new guarantees for bilingualism and the preservation of the French language and culture show that the French have forced Canada to take at least a second language and culture seriously. This is an important step toward pluralism. In the case of the French in Canada, assimilation was tried but failed; amalgamation into Anglo-conformity has not worked either. Neither the cultural nor the structural parts of the Quebec society have followed Gordon's modified assimilation model. The French in Quebec are a clear example of ethnic or national pluralism.

Crean and Rioux (1983:1) recently stated that many people predicted that the referendum on sovereignty-association would not resolve the fundamental questions raised by the separatists in Quebec, and that Canadians and Quebeckers will need to sit down together to work out a new type of association. Their book *Two Nations* assumes that both the British and the French in Canada will not rest until they have sovereignty over their respective languages, cultures, and destinies because they live essentially in two countries. The problem is that even if Quebeckers gain political independence, what will happen to other francophones in Canada and what will happen to the multicultural pluralist model remains unclear. Separatists assume that a uni-ethnic state is the ideal. McNeill (1986) says this state is hardly possible for all groups in our industrial society. A Quebec that stays within Canada can help the pluralist vision, showing that a serious second option is viable. A sovereign Quebec nation might however be tempted to perpetuate Franco-conformity and seek to amalgamate and dominate others as Anglo-conformists have sought to do in the past. Thus, we would be back to attempts at assimilating minorities without concern for their identity as in the colonial past.

HIGHLIGHT 5.1 MY QUEBEC: RENÉ LÉVESQUE

Imagine that the entire continent of North America ought to have been French instead of . . . Neo-Roman. For indeed our beginnings were incredible. From Hudson's Bay and Labrador in the north to the Gulf of Mexico in the south, from the Gaspé near the Atlantic to the Rockies, from which one can almost see the Pacific, there we were—and there you were—as the discoverers and the first European settlers. When Champlain built his home in Quebec and Nouvelle France was born, the Mayflower pilgrims had not even raised anchor on their journey to found New England.

And so, for a hundred and fifty years soldiers and missionaries and colonists and coureurs des bois wrote a good number of the most extraordinary, if not the most famous, pages of the history of the seventeenth and eighteenth centuries.

However, this history, for a century and a half, was ours—and also yours. And I remember that when we arrived at the last chapter, the one which ended with defeat and conquest, we lost the desire to know what followed, and instead returned indefatigably to the beginning; because what followed, with due respect to our British compatriots, seemed in some way to have become the history of another people.

This is not a nostalgic idealization of a tiny society of some tens of thousands of poor people who, in 1760 in the Saint Lawrence Valley, had to submit to a foreign domination which was destined to remain for a long time. As with all the other colonies of the time, this was as yet nothing more than a modest outgrowth of a metropolis which was both natural and distant, and whose power, once its job was done, should have ended with us as it did elsewhere had its continuity not been broken. Already in fact, distance, the climate, contact with the Indian population, the continental experience had fashioned a mentality and a way of life which were becoming more and more different from that of the mother country. This was a nation, and a French nation certainly, but a nation which was just as able to live its own life and to be a presence in the world as any other.

This is what defeat broke up, but it did not manage to dispel the dream. It was a dream which, though normally unacknowledged, was strong enough to nourish, even today, a national identity and a national idea that only numerical weakness and total isolation prevented us from realizing.

The rapid awakening, which we were ourselves the first to find astonishing, we have given the name the 'quiet revolution', which was not ill-founded. Revolutionary it certainly was, if one accepts that a fundamental change can happen without killings and ruins. Quiet, and in consequence marked by a continuity in change, even in the most radical change, which is one of the characteristics of our people. Quietly therefore, but on all levels we saw a liberation which was as sudden as is the breaking of the icepacks on our rivers in the spring. And the ground began to flower and to produce like never before: reform as profound as it was late in the field of education; the initiation of a modern administration, so well organized that it shows signs of a bureaucratic fat which is not exclusively French—but also a jump in social awareness which, on several major points moved rapidly from the back to the foreground; and an increasingly keen consciousness of responsibilities such as the essentials of economic life.

And as is usual, all this was announced by and accompanied by artists, an unprecedented plethora of writers, painters, filmmakers, architects, and in particular some superb popular poets, several of whom are well-known in France, who have created for us a repertory of songs which are reminiscent of your old provincial airs that rocked us in our cradles, and in which we now find our own countenance and our accent of today,

and a precise echo of our successes, our failures, and our plans. It is this new, renewed Quebec which de Gaulle took the trouble to see. Contrary to what some people have thought, he did not have to 'invent' it.

Inevitably this metamorphosis owed it to itself to create an instrument for its political expression and to try to conduct it to its logical conclusion. This instrument is the Parti Quebecois. We were just a few hundred, then a few thousand, to bring it into being in 1967-68, with two objectives which have remained coupled since then: sovereignty and association. This means a sovereign State of Quebec which will accept, or rather offer in advance, new links of interdependence with Canada, but links which will this time be negotiated between equal peoples, as a function of their geographic and other unquestionable common interests.

This, briefly, is the national option, inscribed from the beginning in the heart of a political program in which each paragraph, each word, has been rigorously exposed to the attention of every Quebecker. But like anyone else, certainly, over and above these existential but not very day-to-day questions which we are resolving–for a while–in the Constitution, our people are also experiencing all the problems, the frustrations and the hopes of the men and women of their time. This is why, on the way, we must also try to respond the best we can, with the power the federal regime deigns to give us, to these requirements of our citizens.

SOURCE: René Lévesque, *My Quebec* (Toronto: Methuen, 1979).

LANGUAGE: A FRANCOPHONE SYMBOL SYSTEM

In Chapter 4 we discussed linguistic and cultural factors as the means of differentiating the various regions of Canada. The southern part of Quebec, which we called the Québécois heartland, is one of these distinct regions, and is francophone and francocultural. It includes the largest majority of francophones in Canada: 82 per cent of the population report French as their mother tongue, and 83 per cent speak French in their homes. We also discussed the importance of language as a symbol system into which humans are introduced when they first learn their mother tongue; in turn, how cultural learning is transmitted through the symbolic language code shapes their social worldview. Those who learn French and do not learn another language, for example, are locked into communicating in French and are separated from easy communication with others who do not speak French. Thus, language is a boundaried 'Québécois heritage' system that includes or excludes those who do or do not learn the symbol system (Taylor and Sigal, 1985).

Region may be a form of restriction for people, and regions can become boundaried spaces within which people create their cultures and social interaction. A second important system that humans learn to identify with is language (Lieberson, 1970). More than 80 per cent of Quebec's population is of French origin, and as many also use French as their language of communication as they have now done for almost four hundred years.

The Bilingualism and Biculturalism Commission

For a hundred years after the 1837–8 rebellion the Québécois retreated into a conservative ideology. However, after the Second World War and Duplessis, there was what Rioux (1965) called springtime in Quebec, which began as a quiet revolution in search of greater freedom again. By 1963 the crescendo of discontent had developed to the point that a special 10-person federal Royal Commission on Bilingualism and Biculturalism was established to hear these voices of change, and to assess to what extent other Canadians were willing to allow greater change (Burnet, 1988:175–80). Let us hear how the commission saw the problem:

There have been strains throughout the history of confederation. . . . They have been driven to the conclusion that Canada, without being fully conscious of the fact, is passing through the greatest crisis in its history. . . . The source of the crisis lies in the province of Quebec. . . . Although a provincial crisis at the outset, it has become a Canadian crisis, because of the size and importance of Quebec, and because it has inevitably set off a series of chain reactions elsewhere. . . . The state of affairs established in 1867, and never since seriously challenged, is now for the first time being rejected by the French Canadians in Quebec (Royal Commission on Bilingualism and Biculturalism [RCBB], 1965:13).

In the opinion of the commission, the dominating idea in its terms of reference was 'equal partnership' between the two founding peoples. The commission was appointed, at least to some extent, for the purpose of studying the grievances that French Canadians, and particularly Quebeckers, were voicing more vigorously (Burnet, 1979). As the name of the commission implied, French Québécois thought of equality between the founding peoples as a dual postulate, even though no mention was made in the constitution of such a partnership.

The first preliminary report of the commission said that 'these notions and expressions—"equal partnership", two founding groups, "a compact"—are traditional in French Canada. "Two Nations" is a more recent and vivid way of expressing this desire for a recognition of the dual character of the country' (RCBB, 1965:47). To many people, these expressions of dualism seemed a continuation of the age-old battle of the European British and French nation-states, which could think in terms only of unitary sovereignties and who had faced each other across the Ottawa River for centuries. Did the multi-ethnicity of Canada not matter, and why should the rights of the charter groups be corrected without hearings given to the rights of others as well? Indeed, one of the commissioners, Ukrainian Jaraslov Rudnyckyj, felt so strongly about the rights of 'new Canadians', which supported not duality but a mosaic, that he made a separate statement published in Volume 1 of the Official Languages book (RCBB, 1965:155–69).

Others, however, thought that more than two official languages would lead to Balkanization.

Volume 1 of the Bilingualism and Biculturalism Commission (RCBB) report was devoted entirely to the official languages, English and French. It portrays Canada as a unique state with English and French as two languages of international status:

> English is today the mother tongue of more than 250,000,000 people. To this figure should be added some 200,000,000 who speak English as their second language or who have a good working knowledge of it. French, for its part, is the mother tongue of around 65,000,000 people and is constantly used by another 150,000,000 throughout the world. These two languages thus have worldwide prestige (RCBB, Vol. 1, 1967:15).

The multivolume report involved an enormous amount of research that became a basis of demographic, ecological, economic, political, and social facts sparking a flurry of research on language, culture, ethnicity, and race (Burnet, 1988:175–80; Driedger, 2001; Pendakur, 1990). Volume 1 clearly showed that, even though the mother tongue of over half of all Canadians was English, almost one-third spoke French and a sizeable number had non-charter mother tongues. However, most of these francophones resided in Quebec, where the French dominated, while the rest of Canada was anglophone. The two languages represented the two 'national' solitudes that were separated regionally, politically, and socially. These conclusions later led Prime Minister Trudeau to declare Canada a bilingual nation in 1971 (Crean and Rioux, 1983).

The pressures of Commissioner Rudnyckyj, who made a separate report on languages in Volume 1 based on the outcry of more than one-fourth of the population who then were not charter Canadians, led the commission to publish a fourth volume titled *The Cultural Contributions of Other Ethnic Groups* (RCBB, 1970), a study

which at first they had not commissioned. This no doubt partially contributed to the second part of Trudeau's declaration in 1971 of a bilingual and multicultural Canada, and modified what had originally been a commission on bilingualism and biculturalism. Thus, the commission, which had been asked to explore more than one unitary linguistic and cultural state, actually opened up the arena to the possibility of a broader pluralism beyond charter-group dominance (Burnet, 1979:43–58; Driedger, 2001).

Joy's Bilingual Belt

In the French Canadians Heartland, 82 per cent of the population report French as their mother tongue. French Canadians have lived there for many generations and have become quite distinct from the culture of France, their original mother country. Of the 82 per cent who in 1991 reported French as their mother tongue, 83 per cent speak French at home. English home-language use has declined from 13 per cent in 1971 to 11 per cent in 1991. The French nation has survived in Quebec for almost four centuries. They are a people who have not assimilated, and who clearly represent the pluralism end of our continuum discussed as Cell E.

Richard Joy (1972; 1992) proposed that there is a Bilingual Belt in the south of Quebec (see Figure 4.5). It hugs the southern underbelly of the Heartland, where large numbers of French-speakers reside adjacent to, and in continuity with, the 'mother' core of French Quebec. In our discussion of regions, we plotted this Bilingual Belt and discussed it briefly. Here let us demonstrate how it fits into the total pattern of the French presence in Canada.

Joy's thesis is that the French language and culture has survived and will continue to do so in the Québécois Heartland because there is a sufficient demographic mass of six million French Canadians who have maintained their French language and who are dominant politically in that provincial region. He predicted that French-speaking Canadians in the Bilingual— especially in northern New Brunswick, northeastern Ontario, and the Ottawa area—will also have a very good chance of maintaining their French language because they are adjacent to the Heartland, can remain in contact with this core, and can meet other francophones where their language is of use and can be practised among those who value it. Although there may be somewhat less opportunity to use French than in the French Québécois Heartland, those people in the Bilingual Belt should be able to retain their French.

Joy (1972; 1992) also predicted that as we move farther away from the Quebec core and beyond the Bilingual Belt, it will be increasingly harder to maintain the French language where French communities are smaller, and where support from the Québécois Heartland is less because of distance. Thus, it would be even more difficult to sustain the French language in communities such as Yarmouth, Nova Scotia, an area that used to be a part of French Acadia; Tecumseh, Ontario, near Windsor; Penetanguishene, Ontario, one of the earliest French missions to the Huron on Lake Huron; and St Boniface, Manitoba, even farther away and now part of Winnipeg, where the Northwest French fur trading company and the Hudson's Bay Company had often clashed. Using the 1961 census data, Joy tried to show that the French language was best maintained and even advanced in core parts of the Québécois Heartland, that it was well maintained in the Soo-Moncton Bilingual Belt, and that it declined at points farther away, especially in Atlantic Canada where the population is almost entirely British and anglophone.

Joy summarized seven regions based on the order in which the respective populations speak French: 1) Interior Quebec, where 95 per cent of the population reported French as their mother tongue and only 2 per cent speak English exclusively; 2) southern Quebec and the Ottawa Valley, where 70 per cent of the population report French as their mother tongue, and where French is dominant in government, but English is dominant in industry; 3) northern New Brunswick, where 59 per cent of the population

report French as their mother tongue, but where fewer spoke it; 4) eastern and northern Ontario close to the Quebec border, where French is the mother tongue of 30 per cent of the population; 5) the Atlantic region, where French is spoken by only 5 per cent of the population; 6) the western provinces, where French is the mother tongue of only about 5 per cent of the population and is spoken at home by fewer still; and 7) southern Ontario, the industrial heartland where less than 1 person in 40 gave French as his or her mother tongue. Joy claimed that, although the French language was not declining in the first region, language assimilation progressed increasingly in regions five through seven. Assimilation was proceeding quickly, especially since there are few reinforcements from Quebec. More recently Joy (1992) has updated his original thesis using language use at home rather than only mother tongue, as his measure of the state of French in Quebec and Canada. He has worked on more qualitative assessments saying that "[t]hey're not going to get jobs at age 20 with a 14-year-old's vocabulary' (Joy, 1992:11).

Language Continuity and Shift

To what extent has the language continuity of the French core in the Quebec Heartland extended into the twenty-first century? Do Joy's predictions follow for the regions more distantly removed from this core? How does this affect other language groups, and how does the French language compare with others in Canada?

Of the two million people who experienced a language shift between 1981 and 1991, 70 per cent have mother tongues other than English or French. Twenty per cent switched from French and only 10 percent from English (Statistics Canada, 1993b). Language mobility (i.e., the tendency of persons to speak a language at home that is different than their mother tongue) can be compared. We have developed a language continuity index by calculating the ratio of persons speaking a particular language at home to the number of individuals who have the same language as their mother tongue (deVries, 1990:163–77).

TABLE 5.1 Language Continuity Index for English, French, and Other (Non-official) Languages, Canada, 1991 (%)

Regions	English	French	Other
Canada	113.1	95.8	54.9
Newfoundland	100.7	44.8	60.8
Prince Edward Island	103.3	52.6	25.8
Nova Scotia	103.1	59.5	48.6
New Brunswick	105.6	91.6	47.5
Quebec	121.7	101.2	66.3
Ontario	114.7	63.3	57.1
Manitoba	112.3	49.2	45.6
Saskatchewan	113.3	33.0	33.8
Alberta	112.7	35.6	46.5
British Columbia	113.6	28.3	51.0
Yukon	108.5	44.4	22.7
Northwest Territories	121.1	46.7	75.7

SOURCE: *Home Language and Mother Tongue: The Nation*, Catalogue 93-317, 1991 Census (Ottawa: Statistics Canada, 1993), pp. 16–45,142–219.

In Table 5.1 we see that language mobility favours English (113.1 per cent) for all of Canada, followed by French (95.9 per cent) and the other languages (54.9 per cent). The value larger than 100 per cent means that the English recruited more English-speakers during the decade than they lost, which was the case in each of the regions. The French overall lost more speakers than they recruited, and of the other groups only half (54.9 per cent) continued to use their mother tongues at home. We have the data to examine where these losses for the French and others occur.

In Quebec, which has a language continuity of 101.2 per cent, the French are able to maintain their language continuity and gain some because of their solid French Heartland and their political control over their institutions. There is some loss by the French in New Brunswick (at 91.6 per cent continuity), where they are solidly concentrated in the north but not as much in control as they are in Quebec. In Ontario, French language continuity dropped (to 63.3 per cent); in the other Atlantic Provinces, formerly Acadia, it drops into the fifties; and in Manitoba (including St Boniface) it drops even more, to 49.2 per cent. Joy's theory continues as predicted into the 1990s. It is the non-Quebec French Canadians, not those who live in Quebec, who bring the total French-Canadian continuity index down to 95.9 per cent (Henripin, 1993:316–17).

Even within the province of Quebec, however, there are interesting shifts that deVries and Lewycky (1985), Kalbach and Richard (1990), and Henripin (1993:304–20) have researched. Quebeckers whose mother tongue was English, were able to maintain their continuity until the 1970s. However, by the 1980s the English language continuity percentages began to decline, a considerable difference from the fifties and sixties when they were gaining. The separatist independence drive and Quebec's laws that were favourable to the French language certainly had their impact. The departure of many anglophone Quebeckers for Ontario has also increased francophone ratios in Quebec (Henripin, 1993:310–15).

For other non-official language users, continuity has dropped to 54.9 per cent in Canada.

The aboriginals most often speak their mother tongues at home (75.7 per cent), but language continuity ratios drop to less than 50 per cent in over half the regions (Statistics Canada, 1993b).

The continuity and language shifts vary considerably for non-charter Canadians (as we would expect) since they each represent smaller demographic masses and they do not have political control over territory as charter groups do (Driedger and Hengstenberg, 1986; Herberg, 1989:115–19). In Table 5.2 we see some interesting variations. Over half (54.9 per cent) of these non-charter peoples still speak their mother tongues at home; two-thirds do so in Quebec, and only one-fourth in the Yukon. Interestingly, most of the nine ethnic groups listed have highest language continuity in Quebec. The French Québécois concern for maintaining their own French language seems to also spill over to other groups.

Language continuity varies greatly by ethnic group (Edwards, 1998). North Europeans such as the Dutch and Germans have the lowest continuity; the south and east Europeans such as the Ukrainians, Poles, and Italians, who have been here longer, rank in-between, and the recent south Europeans such as the Portuguese and Greeks (many first generation) rank highest (Herberg, 1989:115–19). Roughly three out of four aboriginals who are segregated in the Northlands speak their mother tongues at home, and the Chinese (86.2 per cent continuity), rank highest with almost all speaking their mother tongues at home. Time of immigration, degree of segregation, demographic mass, and regional residence all influence language continuity rates (Driedger, 1996).

Scholars have devoted considerable attention to the relationship between language and ethnic identity of immigrant groups in multilingual settings and have frequently claimed that preservation and continued use of the traditional mother tongue is one important—if not the most important—component of ethnic identity.

In the 1960s and early 1970s it was mainly social psychologists and psycholinguists who began to study the context and the dynamics of

TABLE 5.2 Language Continuity for Other Non-official Languages by Ethnic Group, Canada and Provinces, 1991 (%)

Regions	Canada Non-Official	Dutch	German	Ukrainian	Italian	Polish	Portuguese	Greek	Aboriginal	Chinese
Canada	54.9	14.4	25.9	26.7	56.4	61.9	71.7	73.8	78.0	86.2
Newfoundland	60.8	29.2	13.4	33.3	37.5	42.1	44.0	77.8	58.5	74.1
Prince Edward Island	25.0	22.8	12.5	50.0	60.0	50.0	55.6	—	—	76.9
Nova Scotia	48.6	14.9	27.3	8.1	39.4	56.2	61.6	74.7	90.5	72.9
New Brunswick	47.5	21.1	25.1	.8	30.6	62.5	77.2	68.1	85.0	77.1
Quebec	66.3	24.2	34.3	49.2	63.2	66.0	74.5	82.6	88.0	91.5
Ontario	57.1	11.0	30.1	40.4	55.6	64.7	74.0	70.5	76.0	87.6
Manitoba	45.6	20.7	36.8	24.7	44.0	48.9	65.1	59.7	78.8	85.9
Saskatchewan	33.8	12.4	21.0	33.0	34.7	31.4	51.3	59.2	76.6	76.8
Alberta	46.5	15.3	32.2	17.6	44.0	58.4	62.2	55.7	70.5	85.2
British Columbia	51.0	12.6	20.2	10.5	42.8	53.6	51.4	55.4	47.0	84.3
Yukon	22.7	12.5	23.1	7.0	—	—	—	75.0	27.3	87.5
Northwest Territories	75.7	9.5	10.6	7.1	40.9	46.2	60.0	40.0	85.6	78.0

SOURCE: *Home Language and Mother Tongue: The Nation*, Catalogue 93-317, 1991 Census (Ottawa: Statistics Canada, 1993), pp. 16–45, 142–219.

language groups. They concentrated mostly on English and French as official languages, dealing with questions of bilingualism, second language learning, and the like (see, e.g., Berry and Wilde, 1972; Edwards, 1985; 1998; Taylor and Gardner, 1970). Similarly, demographic studies based on census data concentrated on the official languages with only passing reference to the non-official language groups that were frequently lumped into a category called 'Others'.

The 1975 study conference 'The Individual, Language and Society in Canada' (Coons, Taylor, and Tremblay, 1977) was an early interdisciplinary effort by psychologists, sociologists, and sociolinguists to deal with different aspects of the languages-in-contrast situation and to include non-official languages. While psychologists brought their research on official languages to the meeting (Berry, 1977; Taylor and Gardner, 1977), sociologists stressed the broader multilingual and regional dimensions of linguistic research in Canada (cf. Driedger, 1977c; Jackson, 1977). These sociologists saw competence in the traditional mother tongue and its continued use as one of a number of ethnic identity factors along with religion, endogamy, parochial education, participation in voluntary associations, etc. (Driedger, 1978b; Isajiw, 1981; Reitz, 1980). Later sociological studies have increasingly focused on language as an important variable related to ethnic identity (Barbaud, 1998; Bourhis, 1983, 1994; Bourhis and Lepicq, 1993; deVries and Lewycky, 1985; deVries and Vallee, 1980; Driedger, 1998; Edwards, 1998; Hammers and Hummel, 1998).

Several Canadian studies have demonstrated the importance of controlling for immigrant generation and community size in the analysis of language maintenance. For the urban context, O'Bryan and colleagues (1976) sampled 10 groups of adult speakers of non-official languages in five Canadian metropolitan centres and found a fairly rapid decline in traditional mother tongue competence from first- to third-generation Canadians. Fluency in the respective languages was fairly high for the first generation (between 56.0 and 80.7 per cent), but had virtually disappeared by the third. These ethnic groups were able to maintain 'some knowledge' of their ethnic language only into the third generation (38.7 per cent; cf. O'Bryan, Reitz, and Kuplowska, 1976:45–6). DeVries and Vallee (1980:132) amply describe this phenomenon as 'the levelling effect of the third generation', and it is also discussed by deVries and Lewycky (1985); Breton et al. (1990); Henripin (1993:316–17); Berry and Laponce (1994); and deVries (1999).

Comparable studies for rural environments have shown that ethnolinguistic or ethnoreligious groups in more segregated rural enclaves have been somewhat more successful in maintaining ethnic language (Anderson, 1980; Anderson and Driedger, 1980a; Driedger and Hengstenberg, 1986). Although an extremely high proportion of all respondents was still competent in an ethnic mother tongue (though most of them were bilingual), actual use and the desire to speak it was consistently lower and varied significantly among the different groups, most markedly among the three German groups (Hutterites, 100 per cent; Mennonites, 68.9 per cent; Catholics, 29.0 per cent). Li and Denis (1983:18–32) studied Gravelbourg, a French community in Saskatchewan, and found that 9 per cent of the French residents spoke French only and 91 per cent were officially bilingual. While most residents in their sixties spoke French at home, less than half under 30 did so.

All these studies support previous observations that ethnolinguistic minorities tend to lose their traditional mother tongue over time, though their capability to resist linguistic assimilation may vary considerably. Language shifts toward the official language(s) do not necessarily imply a complete loss of the heritage language, nor do they mean that a group ceases to exist as an identifiable entity. Therefore, it seems to be more appropriate to describe these processes in terms of linguistic accommodation and to keep in mind that the linguistic factor 'is not always an important, much less the only component of ethnic identity. The varied significance of language, religion and diverse customs as components of ethnic identity can be very complex' (Anderson, 1980:67).

STUDIES IN QUÉBÉCOIS SOLIDARITY AND CHANGE

Having provided the French Québécois setting and the importance of the francophone symbol system, let us turn to early studies that illustrate some of the research done on the traditional habitant village, the industrialization of a small urban community, and French-English power relations. Each will illustrate different features of French-Canadian solidarity and change.

Miner's French Habitants in St Denis

One of the earliest community studies in Canada was done by Horace Miner (1939), which has become a classic (Guindon, 1988; Juteau, 1992: 322–5). Miner was a student of Robert Redfield at Chicago and casts his study in Redfield's peasant or folk society mode. Miner (1939:ix) states that his objectives are to provide an ethnographic description of the old rural French-Canadian folk culture, to analyze the social structure, and to find factors of social change in the direction of urbanization and anglicization. The first two aims are that of an anthropologist; the third is a major focus of the Chicago School. Miner did participant observation for a year (1936–7) and spent some time at McGill. Two chapters were published in *The American Sociological Review* in 1938. In 1949 Miner revisited St Denis and published his findings of change in the *American Journal of Sociology* (1950).

St Denis is a rural French-Canadian parish located on the lower south side of the St Lawrence River between Montreal and Quebec City. When Miner studied St Denis in the 1930s, life there was typical of the French conservative ideology. It was one of many 'sacred' communities symbolized by the steeple of the Roman Catholic Church—located in the centre of each parish like a hen with her brood of chicks. Miner briefly describes some of the historical context that has since been elaborated more fully by French scholars such as Rioux and Martin (1964), Rioux (1965, 1973), and Guindon (1988). St Denis was located in the centre of the agricultural rang system, in which narrow strips of land began at the river and extended inland with the farm buildings bordering the river, forming a long snakelike village.

Miner (1939) describes kinship and the family cycle, the role of religion, the agricultural means of making a living, and patterns of community organization in typical anthropological fashion. The autobiography of a habitant gives insight into experiences such as childhood, schooling, first communion, family reunions, marriage, a death in the family, land improvement, and travel. These ethnographic insights provide a sense of the peasant atmosphere.

Miner compares the changes that had taken place between life in the 1800s and 1936, when he studied St Denis. Flail-threshing was replaced by mechanical tools and hand bucksaws were replaced by circular saws. Local bean-and-barley coffee had been replaced by store-bought tea and coffee. Kerosene lamps replaced candles. Store-bought shoes and clothes replaced homemade clothes and bobsleighs and buggies replaced traineaus and carrioles. Although changes since the 1800s were evident, they escalated in the early 1900s.

Miner returned to St Denis in 1949 to compare the changes since 1936. He found that 'life is now less "like a turning wheel", as an old habitant described it, for the repetitive cycle of life no longer returns to the same point with each succeeding generation' (Miner, 1939:255). In 1949 television had spread to many households; roads once gravelled were now surfaced, and many more automobiles had appeared; easier communication through buses, trucks, and telephones was possible; on farms tractors replaced horses, electricity made electric washers, milkers, refrigerators, electric pumps, and running water possible; store-bought furniture, packaged foods, and clothes no longer required as much home woodwork, cooking, and sewing. We are fortunate that 60 years later, we have such a classic ethnographic study of one French-Canadian parish as an important point of traditional reference.

While Miner's community study of traditional and conservative St Denis was one of the

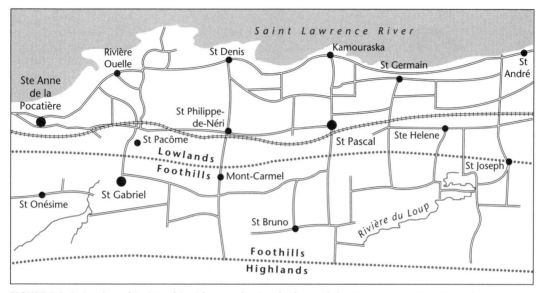

FIGURE 5.1 St Denis and St Pascal Parishes on the South Shore of the St Lawrence River in Quebec

SOURCE: G. Gold, *St Pascal: Changing Leadership and Social Organization in a Quebec Town* (Toronto: Holt, Rinehart and Winston, 1975), p. 23.

first such projects, we have several more to add to our rich understanding of French communities. In 1975, anthropologist Gerald Gold at Laval studied St Pascal, a parish adjacent to St Denis. St Pascal is just southeast of St Denis, located not on the river, but in the second tier of inland rangs. The small map (see Figure 5.1) also shows a dozen Catholic parishes named after saints, which clearly emphasizes 'the sacred' milieu that we are dealing with. Paul Charest (1975:iv) writes in his foreword, 'The non-Québécois reader, familiar with the now classic works of Hughes and Miner, will here find an image of Quebec that is not only different but also much more contemporary and realistic.' Gold (1975) focuses on the changing leadership and social organization of St Pascal. He is concerned with showing the social structure of the town and the influences of industry, combining the interests of both Miner and Hughes. Much more local French control of the economic welfare of the community has developed, and more important linkages have been made with the larger networks outside. Small-town St Pascal

has prospered and joined the larger scene in the twenty-first century. The French are no longer as economically dependent as they were.

Hughes's Industrialized Cantonville

Like Dawson, Everett Hughes was also one of the few sociologists in Canada located at McGill. He too was trained at Chicago, and they each acknowledge the other for support. As we might expect of a Chicago School sociologist, Hughes is interested in the industrialization process in Quebec, an interest illustrated in *French Canada in Transition* (1943). Hughes's study explores charter French-English relations and British-French relations in the Quebec industrial town of Cantonville.

In his preface, Hughes (1943:x, xv) says he chose Cantonville (actually Drummondville) for study because 'it stands in between the two extremes' of Horace Miner's community study of the traditional rural French St Denis parish prototype and Montreal, the largest metropolis in Quebec. Industries, all started and managed by English-speaking people, had both 'enlivened and disturbed' Cantonville. In 1941 Cantonville (near Montreal in southwest Quebec) had a population of 20,000 which was 95 per cent Catholic and French. It was the first of a series of French towns that Hughes had planned to study. The industrial invasion of English-speakers was in many ways alien to French Quebec, and the fact that the English held the top industry positions while the French in their own territory filled in as lower-class workers created potential conflict in French-English relations. These ethnic relations resulted in Hughes's exploring minority-majority relations more than many early sociologists of the day (Juteau, 1992).

Hughes (1943:21) begins his book by sketching the rural Quebec context, the French-Canadian family farm, the centrality of the Catholic parish, the first institution of local self-government, the rural village and parish populations, and the homogeneity for more conspicuous living, clearly showing where the money is. Thus, two ethnic solitudes live side by side, each in its own place encouraged by the differentiation of industrialization.

While the St Denis and St Pascal studies focus on French communities in the Québécois Heartland, Hughes's study of Cantonville shows the impact of industry parachuted into a French community and the need for adjustment and cooperation with those of other ethnic traditions. French communities outside the Quebec Heartland have additional problems with maintaining their identities, because outside Quebec they no longer are a majority who can influence and shape their French destiny. Let us examine several French communities in Ontario and Alberta, to illustrate their struggles.

John Jackson (1975) made a community study of French-English relations in Tecumseh, near Windsor in English-speaking Ontario. The research focused on conflict between the Franco-Ontarians and Anglo-Ontarians over language. In 1921, 86 per cent of the population of Tecumseh was French; by 1971, the French had declined to 48 per cent, still the largest ethnic group (Jackson, 1975:9). Religion

also added to the complexity; in 1921, 94 per cent of the population were Roman Catholic; by 1971 they had declined to 75 per cent, with the French-Ontarians mostly Catholic, and the British and others both Catholic and Protestant. Ethnic origin, language, religion, and social class were all factors that influenced the amount of conflict over social issues such as French-language education and Catholic schools. Jackson (1975:1–15) suggests that, using language as an index, 'Tecumseh Francophones, though not as strong as their confreres in the Ottawa Valley and northeastern Ontario, have maintained an amazing viability against the extreme pressure of anglicization in the Detroit-Windsor metropolitan complex'.

Farther west, Robert Stebbins (1994) made the first metropolitan study of the French outside Quebec in Calgary where some 15,000 represent only 2 per cent of the metropolitan population. Stebbins (1994:113–14) lists four core activities as crucial to their survival: 1) with children, 2) with French schools, 3) routine passive leisure, and 4) interactive leisure. Most are bilingual, 75 per cent speaking French at home, although intermarriage is a problem. These are not highly segregated French communities in Calgary, but many are retaining a modified French identity.

Stebbins (1994:113–21) discusses the future of Franco-Calgarians, saying that they face levels of importance of activities that he classified into core and semi-peripheral activities. He sees their core as centred around the school-community centre that they were planning to construct in 1993 with governmental authorization. This centre will contain space for offices, educational facilities, and room for the performing arts. This they hope will raise the profile of francophones in the surrounding anglophone milieu, which should act as a magnet to draw increased involvement of the 14,490 francophones in the city. Here francophones would have increased opportunities to use their language, and build networks and community where francophones can interact and find each other. Hopefully more of their own kind would marry each other and stem the trends of exogamy. The sizeable flow of francophone immigrants into the city adds to the hopes of a revitalized francophone community (Stebbins, 1994:120). Clearly, the identity maintenance of such a francophone community is more similar to that of other non-charter ethnic communities than French communities supported by a massive regional, demographic, institutional, and political French core in Quebec.

FEDERALIST VERSUS SEPARATIST DIALECTICS

Lord Durham's observation that he found two peoples warring in the bosom of one nation is not surprising in light of our findings in this chapter (Axworthy and Trudeau, 1992:7–50; Denis, 1995:162). New France, created almost four hundred years ago, was designed to be a French Québécois nation, and the original demographic European origin in a distinct region along the St Lawrence was headed that way until the conquest. The various ideologies in Quebec have worked to preserve this French nation whose French-language symbol system is in continuity with its long historical past. The studies by Miner and Hughes just reviewed show both the earlier French parish system that sustained them through their years of conservatism, and the distinct French-English polarities during the time of more recent industrialization. A great deal of research has gone into this English-French power dialectic (Bell and Tepperman, 1979; Breton, Reitz, and Valentine, 1980).

In Chapter 2 our model of conformity and pluralism placed the British and French in opposite corners B and E, with the industrial melting pot and many arrows of conflict between them. The British and French have remained two economic, political, and social solitudes. According to Breton, Reitz, and Valentine (1980:139), 'to a significant degree, anglophones and francophones live separately in their own social circles and institutions. . . . Many Canadians perceive problems of national unity as problems pertaining to English-French relations.' The two are seg-

mented, encircled by institutional boundaries and enclosures, and Breton, Reitz, and Valentine (1980:142–304) describe these in three basic economic, political, and social dimensions. The conflict and dynamics of these dialectics are still unresolved in the nineties.

Trudeau's Federalist Alternative

Two federalist and separatist French-Canadian alternatives for survival were clearly spelled out by Quebeckers Pierre Trudeau and René Lévesque in the 1960s. Trudeau's (1962; 1968) *Federalist alternative* proposes that Quebec's future lies within confederation; Levesque's (1963) *Separatist alternative* (attempted again in the nineties by Jacques Parizeau) is to lead Quebec out of confederation to form a separate sovereign Quebec Nation-state. Both call for the survival of the Québécois as a distinct people, but their models for survival are quite different. Both men are examples of very able modern leaders spawned by Quebec, evidence of changes that have taken place there. Let us look at the federalist and the separatist alternatives briefly.

Pierre Trudeau, the prime minister of Canada for fourteen years (1968–83), was born in Montreal in 1921 and brought up in a bilingual and bicultural home. He was educated at the universities of Montreal, Harvard, Paris, and the London School of Economics, doing postgraduate studies in economics, political studies, and law (Saywell, 1968:viii). During the conservative Duplessis years, to combat Duplessis, Trudeau, Gerard Pelletier, and others founded a new journal, *Cité Libre*, in which they began to expound their visions for change. Later Trudeau, Pelletier, and Jean Marchand—all from Quebec—entered federal politics and became known as the 'three wise men'.

As professor of law at the University of Montreal, Trudeau continued to write. An important article in *Cité Libre* (1962) outlined his position on French nationalism and the need for a multinational state. He rejected any movement toward Quebec's independence, which in the past had failed and which he thought would not succeed but would lead only to further misery. Instead, he proposed a multinational state, rejecting the idea of a nation-state but opting for what he called a 'more civilized goal of polyethnic pluralism . . . dreamed about by Lafontaine, realized under Cartier, perfected by Laurier, and humanized with Bourassa' (Trudeau, 1962:58). Trudeau believed that the *British North America Act* and the constitutionalists had indeed made a first step away from a nation-state toward a multinational option, and that this needed to be refined.

Trudeau had harsh words for 'Separatists and Nationalists of all shapes and sizes baying after independence, who devote all their courage and capabilities to stirring up French-Canadian nationalism in defiance of the Anglo-Canadian variety . . . incessantly promoting the "state-of-siege mentality"' (Trudeau, 1962:59). He felt that French Canadians had failed to make themselves indispensable to Canada's future because of weak leadership and their failure to enter the ranks of senior civil servants. He claimed Anglo-Canadians had been strong because of French weakness, and that the French language had lost its status because Quebeckers had let the language and education be reduced to mediocrity. Trudeau thought that Canada must look for an alternative to a unitary nationalist state because:

A nationalist government is by nature intolerant, discriminatory, and, when all is said and done, totalitarian. A truly democratic government cannot be nationalist, because it must pursue the good of all its citizens, without prejudice to ethnic origin (Trudeau, 1962:63).

These words of Trudeau sound like McNeill's call for polyethnicity that we started with in Chapter 1. Trudeau's call for modification by all sounds much like modified pluralism. He continues:

The die is cast in Canada: there are two main ethnic and linguistic groups; each is too strong and too deeply rooted in the past, too firmly bound to a mother culture, to be able to engulf the other. But if the two will collaborate at the hub of a truly pluralistic State, Canada could become the envied seat of a form of federation that belongs to tomorrow's world. Better than the American melting-pot, Canada could offer an example to all . . . who must discover how to govern their polyethnic populations with proper regard for justice and liberty (Trudeau, 1962:67).

Later, in his books *Federalism and the French Canadians* (1968), and *Toward a Just Society* (1992), Trudeau more systematically argues the federalism case. He argues that the provinces in Canada now have jurisdiction over education and land resources. This jurisdiction provides Quebec and others the opportunity to train and develop their regions. He outlines some necessary constitutional changes, including a Bill of Rights, and the deletion of some of the imperial phraseology, which was done later in the passing of the new Canadian constitution. We will examine the content of the Charter of Rights and Freedoms in more detail in Chapter 12. Trudeau was always very critical of the separatist movement, which he called 'the Wigwam Complex', as a powerless petit-bourgeois minority left behind by the twentieth century.

In 1963, Lester Pearson had appointed the Royal Commission on Bilingualism and Biculturalism to study English-French relations in Canada. In 1965 the three wise men from Quebec—Trudeau, Pelletier, and Marchand—were added to Pearson's Cabinet to bolster French representation. By 1968, when the commission's recommendations began to appear, Trudeau had replaced Pearson as leader and prime minister. Trudeau personally piloted through Parliament new legislation designed to establish English and French as Canada's official languages. The *Official Languages Act* was supported by all political parties and passed in 1969 with few dissenting votes (Bell and Tepperman, 1979:135). At the same time, separatism was also growing in Quebec, led by René

Lévesque, and more recently by Jacques Parizeau and associates (Bouchard and Doucette).

Lévesque's Separatist Solution

While Trudeau stayed in power federally as prime minister of Canada for 14 years to promote his federalism experiment, René Lévesque promoted the separatist option during the seventies through the Parti Québécois, as first minister of the province of Quebec. Lévesque was part of the Liberal Party with Trudeau, but in 1967 he wanted the Liberal Party to favour sovereignty for Quebec within a common market association with Canada. The party did not accept this option (Milner, 1978:153). In 1968, various separatist political groups joined to form the Parti Québécois with René Lévesque as president. It took just eight years (until 1976) for the party to take power in Quebec, with separatism as one of its main goals (Milner, 1978:151–8). The party was considerably to the left of centre, but continually tried to keep the radicals farther to the left in check in order to get elected and to stay in power. Their goal was to rationalize and modernize Quebec and eventually to separate from Confederation with Canada.

'Over 80 per cent of Québécois surveyed in June 1978 wanted either a change in Confederation or outright independence' (Bell and Tepperman, 1979:137). Large numbers, however, considered themselves to be in the middle ground, neither extreme separatists nor extreme federalists. Slowly many Québécois began to see that some third option was needed. Trudeau stopped insisting that Confederation did not need to be altered, and Lévesque increasingly tried to persuade his radical separatists that a more modified sovereignty association was needed. After the Parti Québécois had been in power for four years, a referendum was held in 1980, in which Quebeckers had to choose for or against sovereignty-association. Did they want to separate to become an independent sovereign nation linked and associated with Canada, especially economically, or did they wish to remain in Confederation? Sixty per cent

voted in favour of staying in Confederation. Even a modified form of separatism with sovereignty-association was not acceptable to a majority, even though the Parti Québécois had promoted modified independence extensively (Denis, 1995:166–8).

The defeat of the referendum in Quebec in 1980, put the Quebec drive for separatism on hold; 60 per cent voted against separation. Once again, Quebec had not become an independent sovereign nation as many wished, but this time the Québécois had decided the question internally and without violence. Quebec had passed Bill 101, which strengthened the French language within the province, and the federal bilingual act strengthened French as an official national language in Canada. The nationalist Parti Québécois came to power in 1976 and legislated Bill 101 in 1977, which declared French to be the official language of Quebec for the courts and the legislature (Denis, 1995:167). It made French compulsory in the public service, and restricted access to English schools to children who have one parent educated in English in Quebec, which boosted continuity of the French language in Quebec (Axworthy and Trudeau, 1992).

To many Canadians it seemed unfair, that after great efforts during the Trudeau years to bring about an officially bilingual English and French Canada, Quebec would now legislate French as the only official language in Quebec in Bill 101. From the French Québécois perspective however, Bill 101 was essential. The Quebec population in Canada had dropped from one-third to one-fourth because of the severe drop in birthrates and below-average immigration into the province. Four major factors account for the language-planning efforts in Quebec during the 1950s, 1960s, and 1970s. First, the demographic decline of francophones in Canada meant that Quebec was the last enclave of a French-speaking society. Second, the demographic birthrates in Quebec itself were declining from the highest to the lowest in Canada (Bourhis, 1994:329; Henripin, 1993:304–10). Third, freedom of language choice in Quebec schools meant that immigrants chose English rather than French schools. Fourth, the anglophone dominance of business and economic activity in the province required a more prominent place for the French language. Bill 101 was designed to enhance the status of French generally and it had its intended impact (Bourhis, 1994:330–1). Both anglophones and allophones learned and used more French, and francophone status was enhanced.

Meech Lake and the 1995 Referendum

With the rise of the Parti Québécois and its work such as Bill 101, the French Québécois cause was favourably enhanced. However, when the Canadian constitution was repatriated and signed in 1982, René Lévesque, then first minister of Quebec, did not sign, while the other nine premiers did. Lévesque's refusal to sign was a clear indication that the question of Quebec's integration into Canada had failed (Denis, 1995; Parel, 1988:129–37). The question of a 'Quebec Nation' had not been resolved.

In the 1980s Brian Mulroney, prime minister of Canada, opened up discussions again, trying to get the first ministers to sign an agreement that would include Quebec. The new Liberal Party now in power in Quebec outlined five conditions that had to be met for Quebec to agree: 1) recognition of Quebec as a distinct society, 2) a veto or compensation over constitutional amendments, 3) participation in appointment of three Supreme Court justices from Quebec, 4) Quebec rights to help select immigrants for Quebec, and 5) limitation of Parliament's spending power (Denis, 1995:178–9). The first was a version of the concept of 'nation'. The other four would make Quebec a more active player in Canadian decision-making. These were moves toward sovereignty-association. Quebec was the first to sign the Meech Lake Accord in 1987, and so did seven other provinces. The Canadian Parliament passed the Accord in 1988, but Manitoba and Newfoundland did not, and 'Meech' expired in 1990 (Fournier, 1991).

Another Charlottetown Agreement occurred in 1992, but the Canada-wide referendum on October 26, 1992 was defeated by a vote of 54.5 per cent (Denis, 1995:182). The Charlottetown referendum failed because outside Quebec it appeared that it gave Quebec too much, while inside Quebec, Quebeckers thought it did not give Quebec enough (Russell, 1993:226). In 1994 the separatist Parti Québécois again came into power, with Jacques Parizeau promising to hold another referendum in Quebec in 1995. In early 1995 the public opinion polls in 1995 predicted that a simple question on 'Should Quebec separate from Canada' would be defeated 55–60 to 40–45, similar to the results of the first 1980 referendum to separate. This tended to lull the federalist forces to inactivity. In the meantime politicians argued as to whether some form of sovereignty association should again be proposed (Drache and Perin, 1992).

Figure 5.2 illustrates well the extent to which Quebeckers were split by the 30 October1995 referendum. Basically, metropolitan multi-ethnic Montreal, where 3.1 million or half of all Quebeckers live, voted No and the rest of Quebec, which is much more rural and less metropolitan voted Yes. Quebeckers farthest to the west, near Ottawa and Ontario had voted No, some regions as strongly as three to one. Those farther east, more deeply into the core rural French Catholic heartland voted Yes, as strongly as two to one farthest east. In his agonized concession of defeat, Parti Québécois leader and premier Jacques Parizeau lamented that it was 'money and the ethnic vote' which had brought the separatists down to defeat. What many thought but dared not utter had been said by their leader. It was true that non-francophones had voted No overwhelmingly, but Parizeau's racist remark raised a storm of protest even among his own followers. The next day, on Halloween, Parizeau resigned.

The question that the Parti Québécois posed for the referendum of October, 1995, was not clearcut: 'Do you agree that Quebec should become sovereign, after having made a formal offer to Canada for a new Economic and Political partnership, within the scope of the Bill respecting the future of Quebec and of the agreement

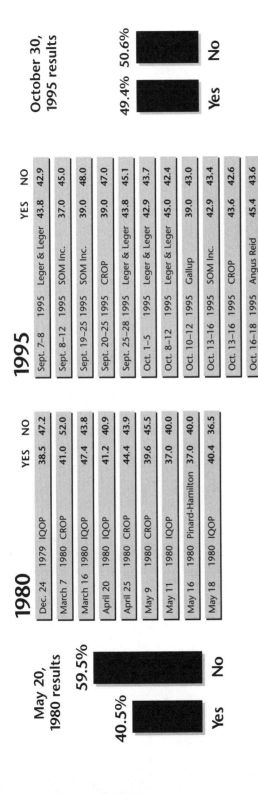

1980

			YES	NO
Dec. 24	1979	IQOP	38.5	47.2
March 7	1980	CROP	41.0	52.0
March 16	1980	IQOP	47.4	43.8
April 20	1980	IQOP	41.2	40.9
April 25	1980	CROP	44.4	43.9
May 9	1980	CROP	39.6	45.5
May 11	1980	IQOP	37.0	40.0
May 16	1980	Pinard-Hamilton	37.0	40.0
May 18	1980	IQOP	40.4	36.5

May 20, 1980 results

Yes 40.5%   No 59.5%

1995

			YES	NO
Sept. 7–8	1995	Leger & Leger	43.8	42.9
Sept. 8–12	1995	SOM Inc.	37.0	45.0
Sept. 19–25	1995	SOM Inc.	39.0	48.0
Sept. 20–25	1995	CROP	39.0	47.0
Sept. 25–28	1995	Leger & Leger	43.8	45.1
Oct. 1–5	1995	Leger & Leger	42.9	43.7
Oct. 8–12	1995	Leger & Leger	45.0	42.4
Oct. 10–12	1995	Gallup	39.0	43.0
Oct. 13–16	1995	SOM Inc.	42.9	43.4
Oct. 13–16	1995	CROP	43.6	42.6
Oct. 16–18	1995	Angus Reid	45.4	43.6
Oct. 16–20	1995	Leger & Leger	45.8	42.2
Oct. 19–23	1995	CROP	44.5	42.2
Oct. 23–25	1995	SOM Inc.	46.0	40.0
Oct. 23–25	1995	Angus Reid	44.0	40.0

October 30, 1995 results

Yes 49.4%   No 50.6%

Official question

The Government of Quebec has made public its proposal to negotiate a new agreement with the rest of Canada, based on the equality of nations; this agreement would enable Quebec to acquire the exclusive power to make its laws, administer its taxes and establish relations abroad—in other words, sovereignty—and at the same time, to maintain with Canada an economic association including a common currency; any change in political status resulting from these negotiations will be submitted to the people through a referendum; on these terms do you agree to give the Government of Quebec the mandate to negotiate the proposed agreement between Quebec and Canada?

Official question

Do you agree that Quebec should become sovereign, after having made a formal offer to Canada for a new Economic and Political Partnership, within the scope of the Bill respecting the future of Quebec and of the agreement signed on June 12, 1995?

FIGURE 5.2 Referendum Polls and Results, 1980 and 1995

SOURCE: Nancy Gill, Canadian Press, 'Referendum Polls and Results, 1980 and 1995', *Winnipeg Free Press*, 28 October 1995, p. A3.

signed on June 12, 1995?' The debate centred around the new division of power (Drache and Perin, 1992:13–19), Quebec-Canadian association (Smith, 1992:61–70), sovereignty and the aboriginals (Turpel, 1992:93–106), a common currency (Donner and Lazar, 1992:127–38), and dividing the debt (Chorney, 1992:156–70). Indeed, just days before the referendum, the Cree of northern Quebec held their own referendum with 97 per cent voting to stay in Canada. With the failure of Meech Lake, federalists had little to offer Quebeckers who wanted to stay. Federalists mostly warned of dire economic consequences for Quebec.

As we can see in Figure 5.3, six of the 1995 polls in the last half of October, two weeks before the vote, had the Yes vote for Quebec sovereignty ahead. The Yes vote gained an enormous boost when charismatic Lucien Bouchard, the leader of the Bloc Québécois, and federal leaders of the official opposition vigorously entered the referendum debate. Whereas polls a month earlier had the No vote leading by as much as 10 points, the race became neck and neck toward the end. The No side won by a narrow 1.2 per cent margin only because the 12 to 15 per cent Undecideds voted four to one No as they had in 1980, and large No crowds rallied in Montreal and cities across Canada. Whereas the No side won by a 20 per cent margin of 59.5 to 40.5 per cent in 1980, by 1995 the margin had been cut to a 49.4 to 50.6 per cent margin of victory. Basically, Quebec voters' opinions split down the middle, where very little had been decided. The survival of Canada had been on the brink, with both sides shaken and dissatisfied!

HIGHLIGHT 5.2 QUEBEC'S FUTURE: DISTINCT OR SOVEREIGN?

The question of what is or what should be the place of Quebec in Canada has been asked since the time of the conquest of New France. The Quebec Act of 1774 and later the British North America Act of 1867 guaranteed that the French in Quebec could keep their culture, language, religion, way of life, and a legal system somewhat different from that of the British. In practice, this has meant that, notwithstanding similarities, Quebec has developed as a society different from that of the rest of Canada. In fact, in many respects, two societies have coexisted side by side in Canada.

Since the 1950's Quebec has developed its own distinct business class of people and its own educated class of people–the intelligentsia. The latter in particular, have heightened the awareness of French Quebec culture, Quebec's history and Quebec's own economic and political interests. The question thus remains: should not the Quebec people take the further step and establish its own full political hegemony over the province? That is,

should it not separate from the rest of Canada and become a sovereign state?

The typical progression among ethnic or cultural groups living on a distinct territory has been from a folk-community to nationally community, to nation, to nation-state. Since the middle of the nineteenth century, Quebec has gone through all these stages, except the last one. Since the middle of the 1970s, each time it came to power, the Parti Quebecois (PQ) has worked to bring about sovereignty. It has tried to accomplish this in a democratic manner, by means of a referendum. Two such referenda were held, in 1980 and 1995, and each time the people of Quebec voted not to separate from Canada, though not by a large margin. In November 1998, in the re-election of the PQ, the popular vote for this separatist party was again almost the same as that for the Liberal party, which is opposed to separation.

This raises the question as to how can one explain this ambiguity among the people of

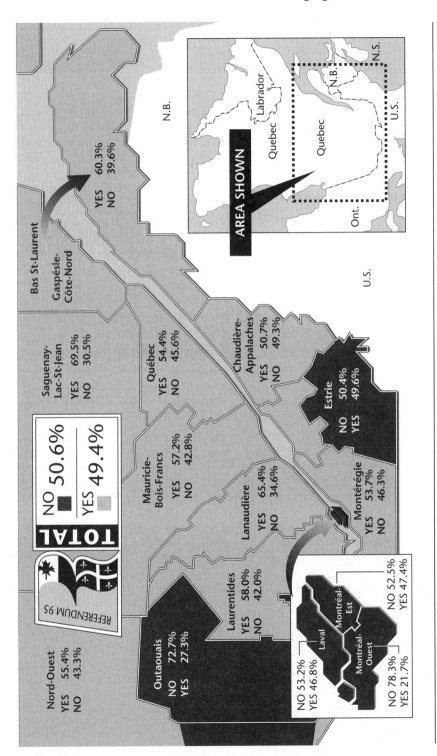

FIGURE 5.3 Quebec Referendum Results by Region, 1995

SOURCE: Canadian Press, '1995 Referendum Results by Region', *Winnipeg Free Press*, 31 October 1995, p. B2.

Quebec toward staying in Canada or separating. Is it, as the Premier of Quebec said after the loss of referendum in 1995, that the 'other' ethnic groups who settled in Quebec vote against separation and this sways the vote? He argued that the other ethnic groups immigrate to Canada not to Quebec and hence they want to remain with the rest of Canada. Is it that the federal government spends a lot of money to keep Quebec in the Confederation? Or, is it that the Quebecois themselves feel more economic security as being part of Canada rather than being independent? Is it that the Quebec business and industry have become so interdependent with the rest of Canadian business and industry that separation may mean a serious disruption of their activities?

Whatever the cause or set of causal factors for this ambiguity, a question can be raised as to how much difference would it make if Quebec were to separate from the rest of Canada. If it stays in Canada, the federal government will have to make more concessions to Quebec, give Quebec more powers, such as taxation, health and welfare, immigration policy, the 'notwithstanding' clause and the amending formula in the constitution, and other powers–things that were envisioned in the failed Meech Lake Accord. In other words, Quebec will most probably be given a status in Canada different from that of the other provinces and one that would make it less dependent on the federal government. On the other hand, if Quebec were to separate what it would have to do immediately afterwards is to negotiate and sign many treaties with Canada in order to maintain normal economic and political relations. This would tie Quebec back with Canada, perhaps even more than it is now, or would be with all the concessions granted.

Yet, how much difference would separation of Quebec make to the rest of Canada? Would Canada be able to maintain a strong economy? Would there not be strong pressures to join the United States? Would Canada be able to maintain its sophisticated social and health policies? Could Canada continue to be a model multicultural country, as it has been for many other nations of the world facing increasing ethnic diversity within their own societies? Would not the world lose a country that presents a unique historical, social and cultural experience?

SOURCE: Wsevolod W. Isajiw, *Understanding Diversity: Ethnicity and Race in the Canadian Context* (Toronto: Thompson Educational Publishing, 1999). Reprinted by permission.

SUMMARY

In Part III we focus on ethnic solidarity and identity. In this chapter we have examined the French in Quebec as the most important evidence of pluralism. In Max Weber's terms, French Québécois are European racially; they have maintained a distinct language, culture, and consciousness of kind for four hundred years; their religious ideology is solidly Roman Catholic; they have definitely remained a distinctive 'people' with the will to fight for their identity; and they think of themselves as a nation. Their macro sociocultural structures are clearly French-Québécois, and they interact extensively with other French Canadians in symbolic interactionist terms.

The regional setting in the province of Quebec has made French solidarity possible. They were the first Europeans to settle in Canada, founding what was to become the nation of New France. Demographically, more than 80 per cent are French, and they speak French in the region of Quebec. During their four hundred years, these Québécois have resorted to a series of colonial, conservative, quiet revolutionary, and separatist ideologies to survive, especially since the conquest by the British.

A francophone symbol system has remained the dominant language of Quebeckers. Recently the recommendations of the Royal Commission on Bilingualism and Biculturalism to make French an official national language along with English have been enacted and promoted nationally. Francophones outside the province of Quebec are struggling more to retain their French identity, but those within the Bilingual Belt adjacent to the French core are maintaining their French-Canadian identity extensively. While fewer others are shifting to speaking French than shifting away, francophones are clearly maintaining themselves in the Quebec core.

Miner's study of the St Denis parish illustrated the rural life of the habitants during the conservative ideological period. Hughes's and Gold's studies illustrate the impact of industrialization and the resulting changes. Quebec is fast becoming more urban and more industrial, but the desire to remain French continues unabated. The recent quiet revolution, the separatist movement, the two Quebec referenda, and Bill 101 have all served to strengthen francoph-

ones and French Québécois, while more and more people are learning French across Canada and accepting Canada as a bilingual nation. French Canadians are the best example of a macro sociocultural 'nation' that has not assimilated, but that has instead fought for an alternative to unitary Canadian nationalism. Plural French identity and solidarity is an empirical fact in Canada. We turn next to ethnic cultural identity, and the extent to which smaller ethnoreligious groups have been able to establish plural ethnic identity and solidarity.

In many ways it is surprising that the French in Quebec have not become a separate nation, but so far they have stayed in Canada. They represent a very solid bloc of people, and show us the extent to which voluntary pluralism (Cell E in our model) can be accomplished—a 'nation' within a nation. Others in Canada, such as aboriginals, Jews, Hutterites, and recent immigrants also try to retain their identities, so in Chapters 6 and 7 we need to explore how they have fared. Can they too retain separate identities, and how do they do this?

CRITICAL THINKING QUESTIONS

1. In what ways is 'the Quebec Nation' a geographic reality in Canada? What indicators should be used to examine this?

2. Why did Quebec not become a separate country? Make a case for separation. Make a case for staying in Canada.

3. How is language a major francophone symbol of the Québécois? Why did the Bi and Bi Commission give Quebeckers such a central place?

4. What is Joy's Bilingual Belt? Discuss the official languages, language shifts, and the language continuity index.

5. Discuss either Miner's French habitant St Denis, or Hughes's industrialized Cantonville, to show traditional French life and the role that industry plays.

6. Compare Pierre Trudeau's federalist and René Lévesque's separatist alternatives for Quebec. Who has won? What has been solved? Where are we now?

SUGGESTED READINGS

Edwards, John (ed.), *Language in Canada* (Cambridge, UK: Cambridge University Press, 1998). An up-to-date account of the linguistic and cultural situation in Canada is presented by 26 experts in the area.

Gagnon, Alain-G. (ed.), *Quebec: State and Society*, 2nd edn (Toronto: Nelson, 1993). Twenty-five essays are presented on the key issues and challenges facing present-day Quebec.

Guindon, Hubert, *Quebec Society: Tradition, Modernity and Nationhood* (Toronto: University of Toronto Press, 1988). Guindon examines the social evolution, political unrest, bureaucratic revolution, and modernization of the Quebec state.

CHAPTER 6

Ethnic Identity and Identification

In Chapter 5 we presented language as an important symbol system, anchored in the distinctive French Québécois territorial 'nation'. The French fact, one of the two founding charter peoples, has been a solid example of voluntary pluralism centring cell E in our theoretical model. To what extent can other ethnic groups also voluntarily perpetuate their heritages even though they may not be as large, or as powerful as the French in Quebec. What is the salience of their ethnic identity? What are some of the cultural indicators of their distinctive identification? How do some minority groups compare to others?

Gordon (1964:24) defines an ethnic group as a group of individuals with a shared sense of peoplehood based on presumed shared sociocultural experience and/or similar physical characteristics. Dashefsky (1975a) defines group identification 'as a generalized attitude involving a personal attachment to a group and a positive orientation toward being a member of a group. Therefore, ethnic identification takes place when the group in question is one with whom the individual believes he has a common ancestry based on shared individual characteristics and/or shared sociocultural experiences' (1976:8). Erikson suggests that 'identity is not only the sum of childhood identifications, but rather a new combination of old and new identification fragments' (1968:90).

'Identity may best be understood if it is viewed first as a higher order concept, i.e., a general organizing referent which includes a number of subsidiary facets' (Dashefsky, 1972:240). Dashefsky has reviewed some of the literature on identity and identification which illustrates the many dimensions of identification:

Foote (1951) and Lindesmith and Strauss (1968) have suggested that identification involves linking oneself to others in an organizational sense (as becoming a formal member of an organization) or in a symbolic sense (as thinking of oneself as a part of a particular group). Stone (1962) argues further that identification subsumes two processes: 'identification of' and 'identification with'. The former involves placing the individual in socially defined categories. This facilitates occurrence of the latter. In Stone's terms it is 'identification with' that gives rise to identity.

Rosen has gone further in arguing that an individual may identify himself (herself) with others on three levels: First, one may identify oneself with some important person in one's life, e.g. a parent or a friend (i.e., a significant other). Second, one may identify with a group from which one draws one's values, e.g. family or coworkers (i.e., reference group). Last, one may identify oneself with a broad category of persons, e.g. an ethnic group or occupational group (i.e., a society category). (1972:242).

THEORIES OF ETHNIC IDENTITY

Because sociologists and psychologists have studied ethnic identity at macro and micro levels there is a great deal of confusion about the nature of ethnic identity. Some of this is due to the different theoretical biases that researchers bring to their studies. Dashefsky (1975a) has tried to systematize some of these macro and micro emphases. He suggests that four frameworks (sociocultural, interactionist, group dynamicist, and psychoanalytic) have generally been used: the first two by sociologists, the second two by psychologists.

Dashefsky (1975a:11) classifies these four theoretical orientations along two axes (shown in Figure 6.1), using ontology (theory of reality) and methodology axes that intersect to form four cells. The first two cells deal with macro and micro sociological orientations, and the second two with macro and micro psychological orientations. Sociological methods of research rely on field study, survey research, and sociohistorical analysis, while psychological methods deal primarily with experimental and clinical studies.

The top left sociocultural cell represents a macro sociological approach in which social structure and culture are the dominant foci of ethnic identity research. In the lower left cell, the interactionist approach is micro sociological and deals with the social-psychological concern with symbols and their importance for social relationships. In the upper right cell, the group dynamicist approach is a macro psychological method in which the group context is important in examinations of ethnic identity. The sociocultural and the group dynamicist traditions are both macro approaches. Both look at the social system, but socioculturalists stress the importance of historical experiences, while group dynamicists focus more on immediate individual and group structures. The lower right cell represents the micro psychological approach often called behaviourist, in which identity is explained in terms of reinformed responses to stimuli (Dashefsky, 1975a:11). Very little research has been done in this behaviourist area of ethnic identity. In this chapter we will confine our theoretical review to the first two sociological macro and micro approaches (sociocultural and interactionist). The interactionist approach is largely an attempt at rebutting the mechanistic image of humans portrayed by behaviourists. Interactionists also want to stress the symbolic dimensions of human behaviour, which structural functionalists tend not to emphasize. The ethnocultural approach can focus so much on structures that the dynamic features of change tend to be overly restrictive and deterministic, squeezing the life out of living too much.

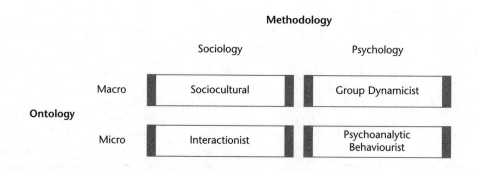

FIGURE 6.1 Theoretical Orientation in the Social Psychology of Ethnicity

SOURCE: Arnold Dashefsky, 'Theoretical Frameworks in the Study of Ethnic Identity', *Ethnicity* 2, 1(1975).

The Macro Sociocultural Approach

Dashefsky (1975a:12) summarized the socioculturalists' assumptions very well. The macro sociocultural framework assumes that individual behaviour is shaped by, and occurs within, social and cultural systems. The social system tends to define the relationships among individuals within the structure, and the cultural system defines the mutual expectations that individuals share and the norms that they hold. The cultural and social system is the result of cumulated historical experiences; individual behaviour is shaped within this context. The study of human behaviour is more important to these socioculturalists than is the study of attitudes, perceptions, and self-conception.

A review of the literature shows that the multidimensional approach to identity has been expounded first by a host of researchers interested mostly in Jewish identity (Levinson, 1962: 375–99; Fathi and Kinsley, 1968; Segalman, 1967:92–111). Many of the factors used by Lazerwitz (1970) include some distinctly Jewish cultural items such as Zionism, although other of his factors such as education, religion, friendships, and dating patterns could be extended to apply to any minority.

Studies show that ethnocultural identity tends to be multidimensional, clustering around a multiplicity of factors, among them language use, religious practice, endogamy, parochial education, choice of ingroup friends, use of ethnic media, and participation in ethnic voluntary organizations (Breton et al., 1990; Burch, 1990; deVries, 1988; Driedger, 1989, 1996, 2000b; Friesen, 1993; Isajiw, 1997; Ishwaren, 1980; Kalbach and Kalbach, 2000; Weinfeld, 1981). Because individuals and ethnic groups vary in the extent to which they emphasize different identity factors, researchers need to sort out the different factors and the patterns or profiles of ethnocultural identity.

Historical, national, and regional experiences also add to Canada's ethnic diversity. Because of the Canadian policy of pluralism, ethnic identity often persists. For some groups, however, shifts of interest reinforce identification and account for greater ethnic identity. This trend may be seen in the French, with the present emphasis on bilingualism, and the Jews, who are concerned with events related to the state of Israel. Glazer and Moynihan (1975), for example, suggest that such events as the Nazi Holocaust, Zionism, and the Catholic School controversy have provided foci for ethnic identification. Charter-group status, entrance status, and ethnic institutional completeness are influential also. Thus, it is reasonable to expect that modes of identification will vary with historically important causes and events. Therefore, the measures of these modes will exhibit a multifactor structure, to distinguish the components that different individuals and groups stress. This raises the problem of selecting crucial elements to measure ethnic identity (Breton et al., 1990; Driedger, 1989; Weinfeld, 1994:238–66).

The Micro Sociological Interactionist Approach

Max Weber assumed that humans live in a symbolic world, are stimulated by symbols, and stimulate others through symbols. Indeed, it is the ability to use symbols in a complex way that makes humans distinctive. Humans learn through symbolic communication—especially language—and become reflective beings who can think abstractly, take roles, and create feelings and values. As a result they learn to predict each other's behaviour and to adjust their behaviour based on these predictions. In this way they define themselves in relationship to other persons and situations (Dashefsky, 1975b:13). It is therefore important to ethnic identity that groups of individuals share symbols and their meanings and values in what we call group identification. Religious institutions, newspapers, and schools can all symbolically reinforce ethnic identification.

Further investigation is needed to determine the relationship between attitudes toward ethnic identification and actual activity based on those attitudes (Edwards and Doucette, 1987).

Lazerwitz (1953:3–24) developed three categories—behavioural, attitudinal, and conceptual—for Jewish identification. He gave the most weight to behavioural items, and middle weight to attitudinal items, and the least weight to conceptual items. According to Segalman, 'the decision to give more weight to the behavioural than to attitudinal data is a matter for continued examination and study' (1967:98).

Kurt Lewin (1948) proposed that individuals need a firm, clear sense of identification with the heritage and culture of their ingroup to find a secure basis for a sense of well-being, and that insufficient ingroup security results in self-hatred and ingroup denial. Rothman's (1960:82) summary of Lewin's theory suggests that such factors as ethnic self-affirmation, ethnic self-denial, and marginality need to be examined as independent but related variables that form a sense of ethnic self-identity for members of a particular ethnic group.

Many social psychologists hold that the preservation and enhancement of the self is a basic human need. To determine the extent to which members of an ethnic group consider their ingroup an essential part of their self-identification, it is necessary to review studies related specifically to ethnic self-identity. Segalman's early extensive review of Jewish identity indicates that few scales include social-psychological items. Since then, some studies have been done (Berry, 1990; Edwards and Doucette, 1987; Mackie and Brinkerhof, 1984; Weinfeld, 1985), a number of these studies have centred around salience of ethnic identity and means of measuring salience. Driedger (1976a) examined ethnic self-identity in Canada and found considerable differences among Winnipeg groups in their real and ideal ethnic affirmation, and their levels of denial and marginality. Isajiw (1981:90) studied symbolic ethnic identity in Toronto, and later Isajiw and Driedger (1987) developed a Symbolic Ethnic Identity (SEI) Index.

Lewin's theory deals with ethnic self-hatred. The first proposition, *ethnic affirmation*, describes the extent to which members identify with the ethnic support provided by their ingroup. It examines whether they are proud of their ingroup, whether it provides them with a rich heritage, and whether they wish to remember it or participate in it if they are given a choice. Ethnic affirmation refers not only to behavioural indicators of identity such as language use, attendance in parochial schools, and choice of ingroup friends, but also to a desire to be affiliated with one's ethnic group. Driedger (1976a) found much Jewish and French ethnic affirmation in Winnipeg.

On the other hand, *ethnic denial* might include feelings of inferiority, of being restricted by or annoyed with the ingroup, or of a desire to hide cultural identity. These feelings of insecurity, inferiority, and discomfort caused by association with the reference group may be due to the negative stereotypes of the ingroup created by members of the majority culture.

Marginality is another important concept derived from Lewin's theory. Sociologically, this term has generally referred to the uncertain position of persons experiencing two cultures but identified with neither; it can also include the idea, at the psychological level, of a *discrepancy* between ingroup members' real and ideal identifications. The format of Worchel's Self Activity Inventory (SAI) (which involves a description of who a person is as well as an assessment of who he *would like to be*) is useful in this connection. The discrepancy between the two is important to a study of student aspirations (Wylie, 1961). A low degree of discrepancy suggests that persons see themselves as consistently successful in meeting their expected needs, while a high degree of discrepancy reveals a sense of being unable to meet expectancy levels. Driedger (1976a) used real and ideal discrepancies as indicators of marginality because ethnic solidarity is perceived as an inferior goal that is not in harmony with the aspirations of the individual showing these discrepancies.

Having reviewed the two major sociological macro and micro perspectives on ethnic identity, let us identify some of the ethnic identification factors evident in the empirical literature. We begin with three structural sociocultural forms of identification (territory, institutions, and culture), and end with three symbolic forms of identification (history, ideology, and leadership). These two theoretical perspectives tend to summarize the many forms of ethnic identification on a structural-symbolic continuum. In the middle of this continuum, the two approaches overlap considerably; the respective poles, in contrast, are clearly distinctive ontologically and methodologically.

HIGHLIGHT 6.1 TRUDEAU'S 1971 MULTICULTURAL CALL

I am happy this morning to be able to reveal to the House that the government has accepted all those recommendations of the Royal Commission on Bilingualism and Biculturalism as contained in Volume IV of its reports directed to federal departments and agencies. Honourable members will recall that the subject of this volume is 'the contribution by other ethnic groups to the cultural enrichment of Canada and the measures that should be taken to safeguard that contribution.'

Volume IV examined the whole question of cultural and ethnic pluralism in this country and the status of our various cultures and languages, an area of study given all too little attention in the past by scholars.

It was the view of the Royal Commission, shared by the government and, I am sure, by all Canadians, that there cannot be one cultural policy for Canadians of British and French origin, another for the original peoples and yet a third for all others. For although there are two official languages, there is no official culture, nor does any ethnic group take precedence over any other. No citizen or group of citizens is other than Canadian, and all should be treated fairly.

The Royal Commission was guided by the belief that adherence to one's ethnic group is influenced not so much by one's origin or mother tongue as by one's sense of belonging to the group, and by what the Commission calls the group's 'collective will to exist'. The government shares this belief.

The individual's freedom would be hampered if he were locked for life within a particular cultural compartment by the accident of birth or language. It is vital, therefore, that every Canadian, whatever his ethnic origin, be given a chance to learn at least one of the two languages in which his country conducts its official business and its politics.

A policy of multiculturalism within a bilingual framework commends itself to the government as the most suitable means of assuring the cultural freedom of Canadians. Such a policy should help to break down discriminatory attitudes and cultural jealousies. National unity, if it is to mean anything in the deeply personal sense, must be founded on confidence in one's own individual identity; out of this can grow respect for that of others and a willingness to share ideas, attitudes and assumptions. A vigorous policy of multiculturalism will help create initial confidence. It can form the base of a society which is based on fair play for all.

The government will support and encourage the various cultures and ethnic groups that give structure and vitality to our society. They will be encouraged to share their cultural expression and values with other Canadians and so contribute to a richer life for us all.

In the past, substantial public support has been given largely to the arts and cultural institutions of English-speaking Canada. More recently, and largely with the help of the Royal Commission's earlier recommendations in Volume I to III, there has been a conscious effort on the government's part to correct any bias against the French language and culture. In the last few months the government has taken steps to provide funds to support cultural-educational centres for native people. The policy I am announcing today accepts the contention of the other cultural communities that they, too, are essential elements in Canada and deserve government assistance in order to contribute to regional and national life in ways that derive from their heritages yet are distinctively Canadian.

In implementing a policy of multiculturalism within a bilingual framework, the government will provide support in four ways.

First, resources permitting, the government will seek to assist all Canadian cultural groups that have demonstrated a desire and effort to continue to develop, a capacity to grow and contribute to Canada, and a clear need for assistance, the small and weak groups no less than the strong and highly organized.

Second, the government will assist members of all cultural groups to overcome cultural barriers to full participation in Canadian society.

Third, the government will promote creative encounters and interchange among all Canadian cultural groups in the interest of national unity.

Fourth, the government will continue to assist immigrants to acquire at least one of Canada's official languages in order to become full participants in Canadian society.

Mr Speaker, I stated at the outset that the government has accepted in principle all recommendations addressed to federal departments and agencies. We are also ready and willing to work cooperatively with the provincial governments towards implementing those recommendations that concern matters under provincial or shared responsibility.

Some of the programs endorsed or recommended by the Commission have been administered for some time by various federal agencies. I might mention the Citizenship Branch, the CRTC and its predecessor the BBG,

the National Film Board and the National Museum of Man. These programs will be revised, broadened and reactivated and they will receive the additional funds that may be required.

Some of the recommendations that concern matters under provincial jurisdiction call for coordinated federal and provincial action. As a first step, I have written to the first ministers of the provinces informing them of the response of the federal government and seeking their cooperation. Officials will be asked to carry this consultation further.

I wish to table details of the government's response to each of the several recommendations.

It should be noted that some of the programs require pilot projects or further short-term research before more extensive action can be taken. As soon as these preliminary studies are available, further programs will be announced and initiated. Additional financial and personnel resources will be provided.

Responsibility for implementing these recommendations has been assigned to the Citizenship Branch of the Department of the Secretary of State, the agency now responsible for matters affecting the social integration of immigrants and the cultural activities of all ethnic groups. An Inter-Agency Committee of all those agencies involved will be established to coordinate the federal effort.

In conclusion, I wish to emphasize the view of the government that a policy of multiculturalism within a bilingual framework is basically the conscious support of individual freedom of choice. We are free to be ourselves. But this cannot be left to chance. It must be fostered and pursued actively. If freedom of choice is in danger for some ethnic groups, it is in danger for all. It is the policy of this government to eliminate any such danger and to 'safeguard' this freedom.

SOURCE: Statement by Prime Minister Trudeau in the House of Commons, 8 October 1971.

ETHNIC IDENTIFICATION FACTORS

In our discussion of ethnic identification, we will touch on six factors: ecological territory, ethnic culture, ethnic institutions, historical symbols, ideology, and charismatic leadership (Driedger, 1989, 1996). We suggest that these factors are some of the basic components that constitute an ethnic community, which Weber referred to as a group of individuals having a shared sense of peoplehood including both structural and symbolic dimensions (Breton, 1991; Weinfeld, 1994).

Identification with a Territory

Both Joy (1972) and Lieberson (1970) argue that the maintenance of an ethnic language and culture is not possible unless there is a sufficiently large number of the same ethnic group concentrated in a territory. Joy demonstrates how Quebec's French were in control of the provincial territory, thus perpetuating their language and culture through religious, educational, and political institutions. Indian reservations also demonstrate ethnic territorial segregation. Most minorities cannot maintain such exclusive control over a territory; however, it is a model to which many minority groups seem to aspire. Ethnic bloc settlements are common, especially in the West. Examples include the French in Quebec, the Germans in the Kitchener-Waterloo area in Ontario, and the Ukrainians in the Aspen Belt stretching from the Manitoba Inter-Lake region to Edmonton. Rural hinterlands often contribute immigrants to the city. These migrants often perpetuate the urban villager way of life, as best illustrated by the North End of Winnipeg—the stronghold of Ukrainians, Poles, and Jews until recently (Driedger and Church, 1974). Balakrishnan and Kralt (1987; Balakrishnan and Selvanathan, 1990; Kalbach, 1990) also found extensive residential segregation in Toronto. Territory is an essential ingredient of any definition of a community (Driedger, 1999). Individuals can identify with a territory, and it is the place within which ethnic activity can take place.

Ethnic Institutional Identification

Breton (1964:193, 194; 1991:125–61) argues that the direction of the immigrant's integration will to a large extent result from the forces of attraction (positive and negative) stemming from three communities: the community of the respondents' ethnicity, the native (receiving) community, and the other ethnic communities. These forces are generated by the social organization of ethnic communities and their capacity to attract and hold members within their social boundaries. Integration into their own ethnic community, supported by institutional completeness of their group, will reinforce solidarity.

The rationale for institutional completeness is that a minority can develop a social system of its own with control over its institutions, and then the social action patterns of the group will take place largely within the system. Breton (1964) suggests that religious, educational, and welfare institutions are crucial, while Joy (1972) adds the importance of political and economic institutions. Vallee (1969) confirmed Breton's claims by summarizing the need for organization of group structures and institutions that influence socialization and ethnic community decision-making. Driedger and Church (1974) found that, in Winnipeg, the French and Jews maintained a more complete set of religious, educational, and welfare institutions than other ethnic groups in the city. These two groups were also the most segregated in St Boniface and the North End respectively, where they established their institutions. Residential segregation and ethnic institutional completeness tend to reinforce each other. The French and the Jews identified with both territory and ethnic institutions.

Identification with Ethnic Culture

Kurt Lewin (1948) proposed that the individual needs to achieve a firm sense of identification with the heritage and culture of the ingroup to find a secure 'ground' for a sense of well-being. We assume that a minority culture can be better groomed within the territorial enclave where an ethnic group can build a concentration of its own institutions. The territory becomes a crucible within which ethnic institutions can be built, and the ethnic culture should flourish within these boundaries that support it.

Ethnic cultural identity factors have been studied by numerous scholars (Berry et al., 1987; Friesen, 1993; Isajiw, 1990; Isajiw, Sev'er, and Driedger, 1993; Richard, 1991; Weinfeld, 1994). Driedger found at least six factors that tended to differentiate group adherence to culture (language use, endogamy, choice of friends, and participation in religion, parochial schools, and voluntary organizations). French and Jewish adherents in Winnipeg, who were residentially segregated and maintained their ethnic institutions to a great degree, also ranked high on attendance at parochial schools (79 and 74 per cent); endogamy (65 and 91 per cent); and choice of ingroup friends (49 and 63 per cent). This would seem to support use of French language at home (61 per cent) and attendance in church (54 per cent) for the French; that was not the case for the Jews. Other ethnic groups such as the Germans, Ukrainians, Poles, Scandinavians, and British supported their ingroup cultures less actively.

Examination of territorial, institutional, and cultural identity factors suggest that these three tend to reinforce each other. When individuals of a given ethnic group identify with their ingroup along these dimensions, they tend to remain more distinctive and this blocks tendencies toward assimilation. Such maintenance of distinctive ethnic features is necessary if the Canadian ethnic mosaic is to remain a distinct reality.

Identification with Historical Symbols

Minority rural villagers may perpetuate their social structures and community as ends in themselves, without much reference to where they came from and their future purpose. Knowledge of their origins and pride in their heritage would seem to be essential for a sense of purpose and direction. Without such knowledge and pride, the desire to perpetuate tradition rap-idly diminishes. The Jews have ritualized their history by placing it before their youth in the form of special days, fasts, candles, and food habits—symbols of their past history. Such historical symbols can create a sense of belonging, a sense of purpose, and a sense of continuing tradition that is important and worth perpetuating. Although tragic for the Jews, the Nazi Holocaust in the 1940s and the present struggles in the Near East may be a reminder of the conflict that is a part of their historical past (Brym and Lenton, 1993; Davis, 1992; Levitt and Shaffir, 1993).

The ethnic heritage of the past can be a positive or negative influence on identity. A comparison of the sense of identity of seven ethnic groups in Winnipeg using a Worchel-type scale indicated strong French and Jewish ingroup affirmation and low ingroup denial, while Scandinavians scored low on both (Driedger, 1976). Jewish and French students were proud of their ingroups, felt strongly bound to them, wished to remember them, and contributed to them. Their ingroups were positive symbols. The French indicated a very low ingroup denial. They did not try to hide their ethnicity, nor did they feel inferior about it. They seldom felt annoyed or restricted by their identity. The Ukrainians, Poles, and Germans felt less positively about their ethnic identity and, at the same time, were more inclined to deny their ethnicity.

Identification with an Ideology

A religious or political ideology can rally followers to a goal beyond cultural and institutional values (Glazer and Moynihan, 1975). For many of the younger generation, territory, culture, and ethnic institutions seem to be means to an end rather than an end to be perpetuated indefinitely. As urban ethnic groups become more sophisticated, it is doubtful that enclavic means will hold them within an ethnic ingroup orbit. A political or religious ideology, however, provides a purpose and impetus for values that are considered more important than cultural and institutional means (Bibby, 1987b; Brym,

Shaffir and Weinfeld, 1993; Kauffman and Driedger, 1991).

In our study of Winnipeg clergymen, we found doctrinal belief, for example, to be an important factor in differentiating attitudes toward a variety of social issues (Driedger and Redekop, 1983). Beliefs had an independent effect on positions taken on issues related to social control, personal morality, use of power by the elite, civil liberties, minority rights, and welfare support. Absolutist clergy, those with a conservative other-worldly focus, were reluctant to change society; clergymen who were more doctrinally liberal were open to change. There is often a very strong correlation between religion and ethnicity in French and Polish Roman Catholics, Orthodox and Catholic Ukrainians, Scandinavian Lutherans, German Lutherans and Baptists, the Jews, and British Anglicans and United Church adherents.

Identification with religious beliefs or a political philosophy provides a more social-psychological dimension, which again emphasizes the importance of decisions to perpetuate or change territory, institutions and ethnic culture (Driedger, 1995, 1996, 1997, 1998, 1999a, 2000a; Driedger and Kraybill, 1994; Friesen, 1993).

Charismatic Leadership and Identification

The importance of charisma is demonstrated in a variety of new minority movements as shown by the leadership of Martin Luther King and Malcolm X among the blacks in the United States, René Lévesque among the Québécois, and especially Nelson Mandela who brought South Africa back into the United Nations. Individuals with a sense of mission often adapt an ideology to a current situation, linking it symbolically with the past and using the media to effectively transform the present into a vision of the future.

Most religious movements began with charismatic leaders as demonstrated by the founders of the great religions: Abraham, Buddha, Confucius, Jesus, and Mohammed. The importance of Martin Luther to the Lutherans, John Calvin to the Presbyterians, Joseph Smith to the Mormons, and Menno Simons to the Mennonites illustrates this also. The same is true of political movements led by Ho Chi Minh of Vietnam, Mao of China, Lenin of Russia, Hitler, Churchill, Castro, Tito, Mahatma Gandhi, Lincoln, Lévesque, and Mandela.

Such charismatic leaders use social-psychological means designed to create trust with which they mould a cohesive loyalty to both leader and ingroup. Look at the havoc Osama bin Laden created in 2001 using terrorism in the name of Islam. They are true believers in a cause that is passed on to their followers, resulting in new potential for change. In the beginning they may be less oriented to territory, institutions, culture, and heritage; as the movement ages, however, such structural features slowly become more important.

Although there may be many more ethnic dimensions of minority identification, we have suggested that territory, institutions, culture, heritage, ideology, and leaders are important. Studies show that some ethnic groups identify more with some of these dimensions than do others, and that some groups are more successful at maintaining a distinct community. The Hutterites are perhaps one of the most obvious groups that have survived in the rural setting, and the Jews have done so effectively in the cities for centuries. The task in this volume is to explore the various dimensions and foci of ethnic identification for various ethnic groups. It will not be possible to explore all of these dimensions with each group; all we can do is provide a small sample of studies to illustrate the multidimensional and multilinear complexity of the ethnic mosaic.

ETHNOCULTURAL IDENTITY DIMENSIONS

It is not easy to measure ethnic identity because we are dealing with a phenomenon that involves many levels, both macro and micro, each of which is multidimensional. A number of studies in search of the macro sociological-sociocultural dimensions have compared the numerous ethnic groups that we wish to examine here. Max Weber often did comparative studies. Anderson first compared rural ethnoreligious identity on the Prairies. Driedger began the urban search by selecting students representing many groups in one university. O'Bryan and colleagues (1976) sampled adults representing 10 groups of non-charter adults in five cities, and Breton and colleagues (1990) took a sample of adults in Toronto. All probed the sociocultural dimensions of ethnic identity, and the findings are fairly consistent and cumulative. Let us begin with rural studies that focus on structure and culture, and end with urban studies that show symbolic identity more.

Rural Ethnoreligious Identity

Anderson (1972) collected 1,000 interviews with adults from 18 rural ethnoreligious bloc settlements (7 French Catholic, 2 Hutterite, 2 Scandinavian Lutheran, 2 Mennonite, and 1 each of German Catholic, Russian Doukhobor, Ukrainian Orthodox, Ukrainian Catholic, and Polish Catholic) located between Saskatoon, North Battleford, and Prince Albert (census divisions 15 and 16) in Saskatchewan. He collected data on church attendance, endogamy, ethnic language ability and use, ethnic food habits, and involvement in ethnic crafts. The French and German Catholics, the Mennonites, and the Doukhobors in Anderson's sample comprise 4 of the 5 prairie groups Dawson studied in 1936.

In Table 6.1 we see that sociocultural identity is high for most of the 9 ethnic groups, although there are considerable variations. More than 9 out of 10 could speak their mother tongue, and two-thirds or more attended church regularly and married their own kind (endogamy). Except for the Germans and Scandinavians, two-thirds or more used their mother tongue at home frequently. Except for the French and German Catholics, a majority cooked and ate traditional ethnic foods. Over half of the groups reported

extensive involvement in making traditional ethnic crafts. Generally, ethnocultural identity was very high in rural northern Saskatchewan.

The Hutterites segregated on colonies, had a perfect score of 100 on all five ethnocultural identity indicators, while the German Catholics had the lowest average identity score of 64. Interestingly, 2 of the Catholic groups (Ukrainian and Polish) scored very high, and 2 (French and German) scored the lowest. This seems to indicate that ethnicity is more important to them than is religion. Religion does, however, seem to be an important factor in maintaining such a generally high rural ethnic identity. Church attendance is generally high. It is somewhat surprising to see that the Mennonites and Doukhobors are in the middle of the church attendance rankings, between the high and low Catholics, when we expected to see them among the highest rankings with the Hutterites.

All of these groups were segregated in rural ethnic enclaves where they could develop some demographic and institutional mass to build their ethnic institutions, although this varied by ethnic group. The Anderson findings confirm the findings of Dawson: the Mennonites and Doukhobors were more sectlike and retained their identity more, while the French and German Catholics, who are more churchlike and somewhat more secularized, did not score as highly on the ethnic identity scale. In general, Anderson's findings show that ethnocultural identity in rural Saskatchewan is high, and that, although it declined somewhat by the third generation for which Anderson and Driedger (1980:166–7) controlled, identity remained high.

A later study of the French Saskatchewan town of Gravelbourg, by Li and Denis (1983: 18–32), does show that there is a language shift to English. Although the majority in Gravelbourg are French, English is used widely in the school board and Board of Trade meetings. Younger, more educated third-generation Gravelbourgians are shifting to English the most. Exogamy is the greatest factor in shifting away from using French in the home (Li and Denis, 1983:26, 27).

TABLE 6.1 Comparison of Nine Rural Ethnoreligious Groups and Ethnic Identity Factors

ETHNIC IDENTITY FACTORS (%): Groups	N	Average Identity	Ability to Speak Mother Tongue	Extent of Endogamy	Regular Church Attendance	Use of Mother Tongue	Frequent Eating Ethnic Foods
Hutterites	(6)	100	100	(6)	100	100	100
Ukrainian Catholic	(154)	86	99	(154)	86	99	88
Polish Catholic	(15)	82	100	(15)	82	100	100
Ukrainian Orthodox	(83)	82	100	83	82	100	89
Mennonite	(244)	81	97	(244)	81	97	98
Doukhobor	(20)	76	95	(20)	76	95	60
Scandinavian Lutheran	(86)	76	90	(86)	76	90	96
French Catholic	(15)	73	99	(15)	73	99	91
German Catholic	(190)	64	93	(190)	64	93	90
Total Sample	(813)	80	97	(813)	80	97	91

SOURCE: Alan B. Anderson and Leo Driedger, 'The Mennonite Family' in K. Ishwaran (ed.), *Canadian Ethnic Variations* (Toronto: McGraw-Hill Ryerson, 1980), pp. 161–80.

Sociocultural Factors in Winnipeg

Numerous samples of ethnocultural identity in urban areas have been made, so we turn now to metropolitan ethnic studies, which we expect will be harder to maintain. A random sample of 1,560 questionnaires was collected by Driedger from 76 classes representing 15 per cent of the undergraduate enrolment on the campus at the University of Manitoba. The following seven groups were represented in sufficient number (50 or more) for the purpose of group comparisons: British (157), French (86), Germans (160), Jews (112), Poles (56), Scandinavians (61), and Ukrainians (188).

Driedger (1974, 1987) was the first to develop an Ethnic Cultural Identity (ECI) index in Canada involving both behavioural and attitudinal items in comparing 7 groups of ethnic university students (French, Jewish, German, Ukrainian, Polish, British, and Scandinavian). A series of behavioural items were designed and analyzed. Six cultural identity factors emerged: religious practice, endogamy, ethnic language use, ethnic organizational participation, atten-

dance in parochial schools, and extent of ethnic best friendships. Religion, endogamy, and language clearly were the most salient factors in that order, but this varied by ethnic group.

In Table 6.2 we see that one-half to three-fourths of the French students scored well on five of the six identity factors. They attended church at least twice a month; all their immediate family members had married French spouses; they spoke French to their parents at home; they participated in French voluntary organizations and attended a French school for at least a year; and a majority of their best friends were French. Their total composite identity score of 55.0 (the sum of the six factor scores divided by six) was the highest of the 7 ethnic groups. Scandinavian students ranked lowest (16.4) with one-fourth or less who scored on any of the five factors excluding endogamy.

The profiles of the 7 ethnic groups vary greatly. The French regularly scored high and the Scandinavians scored low most consistently. Jewish students scored very high on endogamy and attendance at Jewish schools, but very low on religious attendance and ethnic language use. The Germans and Ukrainians scored moderately

TABLE 6.2 Comparison of Ethnic Groups by Six Ethnocultural Factors

BEHAVIOURAL IDENTITY FACTORS (%):

Ethnic Groups	Average Identity Scores	Religious Practise	Church Endogamy	Ethnic Language Use	Ethnic Organizations Participation	Parochial Education Attendance	Best Friends Ethnic
French	55.0	54	65	61	23	79	49
Jewish	44.2	7	91	2	29	74	63
German	40.8	56	63	29	16	44	36
Ukrainian	36.8	44	76	22	23	41	16
Polish	31.5	46	53	14	13	57	5
British	29.3	23	72	—	10	27	45
Scandinavian	16.4	15	67	0	2	25	0

SOURCE: Leo Driedger, 'Ethnic Boundaries' in G.A. Theodorson, (ed.), *Urban Patterns* (University Park, PA: Penn State University Press, 1982).

on most factors. Driedger (1976) concluded that the ethnic cultural identity of the French and Jews was high, and that the sense of identity of the Scandinavians was low. In terms of the theories discussed in Chapter 2, the French and Jews followed the pluralist pattern, retaining their identity; the Scandinavians followed the assimilationist patterns with loss of identity; and the Germans, Ukrainians, and Poles demonstrated varied states of modified pluralism and assimilation. Driedger (1975) found that measures of both behavioural (ECBI scale) and attitudinal (ECAI scale) identity correlated very highly, and these in turn correlated highly with the degree of institutional completeness that ethnic groups had developed (Breton, 1964).

Non-Charter Identity in Five Cities

The Anderson and Driedger studies involved rural adults and urban students in two provinces of the prairie region. O'Bryan, Reitz, and Kuplowska (1976), in contrast, collected data on ethnocultural identity of adults in five cities (Montreal, Toronto, Winnipeg, Edmonton, and Vancouver) that provide us with information from at least three of the Canadian regions discussed in Chapter 4. They also used five ethnocultural identity indicators but confined their study to adults of 10 non-charter groups: Chinese, Dutch, German,

Greek, Hungarian, Italian, Polish, Portuguese, Scandinavian, and Ukrainian. The charter groups (British and French), who represent over half of the Canadian population, were not included.

In Table 6.3 we present comparative data on five ethnocultural indicators: church attendance, language use, ethnic language fluency, listening to ethnic radio, and reading ethnic ingroup newspapers. Except for the Chinese, weekly attendance at church was extensive in all ethnic groups (55 to 86 per cent) as a strong indicator of identity. Ethnic radio and newspapers were the least important; language use and ability were important for respondents of half of the groups (Hungarian, Greek, Chinese, Italian, and Portuguese).

We have ranked the 10 ethnic groups using average ethnic identity scores (the sum of the five indicators divided by five), with the Hungarians on top and the Scandinavians at the bottom. We note that the Chinese and those immigrants who came after the Second World War rank in the top half, indicating the highest identity, while North Europeans who have been in Canada for one hundred years or more rank the lowest. Except for church attendance, the Scandinavians indicate low ethnic identity; this is similar to Driedger's findings in Winnipeg. Interestingly, groups such as the Greeks, Portuguese, Italians, and Chinese (whom Balakrishnan and Kralt found highly segregated in Montreal, Toronto,

TABLE 6.3 Comparison of 10 Non-Charter Urban Ethnic Groups by Five Ethnocultural Factors

Ethnic Group	Average Identity Score	Weekly Ingroup Church Attendance	Frequent Ingroup Language Use	Fluent in Ingroup Language	Regular Ingroup Radio Listening	Regular Ingroup Newspaper Reading
Hungarian	57	75	64	64	58	24
Greek	56	75	92	79	10	26
Portuguese	54	86	95	56	15	18
Italian	51	75	84	60	10	24
Chinese	45	36	88	53	17	34
Polish	42	74	46	36	32	21
German	39	69	46	50	19	19
Ukrainian	39	63	49	31	32	20
Dutch	38	80	40	49	6	13
Scandinavian	29	55	14	23	42	10
Totals		72	63	50	24	21

SOURCE: K.G. O'Bryan, J.G. Reitz, and O.M. Kuplowska, *Non-Official Languages: A Study in Canadian Multiculturalism* (Ottawa: Minister of Supply and Services, 1976), pp. 214–45.

and Vancouver) also show higher ethnic identity. Indeed, Reitz (1980:118) used the same data and found high correlations (Pearson's r) among these ethnic identity indicators ranging from .50 to .56. The Pearson r method correlates high or low statistical correlations between two variables on a scale of zero to unity. The correlation between residential segregation and identity factors was somewhat lower, but still significant.

Comparisons of the five cities from which data were collected show some interesting variations as well. Mother-tongue fluency tended to be highest in Toronto, the most multicultural urban setting. Ethnic language use was most common in Montreal and Toronto. O'Bryan and colleagues (1976) and Breton and colleagues (1990) also controlled for generation, and they found that there was a great decline in language knowledge and use by the third generation, but that church attendance declined only marginally in the same period. This suggests that more indicators of ethnic identity are needed to trace the total ethnic identity profile. These indicators should include controls for generation, size of community, types of indicators, and ethnic groups.

Ethnic Identity in Toronto

Breton, Reitz, and Valentine (1990) did a random survey of 2,338 adult respondents in Toronto. The survey included a series of subprojects, one of which was designed to measure ethnic identity. This is an indepth study of ethnic identity in Toronto, the largest and most multicultural city in Canada.

Isajiw and Driedger (1987) developed two ethnic identity indexes using the Toronto data: one a six-item Ethnic Cultural Identity (ECI) index, and the other a Symbolic Ethnic Identity (SEI) index. In Table 6.4 we show the Ethnic Cultural Identity Index and how 8 ethnic groups (West Indian, Jewish, Chinese, Italian, Ukrainian, Portuguese, British, and German) scored on ethnic cultural items. This ECI index is similar to Driedger's ECI index used to measure ethnocultural identity in Winnipeg.

The average ECI ranking shows that the West Indians, Chinese, and Jews ranked the highest; the Germans and British ranked lowest; and the Italians, Ukrainians, and Portuguese ranked in between. West Indians chose a majority of their

TABLE 6.4 Ethnic Cultural Identity (ECI) in Toronto Using Six Indicators

ETHNIC CULTURAL IDENTITY (ECI) INDEX (%):

Ethnic Groups	ECI Average Scores & Rank	Use Ingroup Language	Consider Endogamy Obligatory	Majority of Friends Ingroup	Use Ingroup Media	Read Ingroup Newspapers	Use Ethnic Foods
West Indian	68.4	—	39	79	66	69	88
Chinese	65.9	83	42	54	49	69	98
Jewish	58.6	0	75	78	29	59	91
Italian	51.6	65	25	68	26	38	86
Ukrainian	44.1	50	33	48	34	39	80
Portuguese	43.5	99	24	17	36	23	63
British	39.3	—	10	70	49	25	42
German	26.5	35	1	49	5	20	50

SOURCE: Breton et al., *Ethnic Identity and Equality: Varieties of Experience in a Canadian City* (Toronto: University of Toronto Press, 1990), pp. 51–83.

friends (79 per cent) from their ingroup and used their media (66 per cent) more than any of the others. The Chinese cooked Chinese foods on holidays (98 per cent) and read Chinese newspapers (69 per cent) more than any of the others, and Jews felt obligated to marry within the group (75 per cent) more than others. The extent of Jewish identity behaviour should be noted, since a majority were second- and third-generation Canadians (Isajiw and Driedger, 1987).

The Germans and British ranked lowest, indicating the least activity in ingroup ethnic cultural behaviour. The Germans ranked last or second-last on all but one of the six indicators; except for cooking German food on holidays (50 per cent), fewer than half were engaged in any ingroup activities. Activities of British respondents were also low, except that 70 per cent indicated that a majority of their best friends were British. Italian, Ukrainian, and Portuguese respondents ranked intermediately. It should be noted that, while the Italian and Ukrainian groups included three generations, the Portuguese were all first generation. We expect that their extensive language use will drop considerably as they proceed through the second and third generations (as it does for most others).

As Driedger found in his sample, different ethnic groups score differently on the six factors. For example, use of ethnic food ranked first for all groups except the Portuguese and British for whom it ranked second. This holds true even for the Jews, Italians, Ukrainians, and Germans, who were represented by many second and third generation members. It seems to be one of the most stable indicators over time. On the other hand, groups that included only first-generation members (such as the Portuguese and Chinese) scored high on language use, which usually declines greatly in succeeding generations. This shows that it is difficult to control for all the variations, and it is most important that a number of indicators of ethnic cultural identity be used in an index so that the different groups have some opportunity to score well.

By using ethnic cultural identity (ECI), we find that West Indians, Chinese, and Jews scored high on ethnic identity, and that Germans and the British scored low. Isajiw and Driedger (1987) turned to symbolic measures of identity to see whether different items measuring another dimension of ethnic identity correlated with the index just designed, and to see how eight ethnic groups in the sample fare with respect to a second index using symbolic items.

HIGHLIGHT 6.2 ETHNIC IDENTITY AND EQUALITY IN TORONTO

The most recent comprehensive and in-depth interview survey was done in Toronto, the largest city in Canada, by four University of Toronto sociologists in the late 1980s. The survey was designed to interview individuals, in at least eight groups so they could be compared. They selected three generations so internal comparisons of identity could also be made over time.

According to conventional wisdom, the United States deals with its diverse cultures by encouraging assimilation in the melting pot, but Canadian society is a cultural mosaic in which diverse cultures are encouraged to maintain their distinctiveness. It has been argued, most notably by John Porter in *The Vertical Mosaic*, that the maintenance of ethnic cultures is a sustaining factor in the Canadian class system.

In recent years Porter's thesis has been challenged by those who maintain that ethnicity in Canada is not a significant factor in determining status. This study addresses the debate with evidence from a major interview survey of eight ethnic groups in Toronto: German, Italian, Jewish, Ukrainian, Chinese, West Indian, Portuguese, British/Irish.

The author focus on the relationship between two aspects of ethnicity: the persistence of individual ethnic cultures and the degree of equality with which ethnic groups participate in the social, economic, and political life of the wider society. They provide in-depth analysis of ethnic-identity retention, residential segregation, occupational and labour-market concentrations, and political organization.

They conclude that the relation between ethnic persistence and inter-ethnic equality is highly variable. Sometimes, and in some respects, ethnic persistence is an obstacle and a liability; sometimes, and in other respects, it is an asset and actually enhances economic and political participation. And sometimes ethnicity does not seem to matter at all.

At a time when racial tensions are rising across Canada, this study offers a new and more comprehensive understanding of the place of ethnic and racial groups and the complex forces that shape them.

SOURCE: Raymond Breton, Wsevolod Isajiw, Warren Kalbach, and Jeffrey Reitz, *Ethnic Identity and Equality* (Toronto: University of Toronto Press, 1990) Reprinted by permission.

Symbolic Interactionalist Ethnic Identification

Max Weber was one of the first to focus on the symbolic features of society. Recently, Raymond Breton (1984:124) followed Weber's lead:

I would like to argue that much of society's activities cannot be adequately understood if we over-emphasize the material dimension to the detriment of the symbolic dimension of social organization. This analysis will apply notions and propositions from Weber, analysts of symbolic behaviour, including symbolic inter-actionists. . . . Attention will be given to the processes involved in attempting to regenerate the cultural-symbolic capital of the society—to restructure the collective identity and the associated symbolic contents.

Breton (1984:127) suggests that, historically, nation-building was symbolically oriented toward the construction of a British type of society in Canada. Being Canadian was defined as speaking English within a British legal, educational, and economic institutional system. However, since the work of the Bilingual and Bicultural Commission in the 1960s, efforts have been made to change the symbolic system to include the French:

> Numerous changes in the symbols themselves were introduced: for instance a Canadian flag was adopted in 1965; Trans-Canada Airlines became Air Canada; the Dominion Bureau of Statistics became Statistics Canada; 'O Canada' was proclaimed as the national anthem; stamps were changed; money was redesigned with more Canadian symbols; and the Constitution was patriated (formerly called the British North America Act) (Breton, 1984:127).

In 1971, when Prime Minister Trudeau proclaimed Canada a multicultural society within a bilingual framework, he was symbolically including all Canadians, especially non-charter groups, when he said, 'Such a policy should help to break down discriminatory attitudes and cultural jealousies. National unity, if it is to mean anything in the deeply personal sense, must be founded on one's own individual identity. Out of this can grow respect for that of others . . . based on fair play for all' (Canada, House of Commons, *Debates*, 1971:8545).

In this section we will examine the extent to which Canadians indeed identify with various 'ethnic', 'hyphenated', or 'Canadian' symbols. So far, relatively few scholars (Berry, Kalin, and Taylor, 1977; Driedger, 1980b; Frideres and Goldenberg, 1977; Mackie, 1978; and O'Bryan, Reitz, and Kuplowska, 1976) have addressed the problems of ethnic, regional, and national identification. Among the studies that have sought to clarify and solve problems of Canadian ethnic identification, and illustrate ethnic identification variations within regions of Canada, are those made by Boyd and colleagues (1981), Berry and colleagues (1977), O'Bryan and colleagues (1976), Mackie (1978), Frideres and Goldenberg (1977), Reitz and Breton (1994), probing Canadian ethnic, regional, and national identification.

National Ethnic Identification

Berry, Kalin, and Taylor (1977) collected a national sample of 1,846 respondents. The survey provided individuals more opportunity to identify both their national and their ethnic identity. The researchers analyzed their data by regional representation and showed the preferences expressed by various ethnic groups. Their study illustrates a richly varied combination of national and/or ethnic preferences.

The sample gave Canadian adults the opportunity to place themselves in one of eight categories (father's ethnic origin, mother's ethnic origin, father's ethnic-Canadian identity, mother's ethnic-Canadian identity, or respondent's choice of English-Canadian, French-Canadian, Quebecois, or Canadian identity). The results are shown in Table 6.5.

Approximately one-fourth (23 per cent) preferred a specific ethnic category, almost one-fifth (18 per cent) preferred a hyphenated identity, and over one-half (59 per cent) preferred the 'Canadian' identification.

More detailed analysis shows that most respondents of British origin (81 per cent) preferred the 'Canadian' category, respondents of French origin (66 per cent) favoured the 'hyphenated' option, and 'other' adults (33 per cent) chose the 'ethnic' category (Berry, Kalin, and Taylor, 1977:36–8). Because ethnic groups are not proportionately represented in all regions of Canada, Berry and colleagues found that 'Canadian' was the most popular in the Atlantic provinces where the population is mainly of British origin; the 'hyphenated' version (French-Canadian) was most popular in Quebec since 80 per cent of the province's population is of French origin and whose ancestors have been in Canada for centuries; the straight 'ethnic' choice was made more often on the Prairies where no group comprises a majority, forming a multicultural pattern.

The data of Berry and associates (1977) show how important it is to get a national sample if we wish to get some sense of preferred ethnic and regional identification in Canada that con-

TABLE 6.5 A Comparison of Four Adult Studies on Ethnic and National Identification

Ethnic Categories of Identification	Berry, et al. National Sample 1974		O'Bryan, et al. 5 cities Sample 1973	Kennedy, et al. Edmonton Sample 1980		Driedger, et al. Winnipeg Sample 1980
ETHNIC	23		18	37		50
Ethnic		16				
Québécois		7				
HYPHENATED	18		46	8		10
French-Canadian		14				
English-Canadian		4				
Ethnic-Canadian					33	
Canadian-Ethnic					13	
CANADIAN	59		36	48		30
Other				7		10
	N= 1849		N= 2433	N= 398		N= 332

SOURCE: Leo Driedger, Charlene Thacker, and Raymond Currie, 'Ethnic Identification: Variations in Regional and National Preferences', *Canadian Ethnic Studies* 14 (1982):57–68.

siders regional differences. A sampling in any one region cannot be presumed to represent the whole of Canada. The Québécois preference shows how intense such ethnic identification can become. On the other hand, it also shows how respondents of British origin chose to relabel their loyalties by adopting the 'Canadian' label. As the largest and most powerful group, the British can afford to abandon the 'ethnic' symbol, hoping that others will join them under a new national symbol strongly influenced by British history, culture, and language (Pendakur and Mata, 2000). In Toronto especially there seemed to be a 1991 'census revolt' where many wanted to be just 'Canadian'.

Ethnic Identification in Cities

O'Bryan, Reitz, and Kuplowski (1976) collected a sample of 10 non-official language groups in five cities (Montreal, Toronto, Winnipeg, Edmonton, and Vancouver). The charter groups (British and French), adults in rural areas, and the Atlantic region were not represented. If the Berry (1977) national study is representative of ethnic and national preferences, then we would expect respondents in the O'Bryan (1976) sample to prefer the straight 'ethnic' symbol more than the 'Canadian' and 'hyphenated' ones that are most popular with the British and French respectively, who are not represented in this sample.

In Table 6.5 we see that, as expected, only 36 per cent chose the 'Canadian' category, and that the 'hyphenated' identification was most popular (46 per cent). This suggests that modifications are taking place as, suggested by modified assimilation and pluralism theories in Chapter 2. Respondents were given four options (ethnic, ethnic-Canadian, Canadian-ethnic, and Canadian). In the Berry sample, the Québécois and rural respondents inflated the 'ethnic' and 'ethnic Canadian' first, indicating the salience of a somewhat modified ethnicity that leans toward pluralism rather than assimilation. The high number in the hyphenated category seems to suggest that urban 'ethnics' have accommodated themselves somewhat as a result of urbanization, although 'ethnic' still precedes 'Canadian'. This clearly shows the need for modified theories of ethnic change.

Jeffrey Reitz (1980:113) based his entire book on the O'Bryan, Reitz, and Kuplowska

TABLE 6.6 Ethnic Preference of Winnipeg and Edmonton Adults, 1980

| | WINNIPEG | | | | EDMONTON | | | |
| | Respondent's Classification of: | | | | Respondent's Classification of: | | | |
Ethnic Categories	Self	Spouse	Mother	Father	Self	Spouse	Mother	Father
Ethnic	50	55	70	70	37	40	57	62
Hyphenated	10	10	8	7	8	9	8	7
Canadian	30	28	15	16	48	45	28	27
Other	10	7	7	7	7	7	7	4
	N 332	198	333	332	398	261	390	394

SOURCE: Leo Driedger, Charlene Thacker, and Raymond Currie, 'Ethnic Identification: Variations in Regional and National Preferences', *Canadian Ethnic Studies* 14 (1982):57–68.

(1976) data and found a direct correlation between ethnic identification and ingroup friends. Nearly two-thirds (64 per cent) of those who reported no ethnic ingroup friends also designated themselves as 'Canadian', while only 7 per cent of those who designated themselves as 'ethnic' reported no ingroup friends. The first group shows assimilation, and the second shows pluralism. The correlations between ethnic identification and language retention (Pearson's r of .53), ingroup interaction (.46), ethnic church affilation (.40), ethnic neighbourhood residence (.32), and endogamy (.31) were all quite significant (Reitz, 1980:116, 118). This shows that identification under such categories (ethnic, ethnic-Canadian, Canadian-ethnic, and Canadian) may well be more a measure of ethnic salience (identity or assimilation) than an objective measure of ethnic heritage. Reitz (1980:20) clearly shows that correlations of ethnic origin and ethnic identification also vary considerably by ethnic categories (Chinese, 82 per cent; South Europeans, 71 per cent; East Europeans, 39 per cent; and North Europeans, 30 per cent).

Identification in the Prairies

In 1980, Edmonton and Winnipeg area studies were coordinated by Driedger, Thacker, and Currie (1982) using the same sampling design, interview schedule, and data collection method. Respondents were given the opportunity to choose their own category of identification without pre-classification. In Table 6.6 we see that most of the respondents in Winnipeg and Edmonton answered the question 'How would you define your ethnicity?' in three categories (ethnic, Canadian, and hyphenated). Most of them also used the same categories to define the ethnicity of their spouse, mother, and father. Overall the 'ethnic' category was the most popular, with 'Canadian' a strong second. The 'hyphenated' category (e.g., Greek-Canadian) was chosen by 10 per cent or less, making it a fairly insignificant category compared to the other two. As expected, these three categories were most popular.

Comparing Winnipeg and Edmonton, we note that one-half (50 per cent) of the respondents in Winnipeg preferred the 'ethnic' category, and about one-third (30 per cent) the 'Canadian' category, while in Edmonton the preferences were reversed (49 per cent 'Canadian' and 37 per cent 'ethnic'). As expected, respondents in the slower growth centre of Winnipeg preferred 'ethnic', while more respondents of the faster-growing Edmonton preferred 'Canadian'.

Third, the respondents' classification of their spouse and parents tended to be more 'ethnic' than the respondents' self-identification in both Winnipeg and Edmonton. This suggests that respondents have the tendency to apply the 'ethnic' criterion more to others than to themselves or that their own ethnic identity is no longer as salient as that of their parents. It is clear that respondents in both Winnipeg and Edmonton classified their parents as highly 'ethnic' (70 and

60 per cent respectively). In Winnipeg, only one-seventh classified their parents as 'Canadian' and in Edmonton only one-fourth did so. Overall, the 'ethnic' category is still very popular (Driedger, Thacker, and Currie, 1982).

We conclude that regionalism must be considered an important variable, and each region deserves to be examined. As the Berry study shows, the British in the Atlantic region prefer to be known as 'Canadian', the French in Quebec prefer hyphenated or ethnolocal (Québécois) categories, and straight 'ethnic' labels are popular in the multicultural West. We cannot assume that preferences in any one region will be uniform. Increasing preferences for 'Canadian' identification in Edmonton and Calgary as compared to Winnipeg suggest that rapid change does wean some people from 'ethnic' identification into assimilation or Anglo-conformity.

The use of adult samples collected randomly is of crucial importance if we wish to get some sense of proportion and the importance of ethnic, regional, and national identification. The national data collected by Berry and associates is clearly preferable.

Free ethnic classification of oneself (as used by Driedger, Thacker, and Currie, 1982) seems to be a more subjective approach and it is difficult to know which criteria guide the respondent's choice. Moreover, free ethnic classification seems to be a measure of identity and assimilation, showing whether the original ethnic milieu or the Canadian context is the more influential cultural pole.

This seems to suggest that the most objective data we can collect is 'ethnic origin' as the census has done for over a century. Other studies suggest the value of additional smaller studies designed to measure the degree to which ethnicity is still salient. If we should abandon the 'ethnic origin' questions, then we would be left only with more subjective data that is less longitudinal, and less consistently and systematically collected.

We recommend that in the future both objective and subjective dimensions of ethnic research are needed. The objective ethnic origin data are useful as a measure of the cultural and social milieu in which respondents were raised; the subjective choice may be more valuable as an assessment of the individual's self-identity and as a measure of assimilation.

SUMMARY

Ethnic identification may be defined as a positive personal attitude and attachment to a group with whom the individual believes he/she has a common ancestry based on shared characteristics and shared sociocultural experiences. Such identification can take place at various levels, ranging from persons to groups and categories such as ethnicity. Similarly there may be identification with a territory, ethnic institutions, culture, historical symbols, ideology, or leaders.

The sociocultural theory of identity deals with a macro ontology and sociological methodology using survey field study, survey research, and sociohistorical analysis focusing on social and cultural items of ethnicity. The interactionist orientation is more micro-sociological, dealing with symbols and their importance for social relationships. A review of the literature shows that more work has been done on sociocultural macro orientation, out of which a multiplicity of factors has developed, demonstrating that sociocultural ethnic identity is multidimensional and complex.

Anderson's ethnoreligious probing of identity of nine groups in rural Saskatchewan showed that some identity factors are more important than others, and that the various ethnic groups also vary in the importance they attach to each of these identity factors. Driedger's study of sociocultural factors in Winnipeg found that of the seven ethnic groups compared, the French and Jews indicated high identity and the Scandinavians low identity, but that all groups scored differently on the six factors used. O'Bryan and associates, comparing the 10 non-charter groups in five Canadian cities, found them similarly diverse of identification; they also found that there was a decline in the use of language by the third generation, but little decline in ethnic food-eating habits. Isajiw's findings on ethnic identity in Toronto using six factors and 8 groups found similar diversity in the importance of the various identity factors and the weight the ethnic groups gave to each.

Studies on symbolic ethnic identification revealed that here, too, there were ethnic group, regional, and other factors that resulted in varied forms of symbolic identification. Berry and colleagues, in their national sample, found that the 'Canadian' designation was most popular, followed by 'ethnic' and 'hyphenated' identification, followed by 'Canadian' and 'ethnic' symbols. Driedger and colleagues found that the 'ethnic' designation was most popular in Winnipeg, but in Edmonton, also a prairie city, scholars found that the 'Canadian' designation was more popular. These findings show that symbolic identification varies by ethnic group, region, city, and generation.

Generally, for some ethnic groups in Canada both ethnocultural and symbolic ethnic identity are clearly present. The diversity of the population makes for a variety of expressions of identity, so that we also found other ethnic groups who no longer expressed high ethnic identity; presumably they had amalgamated or assimilated. Some groups contribute to a multicultural plural society, while others follow the assimilation or modified assimilation models discussed in Chapter 2. Anglo-conformity is also evident for some.

Ethnic identity is always in the process of change, and the modified forms of pluralism and assimilation as discussed in Chapter 2 make for a variety of changes among groups. Sorting and controlling for these many factors makes for interesting but very complex research challenges. The theories and methodologies required to document these changes are too often inadequate.

We are focusing on voluntary ethnic identity, illustrated best in Cell E of our Conformity-Pluralist conceptual model, presented in Chapter 2. In Chapter 5 we found that early French settlers managed to retain their French heritage for four hundred years by continuing a fairly homogeneous large population of more than six million, in one province where they are spatially, politically, religiously (Catholic), institutionally, and increasingly economically dominant. In this chapter we turned to other ethnic groups to explore to what extent they identified with territory, institutions, culture, historical, ideological, and leadership symbols. We found that in rural areas Hutterites, Mennonites, many Catholics and others were able to retain extensive language and cultural identities, especially in the first and second generations. We also found that in urban areas like Winnipeg, Toronto, and Vancouver many ethnic and religious groups were continuing distinct ethnic identities, but some cultural heritage was in decline, in later generations.

CRITICAL THINKING QUESTIONS

1. Distinguish between the macro sociocultural and the micro interactionist theories of ethnic identity.

2. Discuss Driedger's six ethnic identification factors. Identify each and compare.

3. What indicators of rural ethnoreligious identity did Anderson use? How did these differentiate high and low identification?

4. Which indicators of sociocultural identification did Driedger use in Winnipeg? Show how seven ethnic groups scored.

5. What were the ethnic identity findings of Breton and associates in Toronto? How did ethnic groups score there?

6. What do we mean by symbolic interactionist ethnic identification? Discuss how symbolic identity was studied. Discuss.

SUGGESTED READINGS

Breton, Raymond, W.W. Isajiw, Warren E. Kalbach, and Jeffrey G. Reitz, *Ethnic Identity and Equality: Varieties of Experience in a Canadian City* (Toronto: University of Toronto Press, 1990). This survey of eight ethnic groups in Toronto explores the persistence of ethnic identity, and the degree of equal participation there is in the social, economic, and political life.

Isajiw, Wsevolod W. (ed.), *Multiculturalism in North America and Europe: Comparative Perspectives on Interethnic Relations and Social Incorporation* (Toronto: Canadian Scholars Press, 1997). Twenty-five scholars from two continents contribute to a discussion of multiculturalism and identity.

Kallen, Evelyn, *Spanning the Generations: A Study of Jewish Identity* (Toronto: Longman, 1977). Jews have maintained their identities for thousands of years; how have they managed this in the city?

CHAPTER 7

Construction of a Sacred Reality

Chapter 6 outlined Arnold Dashefsky's (1975a) fourfold theoretical classification of ethnic identity, and discussed the two sociocultural and interactionist, macro and micro, forms of sociological ethnic identity.

This chapter will focus on Dashefsky's micro interactionist cell of ethnic identity by considering smaller, less influential ethnic groups such as the aboriginals, the Hutterites, and the Jews. While sociocultural characteristics will again be considered, this time we want to look increasingly at symbolic interactionist characteristics, with a focus on the concept of 'The Sacred' (Bibby, 1993, 1995, 2002). Although religion will be one aspect of 'The Sacred', we need to look at this phenomenon much more broadly to include sociocultural elements as the aboriginals, Hutterites, and Jews all do. We will propose that these three religio-ethnic groups represent three types of development along a traditional-urban continuum into which most other ethnic groups in Canada can be fitted. It is the identity of groups such as these that has led Canadians to consider multiculturalism as an option.

IN SEARCH OF
SACRED SOCIALIZATION

Durkheim was interested in social cohesion and the forms of solidarity that humans developed to stave off anomie and alienation. In his early writings, Durkheim focused on the sacred and profane elements of society and concluded that features such as contract, beliefs, and ritual were important elements of a sense of 'The Sacred'. To study this subtle and profound phenomenon, he changed his methodology from using empirical data collection as he had in *Suicide*, to using the more qualitative methods of inquiry often used by anthropologists: studying whole communities to better gather the quality of relationships found in more primitive religions. He used the latter approach in *Elementary Forms of Religious Life*.

Durkheim went back to a study of pre-modern societies because he wanted to see what the sense of wholeness of life entailed; he concluded that human contact with forces sometimes labelled *mana*, *orenda*, or a totemic principle was always present (Durkheim, 1912 [1945].363). Thus, he concluded that a focus of beliefs on a Sacred force or forces that guides humans is central. Humans then are faced with linking to these forces of belief and developing rituals that direct human action in line with these beliefs. Durkheim concluded that this focus on the Sacred was socially created, thus emphasizing the importance of ritual to reinforce these beliefs in the Sacred. He found that in the pre-industrial societies he studied, all of life became a part of religious ritual and the whole community was seen as a sacred endeavour or enterprise. This, he concluded, brought wholeness and a sense of the sacredness of everything that was done as 'a people'. He thought that this sensibility was partly or largely lost in the process of industrialization, his major concern for modern France. This integration of the all into the Sacred is the means to fight anomie, or normlessness, which often leads to the hopelessness and suicide prevalent in modern industrial society, unless there is a sense of belonging.

Bronislaw Malinowski (1945) was also concerned with similar questions of cohesion and ritual; he found that the most elaborate rituals among the Trobriand Islanders occurred when they prepared for dangerous deep-sea fishing. Religious practitioners engaged in prolonged and elaborate regularized rituals to protect fishermen who were going offshore, but not those who engaged in safer fishing on the shores. He too concluded that the Sacred was an important part in a sense of community and human well-being.

Many anthropologists conclude from their studies that: (1) religion or magic is a vital mechanism in unifying life-giving symbols and integrating humans socially; (2) creeds, beliefs, ritual, and ceremony are enduring elements of community solidarity; and (3) religion is an integral part of social integration as well as a seedbed for social change (Nisbet, 1974:165).

Recent modern sociologists have suggested that becoming Sacred is very much a process which they have called sacralization of identity (Mol, 1976:1). Andrew Greeley (1989:11) said the 'sacralizing tendency' involves a process in which 'the symbols even of a secular faith are so set apart from the profane, and eventually so cloaked with ritual and tradition, that they become in fact 'functionally sacred'. It is in this sense that we will consider the Sacred as more than religion, but as the whole process of setting apart and preserving as special some aspects of life (such as ethnicity or heritage) which are considered very important and which should endure. In line with this trend of thinking, Hans Mol (1976:5, 15) defines sacralization as:

the process by means of which man has preeminently safeguarded and reinforced this complex of orderly interpretations of reality, rules and legitimations. . . . It is a sort of brake applied to unchecked infinite adaptations in symbolic systems . . . for the emotional security of personality and the integration of tribe or community. . . . It safeguards identity, a system of meaning, or a definition of reality; and it modifies, obstructs, or legitimates change.

Thus, it is a process rather than a state.

Max Weber's (1978) concept of charisma has many sacred elements such as being set apart or qualities that seem to be supernatural or not accessible to the ordinary person (Hamm, 1987:14–18). Weber's symbolic emphases have been taken farther by Peter Berger, who suggests that rather than looking at the structural functional outward dimensions of religion, we need to also look within from the standpoint of Weber's *Verstehen* or deep understanding (Berger, 1967). Thus, we need to look at Berger's 'sacred canopy' and the whole idea of nomos-building that has to do with symbolic forms of the Sacred and human experience as part of ethnic identification.

Nomos-Building of Sacred Canopies

Peter Berger (1967:19) writes about the socially constructed world as 'an ordering of experience, into a meaningful order, or *nomos*, which is imposed upon the discrete experiences and meanings of individuals. . . . To participate in the society is to share its "knowledge", that is, co-inhabit its nomos'. He continues:

The socially established nomos may thus be understood, perhaps in its most important aspect, as a shield against terror. Put differently, the most important function of society is nominization. The anthropological presupposition for this is a human craving for meaning that appears to have the force of instinct. Men are congenitally compelled to impose meaningful order upon reality. This order, however, presupposes the social enterprise of ordering world construction. To be separated from society exposes the individual to a multiplicity of dangers which he is unable to cope with himself. . . . The ultimate danger of the individual separation from society is meaninglessness (Berger, 1967:22).

Thus, anomie is normlessness or life without a meaningful construct of reality (Durkheim, 1965; Berger, 1967). Why are we here?

A key element of the Sacred is the 'sharing of society's knowledge and the co-habitation of its nomos'. This suggests the need of humans to belong to a fairly stable community or network where indepth sharing and participating can take place. 'Co-habitation' implies the considerable commitment to a group of people that usually takes place in families, but Berger thinks this must be extended to a larger community, because the nuclear family is no longer a sufficiently large network; like clans used to be. Co-habitation also suggests that considerable quality time be spent within the context of a cohesive *Gemeinschaft*, a meaningful support that satisfies real social needs (Driedger, 1980b:342). 'Sharing of knowledge' implies identification with some ideals and being able to contribute to a sense of richness of belonging that uplifts and challenges. Industrialization usually has a way of detracting from this sense of wholeness and meaning, substituting the drive for materialism. Things seem not to satisfy like social ties do. It is at this point, Berger says, that religion enters significantly into the argument.

Religion is the human enterprise by which a sacred cosmos is established. Put differently, religion is cosmization in a sacred mode. By sacred is meant here a quality of mysterious and awesome power, other than man and yet related to him, which is believed to reside in certain objects of experience (Berger, 1967:25).

The sacred cosmos is confronted by humans as an immensely powerful reality other than

humanity. Some postmoderns are willing to call this 'spiritual' reality.

To bridge the macro and micro realities, we propose to use the concept of a sacred canopy, also introduced by Peter Berger (1967). While Berger speaks of the socially constructed world as an ordering of experience into a meaningful order, or nomos that acts as a shield against terror, he also speaks of a 'sacred canopy'—a tent-like roof used by the Jews as a symbol of protection. It was a large blanket with long stakes attached to each of the four corners to hold it up. This symbolism is useful for our discussion because the blanket can be seen as a roof that protects those who are inside from the onslaughts outside. The stakes are also important because without stakes there would be nothing to hold up the roof. One or two stakes are hardly adequate: four or more provide a better cover. Furthermore, stakes in the canopy can be replaced or substituted by new ones, or better ones, and the various components of the canopy are adjustable. And finally, the canopy is mobile. It can be folded, transported, and pitched again in new places. Nomos-building can be seen as pitching a sacred tent that shields the individual or group from terror or meaninglessness. It houses a 'reality'—a meaningful order or nomos.

Four stakes that hold up the canopy will be considered: (1) an ideology or religion, (2) a community, (3) an ethnic culture, and (4) land or territory in which the group resides (Driedger, 1996). All four components are in a symbiotic relationship. That is, the land will act as a crucible in which the community and culture are formed, and the religious ideology is moulded by these outer circumstances and is a driving force that in turn shapes the community and culture. The task will be to delineate the state of the sacred reality in its original time and place, and to examine how the ideology, community, culture, and territory were either reconstructed, transferred, or transformed as the sacred canopy.

Since there are many ethnoreligious groups in Canada, we need to select several so that we can examine changes in their sacred canopies. Aboriginals (especially the Blackfoot), the

Hutterites, and the Jews have been chosen for specific reasons. As food-gathering people, the Prairie Indians were faced with a complete reconstruction of their sacred canopy when they were forced from the open plains onto reserves. The Hutterites, as food-producing agriculturists, literally transferred their communal society from Europe to the North American Prairies with its ideology and structure intact. The Jews represent yet another form of change because they transformed their east European *shtetl* ghettos into segregated urban communities. We plan to discuss the changes in these three sacred canopies as three different types into which the many other religious and ethnic groups can be fitted. We propose that some canopies provided a better shelter from terror and meaninglessness than others. First, we will examine the original structures of these sacred canopy types, the changes and adaptations made to them, and the social processes involved in these changes.

CONSTRUCTION OF SACRED CANOPIES

Berger's (1967) concept of constructing a nomos to create meaning is directly applicable to the Canadian ethnic scene. Numerous historical events could illustrate the formation of sacred canopies, but we will briefly sketch early aboriginal food-gathering, the coming of the agrarian European immigrants typified by the Hutterites, and the more recent migration to the cities represented best by the Jews, but also the Chinese. Each of these three types was threatened by anomie; however, reconstruction, transferral, and transformation of their social and sacred realities occurred with new identification in various changing situations.

Reconstruction of the Canopy: Aboriginal Food-Gatherers

'An area as large as Europe, bounded on the north by the "Barren lands", on the west by the snow-capped Rockies, and on the south by the arid plains, was transferred by Charles II's sweeping gesture in the overlordship of the Hudson's Bay Company' (Stanley, 1960:3). This happened in 1670, when scattered throughout the area were thousands of aboriginals, who made up three great linguistic groups: the Algonkin, the Athapascan, and the Siouian. Several expeditions were dispatched inland to draw the remote tribes to the trading posts of the Hudson's Bay Company. As early as 1690, Henry Kelsey was sent to visit some of the tribes in the interior, and it appears he reached what is now Saskatchewan. While the English were penetrating Rupert's Land from Hudson Bay, the French also pressed westward. La Verendrye and his sons opened the door to the Northwest during 1732 to 1743, when they discovered the Red River, built Fort Rouge on the site of what is now Winnipeg, and pressed onwards to the Saskatchewan River.

The Indians that the Whites described between 1830 and 1880 had the most highly developed hunting culture in the world. It was a materially rich situation for hunters. A Native population of only 150,000 people was harvesting the herds of millions of buffalo. They were extremely diverse in languages, speaking some 25 languages related to each other in six families, and four phyls. Still, it was a generally uniform culture, as though a few patterns for the region had developed over thousands of years (Price, 1979:165).

Price (1979:167) suggests that the Blackfoot stayed in place in Alberta on the northern plains for approximately 10,000 years, so we will use ethnographic sources by Price, Ponting (1986), Dickason, (1992), Frideres (1996, 1998) and McMillan (1995) as background.

Perhaps the most important stake in the sacred canopy of the aboriginals were the plains, a *land* area which was sometimes referred to by the Europeans as 'The Great American Desert', a myth that persisted because Europeans who populated the Canadian east were used to woodlands territory. In 1700 there were an estimated sixty million buffalo on the plains; they were the major source of food for the plains Indians (Price, 1979). By 1885, because of the earlier introduction of the horse and the excessive hunting that followed, the buffalo had become virtually extinct. The economic base of the prairie Indians was destroyed, causing severe starvation. The eleven treaties made with the prairie Indians beginning in 1871 herded them onto segregated Indian reserves and restricted their lifestyle. They were to become relatively immobile, like the agriculturists, without the will or the skills to eke out a new life. A major stake in the sacred canopy had been severed (Asch, 1984; Cardinal, 1977; Ponting, 1986, 1997).

When the economic base of the plains Indians in the West had been demolished with the demise of the buffalo, the Great Plains lay open for a final onslaught by European agricultural immigrants. A series of treaties numbered 1 to 11 was signed, beginning with Treaty One at Fort Garry, near Winnipeg. In Figure 7.1 we see that a few treaties had been made in southern Ontario or Upper Canada and the West Coast, but none were made in the five most easterly provinces and most of British Columbia (McMillan, 1995; Ponting, 1986). The signing of the 11 treaties began in 1871, a year after Manitoba became a part of the Canadian Confederation. Manitoba became the European foothold in the West once the Selkirk settlement was established. The treaties fanned out in horseshoe fashion westward and then in a northerly and easterly direction as the European immigrants continued to invade the territory. By 1921 these treaties had reached up the Mackenzie Valley into the Yukon and the western Northwest Territories with the signing of Treaty Eleven. The land stake in the sacred canopy of the aboriginals was greatly eroded by herding the aboriginals onto Indian reserves in much of this new treaty territory. Much of Nunavut, eastern Canada, and the west coast still remain untreated (Frideres, 1998; McMillan, 1995).

Price (1979:164) says the *culture* of the prairie and plains Indians had many features in common: 'All the societies had the hide tipi; bows and arrows; leather containers, breech-clothes, leggings, shirts and moccasins, and buffalo robes. Things were light and portable, adapted to a nomadic hunting way of life.' At first they hunted on foot, but later the horse was introduced and greatly increased their effectiveness in buffalo hunting. The Blackfoot farther to the west generally did not make canoes or eat fish, traits that were common almost everywhere else in the Plains. The men were the hunters and warriors and did heavy butchering of meat. They made weapons, shields, drums, pipes, and often their own leggings and coats (McMillan, 1995). This exciting nomadic life and culture was destroyed when the buffalo disappeared and when the Indians were forced onto reserves. Most of the activities centred on the buffalo; and these buffalo-centred activities disappeared in a very short time, so that cultural substitutes were not developed.

> In 1700 there were an estimated 60 million buffalo in North America. When the whites arrived in numbers in 1850 the buffalo had already been reduced to about 20 million animals. By 1885 the buffalo was close to extinction (Price, 1979:165).

Price suggests that the extinction of the buffalo was because of two factors. One of these factors was the introduction of the horse by the Spaniards in the South, which enabled the Indians on horseback to exploit and overkill the buffalo. Previously their hunting was confined largely to buffalo pounds, into which the animals were herded, forced over cliffs, and then butchered. The second factor was the coming of Europeans who slaughtered buffalo for their hides and for pemmican to trade, so that by 1885 the herds were almost extinct. This had radical implications for all plains Indians because their sacred canopy and culture were built around the buffalo. Their whole way of life involved this major means of economic survival. A second major stake in the sacred canopy vanished.

Many horse-related traits died out soon after the extermination of the buffalo. The camps were now permanent, so horses were less use-

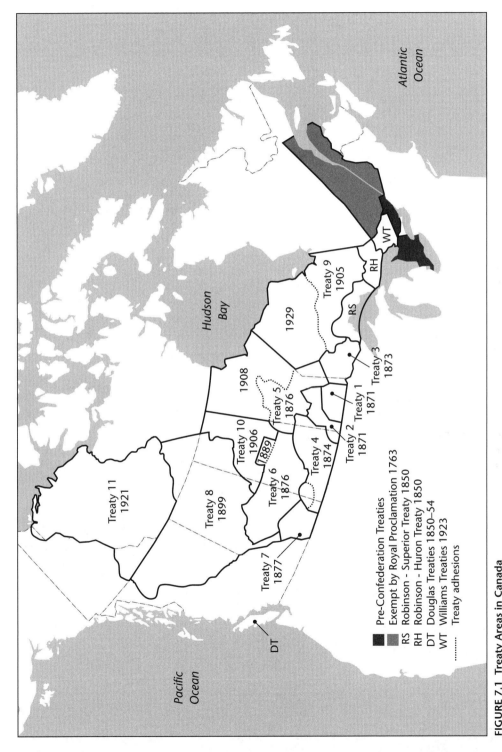

FIGURE 7.1 Treaty Areas in Canada

SOURCE: Alan D. McMillan, *Native Peoples and Cultures of Canada*, 2nd edn, (Vancouver: Douglas & McIntyre, 1995), p. 317.

ful. The Blackfoot were faced with building a new *community* centred on ranching or farming. Price (1979:185) says that many Blackfoot are successful entrepreneurs in ranching, petroleum, mining, and a few in manufacturing. On some reserves, however, especially among the plains Cree and Cheyenne there is a great deal of inertia and despair (McMillan, 1995). While the Indians are still together on reserves as they were in their hunting camps, the buffalo culture is gone, leaving a sense of purposelessness. The foci for nomos-building seem to be gone.

Many Indian chiefs, such as Big Bear in Saskatchewan, did not want to give up their hunting freedoms and resisted confinement on reserves. Although in the United States there were extensive wars between the national government forces and the Indians, this was not usually the case in Canada. However, during the Louis Riel conflict in 1870 in Manitoba and 1885 in Saskatchewan, there was considerable resistance from both the Metis and the Indians (Flanagan, 1991). With the destruction of the buffalo by 1885, the Metis—who were middlemen in the buffalo hunt and trade—were faced with a complete change of lifestyle and culture. The food-gathering Indians, however, were faced with a much greater cultural change: a change to either an agricultural way of life, or to attempts at food-gathering where their territory was almost gone. Reserves were too small for effective hunting and fishing, and much of the land was not very good for farming. The community stake was completely disrupted and had to be reorganized spatially, economically, politically, religiously, and symbolically. Such a drastic community change in so short a time was almost impossible.

Religion, the fourth stake in the sacred canopy, is in many ways a symbolic expression of the total way of life of a people. For food-gathering people especially, religion is fully integrated into the cultural, economic, organizational, and spatial way of life. When the land, culture, and community base had been stripped, the integrating religious expression had no foundation. The Prairie Indians were faced with a vacuum, which in Durkheim's terms was tailored for anomie. Thus, their religious expression no longer symbolized the reality around them.

Many of the religious traits were institutionalized in medicine bundles. These might include feathers, beaks, claws, teeth, or stones that acted as the focus of religious ritual. Rituals and dances were performed and individuals developed relationships with supernatural powers and spirits. After the Blackfoot signed a treaty with the Whites in 1877,

> the White Indian agent and the Anglican missionaries forced the Blackfoot to stop the Sun Dance. They pressured them to substitute tree platform burial with underground burial, though the people were afraid that the spirits would be eternally trapped below the ground. Plural marriages were dissolved and the extra wives sent away. Sacred bundles and regalia or traditional societies were destroyed (Price, 1979:183).

The religious ideological drive for nomos-building was also stripped from them, while the surrounding cultural, community, and territorial context had been destroyed.

Essentially the four stakes (land, culture, community, and ideology) that held up the sacred aboriginal canopy to protect them from normlessness and terror had been destroyed. They were left with a complete reconstruction of a new canopy amidst the ashes of their old sacred reality. As a food-gathering people, many prairie Indians were soon faced with the oncoming agricultural European immigrants who had made the transfer from food-gathering to producing over thousands of years (Dickason, 1992). As if the transition from food-gathering to food producing was not enough, in less than a hundred years many prairie Indians were also faced with entering the industrial urban society as well (Frideres, 1998). By 1991, 44,000 had moved into Winnipeg, 33,000 into Edmonton, and 22,000 into Calgary (1991 census). Very few societies manage to reconstruct canopies that quickly or have the ability to sacralize them into a meaningful nomos.

Transferral of the Canopy: Hutterite Agriculturalists

In contrast to the Native Indians' shattered canopy, the Hutterites transferred their sacred canopy intact from Europe to the North American prairies in Alberta, Saskatchewan, Manitoba, Montana, and North and South Dakota (Driedger, 1996). They were experienced agriculturalists familiar with farming the *land*; they perpetuated a distinctive Germanic *culture* and customs; they were a *communal* society living in colonies; all of this was firmly anchored in a *religious* ideology formed during the Reformation in the sixteenth century. The Hutterites represent one of the most stable types of canopies, anchored firmly in an ideology, community, culture, and land base.

The Hutterite canopy emerged in Moravia in 1528, and shortly thereafter Jacob Hutter, after whom they are named, joined the community (Gross, 1980; Hostetler, 1974). They began as a distinctive *religious* group when a group of refugees pooled their possessions and introduced the practice of the 'community of goods'. Since their community of goods was a unique interpretation that most other Christians did not share, and since they also believed in non-resistance and adult baptism, they became the target for persecution, especially in a Europe that was not tolerant of pluralism (Gross, 1980:26–31). Jacob Hutter, by then their leader, was burned at the stake in 1536, as were many others. Their frequent migrations to escape persecution finally brought them to North America in 1874 (Driedger, 1997; Friesen, 1993; Hofer, 1988; Hostetler, 1974).

Hutterite *communities* are perpetuated in colonies of one hundred or more members, a second stake in the canopy firmly tied to their religious beliefs. Whereas in the past they were engaged in trades in addition to agriculture, they now are mainly agriculturalists (Driedger, 1996; Ryan, 1977). The preacher is the primary leader of the colony, with the farm boss second in authority. The social structure has been developed over many years and has been sanctioned by reli-

gion and tradition. Although some colonies are more economically and politically stable than others, on the whole they compete very well in society and have become an economic threat to neighbours on occasion. While much of their community structure does not change rapidly, they adopt the most modern farming methods, which—together with their simple lifestyle and cooperative work—makes them very competitive economically (Peter, 1987). The community stake is both sacred and functional in Hutterite society, and boundaries are securely maintained (Driedger, 1982a:207–17).

'The Hutterite world view leads to the creation of an earthly environment that is ordered spatially, temporally, socially and symbolically; within this created environment the individual matures and ages' (Hostetler, 1974:155). The Hutterites' colony is the centre of their universe and they sometimes compare the colony to the ark of Noah in the biblical account of the flood, claiming that those within the ark or colony will be rescued from the technological secular flood (Friesen, 1993; Hostetler, 1974:155). Because they spend much time socializing their children to internalize their orderly community, very few of them leave. The whole community is tightly ordered with the preacher at the head, followed by the farm boss, and the subheads of the various chicken, hog, grain, household, and gardening subdivisions. The men work and eat together, the women eat and work separately, and the children eat, study, and play under the supervision of the teacher. Although some colonies now have a separate church building, many still meet in the schoolhouse for worship because the whole colony is their sanctuary, an integral part of their religious life.

While religion and community were the major components of the Hutterite canopy in the beginning, Germanic *culture* was slowly sacralized. In the sixteenth century, their German culture was part of the larger society. Over time, however, traditional forms of female attire such as long dresses, polka-dot kerchiefs, shawls, and parting of the hair in the middle and braiding became sacralized so that now they are required. The men do not wear ties; they wear distinctive hats, suspenders, and hairstyles (including beards) as an essential part of the sacred canopy. A distinctive traditional culture has emerged as a third stake in the sacred canopy (Driedger, 1997; Stephenson, 1991).

The Hutterites speak a German dialect that they adopted in central Europe and transported and used in many parts of Europe before it was transplanted to North America. This dialect also is considered a part of a sacred form of familiar communication and distinguishes them from 'the English' who reside outside in the secular world. These concepts unique to their culture are laden with religious meaning. They live in a *Bruderhof*, or a brotherly yard; they see themselves as a *Gemein*, or a community of believers; they refer to their subdivisions as *Leut*, or people, a practice common among others like the Inuit; their written rules are *Ordnungen*, or rules to be followed, all of which symbolize the sacred canopy in which God's people are sheltered (Hofer, 1988).

Interestingly, their community is so tightly knit that they can afford to adopt the most modern machinery to compete exceedingly well with farmers around them. They can pool and develop their capital, buy in bulk, make the most efficient use of machinery and labour, and, as a larger working unit, act as their own insurance body. They can diversify into all branches of mixed farming on a large scale, which acts as another flexible means of survival in the competitive market.

Agricultural *land* was not an essential part of the Hutterite sacred canopy in the beginning. In addition to agriculture, their early activities included ceramics, cutlery, milling, winemaking, spinning, weaving, tailoring, clock-making, and carriage-making. Hutterite nurses, midwives, and physicians were in great demand (Hostetler and Huntington, 1967:2). By the time they came to the North American Prairies, however, farming agricultural land and raising livestock had become a sacred part of their nomos-building. The norm is to work on the land. Other economic activities are frowned upon and are usually forbidden (Friesen, 1993; Hofer, 1988).

To illustrate the extent of the transferral of the Hutterites from Europe to North America, we see in Figure 7.2 that all of the Hutterites that exist today now reside on the North American Prairies in three provinces of Canada (Alberta, Saskatchewan, and Manitoba) and five states of the United States (Washington, Montana, North and South Dakota, and Minnesota) (Driedger, 1997). None of them exist in Europe any longer. In 1993 there were 262 colonies in Canada and 106 colonies in the United States; of these over half were in Alberta (130) and Manitoba (85) (Driedger, 1997).

In Table 7.1 we see that the Hutterites are divided into three major *Leut* (people): the *Schmiedeleut* (15,855), the *Dariusleut* (10,922), and the *Lehrerleut* (8,544), with a total population of 35,321. The Hutterites of the world are located in a total of 368 prairie colonies, with an average of 96 people in each colony. The Hutterites began in 1528, grew very quickly to about 20,000 just before 1600, then declined; however, today there are more than there ever have been. Since 1874, when they arrived on the Prairies, their numbers have grown due to high birthrates and favourable means of agricultural expansion (Peter, 1987).

In contrast to the aboriginal experience of nomos-building on the Prairies, the Hutterites have built a very stable sacred canopy, firmly staked by religious, communal, cultural, and territorial norms. Tested over time in Europe and transferred intact to the Canadian prairies as a rural ideal type, it appears to be quite functional and protective. The Hutterites illustrate that small groups can survive if they have a clear, ideological symbolic focus to which they are committed, and if they develop tightly knit structures that open and close selectively (Driedger, 1995). They illustrate a micro version of Dashefsky's sociocultural identity and demonstrate the importance of symbolic relations, a major emphasis of Max Weber. They are definitely a tile in the pluralist mosaic.

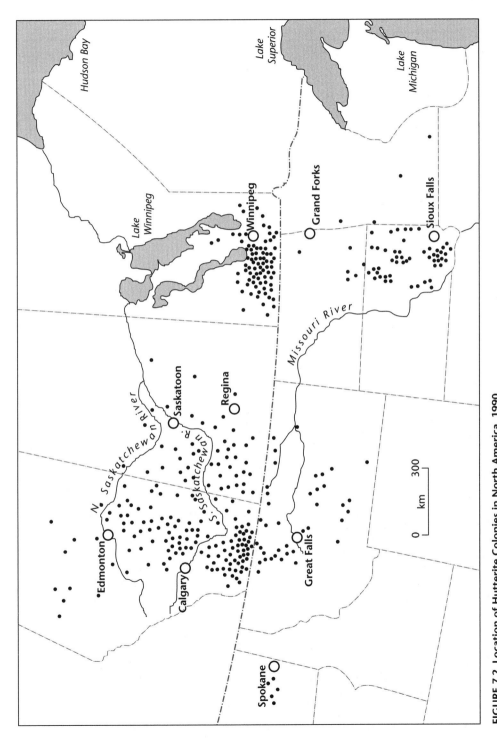

FIGURE 7.2 Location of Hutterite Colonies in North America, 1990
SOURCES: Taken from maps prepared by Lawrence C. Anderson, 1991, and Enco Supply, *Hutterite Colonies of Manitoba* (1993); Leo Driedger, 'The Hutterites', in P.R. Magocsi (ed). *The People of Canada: An Encyclopedia for the Country* (Toronto: University of Toronto Press, 1997).

TABLE 7.1 Hutterite Population in North America by *Leut* Affiliation and Location, 1988

Category	Schmiedeleut	Dariusleut	Lehrerleut	Total
Population	15,855	10,922	8,544	35,321
Number of colonies	146	126	96	368
Mean colony size	105	86	89	93
Location and number of colonies in US				
South Dakota[a]	51	0	0	51
Montana[a]	0	13	27	40
North Dakota[a]	6	0	0	6
Washington	0	5	0	5
Minnesota[a]	4	0	0	4
Total in US	61	18	27	106
Location and number of colonies in Canada				
Alberta[b]	0	84	46	130
Manitoba[c]	85	0	0	85
Saskatchewan	0	23	23	46
British Columbia	0	1	0	1
Total in Canada	85	108	69	262

SOURCES: John Hofer, David Wiebe, and Gerhard Ens, *The History of the Hutterites*, rev. edn. (Altona, MB: D.W. Friesen, 1988), p. 68, plus checks of maps:

[a] Lawrence C. Anderson, 1991
[b] *Hutterite Colonies in Alberta*, June, 1988; and
[c] Enco Supply, *Hutterite Colonies of Manitoba*, 1993

Leo Driedger, 'The Hutterites', in P.R. Magocsi (ed.), *The Peoples of Canada: An Encyclopedia for the Country* (Toronto: University of Toronto Press, 1997).

HIGHLIGHT 7.1 HUTTERITES: RURAL COMMUNAL COLONY

Hutterites are one of 3 major Anabaptist groups (the others are the Mennonites and the Amish) surviving today and the only group to insist rigorously on the communal form of existence. Hutterite history dates to 1528 when to escape religious persecution a group of about 200 Anabaptists established a communal society in Moravia (now a region in the Czech Republic). Under the initial leadership of Jacob Hutter, they established the basic tenets of Hutterian beliefs, which they have followed with little deviation to this day.

These beliefs, based on early Christian teachings and a belief in a strict separation of church and state, include a form of communal living, communal ownership of property, nonviolence and opposition to war, and adult baptism. Also, they have retained the dress, the customs, the language and the simple austere lifestyle of their ancestors.

Migration and Settlement

Because of their beliefs, Hutterites were subjected to periodic persecution, which invariably resulted in migration. They moved from Czechoslovakia to Hungary, Romania, Tsarist Russia, the US, and finally to Canada. They immigrated en masse to Canada in 1918 because of harassment and persecution in the US that resulted from their refusal to participate in any type of military service. Initially, they settled in Manitoba and Alberta; later settlements were established in Saskatchewan and some were re-established in the US. In 1995 the total Hutterite population was about 30,000—more than 66 per cent of whom live in Manitoba, Saskatchewan and Alberta, while the remainder are in the US.

Social and Cultural Life

Hutterites believe that their society can be best preserved in a rural setting, and hence agriculture has become a basic way of life. Their belief in communal living has led them to establish village-type settlements on each of their farms (or colonies, as they are known). In Manitoba the average size of a colony is about 1800 ha, but in Saskatchewan and Alberta, because of drier conditions, the colonies are each about 3600 ha. Despite these relatively large landholdings, each Hutterite family has less than 50 per cent of the land of a typical single-family farm on the prairies. The average colony has about 13 families with a total population of about 90. When the population reaches 125 to 150, the settlements subdivide and form new colonies, on the average every 16 years. In 1995 there were 93 colonies in Manitoba, 54 in Saskatchewan and 138 in Alberta.

The Hutterite respect for the nuclear family is reflected in their provision of private apartments for each family in the row houses they traditionally build. Kindergarten facilities are provided for children from the age of 2 years. The regular curriculum is studied in colony schools by all students, with many now proceeding to the end of grade 12. In recent times computers have become a regular classroom feature in many colonies. A few Hutterites may proceed to take special diploma courses off the colonies such as animal nutrition or veterinary science, and some take teacher training. There are now a number of fully qualified Hutterite teachers.

The structure of Hutterite colonies remains unchanged, although the nature of the particular economic activity in which they are involved may vary. Each colony elects an executive council from the managers of various enterprises, and together with the colony minister the executive deals with important matters that will be brought before the assembly (all baptized male members—in effect, men 20 years of age and older). Although women have an official subordinate status, their informal influence on colony life is significant. They hold managerial positions in the kitchen, kindergarten, the purchase of dry goods, and vegetable production.

Economic Structure

Although there is cooperation among the colonies, each colony operates as an independent economic unit. The Hutterites practise highly mechanized and efficient mixed-farming economy. Because of their well-managed, large-scale operations, when compared to the amount of land they own, the Hutterites produce more than their proportionate share of agricultural produce within the prairie economy. For instance in Manitoba in 1991, Hutterites owned 144,920 hectares, or 1.9 per cent of Manitoba farmland, but they accounted for 9.5 per cent of Manitoba farm population. Hence, on a per capita basis they owned only 20% of their proportionate share of farmland. In 1991 each colony had an average of 1834 h, and on the basis of 15 families per colony, each family had 122 h. Since the average Manitoba farm had 301 h this means that a Hutterite family had only 40.6 per cent of the average.

To put Hutterite agricultural productivity in perspective, on this relatively small amount of land in 1991 Hutterites accounted for over 35 per cent of the laying hens, over 35 per cent of the turkeys and 35 per cent of the hogs in Manitoba. Comparable data are not available for Saskatchewan and Alberta, but the Manitoba comparisons should be basically valid in these areas as well because of the essentially similar Hutterite economic structure.

Until fairly recently, the basic nature of Hutterite settlements had been misunderstood, especially in regard to the relatively small amount of land that they own, and in relation to this their productivity and contribution to the economy had been unappreciated. This had resulted in the past in various restrictions and forms of discrimination against the Hutterites.

Group Maintenance

The survival of the Hutterites and their unique way of life is largely the result of their ability to retain their basic and fundamental beliefs, while simultaneously adopting all the features of contemporary society essential for their economic and social well-being. This strategy of survival includes uncompromising adherence to their religious beliefs and customs, retention of their ancestral German dialect, insistence on their own colony schools and a sound agricultural economy. Although some young people leave the colonies, most return; hence assimilation is not a serious problem for the Hutterites.

SOURCE: John Ryan, 'Hutterites' © 2002 Historica Foundation of Canada/The Canadian Encyclopedia. Reprinted by permission of Historica Foundation of Canada.

Transformation of the Canopy: Jewish Urbanism

While the sacred canopy of many prairie aboriginals was shattered awaiting reconstruction, and the Hutterite canopy was transferred intact and transplanted, the Jewish experience illustrates some of both processes. Like those of the Hutterities, their ideology and community components were transplanted fairly intact, but the cultural and land components, like those of the aboriginals, were changed extensively. Like Glazer and Moynihan's (1975) theory that a shift may take place from traditional identities to new interest foci without losing a sense of a distinctive identity and reality, the Jewish sacred canopy was transformed from a traditional east European *shtetl* community into a segregated urban community located typically in Toronto, Montreal, Vancouver, or Winnipeg (Brym, Shaffir, and Weinfeld, 1993).

While the Jewish community formed one of the most important stakes in the canopy, their *religious* ideology was really the driving force. For nearly 3000 years they found themselves in religiously hostile environments. Within the minority Jewish community, religious (Judaic) law provided the Jewish rules—the worldview and the codes of behaviour—that clearly defined the boundary between insider and outsider (Kallen, 1977:20). Numerous prescriptive and proscriptive commandments regulated religious learning, establishment of the family, and the observation of religious laws. These involved such observances as circumcision, eating Kosher foods, and holding the Sabbath which were transferred to urban settings mostly intact.

Religiously, Jews in Canada can best be discussed under the three categories: Orthodox, Conservative, and Reformed. The Orthodox focus on Jewish religion and customs as their primary reference groups and feel obligated to support their own kind. The Jewish family is of primary importance. Most Orthodox Jews also reside within an Orthodox neighbourhood where they have access to a synagogue, which accounts for the high Jewish residential segregation.

Kallen (1977:72–4) says that Conservative Jews tend to be oriented to the broad ethnic category of Jews as a primary ethnic group, but that they are decidedly more secular and more pragmatic in outlook. Many rituals are still maintained within the home, and they tend to identify strongly with the state of Israel. Like the Conservative Jews, the Reformed Jews have become secular in outlook, but they have become far more critical and questioning about their tradition. Both the Jewish community and the larger society become their dual reference groups, although most Reformed Jews still continue to have their closest friendships with other Jews. Basically, Orthodox Jews attend to boundary maintaining most, while the Reformed Jews do so least (Shaffir, 1993).

Kallen describes the Jewish settlements in Europe as a change from nomadism: 'For almost two hundred years the Jewish people were dispersed throughout the nations of the world where they earned the epithet "wandering Jew" —a migratory people without a national homeland. . . . By the nineteenth century most of the European Jewish population was concentrated in the countries of eastern Europe' (1977:17). Jews have faced pograms and extermination (Brym and Lenton, 1993; Levitt and Shaffir, 1993). A majority lived in small towns and *shtetls* before they came to Canada.

The 318,000 Jews reported by the 1991 census in Canada represent only .9 per cent of the Canadian population, and 98.5 per cent of these are located in cities. Three-fourths of all Canadian Jews live in Toronto (151,000) and Montreal (98,000), where they represent 3 per cent of the city populations. In these two cities the Jews are the most highly segregated of all ethnic groups. Gini indexes of Jewish segregation rank Montreal (.90) the highest followed by Toronto (.78), and Winnipeg (.74) (Balakrishnan and Hou, 1995). About 30 per cent of Jewish households in Toronto and Montreal were foreign-born, which means that many have come to Canada only recently (Shaffir and Weinfeld, 1981:12–13). 'Jews are perhaps the most cosmopolitan, the most internationalist, of all Canadian minority groups' (Weinfeld, Shaffir, and Cotler, 1981:20).

Shaffir and Weinfeld (1981:17–20) discuss the uniqueness of the Jewish *culture* by saying

that they are both an ethnic and a religious group. They have in their cultural portfolio a host of traditions and as many as three languages (Yiddish, Hebrew, and Ladino) (Davids, 1993). Brym, Gillespie, and Gillis (1993) found that density of ingroups' ties and endogamy correlated highly. They are relatively affluent, predominantly of middle and upper-middle class, although that was not always the case when they lived in the East European *shtetls* or small village-towns (Weinfeld, 1993). Many also maintain close ties with Israel, and through radio, television, and newspapers maintained by Jews, they are daily reminded of Israel's problems (Taras and Weinfeld, 1993). Finally, the Holocaust still looms large in their minds, especially for older Jews; it is hard for them to trust others after Hitler's onslaught (Weiman and Winn, 1993; Weinfeld, Shaffir, and Cotler, 1981: 17–20). Thus, Canadian Jews are often obsessed with survival.

Shaffir (1974, 1993) has described in great length the Orthodox culture of the Lubavitcher Chassidim Jews in Montreal, who continue the study of the Jewish Torah, following their traditions transplanted from Poland. They represent a very traditional, back to-the-Torah movement, which lays great emphasis on distinctive dress, study of the scriptures, observance of the traditional rituals, and a general move toward more sacralism and away from secularization. Thus, religious Jewish tradition and culture is again reinforced and new boundaries of separation are strengthened (Brym, Shaffir, and Weinfeld, 1993).

Jewish culture was also transplanted to the Prairies, but there is evidence of a cultural shift as well (Medjuck, 1993). Driedger (1978b) found that third-generation Jewish students in Winnipeg reported high endogamy in their families (81 per cent), one or more years of parochial education (74 per cent), and a majority of ingroup friends (63 per cent). However, other cultural features had declined: only 2 per cent spoke Yiddish at home, just over one-fourth (29 per cent) participated in Jewish organizations, and regular synagogue attendance was minimal (7 per cent). While community practices and religious ideology remained strong, a shift such as Driedger (1996, 2000a) predicted seemed to occur in some of the cultural elements such as a change from the use of Yiddish to English, and less participation in traditional religious and voluntary organizations. The 16,000 Jews in Winnipeg, in 1991 the fourth-largest Jewish community in Canada, continue to perpetuate orthodox and conservative practices in modern synagogues, schools, and organizations. Driedger and Church (1974) found that of all ethnic groups in Winnipeg, the Jews maintained their schools and synagogues as well as any of the others. The religious Jewish reality had been successfully transferred from the east European *shtetls* to the urban prairie. From its early beginnings in the 1900s, the North End of Winnipeg was occupied by East Europeans (Jews, Ukrainians, and Poles). The North End became an enclave of urban ethnic villagers (Driedger, 1987; Gans, 1962). Ecologically it is segregated by river, railroad, and open farmland boundaries; dominated by East Europeans, the area is dotted with Jewish synagogues, and Ukrainian Orthodox and Catholic institutions; culturally, the North End is more akin to the Old World with the maintenance of ethnic languages, endogamy, customs, schools, and clubs (Driedger, 1980b). At first it was a transplantation of the Jews' old communities into the new urban setting, an alternation of their social reality rather than a conversion to the new.

Land seems to have been a fragile stake in the Jewish canopy for a long time. They have been a migratory people, and in many parts of Europe they were not permitted to own land. They certainly have not become agriculturalists like the Hutterites. Jews were forced to live in urban ghettos in Europe and in *shtetls* (Tulchinsky, 1993). This resulted in forced segregation, which they transferred into voluntary segregation in Toronto, Montreal, and Winnipeg. Seventy per cent of all Jews living in Winnipeg in 1941 were located in one part of the North End. By 1961 many had moved out of the North End and 58 per cent formed two new segregated areas in West Kildonan and River Heights (Driedger and

Church, 1974). While segregation seems to be declining somewhat, Jews continue to perpetuate voluntary enclaves. The land stake in the Jewish canopy seems to be in decline, although much still exists. Some of this support seems to be transferred into Zionism, a form of symbolic land identification with Jews in Israel with financial and political support and frequent visits to the Holy Land (Taras and Weinfeld, 1993). Jews are still among the most highly segregated in the largest cities of Toronto, Montreal, and Vancouver (Balakrishnan and Hou, 1995).

Three types of reality structures have been discussed: 1) the Native Indians who were faced with the reconstruction of a meaningful order, 2) the Hutterites who transferred their sacred canopy to the Prairies, and 3) the Jews who transformed their shared knowledge and experience into a viable urban nomos. This involved an ordering of ideology, community, culture, and land into a sacred canopy as a shield against terror. Nomos-building was required so that shared knowledge and ordered experiences could become a meaningful construct of reality. The Hutterites did this effectively in the country, the Jews have struggled to build in the city, but the Native Indians have been faced with almost impossible odds.

Other immigrants who entered Canada can be fitted into these three types. The Mennonites moved onto agricultural reserves in Manitoba and Saskatchewan; the Icelanders sought to reconstruct fishing communities on the shores of Lake Manitoba and Lake Winnipeg; the Ukrainians took up land in the aspen belt where both land and woods provided the environment they were used to (Driedger, 2000a). Like the Hutterites, these groups transferred or transplanted their former communities to a large extent. Like the Jews, more recent immigrants such as the Italians and Chinese have tried to build their nomoses in the city with considerable transformation of parts of their ideology, community, culture, and territory. Other migrants to the city will face similar problems. Like the Indians, the Inuit and other food-gathering peoples will be faced with reconstruction of their sacred canopies.

HIGHLIGHT 7.2 JEWS AND ANTI-SEMITISM

Anti-Semitism in Canada was from the beginning never restricted only to the cranks of society. Rather it has always been part of the mainstream, shared to varying degrees by all elements of the nation, from the top to the bottom. Until the 1950s it had respectability; no one apologized for being anti-Jewish—no one asked them to. It was heard in halls of Parliament, read in the press, taught in the schools and absorbed in most churches. It existed in Canada 100 years ago, when there were scarcely any Jews living here.

The Earliest Manifestation of anti-Jewish sentiment was the expulsion in 1808 of Ezekiel Hart from the Quebec legislature, though this may have been more the result of his politics than his religion. But the major exponent of anti-Semitism in the nineteenth century was the prominent writer and critic Goldwin Smith. A pathological anti-Semite, Smith disseminated his hate in dozens of books, articles and letters. Jews, he charged, were 'parasites', 'dangerous' to their host country and 'enemies of civilization'. His bilious anti-Jewish tirades helped set the tone of a still unmoulded Canadian society and had a profound impact on such young Canadians as Mackenzie King, Henri Bourassa and scores of others. Indeed in 1905 in the most vituperative anti-Jewish speech in the history of the House of Commons, borrowing heavily from Smith, Bourassa urged Canada to keep its gates shut to Jewish immigrants.

Anti-Semitism was particularly acute in Quebec, where the Church associated Jews with modernism, liberalism and a host of other 'dangerous' doctrines. From 1880 through to the 1940s such Catholic journals as *La Verite*, *La Semaine religieuse* and *L'Action sociale* denounced the Jew. And led by people such as J-P. Tardivel a scurrilous anti-Jewish literature spread throughout the province.

There was some violence against Jews, the most notorious incident occurring in Quebec City in 1910 when following a particularly inflammatory address by a well-known anti-semite, Joseph Plamondon, some of the audience attacked Jewish storekeepers and damaged their businesses. The aggrieved Jews launched a civil action against Plamondon. Four years later the courts finally awarded them minimal costs; but the onslaught continued.

Leading the Attack from the 1920s on was the respected French-Canadian intellectual Abbé Lionel Groulx. In many ways what Goldwin Smith was to English Canada in the nineteenth century, Abbé Lionel Groulx was to French Canada in the twentieth. His savage denunciations of the Jews influenced the province's elite—its clerics, politicians, teachers and journalists. Not only were Jews denounced in the Catholic press but popular newspapers also joined in the assault. Out of this was created the 'Achat Chez Nous' movement, an attempt by Church and nationalist leaders to institute a boycott of all Jewish businesses in the province, thus forcing the Jews to leave. As well, since in the view of the Catholic and Protestant clergy Quebec was a Christian society, Jews were barred for years from various school boards. What is most surprising about this concerted campaign against the Jews was that they made up only 1 per cent of Quebec's population.

But anti-Semitism was not the preserve of only one province; it existed—indeed thrived —elsewhere in Canada. In English Canada such organizations as the Social Credit Party, the Orange Order and the Native Sons of Canada were rife with anti-Jewish feeling. For Canadian Jews in the 1920s and 1930s, quotas and restrictions were a way of life. Many industries did not hire Jews; educational institutions such as universities and professional schools discriminated against them, Jewish doctors could not get hospital appointments. There were no Jewish judges, and Jewish lawyers were excluded from most firms. There were scarcely any Jewish teachers and—most notably—no professors. Jewish nurses, engineers and architects had to hide their identity to find jobs in their fields.

Furthermore, there were restrictive covenants on various properties preventing them from being sold to Jews. As well, many clubs, resorts, beaches were barred to Jews. Signs warning 'No Jews or Dogs Allowed' or 'Christians Only!' could be found on Halifax golf courses, outside hotels in the Laurentians and throughout the cottage areas of Ontario, the lake country of Manitoba and the vacation lands of BC.

Worst of all, at least from the point of those Jews desperate to get out of Nazi-infested Europe, anti-semitism had permeated into the upper levels of the Canadian government. While Prime Minister King was worrying that allowing in Jews would 'pollute' Canada's bloodstream, his government was ensuring that no more would be coming. It is perhaps no surprise therefore that Canada had by far the worst record of any Western or immigration country in providing sanctuary to the Jews of Europe in the 1930s and 1940s.

Why was Canada so anti-Semitic? Some hated Jews for religious reasons—after all they had 'killed Christ' and had refused to repent or convert. To others the Jew was the symbol of the millions of aliens who had entered Canada since 1900. They hated Jews because they were the most visible element of this 'mongrelization' of Canada. To the Canadian elite—its leaders, teachers and intellectuals—the Jew did not fit their concept of what a Canadian should be. Theirs was to be a country of farmers and homesteaders, and they believed Jews could not become successful agriculturalists. They saw Jews as city people in a country that wished to build up its rural base.

Since World War II anti-Semitism has been on the decline in Canada. New ideas—and leaders—replaced the old order; attitudes, old habits and traditions were slowly transformed. The creation of the state of Israel changed stereotypes about the Jew. In Canada, following the Holocaust, overt anti-Semitism became the preserve of the crank. In the House of Commons, there was still an occasional outburst from several Social Credit members from Alberta, and from a tiny handful of Parliamentarians from Quebec. But for the most part vocal attacks against Jews had been banished from the public arena—though not necessarily from board rooms and private clubs.

By the 1970s and 1980s most of the earlier barriers had been removed. Human rights commissions, the Canadian Charter of Rights and Freedoms and scores of statutes and judicial decisions guaranteed that the discrimination once so rampant in Canada against Jews—and others—would never reappear. Jews were now playing an increasingly crucial role in all sectors of Canadian society—in politics, law, medicine, arts and business.

Though recent polls indicate that there is still a tiny residue of anti-Semitic feeling in this country, highlighted by the occasional act of anti-Jewish vandalism and by the activities of some right-wing Holocaust-denial groups, for Canadians Jews, anti-Semitism is no longer a major concern. Ironically, what most concerns Jewish leaders is not rates of anti-Semitism but rates of assimilation. That, to many, is the real threat to Jewish survival in the twenty-first century.

SOURCE: 'Anti-semitism' by Irving Abella copyright © 2002 Historica Foundation of Canada/The Canadian Encyclopedia. Reprinted by permission of Historica Foundation of Canada.

SACRED ENCLAVIC COMMUNITIES

With the rural and urban sacred canopy types as the backdrop, let us demonstrate some of the empirical sacred ethnic enclaves found in Canada. While the French who represent one-fourth of the Canadian population, 80 per cent of which are concentrated in the one territory of Quebec, can seriously think of 'nation', smaller groups must resort to smaller territorial enclaves or communities over which they may have some control. Let us first discuss rural means of developing a 'tribe' or 'Volk' as Weber phrased it, to sustain 'a people' in an ethnic 'sacred' territory or community, followed by segregated urban means of doing the same in the city.

Dawson's Sacred Rural Communities

The Chicago School of the 1920s was dominant in the development of sociology in America. Canadian sociology began later than its American counterpart, and early sociologists in Canada such as C.A. Dawson, Everett Hughes, and Horace Miner were Chicago graduates. Dawson and Hughes in particular carried the Chicago tradition to Canada. Because they were both at McGill where early Canadian sociology began in the 1930s, and because they both published studies of ethnic importance, we will begin with their contributions. Roman Catholic Quebec, a very different ethnic milieu from the rest of Canada, served to modify their Chicago assimilationist inclinations and led them to consider ethnic pluralism more.

Dawson's *Group Settlement: Ethnic Communities in Western Canada* (1936) was the seventh volume in the nine-volume Canadian Frontiers of Settlement series, edited by historians Mackintosh and Joerg. To be a sociologist in Canada in the 1930s, to do research on ethnic groups, and to do so in western rather than eastern Canada, was rather astounding. Indeed, the short preface by editor Mackintosh clearly shows the early British bias when he refers to western minorities as 'peculiar peoples' who

have 'formed "cultural islands" which have retarded the progress of assimilation', and when he says Dawson will present them as groups rather than as 'foreigners'. Few present-day scholars would dare include any of the words 'peculiar', 'retarded', 'assimilation progress', or 'foreigners' in any sentence, let alone in a preface to a book on western pluralism.

The Chicago influence clearly shows when Dawson frames his study using 'the main characteristics of sects which have been set forth with insight by Professor R.E. Park' (Dawson, 1936:xiii). The main writings of the 'sect cycle' and the sect-church continuum were actually introduced by the German sociologist Ernst Troeltsch and then adopted and applied by Park in Chicago. The sect cycle implies a secularization process of religious groups (especially Christian groups), where a new group may spring forth out of a larger church because the new believers think the old church does not observe the original intent rigorously enough. However, as this new sect practises with greater fervour and follows the Scriptures more intensely, the concern with purity ages, the commitment again wanes, and slowly it becomes an established sect, then a denomination, and finally a churchlike organization more concerned with structures than original beliefs and practice. This secularization process is similar to the assimilation process we discussed in Chapter 2, only it applies more strictly to religious groups. In this sense, Dawson is a typical Chicago School sociologist, concerned more with the process of change and assuming that solidarity or concern with the Sacred will give way to secularization. All indicators of change are seen as the decline of ethnic identity rather than as change expressed in new forms more adapted to the new social milieu for the sake of survival.

Because Dawson (1936) was interested in the change of ethnoreligious sects, he chose to study the Doukhobors, Mennonites, Mormons, German Catholics, and French Catholics of western Canada. He and his associates made extensive studies of these five groups at the beginning of the Depression (1930–2), and the findings were published in 1936. The West had been settled by European immigrants only 50 years before. Many of these settlers were first- and second-generation immigrants, so their ethnic origins were still very salient. Dawson was one of the first sociologists to study this new frontier. Many of these groups had settled in the West in rural bloc communities, and they could easily be studied as distinct segregated ethnic groups.

Dawson (1936) also chose to study five ethnoreligious groups for comparative purposes, much in the style of Max Weber. His work has not been sufficiently recognized in Canada as one of the first comparative studies. Dawson's methodology includes a combination of qualitative and quantitative means of data collection through ethnographic, survey, interview, community, and census sources. Although he describes each group in 60 to 100 pages, these are not community studies in the sense of having lived and done participant observation in the community in a more qualitative way.

Dawson is mainly concerned with the process of secularization; he uses the Doukhobors and Mennonites as a segregated sacred sect group baseline to see how they have changed, or become more secular (Driedger, 2000a). He also includes the German and French Catholics as non-sectarian religious groups, and compares the sect and church groups to see differences in secularization and assimilation. As expected, he finds that the sects have distinguishing features such as more concern with segregation, maintenance of sect institutions of their own, reluc-

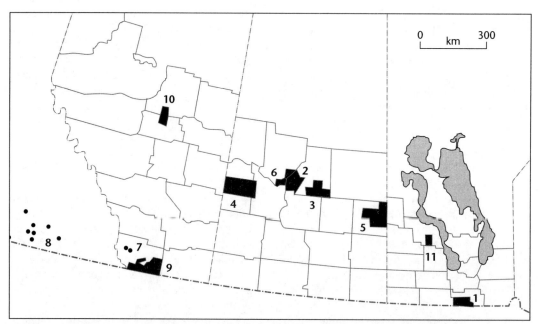

FIGURE 7.3 Location of the 11 Ethnoreligious Reserves and Settlements Studied by Dawson

Map of the Prairie Provinces showing location of group settlements included in the present study; 1, Mennonite West Reserve (Dutch-German); 2, Rosthern Mennonite colony (Dutch-German); 3, St Peter's colony (German); 4, St Joseph's colony (German); 5, North and South colonies and Devil's Lake colony (Doukhobor) (also called Yorkton and Swan River colonies); 6, Saskatchewan (Blaine Lake and Saskatoon) colonies (Doukhobor); 7, Cowley colony (Doukhobor); 8, British Columbia colonies (Doukhobor); 9, Mormon country (Anglo-Saxon); 10, St Albert settlement (French-Canadian); 11, Ste Rose settlement (French-Canadian).

SOURCE: C.A. Dawson, *Group Settlement: Ethnic Communities in Western Canada* (Toronto: Macmillan, 1936), p. xviii.

tance to associate with the outside world, and seeing themselves as distinctive and apart using different dress, languages, morals, and the like. Dawson sees the Doukhobors, Mennonites, and Mormons as more sacred groups and the German and French Catholics as more secularized.

As illustrated in Figure 7.3, Dawson carefully plotted 11 bloc settlements of the five groups and then proceeded to discuss each in detail. Generally, he outlines how each group came to the Prairies and from where, the locale in which they settled, the institutions and organizations they formed, the process of invasion of the area, how in turn the groups were invaded by others, the general social adjustments which were involved, and the resistance to secularization. This is enormously useful data because it describes these multiethnic groups in a very pluralist region more than 50 years ago, a treasure that can no longer be duplicated. These five groups also provide a baseline of religious practices, customs, traditions, and values that can be compared today to see how the means of solidarity have changed, how some groups have indeed integrated, and the extent to which community distinctiveness is still present in changed forms.

Dawson (1936:377–80) concluded that all five rural ethnic communities were changing considerably. Their cultural traditions and the development of their community organizations served as a sacred anchor supported by ecological segregation. Outside forces, however, pressured them to adjust and readjust their economic, community, and educational life considerably. Dawson interpreted these changes as assimilation; today we would see them more as in a modified state of pluralism because all of these communities still exist as changed vibrant rural religio-ethnic communities 60 years later.

Fortunately, E.K. Francis (1955) studied the same Mennonites in southern Manitoba in more depth 20 years later: *In Search of Utopia: The Mennonites in Manitoba*. Francis was among the first in Canada to look at modified forms of pluralism, and he published about 20 articles developing plural ethnic theory in the major sociological journals (Francis, 1947, 1948, 1950,

1954). Driedger (1991, 2000a) has continued the pluralist interpretations since.

The Mennonites originally settled in one hundred villages on the East and West Reserves of southern Manitoba that were reserved for Mennonite rural bloc settlement. The West Reserve was also studied by Dawson and is marked in Figure 7.3, located on the west side of the Red River and on the American border; the East Reserve is on the east side of the Red River centred by Steinbach, 40 miles east of Winnipeg. In 1881, seven years after the first Mennonites arrived, they represented 13 per cent of the Manitoba population, the fourth-largest ethnic group. When Francis studied these two reserves in 1945–7, there were 40,000 Mennonites in Manitoba. They were the sixth-largest ethnic group, representing 5.4 per cent of the provincial population.

Almost all Mennonites in 1955 spoke the Low German dialect at home and in the villages and towns, reserving the High German dialect for church. Families were highly endogamous, schools on the reserves included mostly Mennonite children and teachers, and the business activity in the towns of Steinbach, Winkler, and Altona were mostly in German. Because the Mennonites selected some of the best soil for farming, they had a very good rural economic base. Their prosperity soon resulted in expanded farms and new industry in the towns and villages as well as supporting institutions, schools, and business. Since then, they have moved to cities, and four times as many are in the professions (28 per cent), as are engaged in farming (7 per cent) (Driedger, 2000a; Kauffman and Driedger, 1991). These Mennonites represent an enormous change from segregated sectarian farmers to pluralist professionals more like the urban Jews, half of them who are now living in cities, a modified example of religious pluralism.

Forming Urban Sacred Communities

We were not able to find the same kinds of sacred ethnographic urban community studies that we were able to find on the rural French and

Mennonites, although William Shaffir's (1974) Lubavitcher Chassidim Jews in Montreal, and Stebbins (1994) study of the Franco-Calgarians would be good examples. However, a great deal of literature is available on general ethnic residential concentration of urban ethnic minorities (Balakrishnan and Kralt, 1987, 1995; Driedger, 2000a; Driedger and Church, 1974; Driedger and Kraybill, 1994; Kalbach, 1987).

Using Canada census data, Balakrishnan and Kralt (1987:148) plotted the residential concentration of five minorities in Toronto and Vancouver (see Figure 7.4). They show a small area in Toronto comprising 7 census tracks near the centre of the city where over half of the Catholic Portuguese (56 per cent) live, 7 tracks where the majority of the Jews (53 per cent) live, and 12 tracks where the Catholic Italians (51 per cent) live. The Jews of highest socioeconomic status live the farthest from the centre; the more recent Portuguese immigrants of lowest status are located closest to the business centre, and the Italians in between.

In Vancouver, over half of the Chinese, many of whom are Buddhist, are segregated in Chinatown, closest to the uptown business section, while smaller percentages of other ethnic groups are concentrated farther out. These concentrations need to be examined more closely.

The 1991 census reports 247,000 Portuguese Catholics in Canada, most of whom came after the Second World War and especially during the 1960s. Three-fourths of them live in Ontario, and half live in Toronto (124,000) where they represent 3 per cent of the metropolitan population. Over half (56 per cent) of the Portuguese in Toronto live in 7 small census tracks in the Kensington Market area near downtown Toronto (Balakrishnan and Kralt, 1987:143; Balakrishnan and Hou, 1995; Balakrishnan and Wu, 1992). The Portuguese are among the most segregated ethnic groups in Toronto. They clearly represent immigrants who have come most recently, drawn to the southern Ontario industrial milieu. Race is not a factor, since they are Caucasian, but social class is: most of them came from poor Portuguese-held islands, and they

have little education, and few special occupational skills. Most of them are Roman Catholic.

We are fortunate to have several intensive studies of the Portuguese in Toronto by Grace Anderson (1974) and Anderson and Higgs (1976). Anderson writes:

> When the residents of metropolitan Toronto think of the Portuguese, they usually call to mind the colourful Kensington Market with its Portuguese stores spilling over onto the sidewalks. Chickens can be bought, still alive, from cages. Fresh fruit stores, vegetable stands, and fish shops are there in abundance. The delicious aroma of Portuguese pastries floats from the bakeries. Everywhere there is bustle and animated conversation. The groups jostle each other . . . blocking the free flow of pedestrian traffic on the crowded sidewalks. Occasionally a car attempts to make its way down the road. . . . Many visitors come to the area to see the 'Portuguese district' (1974:167).

Richmond (1972a) has plotted the Portuguese Catholics and other ethnic groups in Toronto on maps to show their relationships, and Balakrishnan and Kralt (1987:148) have done so as well (see Figure 7.4). 'Between 1953 and the mid-sixties, the Portuguese poured into the Kensington Market area' (Anderson and Higgs, 1976:66–9). The Portuguese are located adjacent to Chinatown, and the two business areas complement each other.

In terms of Raymond Breton's 'institutional completeness' of an ethnic group, the Portuguese have their own schools, churches, and voluntary associations. Anderson writes:

> The Portuguese in Toronto now constitute in many ways a very 'institutionally complete' ethnic group. . . . Within the Kensington Market area there are also . . . Portuguese restaurants, real estate agents, printers. Books and records from Portugal can be purchased there. Several newspa-

FIGURE 7.4 Ethnic Concentration in Toronto and in Vancouver, 1981

SOURCE: T.R. Balakrishnan and John Kralt, 'Segregation of Visible Minorities', in Leo Driedger (ed.), *Ethnic Canada* (Toronto: Copp Clark Pitman, 1987), p. 148.

pers are available. . . . A radio station reports Portuguese programmes regularly. In the ethnic press various services are offered in addition to those mentioned above—taxis, driving school . . . a Portuguese bank, and services of immigration consultants, interpreters and income tax specialists(1974:170).

Two Catholic churches specialize in Portuguese services. Several centres provide social activities and social assistance. There are clubs and pool halls, as well as soccer teams with various Portuguese emphases. Religion is an important sacred cohesive factor.

The family is very important, and mutual aid is common. Relatives live within easy reach of each other. The average size of the family is five to six persons, and the average education is three to four years of schooling for those who came from the Azores Islands, where few could go to school beyond grade four (Anderson and Higgs, 1976:71). Half the immigrant men were farmers, so in addition to the cultural changes, life in Toronto is new to them. Most of them are happy to find blue-collar jobs. Owning a home is very important to them, and often families work very hard to save for their own property, which bring status in their Portuguese circles.

The Portuguese in Toronto represent one of the many recent immigrant groups who are highly segregated in the centre of the city, who are cohesive religiously, who are of lower socio-economic status, who have developed their own institutionally complete enclaves, and who communicate at home and in much of their life in Portuguese. As a result, many of them speak a broken form of English. This urban ethnic group will retain its identity for the first several generations. We need to see what changes will take place by the third generation.

Elizabeth Bott was among the first to develop the social network perspective, beginning with the family as a small network unit. Bott suggests that as ethnics move from segregated rural communities or as rural communities become less iso-

lated (Blau, Blum, and Schwartz, 1982:45–62) and move to a more open urban environment, they must make sure that the family as a network remains very tightly knit. All the families she researched 'maintained relationships with external people and institutions—with a place of work, with service institutions such as school, church, doctor, clinic, shops, with voluntary associations such as clubs, evening classes, and recreational institutions. They also maintained more informal relationships with colleagues, friends, neighbours, and relatives' (Bott, 1957: 98). Such a tightly knit family can link with other selected social networks such as a network of extended relatives, an ethnic church, or school, friends, professionals, and others to strengthen itself. Such a 'sacred' network of subnetworks can be sufficiently strong so that linkage with other networks will be less threatening. These networks of beliefs and values can provide guidelines and the opportunities for youth to find ingroup partners. The Jews seem to be most successful in creating such urban networks.

SUMMARY

Nomos-building is a phenomenon creating order for individuals and groups so that life makes sense. Berger's concept of 'sacred canopy' deals with four structural components: ideology, community, culture, and land—stakes that help to uphold the canopy's protective roof or shield against terror, normlessness, and supports meaningfulness. We compared the aboriginal, Hutterite, and Jewish canopies to see how they fared.

While the Jewish sacred canopy is not as secure as that of the Hutterites, it has not succumbed to the devastation of anomie faced by many aboriginals. They appear to have created a nomos in the city, which Hutterites have not attempted, and which aboriginals moving to the city find difficult. It appears that most other subgroups could at least be examined to see which type of structure and process might be most applicable.

Dawson found that religion or sectarianism in the western prairie is an important means of maintaining traditional ethnic enclaves. Francis illustrated that among rural Mennonites there is also considerable change, and that change is easier to integrate in stable communities.

To some extent, segregated ethnic enclaves are also perpetuated in cities. However, recent immigrants of lower socioeconomic status, such as the Catholic Portuguese, continue to establish ethnic enclaves that are segregated and bounded spatially, as illustrated by Anderson.

There is considerable evidence that as ethnic groups move to the city, they are exposed to many more situations where interaction with outgroup members is necessary at work, at play, at school, and in many social situations. Some assimilate but others change and adapt considerably, maintain modified forms of ethnic identity, and therefore save their ethnic identity in a modified sacred form.

We have found strong evidence that ideology in forms like religion, is an important means of perpetuating identity. In Chapter 2 we placed religious groups like Jews and Hutterites in the voluntary identity Cell E, and in this chapter we found much evidence that ideology is a strong supporter of ethnic and religious solidarity. Sacred canopies can be built where land, culture, community, and religion can be combined into a 'sacred' construct, which shelters and supports ethnic identity. The aboriginals have done so on reserves and the Hutterites on agricultural colonies with great success in rural areas. The Jews are excellent examples of how such identity has been perpetuated in cities as well for many millennia. Dawson found such Hutterite, Mennonite, Doukhobor, Mormon, and French Catholic settlements on the Prairies in the 1930s, and recently Alan Anderson still found such communities of ethnic identity in the 1970s in Saskatchewan. Others like Shaffir, Grace Anderson, Driedger, Kalbach, Stebbins, and Balakrishnan have found many 'sacred' communities of religious and ethnic identity in Canadian metropolitan centres. These religious studies remind us that we should not be overly enamoured with only structural-functional findings, and postmodernists would warn us that reason, science and the metanarrative have their limitations, so that deconstruction may be necessary. Spiritual and emotive values need to be considered especially as we see pluralism, diversity and the many differences, not all of which can be dealt with by rational linear science.

CRITICAL THINKING QUESTIONS

1. What does the author mean by a 'sacred reality'? How are ethnicity and 'the sacred' linked? What is a sacred canopy according to Berger?

2. Why did the author propose that the aboriginals have to reconstruct their canopy? Is that a helpful way to proceed? How can reserves become such canopies? Discuss.

3. Why and how did Hutterites transfer their canopy? Discuss how they migrated and changed their identity structurally.

4. In what way has the Jewish canopy been transformed as they became more urban? What do the three major Jewish groupings (Orthodox, Conservative, Reformed) mean? Discuss.

5. Can the three reconstruction, transferral, and transformation processes be thought of as types, and applied to other groups? Which other groups fit these three types?

SUGGESTED READINGS

Brym, Robert J., William Shaffir, and Morton Weinfeld, (eds), *The Jews in Canada* (Toronto: Oxford University Press, 1993). This is a first comprehensive sociological analysis by 24 scholars of Canada's 350,000 Jews showing their economic, political, and social diversity.

Driedger, Leo, *Mennonites in the Global Village* (Toronto: University of Toronto Press, 2000). Driedger discusses the influences of the infor-mation revolution, on Mennonites who are increasingly becoming professional, urban, modern and more institutionalized.

Friesen, John W., *When Cultures Clash: Case Studies in Multiculturalism*, 2nd edn (Calgary: Detselig, 1993). Friesen did studies of Hutterite, Mennonite, Sikh, and Chinese communities and examined their changing identities, and cultural clashes.

PART IV

Stratification: Power, Status, Inequalities

S ociologists for more than a hundred years have been keenly aware of how populations are stratified, and concerned that many minority groups which are small and economically and politically powerless, will be treated by the larger dominant majority. So, first we devote a chapter to social class and socioeconomic status that Karl Marx was most interested in. Next we deal with spatial segregation of minorities especially in cities, where the poor can afford only older cheaper housing usually in the centre, and better-to-do citizens live in the outer suburbs where new housing is available. Thus, they are separated or apart spatially. In the third chapter we deal with the biological factor of race, which separates people who are white and those who are more coloured. Each of these symbols of class, segregation, and race influence the status and power that groups wield, and it creates many inequalities in the competition of making a living.

In Chapter 8, related to socioeconomic status, we deal with the various theories of class and social inequality, proposed by Marx, Weber, Porter, and many others, to gain some perspective on social stratification. We deal with empirical studies such as the formation of the Ontario establishment, how the charter groups became politically dominant, and we sort the various ethnic and racial groups using their incomes, education, and occupations as indicators of status. Finally, we use these three indicators of socioeconomic status to explore how groups have risen to the top, how others are moving toward the top, and how some, such as aboriginals and recent immigrants of more colour, stay at the bottom because they cannot compete.

Class and Socioeconomic Status

Part III focused on voluntary ethnic identity, solidarity, and cohesion; Part IV will focus on differentiation of power and stratification of ethnic groups. This often leads to involuntary differentiations and 'inequalities' as found in Cell D of our model. Clearly, size, regional distribution, length of stay, and influence varied enormously between the various ethnic groups, and some will be in a position of dominance and more powerful than others. Scholars' views differ on the relationships between class and ethnicity, and on the extent to which ethnic identification is a drawback or a resource of social mobility. Chapter 8 focuses on the varying levels of power of the various ethnic groups and on their socioeconomic status. Chapter 9 deals with voluntary and involuntary spatial segregation. Chapter 10 looks at race and its importance for stratification as biological characteristics enter into differentiation of the Canadian population.

THEORIES OF STRATIFICATION

John Porter's sociological study, *The Vertical Mosaic: An Analysis of Social Class and Power in Canada* (1965) sets the stage, which many others have developed since (Clement, 1974; Curtis, Grabb, and Guppy, 1993; Grabb, 1984). Class and power are Porter's major themes, as well as the importance of mobility and migration. He addresses 'ethnicity and class' first (1965: 60–103), giving ethnicity a central and prominent place. Located in Ottawa at Carleton University, Porter was especially aware of the

British-French historical power axis. Ottawa, the national capital, has for generations been the political battleground between these two ethnic blocs. The two groups, each in their respective Ontario and Quebec strongholds, watched each other suspiciously across the Ottawa River. It is not surprising that Porter saw the British-French axis as crucial, and that he was interested in exploring the power relationships and the social-class differentials between the two founding peoples (Elliott and Fleras, 1992: 77–86).

Porter (1965) outlines two important theories that deal with the function and purpose of social classes. The first he calls the functional theory of stratification and the second the Marxian theory; the first he claims is more subjective and the second more objective, based on defined classes. The first claims that inequality is necessary and the second wants to do away with stratification, thinking that social class is unjust and unacceptable.

Class as Functional Inequality

According to Porter (1965:16), the functional theory of stratification reflects the American conservative ideology that inequality is natural and necessary, and that people generally occupy the class positions they deserve. Kingsley Davis and W.E. Moore (1945) suggest that stratification occurs because not all jobs are equally pleasant, though all these jobs need to be done. Social inequality becomes an unconsciously evolved device by which societies ensure that the most important positions are conscientiously filled by the most qualified people (Musynski, 1995:19f). Different jobs require different training and inherited capacity, so the more able and more trained get better, higher-status jobs than others. According to the functional inequality theorists, because of differential ability, opportunity for training, and the will to expend the effort, some people have higher-status jobs than others.

There are many critics of this theory. The theory assumes equality of opportunity, especially education. It does not explain why there are such differential rewards between a corporate president and high-ranking public servants. The theory also does not take sufficiently into account the fact that some jobs and positions are often inherited, eliminating free competition for many jobs. The theory also takes little account of power as a reward itself, where power compensates for monetary reward, as is the case for religious practitioners or politicians (Hunter, 1986). The factor of prestige satisfies many; university professors have relatively higher prestige than their salaries would suggest. Porter (1965:17) claims that class is 'a product of a conservative ideology and a theory to support the status quo. Other variations all assert that social class rests on prestige, derived from occupational roles.'

The Radical Marxian Perspective

Rick Ogmundson (1986:237) has called Porter's second Marxian perspective 'radical' because it emphasizes the divergent interests in society, the conflict that will result, and the coercion that is almost inevitable if things are to change. The Marxian tradition holds that members of a particular class become quite conscious of their class identity and interests, and usually ethnicity and race are seen as part of the powerlessness of the lower classes. This class consciousness is functional because class conflict forces change. In Marxian theory, society comprised owners and non-owners of the productive instruments, an inequality that results from domination and exploitation. The injustice of this inequality must be remedied (Grabb, 1984:13–36).

'It was ironic, that Marx, a radical opponent of capitalism, should find tolerance and refuge within which to express his ideas only in England, the prime example of what he most despised' (Berlin, 1963:181). In Marx's time in England the contrast between rich and poor was especially acute, with child labour, long working hours and weeks, and extremely poor working conditions. Marx himself lived in poverty, although he occasionally had financial help from friends. It was in England that Marx and his lifelong friend Engels helped to form the new Communist League in 1847, and in 1848— the same year that popular revolts against established monarchies occurred in France, Italy, Germany, Austria, and Hungary (Grabb, 1984: 18)—they published the *Communist Manifesto*. The crux of Marx's views is stated clearly in the beginning of the *Manifesto:* 'The history of all hitherto existing society is the history of class struggles' (Marx and Engels, 1948:57). The first volume of *Das Kapital*, the elaboration of their theory, was published by Marx during his lifetime; volumes 2 and 3 were completed by Engels after Marx's death.

In short, Marx saw private property (the capitalists) and alienated labour according to his revised Hegelian dialectic, as antitheses that were in conflict. The earlier theories of the French social thinker Saint-Simon, that economic relationships were the key to explaining historical social change, prevailed in Marx's theory as well. Marx saw the macro society as a struggle between economic classes pitted against each other for power. He was appalled at the small returns labourers got for their long labour, and the disproportionate share of returns that went as profits to owners. Since the small group of bourgeoisie capitalists were in league with governmental power, he saw no other solution than the overthrow of these capitalists by the masses to establish a classless society in which all people would benefit more equitably from their labour.

Marx's focus on economic stratification as the major force of change led him to make short shrift of other forces such as religion, and he wrote nothing about ethnicity. He assumed that religion and ethnicity were only social manifestations of the major power struggle, as some forces such as religious leaders siding with the bourgeoisie and others like ethnic minorities representing the proletariat. According to Marxists, the key to understanding inequality lies in economic factors (Satzewich, 1995:98–121). In addition to land, labour, and capital as resources to earning a living, Marx also added the importance of social technology and the organization of economic activity that he called the mode of production (Ogmundson, 1986:238). Marx saw the dominant capitalist class who owned the means of production as the bourgeoisie, and those who worked for wages as the proletariat. Since the bourgeoisie who owned the capital were primarily concerned with profit, they would try to exploit the workers in order to gain a greater margin of profit. Marx's theory assumes that minority groups are usually among the powerless.

Weber's Functional and Conflict Synthesis

Much of Max Weber's writing was in response to Marx's economic determinism; Weber thought that Marx had not placed enough emphasis on non-economic factors such as ideology, although he agreed that the relations between the propertied and non-propertied were important. However, he thought Marx tended to oversimplify matters and was too rigid on economic materialism as the major factor. Weber argued that the employer-worker relationship was not the only significant one. Other relationships such as those of creditors to debtors, producers to consumers, and questions of usury or high interest rates and just prices all entered into the more complex equation (Ogmundson, 1986:247).

Weber also thought that the social and political bases of human inequality were at least as important as the economic base. He thought that hierarchies based on differing levels of prestige could be independent of economic factors. For example, descendants of aristocrats, confident intellectuals, or members of some ethnic groups might feel themselves superior to other social groups who

merely possess money (Ogmundson, 1986:247). A recent millionaire immigrant might not have as much social status as another Canadian with little money but who is educated and teaching at a university. Race, religion, gender, language, ethnicity, and education could all be factors that might make a difference in social rankings.

Weber thought political hierarchies based on differential power could also be independent of social or economic hierarchies. Weber disagreed with Marx's belief that economic and political power could hardly be separated, arguing instead that each should be considered separately. Whereas Marx thought in terms of one basic economic class hierarchy, Weber argued that there were at least three hierarchies, including class (the economic), status (the social), and power (the political). Weber also saw the bureaucracy as a master trend in the industrialization process that would increasingly control the lives of all, although he argued that social factors such as religion and ethnicity could act as deterrent forces to industrial dehumanization.

We maintain that in Canada ethnic and racial prestige vary considerably and are based on many factors such as occupation and income, which are economic factors. However, social factors such as education, residence, religion, language, gender, age, race, and the like need to be taken into account as well. Historical factors including recency of immigration into Canada are also important. Some ethnic groups will have higher prestige not only because of their economic condition, but also because of different combinations of social factors.

Post-Marxian Industrial Elites

Like Marx, Porter was interested in social class and power, but he argued that modern industrial society no longer requires as much unskilled labour because it has become complex and varied and the labour force has become more skilled. With the development of corporations, managers rather than capitalists run these corporations, which are owned by thousands of shareholders, few of whom ever own the majority of any one stock. Thus, the stockholders or owners are not concentrated in one or several individuals but are dispersed.

Second, these large corporations have concentrated their economic power in the hands of a relatively few large firms that continue to consolidate, resulting in interlocking directorships. Porter (1965:25) contends that ownership or non-ownership of property is no longer the major criterion for class conflict. The power has now shifted to those who make the decisions, who Porter contends are the managers or elites of these large corporations. It is not only the corporations who are now run by managing elites, but labour unions, educational institutions, social agencies, the military, and governmental institutions are now run by managing elites. C. Wright Mills (1956) called these managers the 'power elite'. The struggle is no longer between those who employ or are employed, but between the major decision-makers in their institutional systems. This then raises the question of whether some elites are more heavily drawn from some ethnic groups than others. Porter clearly thought so and proceeded to show that the British were heavily concentrated in the decision-making roles of the economic and political power elite.

In *The Vertical Mosaic*, Porter describes Canada as a stratified mosaic with vast differentiations in social stratification. Whereas the regional mosaic discussed in Chapter 4 focused on the distribution of ethnic groups, Porter's vertical mosaic has to do with vertical strata of status, prestige, and power. Some ethnic groups are much more heavily represented in the lower classes. It is here that Porter's group status and entrance status principles apply.

Charter Group Status

The British North America Act of 1867 gave the founding groups of Canada (the British and French) what has been termed by some as charter group status (Porter, 1965). The act legalized the claims of the two original migrating groups for such historically established privileges as the perpetuation of their separate languages and cultures. The Royal Commission on Bilingualism

and Biculturalism (1970) continued to support and encourage the charter group status of the French, even though by 1991 those of other ethnic origins comprised at least one-third of the Canadian population. Since then the new constitution has entrenched these special rights for all. Though legally of equal status, the French have always been junior partners in the alliance with the British. Though the charter-group status of the French was legally secure, they nevertheless had difficulty matching the numerical, economic, and political strength of the British. They came to rely on regional segregation and their institutions and culture as a means of counteracting British dominance.

The dominance of the charter groups has never been seriously challenged because of natural increase among the French and continuing high levels of British immigration. Also, the ethnic structure of a community in terms of its charter and non-charter groups is determined early and tends to be self-perpetuating. The French made up almost one-third of the Canadian population (although that proportion had declined to 23 per cent by 1991), while the British have always been the largest ethnic group, although their proportion has been steadily dropping from over one-half to 28 per cent in 1991.

At the time of Confederation, the charter groups (91 per cent of the population) in Upper and Lower Canada and the Maritimes formed a bilingual and bicultural nation with few representatives from other countries (9 per cent) (Porter, 1965). The French, however, have been very much junior partners in the charter alliance; the British have dominated economically and politically.

Entrance Group Status

Porter (1965) describes the position to which ethnic groups are admitted and at which they are allowed to function in the power structure of a society as entrance status. For most ethnic groups in Canada, this position is characterized by low-status occupational roles and a subjection to the processes of assimilation laid down by the charter groups. Less preferred immigrants were allowed to enter Canada but were channelled into lower-status jobs and because of their later entrance into Canada were often left with marginal farm lands (Driedger, 1996). German, Dutch, Jewish, and Scandinavian immigrants entered Canada earlier than many of the others, and they could be considered older entrance-status groups. Many of these older immigrants have moved out of an entrance status into higher educational, income, and occupational status. The Jews placed great value on education and entered higher-status occupations; on the average, they have a higher status than any of the other groups, including the charter groups.

Porter suggests that the idea of an ethnic mosaic, as opposed to the idea of the melting pot, impedes the process of social mobility. 'The melting pot with its radical breakdown of national ties and old forms of stratification would have endangered the conservative tradition of Canadian life, a tradition which gives ideological support to the continued high status of the British charter group' (Porter, 1965:71). This seems to be changing, however, as many former entrance groups are gaining status educationally, occupationally, and economically, and nevertheless retain many of their ethnic characteristics (Isajiw, Sev'er, and Driedger, 1993). The Jews would be an excellent example of a group that shows high upward mobility with a high level of maintenance of ethnic identity (Driedger, 1996).

The political and economic power elite, however, is still largely British. The British elite dominates the Canadian economic system with a strong influence in urban industrial Ontario, emerging strength in Alberta, and declining strength in the Maritimes (Porter, 1965). The French dominate the political structure in Quebec, the British dominate in Ontario and the East, and other ethnic groups are becoming increasingly more politically influential in the West. Any theory of Canadian political ethnic relations must deal with these multidimensional regional, economic, and political status structures in order to account for the factors that will influence the Canadian mosaic and the identity of individual ethnic groups (Driedger, 1989).

Class and Social Mobility

Porter (1975a:293–5) found ethnic occupational stratification in his study of the Canadian census and argued that ethnicity serves as a deterrent to social mobility. Porter's vertical mosaic thesis has served as a provocative hypothesis, and numerous scholars have focused their attention on the relationship of ethnicity to social mobility (Agocs and Boyd, 1993; Blishen, 1970; Curtis, Grabb, and Guppy, 1993; Darroch, 1979; Reitz, 1977; Tepperman, 1975). Clement's study (1974) leaves little doubt that non-charter groups have not entered the positions of power extensively, and Blishen (1970) finds considerable evidence of the vertical mosaic. Many others, however, have been highly critical of the 'mobility trap' hypothesis. Among them are Tepperman (1975:156), who concludes that the hypothesis is in many ways 'patently false', and Darroch (1979:22), who found 'it an exaggeration of any data available to date'.

The literature on the interrelationship between class and ethnicity helps to distinguish two traditional theoretical positions: 1) that ethnicity, whatever its cultural origin, is a by-product of the class structure and hence is, in some sense, reducible to class as Marxists assume; and 2) that ethnicity may or may not be reducible to class, but that it is a drawback to social mobility as Porter believed. Marx expounded the first position and so did Oliver Cox (1948:321–52), in his view that race or ethnic relations are merely one aspect of exploitation of labour by the capitalist class. Hence, what are considered to be attributes of ethnicity are simply attributes of the exploited class, and race or ethnic relations are in essence a form of political class conflict.

More recently a much more sophisticated, though similar, position has been taken by advocates of the 'cultural division of labour' approach. There are at least two variants of this approach. One is represented by Edna Bonacich (1972) who suggests that ethnic solidarity is a derivative of dual labour-market exploitation in which the immigrants are funnelled into jobs that are less stable, offer lower wages, and preclude advancement, yet are similar to jobs performed by the indigenous population who receive better wages and have a chance of advancement and upward social mobility.

A second type of the 'cultural division of labour' thinking is Michael Hechter's (1978) theory of 'internal colonialism'. According to Hechter, ethnic solidarity emerges as a reaction of a culturally distinct periphery against exploitation by the centre. This happens especially when there is a division of labour in which the periphery is engaged in an activity which is most advantageous for the centre, but least economically profitable for the periphery. Ethnic solidarity of the periphery is a reaction against exploitation, and the more the periphery is disadvantaged in relation to the centre, the more likely it will develop strong feelings of solidarity.

Wiley (1967) suggests that if a person chooses to move into an ethnic opportunity community rather than that of the society at large, this structure, although it may offer some possibilities for mobility, will ultimately become a mobility trap because it offers a smaller chain of minority opportunities than the mainstream structure outside the ethnic minority group. According to him, being tied to a minority subculture, and hence being socialized to anticipate opportunities within the confines of a minority group, places a low ceiling on a person's career and leaves no easy way into the world at large. Likewise, a psychological commitment to a minority group and its interactional style becomes in itself a mobility trap.

Gordon Darroch (1979:1–25) did an extensive review of the literature on the relationship between ethnicity and social class. He found that three major themes emerged: 1) limited evidence of entrance of non-charter groups into positions of power; 2) evidence (which he suggests is exaggerated) that an ethnic mosaic (maintenance of identities) impedes the processes of social mobility; and 3) evidence that continued ethnic identification (lack of assimilation) can harden so that ethnic groups remain in their original low entrance class, which he seriously questions based on the data he found and could examine. Darroch's (1979:20) review leads him to suggest

'that for some members of a given ethnic population there exist serious "mobility traps", while for others ethnic identity may be of no consequence to mobility whatsoever. Still others may be able to translate their heritage into distinct occupational opportunities.' In other words, ethnicity can be both a resource and a drawback.

Darroch (1979:8–10) also re-examined Porter's 1931, 1941, and 1961 census data, using indexes of dissimilarity for each ethnic group. He found that in the 1931 data dissimilarity differences by ethnic group were considerable for all non-charter groups when compared to the national average. By 1961, however, these differences had almost disappeared for some groups (Germans and Eastern and Other Europeans) and had declined enormously for all but the Native Indians and Inuit. This would suggest that most non-European groups in Canada are rising considerably socioeconomically, compared to the national average.

Tepperman (1975:120–57) explicitly addresses Porter's thesis that some ethnic groups may have been locked into the ethnic statuses they held when they entered Canada, promoting immobility. He doubts that cultural separateness and economic assimilation are incompatible, saying that Canada imports immigrant talent at various levels of the occupational hierarchy. 'All immigrants but the most recent earn more than their native-born ethnic counterparts; Jews and Asiatics are the notable exception of this rule' (Tepperman, 1975:149). He suggests that some immigrant groups enter at higher levels to begin with, that some move faster than others, that some aspire to higher education than others, and that many are willing to enter new sectors of the economy while native Canadians often are not. Tepperman's findings seem to be in direct opposition to the claims of Porter.

EMPIRICAL STUDIES OF POWER AND STATUS

The literature review has suggested a number of interesting possible relationships between social class and ethnicity, and the theories also illustrate many outcomes and interpretations including much potential for conflict.

First, we examine Frederick Armstrong's (1981) study of the rise and formation of the Ontario establishment, the most powerful Anglo-Saxon economic and political force in Canada. Breton, Reitz, and Valentine (1980) review the literature on British-French charter-status relations. Peter Pineo's (1977) discussion of the social standing of ethnic groupings provides a good opportunity to see how ethnic groups rank with respect to social prestige. Fourth, Jeffrey Reitz's (1990) exploration of ethnic inequality, segregation, and control of jobs in Toronto shows considerable ethnic differentiation. Finally, Wsevolod Isajiw, Aysan Sev'er, and Leo Driedger's (1993) study of Toronto adults explores the relationship between ethnic identity and social mobility. These last two empirical studies deal largely with ethnicity in Toronto, the heartland of Canadian industrial power.

Formation of the Ontario Establishment

The 1759 defeat of the French on the Plains of Abraham adjoining Quebec City opened North America to British political dominance. Only a few years later, however, the American Revolution in 1776 took a large section of the colonial empire out of British hands, leaving only Canada as a British colony (Armstrong, 1981). United Empire Loyalists who remained loyal to the crown left the United States for Upper Canada (southern Ontario) beginning in 1784. Thus, the opportunity for the establishment of a British elite began over two hundred years ago.

Since southern Ontario is the heartland of Canada's industrial power, Frederick Armstrong (1981) sought to trace the historical formation of this economic power centred in York, which was renamed Toronto in 1834. By 1981 Toronto had emerged as the largest metropolitan centre in Canada with a population of 3.9 million. The census of 1842 is the first that shows the ethnic composition of southern Ontario. Of the 487,053 population, approximately one-half (247,665) were born as English Canadians and

another third (159,000) were born in the British Isles. Only about 5 per cent were French Canadian or originated in Europe, while the remainder did not report their ethnicity, or were born in the United States. At least 90 per cent were of British origin. Armstrong (1981:23) suggests that with the arrival of the first United Empire Loyalists in 1784, the consolidation of the elite began. The crucial element in gaining power in Upper Canada was the imperial connection with Britain, the colonizing power in Europe. The rulers were usually not Canadian, but representatives sent from Britain to control British interests. The first component of power was the Family Compact of Loyalists who had held important positions in the American colonies. The second component was imperial appointees, who, because of connections in Britain, were granted important political posts that were often perpetuated and kept in the family or among friends. Others, with connections with the governor appointed from England, got influential posts as part of a patronage system. Those who had served in the military were often in line for positions as well (Armstrong, 1981: 26–7). The wealthy were often favoured since they commanded respect and were influential because of their commercial success.

The defeat of the French in Quebec and the arrival of the United Empire Loyalists into new British territory meant that many political positions were available, the basis of creating a British colonial power structure. Many of these appointments were for life, and residency was not required. Plural office-holding was common, as was the tendency to follow hereditary lines in appointments (Armstrong, 1981:28). The office of Justice of the Peace was responsible for handling local and judicial cases, and the opportunity for promotion to higher courts and more responsible positions was always an attraction. With the British in power, and the vast majority of the population of British origin, these positions of power were held mostly by those of British ancestry. It should not be surprising that in the 1960s Porter still found the British heavily represented among the political and economic elite in Canada. The original British power networks have simply been perpetuated.

How did many become wealthy in this new country? The accumulation of land was a common source of wealth, and holding important political offices often helped to accomplish such acquisitions. Much land was available, and land was often paid as bonuses to officials or loyalists. In those days the landed gentry symbolized prestige. Many who held high rank in the military or in government were given special land grants to develop as they wished. Thus, the amassing of large estates was underway (Armstrong, 1981:129). Beyond acquiring wealth through political position and land acquisitions, commerce—and later finance and manufacturing—also provided opportunities. Later acquiring wealth through commerce was most common; some of the elite came to control vast financial empires.

In addition to public office, land, and wealth, there were secondary routes to advancements, such as family connections. The elite tended to intermarry to keep power and wealth within their family, and positions increasingly became hereditary until the oligarchy was entrenched. Armstrong (1981:30) cites 'the Hamiltons of Niagara, Queenston, Hamilton, Kingston and London' as a good example. The city of Hamilton was named after one of them. The Hamiltons were prominent in business, fur trading, and as senators, sheriffs, and magistrates appointed by the Legislature.

Education was another form of mobility open in the early days. Much of the education was in private schools catering to the elite. Religion also played an important role as the state Church of England tried to become dominant in the colonies. The church and its leaders often got special privileges.

The relations between the British ethnic divisions were interesting to observe. The English were initially the largest group and most directly connected with the imperial power; with few exceptions all governors were English (Armstrong, 1981:33). The Irish also formed a large group, but they were split into Catholics and Protestants each division with its own dynamics. The Protestant Irish arrived first, were well off and well connected, and made considerable progress in their quest for power. The Irish Catholics came later, when the power structure had already been formed; they were less well educated and became influential only later. The Scottish Protestants gained a great deal of power in the governance and commerce of the colony. They were early arrivals and worked hard, so they had a great deal of influence. Many Scots gained important political positions.

Armstrong (1981:35–6) concludes that a composite establishment of the British arose in Upper Canada with Toronto as its capital more than two hundred years ago. Various individuals gained power through colonial associations, wealth, education, and the right connections with centres of power. While the British as the senior charter-group partner consolidated their power, the French, as junior charter partners, were faced with less opportunity for power dominance.

Political Dominance of Charter Groups

Although the British establishment clearly developed in Ontario, to what extent do the two British and French charter groups share in the Canadian power relationships? In 1867 the British were almost twice as numerous as the French demographically. Since then the French have slipped to one-fourth, and the British to one-fourth of the single-response Canadian population so that the charter groups still represent half of all Canadians. Breton (1991:2–5) suggests that these charter groups behaved as ethnic political communities, with governance structures and ethnic politics. A study of the two groups' political representation is in order.

Breton and Roseborough (1980) show that the anglophones and francophones have lived separately in their own social circles and institutions in what they call segmentation. They analyze three dimensions (economic, political, and social) of English-French relations, showing that the French, segmented in Quebec with their dominant French language, are often pitted

TABLE 8.1 Years in Which Specified Ministries Were Headed by Representatives of Ethnic Groups, 1867–1966 (%)

Ministries	English	French	Scottish	Irish	Other	N
Policy-making ministries						
Prime Minister	51	23	24	2	–	100
Finance	78	–	4	18	–	100
Agriculture	49	11	27	13	–	100
Fisheries	39	33	23	5	–	100
Mines	33	20	38	3	5	60
Northern Affairs	53	18	29	–	–	17
Trade and Commerce	69	–	26	–	5	74
Transport	40	16	18	26	–	88
National Defence	55	18	18	9	–	100
External Affairs	91	3	–	5	–	58
Total	55	15	20	9	1	797
Human capital ministries						
Interior	60	–	14	25	–	63
Indian Affairs	59	4	16	20	–	69
Veteran Affairs/Health and Welfare	56	23	19	4	–	79
Labour	49	5	23	15	9	66
Immigration and Citizenship	36	44	8	44	3	–
Total	55	9	21	14	1	313
Support ministries						
National Revenue	36	22	15	24	3	145
Receiver General	42	33	–	25	–	12
National Defence	82	–	–	18	–	28
Post Office	34	45	3	18	–	100
Public Works	30	49	16	5	–	100
Total	37	34	11	17	1	385
Coordinative ministries						
President of Privy Council	54	32	11	3	–	91
Justice	31	25	25	19	–	100
Solicitor General	17	54	26	3	–	35
Secretary of State	31	39	–	30	–	100
Total	36	34	14	16	–	326
Ministries without portfolio	45	14	28	13	–	135

NOTE: Total number of years varies by ministry, since each has not lasted the same length of time.

SOURCE: Raymond Breton and Howard Roseborough, 'Ethnic, Religious and Regional Representation in the Federal Cabinet, 1867–1966'. Unpublished manuscript (Toronto: University of Toronto, 1980).

against the English in the rest of Canada. Using Breton and Roseborough's (1980:177–328) findings, let us explore the political differences.

Breton and Roseborough (1980) found that the charter groups did dominate the political elite, as demonstrated by those who headed the various political ministries from 1867 to 1966, shown in Table 8.1. Non-charter groups were hardly represented at all, while the British were heavily overrepresented in all categories during the entire hundred-year period. The British dominated the top policy-making and human capital ministries in particular. Among the policy-making ministries, they dominated consistently in finance, trade and commerce, and external affairs. During this time the French represented about 30 per cent of the Canadian population, but only in the ministry of fisheries were they sufficiently represented, and they were shut out entirely in finance and trade and commerce. French representation in the ministries of human capital was even lower than their representation in policy-making ministries. It is only in the supportive and coordinative ministries that the French were slightly overrepresented at 34 per cent. Non-charter Canadians were shut out of all coordinative ministries for a century and were only briefly represented in 7 of the 25 ministerial portfolios. Clearly, the British political elite have dominated the first century of Canada's political history; the French were underrepresented as junior charter partners, and others were practically unrepresented in the power elite. Unfortunately, we are not aware of similar studies of political influence since 1966.

British dominance of federal cabinet positions also shows in Table 8.2. The French were sufficiently represented during two periods (1927–30 and 1962–6), while other non-charter Canadians were shut out until 1927 and have been grossly underrepresented since. The French were more fairly represented in the House of Commons, but again they were usually underrepresented, although not as badly as in the cabinet (see Table 8.3). Other Canadians still remained very underrepresented.

Breton and Roseborough (1980) show that, while the French were overrepresented in the federal bureaucracy before 1900, for the next 75 years

TABLE 8.2 Years in Which Each Ethnic Group Was Represented in Canadian Cabinet by Political Party in Power, 1867–1966 (%)

Period	Party	English	French	Scottish	Irish	Other	Total Years
1867–1873	Lib.-Cons.	42	23	22	13	–	86
1874–1878	Lib.	52	30	10	8	–	63
1879–1896	Lib.-Cons.	44	21	13	23	–	255
1897–1911	Lib.	46	21	17	17	–	229
1912–1917	Cons.	46	16	0	38	–	108
1917–1921	Unionist	60	6	18	16	–	73
1922–1925	Lib.	27	27	27	20	–	75
1926	Cons.	71	–	14	14	–	7
1927–1930	Lib.	33	33	18	11	6	73
1931–1935	Cons.	43	16	31	11	–	95
1936–1956	Lib.	51	23	21	4	2	303
1957–1962	Cons.	60	14	9	13	5	133
1962–1966	Lib.	44	33	20	–	3	102

SOURCE: Breton and Roseborough, 'Ethnic, Religious and Regional Representation in the Federal Cabinet, 1867–1966'. Unpublished manuscript (Toronto: University of Toronto, 1980).

TABLE 8.3 Ethnic Origin of New Members of House of Commons by Period during Which First Elected, 1867–1964 (%)

Period	French	English	Scottish	Irish	Other	Total	N
1867–1873	24.9	31.5	26.2	14.5	2.8	99.9	317
1874–1877	25.3	16.5	35.2	22.0	1.1	100.1	91
1878–1895	27.2	25.3	23.5	20.9	3.1	100.0	383
1896–1899	24.8	23.9	26.5	20.4	4.4	100.0	113
1900–1910	20.5	26.9	26.9	22.4	3.2	99.9	308
1911–1929	21.7	26.2	29.7	19.5	2.9	100.0	512
1930–1939	30.8	24.2	27.9	14.6	2.5	100.0	240
1940–1953	28.7	32.3	22.5	11.6	4.9	100.0	387
1954–1958	31.3	30.8	15.9	12.6	9.3	99.9	214
1959–1964	48.1	29.1	13.3	5.1	4.4	100.0	158
Total % of Members of Parliament	27.0	27.6	24.9	16.6	3.8	99.9	
Total N	736	751	679	453	104		2,723

NOTE: Because of rounding of numbers, totals do not always correspond to sum of parts.
SOURCE: Ronald A. Manzer, *Canada: A Socio-Political Report* (Toronto: McGraw-Hill Ryerson, 1974).

(until 1975), they were grossly underrepresented. In 1946 French Canadians represented 29 per cent of the Canadian population, but only 13 per cent of the federal bureaucracy was French. During the last 40 years this inequity has been in the process of correction. By the 1970s, when Trudeau and his strong French ministers were in power, the French were better represented. There was a concerted attempt during the Trudeau era to bring the French Canadians to parity in most of these political elite categories, and for the most part it succeeded.

With some variations the charter-group political dominance is also evident in provincial politics. During the period 1961–73 in Quebec, most of the cabinet ministers were French, as expected, and there were a few ministers of British origin, with all the bureaucrats being French. In Ontario, this was reversed with 18 British and 1 French minister, and all the bureaucrats were of British origin; others were not represented at all, even though they represented 31 per cent of the Ontario population. British dominance of provincial government also continued in the West. While the British and others comprised equal numbers in the population (47 per cent), 10 ministers were British, and only 4 were non-charter, while all but 2 of the 24 bureaucrats were British. The same

was true in British Columbia, with the other non-charter Canadians grossly underrepresented.

John Samuel and Aly Karam (2000) have updated these employment equity figures somewhat for 1988–95, using Treasury Board Employment Equity in the Public Service data. They found that in 1988 1.7 per cent of aboriginals were employed in the public service and this had increased to 2.2 per cent in 1995, somewhat higher than their total national population share of 1.7 per cent. Visible minorities in the public service had increased from 2.9 per cent in 1988 to 4.1 per cent in 1995, which was still far below their 10 per cent share in the total population. Women in the public service had gone up from 42.9 per cent in 1988 to 47.4 per cent in 1995.

These findings corroborate the general findings of Porter that the British elite are dominant in political Canada, that the French are junior partners, and that others are hardly represented. During the past 20 years this has changed more in favour of the French and non-charter groups, but it is happening only slowly. Laponce (1994: 179–202) clearly shows that the British, French, and other ethnic groups have their distinctive voting patterns. Future research is needed to update trends into the 1990s, to see whether visible minorities are getting political positions. Rick Ogmundson (1990, 1992a, 1992b) has been following the continued presence of the British elite and generally says the Canadian pattern is in transition, with the Canadian elites becoming less exclusive.

Social Prestige of Ethnic Groups

We would expect that the British establishment, with its political power, would also translate this high profile into high social-prestige rankings, Breton's second dimension of social status.

To what extent do the French, the other charter group, have a similar social standing in the eyes of Canadians, and where do the other ethnic and racial groupings rank in comparison. Are distinctions made between the different racial and religious groups as well? The relative social standing of ethnic groups in Canada should give us some idea of their chances of upward mobility and treatment in Canada. What criteria do respondents use to judge social standing and see whether wealth, power, influence, heritage, colour, and length of residence influence prestige? We will look for correlations between ethnic and occupational prestige.

Peter Pineo (1977) made one of the best studies of the relative social standing of ethnic groups in Canada by comparing the ratings of English and French Canadians as well as English Canadians and Americans. Pineo and Porter (1967) took a national sample of 393 Canadians, asking them to sort the various ethnic groups in hierarchical order, placing the most prestigious at the top, and the less prestigious ones lower. They reported their findings, showing the differences in ranking between English and French Canadians, and compared these rankings with similar rankings made by ethnic groups in the United States. There are both similarities and important differences.

The general ranking of ethnic groups by Pineo's sample of Canadians placed the charter groups first, followed by western and northern Europeans, Mediterranean and central Europeans, and non-Caucasians at the bottom.

Americans tended to rank ethnic groups in the United States in a similar way. These general rankings seem to be similar and the categories are fairly similar; however, specific groups are ranked quite differently by Canadians in English and French Canada. Americans, however, tend to group all ethnic groups more closely together, making the differences between their prestige rankings of northern Europeans and non-Caucasians not nearly as great. Canadians tend to place the British much higher than the rest; as the British have had a greater and longer influence in Canada, this should not be a surprise.

In Table 8.4 we show the hierarchy of ethnic and racial groupings as seen by English and French Canadians using Pineo's data (1977). The differences are more obvious than the similarities. The French and English both ranked their own ethnic backgrounds highest at 74, and they both ranked non-Caucasians at the bottom, ranging from 24 to 35 in the bottom sixth of the hierarchy. English Canadians ranked the Japanese (35) and Chinese (33) a little higher than French Canadians did. Negroes (24) and Coloured (26) were ranked at the very bottom. Canadian Indians (28 and 33) were ranked almost at the bottom. Race seems to be an important factor in prestige and social standing.

The differences in rankings by English and French Canadians are most interesting. First, English Canadians rank English Canadians (83), the English (82), and the British (81) very high; French Canadians do not rank them nearly as high (78, 71, and 66 respectively). Others from the British Isles such as the Scots (75) and Irish (70) are also ranked highly by English Canadians; French Canadians rank them closer together in the middle (57 and 55 respectively). As expected, British origin is ranked highly; because they are the major charter group, they have socioeconomic and political power, and they were also the largest group.

French Canadians rank French Canadians and English Canadians highest (78) and equal in status; the English Canadians rank themselves much higher (83), and French Canadians (56) much lower. While French Canadians see the two

TABLE 8.4 Hierarchy of Ethnic and Racial Groups in English and French Canada

English Canada (N = 300)		French Canada (N = 93)
English Canadians (83.1)	83	
English (82.4)	82	
British	81	
	80	
	79	
	78	
	77	French Canadians, English Canadians
	76	Catholics (77.6)
Protestants (75.3) Scots (75.2)	75	
My own ethnic background (74.4)	74	My own ethnic background (73.7)
	73	
	72	French (72.4)
	71	English (71.0)
Catholics (70.1)	70	
Irish (69.5)	69	
	68	
	67	
	66	British (66.0)
	65	
	64	
	63	
	62	
	61	
French (60.1)	60	
	59	
Dutch (58.4)	58	
Swedes (56.6)	57	Scots (56.5)
French Canadians (56.1) Swiss (55.7)	56	
Norwegians (55.3)	55	Irish (55.2) Protestants (54.8)
	54	
	53	
Danes (52.4)	52	
	51	Italians (51.3)
People of Foreign Ancestry (50.1)	50	Dutch (49.7)
Austrians (49.6) Belgians (49.1)	49	
Germans (48.7) Finns (47.6)	48	
	47	
Jews (46.1) Icelanders (45.6)	46	
	45	Belgians (45.3) Swedes (44.8)
Ukrainians (44.3)	44	Swiss (44.4)
Italians (43.l) Hungarians (42.6)	43	Jews (43.10)
Poles (42.0) Romanians (42.1)	42	
Lithuanians (41.4)	41	
Czecho-Slovaks (41.2)		

TABLE 8.4 Hierarchy of Ethnic and Racial Groups in English and French Canada (continued)

English Canada (N = 300)		French Canada (N = 93)
Greeks (39.9)	40	Germans (40.5) Ukrainians (40.0)
	39	People of Foreign Ancestry (38,9)
	38	Hungarians (38.4) Poles (38.0)
	37	Norwegians (38.0) Austrians (37.5)
Russians (35.8)	36	
Japanese (34.7)	35	
	34	Romanians (33.9) Greeks (33.5)
Chinese (33.1)	33	Russians (33.1) Icelanders (32.9)
	32	Canadian Indians (32.5)
		Czecho-Slovaks (32.4)
	31	Finns (32.3)
	30	Danes (32.2)
	29	Lithuanians (29.1)
Canadian Indians (28.3)	28	Japanese (27.8)
	27	Coloureds (26.5)
Coloureds (26.3)	26	
Negroes (25.4)	25	Chinese (24.9) Negroes (23.5)

SOURCE: Peter Pineo, 'The Social Standing of Ethnic and Racial Groups', *Canadian Review of Sociology and Anthropology* 14 (1977):147–57.

charter groups (French 72 and English 71) as equal partners in status, English Canadians rank French Canadians (56) and the French (60) much lower among northern Europeans. The French actually rank a bit higher than French Canadians. English Canada does not seem to see the two charter groups on the same level (Pineo, 1977).

Interestingly, Catholics (78) are ranked highest—with the French and English Canadians—by French Canadians, and fairly high (70) by English Canadians as well, although they are ranked lower than those of British origin. English Canadians rank Protestants (75) somewhat higher than Catholics; French Canadians rank Protestants much lower in the middle (55). This seems to reflect the high and important status that the Roman Catholic Church has held in Quebec where the vast majority adhere to the Catholic Church; Protestants in Quebec are a very small minority. Since about one-half of all Canadians are Catholic, the Catholics are ranked generally high by all.

English Canadians rank northern Europeans in the middle with the French (60), Dutch (58), Swedes (57), French Canadians (56), Swiss (56), Norwegians (55), and Danes (52). Austrians (50), Belgians (49), and Germans (49) clustered in the fifties. French Canadians tend to rank northern Europeans in the forties. The Germans are at the bottom of the northern European pack, no doubt because of being the enemy during the two world wars (Pineo, 1977).

In the United States the Germans rank on top of the northern European cluster with the French, perhaps because there are so many Germans in the country. Southern and eastern Europeans usually rank after northern Europeans. English Canadians rank the Ukrainians (44), Italians (43), Hungarians (43), Poles (42), Romanians (42), Lithuanians (41), Czecho-Slovaks (41), and Greeks (40) in the forties and the lower middle. French Canadians follow this ranking with two exceptions: they rank the Italians higher (51) at the top of their northern European cluster and they rank the rest after northern Europeans, but generally lower in the thirties. Both groups rank the Russians (36 and 33) low, presumably because of the past cold war. Non-Caucasians rank below the Caucasians.

The Pineo (1977) study just presented (which is quite dated) does not provide us with the answer to why Canadians ranked these groups in the manner that they did. Unfortunately, no comparable recent work has been done. It does not show whether prestige is related to socioeconomic status, political power, size of group, racial biases and preferences, or simply because of familiarity with these groups. We need to document what importance socioeconomic status plays, for example, and this we can do in the next study of ethnic groups in Canada and Toronto.

SOCIOECONOMIC STATUS AND MOBILITY

The information on ethnic power and status provided by Armstrong, Breton, and Pineo leads us to ask whether the Anglo-Saxons who created the industrial concentration in southern Ontario and who also are clearly considered ethnics of the highest prestige actually have more control over education, occupations, and income—the three objective indicators usually used to measure socioeconomic status. Let us look first at comparative income data from the 1991 census, followed by a comparison of ethnic groups in Toronto, using the three socioeconomic indicators.

National Canadian Ethnic Incomes, 1981–91

Using the 1981 and 1991 Canadian National census data, we have ranked 20 ethnic groups by their 1991 annual average incomes in Table 8.5, and we have projected figures to 2001. The top 10 are all of European heritage, and most of them entered Canada a hundred or more years ago. The Jews rank first with average incomes of $72,000 which are more than twice as much as the $33,000 incomes of Latin Americans who rank lowest (Statistics Canada,

1993a). The British rank seventh, a drop from second rank in 1981. The other charter group, the French, do not rank in the top half.

The French charter group ranks in thirteenth place, clearly in the second half of Table 8.5, similar to where they ranked in 1981. The last third of the 20 listed are mostly non-white, so that income clearly separates visible minorities from the rest, many of whom have also come more recently. Aboriginal Peoples and recent Latin American immigrants earn half as much as Jews who rank first.

Comparing 1981 and 1991 rankings, we note that Italians have improved their rank most (from twelfth to tenth), and the British (from second to seventh) have dropped the most between 1981 and 1991. We need to look at other socioeconomic indicators as well.

Using 1994 Survey of Labour and Income Dynamics data, Ellen Gee and Steven Prus (2000) found that using the standard income, education, and occupation indicators of socioeconomic status, that the median total earnings of British men of $31,000 annually was highest, followed by other Europeans ($30,000), French ($29,000), visible Minorities ($24,000), and aboriginals ($22,000). Rankings were similar for British women ($20,000), down to $13,000 annual earnings for aboriginal women. Using higher education as a second indicator, Gee and Prus (2000:245) found that the status rankings were quite different, with 28 per cent of the visible minority men having earned at least a university degree, 19 per cent of the British, 17 per cent other European, 16 per cent French and 8 per cent aboriginals. Rankings of women were similar, with other Europeans (18 per cent) ranking highest, followed by visible minorities (18 per cent), the British (17 per cent), French (16 per cent), and aboriginals (5 per cent). Using a third indicator of occupational status, they found that 28 per cent of visible minority men were in the professions, followed by the British (22 per cent), the French (21 per cent), Other Europeans (18 per cent), and finally aboriginals (10 per cent). Again, the ranking was different for the women with the British highest (29 per cent), followed by

TABLE 8.5 Mean Wage Incomes of Canadian Employed Male Population Aged 20–60 by Ethnic Group, 1981–91

Ethnic Group	Annual Income		
	1981	1991	2001
Jewish	$ 19,054	$ 37,146	$ 72,000
Ukrainian	17,109	34,110	68,000
Other Single	15,510	31,927	65,000
German	16,887	31,506	60,000
Dutch	16,461	30,888	59,000
Multiple British/French	16,556	30,649	59,000
British	17,360	30,420	58,000
Multiple non British/French	16,190	29,928	57,000
Polish	17,095	29,656	57,000
Italian	15,588	29,550	57,000
Grand Mean	16,462	28,946	57,000
Other European	15,776	28,458	56,000
French	15,389	27,222	55,000
Portuguese	14,776	26,926	54,000
Chinese	14,120	26,392	53,000
South Asian	—	25,718	52,000
Other E/SE Asia	—	24,080	48,000
Black/Caribbean	14,442	23,346	46,000
Arab/West Asian	—	21,284	42,000
Aboriginal	—	18,779	38,000
Latin American C/S	—	16,460	33,000

SOURCE: The 1981 and 1991 Census of Canada Public Use Sample Tapes. The 2001 figures are projections.

other Europeans (28 per cent), visible minorities (26 per cent), French (24 per cent), and aboriginals (15 per cent). In summary, using all three indicators, aboriginals always ranked last, men consistently earned more than women, men and women varied on university degree status depending on ethnic status, and women consistently were in higher professions than men, except for the visible minorities. It is clear that the indicators used will influence rankings of ethnic socioeconomic status.

Gee and Prus (2000:252–3) conclude that 'Canada's vertical mosaic has been rearranged or transformed since the time of Porter's research'. Canada displays a 'racial divide' between whites and non-whites, especially in terms of income,

which supports Satzewich and Li's (1987) prediction that race will become more important than ethnicity in the twenty-first century in Canada. This is not the case for education. The racial divide operates more for men than women, also reported by Pendakur and Pendakur (1996) and Li (1999:2).

The differences in earnings between the Canadian-born and immigrant groups using the human capital approach have been well documented (Basavarajappa and Jones, 1999; Bloom, Grenier, and Gunderson, 1995; Boyd, 1992; Miller, 1992). Basavarajappa and Jones (1999: 238–47) published extensive annual mean incomes of Canadian-born and immigrant groups controlling for age, schooling, knowledge of languages, work activity, family size, marital status, religion, birthplace and much more. Basically, they found that Canadian-born non-visible minority males have an income advantage of 18 per cent over their visible minority counterparts; females had a 10 per cent advantage. They found that social mobility comes first in income, then education, and finally occupation. Since many visible minority persons have come to Canada more recently, it takes a while to position themselves so they can compete in all three income, education, and occupation areas. As immigrants, most of them had to have more education to come to Canada, so many have an advantage over the Canadian-born there.

Kazemipur and Halli (2000:107) found similar rankings using poverty rates. They found that more than 40 per cent of Arab and West Asian immigrants lived in poverty, while poverty rates for the Dutch (9 per cent) and British (12 per cent) were lowest. Usually non-immigrant poverty rates were lower. Ravi Verma and Kwok Bun Chan (2000) found similar economic trends for Asian immigrants. Piche, Renaud, and Gingras (1999) found the same in Quebec, and Basavarajappa and Jones (1999) found the same for visible minorities in Canada.

HIGHLIGHT 8.1 THE NEW POVERTY IN CANADA

While common to almost all industrial countries in the Western Hemisphere, the *new poverty* turned out to be more visible in North America (McFate, 1995). During the 1980s and the 1990s, the poverty rate of European countries remained mostly single digit, in clear contrast to the double-digit rates in North America (Danziger and Weinberg, 1994). Let's take Canada as an example. While in the 1980s, except for the recession years of 1983 and 1984, the poverty rate of Canadian families had remained relatively stable and even declined towards the end of the decade (12.1 per cent in 1990, compared to 13.2 per cent in 1980) (National Council of Welfare, 1992:11), this rate rose to 15.8 per cent in 1991 and 16.3 per cent in 1996. In the United States, likewise, the poverty rate was higher in 1993 than in 1973 (Danziger and Weinberg, 1994:18). These poverty rates were high, not only relative to what they had been in the early 1970s, but also relative to what analysts expected and to what they were in other countries with similar standards of living (Danzier and Weinberg, 1994).

Along with the increase in the level of poverty, the racial and ethnic cleavages hardened across the industrial world (Lawson and Wilson, 1995). Some even considered this development to be a result of the increased poverty, arguing that, in an age of shrinking resources, ascribed characteristics such as race, ethnicity, language, and religion might play important roles in the process of resource allocation (Hettne, 1995). The fact that poverty has hit certain racial and/or ethnic minorities harder corroborates that this possibility is not far from reality (hence, the concept of the *racialization* of poverty). In the United States, for instance, while poverty has affected all economically marginal groups, Lawson and Wilson (1995:693) argue 'the urban black poor have been particularly devastated'. They contend that a similar linkage between race or minority status and social exclusion and deprivation has also become increasingly evident in Western Europe. . . .

SOURCE: A. Kazemipur and S. Halli, *The New Poverty in Canada* (Toronto: Thompson Educational Publishing, 2000). Reprinted by permission.

TABLE 8.6 Ethnic Group Means and Socioeconomic Status Using Indices

Ethnic Groups	Composite SES Rank	Education (years)	SES Indices Overall Income (Dollars)	Occupational Status (Blishen)
Jewish	1			
Men		14.2	12,860	51.4
Women		13.9	8,735	49.9
English	2			
Men		13.0	13,481	51.1
Women		12.6	10,017	48.7
Chinese	3			
Men		14.6	12,391	50.4
Women		13.0	10,333	46.1
German	4			
Men		12.8	13,132	46.5
Women		12.8	9,652	48.0
Ukrainian	5			
Men		12.7	12,522	45.3
Women		12.5	10,317	47.3
Italian	6			
Men		10.6	12,278	40.2
Women		11.4	8,840	43.7
West Indian	7			
Men		11.5	12,329	41.4
Women		11.4	8,800	38.9

SOURCE: Aysan Sev'er, W.W. Isajiw, and Leo Driedger, 'Anomie as Powerlessness: Sorting Ethnic Group Prestige, Class and Gender', *Canadian Ethnic Studies* 25 (1993):84–99.

Ethnic Socioeconomic Status in Toronto

John Porter thought the British elite clearly led the way in socioeconomic and political power, and that Canadians of other ethnic backgrounds would need to play down their distinctive ethnicities if they wanted to keep up. Let us look at Toronto, the largest metropolitan centre in Canada, to gain a socioeconomic perspective using education, occupation, and income indicators.

Raymond Breton and associates (1990) collected a sample of 2,338 adults of 10 ethnic groups in Toronto to look at socioeconomic factors. This sample included the English (N of 343), Irish (78), Scottish (76), Germans (321), Ukrainians (354), Italians (351), Jews (348), Portuguese (164), Chinese (153), and West Indians (150). Breton and colleagues compared educational, occupational, and income status, which varied considerably.

In Table 8.6 we have collapsed some of the Toronto data published by Sev'er, Isajiw, and Driedger (1993). We have ranked the 7 ethnic groups by a composite rank that includes a summary of ethnic rankings on education, occupation, and income. Males and females have been controlled for comparison as well. First, we note in general that the Jewish and Majority Canadians rank on top, and the West Indians, and Italians at the bottom.

Comparing the education of males on the three socioeconomic status indicators, Chinese and Jews rank first, while Italians rank last. The other groups tend to be in the middle. West

Indians have a fairly high educational status that is somewhat deviant from their overall socioeconomic ranking. The rankings for females are quite similar to those of the males.

Using Blishen occupational status scores, we find that Jews rank the highest, with the English close behind; Italians and West Indians are at the bottom. Females all rank lower than males in their respective groups, and in most cases the differences are considerable. Italian and West Indian female incomes are very low.

Sev'er, Isajiw, and Driedger (1993) show that ethnic females' status compares well with males on education and least well on income. The range of differences between ethnic groups is enormous; Jews and English Canadians are on top, while the most recent immigrants such as West Indians and Italians are clearly at the bottom of the socioeconomic hierarchy. This may be because they came from poor countries and have not yet had the opportunity to rise in status. More study is required to plot the social mobility of the various ethnic groups to see how they fare over the generations. West Indians are a visible minority.

John Porter feared that if ethnic groups did not shed their ethnic identity, their distinctiveness would keep them from competing in the job market, leaving them in lower-status occupational ghettos. Reitz (in Breton et al., 1990) explored ethnic occupational segregation in Toronto and found, for example, that Italians were usually employed as brick and stone masons (16.8 on index of concentration), barbers and hairdressers (14.4), labourers and construction workers (12.6), plasterers (11.4), and excavation workers (6.0). Jews were concentrated in medicine (10.2), fabric and textiles (8.0), law and notary work (7.9), and as physicians and surgeons (6.0). Others who ranked above a concentration of 5.0 were the Portuguese in labour and construction (9.2), the Chinese in restaurants (5.3), and the British in firefighting (5.0). These data do show that individuals of some ethnic groups concentrate in certain jobs more than others; the Italians and Jews especially did so, representing opposite ends of the socioeconomic scale.

In his own study, Reitz (1982:7) concludes that 'these considerations raise doubts about the extent to which the theory of majority group control can adequately explain all the important variations in allocations of occupational rewards among ethnic and racial groups. Ethnic status does not seem to correlate sufficiently with reward allocation, and it is difficult to explain many of the discrepant cases where they can hardly be attributed to conformity to the larger Canadian culture.' Reitz (1982:9) suggests that ethnic businesses, for example, may serve the clientele of their own ingroup; as a business flourishes, however, it often expands to include customers of the larger population, thus becoming oriented to a more general market. In his analysis, Reitz concludes that anglo-conformity in jobs is hard to document, and although this influence may apply for some groups, it clearly does not for others.

Social Mobility: Ethnicity as a Resource

Isajiw and Driedger (1987) used the same sample of 2,338 adults of 10 ethnic groups in Toronto that Reitz used to explore the relationship between ethnicity and social mobility. Like Van den Berghe, they assumed that ethnicity and class are two different, analytically distinct phenomena, with neither derived from the other. Isajiw and Driedger used ethnic identity scales to measure salience of ethnicity and used income, education, and occupation as socioeconomic indicators to measure social class. They found that Jews, Majority Canadians, and the Chinese cluster in the top socioeconomic status (SES) category; the Germans and Ukrainians rank intermediately; and the Italians, West Indians, and Portuguese cluster in the lowest category for both genders. The Majority Canadian, German, Jewish, and Chinese males attained the highest number of years of schooling (14); the Portuguese (6 years) and Italians (8 years) average the lowest number of years in formal education. The mean income range was not as great for males, but some females (West Indian) earned less than half as much as Jewish females. English Other,

Jewish, and Ukrainian males earn the most, while West Indians and the Portuguese earn the least. The income extremes for both males and females tended to correlate with the high- and low-education clusters as well. The Chinese, Majority Canadians, and Jewish males showed the highest mean job status, while the Portuguese, Italians, and West Indians clustered in the lowest status category.

Isajiw, Sev'er, and Driedger (1993) plotted the socioeconomic mobility of 5 groups (Italians, Ukrainians, Germans, Jews, and the British) beginning with the occupational Blishen scores of the fathers of first-generation respondents and, finally, the Blishen scores of third-generation respondents. Occupational mobility for the 5 groups varied considerably. The extent of mobility between the mean status of the fathers, and the mean status of first-generation respondents varied considerably. It was the greatest for the Italians and Ukrainians, and the least for the Germans. The mobility from first to third generation also varied considerably; it was greatest for Italians and lowest for Jews.

The data showed considerable variation in social mobility between ethnic groups. Isajiw, Sev'er, and Driedger (1993) also explored the direct relationship between ethnic identity and social mobility. They compared degrees of ethnic identity (ECI index) with the respondent's perception of his own social mobility (comparing his own job with the job his father had held while the respondent grew up). They found little correlation between occupational mobility and ethnic identity for the total sample, nor was there any significant correlation when they controlled for the six levels of socioeconomic status (using the Blishen scale) and perceived mobility (see Table 8.7).

The percentages in Table 8.7 show that while roughly two-thirds of the very low and low respondents perceived that they held higher status jobs than their father, about three-fourths of the very high and high-status jobholders thought they were more upwardly mobile. This does not vary by ethnic identity. Isajiw, Sev'er, and Driedger (1993) also controlled for three generations and the results were the same. These findings led them to reject Wiley and Porter's hypothesis. Isajiw, Sev'er, and Driedger concluded, first, that the 8 ethnic groups do not all begin with the same degree of ethnic identity. First-generation West Indians scored highest, while the Germans scored lowest. First-generation ethnic identity ranged from high to medium depending on the group. We cannot assume that all first-generation immigrants start off with high identity scores. Second,

TABLE 8.7 Ethnic Origin Groups and Their Ethnic Cultural Identity (ECI) Using Six Indicators

Respondents' Occupational Status (Blishen Scale) %	ETHNIC CULTURAL IDENTITY INDEX (ECI)						Pearson's r Total
	0	1	2	3	4	5	
Very High	79	88	85	67	100	–	–.07
High	79	84	89	73	88	50	–.04
Medium High	71	75	78	74	71	55	.01
Medium Low	67	66	79	71	70	79	–.04
Low	68	70	66	76	73	76	–.02
Very Low	65	55	70	70	65	61	.00
Total	72	73	78	72	72	68	–.02

the 8 ethnic groups did not all begin at the same socioeconomic level when they arrived as first-generation immigrants. Indeed, their socioeconomic status ranged from very high (the Jews) to very low (the Portuguese). Whereas first-generation Jews because of their high status had limited room for upward mobility, the Portuguese could theoretically move from lowest to highest status.

HIGHLIGHT 8.2 REFUGEE RESETTLEMENT

Although many persons experience dislocation of one kind or another, the experience of refugees is perhaps more extreme than most. According to Tepper, 'refugees are not immigrants, people who voluntarily depart from their homelands to seek a better life. They are emergencies: the homeless, the stateless, the dispossessed' (Tepper, 1980:5). Situations which give rise to refugee movements are generally precipitated by traumatic events such as political upheaval, ideological purges or physical deprivation. Departures are often abrupt and frequently difficult. Refugees seldom have the opportunity to select their final destination and are seldom cognizant of it when they depart. Many are unable to bring material resources with them and often arrive with only the clothes they are wearing. They are seldom able to return to their country of origin or have family and friends visit them. Most experience considerable family disruption, and communication with those left behind is often difficult or impossible. These problems are compounded because refugees, especially in recent times, usually come from countries significantly different from the countries of resettlement. Compared to immigrants, refugees are less prepared for the resettlement process. They maintain a greater commitment to their country of origin and often hope to return to it, no matter how unrealistic such hopes may be. . . .

These participants (studied by Higgitt, 2000) were ethnic Vietnamese (16) and ethnic Chinese (8) men who arrived in Winnipeg from Vietnam between 1975 and 1988. They fled Vietnam primarily to avoid communism and the effects of war. The majority came from Saigon or from small villages surrounding the city. They ranged in age from 22 to 50 years. Almost half (11) were married and living with their spouses, who were either ethnic Vietnamese or ethnic Chinese, except for one who was a Canadian-born Caucasian. One participant was waiting to be reunited with his spouse and another was cohabiting with a female partner. The others were single. Almost all had been separated involuntarily from extended family members. Escape experiences varied but most had suffered some degree of trauma and hardship. Very few participants knew any English on arrival.

Although it was common for participants to live in extended families in Vietnam, their households in Winnipeg were more varied. Three lived in extended family units. Nine lived in nuclear family units consisting of couples with or without children. Nine lived in survival units structured to facilitate the sharing of resources with nonfamily members and three lived in single units. Several participants resided in houses owned by them; however, the majority lived in modest apartments in the central area of the city. Most homes were modestly or sparsely furnished.

Nine participants were employed as blue collar workers and five had white collar jobs. Seven were students and three depended on social assistance. . . .

SOURCE: Nancy Higgitt, 'A Model of Refugee Resettlement' in L. Driedger and S.S. Halli (eds), *Race and Racism* (Kingston and Montreal: McGill-Queen's University Press, 2000). Reprinted by permission.

In the third place, the degree of maintenance of ethnic identity through three generations also varied greatly. Jewish identity remained high with very little change, while Italian identity changed enormously from among the highest to the lowest in three generations. Italians in Toronto were assimilating quickly, while Jews were not.

Finally, Isajiw, Sev'er, and Driedger found that socioeconomic mobility also varied considerably. Since the Jews began on a very high status level when they arrived in Canada, their descendants had very little opportunity for upward mobility. The same was true for the British, who actually dropped slightly by the third generation. Italians ranked low on socioeconomic status. Their opportunities for upward mobility were enormous, and they became the most mobile. These general observations show that the issues of ethnic identity and social mobility are multidimensional, multidirectional, and vary considerably by generations. Starting points vary, and the degree of change from their original identity and status positions vary considerably.

We conclude that class and ethnicity are different phenomena, and each can be a resource or a drawback, depending on social conditions.

SUMMARY

John Porter's work, *The Vertical Mosaic*, outlined two major perspectives: the functional inequality theory, and the radical Marxist theory of social class. The functional theory of stratification, popular with many Americans, assumes that inequality is inevitable where the more able and more trained get higher-status jobs in the process of market competition. Marxists think that the social class system is unjust and unacceptable. Marx and neo-Marxists tend to think that ethnicity is only one variation of the class struggle and give ethnic and race relations little attention.

John Porter also tended to see social class as the major factor of change in the industrial Canadian society, with the majority of power allotted to the two charter groups. The British, being larger numerically, more dominant politically and economically, and having the benefits of the British colonial heritage on their side, have a great advantage over the French, who are junior partners. Ethnic groups who migrated to Canada later were relegated to entrance status, and were faced with fitting into a Canada defined and controlled by the two charter peoples. Porter's empirical studies supported his contention that the British were in the economic, political, and status power positions. Other scholars have contended that social mobility is possible, especially in the socioeconomic area, and that maintenance of ethnic identity need not be a drawback for social mobility; indeed, it may be an asset.

Five empirical studies were examined to illustrate the theoretical discussion. Frederick Armstrong illustrated how the British establishment was formed in Ontario and linked with the British colonial power to attain political and economic power positions, an advantage which the French and others did not have. Thus, southern Ontario has become the Canadian industrial heartland, the most powerful centre of Canada.

Raymond Breton shows that the British have always been politically dominant and that the French—although politically involved—have usually been underrepresented politically. Noncharter Canadians have hardly been represented.

In Peter Pineo's study of the social standing of the various ethnic groups in Canada, the British ranked highest, followed by northern Europeans, eastern and southern Europeans, and finally at the lowest level of prestige, non-Caucasian social minorities. This study clearly shows that the prestige of the various ethnic groups in Canada varies enormously.

Reitz's study of the education, income, and occupations of 8 ethnic groups in Toronto demonstrated that the prestige rankings found by Pineo can indeed be substantiated empirically. Again the English rank on top and West Indians at the bottom; the Chinese and Germans are higher on the socioeconomic scale than in their prestige ranking. This study helps show the importance of socioeconomic status in prestige rankings. Isajiw, Sev'er, and Driedger used the same Toronto sample to show the extent to which socioeconomic status and ethnic identity are related. They found that identity and status vary by groups, that some groups move up faster than others, and that ethnicity and status are both independent factors that need to be considered separately.

Using our model, presented in Chapter 2, we find that when the various populations enter the economic and political areas (Cell A), where they all have to make a living interacting with each other, the British (Cell B) who are the largest group demographically (often with the most income, education, and most prestigious occupations), will be able to compete better than many others. The visible minorities (Cell D) who often represent smaller groups, many of whom are more recent immigrants, live in poorer neighbourhoods, being of lower socioeconomic status, and will find it much harder to compete for good jobs that pay more. Many white Europeans (Cell B) who have been here longer, have learned the languages better and have attained more education, can compete better with the dominant British, and a few will even gain enough status to get elected to political power. Marx a century ago thought too strongly that the political economy was the master metanarrative that created conflict between the haves and have-nots that neo-Marxists have recognized. So postmoderns are an important corrective, to help us see that these processes are much more diverse, that change is not as linear as some think, and that there are multiple narratives, not just one. We need to explore other factors involved in the process of stratification, which we turn to in the next two chapters.

CRITICAL THINKING QUESTIONS

1. Identify class as Functional Inequality and the Radical Marxian class perspectives.

2. What was John Porter's major thesis in his *The Vertical Mosaic*? Compare charter-group and entrance-group status.

3. How does the Ontario establishment fit into Porter's scheme? Do both the British and French charter groups have equal status, and how do they share power?

4. Compare the data in Tables 8.1, 8.2, and 8.3, and compare the political power of the charter groups in Canada.

5. What is the difference between social prestige and social status?

6. Using socioeconomic indicators such as education, income, and occupations, how do ethnic groups in Canada tend to rank? Is ethnicity a resource or a drag on attaining status?

SUGGESTED READINGS

Curtis, James, Edward Grabb, and Neil Guppy (eds), *Social Inequality in Canada*, 2nd ed. (Toronto: Prentice-Hall, 1993). This is a collection of 37 essays that focus on power, class, socioeconomic status, and the consequences of social inequality.

Fleras, Augie, and Jean Leonard Elliott, *Unequal Relations: An Introduction to Race, Ethnic, and Aboriginal Dynamics in Canada*, 3rd edn (Toronto: Prentice-Hall, 1999). A text showing the diversity of Canada's peoples in a multicultural setting where unequal relations abound.

Porter, John, *The Vertical Mosaic* (Toronto: University of Toronto Press, 1965). This is the earliest classic study of economic and political power in Canada, with important treatment of the place of ethnicity.

CHAPTER 9

Apartheid:
Segregation of Minorities

Anthony Richmond, in *Global Apartheid* (1994), suggests that refugees, racism, and the new world order are integrally tied up with social and spatial segregation of peoples:

> The word apartheid literally means 'apart-hood' (cf. neighbor-hood), that is, the separation of people into different areas. . . . From a sociological perspective, these are all actions, structures, and institutions associated with forcible isolation of people who are different. Because of the differences, they are perceived as having actually (potentially) conflicting relationships. Distancing is used to deal with the conflict. When separation is imposed by a dominant group upon a less powerful one, the conflict is only temporarily resolved. Restitution and retribution may be delayed for generations, but the power struggle continues . . . (Richmond, 1994:206).

The principle of separation as a means of social control has a long history in Canada: witness the expulsion of the Acadians from the Maritimes in 1756, the separation of Upper and Lower Canada, the creation of Indian reserves, the formation of separate Catholic and Protestant school systems, and the separation of racial groups.

Power, status and socioeconomic factors tend to segment the rich from the poor, the educated from the illiterate, and white-collar from blue-collar occupational groups. While much of this differentiation seems to follow lines of socioeconomic status, it is clear that recent immigrants and visible minorities are heavily represented among the have-nots. While structural functionalists may see such differences as 'natural' differentiation that will always remain with us, political economy advocates see this as an ongoing source of conflict that must be solved. For good or for ill, social and spatial ethnic residential segregation are means of 'apartheid'.

PERSPECTIVES ON SEGREGATION

The early Chicago sociologists were interested in the ecological segregation of humans in cities. They wanted to plot the spatial arrangements of humans by race, culture, occupation, religion, and the like. Some of these human spatial patterns where segregation happened voluntarily were influenced by political power, but other patterns occurred involuntarily because of coercion. Let us discuss two perspectives on how human ecological segregation may be studied.

Duncans' Zonal Segregation Model

Two well-known models, one developed by the Duncans (1957) and the other by Shevky and Bell (1955; Driedger, 1991), examine urban residential segregation. The Duncans' (1957) model is oriented to social class as the major factor that determines where people live in the city, based on the concentric zone theory of urban growth. The Duncans assume that the lower-class residents live close to the centre where the oldest, cheapest housing is located because socioeconomic status rises towards the outer zones. The Duncans predict that the higher-status families such as the British, other northern Europeans, and Jews will live in the suburbs, and recent immigrants from low-status, non-white racial groups will live near the centre. The Duncans used occupational mobility data as the basis for their study. Much work was devoted to social rank. The Duncans' model is based on the concentric zone model developed by Burgess in Chicago.

Ernest Burgess attempted to order and predict growth patterns of a city, using Chicago as his laboratory. Burgess thought Chicago had grown like a tree, with concentric circles growing around a centre where the main business district was located. These circles grew ever larger as they expanded towards the periphery. Burgess suggested that each of these zones had a different land usage. *The Central Business District* is the innermost zone, the oldest business section; here business first began when the city was small. This concentration of business, commerce, and services meets the needs of downtown shoppers.

The Second Zone of Transition surrounds the business district and is often referred to as the slum. This zone still contains the oldest housing of the early days of the city, housing which has begun to deteriorate, and which is in the immediate path of business and industrial expansion. This area tends to be heavily populated by lower income classes, by Old World immigrants, recent immigrants, racial groups, and social outcasts. Burgess called it the zone of transition because the people living there were often transient, and the housing would soon be demolished to make room for business expansion (Driedger, 1991, 1999b; McGahan, 1995).

The Zone of Workingmen's Homes is the third zone moving out towards the periphery. In fact zones two to five were all residential zones, with the oldest and least desirable housing in zone two and the best housing located in zone five. *The Zone of Middle Class Dwellers,* even farther out

from the centre, consists of professional, small business, managerial, and clerical people. *The Commuters' Zone* is on the outer periphery of the city, often beyond its political boundaries, consists of satellite towns and suburbs that exist in a mutually dependent relationship with the metropolis, as 'bedroom communities'.

In their study, *The Negro Population of Chicago*, the Duncans plotted the distribution of blacks in Chicago in 1920, 1930, 1940, and 1950, using census tract data. The Black Belt, which began between 10th and 40th streets in 1920, spread westwards and extended southwards to 70th street by 1950; it was 99 per cent black. The Duncans preferred to think in zonal terms and tried to fit the Black Belt phenomenon into socioeconomic (income, education, occupation) patterns, directing their attention to invasion and succession trends, thinking that the larger racial patterns had resulted from these trends; more recent immigrants who were non-white and poor would replace older groups who had moved to better places. The Duncans focused on crowding, education, unemployment, home ownership, and rental costs, all of which were socioeconomic factors. While the Duncans were busy looking at blacks in Chicago in socioeconomic terms, trying to fit the racial patterns into the zonal model of Burgess, Shevky and Bell were beginning to follow the multiple nuclei perspective—to predict racial and ethnic patterns.

Shevky and Bell's Multiple Nuclei Model

Shevky and Bell (1955), in their studies of Los Angeles and San Francisco, were able to break out of past thinking based on the zonal theory and to pursue the multiple nuclei theory proposed by Harris and Ullman (McGahan, 1995). Duncan (1955:84–5) recognized their novel, comparative approach and the opportunities it provided for both economic and social research; however, he severely criticized their conceptual framework and their methodological measures. It is true that their methods could have been improved, but their multiple nuclei conceptual framework offered many possibilities, which others have since used with considerable success.

In 1945 Chauncey Harris and Edward Ullman developed another theory that suggested that as a city grew it diversified considerably, and land use diversified as well (Harris and Ullman, 1945). They agreed that a city will begin with a major central business district (CBD), which is an important sector in most cities. This central district however, developed along locational, cultural, and economic lines that the concentric zone theory often did not explain.

> For example, while wholesale and light manufacturing (2) . . . might be near the CBD, low-income residences (3) might be in various separate districts around it. A medium-income residential district (4) might abut the CBD and be bordered on its outer edge by a high-income residential area (5). Between the two might exist a secondary business district (7), and farther out might exist a completely separate residential suburb (8). Heavy manufacturing (6) might be a relatively large distance from the CBD and evolve an industrial-residential suburb (9) near it (Spates and Macionis, 1987:175.)

Why did these more complex patterns develop? Dealing with zones seemed too rigid, especially when the specific land uses were being more carefully considered. Another reason for differentiation of land use is that the various activities are not always compatible and therefore separate themselves into nuclei some distance from each other. Residential and industrial areas become separated and this separation is reinforced by zoning laws.

Third, different racial and ethnic groups such as South Asians and Sikhs may enter a city and begin to concentrate in one area where a cluster of businesses provide specialized foods and clothing, and then become a node attracting more immigrants of the same cultural background.

Fourth, people want to separate themselves for economic and social class reasons. Some can afford only older and less expensive housing and tend to look for the cheapest residential areas. Others can afford newer or better housing and pay more attention to prestige and status, often escaping to the suburbs. Suburbanites also try to locate close to traffic beltways that will permit easy commuting to their work. Industrial suburbs may spring up close to the industries in which blue-collar workers are employed, saving transportation costs as well as traffic hassles (Driedger, 1991, 1999b; McGahan, 1995).

Basically, Harris and Ullman (1945) suggested in their multiple nuclei theory that land use can not always be predicted. Historical, cultural, and socioeconomic values will have differing impacts on cities, and the exact location of an economic or ethnic nucleus cannot be determined for all cities. The formation of these nuclei depends on a variety of factors—topographical, historical, cultural, racial, economic, and political—that do not result in the same combination for each urban area. The Burgess zonal pattern suggested inevitable predetermined patterns of location. Harris and Ullman suggest that these patterns vary depending on circumstances.

By using factor analysis, Shevky and Bell could incorporate and control for more variables. In addition to their three factors of social rank, family status, and ethnicity, Shevky and Bell (1955) developed indices of isolation and segregation that others have found useful (Driedger, 1980b). Shevky and Bell (1955:44) defined ecological isolation as 'the residential concentration of the members of a particular group with other members of the same group'. Their segregation ratio was used to measure a second dimension of interaction, involving the probable interaction between members of a subordinate ethnic group with members of all other subordinate groups in the metropolis. The reasoning here was that minorities within spatial enclaves or minorities in proximity to each other could band together to strengthen their specific interests when negotiating with majority groups. Shevky and Bell's approach is helpful because it shows that ethnicity is an independent influence on spatial location, and results in ethnic nuclei that do not necessarily conform to zonal or sector patterns.

Dawson's Segregation in Montreal

Carl Dawson began his studies at the University of Chicago in 1914, where he also worked with Robert Park (Shore, 1987:xiv). Like many in the Chicago School, Dawson saw the city as a social organism. Dawson went to teach at McGill University in 1922, Montreal was exploding with activity and growth; by 1928 it had at least 1,400 industries, stockyards, and packing houses, so Dawson and his students were among the first in Canada to categorize minorities according to the Burgess concentric zone model learned in Chicago. In 1929 Dawson and Gettys (1929:130) published some of the patterns of growth they had discovered in Montreal; these are shown in Figure 9.1.

Dawson was mostly interested in describing the general growth pattern of Montreal and the extent to which it conformed to the Chicago concentric zone model. He made 'no attempt to account for . . . the division of the city, straight through the centre, into French and anglophone groups' (Shore, 1987:136). Examination of Dawson and Gettys' drawing of Montreal in Figure 9.1 shows that indeed the English are clearly located in the west, segregated by Mount Royal from the French. Immigrants from other countries—Negroes, Italians, Russians, and Chinese—are concentrated near the central business section between the English and French solitudes. Dawson's students later began to examine the effects of transportation lines on population patterns, and the location of ethnic groups such as blacks, Chinese, Italians, and recent immigrants in the city.

Mount Royal dominates Montreal ecologically, so that the concentric zone pattern could not unfold like it did in Chicago (where, by the way, Lake Michigan also interrupts a full circle). Thus, the second image in Figure 9.1 is skewed and distorted out of shape. This suggests that the landscape and topography tend to influence the shape of spatial urban development as it did in Los Angeles where Shevky and Bell did their first study of multiple nuclei, and San Francisco where

hills, bays and coastlines play a similar shaping role. However, Dawson did find blacks in the second zone of transition in the oldest residential section next to downtown in zone two. Since then many other immigrants have come to Montreal, so that it has become a complex mosaic of ethnic and racial groups that resemble the multiple nuclei model (Lazar and Douglas, 1993).

Ethnic Concentration in Winnipeg

One of the simplest ways of plotting ethnic concentrations is to take the Canadian census data and see to what extent persons of one or several groups tend to be concentrated in one area of the city. Driedger and Church (1974) did extensive studies of ethnic groups in Winnipeg, tracing their concentration, segregation, and isolation using 1941, 1951, 1961, and 1971 census data. Their studies showed that the French were concentrated in St Boniface on the east side of the Red River since the early 1800s, the East Europeans were concentrated in the North End (Jews, Ukrainians, Poles) since the late 1800s, and the British were concentrated heavily in the western and southern parts (St James, St Charles, Fort Garry) of the city. As new immigrants arrived, these concentrations have shifted with Jews and some Ukrainians moving out of the North End into the suburbs.

To illustrate some of the recent clusters of ethnic concentration in Winnipeg we present 1991 census data in Figure 9.2 showing four very interesting ethnic concentrations that represent a wide range of variations. The French are still very heavily concentrated in their original St Boniface area where they have now resided for nearly 200 years shown in map A. A hundred years after the East Europeans settled in the Winnipeg North End, we see that many of the Polish Winnipeggers, reinforced by new recent immigrants, are still concentrated in parts of the North End (map B). These were among the early white European immigrants who have been in Winnipeg for a long time, and they are still concentrated in their original separate areas.

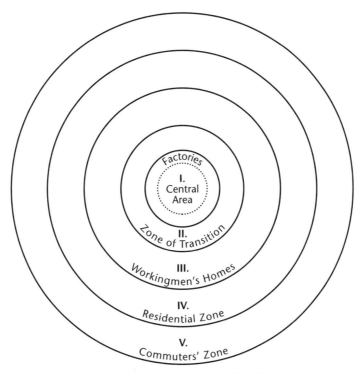

Ideal Concentric Zone Pattern of Urban Expansion

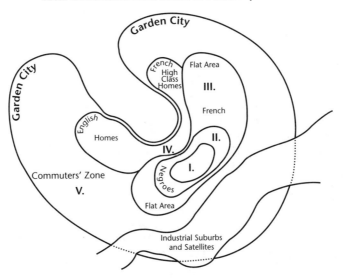

FIGURE 9.1 Dawson's Study of Segregation Patterns in Montreal

SOURCE: Dawson and Gettys, *Introduction to Sociology* (1929), p. 130.

FIGURE 9.2 Ethnic Concentration in Winnipeg, 1991

SOURCES: Statistics Canada, *Ethnic Origin: The Nation*, Catalogue 93–315, and *Home Language and Mother Tongue*, *The Nation*, Catalogue 93–317.

More recently, visible minorities have come to Winnipeg, and they have settled in the inner city (Driedger, 1996, 1999b). The Filipinos (map C) are concentrated in the west end of Winnipeg, just west of the central business district, in Burgess's zone of transition, as well as in the northwest corner near the airport which is also in commercial-industrial transition. Nine percent of Winnipeg's population are aboriginal (map B), the largest population in any metropolitan centre in Canada, and they have moved to the city from northern reserves and areas into the very centre of the city. This is the oldest part of the city, and the least desirable housing located near the central business district and the Canadian Pacific Railway tracks.

These four maps using 1991 census data, show that these four ethnic groups are concentrated in quite different areas. Two white European groups (French and Polish) who have stayed in their original respective areas for a long time, and two visible minority groups (Filipino and aboriginal), who have occupied different inner city areas more recently. Race, social class and immigrant status are important factors that separate these groups, in a multinuclear way as Shevky and Bell predicted.

ETHNIC RESIDENTIAL CONCENTRATIONS

To what extent have the Duncan and Shevky and Bell approaches to research on segregation been applied to Canadian cities? Stanley Lieberson and T.R. Balakrishnan, have done the most work in a national context. Anthony Richmond (1972a) was among the first to focus on segregation in Toronto, and Driedger and Church (1974) did the same in Winnipeg. How have other factors influenced residential segregation in Canadian cities?

National Urban Diversity

Stanley Lieberson (1970) was one of the first sociologists to study residential segregation in Canadian cities; he focussed especially on lan-guage. He used a slightly modified form of the segregation index proposed by Bell (1954), and worked with census data. Comparing 13 metropolitan centres in Canada, he found that there was a considerable correlation between residential segregation and retention of the French language. A score of 1.0 on the index means that the correlation between residential segregation and language maintenance are perfect; a score of 0.0 means that there is no correlation between the two. French language retention was highest in Quebec City (1.0), Montreal (.99), Trois-Rivières (.98), and Ottawa (.81); the concentrations of the French-speaking population in these cities was also highest; in cities where French language retention was low, such as Regina (.18), Calgary (.21), and London (.20), the French populations were also sparse. He concluded that French retention ratios will vary inversely to the degree to which French Canadians encounter people who speak only English (Lieberson, 1970:216).

T.R. Balakrishnan and associates (1982, 1987, 1990, 1995, 1999) have done the most extensive work in Canada on comparing large numbers of ethnic groups in most of the metropolitan areas. Their work is also the most recent and uses the latest available census figures. In their first work (Balakrishnan and Jarvis, 1979:218–27) they used 1961 and 1971 census data to compare all metropolitan centres in Canada; they found very little change (1961 to 1971) in segregation patterns. They also found that socioeconomic status was predominantly sectoral, family status was zonal, and ethnic status followed neither pattern—similar to findings in the United States where ethnic groups seemed to follow multiple nuclei patterns.

Balakrishnan (1995) has now updated his work using a variety of diversity, concentration, dissimilarity, and segregation indexes. Table 9.1, using an ethnic diversity index, indicates that ethnic diversity between 1961 and 1991 has not increased in the Maritimes where (except for Halifax), the population is very homogeneously British. The same is also true for metropolitan centres east of Montreal in Quebec, where the

TABLE 9.1 Indices of Ethnic Diversity for Census Metropolitan Areas of Canada 1961–91

Metropolitan Area	1961	1971	1981	1991
St.John's	.09	.08	.11	.08
Halifax	.45	.38	.42	.47
Saint John	.38	.34	.38	.35
Chicoutimi	—	.12	.08	.07
Quebec	.11	.13	.11	.10
Sherbrooke	—	—	—	.17
Trois-Rivières	—	—	.09	.08
Montreal	.45	.55	.54	.53
Ottawa-Hull	.63	.64	.69	.71
Oshawa	—	—	.51	.68
Toronto	.61	.64	.72	.80
Hamilton	.58	.60	.61	.74
St Catharines-Niagara	—	.68	.67	.76
Kitchener	.69	.66	.67	.75
London	.46	.46	.51	.63
Windsor	.72	.72	.75	.79
Sudbury	.74	.71	.73	.70
Thunder Bay	—	.76	.75	.83
Winnipeg	.75	.76	.79	.85
Regina	.72	.72	.74	.81
Saskatoon	.72	.74	.74	.83
Calgary	.64	.66	.67	.79
Edmonton	.75	.75	.76	.84
Vancouver	.60	.63	.67	.80
Victoria	.39	.43	.46	.59

NOTE: Index of ethnic diversity is defined as $1 - P_i^2$, where P_i, is the proportion of the population in the i th ethnic group. Only single ethnic origin groups are included in the calculation for 1981, and 1991 indices.

population is homogeneously French. Montreal was much more ethnically diverse in 1961 (.45), and has increased somewhat by 1991 (.53).

Urban centres west of Montreal were already ethnically diverse in 1961 ranging from .58 to .75 (exceptions Victoria and London). By 1991 all these centres west had become considerably more ethnically diverse, seven of them ranging

in the seventies and seven in the eighties on the diversity index. Clearly the Maritimes are homogeneously British, Quebec is French, and Ontario and the West multicultural. This diversity needs to be examined more closely, especially the variations in race.

There is an excellent technical discussion of measures of residential segregation in Kazemipur and Halli (2000:66–79), which includes consideration of the patterns of ethnic segregation that prevail in major Canadian cities. This includes the Gini coefficient, the Entropy index, the Atkinson index, the Interaction index, the Isolation index, a Correlation ratio, the Delta index, ACO and RCO indexes, the PCC index, the RCE index, the ACE index, the ACL index, the Spatial Proximity index, the Relative clustering index, the Choice index, for almost any conceivable unit analysis desired.

Concentration of Visible Minorities

Visible minorities have increased from 5 to about 10 percent of the Canadian population between 1971 and 1991. Because of changes in the immigration act in the sixties, visible minorities are now able to compete for entrance into Canada, and those who landed in turn sponsor immediate kin to join them. Visible minorities who came as immigrants during the past two decades came mostly to Canada's cities, especially Toronto and Vancouver.

By 1991 almost one-fourth (22 per cent) of the population of metropolitan Vancouver were visible minorities, and about one-fifth of the population of metropolitan Toronto were visible non-whites. Calgary (15 per cent) and Edmonton (13 per cent) ranked third and fourth, and Winnipeg (10 per cent) approached the national average (Balakrishnan and Hou, 1995). These five metropolitan areas have the highest concentrations of visible minorities, and we would expect that patterns of residential segregation would also be highest there.

In Census Metropolitan Areas (CMAs) east of Montreal, except for Halifax (6 per cent), only 1 or 2 per cent of their populations are non-white. CMAs in the West all have more than 5 per cent of their populations who are visible minorities, largely of Asian and aboriginal descent. Except for Montreal (7 per cent), CMAs in Quebec have almost no visible minorities. Except for Toronto, Ontario CMAs have less than the Canadian average of 10 per cent—closer to 5 per cent or less.

Balakrishnan (2000:130) used the data in the 1996 Canada census and we have presented some of their results in 14 metropolitan centres in Table 9.2. The English, Germans, French, and Italians, a select group of whites, are among the least concentrated (not highly clustered in a few census tracts). English scores are very low (except for Montreal where they are a small minority). Italians who have arrived in Canada more recently are the most concentrated of the whites, but generally lower than visible minorities. The Chinese, blacks, aboriginals, and South Asians who are considered visible minorities, mostly score above .50 in all of the centres. They

are clearly more concentrated than whites. The Jewish Canadians, considered a religious group, are more concentrated residentially than any other group. We conclude that both race and religion are important factors that differentiate ethnic residential concentration.

While concentration of whites is low in Halifax in the east, concentration scores for visible minorities and Jews are similar to that of other centres. The Chinese are the most concentrated in Montreal (.70), blacks in the east (.62), aboriginals (.78) in Toronto, and South Asians (.80) as well as Jews (.93) in Montreal. Overall, Montreal has the most segregated whites, visible minorities and Jews, and Calgary the lowest. Most recently, Balakrishnan and Hou (1999) compared ethnic composition in 14 metropolitan centres using both 1986 and 1991 census data. Thus, the reader could compare the three variables of ethnicity, urban centre, census years, and observe the complexity of changes. Using the same 15 groups in the 14 urban areas, they

TABLE 9.2 Gini Indices of Concentration by Ethnic Group for Major Census Metropolitan Areas of Canada, 1996

	White Europeans				Visible Minorities				Religious
	English	German	French	South Italian	Chinese	Black	Aboriginal	South Asian	Jewish
Halifax	.24	.35	.34	.62	.62	.62	.70	.62	.77
Montreal	.65	.60	.40	.69	.70	.62	.75	.80	.93
Ottawa-Hull	.41	.42	.52	.62	.60	.62	.62	.62	.76
Toronto	.36	.39	.43	.63	.68	.58	.78	.62	.89
Hamilton	.32	.38	.41	.48	.57	.55	.71	.62	.89
St. Catharines	.27	.41	.43	.48	.62	.54	.70	.67	.81
Kitchener-Waterloo	.30	.38	.35	.50	.59	.47	.75	.53	.81
London	.29	.36	.34	.50	.59	.50	.62	.62	.86
Windsor	.26	.33	.37	.47	.58	.49	.65	.60	.77
Winnipeg	.33	.37	.54	.57	.67	.49	.70	.72	.87
Calgary	.22	.26	.30	.51	.57	.59	.59	.67	.78
Edmonton	.29	.34	.36	.63	.58	.50	.69	.68	.86
Vancouver	.30	.33	.40	.55	.56	.49	.69	.65	.72
Victoria	.21	.28	.38	.44	.52	.45	.67	.55	.59

SOURCE: T.R. Balakrishnan, 'Residential Segregation and Canada's Ethnic Groups', in Kalbach and Kalbach (eds), *Perspectives on Ethnicity in Canada* (Toronto: Harcourt Canada, 2000).

also controlled for 50 per cent and 90 per cent concentrations of these groups in the 14 centres. Next, they examined dissimilarities using socio-economic indices for these groups and areas. These numbers help to show complexity, diversity and change, as well as how far sociological methods to measure these phenomena have come (Balakrishnan and Hou, 1999:116–47).

Balakrishnan and Hou (1995) have also presented ethnic concentration comparisons in Toronto and Montreal, in the form of Lorenz curves (Figure 9.3). The Lorenz curve is a simple way of examining concentration to see whether an ethnic group is overrepresented in certain areas of the city compared to others. To plot the curve the census tracts are arranged in descending order of the ethnic group population. Then the cumulative percentage of the ethnic population is plotted. The straight diagonal line from bottom left to top right represents equal distribution, or a score of zero concentration on a 0 to 1 range (Balakrishnan and Hou, 1995). The Gini index measures the proportion of the area above the diagonal between the curve and the diagonal.

For the Jewish population the indices are the highest, reaching values over .90 in the largest centres of Toronto and Montreal. For the visible minorities, including blacks, Chinese and South Asians, the indices range in between around .60. The British in Toronto, and the French in Montreal, who represent white European groups, are closest to the straight diagonal of zero, with low index scores of about .20. The Lorenz curve illustrates comparative degrees of ethnic concentration already plotted in more detail in Table 9.2. Balakrishnan (2000:130) has also done very similar concentration curves using 1996 census data, and the positions of the various ethnic groups have not changed since five years ago, which we would not expect in so short a time.

Race and social class often combine to force many visible minorities to live in deteriorated sections of the city where it is difficult to raise families because of limited resources and disorganized social environments. Early Chinese

bachelors clustered together in Chinatowns to survive and protect themselves against prejudice and discrimination (Lai, 1988). Jews in Montreal, Toronto, Vancouver, and Winnipeg were and still are highly clustered together to support their Jewish institutions, family life, and distinctive religion. However, aboriginals in Canadian cities are forced to live in the inner cities because of unemployment, low incomes, and often discrimination (Winnipeg has the highest concentration). Descendants of northern Europeans usually have the greatest freedom from discrimination because they have the jobs, the means, and therefore the opportunities to live where they choose (Anderson and Frideres, 1981:299–304).

APARTHEID: STUDIES IN SEGREGATION

To get some feel for the diversity of ethnic residential segregation in Canada, we will examine studies of blacks in Nova Scotia and Toronto, and Chinatowns (Richmond, 1994). Blacks and Chinese were among the most concentrated and segregated using indexes (Balakrishnan and Hou, 1995). These studies will show that there are a variety of social reasons why minorities live and work spatially apart and segregated into nuclei.

Blacks in Nova Scotia

Black studies are numerous in the United States where there are more blacks than the entire population of Canada. There are relatively few blacks in Canada; in fact, they comprise less than one per cent of the population. They first settled in Nova Scotia, and a large proportion are still located around Halifax. Blacks have been in Canada at least since 1628, when a young slave was brought to New France; by the mid-eighteenth century there were about 4,000 black slaves in New France (Winks, 1971:26). The United Empire Loyalists brought some slaves with them, but slavery was usually abandoned because it was not profitable in Canada. Slavery was practised in British North America until 1834 when

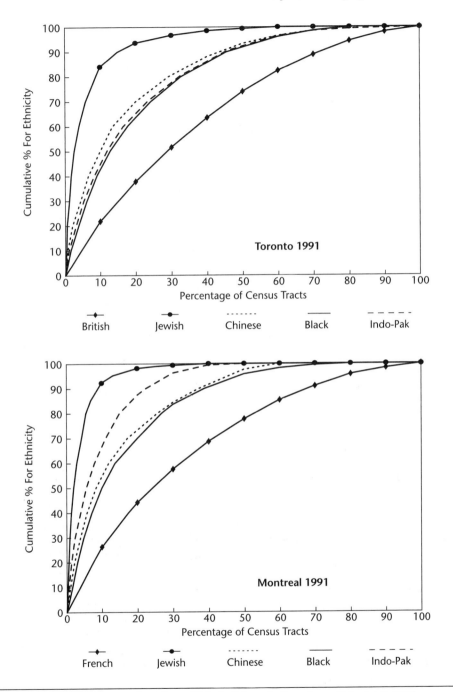

FIGURE 9.3 Concentration Curves for Selected Ethnic Groups in Toronto and Montreal, 1991

SOURCE: T.R. Balakrishnan and Feng Hou, 'The Changing Patterns of Spatial Concentration and Residential Segregation of Ethnic Groups in Canada's Major Metropolitan Areas 1981–1991', paper presented at the Population Association of America meetings in San Francisco, 6–10 April 1995.

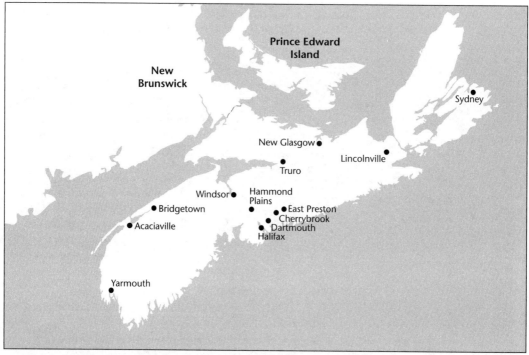

FIGURE 9.4 Location of 13 Black Communities in Nova Scotia

SOURCE: F. Henry, *Forgotten Canadians: The Blacks of Nova Scotia* (Don Mills, ON: Longman Canada, 1973), p. 17. Reprinted by permission of Harcourt Brace Jovanovich, Canada.

all slaves within the British Empire were freed. Although the first blacks came to Nova Scotia, more recently they have entered Toronto and Montreal in larger numbers (Calliste, 1987:1–20).

Fortunately, Frances Henry (1973) researched 13 black rural and urban communities in Nova Scotia, which are located on the map in Figure 9.4. Interviews were conducted by a team of black students in each of these 13 communities, so that in her volume *Forgotten Canadians: Blacks in Nova Scotia*, Henry could provide a general context of black communities showing the rural and urban diversity of the province. Interviews in each of these communities showed that 42 per cent of the blacks had less than a grade school education, that their incomes were very low, that they were employed in the lower-status occupations, that many were unemployed,

that they were pessimistic about chances for upward mobility, and that they often reported prejudice and discrimination.

Henry and associates selected two black communities to study ethnographically in depth. Vale Haven is a small, depressed rural community located 300 miles from Halifax in southeastern Nova Scotia. Far Town is a lower-class semi-urban black community about 10 miles from Halifax. It is also an economically depressed area. These two ethnographic studies qualify for our ethnic community search and demonstrate the life of a visible minority in the Atlantic Region.

The small, rural, black community of Vale Haven lies along a dirt road that is an extension of one of the streets of Sea View (a white coastal town). It has a small primary school, two churches, and a community hall. Vale Haven is entirely dependent upon Sea View's services, which include five grocery stores, a clothing store, a bank, a post office, a funeral parlour, two garages, a hospital, a courthouse, a pool hall, schools, and churches (Henry, 1973:38).

In 1970 Vale Haven had a population of 294. Very little use was made of the land, except that a few residents planted gardens. A few kept a horse and cart; there were 12 cars and 3 or 4 trucks in the town. Most of the houses were ramshackle, unpainted and neglected, although two have inside plumbing and running water. One-third of the houses had no electricity. Few appliances were found, and the furniture was old and sometimes broken. A few houses had telephones, radios, and a television. Most of the people wore poor-quality clothes that were often torn (Henry, 1973:42–3).

Many of Vale Haven's blacks were out of work and were disillusioned about finding work. Younger people tended to leave for work outside the community, leaving the children and the elderly in Vale Haven. The Baptist church was served by a minister who came in occasional rotation, and church attendance was small and sporadic (Henry, 1973:40–5). Vale Haven residents went for supplies to Sea View; there was little interaction between the blacks and whites. Men in Vale Haven tended to meet in the evenings for joking, drinking, and storytelling, and privacy was almost non-existent. Vale Haven, a segregated rural black community, tucked away from general Nova Scotian life and activity, is a good example of rural apartheid.

Far Town, a second black community studied in detail by Henry, was located as a semi-urban string of houses along an unpaved road 10 miles out of Halifax. Three black communities (Far Town, New Town, and East Town) represent the densest population of blacks in Nova Scotia, estimated to be about 3,000 in 1970. Almost all of Far Town's blacks had radios and televisions, and one-third of them owned cars. Far Town's population of 700 comprised 52 households with fairly stable families

(Henry, 1973:57). Recently women were able to get jobs more easily than men by working as domestics in Halifax.

Support for the Baptist church in the community was declining. Politicians tended to visit the area only during election time when they needed black votes, but did little for the community. Far Town's blacks were in need of help but expecting little. There were few militants agitating for change among the blacks, and the community was generally conservative, unwilling to confront the white power structures directly. Blacks and whites were seldom in contact, even when they worked at the same place. Semi-urban Far Town was similar to Vale Haven, only larger with a few more conveniences and opportunities for work in Halifax.

These two ethnographic studies are good rural and semi-urban samples of most of the black communities plotted in Figure 9.4. They all face a life of poverty at the periphery of white society. They are usually segregated, services are lacking, and schools, churches, and social institutions are limited. Blacks in Nova Scotia are marginalized largely because of race.

Donald Clairmont and Dennis Magill (1974) have documented the life and death of Africville, that no longer exists. 'Africville was a Black enclave within the city of Halifax, inhabited by approximately 400 people, comprising 80 families, many of whom were descended from settlers who came over a century ago' (Clairmont and Magill, 1974:19). It was tucked into a corner of Halifax, where it was relatively invisible, and was referred to as 'shack town'. The ghetto was isolated from the rest of Halifax behind the railroad and city dump, and was surrounded on three sides by water (Bedford Basin). Most of the black families had squatter rights; those who did not, rented.

'Slavery was never instituted by statute in Nova Scotia, yet slavery was practised in Halifax a year after the city was founded and, over the next five decades, it was not uncommon in other parts of the province' (Krauter and Davis, 1978:41–68). At the outbreak of the

American Revolution, there were approximately five hundred slaves, many of whom had come with their New England masters. Slave-holding Loyalist immigrants increased the number by approximately a thousand. There were also refugee blacks who settled at Preston near Halifax on small lots of rocky soil and scrubby forest ranging from three to four hectares (Clairmont and Magill, 1974:42).

The area that eventually came to be known as Africville was settled by the slaves who had settled at Preston but could not make a living because of the poor land. They came to the shore of Bedford Basin in the area that is just below the A. Murray MacKay Bridge. This area was convenient for fishing and also near opportunities for wage labour. The Africville population increased tenfold between 1850 and 1964. The people had little education and very low incomes; a third of the adult population was unemployed, another third had irregular work, and the final third worked in low paid jobs as porters, domestics, labourers, clerical workers, and dockworkers. Sewerage, lighting, and other public services were conspicuously absent in Africville (Clairmont and Magill, 1974:19). The people obtained water from improvised wells that were often in a poor state. There were no paved roads.

The Africville land seemed to be a prime site for potential industrial development. The city of Halifax owned properties near it, the railway was close by, and the shoreline was valuable for harbour development. Discussions began after 1955 about removing the black community. After numerous studies and reports it was decided to relocate the residents of the community in 1964 (Clairmont and Magill, 1974:180).

Once relocation was agreed on, the Halifax City Council accepted the responsibility of providing the relocatees with safe, sanitary, and decent housing. About 75 per cent were relocated in urban renewal projects within walking distance of their former dwellings. They received better housing but they were now renters instead of landowners or owners of dwellings; only one-third owned their own homes after relocation. The lack of a

regular income made it difficult to pay mortgages and service and maintenance bills. Most families of Africville were relocated in Uniacke Square; this was two-storey public housing. Clairmont and Magill (1974:223) interviewed many relocatees. Two-thirds said they had more difficulties making ends meet in their new homes. Over half said they were able to stay in contact with their former Africville friends; but over half also thought they could no longer count on their neighbours for help. A majority felt they had lost a feeling of belonging, and that the friendliness and trustworthiness of neighbours had declined. These were the social costs of relocation. Now old Africville is a public park where formerly there was a segregated black community.

Arrival of Caribbeans in Toronto

While the history of blacks in Nova Scotia dates back two hundred years to slavery, the more recent immigration—after a change to the points system—opened Canada up to the arrival of Caribbeans, most of them black. In 1967, 8,400 arrived in Canada, which represented 4 per cent of all arrivals; which grew to a high of 28,000 arrivals in 1974 representing 13 per cent of all immigrants that year (Anderson, 1993:59). By 1990 this had dropped to some 14,000 arrivals, 7 per cent of all newcomers that year (Henry, 1994). Caribbeans are highly visible, coming principally from Jamaica, Guyana, Haiti, and Trinidad and Tobago. Since many of them had to score highly on the immigrant point system, they are much more educated, and skilled than rural Nova Scotia blacks. Since they came from newly independent countries where blacks and non-whites are large majorities, they are also much more self-assured and expect more from their host country than blacks in Nova Scotia who came out of centuries of slavery and oppression.

In Figure 9.5, Anderson (1993:67) has plotted a summary of Caribbeans who arrived in Canada between 1967 and 1989. Of the 301,000 who arrived during these 23 years, representing 9 per

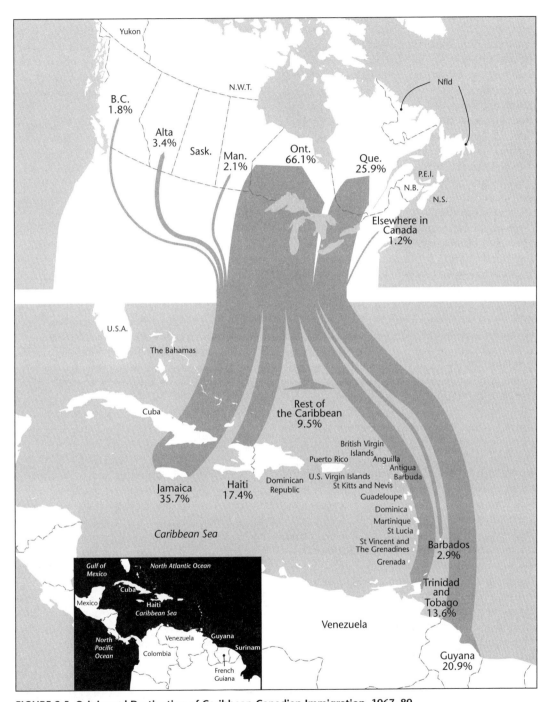

FIGURE 9.5 Origin and Destination of Caribbean-Canadian Immigration, 1967–89

SOURCE: Wolseley W. Anderson, *Caribbean Immigrants: A Socio-Demographic Profile* (Toronto: Canadian Scholars Press, 1993), p. 67.

cent of all immigrant arrivals, 36 per cent came from Jamaica, 21 per cent from Guyana, 17 per cent from Haiti, 14 per cent from Trinidad and Tobago, and 10 per cent from other points in the Caribbean. Two-thirds of these Caribbean immigrants arrived in Ontario (66 per cent) from former British colonies such as Jamaica, Guyana and Trinidad, where they learned English, and most of these arrived in Toronto (Walker, 1984: 14). Immigrants from Haiti who knew French, went mostly to Montreal, representing a large portion of the 26 per cent who went to Quebec.

These Caribbeans who settled mostly in Toronto and Montreal, found jobs in 1987 in services (18 per cent), product fabricating (16 per cent), and clerical (12 per cent) occupations more heavily than the average Canadian (Anderson, 1993:103). Caribbeans were represented about average in medicine and health (3 per cent) and entrepreneural (3 per cent) occupations. They were underrepresented in managerial, administrative, professional and technical occupations that usually require development of social networks over a longer period of time, which new arrivals have not yet been able to build.

Recent arrival of visible minority immigrants into Canada's large metropolitan areas, such as the Caribbeans to Toronto and Montreal since the sixties, illustrate that immigration trends have clearly changed from mostly white Europeans earlier, to largely non-white visible minorities with more diverse cultural, religious, and racial heritages, although Satzewich (1998: 77–9) disputes that racism ceased. Our indices show that blacks in Canadian cities are not as segregated as in the United States, but they are more highly segregated than whites of European origin. Anderson (1993:10) outlines how the paths of Caribbeans have been different: (1) their historical experiences have been different, (2) although from British colonies, their entrance status is determined more by race than by culture, and (3) the creolization process of mixing of cultures, religions, and races has prepared them well for Canadian pluralism.

Canadians must remember that many Caribbeans worked on the sugar cane plantations and factories as slaves where entrepreneurship and private enterprise were prohibited; where rigid dependency and authoritarian structures were total; in a caste system where whites were at the top of the pyramid and blacks at the bottom (Anderson, 1993:11; Henry, 1994). While these immigrants come from a variety of countries in the Caribbean, their experiences of white colonial racism have been similar (Walker, 1984: 3). Caribbeans are not all black, they come from 29 territories, formerly controlled by four white European countries (Britain, France, Spain, Netherlands), where slaves dominated the West Indian population numerically in a highly stratified society, where colour dominated the society (Walker, 1984:4). Maroons—disaffected blacks from Jamaica—had been brought to Nova Scotia as early as 1795.

In Toronto and Montreal, opportunities for housing and jobs have been difficult for visible minorities like the Caribbeans, so that in April 1992 the youth of Toronto rioted (Mata, 1989). Stephen Lewis was commissioned to study the situation. His report to the government read in part:

> What we are dealing with, at root and fundamentally, is anti-black racism . . . wounds of systemic discrimination throughout Southern Ontario. . . It is blacks who are being shot, it is black youth that are underemployed in excessive numbers . . . it is black kids who are disproportionately dropping out (Anderson, 1993:125).

The 37-page Lewis report shows that while Caribbeans are among the most highly educated newcomers, practice of racism against blacks and visible minorities 'have become an escalating staple of news reports on an almost daily basis' (Anderson, 1993:129).

HIGHLIGHT 9.1 TORONTO'S BLACK CARIBBEANS

Frances Henry, professor of anthropology at York University in Toronto, has done research in the Caribbean for 35 years, beginning in Trinidad in 1956. She has written her experiences in the book *The Caribbean Diaspora in Toronto: Learning to Live With Racism* (1994).

The Afro-Caribbean community in Toronto has grown dramatically over the past few decades. Increasingly active as a political and cultural force in the life of the city, the group remains unknown to many of Toronto's other communities and institutions. Frances Henry offers the first intensive ethnographic examination of the community. Based on in-depth interviews and extensive observation, her study provides a richly detailed overview of the major cultural institutions in the lives of Afro-Caribbean residents of Toronto.

Henry begins with an introduction to the Caribbean region, and the cultural and historical origins of its peoples. She focuses on the cultural practices that shape the community in Toronto, and the extent to which they facilitate or impede incorporation in Canadian society. Henry looks closely at such things as male-female relationships, forms of family organization, and patterns of religious practice, and shows that some cultural patterns have been maintained by members of the community whereas others have changed during the migration process.

Two factors emerge as the key to the Afro-Caribbean experience in Toronto. One is the class differences within the community, which play a crucial role in re-creating stratification patterns similar to those in the Caribbean. The other is systemic racism against people of Afro-Caribbean origin, which impacts in all areas of the community's life in Canada.

SOURCE: Frances Henry, *The Caribbean Diaspora in Toronto: Learning to Live with Racism* (Toronto: University of Toronto Press, 1994). Reprinted by permission.

The Chinese: Segregated Chinatowns

Emigration from China to Canada began in 1858 (Anderson, 1991; Tan and Roy, 1985:4). These early Chinese immigrants were mostly men seeking to find jobs in the British Columbia gold rush. In 1881 men were brought in from the United States and Asia to help with the building of the Canadian Pacific Railway (Lai, 1988:3–33). By 1885, there were 10,000 Chinese in Canada, all in British Columbia (Wickberg, 1982:27); more than one-fourth (2,900) in railroad construction. When the building of the railroad ended in the 1880s, thousands of Chinese were left unemployed. While many Chinese settled in Victoria, Vancouver was to be the western terminus of the Canadian Pacific Railway (Li, 1988:11–22). Large groups of Chinese were employed to clear the area, and these workers became a threat to the whites, because they were cheap labour that took much-needed jobs. 'In 1884 the Chinese in Burrard Inlet comprised five merchants, ten store employees, thirty cooks and laundrymen, and one prostitute, as well as sixty sawmill hands' (Wickberg, 1982:61). By 1886 many Chinese in the Burrard Inlet area began to raise vegetable gardens and started truck farming; soon they supplied most of the vegetables for the Vancouver settlement. By 1886 they began to settle in the Pender area; here the oldest and for many years the largest segregated Canadian Chinatown has existed for a hundred years, next to the largest segregated Japantown in Canada (Driedger, 1989:248–50). The Chinese segregated themselves in Chinatowns largely to protect themselves from discrimination and racism (Baureiss, 1987:1–14; Creese, 1987:35–46; Lai, 1987:47–67; Li, 1988:102–13; McEvoy, 1982:24–42; Yu, 1987:114–24).

In 1941 there were 35,000 Chinese in Canada; by 1981 there were 289,000. Their number almost doubled to 58,000 in 1961, more than doubled in 1981 to 289,000, and doubled again in 1991 to 587,000. Before the Second World War the Chinese were centred in British Columbia; after 1945, the many Chinese immigrants spread across Canada. By 1981 about one-third resided in Vancouver, another third in Toronto; the remaining third scattered mostly in other cities across Canada (Lai, 1988:118). The two largest Chinatowns in 1986 were located in Toronto (143,235) and Vancouver (109,370); these were studied in some depth by David Lai (1988).

By 1991, 40 per cent (232,000) of the 587,000 Chinese in Canada resided in Toronto, and 28 per cent (167,000) in Vancouver, which represented two-thirds of all Chinese. Eighty-five per cent (500,000) of the 567,000 lived in the five urban centres of Toronto, Vancouver, Montreal (34,000), Edmonton (33,000), and Calgary (33,000). The dominance of Chinese in these five centres is shown in Figure 9.6. Only 70,000 lived in the remaining centres including 14,000 in Ottawa-Hull, 10,000 in Winnipeg, 5,000 in Hamilton, 3,000 each in Kitchener, Windsor, London, Saskatoon, and less than 2,000 in the rest of the centres.

In 1971 there were little more than 100,000 Chinese in Canada, a number which increased more than fivefold to 567,000 in 1991, in a short 20 years. During this 1971–91 period the Chinese population increased nine times in Toronto from 26,000 to 232,000, in Vancouver fivefold from 36,000 to 167,000, in Montreal 11,000 to 34,000, in Edmonton 5,000 to 33,000, and in Calgary 5,000 to 35,000. So all of these metropolitan centres have seen an enormous increase of Chinese populations in one generation, which makes these new immigrants more visible. Those who are afraid of 'visible minorities' unlike themselves, will tend to feel threatened, especially in centres like Vancouver and Toronto where many other visible minorities are also arriving. Most of these newcomers have not been settled in the Chinatown areas, but scattered in the suburbs, where they are less visible.

While the new Chinese arrivals have located more evenly in a less segregated way in the total city, their increased population mass has also benefited the existing Chinatowns. While the older 'bachelor' Chinese were less well-to-do, Chinese newcomers are better off and are also more educated and politically sophisticated, so that they have helped enhance rehabilitation and new growth in business, schools and institutions, many of which have continued to concentrate in Chinatowns in the centre of the city. Thus, many declining Chinatowns have found new life and have been developed and expanded. In Figure 9.7 (Lai, 1988:127) the old Chinatown in Vancouver is shown as C and D near the newly renovated historic site of Gastown, which has also linked with a development of a historic Chinatown (Lai, 1988:126–35). In many of these cities plans of drastic slum clearance, which would have razed many historic Chinatowns, were stopped by Chinese leaders with lawyers, who persuaded city councils of the importance of a colourful Chinatown. Chinese elderly did not want to leave the community, so new housing was built for them, and in Vancouver a series of redevelopment projects were started. Development of housing projects, new parks, Chinese gardens, cultural centres, and schools and institutions all created a momentum to which new businesses were also attracted. These new Chinese developments were integrated with the historic Gastown and the large development when the Pan American games came to Vancouver. Thus, the redeveloped Chinatown became an important part of Vancouver's city centre, rather than a slum as some had often thought of it. With the influx of new Chinese immigrants, who were of higher status, more integration and less segregation has occurred.

The Vancouver Chinatown comprises some eight city blocks along Pender Street close to the downtown business section, and just off Burrard Inlet. Hundreds of stores, shops, and businesses of all kinds are located in Chinatown, along with all the services that the Chinese need (Lai, 1988:126-35). A number of Chinese newspapers are published here, and movie houses, restaurants, clubs, voluntary organizations, churches

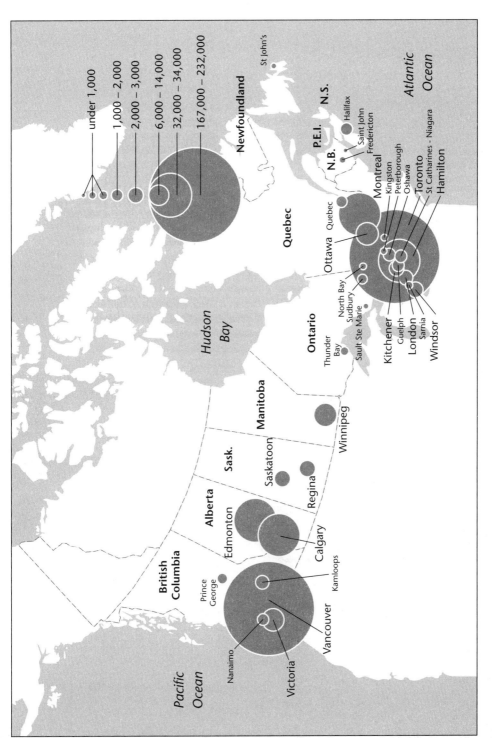

FIGURE 9.6 Distribution of Major Chinese Communities in Canada, 1991

SOURCE: David C. Lai, *Chinatowns: Towns Within Cities in Canada* (Vancouver: University of British Columbia Press, 1988), p. 177 (an adaptation to include 1991 Census of Canada data from *Ethnic Origin: The Nation*, Catalogues 93–31, 93–315).

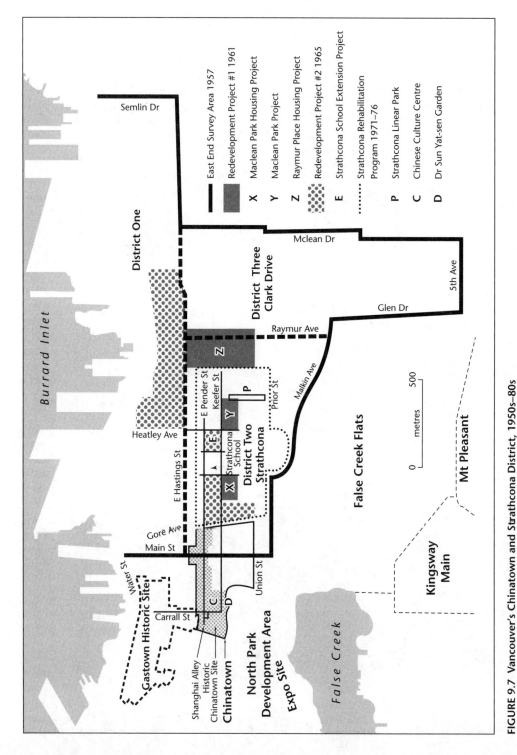

FIGURE 9.7 Vancouver's Chinatown and Strathcona District, 1950s–80s

SOURCE: David C. Lai, *Chinatowns: Towns Within Cities in Canada* (Vancouver: University of British Columbia Press, 1988), p. 127.

and temples, and recreational facilities are located in Chinatown (Wickberg, 1982:254–67). The community puts on annual Chinese festivals and various attractions such as musicals, drama contests, and literary events. Chinese 'bachelors' of the early days live here, as well as many families, so that it is a living Chinese community where activity never ceases (Lai, 1988:126–35). Since Chinatown constitutes a business section that attracts tourists, it has a viable economic base that has survived for more than a hundred years and most likely will continue for the foreseeable future.

The dissimilarity scores for the Chinese in Vancouver (.55), in Toronto (.57), and in Montreal (.67) are still quite high although much lower than they used to be, because of the differing patterns of early and later immigration. Those who still live in Chinatown are as segregated as any other ethnic group, if not more so. The Toronto Chinese community has been moving and has relocated recently, which has not happened in Vancouver (Lai, 1988:146–9). The Vancouver Chinatown is one of the best examples of a segregated urban community near the downtown business district.

Because the first Chinese immigrants were not allowed to bring their families, Chinatowns met the special needs of the Chinese bachelors who relied on each other's social support (Lai, 1988:13–21; Tan and Roy, 1985). The many Chinese immigrants who came to Canada after the Second World War came as families; they were often professional and business people who located freely in urban suburbs, and were therefore relatively accepted and unsegregated. Many are integrating fast, and are experiencing an extensive modification of their culture. Some intermarriage is taking place, but they remain physically visible which is a brake on assimilation for many (Li, 1988).

Kay Anderson's (1991) insightful study of race and racism in Vancouver's Chinatown since 1875, shows how one of Canada's earliest Chinatowns developed over a century. She shows that the very existence of the district—from negative stereotyping of the late nineteenth and early twentieth centuries to its current status an 'ethnic neighbourhood'—is the result of cultural domination that continues to exist today. Anderson (1991) argues that Chinatown was as much a creation of whites as Chinese . . . and she attempts to demystify the concept of Chinatown. The reader cannot help but weep. It is hard to control one's rage at what whites did to 'foreigners', who risked their lives to help build Canada's railroads, and were then marginalized, and maligned as 'outsiders'. Anderson's (1991) empirical study is firmly grounded in history and social theory, which we develop more in Chapter 11.

HIGHLIGHT 9.2 VANCOUVER'S CHINATOWN

'Chinatown' was a concept that belonged to Vancouver's white European community which, like its contemporaries throughout North America, perceived the district of Chinese settlement according to an influential culture of race. For Europeans, Chinatown embodied all those features that seemed to set the Chinese apart. Possible convergences of class, gender, immigrant status, and so on between whites and Chinese were obscured by the overriding beliefs in the natural occurrence of the two races and the superior race and culture of Europeans. Thus, out of the infinity of things that could have been said about the settlers on Vancouver's Pender Street, it was their apparently standard appearance, heathenism, clannishness, propensity to sleep twelve to a room, opium and gambling addiction, eating habits, strange language, odd graveyard practices, and so on that became ingredients of their image. In other words, Chinatown was almost everything white society was not.

This is not to suggest that Chinatown was a fiction; nor does it deny gambling, opium addiction, and unsanitary conditions in the district where Chinese settled in Vancouver. Moreover, there were probably divided opinions among Europeans about the extent of vice and unsanitary behaviour in Chinatown, and such variation in European's responses as existed along class, gender, and other lines should be the subject of further research. The point is that 'Chinatown' was a shared characterization constructed by and for Europeans who—out of conformity toward, and support for, a regime that bestowed on them identity, status, power, and economic advancement—sought to confirm the 'otherness' of the Chinese. That they directed that purpose in large part through the medium of Chinatown attests to the importance of such enclaves in the making of systems of racial classification. That sectors within the Chinatown community also resisted the purpose is testimony to the potential for renegotiation of the forms of dominance we have been describing.

In so defining and targeting Chinatown, the European authorities of early Vancouver ensured that the racial category 'Chinese' would be carried forward in the society and space of their city. 'Chinatown' was their unit of knowledge, and its 'Chineseness' belonged to them. Both notions continued to be reinvented at the symbolic and material levels in the years to come, and while various govern ments were mapping the career of the Chinese they would at the same time be defining the insider community whose boundaries and privilege it was their ambition to protect.

Trouble in Chinatown
BY W.R. GORDON

There's trouble down in chinatown and the
  Chinks are spitting blue;
The cops have yanked old Tai Kee's bank and
  all his layout, too.

The fan-tan game and the py-gow frame and
  the chuck-luck mat all went
In one fell swoop when Sergeant Troop and
  his "bulls" collected rent.

The games were going with a handsome
  showing and a noisy, smoky hum,
While thoughts of raids and police parades
  were far from the yellow scum.
The air was thick as burnt clay brick; the
  smoke you could cut in chunks,
But the monks were gay in their saffron way
  as they bet their hard-earned plunks.

A swell young Chink in a jacket pink lounged
  by the outer door.
His eyes closed and you'd swear he dozed, but
  he saw a whole lot more
Than you or I, if we passed by, would take in at
  a look.
For he was scout for the whole layout and the
  street was his lesson book.

A cop walked by and the Chink's slant eye
  read trouble as he passed,
And before another could follow the other
  that outer door slammed fast.
He pulled a string, and, funny thing, two more
  banged down the hall,
While in the room the noisy hum had
  changed to a heathenish bawl.

But the cops were wise; they had used their
  eyes to size up Tai Kee's joint.
They went at the wall in the dark back hall
  with an axe and a crowbar point.
In a minute or two they laid plain to view the
  murky gambling den;
They swarmed inside and the way they tied
  those Chinks was worth a ten.

Five at a time in a jabbering line, they knotted
  them queue to queue,
While the "muck-a-hai's" and "mo-bing-kai-
  tai's" turned the place an indigo blue.

There were forty odd, too heavy a load for the "Black Maria" van,
So some had to walk for many a block, pig-tailed like a human fan.

Now that is why the big ki-yi is heard in Chinatown.
The row they'll raise will be heard all ways round the streets that they hold down;

But it's all in the game, it's ever the same; they're raided from day to day.
When work is slack the cops fall back on the Chinks for a grandstand play.

SOURCES: Kay Anderson, *Vancouver's Chinatown* (Montreal: McGill-Queen's Press, 1991), pp. 102–3; W.R. Gordon, *British Columbia Magazine*, September 1911.

SUMMARY

Minorities in rural and urban areas do not cluster equally in space, so sociologists have devised various methods to measure class, ethnic, racial and religious concentrations, and segregation. This segregation is often referred to as 'apartheid', where minorities are clustered into separate areas apart from others either voluntarily or involuntarily. Such segregation can be a means of control that has taken a variety of forms.

Two major perspectives in such segmentation in urban areas, focus on Duncan's zonal segregation model, and Shevky and Bell's multiple nuclei model. The Duncan model is based on Burgess' concentric zone model of urban growth which assumes that cities grow in concentric circles like trees, adding to their perimeter each year. Duncan assumed that the smaller older circles in the middle were inhabited by the lower class populations, while the better-off, increasingly moved to the periphery. Thus, social class is a major means of differentiation. Shevky and Bell based their model on Harris and Ullman's multiple nuclei model, where they found that residents cluster more randomly, in class, racial and family status nuclei, based less on predetermined spatial patterns. Dawson found that in early Montreal, groupings seemed to follow Duncan's concentric zone model.

Various measures and indices have been developed to study these complex residential patterns. Balakrishnan and associates developed indices of ethnic diversity and they found that concentration of ethnic minorities varies enormously by cities and by groups. Western Canadian cities are much more ethnically diverse than eastern ones. Visible minorities concentrate heavily in Vancouver and Toronto, and visible minorities are much more concentrated than European whites. Jews, however, who are a religious minority, are most segregated even though they are white. Dissimilarity indices, which measure spatial separation of minorities from larger British and French charter groups, show again that visible minorities are more segregated into their own groupings away from charter groups.

Our several studies of blacks and Chinese in Canada show that there is much evidence of apartheid. Blacks who came to Nova Scotia two hundred years ago were set apart, so that even today they are still segregated in rural black areas or on the periphery of cities. Caribbeans who have come recently, many of whom are black, have concentrated mostly in Toronto and Montreal, where they are also segregated, although not as severely as blacks in the United States. This involves residential, occupational, and social segregation which creates conflict.

Chinese men who came to work in mines and helped build the railroads in Canada, were segregated in workcamps, and again separated themselves in Chinatowns in urban centres for protection against prejudice and discrimination. While immigration laws severely restricted Chinese immigration large numbers of Chinese families have recently come to Canada. These Chinese newcomers are more educated and occupationally specialized so that they are able to compete better with the general population. They increasingly live amongst other Canadians, so that Chinese segregation patterns are diminishing. So far we have shown that social class and residential segregation are major factors in the life patterns of Canada's minorities. A third factor—race—we will explore in the next chapter.

In the last chapter we explored how socioeconomic status varies, and that those with less income, education, and higher-status occupations, will find it harder to compete in the industrial Cell A of our model. When populations are segregated spatially and socially, which Richmond calls apartheid, many ethnic and racial groups find themselves set apart, with less access to opportunities. The better-to-do live in the suburbs spatially (those in Cells A and B), while visible minorities (Cell D), often live in the inner city which is a lower-status area, and where there are older schools, where good teachers are more reluctant to teach, and where

job opportunities are more limited. On the other hand, higher-status Jewish people (Cell E) may segregate themselves voluntarily in some parts of suburbs where they can concentrate and maintain their own schools, which can be an advantage. In rural areas, Hutterites (Cell E) who also wish to voluntarily segregate themselves, create a homogenous population on a few sections of colony land, and maintain their own schools and farming to make a living. Examination of the segregation patterns in several dozen metropolitan centres in Canada by scientific methods and statistics, certainly helps us handle the enormous diversity that postmodern scholars want. Rational, linear comparisons of segregation ratios are helpful, but the more qualitative studies of blacks in Nova Scotia, Caribbeans in Toronto, and Chinese in Vancouver and Toronto, show how the concerns of postmodern scholars add much to our understanding, when we combine both scientific and qualitative studies.

CRITICAL THINKING QUESTIONS

1. Define apartheid and segregation. How are they related?

2. Describe the Duncans' zonal segregation model by plotting the concentric zones of the city. What ethnic and status groups live where? Why?

3. Describe the Shevky and Bell multiple nuclei model. Diagram their spatial model, and compare with the Duncan model. How different are the two?

4. Compare work that Dawson did in Montreal and Driedger and colleagues did in Winnipeg. Which models did they use? How successful were they in using the classical models while studying these cities?

5. Discuss the work that Balakrishnan and associates did on segregation in Canada. Compare cities, time periods, scales used.

6. Compare the work done by scholars on black segregation in Nova Scotia and Toronto. Are these early and late black immigrants the same? Compare.

7. Are Chinatowns a good example of apartheid? Where do Canada's Chinese tend to live in Canada? What proportions live in segregated Chinatowns? Where? How has Chinese segregation changed?

SUGGESTED READINGS

Anderson, Kay J. *Vancouver's Chinatown: Racial Discourse in Canada, 1875–1980* (Montreal: McGill-Queen's, 1991). Anderson examines Vancouver's Chinatown as the creation of whites as much as Chinese; it has become an important tourist attraction.

Bolaria, B. Singh, and Peter S. Li (eds), *Racial Oppression in Canada,* 2nd edn (Toronto: Garamond, 1988). This is a study of the economic and political experiences of aboriginals, Chinese, Japanese, East Indians, and blacks in Canada.

Li, Peter S. *The Chinese in Canada,* 2nd edn (Toronto: Oxford University Press, 1998). This is an account of the history and social development of Chinese in Canada, including legal, demographic, cultural, economic, and political changes over time.

Richmond, Anthony H. *Global Apartheid: Refugees, Racism, and the New World Order* (Toronto: Oxford University Press, 1994). The author examines the impact of postindustrialism, postmodernism, and globalization on international migration, racial conflict, and ethnic nationalism.

CHAPTER 10

Race and Historic Racism

Although power and socioeconomic status are important forms of stratification of ethnic groups in Canada, physical or biological characteristics such as race provide another means of social stratification. Race can be treated from a sociobiological perspective (van den Berghe, 1981), or as socially constructed as seen by Kay Anderson (1991). We will examine the first (van den Berghe) in this chapter, and the second (Anderson 1991) in Chapter 11. Stratification by race is a fairly recent phenomenon perpetuated especially by white Europeans and their ancestors (Boyd, Goldman, and White, 2000; Wargon, 2000). Racial stratification has been especially severe in the United States, where slavery occurred for centuries, but it is also present in Canada and will become more important as increasing numbers of immigrants from the Third World enter (Driedger, 2001).

Kay Anderson begins her discussion of *Vancouver's Chinatown* with a first chapter on "Race and the Power of Definition," where she begins:

While few countries traded as transparently in the currency of race as South Africa, in many countries powerful institutions such as the state ascribe arbitrary racial identities to select groups of people. Classifications of identity—whether of 'West Indians' in Britain, 'Aborigines' in Australia, 'blacks' in the United States, or 'Indians' in Fiji—differ from the South African experience in the degree of

force with which they have been invoked but bear the same stamp of a dominant community conferring identity (Anderson, 1991:8).

She goes on to say that 'the perception of the "Chinese" in Canada as a "different" group is a comparable cultural abstraction that belongs to the beliefs and institutional practices of white European society'. Anderson (1991:9) argues that 'Chinatown' is in part a European creation, where it is seen as 'a colony of the East in the West'. She then proceeds to show that 'race' is a biological notion, as well as a social construct, both of which need to be examined seriously. We will devote Chapter 10 to the first, and Chapter 11 to the second.

Biologists never fully agreed on the criteria for classifying the world's populations, but it is obvious that physical differences among people exist, and some of these differences can be statistically shown. 'The well-known Negroid ('black'), Caucasoid ('white'), and Mongoloid ('yellow') divisions, identified in almost every race typology since the eighteenth century, do have some statistical validity' (Anderson, 1991:11). It is important however, that social scientists be aware of the subtleties and difficulties of this more recent use of the term 'race'.

On the other hand, as W.I. Thomas pointed out many decades ago, if something is defined by people as real—as race has been for decades—it is real in its consequences, so that researchers should pursue these social meanings as well. Social distance, prejudice, discrimination, segregation are 'real' and the researcher must deal with it as well. Anderson (1991:18) introduces the concept of 'racialization' to refer to the process by which attributes such as skin colour, language, birthplace, and cultural practices are given social significance as markers of distinction. She writes a whole book on precisely how the representation of 'Chinese' has been fashioned and recast in Vancouver society in the province of British Columbia. The Chinese were stigmatized and penalized because white British Columbians yearned for a racially homogeneous society—Chinese were targets of white 'yearning' and ostracized as a colony of the East in the West (Anderson, 1991:15). So, our task is to examine the biological implications of race in this chapter, and the social racialization dimensions in the next chapter.

Recently, Pierre van den Berghe (1981) has tried to develop a sociobiological theory of ethnicity and race which again brings physical and biological features into the heart of the ethnicity discussion:

> The view of ethnicity and 'race' does clash with the two dominant ideologies of industrial societies—liberalism and socialism. Ethnicity and 'race,' I will argue, are extensions of kinship, and, therefore, the feelings of ethnocentrism and racism associated with group membership are extensions of nepotism between kinsmen. . . . If my argument is correct, then it follows that ethnocentrism and racism, too, are deeply rooted in our biology and can be expected to persist. . . . In liberal ideology ethnocentrism and racism are archaic, irrational residues of preindustrial societies, which can be expected to yield to univeralism under conditions of 'modernization'. In socialist tradition, these phenomena are seen as the product of the capitalist mode of production and as misguided forms of 'false consciousness' designed to wither away after the advent of socialism. Both ideological traditions have been equally at a loss to explain the persistence, indeed,

the resurgence, of ethnic and racial sentiments (van den Berghe, 1981:xi).

Van den Berghe (1981:1–3) argues that in the second half of the nineteenth century, social Darwinists such as Herbert Spencer and William Sumner tended to perpetuate genetic determinism, which influenced sociology until the 1920s. However, the pendulum began to swing toward an environmentalist direction when Franz Boas and Robert Park emphasized the opposite view of cultural relativism that was expounded by liberals like Adorno, Myrdal, Warner, Allport, Frazier, Klineberg, and Dollard, and which held sway until the 1960s. The liberals played down racial distinctions, which often went hand in hand with the assimilationist ideology and the optimistic notion of a melting pot. Robert Park and many of the Chicago School tended to see little difference between race and ethnicity and used the terms interchangeably. They expected both to disappear by assimilation.

Since the sixties, however, heritage roots, ethnic identity, and 'Black is beautiful' sent scholars looking for black culture, black soul, and black roots clearly based on physical, biological distinctions of the 12 per cent of Americans who were black. Thus, Pierre van den Berghe (1981) began to develop a theory of sociobiology that takes both the social environment and the biological inheritance seriously. He sees race as a special marker of ethnicity, upon which 'dominance orders', 'hierarchies', and 'pecking orders' are based. Racism thus becomes a cultural invention, and ethnicity and class (including race) become two alternative and competing principles of sociality (van den Berghe, 1981:58, 257).

The meaning of the concept of race has evolved and changed over time. Explorers of all these European countries were finding people who looked and behaved somewhat differently, so they became interested in common and distinctive features and invariably began to wonder about the origin of these differences in colour and physical characteristics. At first 'the race of mankind' had been used, generally distinguishing *Homo sapiens* from other animals, but now increasingly people were faced with classifying the varieties of human beings into categories or races. So 'race' today is defined by sociobiologists as an arbitrary biological grouping of people on the basis of physical traits.

The concept 'racism' has been defined by Banton (1967:19) as 'the doctrine that behaviour is determined by stable inherited characteristics deriving from separate racial stocks, having distinctive attributes and usually considered to stand to one another in relations of superiority and inferiority'. As white Europeans increasingly came into contact with peoples around the world, and as the theory of evolution developed, there were many attempts at arranging the varieties of *Homo sapiens* into distinctive groupings. Had some of these humans developed into superior beings? There was often the tendency to identify Europeans as superior and others inferior, especially because white Europeans at the time had a relatively well-developed technology. Racists today believe that some people are inferior or superior biologically; as a result, they often treat people of other races negatively.

While 'racism' is a negative concept, based on the belief that some races are inferior to others, the concept of equality (subtitle of this book) is an attempt at ranking people more objectively on the basis of opportunities to compete in the social, economic, and political spheres of our society. It is assumed that humans have roughly the same abilities, but for many reasons they do not all have the same opportunity to fulfill their potential. In this sense equality is a part of the social structure of a society, rather than a form of biological determinism. While biological features are difficult to change, social structures can be changed, although not easily.

CLASSIFICATION OF HUMANS

The Swedish botanist Carl Linnaeus (1701–78) developed an orderly nomenclature for plants, which soon encouraged biologists similarly to classify organic forms of life. Today it is generally accepted that contemporary mankind belongs to the same *Homo sapiens* species, and

that there is no basic biological or genetic difference between the various human populations. Physical features, however, do vary, and as early as 1745 Linnaeus proposed that mankind be classified into four main races: European, Asiatic, African, and American Indian (Hughes and Kallen, 1974:6). In 1781 the German physiologist Johann Blumenbach proposed a classification of humans based on head and skull shape, forming five races: Caucasian (European), Negro, Mongol, Malayan, and American Indian. There have been many attempts at ordering the complex array of characteristics of humans, as these examples suggest.

During the eighteenth and nineteenth centuries, classification of peoples around the world became popular among physical anthropologists who wished to compare the differences that they encountered. Since evolution was becoming more accepted, many of them attempted to arrange races in a hierarchical order from primitive to highly civilized types. The genetic discoveries of Gregor Mendel (in 1822 to 1824) revolutionized and encouraged further interest in classification (Hughes and Kallen, 1974:8). Slowly the story of human development began to unfold.

Many criteria have been used in the various classifications, and the American physical anthropologist Earnest Hooten expanded the list of physical criteria in his formation of three primary divisions of humans: Caucasian, Mongoloid, and Negroid. Once he had outlined these three major groupings, he subdivided them into intermediate types to account for the complex variations. In Table 10.1 we outline Hooten's (1946) three primary divisions; these have been used fairly extensively in the discussion of race today.

Hooten (1946) used seven criteria including skin colour, eye colour, hair type, nose shape, lip shape, and amount of body hair in the formation of his Caucasoid, Mongoloid, and Negroid racial types. The Caucasoids have the fairest or lightest colour skins and eyes, whereas the Negroids are the darkest, with the Mongoloids falling in between. The nose and lip shapes of the Caucasoids are the narrowest, whereas the Negroids have the broadest and thickest. The

TABLE 10.1 Hooten's Criteria to Distinguish Primary Divisions of Humans

Criteria	Caucasoid (White)	Mongoloid (Yellow)	Negroid (Black)
Skin colour	White, pink or 'ruddy' to light brown	Yellow or yellow-brown	Dark brown to black
Eye colour	All lighter shades, but never black	Medium brown to dark brown	Dark brown to black
Hair type	Straight to wavy, occasionally curled	Straight (coarse in texture), and circular in cross-section	Wooly to frizzy; oval in cross-section
Nose shape	Usually high-bridged and narrow	Low root, short tip, medium width at nostrils	Usually low, depressed, broad tip and nostrils
Lip shape	Thickness, medium to thin; little or no lip eversion	Medium thickness; variable eversion	Usually thick with obvious eversion
Cheek-bone region	Not prominent	Projecting orwards and laterally; may be covered by fat pad	Variable, but usually more obvious than in Caucasoid
Body hair (including beard)	Medium to heavy; very variable	Usually less than Caucasoid and Negroid	Medium to scanty

SOURCE: Modified from Earnest Hooten's *Up From the Ape*, rev. edn (New York: Macmillan, 1946) by David Hughes and Evelyn Kallen (eds), *The Anatomy of Racism: Canadian Dimensions* (Montreal: Harvest House, 1974), p. 9.

Mongoloids have the straightest and coarsest hair texture, whereas the Negroids have the woolliest hair. The Mongoloids also have the most visible cheekbones, whereas these are least prominent among Caucasoids. Caucasoids have the most hair on the body, and Negroids the least.

Classifying *Homo sapiens* into three types makes it quickly apparent that there is a wide range of variation within each of the three types. Many have questioned whether such classification is still useful, but it does appear that Europeans in particular have made much of skin colour and some of the other differential characteristics, so that we are forced to examine the differences and reasons for placing values on such physical characteristics.

Another major problem with this classification is that large numbers of the world's population do not fit the scheme, such as the South Asians of southern Asia, the aboriginals of the two Americas, and most of the Pacific Polynesians and Melanesians. The South Asians from the subcontinent of India represent roughly one-fifth of the population of the world and they seem to fit the Caucasian type in most respects, except that their skin colour is considerably darker. They are classified as Caucasian, but since skin colour is often considered so important by other whites, they are often treated as coloured or visible minorities (Ujimoto and Hirabayashi, 1980). The aboriginals of North and South America (originally two of the six peopled continents) seem to fit between the Caucasoid and Mongoloid types, but are usually classified as Mongoloid. The peoples of the Pacific islands, having somewhat darker skins than the Mongoloids, seem to fit best between the Mongoloid and Negroid categories. It is for reasons such as these that many scholars have created more than three racial types; Hooten, however, suggested that we begin with these three basic types, and then subdivide into more groups as considered necessary.

In summary, the division of the peoples of the world into useful categories or races is difficult, and since all *Homo sapiens* are fundamentally similar, many people suggest that we abandon attempts at classifying humans into races according to their physical characteristics. However, it is a social fact that humans are often stratified and treated differently because of their physical differences, and assimilation has not happened as fast as some hoped, so that we are forced to deal with racial types and inequalities.

Genetic and Skeletal Variations

Physical anthropologists have also analyzed the skeletal characteristics and blood types of the three primary divisions that we have discussed. We can only introduce their work here. There is considerable evidence that *Homo sapiens* evolved over thousands of years, and in the selection process minor skeletal differences evolved in different regions. When skulls are examined, the Europeans have more developed brow ridges than the other two groups. The Caucasoids have a straighter facial profile with small brows and a prominent chin, whereas Asian cheekbones and jaws are more prominent, and African jaws protrude more, with smaller chins and narrower palates (Hughes and Kallen, 1974:14). Europeans have high, narrow nasal apertures, and Asians have versions in between. The body bones of Europeans are thickly constructed with larger joints, while the African bone structure is longer and more slender. Asians

again have intermediate versions. Although the human skeletal structures are basically the same, there are minor variations that again tend to fall into three primary divisions.

Blood types tend to follow a similar pattern of variation, which seems to have emerged from the three major geographical 'breeding grounds' of Africa, Asia, and Europe (Hughes and Kallen, 1974:15). Of the ABO blood group system, Europeans and Africans show moderate evidence of A_2 genes, while in Asians it is virtually absent. B type genes are infrequent among Europeans, frequent among Asians, and intermediate among Africans. The Rh (or Rhesus) factor is high among Europeans, but virtually absent among Asians (Hughes and Kallen, 1974:16). On the other hand, the sickle-cell tendency is high among Africans, but low for the others. Much more could be said about these differences, but it is sufficient to say that there are variations that can be classified into three basic divisions of mankind according to physical characteristics, skeletal types, and blood types. Although *Homo sapiens'* physical evolution seems to have come from one basic source, more recently smaller variations have occurred in the various regions of the world, accounting for differences in skin colour and some variations in skeletal and blood types.

Visible Minorities as Social Reality

Because such a large majority of immigrants came to Canada from Europe, especially from northern Europe, these less pigmented 'whites' set a standard for the visible norm. Thus non-whites, largely from Asia and Africa, look different physically. A hierarchy of values has developed in which lighter-skinned humans are more valued. Differences are even made between northern and southern Europeans; even among blacks, those with lighter coloured skins are valued more. The 'Black is beautiful' call that began in the 1960s has made being black more acceptable, but the value hierarchy based on skin colour tends to continue.

Thus, in this chapter, rather than using Hooten's technical three categories, we will use references to Europeans, Asians, and Africans, as well as the terms 'whites' and 'non-whites' that are in more common usage today. Although Anthony Richmond (1972b) of York University in Toronto published *Readings in Race and Ethnic Relations* in 1972, it included contributions by American scholars on race mostly outside of Canada because very little Canadian research on race existed. So when Ujimoto and Hirabayashi held conferences at the 1977 and 1978 Learneds Society meetings focusing on Asians in Canada, these papers were among the first to deal more seriously with research on Canada's racial minorities. Victor Ujimoto and Gordon Hirabayashi (1980) published these papers in *Visible Minorities and Multiculturalism: Asians in Canada,* which included contributions dealing with Chinese, Japanese, Koreans, Vietnamese, and Filipinos. Since then the concept of 'visible minorities' has gained acceptance to include those who are of Mongoloid and Negroid races. At that time they included 'multiculturalism' in their title, which was becoming more popular. Increasingly, the term 'visible minorities' is gaining acceptance, although some are offended by such a category, because it assumed a 'white' standard in Europe and the Americas; others say that in southern Africa a majority are black, so that is the standard there. In some ways, this category is very general and undefined, based largely on skin colour so that often Arabs and many others are included, depending on how tightly the definition is drawn to include only northern European-origin Canadians.

Since then 'visible minorities' in Canada have doubled to roughly 10 per cent, more problems related to race have emerged, and more research and publication has occurred. These works used bolder titles including words like 'racism' (Bolaria and Li, 1988; Henry et al., 2000; James, 1999; McKague, 1991; Satzewich, 1992), 'oppression' (Bolaria and Li, 1988), and 'apartheid' (Driedger and Halli, 2000; Richmond, 1994) in their titles.

RACISM IN HISTORICAL PERSPECTIVE

If the concept of race is difficult to define, and since it is difficult to classify the many differentiations of humans into racial categories, why do we continue to try? It is because humans need to simplify and order the universe to be able to comprehend it. But more importantly, whites of European Caucasian origin have judged—and continue to judge—others on the basis of skin colour. Racial attitudes and behaviour based on physical characteristics are a fact in North America, and we are forced to deal with the phenomenon of racism (Wargon, 2000). Many North Americans believe that human behaviour is determined by stable, inherited characteristics deriving from separate racial stocks with distinctive attributes that can be ranked as superior or inferior. This is racism.

Aboriginals in North America were slaughtered or placed on reserves. Blacks in America were forced to become slaves; the Japanese in Canada and the United States during the Second World War were forcibly transferred into the interior. Blacks and coloureds in South Africa lived in ghettos and needed passes to enter white territories. These are but a few examples of racism. Let us explore how such thinking developed over time.

White European Dominance

Prior to the sixteenth century, the white Europeans represented only one-sixth of the total world population. However, when the Protestant Reformation began in the 1500s—the same time that Europeans explorers began to discover the rest of the world—ideas, inventions, and technology developed to enhance European power and dominance in the world (van den Berghe, 1981). As European industry flourished, Europe's population exploded and new settlements were established; soon Europeans became one-third of the world's population (Driedger, 1996; Driedger and Halli, 2000).

Europeans had traded with the Chinese, South Asians and others for centuries, facilitated by Arab and other middle entrepreneurs who brought spices and goods across the lands and deserts. After Columbus, however, Europeans soon made direct contacts with the East via the sea. Asians looked physically different; their features were very different. Europeans now had direct contact with these 'different' peoples. As they sought to find a direct passage to the East going west, the Spaniards and Portuguese found South and Central aboriginals; the British, French, and Dutch found more aboriginals in North America. Some, such as the Maya, Aztec, and Inca, had developed great civilizations, but others were in the food-gathering stages. Again, they looked different physically. The same was true when they found the darker peoples on the coasts of Africa. One dominant impression these new experiences left was that other peoples of the world are not white. Skin colour became an easy way of differentiating between white Europeans and others (van den Berghe, 1981).

As these white invaders, who had fairly recently been barbarians themselves, explored the world, many of them were both awed by some of the great and old civilizations that they had found, and hard-pressed to seek ways of justifying their presence there. Since European technology permitted extensive sea travel, technological advances, white physical appearance, and a sense of a superior 'white image' soon appeared around the world. It was only a matter of time before 'white is more beautiful' became popular with the Europeans, first no doubt unconsciously, and later justified by various ideologies.

Colonialism

The patterns of contact varied. In some parts of the world, trading relationships developed, in others exploitation was extensive, and in still other areas pioneer settlers came to possess the land. Trading had taken place overland for centuries, but now the white Europeans made contacts with the Chinese, South Asians, aboriginals in the Americas, and blacks in Africa (van den Berghe, 1981:85–110). Since the Asians had highly developed civilizations, the Europeans

desired their finely crafted cloth, their spices, and many other articles of trade. Europeans created small port enclaves on the coastlines of China, India, Indonesia, and elsewhere to establish trading communities. Raw materials such as furs were also desired, so forts were established across North America where the fur trade flourished. In all of these trading relationships Europeans were a small minority, but they possessed sufficient technological superiority to protect themselves and maintain their white bases amidst peoples of many varieties of colour.

While the temptation to exploit these newly encountered peoples was always present, the great Mayan, Aztec, and Inca civilizations of Latin America provided special opportunities for exploitation (van den Berghe, 1981:85–90). In the 1530s, gold was found by the Spanish among the Inca in what is now Peru. Small groups of powerful Spanish and Portuguese subjugated, often exploited, and sometimes enslaved aboriginals to work in mines. Many European men, away from their families, exploited Native women, and many married them and created families.

Pioneer settlement was a third form of white European contact when North Europeans settled in North America. The French and British created communities on the American and Canadian east coasts and soon began to differentiate between white Europeans and aboriginals. Most of these aboriginals were food gatherers, less technologically advanced, and skin colour or differentiation by physical features became an important means of social differentiation.

IMMIGRATION AND RACE

Immigration Policies

There is no doubt as to who came to the Americas first, and it is well known that many aboriginals had developed civilizations that rivalled white European development. Aboriginals, the first immigrants to the Americas came at least 12,000 years ago. These early *Homo sapiens* possessed the land now called Canada, the United States of

America, Mexico, and Central America twenty-five times as long as any Europeans have lived here. In Canada most of the aboriginals were food gatherers, although food-producing had begun among the Huron and Iroquois in southern Ontario, and large-scale fishing, chiefdoms, and a distinctive art had developed on the northwest coast. In Mexico, Central America, and Peru some of the great civilizations of the Maya, Aztec, and Inca still flourished when Europeans invaded and exploited their land.

After 1600, British, French, Spanish, and Dutch colonies were established in what is now Canada and the United States. Most of these came as families settling permanently, and they needed the land that the aboriginals used for hunting. At first their needs were limited, but slowly white agriculturalists began to crowd out Native food-gatherers. As Indians were increasingly pushed westward, the number of whites and their dominance and power increased, leading to conflicts with the Iroquois, the Huron, and later the Metis battles that took place in 1870 and 1885 at Fort Garry and Batoche (Stanley, 1969). Treaties were signed, and Riel was hanged. The last stand of Indians and Metis had taken place; the white traders and agriculturalists had triumphed.

The white European industrial dominance over coloured Africans and Asians as preindustrial suppliers and servants was a common pattern that emerged around the world (van den Berghe, 1981:111–36). Most countries of Europe created colonies that supplied raw materials for the European industrial revolution. These colonial arrangements always benefited the whites, and in some places took such brutal forms as slavery, especially in colonial America when Blacks were brought mainly from Africa to work in the cotton fields of the Deep South. White dominance had taken the most blatantly inhumane course—the buying and selling of humans as commodities. Ideologies such as the Christian religion of love, professed by many, had to be adjusted in order to present a sense of consistency (van den Berghe, 1981:111–15). The doctrine that blacks were less than human, or subhumans, followed.

Others agreed that God had created some to be dominant and others to be subservient. Still others exploited their fellow humans at will, without thought of morality or justice for all. Always, European whites were the masters, and coloured phenotypes were the servants. We propose that these are some of the historical reasons for the white preoccupation with race.

Europeans have remained 90 per cent of the Canadian population into the twenty-first century. Barely one hundred years ago, the two charter groups laid the foundations of the Canadian confederation, so that white Europeans became the legal and dominant force in the shaping of the dominion. For the most part, Canadian immigrant policy preferred north European immigrants and allowed very few non-Europeans to enter. There were exceptions, however, when Chinese were brought in to build the railroad in British Columbia in the 1880s, or when labourers were needed in mines and factories in the North or southern Ontario. An informal agreement was made with Japan so that few Japanese entered after the initial ones came during the turn of the century. Often head taxes were imposed to discourage 'the yellow hordes of Asia' from entering.

The new point system introduced in the early 1970s was important in Canadian immigration policy. Immigration became possible in three ways: citizens of Canada willing to take responsibility for their care and maintenance could sponsor their parents, brothers, or sisters and have them enter Canada under the category 'Sponsored Dependants' (Richmond, 1994:117–30). Since most Canadians are of northern European ancestry, this opportunity heavily favoured further white European immigration. However, a category for 'Independent' applicants permitted entrance if they could score 50 out of a possible 100 points. This category permitted anyone in the world to compete to enter Canada, especially if they had sufficient educational, occupational, and language skills. The 'Nominated' category is an intermediate version that requires applicants to score some points independently, but prior settlement arrangements and having a relative in

Canada can boost the chances of entrance (Richmond, 1994:117–30).

Since the advent of the point system, the change in the leading source countries of immigrants is quite evident. In 1951 the 10 countries that contributed the largest number of immigrants to Canada were all European except for the United States. By 2000, most of the 10 top contributors were from Asia and the Caribbean. A large proportion of these immigrants were highly visible; many brought with them different religions and cultures, as well as racial differences. Since Canada is a large country with a relatively sparse population, and since the world pressures for living space are increasing, many people expect Canada to take in more refugees and immigrants who have been left homeless. Some, like the Asians, have come by boat illegally. Thus, we can expect that in the future more non-whites will enter Canada and that the proportion of Asians, Africans, and other visible minorities will increase. It is interesting to note that during economic downturns, there are usually pressures from labour unions and others to restrict immigration, based on the argument that there are not enough jobs for everyone. This conflict of interest can lead to changes of laws to restrict immigrants. These changes, some of them very recent, have been part of the changing dynamics of Canada's immigration history (Driedger, 2000b).

Racial Demographic Characteristics

While the proportion of Canadians of Asian and African racial origin was only about 3 per cent in 1971, by 1996 it had increased to nearly 11 per cent (Boyd, Goldman, and White, 2000). This increase in visible minorities was largely due to a change in immigration policy. Whereas Canadian immigration policy clearly preferred northern Europeans until the early 1970s, now the new point system gives immigrants from the Third World a better chance to compete. Many more visible minorities have arrived in the past decade, so let us compare the non-white minorities with those in the American population.

The 1996 census does not show racial divisions in Canada very well, but Table 10.2 shows that about 86 per cent of the Canadian population could be classified as European, 10 per cent as Asian, and about 1 per cent as African or black, and 3 per cent as aboriginal. The rest were of multiple or mixed origins, which requires some interpretation. The census takers indicated that, of the Europeans who married others, most married other non-charter Europeans. The aboriginals who married non-Indians could be classified as Metis. Most likely the Pacific Islanders would be heavily Asian, and the Latin Americans heavily white, with a heavy mixed aboriginal heritage.

With so few non-whites in Canada, we could hardly expect that Asians or Africans would be a majority in any region of Canada. However, the aboriginal peoples in 1996 were a majority in the Northwest Territories and Nunavut (80 per cent Inuit in 1996), representing well over half of the residents there (Hancock, 1995:68). In addition to being a majority in the North, aboriginals are much more concentrated in the five most westerly provinces. In fact, about 7 per cent of the populations of Manitoba and Saskatchewan are aboriginals. There are, however, relatively few aboriginals east of Ontario, living in the five most easterly provinces.

The Chinese represent more than 3 per cent of the Canadian population, and one-fourth of visible minorities, heavily concentrated in Ontario and British Columbia. Three-fourths of all of Canada's Chinese live in Ontario and British Columbia, mostly in Toronto and Vancouver, where the two largest Canadian Chinatowns are also located. The Chinese have been a part of British Columbia history ever since they came to the west coast a hundred years ago, while the Chinese in Ontario have concentrated in Toronto somewhat more recently.

The South Asian Indo-Pakistani visible minority is unique in that they are usually technically classified as Caucasian. They fit most of the Caucasian criteria except skin colour. We discuss them here because they are a visible minority, and whites tend to make much of different phenotypes.

TABLE 10.2 Canadian Visible and Non-visible Racial Populations

Racial/Ethnic Groupings	Canada 1996 N	%
Non-visible Caucasian	24,227,000	86
British	5,582,000	
French	2,665,000	
Other Europeans	3,244,000	
Multiple Responses	7,409,000	
Canadian	5,327,000	
Visible Minorities	3,199,000	11
Chinese	860,000	
South Asian	671,000	
Black	574,000	
Arab	245,000	
Filipino	234,000	
Latin American	177,000	
Southeast Asian	173,000	
Southwest Asian	133,000	
Other visible minorities	70,000	
Multiple visible minorities	62,000	
Aboriginal	1,102,000	3
Native Indian	529,000	
Inuit	40,000	
Metis/Other	533,000	
Total national populations	28,528,000	100

SOURCES: Statistics Canada, *Ethnic Origins*, Census of Canada 1991, 20 Percent Data Base (Ottawa: Statistics Canada, 1993); John R. Weeks, *Population: An Introduction to Concepts and Issues*, 5th edn (Belmont, CA: Wadsworth, 1994), pp. 280–4; Robert Brym, *Canadian Society and the 1996 Census Supplement to Accompany New Society*, 2nd edn (Toronto: Harcourt Brace, 1999), p. 9.

Similar to the Chinese, three-fourths of all Indo-Pakistanis live in Ontario and British Columbia, again mostly in Toronto and Vancouver. Interestingly, 80 per cent of all East Indians in Vancouver are Sikhs from the Punjab. The Indo-Pakistanis represent the third largest visible minority in Canada after the Chinese and aboriginals.

African and Black origin Canadians represent the fourth largest visible minority in Canada.

The African racial group in any case is very small, about 2 per cent of the Canadian population. Well over half of the Africans are located in Ontario, mostly in Toronto. In 1971 about one-third of Canada's blacks resided in Nova Scotia, especially in Halifax, but by 1996 that has changed with many more in Ontario.

The Japanese are similar to the Chinese in that they are Asians racially, and are most heavily located in Ontario and British Columbia; indeed, they were a part of early British Columbia society. A Japantown existed in Vancouver until the Second World War. During the 1940s, however, they were forcibly evacuated into the Canadian interior and today the Japanese total only 68,000, three-fourths of which are scattered in two provinces.

The Indo-Chinese entered Canada mainly during the decade of the 1970s. They represent a multi-ethnic category of Vietnamese, Cambodians, Laotians, Filipinos, and Thais. They speak many languages, represent many traditions, and do not exhibit the same solidarity as the groups discussed so far. Many of them came as boat refugees. One-third of them are located in Quebec, and another third in Ontario. In these two provinces, they are concentrated in the cities of Montreal and Toronto respectively. They add a smaller part to the Canadian Asian racial group.

Thus, Canada's non-white minorities represent about 14 per cent of the total population, and over half of these are Asian racially. They are represented largely by Chinese (Driedger, 1986b: 450). Figure 10.1 shows visible minorities in Canada are distributed proportionately. Of those listed in the table, the Chinese (24 per cent) are the largest group, blacks (20 per cent) the second largest, followed by South Asians (19 per cent), West Asians and Arabs (11 per cent), Filipinos (7 per cent), Southeast Asians including Vietnamese (5 per cent), Latin Americans (5 per cent), and others. Figure 10.1 does not include aboriginals, which would add another 1.7 per cent, which Samuel (1992) who designed this figure did not include. If aboriginals are included, this would raise the proportion of visible minorities in Canada to about 14 per cent in 1996.

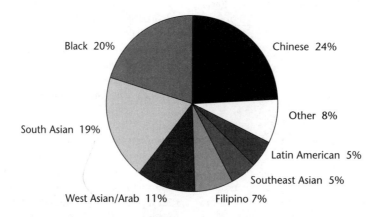

FIGURE 10.1 Ethnicity of Racial Minorities, 1991

SOURCE: T.J. Samuel, *Visible Minorities in Canada: A Projection* (Toronto: Race Relations Advisory Council on Advertising, Canadian Advertising Foundation, 1992).

In contrast to the small non-white Canadian population, there are much larger proportions of non-whites (24 per cent) in the United States population of 250 million in 1990 (Weeks, 1994:280–5). Of these 62 million visible minorities, 12 per cent of the American population are Afro-Americans (Weeks, 1994:280–2). These 31 million blacks are more than the total Canadian population of 30 million. Thus, it is not surprising that Americans are often very preoccupied with the question of race. While in the past, American blacks lived mainly in the Deep South, they have recently moved in large numbers into urban areas, including many northern cities. In 1990 blacks still represented large percentages of the southern state populations in Mississippi, South Carolina, and North Carolina. Although there are many black tenant farmers in the Deep South, their families are beginning to move to the southern cities (Pinkney, 1975:39–53).

Blacks have also moved into many northern American cities. More than 70 per cent of the population of the District of Columbia (mostly metropolitan Washington) is black. Many other northern cities such as Newark, Baltimore, Philadelphia, Cleveland, Detroit, and Chicago are over half black or are nearing a black majority. Many of these cities have black mayors. In many of these cities there are ghettos that are almost exclusively black (Lieberson and Waters, 1990). There are no comparable areas or cities in Canada where people of African or Asian race make up such large numbers, nor such potentially powerful political blocs.

There are also 31 million Americans of other races, representing about 13 per cent of their total population (Weeks, 1994:275–82). Seven million or 3 per cent are Asians. While Canada's proportion of Asians is somewhat larger (6 per cent), the aboriginals make up one-fifth of this category. Not so in the United States: two million American Indians represent less than 1 per cent of the total population. Since the American population is roughly 10 times the Canadian population, the United States should have five million aboriginals, if they were to have a proportionate number compared to Canada. Thus, while Canadians are more preoccupied with aboriginals as a racial group, Americans tend to be much more aware and concerned with their blacks, of which Canada has very few.

But there are also other Canadian and American racial differences. There are 22 million people in the United States of Hispanic origin, representing 9 per cent of their population. They are considered white racially, but are fairly visible physically (Weeks, 1994:282). Most of these Spanish-speaking people are Hispanics from Mexico, who represent a racial mixture of Europeans from Spain and Central and South American aboriginals. Like Canada's South Asians, these Spanish origin peoples are classified as whites, but their darker skin colour makes them more visible and tends to attract prejudice and discrimination.

In summary, a much larger percentage of the American population are from the African (12 per cent) and Asian (3 per cent) races. Along with the visible Hispanic minority (9 per cent) they make up one-fourth of the total American population. In Canada, the non-Caucasian racial percentage is much smaller (about 12 per cent). Therefore we would expect Americans to be more preoccupied with racial categories, problems, and issues. This tends to be true, except that the more open immigration policy of Canada has brought many more visible minorities into Canada, so that Canadians are now becoming increasingly conscious of racial and physical differences, especially in larger cities such as Toronto and Vancouver.

HIGHLIGHT 10.1 'VISIBLE MINORITIES' IN 2016

Of all the issues associated with recent immigration, possibly none is more widely discussed, if not hotly debated, than the sociological impact of increasing numbers of 'visible minorities'.* In a period of economic instability, if not decline, the concern of course is that racial prejudice and scapegoating will gain a greater foothold and that Canadian society will become a less hospitable place to live. Paradoxically, the sheer numbers of visible minorities, and the critical role immigrants play in economic and population growth, may help to ameliorate any widespread racial backlash.

The number of Canadians in 'visible minority' groups is expected to increase to 7.1 million by 2026 from 2.7 million in 1991, according to Statistics Canada projections. As a proportion of the overall population, this represents a doubling to 20 percent in 2016 from 10 percent in 1991. The largest visible minority group in 1991 (as in 1996) was the Chinese (about 666,000 people), and this group will continue to be the largest over the projection period (nearly 2 million by 2016). The proportion of Canadians who are of Chinese ancestry will grow to 5 percent in 2016. Blacks were the third largest visible minority group in 1991 (540,000) but are expected to become the second largest group by 2016 (almost 1.3 million). South Asians will drop from second largest to the third largest group, moving from 543,000 in 1991 to a projected 1.2 million in 2016. West Asians and Arabs will continue to rank as the fourth largest visible minority over this period. However, this group is expected to increase at the fastest rate (217 percent) to approximately 1 million in 2016 from 315,000 in 1991.

The vast majority of visible minority adults live in the large urban areas and large proportions of the populations in each of these CMAs are now visible minorities. In 1991, for example, the adult visible minority population accounted for 24 percent of the adult population in Toronto, 23 percent in Vancouver and 10 percent in Montreal.

Visible minority adults are much more likely to have a university degree and less likely not to have completed high school than are other adults. In 1991, the most recent year for which socio-economic data are available at this time, 18 percent of the visible minority population aged 15 and over had a university degree, compared with 11 percent of other adults. Also 33 percent of visible minorities had less than a high school level education, while this was the case for 39 percent of other adults.

The 1996 census was the first census to ask a direct question on visible minorities. The table above provides counts of the visible minority population as defined for employment equity purposes in the 1996 census.

The impact of this demographic change is still uncertain, but the substantial increase in the visible minority population in recent years is an issue that has already dramatically affected public policy (e.g., multiculturalism and anti-racism policy) and it seems likely to continue to do so in the future.

*NOTE: Statistics Canada uses the term 'visible minorities' rather than the term racially different groups. This term implies a bias. Statistics Canada does not present a clear rationale for singling out such groups instead of analyzing their socio-economic characteristics alongside other ethnic groups. This may be a subject for classroom discussion.

SOURCE: Karen Kelly, 'Projections of Visible Minority Groups, 1991 to 2016', *Canadian Social Trends*, Summer 1995, 37 (Catalogue 11-008E).

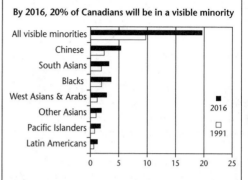

By 2016, 20% of Canadians will be in a visible minority

Visible Minority Population, 1996 (20% sample data)	
Total Population	28,528,125
Total visible minority population	3,197,480
Chinese	860,150
South Asian	670,590
Black	573,860
Arab West Asian	244,665
Filipino	234,195
Southeast Asian	172,765
Latin American	176,970
Japanese	68,135
Korean	64,835
Visible minorities (not included in above)	69,745
Multiple visible minorities	61,575
All others	25,330,645

SOURCE: Statistics Canada, Catalogue Numbers 93F0026XDB96004, 93F0026XDB96005, 93F0026XDB96006, Nation Series.

Socioeconomic Inequality

Sociologists often place individuals or groups into socioeconomic categories and rank them according to high and low status. Occupation, education, and income are the most commonly used indicators of social and economic status (SES). Since the non-white percentage of Canada's population is small, and since none of the groups is large, objective data on socioeconomic inequality tend to be limited.

In Table 8.5 we ranked 20 ethnic groups, showing which ethnic groups ranked above the Canadian mean income of $28,946 in 1991 ($57,000 in 2001), and which ranked below the mean. We found that all visible minorities ranked in the bottom third of the rankings on income. In Table 10.3 we use the three indicators of education, occupation, and income that are usually used as objective measures of socioeconomic status, comparing non-visible (white European) and visible (non-white Asians and Africans).

We have ranked eight non-visible minorities and find the Jewish Canadians on top of the category, ranking the highest on education (mean 14.7 years), white-collar occupational status (56.4 per cent), and income ($37,146). They rank first on a composite ranking of the three indicators combined. The British and French white charter groups who were the first Europeans to arrive,

TABLE 10.3 Socioeconomic Status by Visible Minority Status[a] and Ethnic Origins,[a] Canada, 1991

Ethnic Groups	Composite SES Rank[b]	Rank[c]	Years of Education (Mean)	White-Collar Occupations[d] (%) 1991	Income ($)
Non-visible Minority					
Jewish	1	1	14.7	56.4	37,146
British	2	2	14.0	42.7	29,928
French	3	3	13.5	41.7	27,222
Dutch	4	6	12.4	31.5	30,888
German	5	7	12.4	28.9	31,506
Ukrainian	6	10	11.1	19.0	34,110
Italian	7	12	9.0	15.2	29,550
Portuguese	8	13	7.9	7.7	26,926
Visible Minority					
West Asian	1	4	14.2	43.2	21,284
South Asian	2	5	14.2	36.4	25,718
Chinese	3	8	14.9	34.3	26,392
Southeast Asian	4	9	13.4	29.0	24,080
Black	5	11	13.3	22.9	23,346

NOTES:

a   Single ethnic origin responses only, for males of designated groups age 25–64.

b   Sum of the three ranks divided by three, for each of the non-visible and visible categories.

c   Sum of the three ranks divided by three, combining both non-visible and visible categories.

d   Includes managerial and administrative occupations as well as occupations in the natural sciences, engineering, mathematics, social sciences, teaching, medicine and health, and artistics, literary and realted occupations.

SOURCES: Monica Boyd, 'Gender, Visible Minority, and Immigrant Earnings Inequality', in Vic Satzewich (ed.), *Deconstructing a Nation Immigration, Multiculturalism and Racism in '90s Canada* (Halifax: Fernwood Publishing, 1992), pp. 300–2: The 1991 Census of Canada Public Use Sample Tapes.

rank second and third. The other northern and eastern European entrance groups who followed, rank in the middle, and the Italians and Portuguese who have arrived more recently, rank seventh and eighth in the non-visible category. The Portuguese who rank last, compared to the Jews, who rank first, have half as much education (mean 7.9 years), one-sixth as many in white-collar occupations (7.7 per cent), and earn two-thirds as much ($26,346) as the Jews. There are significant SES differences amongst non-visible minorities.

Comparing five visible minority groups in the second category, we see that the West Asians (Arabs in the Near East, etc.) rank highest in that category on white-collar occupations (43.2 per cent), are tied for first in education (mean 14.2 years), and last in income ($21,284) for an overall ranking of first in the visible minority category. Blacks rank last in education (mean 13.3 years), white-collar occupations (22.9 per cent), and second last in income ($23,346).

Having looked at each of the two non-visible and visible categories separately, we need to compare all 13 groups to see where each ranks overall, using a composite rank score for all three socioeconomic indicators. Whereas the Jews, British, and French rank in the top three overall, the West Asians and South Asians (East Indians, etc.) rank fourth and fifth, and the Chinese and

Southeast Asians (Vietnamese, etc.) eighth and ninth. Overall, it is the non-visible Italians and Portuguese who rank last. Using these objective socioeconomic criteria, we find that visible minorities by no means all rank lower in socioeconomic status. Visible minorities rank especially high on education, because most of them have arrived since the point immigration system established in the 1960s, where they had to have higher education to qualify for entrance into Canada, so they have an educational advantage. With more education, the visible minorities have also been able to get into higher status white-collar occupations on average, than the lower third of the non-visible category. However, this has not translated into comparably higher incomes, which suggest that there are other factors such as discrimination, that operate.

HISTORIC RACISM

The many racial groups in Canada in their many settings cannot be dealt with in depth here. However, two selected types of problems (black slavery and Japanese internment) will show generally the extent of racial stratification and some of its problems.

Slavery of Blacks

The slave trade became an important part of the American economy and social structure and became a caste system unparalleled in North America. The stratification of 31 million blacks who are a sizeable population in many southern states and many large cities of the United States is continuing evidence of inequality based on racial strata (Weeks, 1994:280–4). To a lesser extent, slavery also became a part of the early social structures of Canada. In 1628 a British ship brought a black child, the first known black resident of Canada, to New France (Hill, 1981:3). Although the laws of France forbade slavery, Louis XIV gave his limited approval to slavery because there was a shortage of workers and servants. By 1709 full permission was given, and the long-standing practice of slavery in New France continued.

The British had brought slaves to the New World as early as 1562, selling them to the Spanish-American settlements, and the first shipload of 20 African slaves to reach British North America was landed at Jamestown, Virginia, in 1619. A century later, when the French territory of Acadia was ceded to the British by the Treaty of Utrecht, New England settlers moved north, bringing their slaves to build Halifax in 1749. When the French were defeated by the British in 1759, the French slave system of Quebec passed smoothly into the British regime (Hill, 1981:5–6). Many British officers, prominent citizens, and, on occasion, clergymen owned slaves, and the slave trade was brisk.

The French were not too anxious to promote slavery because they felt that it did not pay and that free labour was more productive. 'Nonetheless, slavery was given a legal formulation in New France between 1689 and 1709' (Winks, 1971:3). By 1759, there were about 4,000 slaves in New France, both Indian and black.

With the Treaty of Paris in 1763, France ceded the whole of its North American territory east of the Mississippi River to Great Britain. One side effect of this was to strengthen the institution of slavery legally and religiously. Not only did the British officials and Protestant sects support slavery, but governmental authorities encouraged the immigration of slave owners (like the New England Loyalists) and their slaves into the country (Krauter and Davis, 1978:48).

When the British Empire Loyalists fled to Canada during the rebellion of the American colonies around 1776, they also brought their slaves to Nova Scotia, and Upper and Lower Canada (Walker, 1992:1–93). Mohawk and Iroquois Indians who had fought with the British also moved north into Canada, some of them bringing with them black slaves whom they owned. Some black Loyalists received land grants. These blacks later formed black settlements in Nova Scotia, the Niagara Peninsula,

York (now Toronto), Kingston, and Prescott. Members of the Legislative Council of Lieutenant-Governor John Graves Simcoe in Upper Canada and members of his Executive Cabinet owned slaves, even though Simcoe himself worked hard to abolish slavery (Hill, 1981:16). Legislation to restrict slavery in 1790 preceded the historic 1803 decision that slavery was inconsistent with democracy. Few slaves were left in Canada when the British Imperial Act of 1833 abolished slavery throughout the empire (Walker, 1992:331–59).

There were also free blacks who entered Nova Scotia. 'Free Blacks had been promised treatment equal to that of their white peers; the British pledge of one hundred-acre grants of land to each Black failed to materialize. Most Blacks received no land at all; if anything was given them it was mainly barren one-acre lots on the edge of white loyalist townships where they were segregated from the main population' (Krauter and Davis, 1978:42). This meant that from the beginning free blacks did not receive the same chances as whites to improve themselves economically, and they were segregated, as they are in Nova Scotia to this day. 'In every instance where acreage was granted to both Black and white settlers, Blacks received less. For example, while Blacks were given one-acre lots in Digby, Whites were granted from one-hundred to four-hundred acre lots throughout the Annapolis County' (Krauter and Davis, 1978:42). Although freed in Canada, most blacks had to go back to work for whites as servants or workers, which kept them from developing their own economic independence. 'Blacks in Nova Scotia had become so disillusioned by 1792 that 1200 of them accepted an offer by the Sierra Leone Company and sailed to Africa' (Krauter and Davis, 1978:43; Walker, 1992:94–114).

While the slavery of blacks and the lack of allocation of free land to free blacks kept them in subjugation, they also were kept in their segregated places by limited education, employment, and housing. Blacks did not enjoy educational opportunities equal to other Nova Scotians, and by the 1850s segregated black schools were operating in both Nova Scotia and Ontario (Winks, 1969:164–91). Educational opportunities for blacks were grossly inadequate: teachers were poorly qualified to teach and were underpaid, and student attendance was irregular (Clairmont, 1965). Many black students left school by the sixth or seventh grade; the high school dropout rate was very high, so very few blacks entered university. This raised the likelihood of poor job opportunities and perpetuated the poverty cycle.

Many blacks who came to Canada became farm labourers, and when the railroads came, many worked on rail construction gangs. When the Maritimes became less competitive economically as forests and fish declined, many blacks became unemployed with little hope of finding jobs. 'More recently, Blacks have occupied the lowest rungs of the urban employment ladder. In 1941, almost half the employed Black males of Montreal were railway porters, while four-fifths of the Black females were domestics' (Calliste, 1988:36–52; Potter, 1961:49). 'A federal government survey of Black workers of the civil service shows that Blacks in Nova Scotia are systematically discriminated against at all levels of employment' (Head, 1975:86).

Our review of blacks in Nova Scotia earlier showed that many of them are rural, and that their houses are substandard with a minimum of heating and plumbing (Henry, 1973). Elsewhere, blacks live mostly in cities; the census shows large numbers in Montreal and Toronto. While in Nova Scotia both rural and urban blacks are segregated, this is not the case in the larger cities in Ontario and Quebec (Anderson, 1993:67). Table 10.3 showed that the income of West Indians is much lower than most other ethnic groups. As a result, they often cannot afford good housing and have to live closer to the centre of the city, where housing is older and less adequate (Bolaria, 1995, 1999:159–62; Fleras, 2001:85–106; James, 1990).

More recently, however, with the change in Canada's new immigration point system, many more West Indian blacks have come to Canada from the Caribbean, and they have come especially to urban areas such as Toronto (Anderson, 1993:69). Ramcharan (1982), and Anderson (1993) have studied black and West Indian communities in Toronto and their social institutions. Recently four Toronto sociologists (Breton, Isajiw, Kalbach, and Reitz, 1990) studied a number of ethnic groups in Toronto (Driedger, 2001). Race relations in Toronto are especially interesting. In 1871, 96 per cent of the population were of British origin, and this has declined to roughly one-half by 2001 (Kalbach, 1980). People of many other origins have entered Toronto so that it is now one of Canada's most multiethnic and multiracial cities. Kalbach (1980) shows that in 1971 there were at least 28,000 blacks in Toronto, although the 1981 census was not able to find that many. Anderson (1993:66–7) reports that two-thirds of the 28,000 Caribbean blacks who arrived in 1974 came to Ontario; the same proportion of 14,000 who came in 1989 also settled in Ontario. Kalbach's (1980:14) measures of discrimination show that in 1971 Jews, Italians, Chinese, and blacks were in many ways less similar to the British than many of the other groups considered. Reitz (1982) found that the West Indians were among the lowest in job status, job security, and mean income of eight groups compared in Toronto.

The recent influx of multiracial groups into Toronto has resulted in racial incidents; as a result, a task force was set up to study the adequacy of the school system to cope with these problems. The task force found that:

> principals and teachers tended to be defensive about the possibility that there were incidents of conflict and confrontation that could be attributed to racist attitudes. Racism in children's lives in Metro Toronto poses a serious challenge not only to the education system but to the future community (Pitman, 1978:183–4).

These findings suggest that blacks and other racial minorities find it difficult to compete in our society; with the history of racism in Canada, it is not surprising. These problems will be discussed again in Chapter 11 (Anderson, 1993; Bolaria, 1995; Christianson and Weinfeld, 1993; Dei, 1993; Fleras, 2001; Henry and Tator, 1994; Henry et al., 2000; James, 1990, 1999).

Japanese Internment

In our discussion of the slavery of blacks, we have suggested that Canadian society has been and still is structured to promote racial inequalities. Lest some think that this happened long ago, the evacuation of Japanese from the Pacific coast to the Canadian interior during the Second World War is a second illustration of structured inequalities in our economic and political systems.

A small number of Japanese began to settle in Canada around 1884, and by 1894 about 1,000 had entered Canada. They had been good fishermen in Japan and found it relatively natural to continue their trade on the Canadian west coast. Indeed, they were able to compete so well that other Canadian fishermen soon saw them as a threat. Cries to stop Japanese immigration increased until, in 1908, Japan and Canada signed a 'gentlemen's agreement' that effectively limited Japanese immigration to less than 1,000 per year. In 1908 alone, 7,985 Japanese entered Canada (Nakamura, 1975:301). Citizens in British Columbia had previously pressured governments to restrict immigrants of Asians in general, excluding especially the Chinese. Political and labour leaders marched into Chinatown in 1907, causing a riot and thousands of dollars of damage. They were stopped by the Japanese from entering the Japanese quarters on Powell Street. Even prior to 1941, discrimination against Asians was commonplace, with many legal restrictions and injustices.

To protect themselves, Chinese and Japanese Canadians established segregated areas where they did their business and where they lived and built their social institutions (Kobayashi, 1987; Sugiman and Nishio, 1993). The largest Chinatown in Canada is still in Vancouver. Prior to the bombing of Pearl Harbor, the majority of Canada's Japanese lived in two large communities: 2,151 lived in Steveston, a fishing community on the coast south of Vancouver, and 8,427 lived in Vancouver (Nakamura, 1975:309). In Steveston, the Japanese were the majority. They owned a fleet of fishing boats, and their various organizations processed and marketed their catch. They had a thriving segregated community where they used their own language and supported their schools, clubs, and religious and social organizations. The same was true on Powell Street in the heart of Vancouver, where Japantown was a growing bustling enclave like many Chinatowns we know today (Broadfoot, 1977).

In 1941, 21,175 of the 23,149 Japanese in Canada were located on the British Columbia coast. A small minority, less than 8 per cent, was scattered throughout the rest of Canada. Ten years later, in 1952, only 12 per cent remained on the West Coast and the majority had been sent inland, 4,527 to the eastern Canadian provinces (Nakamura, 1975:330). Three-fourths of these Japanese Canadians in 1941 were Canadian-born. Many families had lived in Canada for several generations (Sunahara, 1980:93–120).

The evacuation and relocation caused significant changes; it wiped out many of the hard-won economic gains that the Japanese had built up over the years. Most had to start all over again, because before the war they had well over two hundred different Japanese organizations, few of which remained after the war. Kin associations, a traditional Japanese heritage, ceased to function; fathers were separated from families, and families were disbanded; Japanese-language schools and newspapers were closed down. The life, culture, customs, and traditions that were symbolized by Vancouver's Powell Street were over (Nakamura, 1975:330). The evacuation took nine months; the Japanese were sent to road camp projects and old mining towns such as Tashme, Slocan, and New Denver in British Columbia, and to sugarbeet projects in the Prairies. Some were deported to Japan. The property of the Japanese, such as fishing boats, houses, businesses, and public buildings, were confiscated and often sold for a fraction of their value. Some Japanese have returned to the coast, but many have not. Only a block of Japanese

businesses and shops remains on Vancouver's Powell Street today, a remnant of the former thriving Japantown (Petrie, 1982:11–46).

The destruction of the Japanese communities of the West Coast through evacuation and deportment during the Second World War was possible because of the racial hatred and pressures of West Coast Canadians and politicians who themselves were open to condone and/or vote for discriminatory legislation (Kobayashi, 1992). Sunahara (1980:94) lists four major reasons. Mackenzie King and the federal government often sympathized with or yielded to the American government, which may have influenced other Canadian politicians. West Coast labour unions were threatened by the Japanese and pressured politicians to eliminate the Japanese fishermen from the industry, which evacuation did for them. In general, the anti-Asian bias was so strong that very few people objected to the injustices that escalated in evacuation, confiscation, internment, and deportation (Broadfoot, 1977). War hysteria added to the problem. Minority communities were destroyed, social institutions were wiped out, and the Japanese culture was greatly weakened as a result of racism in Canada.

Ujimoto (1983:141) suggests that the Japanese experience can be understood in terms of Daniels and Kitano's (1970:5) minority-majority model, which involves two categories:

By the 'two category' system, they mean 'a system of stratification that is divided into two broad categories: the white and the non-white'. In this system of analysis, it is assumed that the white group is superior to the other group. Although it is recognized that there are other systems of stratification, our analysis of Japanese Canadian historical data indicates that the prejudice, discrimination and concomitant segregation in internment camps inflicted on the Japanese Canadians can be adequately assessed in terms of the simple two category system. . . . It becomes evident how the social and political structures

TABLE 10.4 The Four Stages of Maintaining the Two-Category System of Stratification

	Stages	Beliefs	Action Effects	Primary Mechanisms
Ordinary solutions	1	Prejudice	Avoidance	Stereotyping, informally patterned rules governing interaction
	2	Discrimination	Deprivation	More formal rules, norms, agreements; laws
	3	Segregation	Insulation	If the out-group is perceived as stepping over the line there may be lynchings and other warnings
Extraordinary solutions	4	A. Apartheid concentration	Isolation	A major trigger such as war is necessary;
		B. Expulsion, exile C. Extermination	Exclusion Genocide	out-group perceived as a real threat or danger to the existence of the host culture. Ordinary mechanisms (e.g., Stages 1, 2, and 3) have failed.

SOURCE: Roger Daniels and Harry H.L. Kitano, *American Racism: Exploration of the Nature of Prejudice* (Englewood Cliffs, NJ: Prentice-Hall, 1970) by permission of Roger Daniels and Harry H.L. Kitano, copyright assignees.

were manipulated, often by legislative means, in order to perpetuate the two category system of stratification (Ujimoto, 1983:141).

In Table 10.4, we present Daniels and Kitano's (1970:11) four basic stages of racial separation, which begin as three ordinary solutions, and follow into a fourth drastic extraordinary solution. Research shows (Berger, 1981; Ujimoto, 1983; Ujimoto and Hirabayashi, 1980) that the first stage of prejudice—avoidance and stereotyping—was common in British Columbia before the First World War. There was fertile ground for more serious actions against minorities such as the Japanese, Chinese, and East Indians. Japanese successes in fishing, farming, and lumbering became a serious threat to many who found it hard to compete. 'The anti-Japanese feelings and the eventual culmination of these feelings in the Vancouver Race Riots of 1907 probably best characterize the first stage of the two category system of stratification' (Ujimoto, 1983:144).

It was almost inevitable that the second stage of discrimination—overt action—would move toward deprivation and that more formal rules and laws would follow to restrict this form of economic threat. Many believed that the Japanese would deprive them of the majority of jobs and take away their employment opportunities, so that the political power of the majority would need to stem the Japanese tide. 'The Japanese were believed to constitute a threat to the economic and cultural supremacy of British Protestants and thus a significant threat to the distribution of power' (Baar, 1978:336). By 1908 the gentlemen's agreement with Japan limited Japanese immigration to a trickle. Under the second stage of discrimination, laws had been put into effect to restrict the Japanese minority influence.

Daniels and Kitano (1970:11) suggest that there would be a sequential escalation through the four stages, and indeed, this did happen in British Columbia. Stage three was the segregation and insulation through mass evacuation of

Japanese Canadians from 'protected areas' of British Columbia into interior camps and work projects; it effectively removed the economic threat under the guise of political threat. 'Former mining towns or "ghost towns" in the province were renovated to house the evacuees in Greenwood (1,177 evacuees), Kaslo (964), Sandon (933), New Denver (1,505), and Slocan (4,814)' (Ujimoto, 1983:138). Complete insulation from the rest of society was accomplished by confiscating radios, cameras, and automobiles; freedom of movement was restricted, and letters were censored. During the internment, higher education was not available, thus restricting social mobility; institutionalized discrimination had taken place.

Daniels and Kitano's (1970) fourth extraordinary stage also followed. Subtypes (A), concentration and apartheid through isolation, and (B), exclusion through expulsion and exile, also took place. In the case of Japanese Canadians, Canada called this exile 'repatriation'. The Second World War was the trigger for this extraordinary action. Through an Order-in-Council in December 1945 (after the war had ended), Canada still tried to deport Japanese Canadians (Ujimoto, 1983:140). Arrangements were made to deport 800 in January of 1946, but because many prominent Canadians opposed the deportation, it did not take place. Some Japanese, however, were deported earlier. Since then Canada and its Japanese have agreed to a redress settlement in 1988 as partial compensation for injustices suffered (Kobayashi, 1992:1–19).

These two examples of black and Japanese minorities show that Daniels and Kitano's (1970) four-stage model took place in both the United States and Canada. Canadians are often not aware of the lengths to which we have gone to stratify ethnic minorities in the past. We find it hard to believe that analogs to the Indian caste system and apartheid in South Africa could happen here. These two cases show that they have happened in Canada.

HIGHLIGHT 10.2   IMPLEMENTING THE JAPANESE EVACUATION

At 7:58 a.m., Hawaii time, on December 7, 1941—a quiet, sunlit Sunday—there flashed from headquarters of the great American naval base of Pearl Harbor this message to Washington:

Air Raid Pearl Harbor—This Is No Drill.

It was true. Dive bombers and fighters from six aircraft carriers commanded by Admiral Yamamoto of the Japanese Navy struck without warning and devastated the huge US Pacific battleship fleet.

From that moment forward and, yes, until even today, that act of war had one extraordinary and terrible effect upon more than 22,000 persons of Japanese ancestry then living in British Columbia, Canada. All that they had achieved in the sixty-four years since the first Japanese had arrived in Canada—all was blasted away and nothing again would be as it had been before. They became 'enemy aliens'.

Confusion and panic mounted as rumours spread. The Japanese had always been a prime target for racist sentiment; now they were viewed as a threat, a potential fifth column. Secret government plans came out of dusty drawers, orders-in-council were passed, the 1914 War Measures Act was used against them and the entire Japanese population on the West Coast was uprooted in the name of 'national security'. There were some Japanese nationals, many of whom had been in Canada as long as fifty years, but most were Canadians, born in Canada of Japanese parents, or Japanese who were naturalized citizens. Yet between Pearl Harbor Day and V-J Day in 1945, they literally became Canada's Forgotten People.

Regulations of Minister of Justice

1. Every person of the Japanese race, while within the protected area aforesaid, shall hereafter be at his usual place of residence each day before sunset and shall remain therein until sunrise on the following day...
2. No person of the Japanese race shall have in his possession or use in such protected area any motor vehicle, camera, radio transmitter, radio receiving set, firearm, ammunition or explosive;
3. It shall be the duty of every person of the Japanese race having in his possession or upon his premises any article mentioned in the next preceding paragraph, forthwith to cause such article to be delivered up to any Justice of the Peace...
4. Any Justice of the Peace or officer or constable receiving any article mentioned in paragraph 2 of this order shall give to the person delivering the same a receipt therefore . . .
5. Any peace officer or any officer or constable of the Royal Canadian Mounted Police having power to act as such peace officer or officer or constable in the said protected area, is authorized to search without warrant the premises . . .
6. Every person of the Japanese race shall leave the protected area aforesaid forthwith;
7. No person of the Japanese race shall enter such protected area except under permit issued by the Royal Canadian Mounted Police;

Dated at Ottawa this 26th day of February, 1942.

Louis S. St.Laurent
Minster of Justice

SOURCES: Barry Broadfoot, *Years of Sorrow, Years of Shame*, copyright © 1977 by Barry Broadfoot. Used by permission of Doubleday, a division of Random House, Inc., *Canadian Gazette*, 7 March 1942.

SUMMARY

What is unique about humans is that they are so much the same throughout the world. However, visual differences do exist, so that *Homo sapiens* are most often classified into groupings of Caucasians, Mongoloids, and Negroids, based on such characteristics as skin colour, facial features, and head and body forms. These physical, genetic, and skeletal differences are attributed largely to evolutionary variations.

If these differences are minor compared to human similarities, then why do we attempt a discussion on racial inequalities? Historically, whites from Europe have developed a sense of white superiority and dominance over Asians and Africans that has resulted in colonialism, invasion, exploitation, and slavery. The belief in racial superiority has led to racism, which still exists in many parts of the world.

In Canada's history there are many examples of the social structure's promotion of injustices, slavery, and deportation. Aboriginals were slaughtered, Europeans invaded aboriginal lands without compensation, treaties were made and broken, and many Native claims are not settled while industry and technology continue to exploit their rights. Blacks were bought and sold and slavery was accepted; even today many people complain that those who are not white find it difficult to compete. The Japanese during the Second World War were freely evacuated, their property confiscated, and their communities destroyed without adequate compensation.

Racial inequalities are a reality in Canada, even though many Canadians claim that all humans are physically equal. Social stratification in Canada means that the political and socioeconomic power clearly remains in the hands of European whites. Because of strong recent immigration from the Third World, more non-whites have arrived, but they still remain a small proportion of the total population. In Part V we explore the extent to which conflict and social injustice prevail because of inequality and stratification, and the provisions made for human rights in Canada.

Chapter 10 clearly deals mostly with those plotted in Cell D of our Conformity-Pluralist model, where visible minorities and aboriginals are heavily located. These are often newcomers who immigrated to Canada recently, they are classified as Mongoloid and Negroid, visible because they are not white in a largely Caucasoid country. They are faced with racism when they enter the industrial arena to make a living (Cell A), where prejudice and discrimination can be blatant, which we will discuss in the next chapter. There is also potential conflict between those in Cell D and Cell B, because the dominant British who are white, see them as being without power politically and economically, so they pose little threat to their dominance. There is also potential conflict between those who are visible (Cell D) and those who wish to voluntarily segregate themselves (Cell E), because Voluntary Pluralists like Hutterites, Jews, and the French, wish to retain their distinctiveness, and retreat from potential intermarriage and interaction from visible minorities in Cell D. Let us examine this potential for conflict in the next chapter. Dealing with race and racism, we become especially aware that reason, and linear methods of science are often quite limited in getting at more social psychological motives, feelings, emotions, motives, values, and attitudes. Diversity in a plural society leads into many directions amongst the cultures and races represented, and objective linear methods often have to give way to contexts and stories which are hard to classify rationally, because we are dealing with intense emotion.

CRITICAL THINKING QUESTIONS

1. Define race and racism.

2. To what extent is Hooten's way of comparing biological and physical human characteristics still used? Discuss his criteria and his three types.

3. What percentage of Canada's population is non-white? Discuss these visible minorities beginning with the largest group. Use some statistics.

4. Discuss historic racism focusing on the slavery of blacks. How pervasive was slavery in Canada? When was it abolished?

5. Why did the Canadian government intern Japanese Canadians during the Second World War? What do we think of what we did then? Have we made things right?

6. Discuss Daniels and Kitano's four stages of stratification. What is meant by the two-category system?

SUGGESTED READINGS

Driedger, Leo, and Shiva Halli (eds), *Race and Racism: Canada's Challenge* (Montreal: McGill-Queen's, 2000). *Race and Racism* brings together contributions by 20 sociologists, social psychologists, demographers, and anthropologists who discuss the new challenges of race.

Henry, Frances, Carol Tator, Winston Mattis, and Tim Rees, *The Colour of Democracy: Racism in Canadian Society,* 2nd edn (Toronto: Harcourt, 2000). This text demonstrates how racist attitudes are embedded in the policies and practices of Canadian institutions, organizations, and the media.

Li, Peter S. (ed.), *Race and Ethnic Relations in Canada*, 2nd edn (Toronto: Oxford University Press, 1999). Twelve authors discuss a variety of perspectives on race and multiculturalism in Canada.

PART V

In Search of Human Rights and Freedoms

When peoples of many backgrounds migrate to the same place like Canada, there is much opportunity for conflict. Political and religious systems have been developed over many millennia to try to order fair play so all humans have the right to exercise their freedoms. Also, prejudice, discrimination, stereotypes, and racism can be found everywhere. In Chapter 11 we review the tenets of political democracy, designed to give all a fair chance. Attitudes toward pluralism are measured, we sort the indicators of racism such as stereotypes, prejudice, and discrimination, and we discuss historical examples of unfair treatment. For many years societies have tried to respond to the quest for human rights by enacting the American Bill of Rights, the United Nations Declaration of Human Rights, and the more recent Canadian Charter of Rights and Freedoms. We are reminded how bad historical mistreatment can get, by reviewing the expulsion of Acadians in the East, ignoring the aspirations of the Metis on the Prairies by executing Louis Riel, procrastinating in the call to settle Aboriginal land claims, and watching the Jewish Holocaust in Europe. It is amazing what humans will do to each other!

In Chapter 11 we explore the dimensions of racism, by finding the extent to which Canadians are willing to build a mosaic rather than a melting pot. How do Canadians feel about being with minorities who look different? Each of the indicators of social distance, stereotypes, prejudice, and discrimination are defined and illustrated. We find that racism exists where there are differences in ethnicity, race, and religion. There is much evidence of unfair treatment, and inequality.

Racism: Prejudice and Discrimination

Chapter 11 reviews the total effects of ethnic and race relations on Canadian attitudes and behaviour. Chapter 12 reviews the rights and freedoms outlined by the American, United Nations, and Canadian charters. The two chapters together are a search for human freedoms in Canada and the extent to which human rights are feasible.

Let us begin with the ideology of democratic racism and explore the extent to which multiculturalism is indeed viable. We will examine whether Canadians prefer the mosaic to the melting pot, and whether they are comfortable with a diversity of minorities. We will also examine how minorities are, or are not, positively accepted in Canadian society. These general attitudes will provide a background for understanding the perceptual ethnic hierarchies that exist and the extent to which there are negative attitudes of prejudice and discriminatory behaviour based on negative ethnic stereotypes.

DEMOCRATIC RACISM

Frances Henry and Carol Tator (1994:1) present the ideology of 'democratic racism', which resists equal access to opportunities in Canada. This perspective assumes that racism is socially constructed, where minorities are dominated by majorities under the pretext of difference.

The conflict between the ideology of democratic liberalism and the racist ideology

present in the collective belief system of the dominant culture of Canada creates a fundamental dissonance. Although lip service is paid to the need to ensure equality in a pluralistic society, in reality individuals, organizations and institutions are far more committed to maintaining the status quo in order to stabilize or increase their power.

This paper identifies the concept of 'democratic racism', an ideology that permits and justifies the maintenance of two apparent conflicts of values. One set consists of a commitment to a democratic society motivated by egalitarian values of fairness, justice and equality. In conflict with these liberal values, a second set of attitudes and behaviours includes negative feelings about people of colour that carry the potential for differential treatment or discrimination. In its simplest form, democratic racism reduces this conflict between egalitarian and non-egalitarian values.

Henry, Tator, Mattis, and Rees (2000) expound on these basic premises in their recently published *The Colour of Democracy: Racism in Canadian Society*.

In the United Kingdom, Henry and Tator (1994:5–9) define democratic racists as 'distancing themselves from the crude ideas of biological inferiority and superiority' and 'defining a national

British culture which is homogeneous and white' (Henry et al., 2000:17–19). Mechanisms of inclusion and exclusion, who belongs and who does not, have been set in motion to protect the 'authentic' against the 'alien' characteristics of culture related to the national weakness and decline (Gilroy, 1987:45–46; Richmond, 1994:155–69).

Recently Gaertner and Dovidic (1986:208) have explored 'aversive racism' in the United States. Their findings are based on social psychological research that suggests that some Americans are prejudiced but do not act out their beliefs in actual discriminatory behaviour. They may avoid racial minorities, or if contact is unavoidable, assume a demeanour of formal politeness (Elliott and Fleras, 1992:59). Others who are liberals may have a strong social conscience, believe in fairness and equality for all, but it is a superficial favourableness that does little to change things. They may pride themselves in being open-minded and prejudice free, but feel ambivalent about how things are changing (Henry and Tator, 1994:6–7).

Henry and Tator (1994:9) suggest that democratic racism applies to Canada, that it may combine the British and American versions of 'new racism', 'aversive racism', and 'symbolic racism' because it involves value conflict:

'Democratic racism', therefore, is defined as an ideology in which two conflicting sets of values are made congruent to each other. Commitments to democratic principles, with their egalitarian notions of justice, equality, and fairness, are valued positively. These are in conflict, however, with those attitudes and behaviours that include negative feelings about minority groups and the potential for differential treatment or discrimination against them.

As a consequence there is a lack of support for policies and practices that ameliorate existing racial problems. Interventions are seen as conflicting with liberal notions of democracy, so democratic racists are reluctant to change basic structures (Henry, Tator, Mattis, Rees, 2000).

Table 11.1 lists the 13 expressions Henry and Tator (1994:9–12) discuss as evidence of democratic racism. Some believe racism cannot exist in a democratic society, but discrimination happens to all. Others believe that immigration policies are at fault, or minorities don't want to adapt, or that these are cultural problems. Others feel new immigrants lack skills to succeed, that multicultural policies are sufficient and that more education is the answer. Still others say it is a problem for non-whites, that fair treatment will solve the problems, and that individual rights and free speech must remain paramount. Deeper forms of racism resist action by innuendo opposing anti-racism initiatives, claiming that such action is racism in reverse. Let us examine some of these empirical studies that explore the extent of some of these racist attitudes and behaviour (Henry et al., 2000).

TABLE 11.1 Values and Myths Associated With Democratic Racism

Expressions by Canadians

1. Racism cannot exist within a democratic society.

2. Discrimination is a problem faced by all from time to time.

3. Racism is a consequence of immigration and increased diversity.

4. Minority groups refuse to fit in and adapt.

5. These are cultural not racial problems.

6. Non-whites lack the skills to succeed.

7. Multicultural policies are sufficient.

8. Education will change ignorance and attitudes of people.

9. Race is a problem for non-whites mostly.

10. What we need to do is treat everyone equally.

11. Individual rights are primary, including free speech.

12. Smear and innuendo are used to undermine anti-racism initiatives.

13. Anti-racism initiatives are racism in reverse.

SOURCE: Frances Henry and Carol Tator, 'The Ideology of Racism: "Democratic Racism"', *Canadian Ethnic Studies* 26 (1994):9–12.

ATTITUDES TOWARD PLURALISM

Since charter Canadians are clearly dominant in Canada numerically, it is important to study what is happening to other minorities and their place in Canada. We will examine whether Canadians prefer the melting pot over the mosaic, what their attitudes are toward pluralism and multiculturalism, and whether they feel at ease with the growing numbers of visible non-charter minorities.

Mosaic and Melting Pot Preferences

Reginald Bibby (1987a:161) asked his 1985 national sample of Canadians whether they preferred the mosaic or melting-pot models. He found that well over one-half (56 per cent) preferred the mosaic, and that over one-fourth (27 per cent) opted for the melting-pot model. These preferences varied by region, age, and education of the respondent. Bibby (1995) found that by 1995, preference for the mosaic had fallen to 44 per cent, however, and had risen to 40 per cent in favour of the melting pot. So these attitudes change over the decades.

Preference for the model of the mosaic was strongest in the Prairies, Ontario, and Quebec (58 per cent), and weaker in British Columbia (53 per cent) and the Atlantic region (49 per cent). Interestingly, the melting pot, in which all groups would lose their ethnic identity, was least preferred by Canadians in Quebec (16 per cent) and Ontario (29 per cent). The mosaic has considerable support from the most populous regions, the central provinces, where charter-group strength also lies. To what extent does this support include the rights of minorities and positive attitudes toward minorities?

Younger Canadians aged 18 to 34 (61 per cent) also support the mosaic more than those over 55 (54 per cent), while the reverse is true for the melting-pot model. Not nearly as many young Canadians (20 per cent) support the melting-pot model as older Canadians (33 per cent). The trend in the future is clearly toward the mosaic. The more educated respondents with university degrees (70 per cent) also favour the

mosaic, while very few (17 per cent) favour the melting-pot model. The better-educated people will likely have more influence in shaping the direction toward the mosaic as well. The social climate definitely favours diversity and pluralism; will this also translate into acceptance of diverse racial and ethnic minorities?

In 1991, the multicultural and citizenship branch of the Government of Canada commissioned the Angus Reid organization to undertake a national poll on the extent to which Canadians favoured diversity in Canada. Some of these results are presented in Table 11.2 (Angus Reid, 1991:4–5). We note that a large majority of Canadians favoured a federal governmental policy that promotes and ensures equality, eliminates racial discrimination in education, health care, and justice systems, helps police to improve their services and new immigrants to acquire skills to integrate. Indeed over half to three-fourths of the respondents gave their strongest support (a 7 on a 7-point scale), for the top 11 items. Driedger and Reid (2000) have summarized some of these findings since.

Eight out of 10 also favoured proactive moves such as developing helpful school materials that recognize that diversity is acceptable, and helping organizations reflect Canadian diversity.

There was less enthusiasm for funding festivals, special events, and helping minorities preserve their heritages, with roughly 6 out of 10 favouring such action. Very strong support (7 on the scale) dropped to below one-third for items 12 and 13. The questions usually included both 'ethnic' and 'racial' designations, and most respondents seemed to favour strong support for both categories.

Feeling at Ease with Visible Minorities

The multicultural attitudes of Canadians suggest that there is considerable goodwill toward a variety of ethnic expressions, although a minority has negative attitudes toward pluralization. To what extent do Canadians feel at ease with visible minorities? Reginald Bibby (1995:57, 59) asked the 'at ease' questions of Canadians in his national

TABLE 11.2 Canadian Attitudes Toward Immigration, Ethnic and Racial Diversity, Angus Reid Poll, 1991

Canadian Federal Policy should:	General Disagreement	Neither Agree nor Disagree	General Agreement
		(%)	
1. Promote equality among all Canadians regardless of racial or ethnic origin	4	5	91
2. Ensure equal access to jobs regardless of ethnic or racial background	4	6	90
3. Eliminate racial discrimination through public education	5	7	88
4. Eliminate racism in health care, the justice and education systems	6	7	87
5. Help police to improve their ability to deal with different ethnic/racial groups.	6	7	87
6. Help citizens who are immigrants to acquire skills/knowledge to integrate	6	9	85
7. Have people from different ethnic/racial groups live in the same country	5	11	84
8. Help everyone deal with ethnic, cultural and racial diversity	6	7	83
9. Develop school materials to teach children and teachers about other cultures/life	11	9	80
10. Recognize that cultural/racial diversity is fundamental to Canadian society	10	14	76
11. Ensure that organizations reflect the cultural and racial diversity of Canadians	9	12	79
12. Fund festivals and special events celebrating different cultures	26	16	58
13. Help ethnic and racial minorities maintain their cultural heritages in Canada	25	17	58

SOURCE: Angus Reid Group, 'Multiculturalism and Canadians: National Attitude Study 1991' (Ottawa: Multiculturalism and Citizenship Canada, 1991), pp. 4–5.

samples in 1975, 1980, 1985, 1990, and 1995.

Bibby found that in 1975 a majority of Canadians (ranging from 84 to 91 per cent) felt at ease with Jews, Canadian Indians, Orientals, and blacks. In 1995 feelings of ease had increased slightly to 85 to 94 per cent. There is some difference in attitudes toward the five visible-minor-ity groups, with only 6 per cent feeling uneasy with Jews and 15 per cent uneasy with East Indians. The differences also varied very little regionally, although in 1995 Quebeckers (22 per cent) and British Columbians (19 per cent) felt most uneasy with Asians, and Quebec (14 per cent) and Prairie (11 per cent) residents felt most uneasy with aboriginals (Bibby, 1995:57–8). More educated respondents again were more at ease with these minorities than were those respondents with less than a high school education; but this did not vary by gender or age. The percentages are so high that very few 'ill at ease' respondents remained; however, there were roughly 10 per cent, depending on the group. From Bibby's work we conclude that there is enough comfort with visible minorities that we would expect considerable goodwill on the part of most people in Canada, but there is always a small minority who are uncomfortable.

The Angus Reid Group did a national poll in 1991 asking their respondents 'How comfortable would you feel being around recent immigrants?' listing 13 groups on a 7-point scale where zero meant not comfortable, and 7 very comfortable. Table 11.3 plots their responses. Out of 10 respondents, 7 or 8 felt very comfortable with the 6 white European groups listed, and almost none felt uncomfortable around these groups. Two-thirds still felt very comfortable with Chinese, Jewish, and West Indian blacks, but more placed themselves in the middle between comfort and discomfort, although still very few claimed they were very uncomfortable in the presence of these groups.

Only a minority felt comfortable around Arabs, Muslims, Indo-Pakistanis, and Sikhs that would clearly be visible religious and ethnic minorities. Ten to 20 per cent felt uncomfortable around these 4 groups, and more than one-third checked the middle range of the scale (3, 4, 5). These data show that discomfort clearly increased as respondents moved from feelings about white European Christian groups to other minorities.

Social Distance

Our discussion so far suggests that some Canadians place themselves closer to some groups than to others. The Anglocelts, for

TABLE 11.3 Degree of Comfort Canadians Feel Around a Variety of Recent Immigrants in Canada, 1991

Feel Comfortable Around	Not Comfortable 1,2	3,4,5	Very Comfortable 6,7
British	3	14	83
Italians	2	11	77
French	5	11	74
Ukrainians	3	14	73
Germans	4	14	72
Portuguese	3	17	70
Chinese	5	16	69
Jews	4	22	64
West Indian Blacks	8	31	61
Arabs	11	37	52
Muslims	11	40	50
Indo-Pakistanis	13	39	48
Sikhs	17	40	43

SOURCE: Angus Reid Group, 'Multiculturalism and Canadians: National Attitude Study 1991' (Ottawa: Multiculturalism and Citizenship Canada, 1991), pp. 7–8.

instance, express a sense of nearness to the French and a sense of distance from Doukhobors and Hutterites. This suggests that we could order ethnic groups along a nearness-farness continuum, or a social distance scale.

According to Levine, Carter, and Gorman (1976), Simmel's utilization of the metaphor distance constitutes a pervasive and distinctive feature of his sociology as a whole. They summarize Simmel's meanings as: 1) ecological attachment and mobility, 2) emotional involvement and detachment, and 3) the extent to which persons share similar qualities and sentiments. Simmel himself thought that distance could be expressed in many ways. Recent work on social distance has attempted to sort out the many meanings of the concept and to devise ways of measuring it (Driedger and Peters, 1977:161). Westie (1959) includes the dimensions of residential distance, positional distance, interpersonal physical distance, and interpersonal interaction distance. Banton (1960) distinguishes four forms of social distance (attitudinal, positional, qualitative, and ecological). Kadushin (1962) speaks of normative distance, interactive distance, cultural or valuational distance, and personal distance. Laumann (1965) seeks to measure subjective social distance and objective social distance. It is apparent that the metaphor 'distance' can be widely used and must be adapted to specific study situations.

Bogardus (1959) expands Park's personal dimension of social distance and chooses to use 'the degree of sympathetic understanding that functions between person and person, between person and group, and between group and group as his measure of social distance. Sympathy refers to feeling reactions of a favourable responsive type, and understanding involves that knowledge of a person which also leads to favourably responsive behaviour'. Bogardus selects one component of Simmel's notion of social distance and substitutes an operational continuum for Park's informal observations. Krech, Crutchfield, and Ballachey (1962:154) note that 'with appropriate modifications, the scale can be adapted to measure attitudes toward any category of persons'.

We wish to use the Bogardus scale to measure the associational component—the social distance of personal relationships.

Although the Bogardus social distance scale has been used in scores of studies in countries around the world, very little use has been made of the scale for social distance research in Canada. However, Driedger and Peters (1977) did a revealing study of students in nine Winnipeg high schools, and found that a sample of 2,328 high school students in Winnipeg are much more willing to marry persons of European origin than of non-European origin. They appear to make racial distinctions between whites and non-whites in their marriage preferences (Driedger and Mezoff, 1981:7). It is also clear that nearness differentiations made within the European category are great. Three times as many high school students are willing to marry Americans as are willing to marry Jews. In fact, the Jews are classified more like non-Europeans; only one-fifth to one-fourth of the sample were willing to consider them as eligible partners.

Bogardus's instrument is a 7-point scale indicating nearness at the low end and farness at the top. Driedger and Mezoff found, looking at the farness (6 and 7) end of the scale, that a small proportion of the students wished to debar certain groups and permit only visits to Canada. About 50 students (2 per cent) were in favour of excluding the Dutch and the blacks (the least restricted group), while 200 students (11 per cent) wished to restrict the Jews. The restrictions of the Jews by 11 per cent of the sample appears to be clear ethnic or religious prejudice; let us examine these negative attitudes more closely.

INDICATORS OF RACISM

'Somewhere in Canada, a fellow leans across a beer-laden table to ask his comrades, "Why does it take a Ukrainian three days to fill the salt shaker?" The punch line ("The salt is forced through the little holes") reflects the "dumb" jokes' (Mackie, 1984:219). Ethnic jokes are but one way of keeping minorities 'in their place' away from the status and prestige of the majority. Let us discuss common forms of racism such as stereotypes, prejudice, and discrimination, and the extent to which they exist in Canada to see how well Canadians have been able to follow their ideals of rights and freedoms for all.

Ethnic Stereotypes

Walter Lippmann (1922) was the first to use the concept 'stereotype' in his book *Public Opinion* in 1922. Since then, stereotype has become a major concept in the vocabulary of the social sciences. Canadian research on ethnic stereotypes has been extensive (Anderson and Frideres, 1981; Mackie, 1984; Taylor, 1981). More study of the complexity of stereotypes is needed; there are virtually no analyses of autostereotypes (how people or groups stereotype themselves) and there are few evaluations of the reciprocity of ethnic stereotypes (Driedger and Clifton, 1984; Driedger and Halli, 2000; James, 1999:134–41; Taylor, 1981). This is particularly important in the Canadian context because the preservation of ethnic identities that may precede the development of ethnic stereotypes is now enshrined in a federal policy on multiculturalism.

In his discussion of stereotypes, Lippmann assumes that his readers are familiar with the concept as it is used in the printing industry. In this context, a stereotype is a plate made by moulding a matrix of a printing surface to be used in casting a metal typeface. That is, a stereotype is a uniform matrix of type that is moulded so that the printing is standard and unchanging. The printer's stereotype was obviously in Lippmann's mind when he coined the concept of social stereotypes:

The problem of the acquisition of meaning of things, or of forming habits of simple comprehension, is thus the problem of introducing: 1) definiteness and distinction and 2) consistency or stability of meaning into what is otherwise vague and wavering. In the great booming, buzzing confu-

sion of the outer world we pick out what our culture has already defined for us, and we tend to perceive that which we have picked out in the form stereotyped for us by our culture (Lippmann, 1922:81).

Lippmann continues his images of the printer's stereotype using phrases such as these: 'stereotyped ideas accumulated and hardened', 'series of images', 'stereotyped shapes', 'habit of molding', 'substitution of American for European stereotypes', 'to see all things freshly and in detail, rather than as types and generalities', 'uniformities', and 'economizing attention' (Lippmann, 1922:79–94).

Anderson and Frideres (1981:57–78) reviewed the conceptualization of stereotypes by such American scholars as Simpson and Yinger, who characterize the concept as a highly exaggerated picture, the invention of supposed traits, and the formation of incomplete images leaving little room for change or individual variation. This raises additional questions of myth versus reality, and the problem of evaluating the content of stereotypes (Anderson and Frideres, 1981). Canadian studies have dealt extensively with stereotypes of English- and French-speaking groups. Lambert and associates (1960) found that English speakers were more favourably evaluated than speakers of French. These studies show that stereotypes vary by group, situation and time. There has been considerably less research on 'other' ethnic groups in Canada and their stereotypes, although Driedger and Clifton (1984) explore this new field.

Taylor (1981:161) lists two important functions of stereotyping. First, stereotypes involve categorization; when little is known about a group, there is a tendency to 'fill in' missing information. There may also be too much information, and therefore a need to simplify it. What is included and left out in the process of selecting information leaves much room for misinformation, bias, and prejudice. On the other hand, while the self is bombarded by stimuli, it is continually shaping and forming its own self-image. Emotions are an important part of this image and, depending on past experiences, may involve negative or positive tendencies and preferences. In this process of perception and cognition, most people are inclined to rate themselves positively, and often may not give enough credit to others.

These examples suggest that cognitive and affective dimensions of social interaction are involved in the formation of stereotypes. People form a *gestalt* that may be fairly accurate or very biased and inaccurate. The assumption that when we know the facts about another person or group, we will act on those facts is not necessarily true. Reason does not always prevail: emotions often impose positive and negative evaluations. When images of others become rigid, like the printer's stereotype, and when they produce the same reaction automatically without further examination, then we have a social stereotype.

Edwards (1985) developed four dimensions that include *content*, the traits which make up the stereotypes; *uniformity*, the degree of agreement of these traits; *direction*, the favourableness or unfavourableness of these traits; and *intensity*, the degree of favourableness or unfavourableness of responses to these traits.

Content can be seen as the matrix in the printer's stereotype. It is the linotype grid, the raw materials from which clusters of meaning spring. For example, Jews can be seen as shrewd, industrious, grasping, intelligent, and ambitious (Cauthen, Robinson, and Kraus, 1971).

Uniformity is a second important dimension of stereotypes in which the printer clamps the matrix into a rigid form. Common images that are held by many individuals and groups may emerge from the matrix. There may not be perfect agreement as to which traits apply to certain ethnic groups, but we expect clusters to emerge. We expect that uniformity is determined by cultural factors. Thus, it is reasonable to assume that ethnic stereotypes will vary. Most ethnic groups in Canada have come from different cultural contexts, and they have brought to Canada various traditions and attitudes. Two questions arise: first, will all of these groups have uniform images of themselves, or will there be more

internal variation in some than in others? Second, how uniformly will others view specific groups? Fairly uniform images of some groups may already have been moulded in their mother countries and may be transplanted and perpetuated in Canada. When Germans, for example, are viewed as being aggressive, when this assessment is common in many groups, then we have evidence of a uniform attitude toward Germans. If Germans view themselves as aggressive as well, then the autostereotype and the stereotypical view of others is uniform.

Direction of stereotypes can be either positive or negative as Taylor (1981) stresses. Moreover, he suggests that 'stereotypes can be an important mechanism for recognizing and expressing ethnicity, and to the extent that they are accurate reflections, and refer to positive attributes of the stereotyped group, stereotypes can play a constructive role in intergroup relations' (1981:163). Actually, ethnocentrism is a stereotype if the ingroup evaluates itself fairly rigidly, and if it does not change its attitudes when new evidence requires re-evaluation. There may be a tendency for individuals to evaluate themselves more positively than others may evaluate them. The gap between ingroup evaluations and the evaluations of others may be either positive or negative. The ingroup may evaluate itself positively, a tendency that is often labelled ethnocentrism, and it may be evaluated negatively by others, a tendency that is often labelled prejudice.

Taylor (1981:163–4) argues that in ethnic relations it is important that 1) the stereotype an ingroup has of itself and that others have of it match, and 2) that these stereotypes are positive and not negative. If this is true, then the assumption inherent in the policy of multiculturalism would be that positive relations would result in each group's retaining its own cultural distinctiveness. We expect that ingroup evaluations will be generally positive, but we also expect that there will be significant variations on some of the scales. While autostereotypes are expected to be positive, each group is expected to evaluate itself significantly higher on some attributes than others.

Intensity, Edwards's fourth dimension, has to do with the degree of favourableness or unfavourableness of a response. Thus, the dimension implies both the direction and the degree of a response.

When autostereotyping is positive and outgroup stereotyping is negative, the gap between the two evaluations may be so great that expectations from both sides will not conform to reality. There can also be counter stereotyping. Deroche and Deroche (1991:69) found that on television black police were portrayed as more level-headed and correct than their co-workers. When the expectations of both sides coincide, then the stereotype can satisfy the desires of both groups involved, and ethnicity, for example, can take a constructive rather than a destructive form. Negative evaluations of a group, if they do not reflect reality, indicate prejudice. It is at this point that stereotypes and prejudice become synonymous. Too often the distinction between stereotype and prejudice becomes blurred and stereotypes merely become negative attitudes (Driedger, 1989:346).

Driedger and Clifton (1984) also derived findings from their Winnipeg high school sample. Individual semantic differential scales comparing Jewish and non-Jewish students indicated stereotypes that ranged from positive to negative. The Jewish autostereotype of the intellectual, good, valuable, interesting, friendly, and kind Jew in Part A was positive, but students from the other three groups evaluated Jews much less positively. Part B indicated considerable ingroup and outgroup consensus that Jews were excitable, domineering, competitive, emotional, religious, wealthy, and talkative. If Jews and the three other groups are indeed different in beliefs, values, customs, and culture, then these differences did not seem to have an effect upon this consensual stereotype. Is this a stereotype that is a fair assessment of Jews by all and that is accepted by all? Only three scales indicated the negative stereotype of Jews held by respondents of the three other groups. There were only three scales in which the ratings fell below the neutral point, indicating slight negative ten-

dencies to form a traditional stereotype of materialism and dishonesty. Jewish students did not agree with the other three groups' stereotypes of them—especially on the dishonest and materialist variables—and rated themselves more positively. The data in Part C suggest that dissimilarity may breed negative evaluations. It is important to note, however, that these are only three of seventeen scales; the other fourteen scales are not negative.

Overall, the results of Driedger and Clifton (1984) indicate that students have more positive self-identities than their evaluations of others, that they have neutral or slightly positive evaluations of students from other ethnic groups, and that generally the more positive the student's self-identities are, the more positive their evaluations of other groups will be. Let us turn next to a discussion of prejudice or negative attitudes.

Ethnic Prejudice

Allport (1954) suggests that prejudice refers to attitudes while discrimination refers to action. Both phenomena are subject to irrational emotions that often lead to attitudes and behaviours inconsistent with the values of freedom and equality legitimized by a democratic society. Francis (1976:268–70) defines prejudice as illegitimate categorization and discrimination as illegitimate differential treatment. Illegitimate forms of categorization and differential treatment have preoccupied many scholars of ethnic prejudice and discrimination (Berry and Kalin, 2000; Driedger and Reid, 2000; Francis, 1976; Hagan, 1977; Henry et al., 2000; Mackie, 1984). Since humans all need to classify their experiences, this process of categorization involves valuations that may or may not be legitimate, depending on the norms of a particular society. In democracies, where freedom and equality are highly valued, there are many discrepancies between ideal and real attitudes and behaviour.

But the problem is more complex because actions and attitudes that are considered legitimate for all may be based on a society's expectations of what should happen to minorities or immigrants in that society. Assimilationists would expect that all people should fuse in a cultural 'melting pot', while pluralists would deem differentiation and a multitude of sub-identities as the legitimate right of minorities. A question arises about the rights of members of a society to extend their political and religious diversity to ethnic pluralism. In Canada such a legal right has been extended to the two founding people (the British and the French), but the extent to which a distinctive identity is the right of others in a multicultural society is problematic. In the United States, multiculturalism appears to be less 'legitimate' than in Canada, although pluralism seems to be on the rise there. In most societies some groups have more rights than others (officially or unofficially), even though the equality of all may be the official ideal (Berry and Kalin, 2000; Driedger and Reid, 2000; Taylor, Wright, and Ruggiero, 2000).

Hagan (1977:168) suggests that *differential treatment* can be a predisposition to discrimination. All humans have to categorize their experiences, but some categories may promote the norms of a society more clearly than others. Canadians, for example, hold to the ideal of the right to equal treatment in a democratic society. In reality, not all people are treated equally and differentiation that does not provide equal distribution of opportunities or rewards can be seen as discriminatory.

Francis (1976:269–70) adds the dimension of functional and dysfunctional differentiation, which further complicates the matter. 'Foreigners are admitted on the, at least tacit, assumption that relations with their hosts will be governed by particularistic norms specified by the terms of their admission. Thus, participation in the host society is, on principle, contractual and valid until further notice'. The situation is different when a newcomer is expected to settle permanently in a modern state:

> Although he is not a member upon arrival, he is a prospective member supposed to acquire, in due course, all the qualifica-

tions necessary for regular membership. Whereas the hosts expect him to comply with the conditions under which he has been admitted as a prospective member, the ethnic in turn expects that, upon assuming his obligations, he will be granted all the benefits the host society has to offer to its charter members in accordance with generally accepted 'universalist' rules. We conclude that under certain conditions the differential treatment of ethnics may be not only functional but also legitimate, and that this is, as a rule, recognized by both the natives and the ethnics themselves (Francis, 1976:269).

The definition of prejudice should be confined to attitudes of illegitimate differentiation between members of a democratic society that are due solely to ethnicity and that prevent the victims from competing with other aspirants on equal terms. It is difficult to determine how much differentiation is illegitimate; we need to sort out legitimate and illegitimate differential attitudes to citizens' rights.

Prejudicial treatment is viewed by Hagan (1977:170) as a negative predisposition to behaviour that could lead to discrimination. Francis (1976:264) says, 'Prejudice is a legal term referring to the anticipation of judicial decision without due process.' Prejudice is a prejudgement insofar as preconceived opinions have been assumed to be true before having been put to the test. What makes identifying prejudice difficult is that prejudice is made of the same stuff as categorization (which we are all involved in), but that prejudice is based on invalid negative attitudes.

We need to see whether some people are more prone to evaluate others negatively, and then infer whether this connotes a disposition to prejudice that may, in turn, lead to discrimination. Unfortunately, there is not always a constant relationship between opinions, attitudes, and discrimination, but this assumed cause-and-effect relationship is only one of numerous types of problems in finding prejudice.

HIGHLIGHT 11.1 COMMENTS BY YOUTH ABOUT PREJUDICE

Let us look at some of the comments made by youth as they reflect on their attitudes, philosophies and actions after discussing the issues of prejudice, racism, ethnocentrism, discrimination and stereotyping.

Nicole: *'Canadians tend to be rather ethnocentric . . .'*

I know that if I were to enter a foreign country I would want to continue practising my usual traditions, such as Christmas, because this is important and something I would not like to live without. We Canadians tend to be rather ethnocentric and don't realize that immigrants have these same beliefs.

Jody: *'Two different teachings . . .'*

'Jesus loves the little children; all the little children of the world. Red and yellow; Black and White; they are precious in his sight. Jesus loves the little children of the world.'

This song, which I sang in Sunday School as a child, never gave me the message that was intended! As Southern Baptists we sang about people being equal but never believed it. People were only equal if they were White. When reflecting back over our discussions, I realize that I received two very different teachings as a child. My Christian faith taught me the love of all mankind, but my society taught me to love only the White sector of mankind.

Andy: *'Awareness is of crucial importance . . .'*

It is my conviction that, although we are not born with racial and prejudicial concerns, through experience, observation, learning and interactions with society as a whole, we soon develop these characteristics and they become ingrained into our personalities whether we realize it or not. I was never told outright that one race was superior to another or that I should not like a certain individual because of their cultural and/or racial heritage. Nevertheless, I have been influenced by media stereotypes, by interactions with specific individuals whose behaviour I have subsequently generalized to their whole culture and by the thoughts and opinions of people I consider important. All these factors have contributed to the manner in which I view different races and cultures.

SOURCE: Carl E. James, Seeing Ourselves: Exploring Race, Ethnicity and Culture (Toronto: Thompson Educational Publishing, 1995). Reprinted by permission.

Discrimination: Illegitimate Treatment

Discrimination is related to illegitimate behaviour. Hagan (1977:170–1) suggests that *denial of desire* can be a form of discrimination if we assume that all persons should be allowed equal preference and the freedom to choose. 'Restrictions on immigration and naturalization have been common, yet once ethnics have been admitted to potential regular membership, their differential treatment is relatively soon recognized as illegitimate' (Francis, 1976:272). Lately, these egalitarian democratic principles may also be expanded to broader spheres of social life such as club membership or intermarriage. This raises the question of how open or closed a society or community may be with regard to access to its institutions and places of social, economic, and political life.

Many ethnic minorities such as the Hutterites choose to be segregated and do not wish to avail themselves of what an open society has to offer. Those who seek greater freedom and equality, however, are presumed to be discriminated against if they are denied such opportunities as jobs, open housing, or access to leisure and institutional activities. It should be possible to measure how open respondents perceive our society to be and whether opportunities are equal, as

Canadian society says they are supposed to be. Discrimination comes about only when we deny to individuals or groups of people equality of treatment that they may wish.

Hagan (1977:17) denotes *disadvantaged treatment* as a clear form of discrimination. Discrimination occurs when the object of prejudice is placed at some disadvantage not merited by his own misconduct. Discrimination may be defined as the effective injurious treatment of persons on grounds rationally irrelevant to the situation (Driedger, 1996; James, 1999:141–7).

The definition of disadvantage and the level of disadvantage induced are important to studies of prejudice and discrimination. Freedom to compete for the rewards of society and equal opportunity to attain these rewards have already been designated as 'rights' in a democratic society. When members of groups are abused verbally, this presumably would be disadvantageous over time to their attaining respect and status, which, in turn, are important for equal competition. However, are ethnic jokes sufficiently disadvantageous in a high school setting to result in discriminatory disadvantage? Different ethnic groups could interpret such a mild form of negative language usage differently. Jokes may mean different things to different people, depending on the intention of the speaker, and the context of the situation. While the disadvantage of ethnic jokes is difficult to discern, more severe forms of action such as receiving hate literature, being vandalized, or being attacked physically can certainly be designated as discriminatory disadvantage. Thus we are forced to examine a wide range of disadvantageous action. Severe forms will be relatively easy to designate as discrimination; we will need to see how well we can interpret milder forms of disadvantage and whether these represent discrimination or not.

The four denotations of prejudice and discrimination (differential, prejudicial, disadvantageous treatment, and denial of desire) form a useful continuum. The differentiation end represents only predisposition to prejudice, while the disadvantageous treatment end represents blatant forms of discrimination.

Driedger and Mezoff (1981:1–17) asked students to report whether they had been discriminated against in various situations, and what types of discrimination were involved. In Table 11.4 we see that about one-third (35.5 per cent) of the high school students in the sample reported discrimination at some time in a given place. Table 11.4 reports six types, ranging from ethnic jokes (a fairly minor form of disadvantage) to vandalism (a serious form of destruction). The six types of discrimination form a type of Guttman scale: about one-fourth (27.5 per cent) of the respondents reported discrimination in the form of ethnic jokes; about one-fifth (18.3 per cent) reported verbal abuse; one-sixth (15.7 per cent) reported language ridicule; and 3 to 5 per cent were victims of hate literature.

More than two-thirds (68 per cent) of the Jewish students perceived discrimination; about one-half of the Polish (51 per cent), Italian (46 per cent), and French (45 per cent) students also perceived discrimination; about one-third of the Ukrainian (36 per cent) and German (33 per cent) students reported discrimination; less than one-fifth of the Scandinavians (19 per cent) and British (18 per cent) reported disadvantageous treatment. The data in Table 11.4 also show that most discrimination seems to take the form of jokes, ridicule, and verbal abuse. Except for the Jews, most of the students did not report severe attacks, hate literature, or vandalism. Driedger and Mezoff (1981) concluded that evidence in four distinct areas—differential treatment, prejudicial treatment, denial of desire, and disadvantageous treatment (as described in Hagan)—shows that prejudice and discrimination occur among students in Winnipeg.

Differential treatment was clearly shown by the fact that three times as many students were willing to marry northern Europeans as non-Europeans and Jews. More than 10 per cent of the students wished to debar Jews or restrict them to visits to Canada.

A majority of students agreed that openness in leisure activity, semantic expression, public

TABLE 11.4 Type of Discrimination Reported by High School Students by Ethnic Groups

Form of Discrimination (N=2408)	Jews (N=290)	Poles (227)	Italians (65)	French (396)	Ukrainians (517)	Germans (333)	Scandinavians (78)	British (502)	Total
				DISCRIMINATION BY REPORTING GROUPS					
				(%)					
Total[a]	68	51	46	45	36	33	19	18	35.5
Ethnic jokes	50	45	37	33	30	23	9	8	27.5
Verbal abuse	53	17	19	21	13	19	8	4	18.3
Language ridicule	27	15	30	29	13	13	4	8	15.7
Hate literature	19	2	6	4	3	5	0	2	5.0
Physical attack	21	2	3	4	3	3	1	2	4.7
Vandalism	13	1	2	1	2	3	1	0	2.7

NOTE: [a] The percentage in this row represent the proportion of students in each category who reported at least one type of discrimination, or reported discriminations in a given place.
SOURCE: Leo Driedger and Richard Mezoff, 'Ethnic Prejudice and Discrimination in Winnipeg High Schools', *Canadian Journal of Sociology* 6 (1981):1–17.

places, and public communication was desirable. However, Driedger and Mezoff (1981) again found that a minority who could not agree to equal treatment and openness of parties, sports, restaurants, clubs, oral expressions, and communication.

Denial of the desire for equality took place mostly in the school. The Jews, Italians, Poles, and Germans perceived the greatest discrimination in the classroom and in textbooks. Less than 10 per cent of the students, however, reported being denied open access to all types of places.

Wilson Head (1981) conducted a study of racial minorities in Toronto related to discrimination in housing, employment, and community services and found that 90 per cent of blacks and 72 per cent of South Asians felt 'some' or a 'great deal of' discrimination, in contrast to only 35 per cent of European respondents who reported discrimination. Henry and Ginzberg (1984) in *Who Gets the Work?* matched black and white job seekers applying for jobs advertised in a major newspaper in

Toronto, and found that whites received three times as many job offers. They also found that telephone callers with accents, especially South Asian and Caribbean, were more often screened out when they inquired about job vacancies. In a follow-up study of employers who advertised these jobs, Billingsley and Musynski (1985) found that 28 per cent of the respondents felt that racial minorities did not have the ability to meet their performance criteria. Jain (1988) concluded that visible minorities face pay and employment discrimination. Ponting (1983: 57–76) found that blacks in Calgary encountered similar discrimination in areas of employment and housing, results also reported by Christianson and Weinfeld (1993: 26–44) and Henry (1989). Similar problems were found among black students in school by Dei (1993:45–65) and, as a black teacher, Dei (1993: 38–51) outlines challenges which teachers face in anti-racist teaching (Tuzlak, 1989:103–19). Taylor, Wright, and Ruggiero (2000) describe discrimination as an invisible evil.

HIGHLIGHT 11.2 EMPLOYMENT DISCRIMINATION

One of the clearest demonstrations of racism in a society is the lack of access and equity experienced by people of colour in the workplace. A number of studies over the past two decades have documented the nature and extent of racial bias and discrimination in employment. One study, Who Gets the Work? (Henry and Ginzberg, 1984), examined access to employment. In this field research, evenly matched Black and White jobseekers were sent to apply for entry positions advertised in a major newspaper. An analysis of the results of several hundred applications and interviews revealed that White applicants received job offers three times more often than did Black applicants. In addition, telephone callers with accents, particularly those from South Asia and the Caribbean, were more often screened out when they phoned to inquire about a job vacancy.

A follow-up study to Who Gets the Work? focussed on the attitude, hiring, and management practices of large businesses and corporations in Toronto. This report, No Discrimination Here, documented the perceptions of employers and personnel managers in these organizations. In personnel interviews, recruitment, hiring, promotion, training, and termination practices, a high level of both racial prejudice and discrimination was demonstrated; 28 per cent of the respondents felt that racial minorities did not have the ability to meet performance criteria as well as Whites did (Billingsley and Musynski, 1985).

SOURCE: Frances Henry, Carol Tator, Winston Mattis, and Tim Rees, *The Colour of Democracy*, 2nd edn (Toronto: Harcourt Brace, 2000).

National Perceived Discrimination 1980–95

Reginald Bibby (1995) has been taking national samples every five years between 1980 and 1995, asking 'Do you feel that racial and cultural groups in your community are discriminated against?' Table 11.5 shows that while in 1980 about one-half felt that some groups were discriminated against, by 1995 two-thirds thought so. Since 1980, the percentage who think discrimination is getting worse has averaged about 15 per cent; those who think it is better has risen from 15 to 20 per cent, and those who think it is about the same has decreased from 45 to 33 per cent (Bibby, 1995:52).

In 1995 Quebeckers (75 per cent) are most likely to report discrimination and residents of the Atlantic region (58 per cent) least likely. Residents in all regions except British Columbia are reporting increases in discrimination since 1980 with exceptionally high increases in Ontario and the Atlantic region. One-fourth of British Columbians think it is getting worse (much more than the others), while one-fourth of Quebeckers (the highest), think it is getting better now. Acknowledgement that discrimination exists varies little by ethnic group.

One measure of the acceptance of each other is approval of intergroup marriage. There has been a gradual increase in the approval of marriage between different Canadians, ranging from a low of 57 per cent in 1975 approving of marriage between whites and blacks, to 81 per cent in 1995 (Bibby, 1995:54), very similar to that of intermarriage of whites and East Indians/Pakistanis. In 1995 most respondents (80 to 84 per cent) approve of whites marrying East Indians, blacks, Asians and aboriginals. There was more readiness to intermarry between the religious groups in 1975 (78 to 86 per cent range) and this has increased by 1995 (89 to 92 per cent range). Still, 10 to 20 per cent are opposed to some forms of intermarriage depending on type.

TABLE 11.5   National Perceived Discrimination, 1980–95

Region and Year		Do you feel that any racial or cultural groups in your community are discriminated against?	
		Yes	No
		(%)	
National	1995	67	33
	1990	59	41
	1985	54	46
	1980	55	45
BC	1995	67	33
	1980	71	29
Prairies	1995	64	36
	1980	55	45
Ontario	1995	63	37
	1980	49	51
Quebec	1995	75	25
	1980	65	35
Atlantic	1995	58	42
	1980	32	68

SOURCE: Reginald Bibby, *The Bibby Report: Social Trends Canadian Style* (Toronto: Stoddart, 1995), pp. 52–4.

DIFFERENTIAL AND UNFAIR TREATMENT

Our discussion of stereotype, prejudice, and discrimination strongly suggests that the symbolic status we attribute to groups varies along at least three dimensions. In Canada we treat people differently on the basis of ethnicity, race, and religion. Canadians are not all of equal status; although our ideals (as seen in the Charter of Rights and Freedoms) say that all people must be treated with respect and equality, but for a variety of reasons this seldom happens. Let us summarize by reviewing these three symbolic status indicators.

Ethnic Origin

In Chapter 8 we found that the British score among the highest on socioeconomic status, with higher levels of income, education, and occupational status than most people in Canada. These indicators are highly valued in a technological, industrial soci-ety, and present a model of success to which many aspire. Because the British are numerically the largest ethnic group (as well as one of the two founding charter peoples) and are politically most powerful, they are a considerable force to be reckoned with when studying status and prestige as illustrated in our model (Cell B) in Chapter 2.

The French, the other charter group, have been settled in Canada even longer than the British. They have consolidated their strength spatially in Quebec, and they are numerically the second largest ethnic group. They, too, have extensive political influence. As we will discuss in Chapter 12, the Canadian Charter of Rights and Freedoms has provided special status and privileges to both charter groups, raising their languages to official status and guaranteeing the survival of their respective cultures. These privileges have been more entrenched during the past several decades. The Canadian constitution symbolically, as well as legally, places the two charter groups above all others in Canada.

On the other hand, the aboriginals of Canada have been placed symbolically at the bottom of this hierarchy of status and privilege because of treaties that place them in a subservient position. Historically, large stretches of land were surrendered for a minimal return. Aboriginals were shunted onto special reserves, making it difficult to compete in the Canadian mainstream. The Indian Act and federal agencies still relate to them in paternal ways, giving them little control over their destiny. In non-treatied territories, Canada has not yet dealt with Indian and Inuit land claims, and there is considerable procrastination in settling these rights. Furthermore, only limited aboriginal rights have been entrenched in the Canadian constitution for the aboriginals because the aboriginals represent less than 2 per cent of our population and are very weak economically and politically.

Race and Racism

While ethnic origin has been solidified into high (charter group) and low (aboriginal) ethnic status polarities, race and skin colour also enter the equation of stereotypes, prejudice, and discrimination. In Chapter 10 we clearly showed the socioeconomic racial differentiations in Canada. Whites, largely of European origin tend to rank high, while aboriginals, blacks, and some Asians who are visible minorities rank low. Whites are an overwhelming majority in Canada, and the proportion of visible minorities is small compared to comparable proportions in the United States.

To some extent it is surprising that such large numbers of Canadians feel relatively comfortable with East Indians, aboriginals, blacks, Asians, and Jews (Table 11.3). It is not surprising to see (Table 11.4) that Canadians of European origin (all white) were much more preferred for marriage partners than were non-Europeans of Asian and African racial origin. Ramcharan's (1982) findings on racism toward non-whites documents some of the discrimination of West Indians, Chinese, Japanese, East Indians, Filipinos, and Arabs.

Ramcharan (1982:88) proposes that discriminatory behaviour in Canada can be analyzed from two perspectives—the colour-class and the stranger theses:

> With regard to the colour-class thesis, the supposition is that the majority groups in the society identify nonwhites with the lowest social class mainly because of the historical relationships between whites and nonwhites. The Stranger thesis sees the nonwhite immigrants as archetypal stranger both in appearance and behaviour, and react to them with distrust, antipathy, and a resultant negative attitude (Ramcharan, 1982:88).

Ramcharan suggests that both of these perspectives may be operating for many people. As a result, non-whites may be seen as both outsiders and strangers, marginal to society but also relegated to an inferior socioeconomic status. What remains to be seen is whether the above has been institutionalized in Canada, and whether these attitudes can still be changed.

Recently there has been a much larger influx of non-white immigrants so that colour and racial factors are creating larger visible minority sectors, especially in some of the larger cities such as Toronto, Montreal, and Vancouver. A very large proportion of recent immigrants entering Canada come to Toronto; many of these are non-whites. Studies by Frances Henry (1978:383; 1994) show that the black presence in Toronto is resulting in more racism. Toronto discriminates in employment and access to housing four to eight times as often as whites (James, 1995:135–46). Ramcharan's (1982:89) study of West Indians in Toronto shows that 58 per cent reported discrimination in housing, 38 per cent in access to housing, and 16 per cent in hotels, bars, and relations with the police. The Ontario Human Rights Commission reports that in 1977 over half of their complaints were from visible minorities. Since then Toronto has commissioned the Task Force on Race Relations to look into the problem.

Ramcharan (1982:90) suggests that there are also differences among visible minorities; his suggestion is supported by the Toronto Task Force:

> The report believes, however, that it was not a phenomenon of institutional racism but rather of 'culture shock' with the white majority being unable to adjust to the fact that Toronto had become a multicultural entity. . . . It notes that the Asian migrant is usually a professional and skilled worker, and as a result has not started at the bottom of the stratification system as was expected. The immigrants' sudden emergence above the expected level shocked and surprised many majority group members who were born here and have not risen to the upper echelons of the economic system (Pitman, 1978:38–41).

Ramcharan (1982:90) suggests this shows the combination of the stranger and colour-class theses. Some visible minorities are discriminated against because their cultural traditions are considered inferior, and others are discriminated against because higher status visible immigrants have not accepted a low ascribed entrance status.

Frances Henry classifies racism in three categories: 'Individual racism refers to conscious prejudice; institutional racism is that which is carried out by an individual because of others who are prejudiced; and structural racism has its base in the inequalities rooted in the operations of society at large'. Henry and associates (Henry et al., 2000) found that roughly half of their sample in Toronto expressed some degree of racism; approximately 16 per cent were considered very racist, 35 percent somewhat racist, 30 per cent somewhat liberal, and 19 per cent very liberal. They found that younger Torontonians were less racist, and that the more educated also were less racist, which confirms Bibby's (1987:160) national findings. Again we must ask, what affirmative action should be initiated? Studies by Satzewich (1998), Fleras and Elliott (1999), Ralston (2000), Wong (2000), and Tian (2000) all show that Asian women, Chinese youth, and refugees all struggle with problems of race.

Religion and Anti-Semitism

In addition to ethnic origin and race, religion is also a means of differentiating status. John Berry et al. (1977) found that both Angloceltic and French Canadians placed Doukhobors, Hutterites, and Mennonites at the bottom of the social distance scale (Friesen, 1993). These religious minorities ranked lower than visible minorities (1995).

Reginald Bibby (1995) found that his national samples felt about as at ease with Jews as with East Indians, Canadian Indians, blacks, and Asians. Driedger's Winnipeg high school students placed Jews roughly at a par with the non-European origin category with respect to social distance (Table 11.4). Only one-fourth were willing to marry Jews, 7 per cent wanted them only as visitors to Canada. Lambert and Curtis (1984:30–46) compared four samples of Canadians and found that opposition to mixed racial and religious marriages declined between 1968 and 1983. These data suggest that many Canadians place considerable distance between themselves and some religious minorities.

Howard Palmer (1982) found that during the Second World War, German-speaking Canadians were associated with the enemy; this association led to the 1940 burning of two Mennonite churches in Vauxhall, Alberta. Similar reports can be found with regard to Jehovah's Witnesses. In Chapter 12 we will discuss the Jewish Holocaust, the attitudes of Canadians toward the Jews, and the degree of prejudice and discrimination based on anti-Semitism in Canada (Elliott and Fleras, 1992:51).

In Winnipeg, Driedger and Mezoff (1981: 11–15) found that Jewish high school students reported the greatest discrimination. About half of the Jewish and Polish students reported being subjected to ethnic jokes. Twenty Jewish students interpreted some of the joking as malicious. Verbal abuse, a more serious form of negative expression, was reported by about one-sixth (18.3 per cent) of the total sample of students. In contrast, half of the Jews reported verbal abuse. 'Dirty Jews' was reported by 31 Jewish students as the most common verbal abuse, followed by reference to 'cheap and rich Jews' (11) and 'bloody Jews' (4). Less than 5 per cent also reported more serious forms of discrimination, such as receiving hate literature, physical attack, and vandalism. Over half of this form of abuse was reported by the Jewish students. One-fifth of the Jewish students had received hate literature; a similar proportion also reported physical attacks, but it was not always clear whether they were assaulted because they were Jewish. Their reports included the following comments: 'I was hit', 'attacked at school', 'beat up because I was Jewish', 'kids threw sticks and leaves at one', 'physical attack in younger years', 'fights in high school', 'got into a fight', 'attacked in Grade 5', 'kicked and punched in school', 'boys came to private school to pick fights', 'attacked in school halls', 'attacked by drunks', 'pushed down in park', 'beaten up by Protestants', and 'gang bullied me'. Vandalism was reported by 13 per cent of the Jewish students in the following places: 'at the Jewish cemetery', 'house broken into', 'against religious property', 'family plot in cemeteries', 'swastikas on the walls of synagogues', '"Dirty Jew" written on garage door', and 'Jewish school broken into'. There is little doubt that the hate literature, physical attacks, and vandalism reported and confirmed by citation of places and events are forms of discriminatory abuse.

Canadians clearly differentiate between others on the basis of ethnicity, race, and religion. Canadians make and use symbolic differentiations as a basis of discrimination. There is considerable evidence that prejudice and discrimination do exist, even though more thorough documentation would be desirable. John Porter was keenly aware of this potential for disadvantage, and favoured less stress on ethnic differentiation so that all could compete in the labour market on the same basis. With the increase of a more pluralist ethnic, racial, and religious mosaic, it is also essential that Canadians increasingly accept variety and diversity as the norm. As long as expectations of ethnic minority assimilation and amalgamation survive, minorities will be viewed as inferior and second-class citizens. Affirmative action to fight discrimination and racism again seems appropriate.

SUMMARY

With stratification and increased pluralism come a variety of attitudes and behaviours. Some Canadians are 'much more equal' than others, and that there is considerable evidence of social distance in the form of ethnic stereotypes, prejudice, and discrimination.

The charter groups have received special privileges in the Canadian constitution to preserve their languages and culture. The British and French also reinforce their higher status and privilege by supporting their charter status and ranking others in lesser positions. The majority in Canada now supports bilingualism, although this support is greater in Quebec, where the French are a large majority, than in the West, where the ethnic mosaic is more diversified. Generally the prestige of the charter Canadians is set and is increasingly recognized.

Attitudes toward a plural society are also growing, with a majority favouring the mosaic over the melting pot. Attitudes of Canadians show that immigrants are welcome, and that they may retain their cultures. There is considerable recognition that such pluralism may not be easy, with a sizeable minority who would rather dispense with multiculturalism. A huge majority claim that they feel relatively at ease with visible minorities, an openness that appears hopeful for Canada's multicultural future.

However, there is also considerable social distance or racism in the form of stereotyping, prejudice, and discrimination. Two to three times as many Canadians would rather marry European-origin than non-European-origin Canadians. Negative stereotypes of Jews persist, and there is considerable evidence that visible minorities are also subject to abuse by a minority of Canadians who do not wish them well. Aboriginals are continually shunted to the periphery and given inferior opportunities and status. In large cities there is evidence of racism based on skin colour, especially as visible minorities try to compete for jobs and better housing. There are also religious differentiations, focused mainly on anti-Semitism.

Canada is becoming an increasingly pluralist society, there is progress in the acceptance of multiculturalism and diversity of colour, race, and beliefs. A sizeable minority, however, neither accepts ethnic diversity nor complies with the ideals of minority rights and freedoms. This is especially evident in repeated incidents of racism and anti-Semitism. It will not be easy to build a pluralist ethnic, racial, and religious society. Attitudes and behaviour do not easily conform to ideal norms set on paper. A just society based on equality and freedom seems always a step away. We are dealing here with those located in Cell D, who are visible minorities in our Conformity-Pluralist model. We have found much conflict between racial minorities and dominant whites (Cell B), voluntary pluralists (Cell E), and especially those who have gathered at the watering hole (Cell A) where all have to make a living. Let us turn finally, for guidance on how we might facilitate the quest of all Canadians for human rights in Chapter 12.

CRITICAL THINKING QUESTIONS

1. What do Frances Henry and Carol Tator mean by 'democratic racism'? List some of the values and myths associated with democratic racism.

2. What did the Angus Reid poll of 1991 discover with respect to attitudes toward immigration, racial diversity, and the degree of comfort with diversity?

3. Define what Bogardus meant by social distance. What did Driedger and Mezoff find when they used the Bogardus scale with high school students in Winnipeg?

4. What did Lippmann mean by ethnic stereotype, and what did Driedger and Clifton find in their Winnipeg student sample? Compare groups.

5. What is the difference between prejudice and discrimination? Discuss Hagan's four types of illegitimate treatment.

6. What national perceived discrimination did Reginald Bibby find between 1980-1995? Did discrimination increase or decrease? Where?

SUGGESTED READINGS

Henry, Frances, *The Caribbean Diaspora in Toronto: Learning to Live with Racism* (Toronto: University of Toronto Press, 1994). This is a study of mostly black Caribbeans who emigrated to Toronto and their experiences with racism.

Reid, Angus, Multiculturalism and Canadians: Attitude Study, A National Report (Ottawa: Ministry of Multiculturalism, 1991). This national survey follows up on Berry's earlier 1977 survey, comparing changing attitudes on prejudice and discrimination in Canada.

Satzewich, Victor (ed.), *Racism and Social Inequality in Canada: Concepts, Controversies and Strategies of Resistance* (Toronto: Thompson Publishing, 1998). Fifteen contributors explore the extent to which institutional arrangements shape individual attitudes and state policies toward race.

CHAPTER 12

The Quest for Human Rights

While multiethnicity is normal in civilized societies, the ideal of one ethnically unitary state, perpetuated by British and French nationalism until the 1920s, was rarely approached in practice. The unitary national state simplified the wielding of power by a majority because such nationalism seeks to justify the power relations discussed in Part IV. The settlement and invasion of the Americas by Europeans since the early 1500s was fraught with numerous wars among the British, French, Spanish, and Portuguese. These nations wished to extend their power as colonizers of weaker peoples and to entrench their own political dominance and economic advantage.

Karl Marx's main concern was with these macro political-economy power issues and he hoped for a 'classless society' in which all people could survive under more equal relations. Unfortunately, he spent little time spelling out the fine points of how such relations on a micro level might work. Max Weber focused more on multidimensional factors of human relations that operated on the micro level, which he had experienced firsthand in the Austro-Hungarian Empire. His concern for individuals and their needs, allowed him to consider economic and political factors, and also the religious and value systems that often motivate humans in a variety of directions. In Part IV we focused on macro power relations; in Part V we wish to see how they affect minorities and their rights and freedoms.

HIGHLIGHT 12.1 MULTICULTURAL CITIZENSHIP

The late twentieth century has been described as the age of migration. Massive numbers of people are moving across borders, making virtually every country more polyethnic in composition. This has also been described as 'the age of nationalism', as more and more national groups throughout the world mobilize and assert their identity. As a result, the settled rules of political life in many countries are being challenged by new 'politics of cultural difference'. Indeed, with the end of the Cold War, the demands of ethnic and national groups have taken over cen-tre stage in political life, both domestically and internationally.

Many people see this new 'politics of difference' as a threat to liberal democracy. I have presented a more optimistic view. I have tried to show that many (but not all) of the demands of ethnic and national groups are consistent with liberal principles of individual freedom and social justice. I would not say that these issues can be 'resolved' in any final sense. The issues are too complicated for that. But they can be 'managed' peacefully and fairly, assuming there is some level of goodwill.

Of course, in many parts of the world, groups are motivated by hatred and intolerance, not justice, and have no interest in treating others with goodwill. Under these circumstances, the potential for ethnic and national groups to abuse their rights and powers is very high. Yugoslavia and Rwanda are only the most recent reminders of the injustices which have been committed in the name of ethnic and national differences, from racial segregation and religious pogroms to ethnic cleansing and genocide.

Given these potential abuses, many people feel a strong temptation to push the issue of minority rights off to the side. Why, they ask, can we not simply 'treat people as individuals', without regard for their ethnic or national identity? Why can we not focus on the things we share as humans, rather than what distinguishes us? I suspect that most of us have had that reaction at some point when dealing with the new and complicated 'politics of difference'.

However, that response is misguided. The problem is not that it is too 'individualistic'. In many parts of the world, a healthy dose of individualism would provide a welcome respite from group-based conflict. The problem, rather, is that the response is simply incoherent. As I have tried to show, political life has an inescapably national dimension, whether it is in the drawing of boundaries and distributing of powers, or in decisions about the language of schooling, courts, and bureaucracies, or in the choice of public holidays. Moreover, these inescapable aspects of political life give a profound advantage to the members of majority nations.

We need to be aware of this, and the way it can alienate and disadvantage others, and take steps to prevent any resulting injustices. These steps might include polyethnic and representation rights to accommodate ethnic and other disadvantaged rights to enable autonomy for national minorities alongside the majority nation. Without such measures, talk of 'treating people as individuals' is itself just a cover for ethnic and national injustice.

It is equally important to stress the limits on such rights. In particular, I have argued that they must respect two constraints: minority rights should not allow one group to dominate other groups; and they should not enable a group to oppress its own members. In other words, liberals should seek to ensure that there is equality between groups, and freedom and equality within groups. Within these limits, minority rights can play a valuable role within a broader theory of liberal justice. In deed, they must play a role if liberalism is not to be condemned to irrelevance in many parts of the world.

In the traditional birthplace(s) of liberal theory–Britain, France, and the United States–minority rights have been ignored, or treated as mere curiosities or anomalies. This is particularly true of the claims of indigenous peoples. But it has become increasingly clear that minority rights are central to the future of the liberal tradition throughout the world. In many countries of the world—including the emerging democracies in Eastern Europe, Africa, and Asia—the status of national minorities and indigenous peoples is perhaps the most pressing issue.

People in these countries are looking to the works of Western liberals for guidance regarding the principles of liberal constitutionalism in a multination state. But the liberal tradition offers only confused and contradictory advice on this question. Liberal thinking on minority rights has too often been guilty of ethnocentric assumptions, or of over-generalizing particular cases, or of conflating contingent political strategy with enduring moral principle. This is reflected in the wide range of policies liberal states have historically adopted regarding ethnic and national groups, ranging from coercive assimilation to coercive segregation, from conquest and colonization to federalism and self-government.

The result has often been grave injustices against the ethnic and national minorities in many Western democracies. But the failure to develop a consistent and principled approach to minority rights may have even greater costs in the newly emerging democracies. At present, the fate of ethnic and national groups around the world is in the hand of xenophobic nationalists, religious extremists, and military dictators. If liberalism is to have any chance of taking hold in these countries, it must explicitly address the needs and aspirations of ethnic and national minorities.

SOURCE: Will Kymlicka, Multicultural Citizenship (Oxford: Oxford University Press, 1995).

INDIVIDUAL RIGHTS AND FREEDOMS

The American Bill of Rights

The two Americas were settled mainly by the Spaniards, Portuguese, British, and French. The Spanish and Portuguese explorers who settled Central and South America came from homelands where Roman Catholicism was the state religion. They propagated their religion in Latin America, and all these countries are now also dominantly Roman Catholic. The state religion was considered an integral part of power politics, when the aboriginals were conquered and subdued. Catholicism replaced aboriginal religions, although in greatly modified forms.

North American settlement, however, did not follow the pattern established in Latin America. The 13 American colonies on the East Coast began in a more heterogeneous manner. Jamestown, the first permanent English settlement in North America, was established in 1607 in what is now Virginia. One year later in 1608, Champlain established the first French settlement on the St Lawrence River at Quebec. The Pilgrim Fathers, a group of separatists from the Church of England who founded Plymouth Colony near Boston, came to America in 1620 on the *Mayflower*. In 1624, the Dutch West Indies Company established the colony of New Amsterdam, which in 1664 was surrendered to the English and renamed New York. In 1681 William Penn, an English Quaker who had ear-lier been jailed for his writings on religious freedom and his defence of the doctrine of toleration, received a grant of territory later to be named Pennsylvania after him. These varied settlements were founded because refugees and settlers left their European states for more freedom and tolerance, particularly of religious beliefs.

It is not surprising that when the American constitution was drafted and signed in 1787, shortly after independence from British rule, it guaranteed freedom of religion, speech, and assembly. Many of the new settlers were dissenters who could not freely practise their beliefs in the normal context of European state religions. They came from a variety of situations with a variety of aspirations that could prosper only under norms of freedom and toleration.

The First Amendment of the Constitution of the United States of America reads: Congress shall make no law respecting an establishment of religion, or prohibiting the free exercise thereof; or abridging the freedom of speech or of the press; or of the right of the people peaceably to assemble, and to petition the government for a redress of grievances.

Congress's first concern was that there should not be an official state religion, and that all people should have the right to practise their religions freely. Freedom of speech and of the press were important for maintaining and propagating

Americans' beliefs, and the ability to meet and assemble as the people saw fit was an important part of these freedoms. The constitution was ratified by the states only after the promise of amendments that related directly to human rights. The first 10 amendments, known as the Bill of Rights, were passed in 1791.

After the bloody Civil War between the North and the South, 75 years later, the Thirteenth, Fourteenth, and Fifteenth Amendments abolished slavery, conferred citizenship on former slaves, and established the principle that the state cannot deprive any person of life, liberty, and/or property, without due process of law. Section One of the Thirteenth Amendment reads:

> Neither Slavery, nor involuntary servitude, except as a punishment for crime whereof the party shall have been duly convicted, shall exist within the United States, or any place subject to their jurisdiction.

Section One of the Fifteenth Amendment reads:

> The right of citizens of the United States to vote shall not be denied or abridged by the United States or by any State on account of race, color, or previous condition of servitude.

Although religious rights were entrenched two hundred years ago, it was almost a century later, after a civil war, that equality of race was entrenched. To this day, problems of racial inequality exist.

It was not until 1920 that women received the right to vote under Section One of the Nineteenth Amendment, which reads:

> The right of citizens of the United States to vote shall not be denied or abridged by the United States on account of sex.

These are not, however, articles or amendments that relate directly to ethnicity except the Fifteenth Amendment's guarantee of voting to all races. All these articles protect individual rights; none deal with group rights. Individual religions, races, or ethnic groups are not provided any specific rights. The United States is one of the first modern states to entrench human rights and freedoms by restricting state powers. It has been a struggle, but in the process America has been held up by many as the land of liberty and freedom. The drive for religious freedom was an important part of this historical quest and played an important part in setting these standards.

The Western World has been profoundly influenced by Judeo-Christian religious ideology. Although secularization has ensured that this ideology is no longer as dominant as it was in Europe during the Middle Ages, a large majority of North Americans claim to be Christian. Christianity is an ideology that grew out of the Jewish religion, which is based on the law and the prophets. Prophets such as Amos proclaimed the concept of justice based on the fundamental tenet that all human beings are of equal worth. Justice implies that there are standards for the treatment of human beings, and that these must be applied fairly in accordance with principles based on what is 'right'. The prophets proclaimed these standards and appealed to Israel to comply.

The Christian religion grew out of this Jewish tradition, confirmed the law and the prophets, and extended the ideology to embrace and promote 'love' (see, for instance, Matthew 5, the Sermon on the Mount). Again the worth of every human being was stressed and was extended to include even the enemy. The 'brotherhood of man' applied to all people, nations, and races. Everyone was considered worthy of love. It was a message not only for the Jews, but for Gentiles as well.

Western political ideology (especially in the democracies) is based on principles quite in line with Western religious ideology. Although in Britain freedom was at first mainly for the elite, slowly freedom for all citizens was recognized and affirmed. The French call for 'liberty, equality and fraternity' was also intended for the masses. The conclusion of Abraham Lincoln's Gettysburg Address (19 November 1863)—calling for government for, by, and of the people—perhaps summarized this ideology best, giving notice that all citizens have the franchise and deserve a voice in the affairs of the nation. This was enshrined in the constitution and its subsequent amendments, so that freedom of speech, freedom of assembly, and the pursuit of life, liberty, and happiness were legal rights upheld by the law.

While North American religious and political ideologies generally aim in the same direction, our economic ideologies often pull in opposite directions. Laissez-faire capitalism had as its basic tenets freedom of individual enterprise, ownership of private property, rights to inheritance, and the need for competition under minimal government interference. Capitalism tends to embrace some of the individual freedoms of Christianity and democracy, but it is much less open to the group and social responsibilities of our religious and political ideologies. Early capitalism tended to promote individual rights and often sacrificed the welfare of others, usually the workers and the masses.

Since then, capitalism in Canada has been greatly modified to accommodate more social needs. This seems to have come about because of socialist philosophies that advocated greater emphasis on state control of some of the basic economic industries. These philosophies hold that the basic and common needs of education, welfare, health, transportation, and communication should be operated or controlled by the government for the benefit of all. Thus we have a modified sociocapitalist economy that tries to hold together individual freedoms and collective responsibility. Access to economic management and control, however, lies mostly in the hands of those of northern European (especially British) origin. Not all Canadians have an equal chance to compete within the economic structure.

Thus, we are faced with individual, institutional, and structural inequalities in the social order that need to be addressed. Kallen (1995: 13–40) points out that despite a proliferation of human rights legislation, racism persists. Some people call for the restructuring of our social institutions so that schools, churches, governments, and the workplace articulate and promote equal human rights, the only foundation

upon which legislation can be justly based and enforced. In the 1960s such restructuring related to the equal freedom of blacks in the United States was the major issue which many feel needs to be continued in the nineties.

The United Nations Universal Declaration of Human Rights

The Universal Declaration of Human Rights was unanimously adopted in 1948 by the General Assembly of the United Nations (Kallen, 1995: 286–91). Canadian John Humphrey, a native of New Brunswick, played a major role in writing this United Nations Declaration. The Declaration's main objective is to promote and encourage respect for human rights and freedoms. Thirty articles proclaim the personal, civil, political, economic, social, and cultural rights of humans. It goes considerably farther than the American constitution's guarantee of individual rights. It is amazing that the nations of the world were able to agree on such far-reaching freedoms for all world citizens; exercising these ideals is another matter.

Article One declares that 'all humans are born free and equal in dignity and rights' and should act 'towards each other in a spirit of brotherhood.' Article Two states that these 'freedoms are set forth without distinction of any kind, such as race, color, sex, language, religion, political . . . national or social . . . origin'. Article Two clearly declares that racial, ethnic, and religious equality must be respected. In Article Three the right to 'life, liberty and security of person' is articulated and Article Four says that 'no one shall be held in slavery or servitude'. These four articles certainly cover the basic rights of all humans.

The remaining articles continue to spell out rights related to freedom from torture, recognition before the law, and protection by the law. No one shall be subjected to arbitrary arrest and detention; everyone shall have equality in a fair hearing in the case of criminal charges, and shall be tried under the presumption of innocence. Privacy, family, home, honour, and reputation must be protected by law. There should be rights to freedom of movement, and all people should have the right to asylum when persecuted.

Articles Fifteen through Thirty each elaborate briefly on a series of rights and freedoms including the right to nationality, the right to marry and to found a family, the right to own property, freedom of opinion and expression, freedom of assembly and participation in government, and the right to social security, which includes work, rest and leisure, health, education, and the cultural life of a community. Social and international order are noted as being necessary to make these rights possible. The articles also declare the nations' duty to help create communities in which such rights and freedoms are possible. The list of rights and freedoms is so extensive that few societies are able to fulfill all these obligations, especially in Third World countries where the capacity to provide educational, work, and economic opportunities are limited. Presumably the rights and freedoms are spelled out in detail as a goal to which all nations may aspire.

While these rights and freedoms are all related and relevant to ethnic relations, Articles Two, Four, Seven, Sixteen, and Eighteen are more specifically focused on race, ethnicity, and religion (Kallen, 1995:287–9). Article Two clearly states that the rights and freedoms are universal:

> Everyone is entitled to all the rights and freedoms set forth in this Declaration, without distinction of any kind, such as race, sex, language, religion, political or other opinion, national or social origin, property, birth or other status.

The foundation for freedoms clearly extends to persons of any race, language, religion, or national origin. Article Four is clear on slavery:

> No one shall be held in slavery or servitude, slavery and slave trade shall be prohibited in all their forms.

This goes farther than the American Bill of Rights did originally. Although the United States waited 78 years after the first states ratified the constitution before they outlawed slavery, they ratified the Thirteenth Amendment in 1865, 83 years before the United Nations Declaration. The definition of slavery might be subject to interpretation. While ownership of persons might not be direct, they could still be subject to circumstances such as those in which black South Africans recently lived, which amounts to informal forms of slavery where a white minority is subjugating a black majority.

> Article Seven addresses the issue of equality before the law:
> All are equal before the law and are entitled without discrimination to equal protection of the law. All are entitled to equal protection against any discrimination in violation of this Declaration and against any incitement to such discrimination.

We know, of course, that not all accused have equal access to a fair hearing or legal help; some can afford it better than others. The fact that a highly disproportionate number of aboriginals are found in Canadian prisons indicates inequality; the same is true for Afro-Americans in the United States. These Natives may be less knowledgeable about legal matters, may not have the means to secure bail, and may be more vigorously pursued by the police because of their visibility. This kind of discrimination can be subtle.

The first part of Article Sixteen clearly mentions ethnicity and the rights to marriage and a family:

> 1) Men and women of full age, without any limitation due to race, nationality or religion, have the rights to marry and to found a family. They are entitled to equal rights as to marriage, during marriage and at its dissolution . . .

Marriage to a partner who wishes to perpetuate similar beliefs and values is important for ethnic identity. Thus, no one should be forced to marriage outside these restrictions. On the other hand, persons are also free to marry across racial, national, and religious lines if they wish to do so. Thus, both freedom to maintain ethnic solidarity and to move beyond it are assured (Kallen, 1995:288). Article Eighteen deals with freedom in religion:

> Everyone has the right to freedom of thought, conscience and religion; this right includes freedom to change his religion or belief, and freedom, either alone or in community with others and in public or private, to manifest his religion or belief in teaching, practice, worship and observance.

For minorities such as Jews, Hutterites, Mennonites, Doukhobors, Hindus, Muslims, and others, ethnicity and religion are closely intertwined; their religion must be safeguarded to protect their ethnicity. However, this freedom is also important for larger groups: the French, Italians, and Poles are usually Roman Catholics; the British are largely Anglican, United Church, or Presbyterian. Religious freedom for minorities is crucial in India, Pakistan, Northern Ireland, the Arab countries, Israel, and most Latin American countries where the majority belongs to one religion.

The freedoms stated in the American constitution and its amendments are confined to individual rights, and that is also largely the case for the rights stated in the United Nations Declaration. However, the Universal Declaration of Human Rights does provide more social context to support individual rights. Article Twelve speaks against family and home interference. Article Thirteen deals with freedom of residence and movement, and Article Twenty supports the right of peaceful assembly. Both documents speak to social group supports. Article Twenty supports the right to take part in government, and Articles Twenty-Two through Twenty-Nine all support rights to associations such as social security, work, leisure, health services, education, community, and international order. Thus, the United Nations Declaration protects the social context and supports much more freedom in a greater holistic fashion.

Evelyn Kallen has evaluated the United Nations Declaration and suggests that it supports individual rights, but offers little support for ethnic collectivities living within the boundaries of a nation. Kallen (1995:9–12) suggests that if multiculturalism in Canada is to mean anything, rights will have to reach beyond individual levels, to subnational ethnic collectivities. For example the Québécois, the Dene Nation, and the Inuit of Nunavut movements will be dealt with as peoples who deserve special rights within the nation-state. Indeed, by 1992 the United Nations General Assembly made a 'Declaration on the Rights of Persons Belonging to National or Ethnic, Religious and Linguistic Minorities', which we present under Appendix C in this volume. The nine articles deal with issues of protection, participation, favourable conditions, information, in order to provide full opportunities for minority groups.

The Canadian Charter of Rights and Freedoms

Whereas the United States was concerned with protecting individual rights and freedoms two hundred years ago, the British North America (BNA) Act of 1867, created in Britain, made no specific reference to human rights. Aside from provisions to protect the English and French languages, and the rights to Protestants and Catholics to have their own denominational schools, the BNA Act did not address human rights. This seems to have been a reflection of the dominance of two colonial powers that shaped the Canadian nation. Aside from the aboriginals in Canada, the two charter European founding peoples represented more than 90 per cent of the population in 1867.

The BNA Act virtually ignored Canada's aboriginals, and recognized almost no rights for them.

> For almost a century after the British Emancipation Act of 1833, which marked the official demise of slavery in Canada, the trend at the federal, provincial and municipal levels of Canadian government was to enact discriminatory legislation.

Among the most pernicious pieces of legislation was the Indian Act, whereby Indians were virtually denied all of their fundamental rights; but many other discriminatory laws impeded the rightful participation of Asians, Blacks and other ethnic minorities from anything like full participation in Canadian society (Kallen, 1995:43).

Questions of human rights and discrimination began to be considered seriously only after the Second World War, most likely due to the atrocities of the Nazis and the concerns of the increasingly larger immigrant population who considered themselves other than charter Canadians.

Legal rights, some of which are formally stated (charter status and treaty status) and others of which are assumed (entrance status), have evolved during the last 135 years. The British North America Act of 1867 gave the founding groups of Canada charter-group status (Porter, 1965). The Act legalized the claims of the two groups to such historical privileges as the perpetuation of their separate languages and cultures. Though legally of equal status, the French have always been junior partners in their alliance with the English, especially where British political, economic, educational, and demographic influences have been dominant outside Quebec.

The presence of two major European linguistic and cultural groups from the beginning of Confederation has in some ways set a precedent for the recognition of more than one ethnic presence. Most nations assume one dominant culture to which others must conform, although all nations do have a variety of subgroups (French and Flemish in Belgium; German, French, and Italian in Switzerland; English, Scottish, Irish, and Welsh in Great Britain; etc.). Even in the new constitution two official languages are recognized and legally entrenched. French Canadians in Quebec have moulded their curricula to emphasize their long 350-year history, and the British have done the same in the rest of Canada. The two often interpret the same events quite differ-

ently to cast their respective histories in the best light. In the process, minority languages and heritages were often legislated against by both the British (e.g., the Manitoba School Question) and the French (e.g., Bill 101). Canada is seeking to correct some of these injustices and inequalities, and to recognize the contributions of non-charter Canadians now that multiculturalism within a bilingual framework has been recognized.

While the legal rights and special privileges of the charter groups became a part of the social structure early in Canada's history, the structure created by treaties with Canadian Indians often placed aboriginals in underprivileged positions. About one-half of Canada's aboriginals were forced onto reserves to free the land for white European settlers and to provide a more convenient administrative arrangement of control. Indians on the Prairies in particular did not yet have a concept of private property and the value of land, which aboriginals on the West Coast, for example, had developed. Thus, most West Coast aboriginals have not yet signed treaties, while Prairie Indians signed away their lands for a pittance in Treaties 1–11. These reserves, often in marginal regions, have been mostly noncompetitive in today's industrial society. As a result we find large numbers of young aboriginals leaving the reserves in search of jobs and many are coming to Canada's cities. In the meantime, new questions arise as to whether the treaties still apply, how they should be interpreted, and what land rights can be negotiated where treaties have not been made. A wide range of interpretations can be given to the present plight of Canada's 'first peoples', what rights they have, and what they deserve in the future.

Now that the rights of the charter groups and some of the rights of half of our aboriginal people have been partly clarified, we turn to the rights of the one-third of Canada's population who are neither British, French, nor aboriginal. This proportion of population has been growing steadily and is trying to find its place in a multicultural society. Advocates of pluralism often complain that the contributions of these groups have not been sufficiently recognized and taught.

In the past decade a point system of desired traits has resulted in an increase of many more immigrants from the Third World, including Asians, South Americans, Africans, and other visible minorities, often of other religions and non-European cultures. Many of these new immigrants are also well educated, and thus increasingly demand equal rights and just treatment. How can we integrate their contribution into our social system so that their voices may be heard as equals?

Canada passed its Charter of Rights and Freedoms in 1982 (see Appendix B), when it became a part of the new Canadian Constitution that replaced the BNA Act (Kallen, 1995:292–8). Article 2 lists four fundamental freedoms: '(a) freedom of conscience and religion; (b) freedom of thought, belief, opinion, . . . the press and other media of communication; (c) freedom of peaceable assembly; and (d) freedom of association: (Constitution Act, 1982, Appendix 1). Articles 2 through 15 have to do with individual rights. Article 3 deals with the right to vote, and Article 6 with the right to mobility inside and outside Canada. Articles 7 through 14 provide legal rights: the right to life, liberty, and security, and freedom from unreasonable seizure, arbitrary imprisonment, and cruel punishment (Driedger, 1996:291–3).

Article 15 specifically spells out individual equality of rights:

1) Every individual is equal before and under the law and has the right to the equal protection and equal benefits of the law without discrimination and, in particular, without discrimination based on race, national or ethnic origin, colour, religion, sex, age or mental or physical disability.

This is the first of the three documents to include ethnic origin. The traits protected from discrimination, including ethnicity, are again mentioned in subsection two. Thus, the multicultural nature of Canada is recognized beyond racial and religious variations.

Articles 16 through 35 deal with collective rights, which are also found only in the Canadian Constitution. Articles 16 through 22 deal with the two official languages, English and French. Article 16 declares English and French the official languages of Canada, and Article 17 states that the official languages may be used in the Canadian parliament and in the New Brunswick legislature. Article 18 says that statues and records must be in both official languages, Article 19 says the same applies to the courts, and Article 20 says that the public may communicate in both languages when dealing with government services. Articles 21 and 22 solidify these rights as pre-eminent. Thus, the languages of the original European charter peoples have been entrenched (Driedger, 1989:373).

Article 23 spells out minority language educational rights. In Quebec, for example, minorities such as the British or others, when of a sufficient number, have the right to learn in English; the same applies to the French minorities in the rest of Canada.

Article 25 deals with aboriginal and treaty rights:

The guarantee in this Charter of certain rights and freedoms shall not be construed so as to abrogate or derogate from any aboriginal, treaty or other rights or freedoms that pertain to the aboriginal peoples of Canada including:
(a) any rights of freedoms that have been recognized by the Royal Proclamation of 1763; and
(b) any rights or freedoms that may be acquired by the aboriginal peoples of Canada by way of land claims settlement.

Article 35 reinforces the treaty rights of the aboriginal peoples of Canada:

(1) The existing aboriginal treaty rights of the aboriginal peoples of Canada are hereby recognized and affirmed.
(2) In this Act, 'Aboriginal peoples of Canada' includes the Indian, Inuit and Metis peoples of Canada.

The meeting of aboriginal peoples and the governments has not, however, been able to clarify numerous issues that apply to the contemporary scene. Three official meetings held in the mid-eighties have not been able to resolve the differences; therefore, the aboriginal peoples are still very unsatisfied with the wording.

The rights of the non-charter and non-aboriginal one-third of Canadians have been recognized, as outlined in Article 27:

This Charter shall be interpreted in a manner consistent with the preservation, and enhancement of the multicultural heritage of Canadians.

This ethnic segment of Canada has been growing the fastest, and although they have gained recognition in the Constitution, there are no specific guarantees to any particular group. The Manitoba School Question in the early 1900s would likely not have happened had we had rights of non-charter groups spelled out more clearly. Bill 101, which declares French as dominant in Quebec, is again a more recent issue that needs clarification.

Our discussion of these three declarations of rights and freedoms shows the common search for individual rights and freedoms, and also the willingness in Canada to begin to consider group rights. However, group rights are still not clearly entrenched, and multicultural rights are only recognized, but not elaborated.

Typology of Human Rights

Evelyn Kallen (1995:10) presents and summarizes these human rights shown in Table 12.1. She moves from micro individual rights to more macro group rights, and then spells out the principles, violations and claims of cultural, national and aboriginal rights. Kallen's typology helps sort some of the important categories dealt with in Chapters 8 through 12: 1) *Individual rights* to life, freedom, opportunity, and dignity; 2) *Group or category* rights to life, freedom, opportunity, and dignity; 3) *Collective*

cultural rights to ethnocultural distinctiveness, design for living, language, religion, institutions, and customs; 4) *Collective national rights* to self-determination, ancestral territory, nation; and 5) *Collective Aboriginal rights* to land, occupancy, and use. All individuals are covered by the first, religious groups by the second, ethnic groups by the third, Québécois by the fourth and aboriginals by the fifth.

Individual rights can be violated by neglect, diminution, oppression, and finally homicide, which we have illustrated. Group rights can be violated by inequality, defamation, oppression and—worst of all—genocide, typified by the Jewish Holocaust and more recently the atrocities in Rwanda and Bosnia-Herzegovina. Deculturation, discrimination, and cultural genocide can be inflicted by those who are dominant, illustrated by European treatment of Canada's aboriginals (Kallen, 1995:10). Collective rights could be violated, if Quebeckers decided to separate and the rest of Canada denied them nationhood status; so far, a majority have not called for such separation. Aboriginal rights can be violated when land settlements have not been made, as they have not in half of Canada. Let us examine some of these collective violations of human rights.

ETHNICITY AND COLLECTIVE RIGHTS

The three declarations of human rights we have reviewed focus largely on individual rights, although the Canadian Charter of Rights and Freedoms does spell out the rights of the majority charter groups, and recognizes some aboriginal and multicultural rights. In Chapter 9 we highlighted examples of racial atrocities by showing how blacks were enslaved and the Japanese were interned in North America. Here we wish to add the expulsion of the Acadians, the demise of the Metis nation, the settling of aboriginal land claims, and the Jewish Holocaust to further portray the need for minority rights. Canadians are not sufficiently aware of their own sordid history, and what they have done to many minorities in the past.

TABLE 12.1 A Typology of Human Rights Principles, Violations, and Claims

Principles	Violations	Claims
Fundamental Human Rights		
Individual		Individual claims
Right to life	Homicide	
Freedom (self-determination)	Oppression	
Equal opportunity	Neglect	
Dignity of person	Diminution	
Group or Category		
Right to life	Genocide	
Freedom (group autonomy)	Group oppression	
Equal opportunity	Group inequity	
Group dignity	Group defamation	
Collective Cultural Rights		Collective claims
Distinctive ethnocultural	Cultural discrimination	
design for living (language, religion,	(deculturation/cultural genocide)	
institutions, customs)		
Collective National Rights		Nationhood claims
Self-determination as	National discrimination	
a distinctive nation within	(denial of nationhood status)	
own ancestral/territorial bounds		
Collective Aboriginal Rights		Aboriginal rights claims
Right and title to aboriginal lands	Land entitlement	
based on collective use and occupancy	discrimination	
by aboriginal ethnic group 'from		
time immemorial'		

SOURCE: Evelyn Kallen, *Ethnicity and Human Rights in Canada,* 3rd edn (Toronto: Oxford University Press, 2003).

Expulsion of the Acadians

In his book *Fragile Freedoms* (1981), Thomas Berger describes the descent of many minority groups, and we are indebted to his concise portrayal of the expulsion of the Acadians in 1755 from the earliest European settlement in Canada.

The nation states of Britain and France were traditionally and ethnically well defined by the time Columbus discovered America in 1492. They had their own internal ethnic struggles earlier, and by 1500 diversity was anathema to the rulers of these nation-states. They were more preoccupied with consolidating their sovereignty in the newly discovered lands (where power relations led to much conflict and many wars) than worrying about rights for minorities in the path of their conquests. Ever since, the central issue of Canadian history has been the working out of the relations between these two societies (Berger, 1981:xiv). The final conquest of New France by the British led to a series of attempts to assimilate the people of Quebec. The struggle of French Canadians epitomizes the struggle of minorities everywhere. Confederation in 1867 was the accommodation of these two communities.

The Sieur de Monts' French expedition first wintered at the mouth of the St Croix River in 1604–5. In 1605 they moved to Port Royal on the Annapolis River on the south shore of the Bay of Fundy where they established the Order of Good Cheer. Later known as Acadia, this was the first permanent European settlement in North America north of Florida. In 1608 Champlain started the new settlement in Quebec and the centre of French activities shifted to the St Lawrence.

Although Champlain abandoned the new Acadia, others continued to build the French settlement. Argall, governor of Virginia, looted and burned their buildings in 1613. In 1671 King James I of England granted the whole of Acadia to the Earl of Stirling, making it part of New Scotland, or Nova Scotia (Berger, 1981:4–5). In 1627 the Earl seized the small French community at Port Royal; by a later British and French treaty, Acadia reverted to the French and several hundred new French settlers came to the Port Royal area. The boundaries of Acadia were never well defined (Dinwoodie, 1986:15–20), but it became a centre of English-French conflict:

It lay as a wedge between the expanding empires of New France on the St. Lawrence and of New England on the Atlantic seaboard farther to the south. France and England were in constant conflict over Acadia. In just over a century, Port Royal changed hands nine times, six times by force of arms, three times by treaty (Berger, 1981:6).

By 1701, when the Acadians had lived around the Bay of Fundy for almost a century, they numbered 1,134; their relations with the aboriginals were harmonious, and they felt more attached to North America than to the whims of the European powers. 'In 1713, by the Treaty of Utrecht, the colony passed permanently into the hands of the British. . . . There were now 2,500 Acadians . . .' (Berger, 1981:8). While the treaty provided that they could emigrate to French soil, they were unwilling to give up their fertile farms and abandon what had been their home for over a century. Thus, the British were faced with attempting to rule a people whose language, religion, and cultural heritage were those of their major European enemy.

The Acadians were peaceful until the British insisted that they take an oath of allegiance to the King of England. The Acadians—with their roots in the French tradition and remembering that their territory had changed hands many times—could not pledge allegiance to the British crown. Increasingly, the British were nervous about having the Acadians on their territory, and felt that they needed to secure Halifax and Nova Scotia from a potential uprising of these French-speaking Acadians. Colonel John Winslow, a British officer, wrote in his journal:

We are now hatching the noble and great project of banishing the French neutrals from the Province. . . . If we accomplish this expulsion, it will have been one of the greatest deeds the English in America have ever achieved, for among other considerations, the part of the country which they occupy is one of the best soil in the world, and, in this event, we might place some good farmers on their homesteads (Berger, 1981:12).

In 1755 the governor ordered the Acadians to take an oath of allegiance to the king; when they refused, they were ordered to be dispersed among the British colonies on the continent. The order added that if the Acadians resisted, force should be used and their houses and farms were to be destroyed. They forfeited their lands, tenements, cattle, and other livestock to the Crown after the men had been locked up under guard in the church and their families herded into ships of transport (Berger, 1981:14, 15). Many families were dispersed, never to be reunited; the British burned their barns and houses and turned their cattle loose. 'Altogether, the British forcibly removed and transported around 6,000 Acadians

in 1755, and perhaps 2,000 more in the following years, out of a total population of about
10,000. Some Acadians took refuge in the
forests, just as their ancestors had when Argall
destroyed Port Royal a century and a half before'
(Berger, 1981:14). Longfellow's narrative poem,
Evangeline, A Tale of Acadie, describes the woes
and sorrows of two Acadian lovers separated in
the expulsion.

A few Acadians from Port Royal went to Ile
St. Jean (now Prince Edward Island) under
French control; however, by 1758 the British
occupied the island and the Acadians were again
deported—many of them drowned at sea. When
Louisbourg fell in 1758, the British were masters
of Acadia and the whole region of the St
Lawrence (Daigle, 1982). After the 1755 deportation of Acadians from Port Royal, some
returned; by 1764 Acadians were once again
allowed to own land in Nova Scotia. Most of
them, however, re-established themselves on new
land on the east coast of New Brunswick; more
than a third of the province now speaks French.
When the British Empire Loyalists arrived in
southern New Brunswick, some Acadians had
to move further north. Until recently, there
has been little communication between the
Protestant British Loyalists in the south, and the
Catholic Acadians in the north of the province.

Although the British North America Act provided for parochial schools in Quebec, this was
not the case in New Brunswick. In 1871, four
years after Confederation, New Brunswick
passed the Common Schools Act, denying funds
to denominational schools (Berger, 1981:20).
The Acadians challenged the law in the courts
but they were unsuccessful. By 1969, the New
Brunswick Legislature did pass a law making it a
bilingual province. This bilingualism has also
been entrenched in the Charter of Rights and
Freedoms in the new Constitution of Canada in
1982. Despite much persecution, deportation,
explusion, and sorrow, the French Acadians have
survived in New Brunswick and Nova Scotia, as
a people who are neither Québécois, nor French,
but Acadian. Much too late, some of their minority group rights have been entrenched.

The Metis Nation of the Prairies

The Hudson's Bay Company began trading in
the great Canadian northwest in 1670 by waiting for furs at their posts located on the shores
of Hudson Bay. As La Verendrye, born in Trois-
Rivières, explored the prairie interior in the
1740s for the French fur traders operating out of
Quebec, the British also increasingly began to
follow the rivers westward in search of furs.
Many of the French traders, or voyageurs, of the
Northwest Trading Company wintered among
the Indians and returned with their furs to
Montreal the next summer. These traders often
took Indian wives, so that by 1775 the 'half-
breeds' (as they were often called), or Metis,
emerged as a new people, bridging the white and
Indian populations (Flanagan, 1991).

The buffalo hunt lay at the heart of the new
Metis culture as pemmican, the staple food of
the canoe brigades, emerged as a major com-
modity. The voyageurs did not have time to hunt
the buffalo, and the Montreal-based fur trade
became increasingly dependent on a supply of
pemmican. As the demand grew, the Metis
began to organize elaborate expeditions westward on horseback to hunt buffalo. While the
men hunted, the women skinned the animals
and cut the meat to dry in the sun.

> In 1820, 540 carts left Red River to carry
> buffalo meat back from the plains. The
> expedition of 1840 included 403 horses,
> 536 draught oxen, 1,240 carts and horses,
> 740 guns and 1,600 men, women and chil-
> dren. When they returned, they had killed
> 2,500 buffalo and loaded 800 carts with
> pemmican, dried meat and buffalo hide
> (Berger, 1981:32).

The buffalo hunt was a large organization with
an elected president, councillors, guides, and
captains, each of whom was in command of 10
hunters. This organization made the Metis the
strongest military force in the West. For 50 years
the Metis prospered in their settlement at the
forks of the Assiniboine and Red rivers, where

they lived in cabins on their long river lots (similar to Quebec lots), raising gardens and cattle (McMillan, 1995:312–13). This way of life lasted until the last buffalo were destroyed by about 1885, when the railroad also arrived on the Prairies. The Metis spoke French, were Roman Catholic, and were inclined to follow the life of their aboriginal mother's people, who considered the Prairies their homeland. A new people had been born because of aboriginal European contacts.

'In 1811, the Hudson's Bay Company granted 116,000 square miles of its territory, centred on the junction of the Red and Assiniboine rivers, to Thomas Douglas, the young Earl of Selkirk' (Berger, 1981:28). Selkirk wanted to establish an agricultural colony for impoverished Scots, but the Hudson's Bay Company wanted this settlement located precisely at the confluence of the two rivers to thwart and interrupt the canoe route of the Northwest Company's fur trade and line of communication. This settlement would also control the pemmican trade.

In January, 1814, Miles Macdonnell, governor of the Selkirk colony, prohibited the export of pemmican and forbade the Northwest Company to occupy forts within the new District of Assiniboia, as the lands granted to Selkirk had been called. In June, 1815, the Nor'Westers and the Metis arrested Macdonnell and ran the settlers out of the Red River—although in the fall they returned (Berger, 1981:30).

Now the British-French wars begun in the Atlantic region and Acadia had also reached the prairies. The French and the British began to see this as another struggle for sovereignty. First, Fort Gibraltar, the Nor'Westers' fort at the forks was burned; next Semple and 20 settlers were killed at the Battle of Seven Oaks. The Metis saw this as an invasion by agricultural settlers of their pemmican industry. The Selkirk white settlement soon folded.

In 1867, the Confederation of Canada involved only small segments of what is now southern Ontario and Quebec, Nova Scotia, and New Brunswick. The vast territory west and north of the Great Lakes was an unorganized, unsurveyed territory used for fur trading. The Metis buffalo culture and trade dominated the plains area. By 1871, when the census was taken, there were '5,420 French-speaking half-breeds, 4,080 English-speaking half-breeds and 1,600 white settlers' in the Red River settlement surrounding present-day Winnipeg (Stanley, 1960:13). Only three years after the 1867 Confederation, the Red River settlement entered Canadian history with the transfer of the rights to the vast northwest territories from the Hudson's Bay Company to the Canadian government. The plan was to make the transfer between Ottawa and the British without consulting the Red River residents. The inhabitants of the Red River settlement were incensed that the transfer of the Northwest Territory would take place without any consultation with the Red River inhabitants involved (Driedger, 1996).

The 10,000 inhabitants of the Red River settlement had developed strong transportation ties between themselves and St Paul, Minnesota. 'In 1865 on one trip alone, Norbert Welsh travelled with a train of 300 carts; and by 1869 some 2,500 Red River carts lunged and screeched their ungreased way behind the ponderous ox-teams that hauled them along the road to St. Paul' (Stanley, 1969:37). In 1859 merchants of St Paul launched the first steamboat north to Fort Garry. The United States seemed close by, and Canada and Britain seemed far away. All this was happening when Canada was a new-born nation, greatly preoccupied with holding together the French and English cultures in Upper and Lower Canada.

While more and more settlers came, the Metis, who were a majority, wondered whether the influx of white settlers would swamp their aboriginal and Metis way of life. They were particularly concerned about the fur trade. This was the Red River settlement into which Louis Riel came in 1868. His French-Canadian mother was a daughter of the first white woman in western Canada and his father was a French Metis leader. Riel was born in the settlement and was sent to Montreal to train for the Catholic priesthood; when he returned, he became one of the leaders of the settlement. When in 1869 the Canadian government sent a team of surveyors to stake the land in preparation for the federal takeover from the Hudson's Bay Company (which would severely interrupt the Metis riverfront strip system), the Metis under the leadership of Riel stopped them (Stanley, 1969). They also stopped the new Lieutenant-Governor McDougall, sent from the East, from taking his seat at Fort Garry.

These events resulted in a Metis provisional government headed by Riel, which outlined a series of points it wished to negotiate with the government before the area would become a new province. The settlement requests included the right to elect their own legislature, magistrates, and sheriffs; a free homestead for each family; a rail connection with the East; the right to use English and French languages in the courts and legislature; and the right to be represented in the Canadian government (Stanley, 1969). Canada agreed to most of their requests and Manitoba became the fifth province of Canada in 1870, but not before an army from the East was sent to deal with Riel and his provisional government (Driedger, 1972:294). Riel fled to the United States uncertain about the army's intentions. As a refugee he was thrice elected to the Ottawa Parliament by his constituents, but he was never able to take his seat because of Scottish resentment against him in Ontario. Although he should have become the first Manitoba premier, he was exiled and never given amnesty. Power politics and nation-state dominance again missed a chance for Canada's first Metis premier elected by the people from the Red River settlement. Once more, multiculturalism was not given a chance.

Many Metis of the Red River community left after 1870 and settled in the Duck Lake area on the South Saskatchewan River. Fifteen years later the Metis called Riel to help them gain rights for their new settlement, but in 1885 the federal government once more sent troops,

this time via the CPR, the new railroad to crush the Metis and Louis Riel. Riel was hanged for treason in that same year, and his grave is located in St Boniface, now Winnipeg. Two chances for the recognition of a Metis nation had been crushed, because Easterners saw these French Metis uprisings as a threat, rather than as an opportunity for aboriginal and Metis representation of the majority of the northwest region. Macdonald refused to recognize in them the people of a New Nation. 'If they are Indians,' Macdonald said, 'they go with the tribe; if they are half breeds, they are white' (Berger, 1981: 52). The categories into which people were fitted were still limited—either white or Indian racially, or French or British ethnically.

A century later, in Section 35 of the 1982 Charter of Rights and Freedoms, the Metis people are listed with Indian and Inuit people as 'aboriginal peoples of Canada'. There is a great deal of confusion as to whether they all received their land claims or scrip; many claim they did not. In any case, had their leader Riel become the father of Manitoba and its first premier, as many now think he should have, most Metis would likely have stayed and settled in the Fort Garry area and Manitoba would now be a much different multicultural province. Since then, both Manitoba and Saskatchewan have erected monuments on their provincial legislative grounds honouring Riel, but a century too late.

Settling Indian Land Claims

Chapter 3 provided some of the demographic data to show where the aboriginal (Inuit, Metis, Non-Status Indian, and Status Indian) populations are located. Of the 532,060 aboriginals in 1991, 3.8 per cent were Inuit, two-thirds of whom were located in the Territories; 22.5 per cent were Metis, two-thirds of whom were located on the Prairies; 21.6 per cent were Non-Status Indians, almost two-thirds of whom were located in Ontario and British Columbia; and over half (52.1 per cent) were located on the Prairies and northern Ontario. Aboriginals are a majority (51.2 per cent) in the Northwest

Territories and Nunavut, and the largest number are located on the Prairies with well over half of their population in the four most westerly provinces in 1991. Treaties have not been made with almost half of these aboriginals, and there are problems with the treaties made with some of the Status Indians. Thus, numerous aboriginal land claims have not yet been settled.

In Figure 7.1 we saw that treaties have not been made (except for the James Bay area) in the five most easterly provinces (Quebec and the Maritimes), in most of British Columbia, and the Yukon (Frideres, 1998; Ponting, 1986). The earliest treaties, known as the Robinson Huron and Robinson Superior treaties, were made in northern Ontario in 1850. The Williams treaties were made a little farther to the south of Ontario in 1923. Minor treaties, known as the Douglas treaties (1850–4), were also made in parts of Vancouver Island (Frideres, 1998).

The 11 major treaties, known as Treaties 1–11 were made in the West, beginning in 1871 at the forks of the Red and Assiniboine rivers, the heart of the Metis region (Dickason, 1992:273–89). Treaty 1 was signed in Fort Garry, the stone fort north of Winnipeg, one year after Manitoba became a province. The Metis Nation had been dislodged from their power base, European settlers were about to enter the territory en masse, and the Indians and Metis had to be dealt with to make room for the white Europeans. As the white settlers moved westward from the forks, more treaties were signed as needed. They were signed in 1874 in southern Saskatchewan, in 1876 and 1877 in southern Alberta, and then the last treaty was signed in 1921 in the Mackenzie Valley region reaching into the Northwest Territories (Frideres, 1998). These later treaties were signed as mining interests moved up the Mackenzie River.

The paternalism conveyed in the wording of these treaties shows the colonialist stance of a majority power dealing with 'poor uncivilized aboriginals who need to be cared for':

And with a view to show the satisfaction of Her Majesty with the behaviour and good conduct of Her Indians parties to this treaty,

She hereby, through Her Commissioner, makes them a present of three dollars for each Indian man, woman and child belonging to the bands here represented. And further, Her Majesty agrees to maintain a school on each reserve hereby made whenever the Indians of the reserve should desire it (Treaty No. 1:10).

In essence, since they are 'good children', she is taking all their land and will, out of her gracious spirit, 'give them a present': three dollars each annually and a reserve. Treaties 1–11 vary somewhat, but each family of five Metis received 160 acres on the reserve in the early treaties. However, reserves have not been established in the Northwest Territories as they were farther south.

Since Treaty 11 was signed in 1921, numerous attempts have been made to deal with aboriginal land claims; however, there have been many difficulties (Frideres, 1998:66–121). The Department of Indian Affairs and Northern Development has plotted 11 major areas of aboriginal land claims presented in Figure 12.1. Claim 1 deals with Indians in the Yukon. Claims 2 to 4 made by Indian and Metis organizations cover all of the Northwest Territories. Treaty 5 covers mostly what is now the new territory of Nunavut. Claims 6 and 7 by the Inuit and Innu associations cover most of Labrador, where no treaties had been made. The James Bay agreements with the Inuit and Cree deal with Claim 8. Claims 9 and 10 deal with the rest of Quebec, where again no treaties have been made. Claim 11, the Nisga' a claim in British Columbia, is but a small claim in the whole of British Columbia where except for the small Douglas treaties, no treaties have been made either.

Only about half of the Canadian territory is covered by aboriginal treaty. Land claims currently under review involve mostly northern territory, where it should be relatively easier to come to treaty agreement and a resolution of native land rights. However, settlement involves large sums of money, and increasingly, aboriginals are asking for sovereignty or some say in how these lands should be used and adminis-

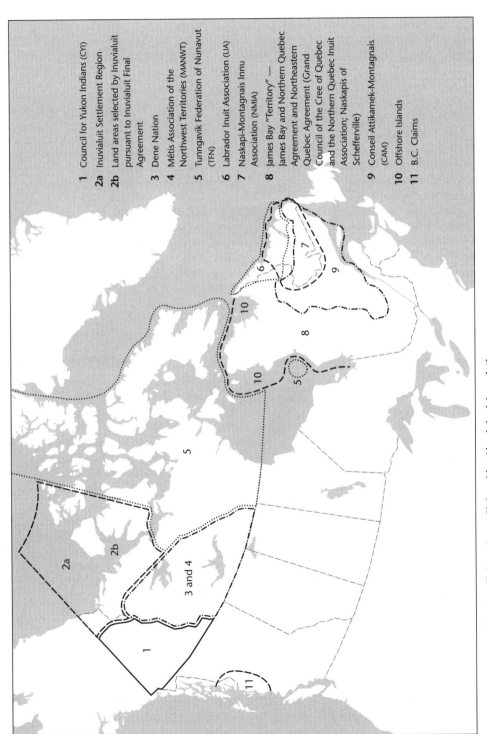

1 Council for Yukon Indians (CYI)
2a Inuvialuit Settlement Region
2b Land areas selected by Inuvialuit pursuant to Inuvialuit Final Agreement
3 Dene Nation
4 Métis Association of the Northwest Territories (MANWT)
5 Tunngavik Federation of Nunavut (TFN)
6 Labrador Inuit Association (LIA)
7 Naskapi-Montagnais Innu Association (NMIA)
8 James Bay "Territory" — James Bay and Northern Quebec Agreement and Northeastern Quebec Agreement (Grand Council of the Cree of Quebec and the Northern Quebec Inuit Association; Naskapis of Schefferville)
9 Conseil Attikamek-Montagnais (CAM)
10 Offshore Islands
11 B.C. Claims

FIGURE 12.1 Comprehensive Claims: Areas Claimed by Aboriginal Associations

SOURCE: James S. Frideres, *Native People in Canada: Contemporary Conflicts*, 2nd edn. (Scarborough, ON: Prentice-Hall, 1993), p. 79.

tered (Asch, 1984). Many of these claims are in territories where the federal government has jurisdiction, which also makes the process easier, since few whites have moved into these regions and would have to be displaced. Claims 1, 6, 7, 8, and 9, however, are located in three provincial regions. This involves provincial governments and further complicates matters (Frideres, 1998: 108–21). This is the case in British Columbia, which has historically not recognized the right of aboriginals to claim land. Even more difficult will be the settlement of treaty claims in Quebec, and the southern parts of the four maritime provinces, where white settlement has a long history, but where treaties have still not been made. Many of these areas are urban, with dense populations.

While we may be inclined to criticize those of the past for not attending to the rights and freedoms of the Acadians and Metis, we today still have much difficulty in dealing with aboriginal land claims. So far these claims have been dealt with only haphazardly. The fact that few treaties have been made on either coast, can again be attributed to the early power politics of nation-state colonialists who had little concern for minority rights and freedoms. To our credit, we have recognized aboriginal land rights in the western interior by signing Treaties 1–11, but these treaties are fraught with many difficulties, ambiguities, and problems. Much still remains to be done, and we are not moving very quickly in resolving these injustices, although the recent Nunavut settlement in what was the eastern Northwest Territories in 1993 is an important recent agreement.

The Jewish Holocaust

The furore over Salman Rushdie's *The Satanic Verses* raises the extent to which rights and freedoms are respected in the world today. The extermination of six million Jews by the Nazis during the Second World War was an event that showed that the freedoms we have are fragile, and that they continue to be attacked by those who consider themselves 'civilized'. The Jewish Holocaust happened in the land that spawned Einstein, Beethoven, Mozart, Freud, and Marx. How could modern people who claim to hold to ideologies of Christianity and democracy allow such atrocities to happen? The roots of such holocausts continue to linger, as illustrated by several Canadian examples.

Levitt and Shaffir (1986) have documented the Christie Pits riot that occurred in Toronto in 1933, between Jews and Gentiles. On the evening of August 16, 1933, a riot occurred after a semifinal series of the Toronto Amateur Softball Association championship between Harbord (with mostly Jewish members) and St Peter's (a Gentile team). A number of factors led up to the riot. Toronto's eastern beaches and parks were a favourite picnic area for thousands of Jewish immigrants and their families, whose customs, cuisine, and language were different from those of the residents near these beaches, who were concerned about the increasing presence of Jews.

Life was not easy for Toronto's Jews in 1933: they were barred from certain jobs, they were not welcome in some recreation and social circles, and on occasion they were beaten up (Levitt and Shaffir, 1986:3–4). Discrimination seemed routine, and swastika signs (which symbolized suffering, torture, and death to these Jews) were increasingly found in the parks. When a Swastika Club was formed and displayed the swastika, Jewish youths countered by organizing parades on the beaches' boardwalks. Mayor Stewart of Toronto tried to crack down on these Nazi groups and the display of their symbols, but without avail.

The riot began immediately after the game in the park. A huge swastika was unfurled with shouts of 'Heil Hitler', and when a group of Jewish youths stormed the swastika group. There had already been several clashes at the game, but police had been able to restore order. The fighting lasted for several hours and scores of people were injured. Later 22 members of the Pit Gang that unfurled the swastika were questioned. Three were taken into custody, but none were charged (Levitt and Shaffir, 1986:17–18). The riot showed that anti-Jewish feelings often lay close to the surface, and that there was always a potential for violence. This riot occurred just as Hitler was beginning his political drive in Germany leading to the Holocaust taking six million Jewish lives.

In a more modern example, David Elliott (1985:78–89) has tried to document some of the intellectual roots of the Keegstra affair, and concludes that some anti-Semitism has its roots in the early Social Credit movement in Canada. Criminal charges were laid against James Keegstra, a high school social studies teacher (and former mayor) in Eckville, Alberta, because he taught that the holocaust was a myth and that the Jews were conspiring to rule the world (Elliott, 1985:78). Keegstra was also a member of the national Social Credit Party Executive, which was unwilling to censure him. The Keegstra affair became a national issue. Elliott claims Major C.H. Douglas, the founder of the Social Credit Party, believed that Canada was menaced by a Jewish conspiracy to acquire key positions in the economic and political fields. 'The full scope of Douglas's anti-Semitic paranoia was found in his *Brief for the Prosecution* published in 1945' (Elliott, 1985:82).

Keegstra lived in southern Alberta during the Aberhart and Manning Social Credit administrations and his parents were ardent Social Credit supporters. Keegstra immersed himself in the writings of Douglas, and was generally influenced by anti-communist and anti-Semitic writings. Keegstra taught his beliefs of an all-powerful Jewish conspiracy in the Eckville High School for 14 years. Elliott (1985:86) claims that although Aberhart denounced anti-Semitism publicly, there were anti-Semitic undertones in many of his speeches. Later Premier Manning clearly purged his Social Credit Party of anti-Semitic people. The Keegstra affair shows the extent to which anti-Semitism is present in individuals, and the extent to which it can invade legitimate Canadian institutions. The Zundel affair is another (Weiman and Winn, 1993: 97–111).

Yaacov Glickman and Alan Bardikoff (1982) published a book on the degree to which Cana-

dian history and social science textbooks inform and sensitize Canadian students to the events of the Holocaust. They examined 72 textbooks authorized for use in Canada's secondary schools, and found inadequate treatment of the Jewish Holocaust. They did a content analysis of the texts, using a panel of eight judges. They used seven criteria including inclusion, validity, balance, comprehensiveness, concreteness, unity, and realism in their evaluation of published presentations of the holocaust. They found that 29 per cent of the textbooks excluded the subject matter entirely, and 42 per cent were judged to have treated it inadequately; only 4 per cent were judged to have presented it well. These 72 texts were rated as being poor on validity (43 per cent), comprehensiveness (71 per cent), balance (65 per cent), concreteness (53 per cent), and unity (57 per cent) (Glickman and Bardikoff, 1982:17).

While the Jewish Holocaust—the destruction of one-third of a people—occurred in Europe more than 50 years ago, we still cringe at the extent to which modern Nazis were willing to go to follow their Aryan ideology. It is clear that the Holocaust has affected Canada directly, because the Christie Pits riots and Keegstra affair demonstrate that anti-Semitic tendencies continue in our midst. Elderly Jews who experienced and escaped the European Holocaust will always fear the danger of similar threats in the future (Driedger and Chappell, 1987). The rights and freedoms of minorities are indeed fragile, to which the Jews can attest from several millennia's experience.

Will Kymlicka, especially in the last decade, has published a half-dozen books that are deeply concerned with the diversity that we are headed into. These publications focus on liberalism, community, and culture (1989), multicultural citizenship (1995a), the rights of minority cultures (1995b), finding our way in rethinking ethnocultural relations (1998), and citizenship in diverse societies (2000). These political issues will become more complex as we increasingly move from commitments to ideologies and science, to postmodern values of freedom, individualism, skepticism about linear thinking, with more openness to diversity and pluralism.

SUMMARY

We began by saying that nation-states in the past tried to establish unitary ethnic sovereign states that, nevertheless, always included numerous minorities that were often ignored or forced into assimilation. The polyethnic or pluralist ethnic view is also concerned with the rights and freedoms of minorities, so that the rights of all can be perpetuated. In Canada's past there are many examples of how collective minority rights have been trampled upon.

First, we examined three bills, declarations, or charters—sets of standards or norms that might guide us in establishing rights and freedoms. As early as two hundred years ago, the American constitution declared the free exercise of religion as a right of all. Eighty years later they recognized the equality of race and abolished slavery. The United Nations extended these rights to freedoms of language, religion, politics, national origin, and property. Most recently, the Canadian Charter of Rights and Freedoms, although belatedly, also extended these individual rights in Canada. In addition, the two charter groups were given certain group rights, and the rights of aboriginals and others of the multicultural community were also recognized.

We reviewed the fate of four tragic communities whose rights and freedoms were stripped in Canada in the past. The Acadians were forcibly expelled from their homeland in Acadia and were scattered throughout North America because they were French. The Metis Nation formed on the Prairies and was twice routed by armies from the East when Riel, their leader, should have become a part of the prairie political establishment. Treaties have been made with aboriginals, but to this day half of their territory has not yet been settled by treaties. The tragedy of the Jewish Holocaust is remembered by many, yet Jews continue to be mistreated in Canada, and their rights and freedoms are often restricted.

While our standards and norms for minority rights and freedoms have evolved, these rights have been grossly neglected and misused in the past, and much more is needed in the present to correct injustices. How these injustices are dealt with will depend greatly on the change of perspective discussed in Chapter 2. If we want a unitary state with a homogeneous language, culture, and institutions, then obviously assimilation is the way to proceed as was attempted in the past. Many minorities will then be forced to comply to the majority culture; some will need to change too quickly with disorganizational results, while still others will resist so that there will be conflict. The French in Quebec have always resisted assimilation and will continue to fight for their identity; so will the aboriginals, religious groups like the Jews, Mennonites, and Hutterites, and recent Muslim immigrants. As more visible minorities enter Canada, there will be increasing resistance to their integration.

For a long time Canadian immigration policy has worked against a unitary melting pot and the population has become increasingly more heterogeneous. Northern European immigrants no longer dominate the top 10 largest groups that enter Canada. With recent heavy Asian immigration, Canada's population is becoming more heterogeneous, so a pluralist policy makes a great deal of sense and is more compatible with Canada's democratic and religious ideology which is diverse. As immigrants adjust with succeeding generations, modified forms of pluralism or assimilation seem logical as the various groups adjust to form a Canadian whole. Some groups will be given more opportunity to participate than others, and visible minorities should be given equal opportunities to participate. Many laws in the past were passed to keep some groups segregated and in inferior places, which again is not compatible with our Charter of Rights and Freedoms. Building a modern industrial pluralist Canada will not be easy because the regions vary considerably with respect to cultural, religious, racial, and national aspirations.

Quebec has always wanted to be a nation with aspirations for increased sovereignty in determining French-Canadian interests. Discussions on the Meech Lake Accord illustrate the differences of opinion on how special Quebec is. To what extent this uniqueness will be entrenched in the constitution remains to be seen. Like the Québécois, many groups, such as the Jews, Mennonites, Hutterites, and others with less demographic and political power also wish to construct unique 'sacred realities'. We discussed the identities of Quebec and other minorities in Chapters 6 and 7, illustrating the various micro and macro levels of sociocultural and symbolic identity to which many ethnic groups in Canada aspire. Segregated rural ethnic enclaves use very different means of constructing solidarity than urbanites who increasingly turn to social networks and symbolic means of identification. In Part III we devoted three chapters to the complexity of ethnic solidarity and identification consistent with Weber's multidimensional and comparative analysis.

While pluralists more than assimilationists tend to look for ethnic and racial diversity and identity, there is also much evidence that there is considerable socioeconomic and racial stratification. There is much social inequality: some groups are more powerful than others, and many minorities are 'less equal' than others. While some people would call for the elimination of social ethnic distinction so all people would have a better chance to compete in the labour market, others look for greater tolerance toward ethnic, racial,

and religious diversity, so everyone can compete without prejudice or discrimination based on colour, race, creed, or gender. It is true that diversity also poses more risks for conflict, but heterogeneous populations can also create more variety and interest for a more dynamic society.

There is much evidence of social distance, stereotypes, prejudice, and discrimination in Canada. However, the United Nations' and Canadian charters of rights and freedoms clearly show the way that a majority of Canadians would like to go. Canada is a pluralist multiethnic society, and there is much evidence that more and more Canadians are willing to accept and work for equality, justice, and opportunity for all.

In the end we can say that the British and French charter groups began five hundred years ago to colonize eastern Canada, like they had done in other parts of the world expecting everyone else to assimilate into their ways. By 2003 these limited visions of colonial dominance, had changed to a much more plural vision of many participating together in a more equal way. These diverse Canadians seek to work together to form a plural mosaic, which all can identify with and be proud of. It is the Canadian ethnic and racial experiment!

HIGHLIGHT 12.2 MULTICULTURALISM POLICY OF CANADA

WHEREAS the Constitution of Canada provides that every individual is equal before and under the law and has the right to the equal protection and benefit of the law without discrimination and that everyone has the freedom of conscience, religion, thought, belief, opinion, expression, peaceful assembly and association and guarantees those rights and freedoms equally to male and female persons;

WHEREAS the Constitution of Canada recognizes rights of the aboriginal peoples of Canada;

WHEREAS the Constitution of Canada and the Official Languages Act provide that

English and French are the official languages of Canada and neither abrogates or derogates from any rights or privileges acquired or enjoyed with respect to any other language;

AND WHEREAS the Citizenship Act provides that all Canadians, whether by birth or by choice, enjoy equal status, are entitled to the same rights, powers and privileges and are subject to the same obligations, duties and liabilities;

AND WHEREAS the Canadian Human Rights provides that every individual should have an equal opportunity with other individuals to make the life that the individual is able and wishes to have, consistent with the duties and obligations of that individual as a member of society, and, in order to secure that opportunity, establishes the Canadian Human Rights Commission to redress any proscribed discrimination, including discrimination on the basis of race, national or ethnic origin or colour;

AND WHEREAS Canada is a party to the International Convention on the Elimination of All Forms of Racial Discrimination, which Convention recognizes that all human beings are equal before the law and are entitled to equal protection of the law against any discrimination and against any incitement to discrimination, and to the International Covenant on Civil and Political Rights, which Covenant provides that persons belonging to ethnic, religious or linguistic minorities shall not be denied the right to enjoy their own culture, to profess and practise their own religion or to use their own language.

AND WHEREAS the Government of Canada recognizes the diversity of Canadians as regards race, national or ethnic origin, colour and religion as a fundamental characteristic of Canadian society and is committed to a policy of multiculturalism designed to preserve and enhance the multicultural heritage of Canadians while working to achieve the equality of all Canadians in the economic, social, cultural and political life of Canada;

(1) It is hereby declared to be the policy of the Government of Canada to:

(a) recognize and promote the understanding that multiculturalism reflects the cultural and racial diversity of Canadian society and acknowledges the freedom of all members of Canadian society to preserve, enhance and share their cultural heritage;

(b) recognize and promote the understanding that multiculturalism is a fundamental characteristic of the Canadian heritage and identity and that it provides an invaluable resource in the shaping of Canada's future;

(c) promote the full and equitable participation of individuals and communities of all origins in the continuing evolution and shaping of all aspects of Canadian society and assist them in the elimination of any barrier to such participation;

(d) recognize the existence of communities whose members share a common origin and their historic contribution to Canadian society, and enhance their development;

(e) ensure that all individuals receive equal treatment and equal protection under the law, while respecting and valuing their diversity;

(f) encourage and assist the social, cultural, economic and political institutions of Canada to be both respectful and inclusive of Canada's multicultural character;

(g) promote the understanding and creativity that arise from the interaction between individuals and communities of different origins;

(h) foster the recognition and appreciation of the diverse cultures of Canadian society and promote the reflection and the evolving expressions of those cultures;

(i) preserve and enhance the use of languages other than English and French, while strengthening the status and use of the official languages of Canada; and

(j) advance multiculturalism throughout Canada in harmony with the national commitment to the official languages of Canada.

(2) It is further declared to be the policy of the Government of Canada that all federal institutions shall:

(a) ensure that Canadians of all origins have an equal opportunity to obtain employment and advancement in those institutions;

(b) promote policies, programs and practices that enhance the ability of individuals and communities of all origins to contribute to the continuing evolution of Canada;

(c) promote policies, programs and practices that enhance the understanding of and respect for the diversity of members of Canadian society;

(d) collect statistical data in order to enable the development of policies, programs and practices that are sensitive and responsive

to the multicultural reality of Canada;

(e) make use, as appropriate, of the language skills and cultural understanding of individuals of all origins; and

(f) generally, carry on their activities in a manner that is sensitive and responsive to the multicultural reality of Canada.

SOURCE: Excerpts from the Canadian Multiculturalism Act, July 1988.

CRITICAL THINKING QUESTIONS

1. Compare the American, United Nations, and Canadian charters of rights. How do they vary on focus and content?

2. Is the American Bill of Rights still relevant for today, since it was designed over two hundred years ago? What are some areas of emphasis?

3. Does the United Nations Declaration of Rights speak to specific Canadian needs, or is it very general to fit the situations of many nations who signed it? How comprehensive is it?

4. Why would Canada have waited so long to pass its own charter, when its neighbour did so more than two hundred years earlier? Is Canada's charter more relevant to today's needs?

5. What do you see as the major features of Kallen's human rights typology? Discuss and evaluate.

6. Why might collective rights be needed? Using examples of the Acadians, Metis, Indians, and Jews, how well have Canadians managed such collective claims? Discuss.

SUGGESTED READINGS

Axworthy, Thomas S., and Pierre Elliott Trudeau (eds), *Towards a Just Society: The Trudeau Years* (Toronto: Penguin,1992). This collection of essays explores the extent to which Trudeau's vision for a just society became a reality.

James, Carl E., Making it: *Black Youth, Racism and Career Aspirations in a Big City* (Oakville, ON: Mosaic, 1990). This is an in-depth attempt to explore and comprehend the world of Black youth in a large urban environment.

Kallen, Evelyn, *Ethnicity and Human Rights in Canada,* 2nd edn (Toronto: Oxford University Press, 1995). The comparative strength of legal protection for the human rights of members of each of Canada's three aboriginal, charter, and minority constituencies is examined and evaluated.

Kymlicka, Will, and Wayne Norman (eds), *Citizenship in Diverse Societies*. (Oxford: Oxford University Press, 2000). This is a collection of readings on citizenship, political participation, immigration and multiculturalism, diversity, rights, nationalism, and federalism.

APPENDIX A

UNIVERSAL DECLARATION OF HUMANS RIGHTS

Adopted by United Nations General Assembly, December 10, 1948.

WHEREAS recognition of the inherent dignity and of the equal and inalienable rights of all members of the human family is the foundation of freedom, justice and peace in the world,

WHEREAS disregard and contempt for human rights have resulted in barbarous acts which have outraged the conscience of mankind, and the advent of a world in which human beings shall enjoy freedom of speech and belief and freedom from fear and want has been proclaimed as the highest aspiration of the common people,

WHEREAS it is essential, if man is not to be compelled to have recourse, as a last resort, to rebellion against tyranny and oppression, that human rights should be protected by the rule of law,

WHEREAS it is essential to promote the development of friendly relations between nations.

WHEREAS the peoples of the United Nations have in the Charter reaffirmed their faith in fundamental human rights in the dignity and worth of the human person and in the equal rights of men and women and have determined to promote social progress and better standards of life in larger freedoms,

WHEREAS Member States have pledged themselves to achieve, in co-operation with the United Nations, the promotion of universal respect for and observance of human rights and fundamental freedoms,

WHEREAS a common understanding of these rights and freedoms is of the greatest importance for the full realization of this pledge,

NOW THEREFORE, THE GENERAL ASSEMBLY PROCLAIMS

THIS UNIVERSAL DECLARATION OF HUMAN RIGHTS as a common standard of achievement for all peoples and all nations to the end that every individual and every organ of society, keeping this Declaration constantly in mind, shall strive by teaching and education to promote respect for these rights and freedoms and by progressive measures, national and international, to secure their universal and effective recognition and observance, both among the peoples of Member States themselves and among the peoples of territories under their jurisdiction.

Article 1
All human beings are born free and equal in dignity and rights. They are endowed with reason and conscience and should act towards one another in a spirit of brotherhood.

Article 2
Everyone is entitled to all the rights and freedoms set forth in this Declaration, without distinction of any kind, such as race, colour, sex, language, religion, political or other opinion, national or social origin, property, birth or other status. Furthermore, no distinction shall be made on the basis of the politicial, jurisdictional or international status of the country or territory to which a person belongs, whether it be independent, trust, non-selfgoverning or under any other limitation of sovereignty.

Article 3
Everyone has the right to life, liberty and security of person.

Article 4
No one shall be held in slavery or servitude; slavery and the slave trade shall be prohibited in all their forms.

Article 5

No one shall be subjected to torture or to cruel, inhuman or degrading treatment or punishment.

Article 6

Everyone has the right to recognition everywhere as a person before the law.

Article 7

All are equal before the law and are entitled without any discrimination to equal protection of the law. All are entitled to equal protection against any discrimination in violation of this Declaration and against any incitement to such discrimination.

Article 8

Everyone has the right to an effective remedy by the competent national tribunals for acts violating the fundamental rights granted him by the constitution or by law.

Article 9

No one shall be subjected to arbitrary arrest, detention or exile.

Article 10

Everyone is entitled in full equality to a fair and public hearing by an independent and impartial tribunal, in the determination of his rights and obligations and of any criminal charge against him.

Article 11

(1) Everyone charged with a penal offence has the right to be presumed innocent until proved guilty according to law in a public trial at which he has had all the guarantees necessary for his defence.

(2) No one shall be held guilty of any penal offence on account of any act or omission which did not constitute a penal offence, under national or international law, at the time when it was committed. Nor shall a heavier penalty be imposed than the one that was applicable at the time the penal offence was committed.

Article 12

No one shall be subjected to arbitrary interference with his privacy, family, home or correspondence, nor to attacks upon his honour and reputation. Everyone has the right to the protection of the law against such interference or attacks.

Article 13

(1) Everyone has the right to freedom of movement and residence within the borders of each state.

(2) Everyone has the right to leave any country, including his own, and to return to his country.

Article 14

(1) Everyone has the right to seek and to enjoy in other countries asylum for persecution.

(2) This right may not be invoked in the case of prosecutions genuinely arising from non-political crimes or from acts contrary to the purposes and principles of the United Nations.

Article 15

(1) Everyone has the right to a nationality.

(2) No one shall be arbitrarily deprived of his nationality nor denied the right to change his nationality.

Article 16

(1) Men and women of full age, without any limitation due to race, nationality or religion, have the right to marry and to found a family. They are entitled to equal rights as to marriage, during marriage and at its dissolution.

(2) Marriage shall be entered into only with the free and full consent of the intending spouses.

(3) The family is the natural and fundamental group unit of society and is entitled to protection by society and the State.

Article 17

(1) Everyone has the right to own property alone as well as in association with others.

(2) No one shall be arbitrarily deprived of his property.

Article 18

Everyone has the right to freedom of thought, conscience and religion; this right includes freedom to change his religion or belief, and freedom, either alone or in community with others and in public or private, to manifest his religion or belief in teaching, practice, worship and observance.

Article 19

Everyone has the right to freedom of opinion and expression; this right includes freedom to hold opinions without interference and to seek, receive and impart information and ideas through any media and regardless of frontiers.

Article 20

(1) Everyone has the right to freedom of peaceful assembly and association.
(2) No one may be compelled to belong to an association.

Article 21

(1) Everyone has the right to take part in the government of his country, directly or through freely chosen representatives.
(2) Everyone has the right of equal access to public service in his country.
(3) The will of the people shall be the basis of the authority of government; this will shall be expressed in periodic and genuine elections which shall be by universal and equal suffrage and shall be held by secret vote or by equivalent free voting procedures.

Article 22

Everyone, as a member of society, has the right to social security and is entitled to realization, through national effort and international cooperation and in accordance with the organization and resources of each State, of the economic, social and cultural rights indispensable for his dignity and the free development of his personality.

Article 23

(1) Everyone has the right to work, to free choice of employment, to just and favorable conditions of work and to protection against unemployment.
(2) Everyone, without any discrimination, has the right to equal pay for equal work.
(3) Everyone who works has the right to just and favorable remuneration insuring for himself and his family an existence worthy of human dignity, and supplemented, if necessary, by other means of social protection.
(4) Everyone has the right to form and to join trade unions for the protection of his interests.

Article 24

Everyone has the right to rest and leisure, including reasonable limitation of working hours and periodic holidays with pay.

Article 25

(1) Everyone has the right to a standard of living adequate for the health and well-being of himself and of his family, including food, clothing, housing and medical care and necessary social services, and the right to security in the event of unemployment, sickness, disability, widowhood, old age or other lack of livelihood in circumstances beyond his control.
(2) Motherhood and childhood are entitled to special care and assistance. All children, whether born in or out of wedlock, shall enjoy the same social protection.

Article 26

(1) Everyone has the right to education. Education shall be free, at least in the elementary and fundamental stages. Elementary education shall be compulsory. Technical and professional education shall be made generally available and higher education shall be equally accessible to all on the basis of merit.
(2) Education shall be directed to the full development of the human personality and to the strengthening of respect for human rights and fundamental freedoms. It shall promote understanding, tolerance and friendship among all nations, racial or religious groups,

and shall further the activities of the United Nations for the maintenance of peace.

(3) Parents have a prior right to choose the kind of education that shall be given to their children.

Article 27

(1) Everyone has the right freely to participate in the cultural life of the community, to enjoy the arts and to share in scientific advancement and its benefits.

(2) Everyone has the right to the protection of the moral and material interests resulting from any scientific, literary or artistic production of which he is the author.

Article 28

Everyone is entitled to a social and international order in which the rights and freedoms set forth in this Declaration can be fully realized.

Article 29

(1) Everyone has duties to the community in which alone the free and full development of his personality is possible.

(2) In the exercise of his rights and freedoms, everyone shall be subject only to such limitations as are determined by law solely for the purpose of securing due recognition and respect for the rights and freedoms of others and of meeting the just requirements of morality, public order and the general welfare in a democratic society.

(3) These rights and freedoms may in no case be exercised contrary to the purpose and principles of the United Nations.

Article 30

Nothing in this Declaration may be interpreted as implying for any State, group or person any right to engage in any activity or to perform any act aimed at the destruction of any of the rights and freedoms set forth herein.

APPENDIX B

CANADIAN CHARTER OF RIGHTS AND FREEDOMS

CONSTITUTION ACT, 1982

WHEREAS Canada is founded upon principles that recognize the supremacy of God and the rule of law:

Guarantee of Rights and Freedoms

1. The Canadian Charter of Rights and Freedoms guarantees the rights and freedoms set out in it subject only to such reasonable limits prescribed by law as can be demonstrably justified in a free and democratic society.

Fundamental Freedoms

2. Everyone has the following fundamental freedoms:
(a) freedom of conscience and religion;
(b) freedom of thought, belief, opinion and expression, including freedom of the press and other media of communication;
(c) freedom of peaceful assembly; and
(d) freedom of association.

Democratic Rights

3. Every citizen of Canada has the right to vote in an election of members of the House of Commons or of a legislative assembly and to be qualified for membership therein.

4. (1) No House of Commons and no legislative assembly shall continue for longer than five years from the date fixed for the return of the writs at a general election of its members.
(2) In time of real or apprehended war, invasion or insurrection, a House of Commons may be continued by Parliament and a legislative assembly may be continued by the legislative beyond five years if such continuation is not opposed by the votes of more than one-third of the members of the House of Commons or the legislative assembly, as the case may be.

5. There shall be a sitting of Parliament and of each legislature at least once every twelve months.

Mobility Rights

6. (1) Every citizen of Canada has the right to enter, remain in and leave Canada.
(2) Every citizen of Canada and every person who has the status of a permanent resident of Canada has the right
(a) to move to and take up residence in any province; and
(b) to pursue the gaining of a livelihood in any province.
(3) The rights specified in subsection (2) are subject to
(a) any laws or practices of general application in force in a province other than those that discriminate among persons primarily on the basis of province of present or previous residence; and
(b) any laws providing for reasonable residency requirements as a qualification for the receipt of publicly provided social services.

Legal Rights

7. Everyone has the right to life, liberty and security of the person and the right not to be deprived thereof except in accordance with the principles of fundamental justice.

8. Everyone has the right to be secure against unreasonable search or seizure.

9. Everyone has the right not to be arbitrarily detained or imprisoned.

10. Everyone has the right on arrest or detention
(a) to be informed promptly of the reasons therefor;
(b) to retain and instruct counsel without delay and to be informed of that right; and
(c) to have the validity of the detention determined by way of habeas corpus and to be released if the detention is not lawful.

11. Any person charged with an offence has the right

(a) to be informed without unreasonable delay of the specific offence;

(b) to be tried within a reasonable time;

(c) to not be compelled to be a witness in proceedings against that person in respect of the offence;

(d) to be presented innocent until proven guilty according to law in a fair and public hearing by an independent and impartial tribunal;

(e) not to be denied reasonable bail without just cause;

(f) except the case of an offence under military law tried before a military tribunal, to the benefit of trial by jury where the maximum punishment for the offence is imprisonment for five years or a more severe punishment;

(g) not to be found guilty on account of any act or omission unless, at the time of the act or omission, it constituted an offence under Canadian or international law or was criminal according to the general principles of law recognized by the community of nations;

(h) if finally acquitted of the offence, not to be tried for it again and, if finally found guilty and punished for the offence, not to be tried or punished for it again; and

(i) if found guilty of the offence and if the punishment for the offence has been varied between the time of commission and the time of sentencing, to the benefit of the lesser punishment.

12. Everyone has the right not to be subjected to any cruel and unusual treatment or punishment.

13. A witness who testifies in any proceedings has the right not to have any incriminating evidence so given used to incriminate that witness in any other proceedings, except in a prosecution for perjury or for the giving of contradictory evidence.

14. A party or witness in any proceedings who does not understand or speak the language in which the proceedings are conducted or who is deaf has the right to the assistance of an interpreter.

Equality Rights

15. (1) Every individual is equal before and under the law and has the right to the equal protection and equal benefit of the law without discrimination and, in particular, without discrimination based on race, national or ethnic origin, colour, religion, sex, age or mental or physical disability.

(2) Subsection (1) does not preclude any law, program or activity that has as its object the amelioration of conditions of disadvantaged individuals or groups including those that are disadvantaged because of race, national or ethnic origin, colour, religion, sex, age or mental or physical disability.

Official Languages of Canada

16. (1) English and French are the official languages of Canada and have equality of status and equal rights and privileges as to their use in all institutions of the Parliament and government of Canada.

(2) English and French are the official languages of New Brunswick and have quality of status and equal rights and privileges as to their use in all institutions of the legislative and government of New Brunswick.

17. (1) Everyone has the right to use English or French in any debates and other proceedings of Parliament.

(2) Everyone has the right to use English or French in any debates and other proceedings of the legislature of New Brunswick.

18. (1) The statues, records and journals of Parliament shall be printed and published in English and French and both language versions are equally authoritative.

(2) The statues, records and journals of the legislature of New Brunswick shall be printed and published in English and French and both language versions are equally authoritative.

19. (1) Either English or French may be used by any person in, or in any pleading in or process issuing from, any court established by Parliament.

(2) Either English or French may be used by any person in, or in any pleading in or process issuing from, any court of New Brunswick.

20. (1) Any member of the public in Canada has the right to communicate with, and to receive available services from, any head or central office of an institution of the Parliament or government of Canada in English or French, and has the same right with respect to any other office of any such institution where

(a) there is a significant demand for communications with and services from that office in such language; or

(b) due to the nature of the office, it is reasonable that communications with and services from that office be available in both English and French.

(2) Any member of the public in New Brunswick has the right to communicate with, and to receive available services from, any office of an institution of the legislature or government of New Brunswick in English and French.

21. Nothing in sections 16 to 20 abrogates or derogates from any right, privilege or obligation with respect to the English and French languages, or either of them, that exists or is continued by virtue of any other provision of the Constitution of Canada.

22. Nothing in sections 16 to 20 abrogates or derogates from any legal or customary right or privilege acquired or enjoyed either before or after the coming into force of this Charter with respect to any language that is not English or French.

Minority Language Educational Rights

23. (1) Citizens of Canada

(a) whose first language learned and still understood is that of the English or French linguistic minority population of the province in which they reside, or

(b) who have received their primary school instruction in Canada in English or French and reside in a province where the language in which they received that instruction is the language of the English or French linguistic minority population of the province, have the right to have their children receive primary and secondary school instruction in that language in that province.

(2) Citizens of Canada of whom any child has received or is receiving primary or secondary school instruction in English or French in Canada, have the right to have all their children receive primary or secondary school instruction in the same language.

(3) The right of citizens of Canada under subsections (1) and (2) to have their children receive primary and secondary school instruction in the language of the English or French linguistic minority population of a province

(a) applies wherever in the province the number of children of citizens who have such a right is sufficient to warrant the provision to them out of public funds of minority language instruction; and

(b) includes, where the number of those children so warrants, the right to have them receive that instruction in minority language educational facilities provided out of public funds.

Enforcement

24. (1) Anyone whose rights or freedoms, as guaranteed by this Charter, have been infringed or denied may apply to a court of competent jurisdiction to obtain such remedy as the court considers appropriate and just in the circumstances.

(2) Where, in proceedings under subsection (1), a court concludes that evidence was obtained in a manner that infringed or denied any rights or freedoms guaranteed by this Charter, the evidence shall be excluded if it is established that, having regard to all the circumstances, the admission of it in the proceedings would bring the administration of justice into disrepute.

25. The guarantee in this Charter of certain rights and freedoms shall not be construed

so as to abrogate or derogate from any aboriginal, treaty or other rights or freedoms that pertain to the aboriginal peoples of Canada including

(a) any rights or freedoms that have been recognized by the Royal Proclamation of October 7, 1763; and

(b) any rights or freedoms that may be acquired by the aboriginal peoples of Canada by way of land claims settlement.

26. The guarantee in this Charter of certain rights and freedoms shall not be construed as denying the existence of any other rights or freedoms that exist in Canada.

27. This Charter shall be interpreted in a manner consistent with the preservation and enhancement of the multicultural heritage of Canadians.

28. Notwithstanding anything in this Charter, the rights and freedoms referred to in it are guaranteed equally to male and female persons.

29. Nothing in this Charter abrogates or derogates from any rights or privileges guaranteed by or under the Constitution of Canada in respect of denominational, separate or dissentient schools.

31. Nothing in this Charter extends the legislative powers of any body or authority.

Application of Charter

32. (1) This Charter applies

(a) to the Parliament and government of Canada in respect of all matters within the authority of Parliament including all matters relating to the Yukon Territory and Northwest Territories; and

(b) to the legislature and government of each province in respect of all matters within the authority of the legislature of each province.

(2) Notwithstanding subsection (1), section 15 shall not have effect until three years after this section comes into force.

33. (1) Parliament or the legislature of a province may expressly declare in an Act of Parliament or of the legislature, as the case may be, that the Act or a provision thereof shall operate notwithstanding a provision included in section 2 or sections 7 to 15 of this Charter.

(2) An Act or a provision of an Act in respect of which a declaration made under this section is in effect shall have such operation as it would have but for the provision of this Charter referred to in the declaration.

(3) A declaration made under subsection (1) shall cease to have effect five years after it comes into force or on such earlier date as may be specified in the declaration.

(4) Parliament or a legislature of a province may re-enact a declaration made under subsection (1).

(5) Subsection (3) applies in respect of a re-enactment made under subsection (4).

34. This Part may be cited as the Canadian Charter of Rights and Freedoms.

35. (1) The existing aboriginal and treaty rights of the aboriginal peoples of Canada are hereby recognized and affirmed.

(2) In this Act, 'aboriginal peoples of Canada' includes the Indian, Inuit and Metis peoples of Canada.

(3) For greater certainty, in subsection (1) 'treaty rights' includes rights that now exist by way of land claims agreements or may be so acquired.

(4) Notwithstanding any other provinces of this Act, the aboriginal and treaty rights referred to in subsection (1) are guaranteed equally to male and female persons.

APPENDIX C

DECLARATION ON THE RIGHTS OF PERSONS BELONGING TO NATIONAL OR ETHNIC, RELIGIOUS AND LINGUISTIC MINORITIES

Adopted by United Nations General Assembly, in plenary, December 18, 1992.

Article 1

1. States shall protect the existence and the national or ethnic, cultural, religious or linguistic identity of minorities within their respective territories, and shall encourage conditions for the promotion of that identity.
2. States shall adopt appropriate legislative and other measures to achieve these ends.

Article 2

1. Persons belonging to national or ethnic, religious and linguistic minorities (hereinafter referred to as persons belonging to minorities) have the right to enjoy their own culture, to profess and practise their own religion, and to use their own language, in private or in public, freely and without interference, or any form of discrimination.
2. Persons belonging to minorities have the right to participate effectively in cultural, religious, social, economic and public life.
3. Persons belonging to minorities have the right to participate effectively in decisions on the national and, where appropriate, regional level concerning the minority to which they belong or the regions in which they live, in a manner not incompatible with national legislation.
4. Persons belonging to minorities have the right to establish and maintain their own associations.
5. Persons belonging to minorities have the right to establish and maintain, without any discrimination, free and peaceful contacts with other members of their group, and with persons belonging to other minorities, as well as contacts across frontiers with citizens of other States to whom they are related by national or ethnic, religious or linguistic ties.

Article 3

1. Persons belonging to minorities may exercise their rights, including those set forth in this Declaration, individually as well as in community with other members of their group, without any discrimination.
2. No disadvantage shall result for any person belonging to a minority as the consequence of the exercise or non-exercise of the rights set forth in this Declaration.

Article 4

1. States shall take measures where required to ensure that persons belonging to minorities may exercise fully and effectively all their human rights and fundamental freedoms without any discrimination and in full equality before the law.
2. States shall take measures to create favourable conditions to enable persons belonging to minorities to express their characteristics and to develop their culture, language, religion, traditions and customs, except where specific practices are in violation of national law and contrary to international standards.
3. States should take appropriate measures so that, wherever possible, persons belonging to minorities have adequate opportunities to learn their mother tongue or to have instruction in their mother tongue.
4. States should, where appropriate, take measures in the field of education, in order to encourage knowledge of the history, traditions, language and culture of the minorities existing within their territory. Persons belonging to minorities should have adequate opportunities to gain knowledge of the society as a whole.
5. States should consider appropriate measures so that persons belonging to minorities may participate fully in the economic progress and development in their country.

Article 5

1. National policies and programmes shall be planned and implemented with due regard for the legitimate interests of persons belonging to minorities.
2. Programmes of cooperation and assistance among States should be planned and implemented with due regard for the legitimate interests of persons belonging to minorities.

Article 6

States should cooperate on questions relating to persons belonging to minorities, including exchange of information and experiences, in order to promote mutual understanding and confidence.

Article 7

States should cooperate in order to promote respect for the rights set forth in this Declaration.

Article 8

1. Nothing in this Declaration shall prevent the fulfillment of international obligations of States in relation to persons belonging to minorities. In particular, States shall fulfil in good faith the obligations and commitments they have assumed under international treaties and agreements to which they are parties.
2. The exercise of the rights set forth in this Declaration shall not prejudice the enjoyment by all persons of universally recognized human rights and fundamental freedoms.
3. Measures taken by States to ensure the effective enjoyment of the rights set forth in this Declaration shall not prima facie be considered contrary to the principle of equality contained in the Universal Declaration of Human Rights.
4. Nothing in this Declaration may be construed as permitting any activity contrary to the purposes and principles of the United Nations, including sovereign equality, territorial integrity and political independence of States.

Article 9

The specialized agencies and other organizations of the United Nations system shall contribute to the full realization of the rights and principles set forth in this Declaration, within their respective fields of competence.

REFERENCES

Abella, Irving. 2000. 'Anti-Semitism'. *The Canadian Encyclopedia, Year 2000 Edition*. Toronto: McClelland & Stewart.

Abu Laban, Baha, Tracey Derwing, Harvey Krahn, Marlene Mulder, and Lori Wilkinson. 1998. *The Resettlement of Refugees in Alberta, 1992–1997*. Edmonton: Citizenship and Immigration Canada.

Abbott, Andrew. 1997. 'Transcending General Linear Reality'. *Sociology Theory* 6:169–86.

Adachi, Ken. 1976. *The Enemy That Never Was*. Toronto: McClelland and Stewart.

Agocs, Carol, and Monica Boyd. 1993. 'The Vertical Mosaic Revisited'. In Jim Curtis (ed.), *Social Inequality*, 2nd edn. Scarborough, ON: Prentice-Hall.

Akbari, Ather H. 1989. 'Economics of Immigration and Racial Discrimination: A Literature Survey (1970–1989)'. Ottawa: Policy and Research, Multiculturalism and Citizenship.

Allport, Gordon. 1954. *The Nature of Prejudice*. New York: Doubleday.

Anderson, Alan B. 1972. 'Assimilation in the Bloc Settlements of North-Central Saskatchewan: Comparative Study of Identity Change Among Seven Ethno-Religious Groups in a Canadian Prairie Region'. Ph.D. dissertation (University of Saskatchewan).

———. 1980. 'The Survival of Ethnolinguistic Minorities: Canadian and Comparative Research'. In Howard Giles et al. (eds), *Language and Ethnic Relations*. New York: Pergamon Press.

——— and J.S. Frideres. 1981. *Ethnicity in Canada: Theoretical Perspectives*. Toronto: Butterworths.

——— and Leo Driedger. 1980. 'The Mennonite Family: Culture and Kin in Rural Saskatchewan'. In K. Ishwaran (ed.), *Canadian Families: Ethnic Variations*. Toronto: McGraw-Hill Ryerson.

Anderson, Grace. 1974. *Networks of Contact: The Portuguese and Toronto*. Waterloo, ON: Wilfrid Laurier University Press.

——— and David Higgs. 1976. *A Future to Inherit: The Portuguese Communities of Canada*. Toronto: McClelland and Stewart.

Anderson, Kay J. 1991. *Vancouver's Chinatown: Racial Discourse in Canada, 1875–1980*. Montreal: McGill-Queen's University Press.

Anderson, Wolseley W. 1993. *Caribbean Immigrants: A Socio-Demographic Profile*. Toronto: Canadian Scholars' Press.

Angus Reid Group. 1991. 'Multiculturalism and Canadians: National Attitude Survey 1991'. Ottawa: Multiculturalism and Citizenship Canada.

Armstrong, Frederick H. 1981. 'Ethnicity in the Formation of the Family Compact: A Case Study in the Growth of the Canadian Establishment'. In Jorgen Dahlie and Tessa Fernando (eds), *Ethnicity, Power and Politics in Canada*. Toronto: Methuen.

Asch, Michael. 1984. *Home and Native Land: Aboriginal Rights and the Canadian Constitution*. Toronto: Methuen.

Axworthy, Thomas S., and Pierre Elliott Trudeau. 1992. *Towards a Just Society: The Trudeau Years*. Toronto: Penguin.

Baar, Ellen. 1978. 'Issei, Nisei and Sansei'. In Daniel Glenday, Hubert Guidon, and Alan Turowetz (eds), *Modernization and the Canadian State*. Toronto: Macmillan.

Badets, Jane, and Tina W.L. Chiu. 1994. *Canada's Changing Immigrant Population*, Catalogue 96-311E. Ottawa: Statistics Canada and Prentice-Hall.

Balakrishnan, T.R. 1982. 'Changing Patterns of Ethnic Residential Segregation in the Metropolitan Areas of Canada'. *Canadian Review of Sociology and Anthropology* 19:92–110.

———. 2000. 'Residential Segregation and Canada's Ethnic Groups'. In M.A. Kalbach and W.E. Kalbach (eds), *Perspectives on Ethnicity in Canada*. Toronto: Harcourt Canada.

——— and Feng Hou. 1995. 'The Changing Patterns of Spatial Concentration and Residential Segregation of Ethnic Groups in Canada's Major

Metropolitan Areas 1981–1991', paper presented at the Population Association of America meetings in San Francisco, 6–10 April.

—— and Feng Hou. 1999. 'Residential Patterns in Cities'. In S. Halli and Leo Driedger (eds), *Immigrant Canada*. Toronto: University of Toronto Press.

—— and George K. Jarvis. 1979. 'Changing Patterns of Spatial Differentiation in Canada, 1961–1971'. *Canadian Review of Sociology and Anthropology* 16:218–27.

—— and John Kralt. 1987. 'Segregation of Visible Minorities in Toronto, Montreal and Vancouver'. In Leo Driedger (ed.), *Ethnic Canada: Identities and Inequalities*. Toronto: Copp Clark Pitman.

—— and K. Selvanathan. 1990. 'Ethnic Residential Segregation in Metropolitan Canada'. In Shiva Halli, Frank Trovato, and Leo Driedger (eds), *Ethnic Demography*. Ottawa: Carleton University Press.

—— and Zheng Wu. 1992. 'Home Ownership Patterns and Ethnicity in Selected Canadian Cities'. *Canadian Journal of Sociology* 17: 389–403.

Banton, Michael. 1960. 'Social Distance: A New Appreciation'. *Sociological Review* 8:169–83.

——. 1967. *Race Relations*. London: Tavistock.

Barbaud, Philippe. 1998. 'French in Quebec'. In J. Edwards (ed.), *Language in Canada*. Cambridge, UK: Cambridge University Press.

Basavarajappa, K.G., and Frank Jones. 1999. 'Visible Minority Income Differences'. In S. Halli and Leo Driedger (eds), *Immigrant Canada*. Toronto: University of Toronto Press.

Baureiss, Gunter. 1987. 'Chinese Immigration, Chinese Stereotypes, and Chinese Labour'. *Canadian Ethnic Studies* 19:15–34.

Beaujot, Roderic P. 1999. 'Immigration and Demographic Structures'. In S.S. Halli and Leo Driedger (eds), *Immigrant Canada*. Toronto: University of Toronto Press.

—— and Feng Hou. 1993. *Projecting the Visible Minority Population of Canada: The Immigration Component*. Ottawa: Statistics Canada.

Beavis, Mary Ann. 1995. *Housing and Ethnicity: Literature Review and Select, Annotated Bibliography*. Winnipeg: Institute of Urban Studies, University of Winnipeg.

Bell, David, and Lorne Tepperman. 1979. *The Roots of Disunity: A Look at Canadian Political Culture*. Toronto: McClelland and Stewart.

Bellah, Robert N. 1973. *Emile Durkheim on Morality and Society*. Chicago: University of Chicago Press.

Bendix, Reinhard. 1977. *Max Weber: An Intellectual Portrait*. Berkeley, CA: University of California Press.

Berger, Peter L. 1967. *The Sacred Canopy: Elements of a Sociological Theory of Religion*. Garden City, NY: Doubleday and Company.

Berger, Thomas R. 1981. *Fragile Freedoms: Human Rights and Dissent in Canada*. Toronto: Clarke, Irwin.

Berlin, Isaiah. 1963. *Karl Marx: His Life and Environment*. Oxford: Oxford University Press.

Berry, John W. 1990. 'Psychology of Acculturation'. In J. Berman (ed.), *Nebraska Symposium on Motivation*, 37:201–34. Lincoln: University of Nebraska Press.

—— and G.J.S. Wilde. 1972. *Social Psychology: The Canadian Context*. Toronto: McClelland and Stewart.

—— and J.A. Laponce. 1994. *Ethnicity and Culture in Canada: The Research Landscape*. Toronto: University of Toronto Press.

——, R. Kalin, and D.M. Taylor. 1977. *Multiculturalism and Ethnic Attitudes in Canada*. Ottawa: Minister of Supply and Services.

—— and Rudolf Kalin. 2000. 'Racism: Evidence from National Surveys'. In L. Driedger and S. Halli (eds), *Race and Racism: Canada's Challenge*. Montreal: McGill-Queen's University Press.

——, U. Kim, S. Power, M. Young, and D. Mok. 1987. 'Comparative Studies of Acculturation Stress'. *International Migration Review* 21: 491–511.

Bibby, Reginald W. 1987a. 'Bilingualism and Multiculturalism: A National Reading'. In Leo Driedger (ed.), *Ethnic Canada: Identities and Inequalities*. Toronto: Copp Clark Pitman.

——. 1987b. *Fragmented Gods: The Poverty and Potential of Religion in Canada*. Toronto: Irwin.

——. 1993. *Unknown Gods: The Ongoing Story of Religion in Canada*. Toronto: Stoddart.

———. 1995. *The Bibby Report: Social Trends Canadian Style.* Toronto: Stoddart.

———. 2002. *Restless Gods: The Renaissance of Religion in Canada.* Toronto: Stoddart.

Bienvenue, Rita, and Jay Goldstein. 1985. *Ethnicity and Ethnic Relations in Canada: A Book of Readings,* 2nd edn. Toronto: Butterworths.

Billingsley, B., and L. Musynski. 1985. *No Discrimination Here.* Toronto: Social Planning Council of Metro Toronto and the Urban Alliance on Race Relations.

Blishen, Bernard R. 1970. 'Social Class and Opportunity in Canada'. *Canadian Review of Sociology and Anthropology* 7:110–27.

Blau, Peter M., Jerry C. Blum, and Joseph E. Schwartz. 1982. 'Heterogeneity and Intermarriage'. *American Sociological Review* 47:45–61.

Bloom, D.E., G. Grenier, and M. Gunderson. 1995. 'The Changing Labor Market Position of Canadian Immigrants'. *Canadian Journal of Economics* 28:987–1001.

Bogardus, Emory S. 1959. *Social Distance.* Los Angeles: Antioch Press.

Bolaria, B. Singh. 1995. *Social Issues and Contradictions in Canadian Society,* 2nd edn. Toronto: Harcourt Brace Canada.

——— and Peter S. Li 1988. *Racial Oppression in Canada,* 2nd edn. Toronto: Garamond Press.

Bonacich, Edna. 1972. 'A Therapy of Ethnic Antagonism: The Split Labour Market'. *American Sociological Review* 37:547–59.

Bothwell, R. 1996. *Canada and Quebec.* Vancouver: University of British Columbia Press.

Bott, Elizabeth. 1957. *Family and Social Network,* 2nd edn. New York: Free Press.

Bourhis, R.Y. 1983. 'Language Attitudes and Self-Reports of French-English Language Usage in Quebec'. *Journal of Multilingual and Multicultural Development* 4:163–79.

———. 1994. 'Ethnic and Language Attitudes in Quebec'. In J. Berry and J.A. Laponce (eds), *Ethnicity and Culture in Canada: The Research Landscape.* Toronto: University of Toronto Press.

——— and D. Lepicq. 1993. 'Quebec French and Language Issues in Quebec'. In R. Posner and J.N. Green (eds), *Trends in Romance Linguistics and Philology,* Vol. 5: *Bilingualism and*

Linguistic Conflict in Romance. The Hague and Berlin: Mouton de Gruyter.

Boyd, Monica. 1992. 'Gender, Visible Minority, and Immigrant Earnings Inequality: Reassessing an Employment Equity Premise'. In Vic Satzewich (ed.), *Reconstructing a Nation.* Halifax: Fernwood.

———. 1999. 'Integrating Gender, Language and Race'. In S. Halli and L. Driedger (eds), *Immigrant Canada.* Toronto: University of Toronto Press.

———, Gustave Goldman, and Pamela White. 2000. 'Race in the Canadian Census'. In L. Driedger and S. Halli (eds), *Race and Racism: Canada's Challenge.* Montreal: McGill-Queen's University Press.

———, John Goyder, Frank E. Jones, Hugh A. McRoberts, Peter Pineo, and John Porter. 1981. 'Status Attainment in Canada: Findings of the Canadian Mobility Study'. *Canadian Review of Sociology and Anthropology* 18:657–73.

Breton, Raymond. 1964. 'Institutional Completeness of Ethnic Communities and Personal Relations to Immigrants'. *American Journal of Sociology* 70:193–205.

———. 1984. 'The Production and Allocation of Symbolic Resources: An Analysis of the Linguistic and Ethnocultural Fields in Canada'. *Canadian Review of Sociology and Anthropology* 21:123–44.

———. 1991. *The Governance of Ethnic Communities: Political Structures and Processes in Canada.* New York: Greenwood Press.

———. 1999. 'Ethnic and Race Relations'. *The Canadian Encyclopedia, Year 2000 Edition.* Toronto: McClelland & Stewart.

——— and Howard Roseborough. 1980. 'Ethnic, Religious and Regional Representation in the Federal Cabinet, 1869–1966' (University of Toronto).

———, Jeffrey Reitz, and Victor Valentine. 1980. *Cultural Boundaries and the Cohesion of Canada.* Montreal: The Institute of Research and Public Policy.

——— and Pierre Savard. 1982. *The Quebec and Acadian Diaspora in North America.* Toronto: The Multicultural Society of Ontario.

———, Wsevolod, W. Isajiw, Warren W. Kalbach, and Jeffrey G. Reitz. 1990. *Ethnic Identity and*

Equality: Varieties of Experience in a Canadian City. Toronto: University of Toronto Press.

Broadfoot, Barry. 1977. *Years of Sorrow, Years of Shame: The Story of the Japanese in World War II.* Toronto: Doubleday Canada.

Brown, R. 1995. *Prejudice: Its Social Psychology.* Oxford: Blackwell.

Brym, Robert. 1993. 'The Distribution of Anti-Semitism in Canada in 1984'. In Robert Brym et al. (eds), *The Jews in Canada.* Toronto: Oxford University Press.

———, Michael Gillespie, and A.R. Gillis. 1993. 'Anomie Opportunity, and the Density of Ethnic Ties: Another View of Jewish Outmarriage in Canada'. In Robert Brym et al. (eds), *The Jews in Canada.* Toronto: Oxford University Press.

——— and Rhonda Lenton. 1993. 'The Distribution of Anti-Semitism in Canada in 1984'. In Robert Brym et al. (eds), *The Jews in Canada.* Toronto: Oxford University Press.

———, William Shaffir, and Morton Weinfeld. 1993. *The Jews in Canada.* Toronto: Oxford University Press.

Burch, Thomas K. 1990. 'Family Structure and Ethnicity'. In Shiva Halli, Frank Trovato, and Leo Driedger (eds), *Ethnic Demography.* Ottawa: Carleton University Press.

Burnet, Jean. 1979. 'Myths and Multiculturalism'. *Canadian Journal of Education* 4:43–58.

———. 1988. *'Coming Canadians': An Introduction to a History of Canada's Peoples.* Toronto: McClelland and Stewart.

Cahoone, Lawrence (ed.). 1996. *From Modernism to Postmodernism: An Anthology.* Oxford: Blackwell.

Caldwell, Gary, and Daniel Fournier. 1987. 'The Quebec Question: A Matter of Population'. *Canadian Journal of Sociology* 12:16–41.

Calliste, Agnes. 1987. 'Sleeping Car Porters in Canada: An Ethnically Submerged Labour Market'. *Canadian Ethnic Studies* 19:1–20.

———. 1988. 'Blacks on Canadian Railroads'. *Canadian Ethnic Studies* 20:36–52.

Cameron, Duncan. 1992. 'A Constitution for English Canada'. In Daniel Drache and Roberto Perin (eds), *Negotiating Within a Sovereign Quebec.* Toronto: James Lorimer.

Canada. Parliament. House of Commons. *Debates.* 1971: 8545.

Cardinal, Harold. 1977. *The Rebirth of Canada's Indians.* Edmonton: Hurtig.

Cauthen, N.R., I.E. Robinson, and H.H. Kraus. 1971. 'Stereotypes: A Review of the Literature 1926–1968'. *The Journal of Social Psychology* 84:103–25.

Census of Canada. 1981. Catalogues 92-910, 92-912.

Chard, A., and S. Renaud. 2001. 'Visible Minorities in Toronto, Vancouver and Montreal'. *Canadian Social Trends.* Toronto: Thompson Educational Publishing.

Charest, Paul. 1975. 'Foreword'. In Gerald Gold, *St. Pascal.* Toronto: Holt, Rinehart and Winston.

Chevrier, Richard. 1983. *Le français au Canada: situation à l'extérieur du Quebec.* Quebec: Conseil de la langue français.

Chorney, Harold. 1992. 'Dividing the Debt: More than Bean Counting'. In Daniel Drache and Roberto Perin (eds), *Negotiating Within a Sovereign Quebec.* Toronto: James Lorimer.

Christianson, Carole P., and Morton Weinfeld. 1993. 'The Black Family in Canada: A Preliminary Exploration of Family Patterns and Inequality'. *Canadian Ethnic Studies* 25:26–44.

Citizenship and Immigration Canada. 1992. *Immigration Statistics 1992,* Catalogue MP22-1/1992. Ottawa: Public Works and Government Services.

———. 2002. *Pursuing Canada's Commitment to Immigration.* Ottawa: Public Works and Government Services.

Clairmont, Denis H. et al. 1965. *A Socio-Economic Study and Recommendations: Sunnyville, Lincolnville and Upper Big Tracadie, Guysborough County.* Halifax: Institute of Public Affairs, Dalhousie University.

Clairmont, Donald H., and Dennis W. Magill. 1974. *The Life and Death of a Canadian Black Community.* Toronto: McClelland and Stewart.

Clark, S.D. 1968. *The Developing Canadian Community.* Toronto: University of Toronto Press.

Clement, Wallace. 1974. *The Canadian Corporate Elite: An Analysis of Economic Power.* Toronto: McClelland and Stewart.

Comeau, Larry, and Leo Driedger. 1978. 'Opening and Closing in an Open Society'. *Social Forces* 57:600–20.

Coons, W.H., Donald W. Taylor, and Marc-Adelard Tremblay. 1977. *The Individual, Language and Society in Canada.* Ottawa: The Canada Council.

Coser, Lewis. 1956. *The Functions of Social Conflict.* New York: Free Press.

Cox, Oliver C. 1948. *Caste, Class and Race: A Study in Social Dynamics.* Garden City, NY: Doubleday.

Crean, Susan, and Marcel Rioux. 1983. *Two Nations: An Essay on the Culture and Politics of Canada and Quebec in a World of American Pre-eminence.* Toronto: James Lorimer.

Creese, Gillian. 1987. 'Organizing Against Racism in the Workplace: Chinese Workers in Vancouver Before the Second World War'. *Canadian Ethnic Studies* 19:35–46.

Cummins, Jim. 1994. 'Heritage Language Learning and Teaching'. In J.W. Berry and J.A. Laponce (eds), *Ethnicity and Culture in Canada: The Research Landscape.* Toronto: University of Toronto Press.

Cuneo, Carl J., and James E. Curtis. 1975. 'Social Ascription in the Educational and Occupational Status Attainment of Urban Canadians'. *Canadian Review of Sociology and Anthropology* 12:6–24.

Curtis, James, Edward Grabb, and Neil Guppy (eds). 1993. *Social Inequality in Canada: Patterns, Problems, Policies,* 2nd edn. Scarborough, ON: Prentice-Hall.

Dahrendorf, Rolf. 1959. *Class and Class Conflict in Industrial Society.* Palo Alto, CA: Stanford University Press.

Dai, S.Y., and M.V. George. 1996. *Projections of Visible Minority Groups, Canada, Provinces and Regions, 1991,* Catalogue 91-541. Ottawa: Statistics Canada.

Daigle, Jean. 1982. 'The Acadians: A People in Search of a Country'. In Raymond Breton and Pierre Savard (eds), *The Quebec and Acadian Diaspora in North America.* Toronto: The Multicultural History Society of Ontario.

Daniels, Roger, and Harry H.L. Kitano. 1970. *American Racism: Exploration of the Nature of Prejudice.* Englewood Cliffs, NJ: Prentice-Hall.

Danziger, Sheldon H., and Daniel H. Weinberg. 1994. 'The Historical Record: Trends in Family Income, Inequality, and Poverty'. In S.H. Danziger, G.D. Sandefur, and D.H. Weinberg (eds), *Confronting Poverty Prescriptions for Change.* New York: Harvard University Press.

Darroch, Gordon A. 1979. 'Another Look at Ethnicity: Stratification and Social Mobility in Canada'. *Canadian Journal of Sociology* 4:1–25.

Dashefsky, Arnold. 1972. 'And the Search Goes on: Religio-Ethnic Identity and Identification in the Study of Ethnicity'. *Sociological Analysis* 33:239–45.

———. 1975a. *Ethnic Identity in Society.* Chicago: Rand McNally.

———. 1975b. 'Theoretical Frameworks in the Study of Ethnic Identity'. *Ethnicity* 2:1–15.

Davids, Leo. 1993. 'Yiddish in Canada: Picture and Prospects'. In Robert Brym et al. (eds), *The Jews in Canada.* Toronto: Oxford University Press.

Davis, Alan. 1992. *Anti-Semitism in Canada: History and Interpretation.* Waterloo, ON: Wilfrid Laurier University Press.

Davis, Kingsley. 1950. *Human Society.* New York: Free Press.

——— and W.E. Moore. 1945. 'Some Principles of Stratification'. *American Sociological Review* 10:242–9.

Dawson, C.A. 1936. *Group Settlement: Ethnic Communities in Western Canada.* Toronto: Macmillan.

——— and W.E. Gettys. 1929. *Introduction to Sociology.* New York: Ronald Press.

Deffontaines, Pierre. 1965. 'The Rang: Pattern of Rural Settlement in French Canada'. In Marcel Rioux and Yves Martin (eds), *French-Canadian Society,* Vol. 1. Ottawa: Carleton Library.

Dei, George J. Sefa. 1993. 'Narrative Discourses of Black/African-Canadian Parents and the Canadian Public School System'. *Canadian Ethnic Studies* 25:45–65.

Denis, Wilfrid B. 1995. 'The Meech Lake Shuffle: French and English Language Rights in Canada'. In Singh Bolaria (ed.), *Social Issues and Contradictions in Canadian Society,* 2nd edn. Toronto: Harcourt Brace Canada.

———. 1999. 'Language Policy in Canada'. In P. Li (ed.), *Race and Ethnic Relations in Canada.* Toronto: Oxford University Press.

Department of Employment and Immigration Canada. 1985. *Annual Report to Parliament on Future Immigration Levels*. Ottawa: Minister of Supply and Services Canada.

———. 1989. *Immigration to Canada: A Statistical Overview*. Ottawa: Employment and Immigration Canada.

Department of Indian Affairs and Native Development. 1987. *Indian Register, 1961–87*. Ottawa: Minister of Supply and Services.

———. 1992. *Basic Departmental Data—1991*. Ottawa: Minister of Supply and Services.

Department of Manpower and Immigration. 1974. *A Report of the Canadian Immigration and Population Study*. Ottawa: Information Canada.

Deroche, Constance, and John Deroche. 1991. 'Black and White: Racial Construction in Television Police Dramas'. *Canadian Ethnic Studies* 23:69–91.

Derrida, Jacques. 1974. 'The End of the Book and the Beginning of Writing'. In Jacques Derrida, *Of Grammatology*. Baltimore: Johns Hopkins University Press.

deSilva, Arnold. 1996. 'Discrimination Against Visible Minority Men', Working Paper #W-96-6E. Ottawa: Human Resources Development Canada.

deVries, John. 1980. *Language Use in Canada*. Ottawa: Ministry of Supply and Services.

———. 1988. *The Integration of Ethno-Cultural Communities into Canadian Society: A Selected Bibliography*. Ottawa: Policy and Research, Multiculturalism and Citizenship.

———. 1990. 'Language and Ethnicity: Canadian Aspects'. In Peter Li (ed.), *Race and Ethnic Relations in Canada*. Toronto: Oxford University Press.

———. 1999. 'Foreign Born Language Acquisition and Shift'. In Shiva Halli and Leo Driedger (eds), *Immigrant Canada: Demographic, Economic and Social Challenges*. Toronto: University of Toronto Press.

——— and Frank Vallee. 1980. *Language Use in Canada*. Ottawa: Ministry of Supply and Services.

——— and Laverne Lewycky. 1985. 'Data Book on Canadian Official Language Minorities, Second Edition'. Ottawa: Centre for Research and on Ethnic Minorities, Carleton University Press.

Dickason, Olive Patricia. 2002. *Canada's First Nations: A History of Founding Peoples From Earliest Time*, 3rd edn. Toronto: McClelland and Stewart.

Dinwoodie, Catriona. 1986. 'Where Is Acadia?' *British Journal of Canadian Studies* 1:15–30.

Dion, Leon. 1975. 'French as an Adopted Language in Quebec'. In P. Migus (ed.), *Sounds Canadian: Languages and Culture in Multi-Ethnic Society*. Toronto: Peter Martin Associates.

Donner, Arthur, and Fred Lazar. 1992. 'The Case for a Single Currency and a Reformed Central Bank'. In D. Drache and R. Perin (eds), *Negotiating with a Sovereign Quebec*. Toronto: James Lorimer.

Drache, Daniel, and Roberto Perin (eds). 1992. *Negotiating with a Sovereign Quebec*. Toronto: James Lorimer.

Driedger, Leo. 1972. 'Native Rebellion and Mennonite Invasion: An Examination of Two Canadian River Valleys'. *Mennonite Quarterly Review* 46:290–300.

———. 1974. 'Doctrinal Belief: A Major Factor in the Differential Perception of Social Issues'. *Sociological Quarterly* 15:66–80.

———. 1975. 'In Search of Cultural Identity Factors: A Comparison of Ethnic Minority Students in Manitoba'. *Canadian Review of Sociology and Anthropology* 12:150–62.

———. 1976. 'Ethnic Self-Identity: A Comparison of Ingroup Evaluations'. *Sociometry* 39:131–41.

———. 1977a. 'The Anabaptist Identification Ladder: Plain-Urban Continuity in Diversity'. *Mennonite Quarterly Review* 51:278–91.

———. 1977b. 'Structural, Social and Individual Factors in Language Maintenance in Canada'. In W.H. Coons, Donald W. Taylor, and Marc-Adelard Tremblay (eds), *The Individual, Language and Society in Canada*. Ottawa: The Canada Council.

———. 1977c. 'Toward a Perspective on Canadian Pluralism: Ethnic Identity in Winnipeg'. *Canadian Journal of Sociology* 2:77–95.

———. 1978a. *The Canadian Ethnic Mosaic: A Quest for Identity*. Toronto: McClelland and Stewart.

———. 1978b. 'Ethnic Boundaries: A Comparison of Two Urban Neighbourhoods'. *Sociology and Social Research* 62:193–211.

———. 1980a. 'Jewish Identity: Maintenance of Urban Religious and Ethnic Boundaries'. *Ethnic and Racial Studies* 3:67–81.

———. 1980b. 'Nomos-Building on the Prairies: Construction of Indian, Hutterite and Jewish Sacred Canopies'. *Canadian Journal of Sociology* 5:341–56.

———. 1982a. 'Ethnic Boundaries: A Comparison of Two Urban Neighborhoods'. In George A. Theodorson (ed.), *Urban Patterns: Studies in Human Ecology*. University Park, PA: Pennsylvania State University Press.

———. 1982b. 'Individual Freedom vs. Community Control: An Adaptation of Erikson's Ontogeny of Ritualization'. *Journal for the Scientific Study of Religion* 21:226–41.

———. 1984. 'Multicultural Regionalism: Toward Understanding the Canadian West'. In Tony Rasporich (ed.), *Making of the Modern West: Western Canada Since 1945*. Calgary: University of Calgary Press.

———. 1986a. 'Community Conflict: The Eldorado Invasion of Warman'. *Canadian Review of Sociology and Anthropology* 23:247–69.

———. 1986b. 'Inequalities of Race'. In K. Ishwaran (ed.), *Sociology: An Introduction*. Don Mills, ON: Addison-Wesley.

———. 1987. *Ethnic Canada: Identities and Inequalities*. Toronto: Copp Clark Pitman.

———. 1989. *The Ethnic Factor: Identity in Diversity*. Toronto: McGraw-Hill Ryerson.

———. 1991. *The Urban Factor: Sociology of Canadian Cities*. Toronto: Oxford University Press.

———. 1995. 'Alert Opening and Closing: Rural-Urban Changes'. *Rural Sociology* 60:323–32.

———. 1996. *Multi-Ethnic Canada: Identities and Inequalities*. Toronto: Oxford University Press.

———. 1997. 'The Hutterites'. In P.R. Magocsi, (ed.), *The Peoples of Canada: An Encyclopedia for the Country*. Toronto: University of Toronto Press.

———. 1998. 'Language in Manitoba'. In John Edwards (ed.), *Language in Canada*. Cambridge, UK: Cambridge University Press.

———. 1999a. 'Hutterites'. In Paul R. Magocsi (ed.), *Encyclopedia of Canada's People*. Toronto: University of Toronto Press.

———. 1999b. 'Immigrant/Ethnic/Racial Segregation: Big Three and Prairie Metropolitan Comparisons'. *Canadian Journal of Sociology* 24:485–509.

———. 2000a. *Mennonites in the Global Village*. Toronto: University of Toronto Press.

———. 2000b. 'Postmodern Experiments: Blips or New Revolution?' In Susan Biesecker-Mast and Gerald Biesecker-Mast (eds), *Anabaptists and Postmodernity*. Telford, PA: Pandora Press US.

———. 2001. 'Changing Visions in Ethnic Relations'. *Canadian Journal of Sociology* 26:421–51.

——— and Angus Reid. 2000. 'Public Opinion on Visible Minorities'. In L. Driedger and S. Halli (eds), *Race and Racism: Canada's Challenge*. Montreal: McGill-Queen's University Press.

——— and Calvin Redekop. 1983. 'Sociology of Mennonites: State of the Art and Science'. *Journal of Mennonite Studies* 1:33–63.

———, Charlene Thacker, and Raymond Currie. 1982. 'Ethnic Identification: Variations in Regional and National Preferences'. *Canadian Ethnic Studies* 14:57–68.

——— and Conrad G. Kanagy. 1996. 'Changing Mennonite Values: Attitudes on Women, Politics and Peace, 1972–1989'. *Review of Religious Research* 37:89–103.

——— and Donald B. Kraybill. 1994. *Mennonite Peacemaking: From Quietism to Activism*. Scottdale, PA: Herald Press.

——— and Glenn Church. 1974. 'Residential Segregation and Institutional Completeness: A Comparison of Ethnic Minorities'. *Canadian Review of Sociology and Anthropology* 11:30–52.

——— and Jacob Peters. 1976. 'Ethnic Identity of Students of Mennonite and German Heritage'. In Stewart Crysdale and Les Wheatcraft (eds), *Religion in Canadian Society*. Toronto: Macmillan.

——— and Jacob Peters. 1977. 'Identity and Social Distance: Towards Understanding Simmel's "The Stranger"'. *Canadian Review of Sociology and Anthropology* 14:158–73.

——— and Neena Chappell. 1987. *Aging and Ethnicity: Toward an Interface*. Toronto: Butterworths.

────── and Paul Redekop. 1998. 'Testing the Innis and McLuhan Theses: Mennonite Media Access and TV Use'. *Canadian Review of Sociology and Anthropology* 35:43–64.

────── and Peter Hengstenberg. 1986. 'Non-Official Multilingualism: Factors Affecting Language Competence, Use and Maintenance'. *Canadian Ethnic Studies* 60:374–86.

────── and Richard Mezoff. 1981. 'Ethnic Prejudice and Discrimination in Winnipeg High Schools'. *Canadian Journal of Sociology* 6:1–17.

────── and Rodney Clifton. 1984. 'Ethnic Stereotypes: Images of Ethnocentrism, Reciprocity of Dissimilarity?' *Canadian Review of Sociology and Anthropology* 21:287–301.

────── and Shiva S. Halli. 1997. 'Pro-Life and Pro-Choice: Politics of Career and Homemaking'. *Population Studies* 51:129–37.

────── and Shiva S. Halli. 2000. *Race and Racism: Canada's Challenge.* Montreal: McGill-Queen's University Press.

Ducharme, Michele. 1986. 'The Segregation of Native People in Canada: Voluntary or Compulsory'. *Currents* (Summer):2–3.

Duncan, Otis Dudley. 1955. 'Review of Social Area Analysis'. *American Journal of Sociology* 61:84–5.

────── and Beverly Duncan. 1957. *The Negro Population of Chicago: A Study of Residential Segregation.* Chicago: University of Chicago Press.

Durkheim, Emile. 1897 [1981]. *Suicide,* trans. John A. Spaulding and George Simpson. Glencoe, IL: Free Press.

──────. 1912 [1945]. *The Elementary Forms of Religious Life.* New York: Free Press.

Edwards, John. 1985. *Language, Society and Identity.* London: Basil Blackwell.

────── (ed.). 1998. *Language in Canada.* Cambridge, UK: Cambridge University Press.

────── and Lori Doucette. 1987. 'Ethnic Salience, Identity and Symbolic Ethnicity'. *Canadian Ethnic Studies* 19:53–62.

Elliott, David R. 1985. 'Anti-Semitism and the Social Credit Movement: The Intellectual Roots of the Keegstra Affair'. *Canadian Ethnic Studies* 17:78–89.

Elliott, Jean Leonard, and Augie Fleras. 1992. *Unequal Relations: An Introduction to Race and Ethnic Dynamics in Canada.* Scarborough, ON: Prentice-Hall Canada.

Erikson, Erik. 1968. *Identity: Youth in Crisis.* New York: W.W. Norton.

Fairbairn, Kenneth J., and Hafiza Khatun. 1989. 'Residential Segregation and the Intra-Urban Migration of South Asians in Edmonton'. *Canadian Ethnic Studies* 21:45–64.

Fathi, Asghar, and Brian L. Kinsley. 1968. 'The Changing Identity of Jewish Youth in Canada', paper presented at the Canadian Sociology and Anthropology Association meetings.

Flanagan, Thomas. 1991. *Metis Lands in Manitoba.* Calgary: University of Calgary.

Fleras, Augie. 1995. '"From Culture to Equality: Multiculturalism as Ideology and Policy'. In J. Curtis, E. Grabb, and N. Guppy (eds). *Social Inequality in Canada,* 2nd edn. Scarborough, ON: Prentice-Hall.

──────. 2001. *Social Problems in Canada: Conditions, Constructions, and Challenges.* Toronto: Prentice-Hall.

────── and Jean Leonard Elliott. 1992a. *Multiculturalism in Canada: The Challenge of Diversity.* Toronto: Nelson Canada.

────── and Jean Elliott. 1992b. *The Nations Within: Aboriginal-State Relations in Canada, The United States, and New Zealand.* Toronto: Oxford University Press.

────── and Jean Elliott. 1996. *Unequal Relations: An Introduction to Race, Ethnic, and Aboriginal Relations in Canada,* 2nd edn. Scarborough, ON: Prentice-Hall.

────── and Jean Elliott. 1999. *Unequal Relations: An Introduction to Race, Ethnic and Aboriginal Dynamics in Canada,* 3rd edn. Scarborough, ON: Prentice-Hall.

Foster, L. 1998. *Turnstile Immigration.* Toronto: Thompson Educational Publishing.

Fournier, Pierre. 1991. *A Meech Lake Post-Mortem.* Montreal: McGill-Queen's University Press.

Francis, E.K. 1947. 'The Nature of the Ethnic Group'. *American Sociological Review* 52:393–400.

──────. 1948. 'The Russian Mennonites: From Religious to Ethnic Group'. *American Journal of Sociology* 54:101–6.

———. 1950. 'The Russian Mennonites: From Religious Group to Ethnic Group'. *American Journal of Sociology* 50:101–7.

———. 1954. 'Variables in the Formation of So-Called Minority Groups'. *American Journal of Sociology* 60:6–14.

———. 1955. *In Search of Utopia: The Mennonites in Manitoba*. Altona, MB: D.W. Friesen Publishers.

———. 1965. *Ethnos and Demos*. Berlin: Duncher and Humblot.

———. 1976. *Interethnic Relations: An Essay in Sociological Theory*. New York: Elsevier.

Frideres, James. 1993. *Native Peoples in Conflict*. Scarborough, ON: Prentice-Hall.

———. 1998. *Aboriginal People in Canada: Contemporary Conflicts*. Scarborough, ON: Prentice-Hall Allyn Bacon Canada.

——— and Sheldon Goldenberg. 1977. 'Hyphenated Canadians: Comparative Analysis of Ethnic, Regional and National Identification of Western Canadian University Students'. *Journal of Ethnic Studies* 5:91–100.

Friesen, John W. 1993. *When Cultures Clash: Case Studies in Multiculturalism*, 2nd edn. Calgary: Detselig Enterprises.

Fromm, Erich. 1956. 'Introduction'. In T.B. Bottomore and Maximilien Rubel (eds), *Karl Marx*. New York: McGraw-Hill.

Gaertner, S.L., and J.F. Dovidic. 1986. 'The Aversive Forms of Racism'. In S.L. Gaertner and J.F. Dovidic (eds), *Prejudice, Discrimination and Racism*. New York: Academic Press.

Gagnon, Alain-G. 1993. *Quebec: State and Society*, 2nd edn. Scarborough, ON: Nelson Canada.

Gagnon, M. 1974. 'Quelques facteurs determinant l'attitude vis-à-vis l'anglais, langue seconde'. In R. Darnell (ed.), *Linguistic Diversity in Canadian Society*. Vol. 2. Edmonton: Linguistic Research Inc.

Gans, Herbert. 1962. *The Urban Villagers*. Glencoe, IL: Free Press.

———. 1979. 'Symbolic Ethnicity: The Future of Ethnic Groups and Cultures in America'. *Ethnic and Racial Studies* 2:1–20.

Gardner, Robert C. 1977. 'Social Factors in Second Language Acquisition and Bilinguality'. In W.H. Coons et al. (eds), *The Individual, Language and Society in Canada*. Ottawa: The Canada Council.

——— and P.C. Smythe. 1975. 'Motivation and Second Language Acquisition'. *Canadian Modern Language Review* 21:218–30.

Gee, Ellen M., and Steven G. Prus. 2000. 'Income Inequality in Canada: A "Racial Divide"'. In M. Kalbach and W.E. Kalbach (eds), *Perspectives on Ethnicity in Canada*. Toronto: Harcourt Canada.

Gill, Rajesh. 2000. 'Cities and Ethnicity: A Case of De-ethnicization or Re-ethnicization?' *Sociological Bulletin* 49:213–28.

Gilroy, P. 1987. *There Ain't No Black in the Union Jack*. Chicago: University of Chicago Press.

Glazer, Nathan, and Daniel P. Moynihan. 1975. *Beyond the Melting Pot*. Cambridge, MA: Massachusetts Institute of Technology.

Glickman, Yaacov, and Alan Bardikoff. 1982. *The Treatment of the Holocaust in Canadian History and Social Science Textbooks*. Downsview, ON: League for Human Rights of B'nai Brith.

Gold, Gerald L. 1975. *St. Pascal: Changing Leadership and Social Organization in a Quebec Town*. Toronto: Holt, Rinehart and Winston.

Gordon, Milton M. 1964. *Assimilation in American Life*. New York: Oxford University Press.

Grabb, Edward G. 1984. *Social Inequality: Classical and Contemporary Theorists*. Toronto: Holt, Rinehart and Winston.

Greeley, Andrew. 1989. *Religious Change in America*. Cambridge, MA: Harvard University Press.

Green, Alan G. 1995. 'A Comparison of Canadian and U.S. Immigration Policy in the Twentieth Century'. In D.J. DeVortez (ed.), *Diminishing Returns: The Economics of Canada's Recent Immigration Policy*. Ottawa: Renouf Publications for C.D. Howe.

——— and David A. Green. 1995. 'Canadian Immigration Policy: The Effectiveness of the Point System and Other Instruments'. *Canadian Journal of Economics* 28:4–20.

Grenz, Stanley J. 1996. *A Primer on Postmodernism*. Grand Rapids, MI: W.B. Eerdmans Publishing.

Grindstaff, Carl F., and Frank Trovato. 1994.

'Canada's Population in the World Context'. In Frank Trovato and Carl Grindstaff (eds), *Perspectives on Canada's Population: An Introduction to Concepts and Issues*. Toronto: Oxford University Press.

Gross, Leonard. 1980. *The Golden Years of the Hutterites*. Scottdale, PA: Herald Press.

Guindon, Hubert. 1988. *Quebec Society: Tradition, Modernity, and Nationhood*. Toronto: University of Toronto Press.

Habermas, Jurgen. 1996. 'An Alternative Way Out of the Philosophy of the Subject: Communicative Versus Subject-Centered Reason'. In Jurgen Habermas, *The Philosophical Discourse of Modernity*. Cambridge, MA: MIT Press.

Hagan, John. 1977. 'Finding "Discrimination": A Question of Meaning'. *Ethnicity* 4:167–76.

Hall, David. 1991. 'Modern China and the Postmodern'. In Eliot Deutsch (ed.), *Culture and Modernity: East-West Philosophic Perspectives*. Honolulu: University of Hawaii Press.

Halli, Shiva S., Frank Trovato, and Leo Driedger. 1990. *Ethnic Demography: Canadian Immigrant, Racial and Cultural Variations*. Ottawa: Carleton University Press.

Halli, Shiva, and Leo Driedger. 1999. *Immigrant Canada: Demographic, Economic and Social Changes*. Toronto: University of Toronto Press.

Hamm, Peter M. 1987. *Continuity and Change*. Waterloo, ON: Wilfrid Laurier University Press.

Hammers, Josiane F., and Kirsten M. Hummel. 1998. 'Language in Quebec: Aboriginal and Heritage Varieties'. In John Edwards (ed.), *Language in Canada*. Cambridge, UK: Cambridge University Press.

Hancock, Lyn. 1995. *Nunavut*. Markham, ON: Fitzhenry and Whiteside.

Harris, Chauncey, and Edward L. Ullman. 1945. 'The Nature of Cities'. *Annuals* 242:7–17.

Harrison, Brian E. 1996. *Youth in Official Language Minorities: 1971–1996*, Catalogue 91-545. Ottawa: Statistics Canada.

———. 1999. 'Intergenerational Language Learning'. In L. Driedger and S. Halli (eds), *Race and Racism: Canada's Challenge*. Montreal: McGill-Queen's University Press.

——— and Louise Marmen. 1994. *Languages in Canada*, Catalogue 96-313E. Ottawa: Statistics Canada.

Havel, Vaclav. 1994. 'The Need for Transcendence in the Postmodern World'. Philadelphia: The Home Systems Home Page.

Head, Wilson. 1975. *The Black Presence in the Canadian Mosaic*. Toronto: Human Rights Commission.

———. 1981. *Adaptation of Immigrants: Perceptions of Ethnic and Racial Discrimination*. North York, ON: York University.

Hechter, Michael. 1978. 'Group Formation and the Cultural Division of Labor'. *American Journal of Sociology* 84:293–318.

Helly, D. 1994. 'Politique quebecoise face en pluralisme/culturel et pistes de recherche: 1977–1990'. In J. Berry and J. Laponce (eds), *Ethnicity and Culture in Canada: The Research Landscape*. Toronto: University of Toronto Press.

Henripin, Jacques. 1974. 'Immigration and Language Imbalance'. *Canadian Immigration and Population Study*. Ottawa: Information Canada.

———. 1993. 'Population Trends and Policies in Quebec'. In Alain-G. Gagnon (ed.), *Quebec: State and Society*, 2nd edn. Scarborough, ON: Nelson Canada.

Henry, Frances. 1973. *Forgotten Canadians: The Blacks of Nova Scotia*. Toronto: Longman Canada.

———. 1989. 'Housing and Racial Discrimination in Canada: A Preliminary Assessment of Current Initiatives and Information'. Ottawa: Policy and Research, Multiculturalism and Citizenship.

———. 1994. *The Caribbean Diaspora in Toronto: Learning to Live with Racism*. Toronto: University of Toronto Press.

——— and Carol Tator. 1994. 'The Ideology of Racism: "Democratic Racism"'. *Canadian Ethnic Studies* 26:1–14.

———, Carol Tator, Winston Mattis, and Tim Rees. 2000. *The Colour of Democracy: Racism in Canadian Society*. Toronto: Harcourt Brace Canada.

——— and E. Ginzberg. 1984. *Who Gets the Work? A Test of Racial Discrimination in Employment*. Toronto: Urban Alliance on Race Relations.

Herberg, Edward N. 1989. *Ethnic Groups in Canada: Adaptations and Transitions*. Scarborough, ON: Nelson Canada.

Herberg, Will. 1955. *Protestant, Catholic, Jew.* New York: Doubleday.

Hettne, Björn. 1995. *Development Theory and the Three Worlds*, 2nd edn. Essex, UK: Longman, Scientific and Technical.

Higgitt, Nancy. 2000. 'A Model of Refugee Resettlement'. In L. Driedger and S.S. Halli (eds), *Race and Racism*. Montreal: McGill-Queen's University Press.

Hill, Daniel G. 1981. *The Freedom-Seekers: Blacks in Early Canada*. Agincourt, ON: Book Society of Canada.

Hintze, Otto. 1931. 'Kalvinismus und Statsrazon in Brandenburg zu Beginn des 17ten Jahrhunderts'. *Historische Zeitschrift* 144:232.

Hofer, John. 1988. *The History of the Hutterites*, rev. edn. Altona, MB: D.W. Friesen Publishers.

Hooton, E.A. 1946. *Up From the Ape*, rev. edn. New York: Macmillan.

Hostetler, John A. 1974. *Hutterite Society*. Baltimore: Johns Hopkins University Press.

——— and Gertrude Huntington. 1967. *The Hutterites in North America*. New York: Holt, Rinehart and Winston.

Hou, Feng, and T.R. Balakrishnan. 1996. 'The Integration of Visible Minorities in Contemporary Canadian Society'. *Canadian Journal of Sociology* 21:307–26.

Hughes, David R., and Evelyn Kallen. 1974. *The Anatomy of Racism: Canadian Dimensions*. Montreal: Harvest House.

Hughes, Everett C. 1943. *French Canada in Transition*. Chicago: University of Chicago Press.

——— and Helen M. Hughes. 1952. *Where Peoples Meet: Racial and Ethnic Frontiers*. Glencoe, IL: Free Press.

Hunter, Alfred. 1986. *Class Tells: On Social Inequality in Canada*. Toronto: Butterworths.

Isajiw, Wsevolod W. 1978. 'Olga in Wonderland: Ethnicity in Technological Society'. In Leo Driedger (ed.), *The Canadian Ethnic Mosaic*. Toronto: McClelland and Stewart.

———. 1981. 'Ethnic Identity Retention', Research Paper No. 125. Toronto: Centre for Urban and Community Studies.

———. 1990. 'Ethnic Identity Retention'. In Breton et al. (eds), *Ethnic Identity and Inequality*. Toronto: University of Toronto Press.

——— (ed.). 1997. *Multiculturalism in North America and Europe: Comparative Perspectives on Interethnic Relations and Social Incorporation*. Toronto: Canadian Scholars Press.

———. 1999. *Understanding Diversity: Ethnicity and Race in the Canadian Context*. Toronto: Thompson Educational Publishing.

———, Aysan Sev'er, and Leo Driedger. 1993. 'Ethnic Identity and Social Mobility: A Test of the "Drawback Model" and Resources'. *Canadian Journal of Sociology* 18:177–96.

——— and Leo Driedger. 1987. 'Ethnic Identity: Resource or Drawback for Social Mobility', paper presented at the American Sociological Association meetings, Chicago, 17–21 August.

Ishwaran, K. 1980. *Canadian Families: Ethnic Variations*. Toronto: McGraw-Hill Ryerson.

Jackson, John D. 1975. *Community and Conflict: A Study of French-English Relations in Ontario*. Montreal: Holt, Rinehart and Winston.

———. 1977. 'The Functions of Language in Canada: On the Political Economy of Language'. In W.H. Coons et al. (eds), *The Individual, Languages and Society in Canada*. Ottawa: The Canada Council.

Jain, Harish C. 1988. 'Employment Discrimination Against Visible Minorities and Employment Equity'. Hamilton: McMaster University.

James, Carl E. 1990. *Making It: Black Youth, Racism and Career Aspirations in a Big City*. Oakville, ON: Mosaic Press.

——— (ed.). 1996. *Perspectives on Racism and the Human Services Sector: A Case for Change*. Toronto: University of Toronto Press.

———. 1999. *Seeing Ourselves: Exploring Race, Ethnicity and Culture*. Toronto: Thompson Educational Publishing.

——— and Adrienne Shadd (eds). 2001. *Talking About Differences: Encounters in Culture, Language and Identity*. Toronto: Between the Lines.

Jensen, J. 1996. 'When Identities Collide'. *Canadian Forum* 74:846.

Joy, Richard J. 1972. *Languages in Conflict*. Toronto: McClelland and Stewart.

———. 1992. *Canada's Official Languages: The Progress of Bilingualism*. Toronto: University of Toronto Press.

Juteau, Danielle. 1992. 'The Sociology of Ethno-National Relations in Quebec'. In Vic Satzewich (ed.), *Deconstructing a Nation*. Halifax: Fernwood.

Juteau-Lee, D., and Jean Lapointe. 1977. 'School Conflict in a Multi-Ethnic Community: A Case Study'. In R.R. Carlton, L.A. Colley, and N.J. McKinnon (eds), *Education in a Changing Society*. Toronto: Gage.

Kadushin, Charles. 1962. 'Social Distance Between Client and Professional'. *American Journal of Sociology* 67:517–31.

Kalbach, Warren E. 1980. 'Historical and Generational Perspectives of Ethnic Residential Segregation in Toronto, Canada: 1851–1971', Research Paper No. 118. Toronto: University of Toronto, Centre for Urban and Community Studies.

———. 1987. 'Growth and Distribution of Canada's Ethnic Population, 1871–1981'. In Leo Driedger (ed.), *Ethnic Canada: Identities and Inequalities*. Toronto: Copp Clark Pitman.

———. 1990. 'A Demographic Overview of Racial and Ethnic Groups in Canada'. In Peter Li (ed.), *Race and Ethnic Relations in Canada*. Toronto: Oxford University Press.

——— and Mary Richard. 1990. 'Ethno-Religious Identity and Acculturation'. In Shiva Halli, Frank Trovato, and Leo Driedger (eds), *Ethnic Demography*. Ottawa: Carleton University Press.

Kalbach, Madeline, and Warren E. Kalbach (eds). 2000. *Perspectives on Ethnicity: A Reader*. Toronto: Harcourt Canada.

Kalin, Rudolf. 1996a. 'Ethnic Attitudes as a Function of Ethnic Presence'. *Canadian Journal of Behavioural Science* 28:262–80.

———. 1996b. 'Interethnic Attitudes in Canada: Ethnocentrism, Consensual Hierarchy and Reciprocity'. *Canadian Journal of Behavioural Science* 28:262–80.

Kallen, Evelyn. 1977. *Spanning the Generations: A Study in Jewish Identity*. Don Mills, ON: Longman.

———. 1982. *Ethnicity and Human Rights in Canada*. Toronto: Gage.

———. 1995. *Ethnicity and Human Rights in Canada*, 2nd edn. Toronto: Oxford University Press.

Kallen, Horace M. 1924. *Culture and Democracy in the United States*. New York: Liverright.

Kauffman, J. Howard, and Leland Harder. 1975. *Anabaptists: Four Centuries Later*. Scottdale, PA: Herald Press.

Kauffman, J. Howard, and Leo Driedger. 1991. *The Mennonite Mosaic: Identity and Modernization*. Scottdale, PA: Herald Press.

Kazemipur, A., and S.S. Halli. 2000. *The New Poverty in Canada: Ethnic Groups and Ghetto Neighbourhoods*. Toronto: Thompson Educational Publishing.

Kelly, Karen. 1995. 'Projections of Visible Minority Groups, 1991 to 2016', Catalogue 11-0083. *Canadian Social Trends* (Summer).

Keyfitz, Nathan. 1965. 'Population Problems'. In Marcel Rioux and Yves Martin (eds), *French-Canadian Society*, Vol. 1. Ottawa: Carleton University Press.

Khubchandoni, Lachman M. 1976. 'Language Factor in Census'. In A. Verdoodt and R. Kjolseth (eds), *Language in Sociology*. Louvain: Editions Peeters.

Kobayashi, A. 1987. 'From Tyranny to Justice: The Uprooting of the Japanese Canadians in 1941'. *Tribune Juive* 5:28–35.

Krauter, Joseph F., and Morris Davis. 1978. *Minority Canadians: Ethnic Groups*. Toronto: Methuen.

Krech, David, Richard S. Crutchfield, and Egerton L. Ballachey. 1962. *The Individual in Society: A Textbook of Social Psychology*. New York: McGraw-Hill.

Krotki, Karol J., and Colin Reid. 1994. 'Demography of Canadian Population by Ethnic Group'. In John Berry and J. Laponce, *Ethnicity and Culture in Canada*. Toronto: University of Toronto Press.

Kymlicka, Will. 1989. *Liberalism, Community and Culture*. Oxford: Oxford University Press.

———. 1995a. *Multicultural Citizenship: A Liberal Theory of Minority Rights*. Oxford: Oxford University Press.

———. 1995b. *The Rights of Minority Cultures*. Oxford: Oxford University Press.

———. 1998. *Finding Our Way: Rethinking Ethnocultural Relations in Canada*. Toronto: Oxford University Press.

——— and Wayne Norman (eds). 2000. *Citizenship in Diverse Societies*. Oxford: Oxford University Press.

Lachapelle, R. 1979. *La Situation demolinguistique au Canada: evolution passée et prospective*. Montreal: Institute for Research on Public Policy.

Laczko, Leslie. 1995. *Pluralism and Inequality in Quebec*. Toronto: University of Toronto Press.

Lai, David Chuenyan. 1987. 'The Issue of Discrimination in Education in Victoria, 1901–1923'. *Canadian Ethnic Studies* 19:47–67.

———. 1988. *Chinatowns: Towns within Cities in Canada*. Vancouver: University of British Columbia Press.

Lambert, Ronald D., and James E. Curtis. 1984. 'Quebecois and English Canadian Opposition to Racial and Religious Intermarriage, 1968–1983'. *Canadian Ethnic Studies* 16:31–46.

Lambert, W.E., R.C. Hodgson, R.C. Gardner, and S. Fillenbaum. 1960. 'Evaluation Reactions to Spoken Languages'. *Journal of Abnormal and Social Psychology* 60:44–51.

Laponce, J.A. 1994. 'Ethnicity and Voting Studies in Canada: Primary and Secondary Sources 1970–1991'. In John Berry and J.A. Laponce, *Ethnicity and Culture in Canada*. Toronto: University of Toronto Press.

Laumann, E.O. 1965. 'Subjective Social Distance and Urban Occupational Stratification'. *American Journal of Sociology* 71:26–36.

Lawson, Roger, and William J. Wilson. 1995. 'Poverty, Social Rights, and the Quality of Citizenship'. In K. McFate, R. Lawson, and J. Wilson (eds), *Poverty, Inequality, and the Future of Social Policy*. New York: Russell Sage Foundation.

Lazar, Barry, and Tamsin Douglas. 1993. *Guide to Ethnic Montreal*, rev. edn. Montreal: Vehicule Press.

Lazerwitz, Bernard. 1953. 'Some Factors in Jewish Identification'. *Jewish Social Studies* 15:24.

———. 1970. 'An Approach to the Components and Consequences of Religio-Ethnic Indentification', unpublished manuscript.

Lévesque, René. 1979. *My Quebec*. Toronto: Methuen.

Levine, Donald N., Ellwood B. Carter, and Eleanor Miller Gorman. 1976. 'Simmel's Influence on American Sociology'. *American Journal of Sociology* 81:813–45.

Levinson, B.M. 1962. 'Yeshiva College Sub-Cultural Scale: An Experimental Attempt to Devise a Scale of the Internalization of Jewish Traditional Values'. *Journal of Genetic Psychology* 101:375–99.

Levitt, Cyril, and William Shaffir. 1986. 'The Christie Pits Riot: A Case Study in the Dynamics of Ethnic Violence'. Hamilton: McMaster University.

———. 1993. 'The Swastika as Dramatic Symbol: A Case-Study of Ethnic Violence in Canada'. In Brym et al. (eds), *The Jews in Canada*. Toronto: Oxford University Press.

Lewin, Kurt. 1948. *Resolving Social Conflicts*. New York: Harper and Brothers.

Li, Peter S. 1987. 'The Economic Cost of Racism to Chinese-Canadians'. *Canadian Ethnic Studies* 19:102–13.

———. 1988. *The Chinese in Canada*. Toronto: Oxford University Press.

———. 1992. 'Race and Gender as Bases of Class Fractions and Their Efforts on Earnings'. *Canadian Review of Sociology and Anthropology* 29:488–510.

———. 1994. 'A World Apart: The Multicultural World of Visible Minorities and the Art World in Canada'. *Canadian Review of Sociology and Anthropology* 31:365–91.

——— (ed.). 1999. *Race and Ethnic Relations in Canada*, 2nd edn. Toronto: Oxford University Press.

——— and B. Singh Bolaria. 1993. *Contemporary Sociology: Critical Perspectives*. Mississauga, ON: Copp Clark Pitman.

——— and Wilfrid B. Denis. 1983. 'Minority Enclave and Majority Language: The Case of a French Town in Western Canada'. *Canadian Ethnic Studies* 15:18–32.

Lieberson, Stanley. 1966. 'Bilingualism in Montreal: A Demographic Analysis'. *American Journal of Sociology* 71:10–25.

———. 1970. 'Residence and Language Maintenance in a Multilingual Society'. *South African Journal of Sociology* 1:14–23.

——— and Mary Waters. 1990. *From Many Strands: Ethnic and Racial Groups in Contemporary America*. New York: Russell Sage Foundation.

Lippmann, W. 1922. *Public Opinion*. New York: Harcourt Brace.

Lyon, David. 1994. *Postmodernity*. Minneapolis: University of Minnesota Press.

McEvoy, F.J. 1982. '"A Symbol of Racial Discrimination": The Chinese Immigration Act and Canada's Relations With China, 1942–1947'. *Canadian Ethnic Studies* 14:24–42.

McFate, Katherine. 1995. 'Introduction: Western States in the New World Order'. In K. McFate, R. Lawson, and J. Wilson (eds), *Poverty, Inequality, and the Future of Social Policy*. New York: Russell Sage Foundation.

McGahan, Peter. 1995. *Urban Sociology in Canada*, 3rd edn. Toronto: Harcourt Brace Canada.

McKague, Ormond. 1991. *Racism in Canada*. Saskatoon: Fifth House Publishers.

Mackie, Marlene. 1978. 'Ethnicity and Nationality: How Much Do They Matter to Western Canadians?' *Canadian Ethnic Studies* 10:118–29.

———. 1984. 'Stereotypes, Prejudice, and Discrimination'. In Rita Bienvenue and Jay Goldstein (eds), *Ethnicity and Ethnic Relations in Canada*. Toronto: Butterworths.

——— and Merlin Brinkerhof. 1984. 'Measuring Ethnic Salience'. *Canadian Ethnic Studies* 16:114–31.

McLuhan, Marshall. 1964. *Understanding the Media: The Extensions of Man*. New York: McGraw-Hill.

McMillan, Alan D. 1995. *Native Peoples and Cultures of Canada*, 2nd edn. Vancouver: Douglas and McIntyre.

McNeill, William H. 1986. *Poly-Ethnicity and National Unity in World History*. Toronto: University of Toronto Press.

McRoberts, Kenneth. 1990. 'Quebec: Province, Nation, or "Distinct Society"?' In M.S. Whittington and G. Williams (eds), *Canadian Politics in the 1990s*, 3rd edn. Scarborough, ON: Nelson.

McVey, W.W., and W.E. Kalbach. 1995. *The Population of Canada*. Toronto: Nelson Canada.

Magosci, Paul Robert (ed.). 1999. *Encyclopedia of Canada's Peoples*. Toronto: University of Toronto Press.

Makabe, Tomoko. 1978. 'Ethnic Identity and Social Mobility: The Case of the Second Generation Japanese in Metropolitan Toronto'. *Canadian Ethnic Studies* 10:106–23.

———. 1981. 'Theory of the Split Labor Market: A Comparison of the Japanese Experience in Brazil and Canada'. *Social Forces* 59:786–809.

Malinowski, Bronislaw. 1945. In Phyllis M. Kaberry (ed.), *The Dynamics of Culture Change*. New Haven: Yale University Press.

Manzer, Ronald A. 1974. *Canada: A Socio-Political Report*. Toronto: McGraw-Hill Ryerson.

Marchi, Sergio. 1996. *A Broader Vision: Immigration Plan, 1996 Annual Report to Parliament*. Ottawa: Citizenship and Immigration Canada.

Markides, Kyriakos, and Sandra A. Black. 1996. 'Race, Ethnicity, and Aging: The Impact of Inequality'. In R.H. Binstock and L.K. George (eds), *Handbook of Aging and the Social Sciences*, 4th edn. New York: Academic Press.

Marx, Karl. 1867. *Das Kapital*. Vol. 1. Hamburg.

———. 1963. *Early Writings*. London: Watts.

——— and Friedrich Engels. 1841–48. *Marx-Engels Gesamtausgabe*, I (MEGA). Vols. 1–6.

——— and Friedrich Engels. 1948. *Communist Manifesto*. London: George Allen and Unwin.

Massey, D.S. 1995. 'The New Immigration and Ethnicity in the United States'. *Population and Development Review* 21:103–21.

Mata, Fernando G. 1989. 'The Black Youth of Toronto: Exploration of Issues'. Ottawa: Policy and Research, Multiculturalism and Citizenship.

Matthews, Ralph. 1980. 'The Significance and Explanation of Regional Divisions in Canada: Toward a Canadian Sociology'. *Journal of Canadian Studies* 15:43–61.

Medjuck, Sheva. 1993. 'Jewish Survival in Small Communities in Canada'. In Robert Brym et al. (eds), *The Jews in Canada*. Toronto: Oxford University Press.

Mercer, John. 1995. 'Canadian Cities and Their Immigrants: New Realities'. *Annals of the American Academy of Political Social Science* 538:169–84.

Miller, Paul W. 1992. 'The Earnings of Asian Male Immigrants in the Canadian Labor Market'. *International Migration Review* 26:122–47.

Mills, C. Wright. 1956. *The Power Elite*. New York: Oxford University Press.

Milner, Henry. 1978. *Politics in the New Quebec*. Toronto: McClelland and Stewart.

Miner, Horace. 1939. *St. Denis: A French-Canadian Parish*. Chicago: University of Chicago Press.

Mol, Hans. 1985. *Faith and Fragility: Religion and Identity in Canada*. Burlington, ON: Trinity Press.

Mulroney, Brian. 1988. Excerpts from the Canadian Multiculturalism Act, 1988.

Musynski, Alicja. 1995. 'Social Stratification: Class and Gender Inequality'. In Singh Bolaria (ed.), *Social Issues and Contradictions in Canadian Society*, 2nd edn. Toronto: Harcourt Brace Canada.

Nagel, Joane. 1984. 'The Ethnic Revolution: Emergence of Ethnic Nationalism'. *Sociology and Social Research* 69:417–34.

Nakamura, Mark. 1975. 'The Japanese'. In Norman Sheffe (ed.), *Many Cultures, Many Heritages*. Toronto: McGraw-Hill Ryerson.

National Council of Welfare. 1992. *Poverty Profile: 1980–1990*. Ottawa: Minister of Supply and Services.

Newhold, K. Bruce. 1995. 'Internal Migration of the Foreign-Born in Canada'. *International Migration Review* 30:728–47.

Newman, William M. 1973. *American Pluralism: A Study of Minority Groups and Social Theory*. New York: Harper and Row.

Nietzsche, Friedrich. 1966. *Beyond God and Evil: Prelude to a Philosophy of the Future*, trans. Walter Kaufmann. New York: Vintage Press.

Nisbet, Robert A. 1974. *The Sociology of Emile Durkheim*. New York: Oxford University Press.

O'Bryan, K.G., Jeffrey G. Reitz, and O. Kuplowska. 1976. *Non-Official Languages: A Study in Canadian Multiculturalism*. Ottawa: Department of the Secretary of State.

Odum, Howard W. 1936. *Southern Regions of the United States*. Chapel Hill: University of North Carolina Press.

Ogmundson, Rick. 1986. 'Social Inequality'. In Robert Hagedorn (ed.), *Sociology*. Toronto: Holt, Rinehart and Winston.

———. 1990. 'Perspectives on the Class and Ethnic Origins of Canadian Elites'. *Canadian Journal of Sociology* 15:165–77.

———. 1992. 'Perspectives on the Class and Ethnic Origins of Canadian Elites: A Reply to Clement and Rich'. *Canadian Journal of Sociology* 17:313–21.

——— and J. McLaughlin. 1992. 'Trends in the Ethnic Origins of Canadian Elites: The Decline of the Brits?' *Canadian Review of Sociology and Anthropology* 29:227–42.

Palmer, D. 1996. 'Determinants of Canadian Attitudes Toward Immigration: More Than Just Racism?' *Canadian Journal of Behavioural Science* 28:180–92.

Palmer, Howard. 1982. 'Ethnic Relations in Wartime: Nationalism and European Minorities in Alberta During the Second World War'. *Canadian Ethnic Studies* 14:1–23.

Paquet, G. 1994. 'Political Philosophy of Multiculturalism'. In J. Gerry and J. Laponce (eds), *Ethnicity and Culture in Canada*. Toronto: University of Toronto Press.

Parel, Anthony. 1988. 'The Meech Lake Accord and Indo-Canadians'. *Canadian Ethnic Studies* 20:129–37.

Park, Robert. 1922. *The Immigrant Press and Its Control*. New York: Harper.

———. 1928. 'Human Migration and Modern Man'. *American Journal of Sociology* 33:881–93.

———. 1950. *Race and Culture*. Glencoe, IL: Free Press.

———. 1967. 'The City: Suggestions for the Investigation of Human Behavior in the Urban Environment'. In Robert Park and Ernest W. Burgess (eds), *The City*. Chicago: University of Chicago Press.

Parsons, John. 1985. 'John Cabot'. In *The Canadian Encyclopedia*. Edmonton: Hurtig.

Pendakur, K., and Ravi Pendakur. 1996. *Earnings Differentials Among Ethnic Groups in Canada*. Ottawa: Strategic Research and Analysis, Department of Canadian Heritage.

Pendakur, Ravi. 1990. *Speaking in Tongues: Heritage Language Maintenance and Transfer in Canada*. Ottawa: Policy and Research, Multiculturalism and Citizenship.

———. 1995. *The Changing Role of Post-War Immigrants in Canada's Labour Force: An Examination Across Four Census Periods*. Ottawa: Patrimonine Canadien.

——— and Fernando Mata. 2000. 'Patterns of Ethnic Identification and the "Canadian

Response"'. In M.A. Kalbach and W.E. Kalbach (eds), *Perspectives on Ethnicity in Canada*. Toronto: Harcourt.

Persons, Stow. 1987. *Ethnic Studies at Chicago, 1905–45*. Urbana: University of Illinois Press.

Peter, Karl A. 1987. *The Dynamics of Hutterite Society: An Analytical Approach*. Edmonton: University of Alberta Press.

Petrie, Anne. 1982. *A Guidebook to Ethnic Vancouver*. Surrey, BC: Hancock House.

Piche, Victor, Jean Renaud, and Lucie Gingras. 1999. 'Comparative Immigrant Economic Integration'. In S. Halli and L. Driedger (eds), *Immigrant Canada*. Toronto: University of Toronto Press.

Pineo, Peter. 1977. 'The Social Standing of Ethnic and Racial Groups'. *Canadian Review of Sociology and Anthropology* 14:147–57.

——— and John Porter. 1967. 'Occupational Prestige in Canada'. *Canadian Review of Sociology and Anthropology* 14:24–40.

Pinkney, Alphonso. 1975. *Black Americans*, 2nd edn. Toronto: Prentice-Hall.

Pitman, W. 1978. *Report on Race Relations in Metropolitan Toronto: The Pitman Report*. Toronto: Metropolitan Toronto Council.

Ponting, J. Rick. 1983. 'Blacks in Calgary: A Social and Attitudinal Profile'. *Canadian Ethnic Studies* 15:57–76.

———. 1986. *Arduous Journey: Canadian Indians and Decolonization*. Toronto: McClelland and Stewart.

———. 1997. *First Nations in Canada: Perspectives on Opportunity, Empowerment, and Self-Determination*. Toronto: McGraw-Hill Ryerson.

——— and Roger Gibbons. 1980. *Out of Irrelevance: A Socio-Political Introduction to Indian Affairs in Canada*. Toronto: Butterworths.

Porter, John. 1965. *The Vertical Mosaic*. Toronto: University of Toronto Press.

———. 1975a. 'Ethnic Pluralism in Canadian Perspective'. In N. Glazer and D.P. Moynihan (eds), *Ethnicity, Theory and Experience*. Cambridge, MA: Harvard University Press.

———. 1975b. 'Plenary Address'. Annual meeting of the Canadian Sociology and Anthropology Association, Edmonton.

Potter, Harold H. 1961. 'Negroes in Canada', *Race* 3:49.

Price, John. 1979. *Indians of Canada: Cultural Dynamics*. Toronto: Prentice-Hall.

Ralston, Helen. 1995. 'Organizational Empowerment Among South Asian Immigrant Women in Canada', *International Journal of Canadian Studies* 1:121–46.

———. 2000. 'Redefinitions of South Asian Women'. In L. Driedger and S. Halli (eds), *Race and Racism: Canada's Challenge*. Montreal: McGill-Queen's University Press.

Ramcharan, Subhas. 1982. *Racism: Nonwhites in Canada*. Toronto: Butterworths.

Raushenbush, Winifred. 1979. *Robert E. Park: Biography of a Sociologist*. Durham, NC: Duke University Press.

Redfield, Robert. 1953. 'The Folk Society', *American Journal of Sociology* 52:293–308.

Reid, Angus. 1991. *Multiculturalism and Canadians: Attitude Study, A National Report*. Ottawa: Ministry of Multiculturalism.

Reitz, Jeffrey G. 1977. 'Analysis of Changing Group Inequalities in a Changing Occupational Structure'. In P. Krishnan (ed.), *Mathematical Models in Sociology*, Sociological Review Monograph, No. 24. Keele, Staffordshire: University of Keele.

———. 1980. *The Survival of Ethnic Groups*. Toronto: McGraw-Hill Ryerson.

———. 1982. 'Ethnic Group Control of Jobs', Research Paper No. 133. Toronto: Centre for Urban and Community Studies, University of Toronto.

———, Liviana Calzavara, and Donna Dasko. 1981. 'Ethnic Inequality and Segregation in Jobs', Research Paper No. 123. Toronto: University of Toronto, Centre for Urban and Community Studies.

——— and Raymond Breton. 1994. *The Illusion of Difference: Realities of Ethnicity in Canada and the United States*. Toronto: C.D. Howe Institute.

——— and Sherrilyn M. Sklare. 1997. 'Culture, Race, and the Economic Assimilation of Immigrants'. *Sociological Forum* 12:233–77.

Renaud, J., V. Piche, and L. Gingras. 1996. Immigration et integration economique à Montreal: le role de l'origine nationale. Revised version of a communication presented at the Huitièmes Entretiens du Centre Jacques Cartier, December 1995.

Richard, Madeline A. 1991. *Ethnic Groups and Marital Choices: Ethnic History and Marital Assimilation in Canada, 1871 and 1971.* Vancouver: University of British Columbia Press.

Richmond, Anthony H. 1972a. *Ethnic Residential Segregation in Metropolitan Toronto.* Toronto: Institute for Behavioural Research, York University.

———. 1972b. *Readings in Race and Ethnic Relations.* Toronto: Pergamon Press.

———. 1994. *Global Apartheid: Refugees, Racism, and the New World Order.* Toronto: Oxford University Press.

——— and Warren E. Kalbach. 1980. *Factors in the Adjustment of Immigrant and Their Descendants.* Ottawa: Minister of Supply and Services.

Riesman, David. 1950. *The Lonely Crowd.* New Haven, CT: Yale University Press.

Rioux, Marcel. 1971. *Quebec in Question.* Toronto: James Lewis and Samuel.

———. 1973. 'The Development of Ideologies in Quebec'. In Gerald Gold and Marc-Adelard Tremblay (eds), *Communities and Cultures in French Canada.* Toronto: Holt, Rinehart and Winston.

——— and Yves Martin. 1964. *French-Canadian Society*, Vol. 1. Ottawa: Carleton University Press.

Rothman, Jack. 1960. 'In-Group Identification and Out-Group Association: A Theoretical and Experimental Study'. *Journal of Jewish Communal Service* 37:81–93.

Royal Commission on Bilingualism and Biculturalism. 1965. *A Preliminary Report.* Ottawa: Queen's Printer.

———. 1967. *The Official Languages.* Vol. 1 of the *Report of the Royal Commission on Bilingualism and Biculturalism.* Ottawa: Queen's Printer.

———. 1970. *The Cultural Contributions of Other Ethnic Groups.* Vol. 4 of the *Report of the Royal Commission on Bilingualism and Biculturalism.* Ottawa: Queen's Printer.

Ruggiero, K.M., and Donald M. Taylor. 1997. 'Coping with Discrimination: How Disadvan-

taged Group Members Perceive the Discrimination That Confronts Them'. *Journal of Personality and Social Psychology* 68:826–38.

Russell, P. 1993. *Constitutional Odyssey.* Toronto: University of Toronto Press.

Ryan, John. 1977. *The Agricultural Economy of Manitoba Hutterite Colonies.* Ottawa: McClelland and Stewart.

———. 2000. 'Hutterites'. *The Canadian Encyclopedia, Year 2000 Edition.* Toronto: McClelland & Stewart.

Safron, W. 1996. 'Rebuilding the Unity of Divided Nations and Ethnicities: Possibilities, Incentives, and Constraints'. *Australian Journal of International Affairs* 50:5–21.

Sallee, D. 1995. 'Identities in Conflict: The Aboriginal Question and the Politics of Recognition in Quebec'. *Ethnic and Racial Studies* 18:277–314.

Samuel, T.J. 1992. *Visible Minorities in Canada: A Projection.* Toronto: Advertising Foundation.

———. 1997. 'Visible Minorities and the Public Service in Canada'. Ottawa: Canadian Human Rights Commission.

——— and Aly Karam. 2000. 'Employment Equity for Visible Minorities'. In L. Driedger and S. Halli (eds), *Race and Racism.* Montreal: McGill-Queen's University Press.

Sapir, Edward. 1949. *Language.* New York: Harcourt Brace World.

Satzewich, Victor Nicholas. 1992. *Deconstructing a Nation: Immigration, Multiculturalism and Racism in '90s Canada.* Halifax: Fernwood.

———. 1995. 'Social Stratification: Class and Racial Inequality'. In Singh Bolaria (ed.), *Social Issues and Contradictions in Canadian Society*, 2nd edn. Toronto: Harcourt Brace Canada.

——— (ed.). 1998. *Racism and Social Inequality in Canada: Concepts, Controversies and Strategies of Resistance.* Toronto: Thompson Educational Publishing.

——— and Peter S. Li. 1987. 'Immigrant Labour in Canada: The Cost and Benefit of Ethnic Origin in the Job Market'. *Canadian Journal of Sociology* 12:229–41.

Saywell, John T. 1968. 'Introduction'. In Pierre Trudeau, *Federalism and the French Canadians.* Toronto: Macmillan.

Secretary of State. 1972. *Revised Handbook of Selected Ethnic Organization in Canada*. Ottawa: Canadian Citizenship Branch.

Segalman, Ralph. 1967. 'Jewish Identity Scales: A Report'. *Jewish Social Studies* 29:92–111.

Seidman, Steven. 1994. *Contested Knowledge: Social Theory in the Postmodern Era*. Oxford: Blackwell.

Sev'er, Aysan, W.W. Isajiw, and Leo Driedger. 1993. 'Anomie as Powerlessness: Sorting Ethnic Group Prestige, Class and Gender'. *Canadian Ethnic Studies* 25:86–99.

Shaffir, William. 1974. *Life in a Religious Community: The Lubavitcher Chassidim in Montreal*. Toronto: Holt, Rinehart and Winston.

———. 1993. 'The Hassidic Community of Tash'. In Robert Brym et al. (eds), *The Jews in Canada*. Toronto: Oxford University Press.

——— and Morton Weinfeld. 1981. 'Canada and the Jews: An Introduction'. In Morton Weinfeld et al. (eds), *The Canadian Jewish Mosaic*. Toronto: John Wiley and Sons.

Shevky, Eshref, and Wendell Bell. 1955. *Social Area Analysis*. Stanford, CA: University of Stanford Press.

Shibutani, Tamotsu, and Kian M. Kwan. 1965. *Ethnic Stratification: A Comparative Approach*. New York: Macmillan.

Shore, Marlene. 1987. *The Science of Social Redemption: McGill, the Chicago School, and the Origins of Social Research in Canada*. Toronto: University of Toronto Press.

Simeon, Richard. 1979. 'Regionalism and Canadian Political Institutions'. In Richard Schultz et al. (eds), *The Canadian Political Process*. Toronto: Holt, Rinehart and Winston.

——— and David J. Elkins. 1979. 'Regional Political Cultures in Canada'. In Richard Schultz et al. (eds), *The Canadian Political Process*. Toronto: Holt, Rinehart and Winston.

Simmel, Georg. 1950. *The Sociology of Georg Simmel*. Kurt Wolff (ed.). Glencoe, IL: Free Press.

———. 1955. *Conflict and the Web of Group Affiliations*. Glencoe, IL: Free Press.

Simmons, Alan. 1995. 'Economic Globalization and Immigration Policy: Canada Compared to Europe'. *Organizing Diversity: Migration Policy and Practice, Canada and Europe*.

Toronto: Oxford University Press.

Smith, Miriam. 1992. 'Quebec-Canada Association: Divergent Paths to a Common Economic Agenda'. In Daniel Drache and Roberto Perin (eds), *Negotiating within a Sovereign Quebec*. Toronto: James Lorimer.

Spates, James L., and John J. Macionis. 1987. *The Sociology of Cities*, 2nd edn. Belmont, CA: Wadsworth.

Stafford, James. 1992. 'The Impact of the New Immigration Policy on Racism in Canada'. In Vic Satzewich (ed.), *Deconstructing a Nation: Immigration, Multiculturalism and Racism in '90s Canada*. Halifax: Fernwood.

Stanley, F.G. 1960. *The Birth of Western Canada: A History of the Riel Rebellions*. Toronto: University of Toronto Press.

———. 1969. *Louis Riel: Rebel of the Western Frontier or Victim of Politics and Prejudice?* Toronto: Copp Clark.

Statistics Canada. 1983. *1981 Census of Canada: 20 Percent Data Base*. Ottawa: Supply and Services.

———. 1984a. *Canada's Native People*. Ottawa: Statistics Canada.

———. 1984b. *1981 Census of Canada*, Catalogue 92-911. Ottawa: Minister of Supply and Services.

———. 1985. *Languages in Canada*. Ottawa: Minister of Supply and Services.

———. 1993a. *Ethnic Origin: The Nation*, Catalogue 93-315. Ottawa: Statistics Canada.

———. 1993b. *Home Language and Mother Tongue: The Nation*, Catalogue 93-317.

———. 1994. *Profile of Urban and Rural Areas*, Part B. Ottawa: Statistics Canada.

———. 2001. *Canada Yearbook, 2001*. Ottawa: Statistics Canada.

Stebbins, Robert A. 1994. *The Franco-Calgarians: French Language, Leisure, and Linguistic Life-Style in an Anglophone City*. Toronto: University of Toronto Press.

Stephenson, Peter H. 1991. *The Hutterian People: Ritual, Rebirth and the Evolution of Communal Life*. Lanham, NY: University Press of America.

Sugiman, Pamela, and H.K. Nishio. 1993. 'Socialization and Cultural Duality Among Aging Japanese Canadians'. *Canadian Ethnic Studies* 15:17–35.

Sunahara, M. Ann. 1980. 'Federal Policy and the Japanese Canadians: The Decision to Evacuate, 1942'. In K.V. Ujimoto and G. Hirabayashi (eds), *Visible Minorities and Multiculturalism: Asians in Canada*. Toronto: Butterworths.

Tan, Jin, and Patricia E. Roy. 1985. *The Chinese in Canada*. Ottawa: Canadian Historical Association.

Taras, David, and Morton Weinfeld. 1993. 'Continuity and Criticism: North American Jews and Israel'. In Robert Brym et al. (eds), *The Jews in Canada*. Toronto: Oxford University Press.

Tator, Carol, Frances Henry, and Winston Mattis. 1998. *Challenging Racism in Cultural Production in Canada: Six Case Studies*. Toronto: University of Toronto Press.

Taylor, D.M. 1981. 'Stereotypes and Intergroup Relations'. In R.C. Gardner and R. Kalin (eds), *A Canadian Social Psychology of Ethnic Relations*. Toronto: Methuen.

——— and R.C. Gardner. 1970. 'Bicultural Communications: A Study of Communicational Efficiency and Person Percepetion'. In J.W. Berry and G.J.S. Wilde (eds), *Social Psychology: The Canadian Context*. Toronto: McClelland and Stewart.

——— and R. Sigal. 1982. 'Defining "Quebecois": The Role of Ethnic Heritage, Language, and Political Orientation'. *Canadian Ethnic Studies* 14:59–70.

———, Stephen Wright, and Karen Ruggiero. 2000. 'Discrimination: An Invisible Evil'. In L. Driedger and S. Halli (eds), *Race and Racism: Canada's Challenge*. Montreal: McGill-Queen's University Press.

Taylor, K.W. 1991. 'Racism in Canadian Immigration Policy'. *Canadian Ethnic Studies* 23:1–20.

Tepper, Elliot L. 1980. 'Changing Canada: The Institutional Response to Polyethnicity'. *The Review of Demography and Its Implications for Economic and Social Policy*. Ottawa: Carleton University.

Tepperman, Lorne. 1975. *Social Mobility in Canada*. Toronto: University of Toronto Press.

Theberge, Raymond. 1987. 'Scandale nationale: meme la ou le nombre le justifie'. Commission nationale des parents francophones, Actes du colloque tenu a Montreal, 13–15 novembre.

Thomas, William I. 1921. *Old World Traits Transplanted*. New York: Harper.

——— and Florian Znaniecki. 1918–20. *The Polish Peasant in Europe and America*. Vols. 1–4. Boston: The Gorham Press.

Tian, Guang. 2000. 'Chinese Refugees Coping with Stress in Toronto'. In L. Driedger and S. Halli (eds), *Race and Racism: Canada's Challenge*. Montreal: McGill-Queen's University Press.

Tilly, Charles. 1967. 'Anthropology on the Town'. *Habitat* 10:20–5.

Toennies, Ferdinand. 1957. *Community and Society*, translated by Charles P. Loomis. East Lansing, MI: Michigan State University Press.

Toffler, Alvin, and Heidi Toffler. 1995. *Creating a New Civilization: The Politics of the Third Wave*. New York: Bantam Books.

Toynbee, Arnold J. 1954. *A Study of History*. London: Oxford University Press.

Trovato, Frank, and Carl F. Grindstaff. 1994. *Perspectives on Canada's Population: An Introduction to Concepts and Issues*. Toronto: Oxford University Press.

Trudeau, Pierre. 1962. 'The Conflict of Nationalism in Canada'. *Cité Libre*, April.

———. 1968. *Federalism and the French Canadians*. Toronto: The Macmillan Company.

———. 1971. Statement by the Prime Minister in the House of Commons, 8 October 1971.

Trudel, Marcel. 1985. 'Jacques Cartier'. In *The Canadian Encyclopedia*. Edmonton: Hurtig.

Tulchinsky, Gerald. 1993. 'The Contours of Canadian Jewish History'. In Robert Brym et al. (eds), *The Jews in Canada*. Toronto: Oxford University Press.

Turpel, Mary Ellen. 1992. 'Does the Road to Quebec Sovereignty Run Through Aboriginal Territory?' Daniel Drache and Roberto Perin (eds), *Negotiating within a Sovereign Quebec*. Toronto: James Lorimer.

Tuzlak, Aysan Sev'er. 1989. 'Joint Effects of Race and Confidence on Perceptions and Influence: Implications for Blacks in Decision-Making Positions'. *Canadian Ethnic Studies* 21:103–19.

Ujimoto, K. Victor. 1983. 'Institutional Controls and Their Impact on Japanese Canadian Social Relations, 1877–1977'. In Peter S. Li and B. Singh Bolaria (eds), *Racial Minorities in Multicultural Canada*. Toronto: Garamond Press.

—— and Gordon Hirabayashi. 1980. *Visible Minorities and Multiculturalism: Asians in Canada*. Toronto: Butterworths.

Vallee, Frank G. 1969. 'Regionalism and Ethnicity: The French-Canadian Case'. In Gard (ed.), *Perspectives on Regions and Regionalism*. Edmonton: University of Alberta Press.

——. 1981. 'The Sociology of John Porter: Ethnicity as Anachronism'. *Canadian Review of Sociology and Anthropology* 8:639–50.

—— and Albert Dufour. 1974. 'The Bilingual Belt: A Garrotte for the French?' *Laurentian University Review* 6, 2.

—— and John deVries. 1975. *Data Book for the Conference on Individual, Language and Society*. Ottawa: The Canada Council.

—— and John deVries. 1978. 'Issues and Trends in Bilingualism in Canada'. In J.A. Fishman (ed.), *Advances in the Study of Societal Multilingualism*. The Hague: Mouton.

van den Berghe, Pierre L. 1981. *The Ethnic Phenomenon*. New York: Elsevier.

Verma, Ravi B.P., and Kwok Bun Chan. 2000. 'Economic Adaptation of Asian Immigrants'. In L. Driedger and S. Halli (eds), *Race and Racism: Canada's Challenge*. Montreal: McGill-Queen's University Press.

Wade, Mason. 1968. *The French Canadians*, Vols. 1 and 2. Toronto: Macmillan.

Walker, James W. St. G. 1984. *The West Indians in Canada*. Ottawa: Canadian Historical Association.

——. 1992. *The Black Loyalists: The Search for a Promised Land in Nova Scotia and Sierra Leone 1783–1870*. Toronto: University of Toronto Press.

Wallace, Samuel B. 1981. 'Regional Sociology: The South'. *Sociological Spectrum* 14:429–42.

Wargon, Sylvia. 2000. 'Historical and Political Reflections on Race'. In L. Driedger and S. Halli (eds), *Race and Racism: Canada's Challenge*. Montreal: McGill-Queen's University Press.

Weber, Max. 1894. Speech made at the Evangelisch-Soziale Kongress in the biography written by Marianne Weber.

——. 1904 [1958]. *The Protestant Ethnic and the Spirit of Capitalism,* trans. Talcott Parsons. New York: Scribner.

——. 1978. *Economy and Society,* Vols. 1 and 2. Guenther Roth and Claus Wittich (eds).

Berkeley, CA: University of California Press.

Weeks, John R. 1994. *Population: An Introduction to Concepts and Issues,* 5th edn. Belmont, CA: Wadsworth.

Weinfeld, Morton. 1985. 'Myth and Reality in the Canadian Mosaic: "Affective Ethnicity"'. In Rita Bienvenue and Jay Goldstein (eds), *Ethnicity and Ethnic Relations*. Toronto: Butterworths.

——. 1993. 'The Ethnic Sub-Economy: Explication and Analysis of a Case Study of the Jews of Montreal'. In Robert Brym et al. (eds), *The Jews in Canada*. Toronto: Oxford University Press.

——. 1994. 'Ethnic Assimilation and the Retention of Ethnic Cultures'. In John Berry and J.A. Laponce (eds), *Ethnicity and Culture in Canada*. Toronto: University of Toronto Press.

——, William Shaffir, and I. Cotler. 1981. *The Canadian Jewish Mosaic*. Toronto: John Wiley and Sons.

Weiman, Gabriel, and Conrad Winn. 1993. 'Hate on Trial: The Zundel Affair, The Media, Public Opinion in Canada'. In Brym et al. (eds), *The Jews in Canada*. Toronto: Oxford University Press.

Westie, Frank R. 1959. 'Social Distance Scales: A Tool for the Study of Stratification'. *Sociology and Social Research* 43:251–8.

Wickberg, Edgar (ed.). 1982. *From China to Canada: A History of the Chinese Communities in Canada*. Toronto: McClelland and Stewart.

Wiley, Norbert F. 1967. 'The Ethnic Mobility Trap and Stratification Theory'. *Social Problems* 15:147–59.

Winks, Robin W. 1969. 'Negro School Segregation in Ontario and Nova Scotia'. *Canadian Historical Review* 50:164–91.

——. 1971. *The Blacks in Canada: A History*. Montreal: McGill-Queen's University Press.

Wirth, Louis. 1928. *The Ghetto*. Chicago: University of Chicago Press.

Wong, Siu Kwong. 2000. 'Acculturation and Chinese Delinquency'. In L. Driedger and S. Halli (eds), *Race and Racism: Canada's Challenge*. Montreal: McGill-Queen's University Press.

Wylie, Ruth C. 1961. *The Self Concept*. Lincoln: University of Nebraska Press.

Young, Donald R. 1971. 'Introduction to the Republished Edition'. In W.I. Thomas, *Old World Traits Transplanted*. Montclair, NJ: Patterson Smith.

Yu, Miriam. 1987. 'Human Rights, Discrimination, and Coping Behavior of the Chinese in Canada'. *Canadian Ethnic Studies* 19:114–21.

Yuzyk, Paul. 1975. 'Canada as a Multi-Cultural Society', paper presented at the Conference on Multiculturalism and Third World Immigrants, University of Alberta, Edmonton, 3–6 September.

Zarbaugh, Harvey. 1929. *The Gold Coast and the Slum*. Chicago: University of Chicago Press.

INDEX